SAS® Macro Facility Tips Techniques

Version 6
First Edition

SAS Institute Inc.
SAS Campus Drive
Cary, NC 27513

The correct bibliographic citation for this manual is as follows: *SAS® Macro Facility Tips and Techniques, Version 6, First Edition*, Cary, NC: SAS Institute Inc., 1994. 319 pp.

SAS® Macro Facility Tips and Techniques, Version 6, First Edition

ISBN 1-55544-605-1

1st printing, March 1994

Doc S19, 021794

Contents

Credits

Documentation

Design and Production	Design, Production, and Printing Services
Style Programming	Publications Technology Development
Writing and Editing	Patsy P. Blessis, Brenda C. Kalt, and Jason R. Sharpe

Acknowledgments

The SAS software users who presented papers on the SAS macro facility at SUGI 14 through SUGI 18 made this book possible. Many thanks go to the following people for the papers listed:

Bercov, Mark, "SAS Macros - What's Really Happening?" *Proceedings of the Eighteenth Annual SAS Users Group International Conference*, Cary, NC: SAS Institute Inc., 1993.

Bergstralh, Erik J., "PLOTCORR: A SAS Macro for Appending Correlation and Regression Statistics to the PLOT or GPLOT Procedures," *Proceedings of the Fifteenth Annual SAS Users Group International Conference*, Cary, NC: SAS Institute Inc., 1990.

Blood, Nancy K., "Using SAS Macros to Generate Code (So Your Program Can Figure Out What to Do for Itself)," *Proceedings of the Seventeenth Annual SAS Users Group International Conference*, Cary, NC: SAS Institute Inc., 1992.

Broder, Benjamin I. and Chou, Shih-Ping, "A SAS Macro Procedure to Summarize the Output of Logistic Regression Models," *Proceedings of the Eighteenth Annual SAS Users Group International Conference*, Cary, NC: SAS Institute Inc., 1993.

Brown, Michael M., "Macros - A Few Uses to Get You Started," *Proceedings of the Fourteenth Annual SAS Users Group International Conference*, Cary, NC: SAS Institute Inc., 1989.

Cassidy, Deb, "Writing SAS Code Behind the Scenes: A Conversational Macro Example," *Proceedings of the Eighteenth Annual SAS Users Group International Conference*, Cary, NC: SAS Institute Inc., 1993.

Culp, Jennifer C., "Using SAS Macros with SAS/AF and SAS/FSP Software in Developing User-Friendly Applications," *Proceedings of the Sixteenth Annual SAS Users Group International Conference*, Cary, NC: SAS Institute Inc., 1991.

DeFoor, Jim, "A Macro Program for Generating Customized Reports from User-Specified Column Variables and Page-Sort Variables," *Proceedings of the Sixteenth Annual SAS Users Group International Conference*, Cary, NC: SAS Institute Inc., 1991.

Edwards, Kathleen D. and King, John Henry, "MACPAGE - A SAS Macro for Enhancing Reports," *Proceedings of the Fourteenth Annual SAS Users Group International Conference*, Cary, NC: SAS Institute Inc., 1989.

Forster, Christian M., "Generic Applications Development Using the SAS Macro Language," *Proceedings of the Eighteenth Annual SAS Users Group International Conference*, Cary, NC: SAS Institute Inc., 1993.

Frankel, David S. and Kochanski, Mark A., "A Debugging Facility for SAS Macro Systems," *Proceedings of the Sixteenth Annual SAS Users Group International Conference*, Cary, NC: SAS Institute Inc., 1991.

Gilmore, Jodie and Helwig, Linda, "Debugging Your SAS Macro Application under VMS: A Practical Approach," *Proceedings of the Fifteenth Annual SAS Users Group International Conference*, Cary, NC: SAS Institute Inc., 1990.

Hubbell, Katie A., "Conquering the Dreaded Macro Error," *Proceedings of the Fifteenth Annual SAS Users Group International Conference*, Cary, NC: SAS Institute Inc., 1990.

Huffman, Cam; Arneson, Carl P.; Horton, John; and King, John H., "Using the SAS System in the Pharmaceutical Industry: Project Setup and Standardization for the Analysis of Clinical Trial Data," *Proceedings of the Eighteenth Annual SAS Users Group International Conference*, Cary, NC: SAS Institute Inc., 1993.

Ison, Barbara M. and Ferguson, Dania P., "The Mighty Macro versus the Lowly Link," *Proceedings of the Seventeenth Annual SAS Users Group International Conference*, Cary, NC: SAS Institute Inc., 1992.

Jackson, Barbara L., "SAS Macros for Converting between ARC/INFO Import/Export Files and SAS Data Sets," *Proceedings of the Sixteenth Annual SAS Users Group International Conference*, Cary, NC: SAS Institute Inc., 1991.

Jair, Joy Y. S. and Wu, Rex C.T., "A Menu-Driven Table Generator," *Proceedings of the Seventeenth Annual SAS Users Group International Conference*, Cary, NC: SAS Institute Inc., 1992.

Jane, Lee-Hwa and McCormick, Maureen, "Automated Generation of Statistical Tables: Integration of Structure Programming and SAS Macros," *Proceedings of the Sixteenth Annual SAS Users Group International Conference*, Cary, NC: SAS Institute Inc., 1991.

Johnson, Robert E., "The SAS Macro: An Aid to the User," *Proceedings of the Fifteenth Annual SAS Users Group International Conference*, Cary, NC: SAS Institute Inc., 1990.

Katsanis, Gary L., "An Introduction to the SAS Macro Language," *Proceedings of the Sixteenth Annual SAS Users Group International Conference*, Cary, NC: SAS Institute Inc., 1991.

Keene, Tina, "Macro Windows: Creating a User-Friendly Application," *Proceedings of the Sixteenth Annual SAS Users Group International Conference*, Cary, NC: SAS Institute Inc., 1991.

Kenny, Susan J., "The Generation of a Series of Annotated and Templated Statistical Graphs Using SAS Macros," *Proceedings of the Eighteenth Annual SAS Users Group International Conference*, Cary, NC: SAS Institute Inc., 1993.

King, John Henry and Goldstein, Donna S., "SAS Macros for Source Program Tracking," *Proceedings of the Fifteenth Annual SAS Users Group International Conference*, Cary, NC: SAS Institute Inc., 1990.

Knoop, Jim C., "Putting the Pieces Together: Applying Advanced SAS Macro Techniques to Everyday Problems," *Proceedings of the Eighteenth Annual SAS Users Group International Conference*, Cary, NC: SAS Institute Inc., 1993.

Kreamer, Anthony B., "Macro-Based Report Generator," *Proceedings of the Fourteenth Annual SAS Users Group International Conference*, Cary, NC: SAS Institute Inc., 1989.

Kretzman, Peter, "Ifs, Ands, and Buts: A Case Study in Advanced Macro Implementation," *Proceedings of the Seventeenth Annual SAS Users Group International Conference*, Cary, NC: SAS Institute Inc., 1992.

Levine, Howard, "Building Macro-Based Systems," *Proceedings of the Fourteenth Annual SAS Users Group International Conference*, Cary, NC: SAS Institute Inc., 1989.

Luedke, Kurt and Keene, Jeffrey, "Dynamic Code Replaces Itself Every 3,000 Executions or Less," *Proceedings of the Sixteenth Annual SAS Users Group International Conference*, Cary, NC: SAS Institute Inc., 1991.

MacHose, William R., "Make a Date with the SAS System," *Proceedings of the Fourteenth Annual SAS Users Group International Conference*, Cary, NC: SAS Institute Inc., 1989.

Mauromoustakos, Andy and Thompson, Kevin, "A Macro for a Multiple Stars Plot," *Proceedings of the Eighteenth Annual SAS Users Group International Conference*, Cary, NC: SAS Institute Inc., 1993.

Norton, Andrew A., "Screen Control Language versus Macros in Batch Environments," *Proceedings of the Sixteenth Annual SAS Users Group International Conference*, Cary, NC: SAS Institute Inc., 1991.

O'Connor, Susan M., "A Roadmap to Macro Facility Error Messages and Debugging," *Proceedings of the Sixteenth Annual SAS Users Group International Conference*, Cary, NC: SAS Institute Inc., 1991.

O'Connor, Susan M., "Macros Invocation Hierarchy: Session Compiled, Autocall, and Compiled Stored Macros," *Proceedings of the Seventeenth Annual SAS Users Group International Conference*, Cary, NC: SAS Institute Inc., 1992.

Patrick, Lynn, "Macro: Bells and Whistles for Version 6," *Proceedings of the Fourteenth Annual SAS Users Group International Conference*, Cary, NC: SAS Institute Inc., 1989

Perry, Michael F., "Menu-Driven Interfaces Using SAS/FSP Software and the SAS Macro Language," *Proceedings of the Fifteenth Annual SAS Users Group International Conference*, Cary, NC: SAS Institute Inc., 1990.

Phillips, Jeff; Walgamotte, Veronica; and Drummond, Derek, "Warning: Apparent Macro Invocation Not Resolved... Techniques for Debugging Macro Code," *Proceedings of the Eighteenth Annual SAS Users Group International Conference*, Cary, NC: SAS Institute Inc., 1993.

Pratter, Frederick, "Two or Three Neat Things You Can Do with SAS Software," *Proceedings of the Fourteenth Annual SAS Users Group International Conference*, Cary, NC: SAS Institute Inc., 1989.

Ransom, Ray L.; Hightower, Allen W.; and Plikaytis, Brian D., "A Multi-Site Data Collection and Analysis System Based on the SAS System," *Proceedings of the Fifteenth Annual SAS Users Group International Conference*, Cary, NC: SAS Institute Inc., 1990.

Remsburg, Madelyn A., "Producing Multiple Graphs Using Macros: 60% Code Reduction," *Proceedings of the Fourteenth Annual SAS Users Group International Conference*, Cary, NC: SAS Institute Inc., 1989.

Schilling, Michael J., "A Macro to Separate Records into Output Datasets by Date and Create Dataset Names with Date as a Part," *Proceedings of the Fourteenth Annual SAS Users Group International Conference*, Cary, NC: SAS Institute Inc., 1989.

Thompson, Paul A., "A Cross-Reference Listing Program for SAS Software Macros," *Proceedings of the Fifteenth Annual SAS Users Group International Conference*, Cary, NC: SAS Institute Inc., 1990.

Tindall, Bruce M. and O'Connor, Susan M., "Macro Tricks to Astound the Folks on Thursday Morning: Ten Immediately Useful Macro Techniques," *Proceedings of the Sixteenth Annual SAS Users Group International Conference*, Cary, NC: SAS Institute Inc., 1991.

Tsien, Aileen L., "Shortcuts to Customize Clinical Trial Reports," *Proceedings of the Fifteenth Annual SAS Users Group International Conference*, Cary, NC: SAS Institute Inc., 1990.

Wang, Eric Yu I; Gong, Aili; and MacKinnon, David P., "A Program to Compute Odds Ratios and Confidence Intervals from LOGISTIC Output," *Proceedings of the Sixteenth Annual SAS Users Group International Conference*, Cary, NC: SAS Institute Inc., 1991.

Westerlund, Earl R., "SAS Macro Language Features for Application Development," *Proceedings of the Sixteenth Annual SAS Users Group International Conference*, Cary, NC: SAS Institute Inc., 1991.

Whitaker, Ken, "Using Macro Variable Lists," *Proceedings of the Fourteenth Annual SAS Users Group International Conference*, Cary, NC: SAS Institute Inc., 1989.

Whitlock, H. Ian, "A Study in Repetition Resulting in a Utility Macro for Substitution," *Proceedings of the Fifteenth Annual SAS Users Group International Conference*, Cary, NC: SAS Institute Inc., 1990.

Whitlock, H. Ian, "A Macro to Make External Flat Files," *Proceedings of the Eighteenth Annual SAS Users Group International Conference*, Cary, NC: SAS Institute Inc., 1993.

Williams, Edmond, "TRAVERSE: The Macros' Macro," *Proceedings of the Sixteenth Annual SAS Users Group International Conference*, Cary, NC: SAS Institute Inc., 1991.

Yeh, Shi-Tao, "A Supplemental SAS Function for Computing Moving Average," *Proceedings of the Seventeenth Annual SAS Users Group International Conference*, Cary, NC: SAS Institute Inc., 1992.

Using This Book

Purpose

SAS Macro Facility Tips and Techniques, Version 6, First Edition answers users' requests for more information on and examples of using the SAS macro facility. A valuable source of information has always been the *Proceedings* of the SAS Users Group International (SUGI) conference each year. To make that information more accessible, *SAS Macro Facility Tips and Techniques* reprints selected papers on the SAS macro facility from SUGI 14 through SUGI 18 (1989-1993). The papers are now organized by topic in a single volume.

Audience

The audience for *SAS Macro Facility Tips and Techniques* is users of the SAS macro facility at all levels of experience.

Prerequisites

The papers in *SAS Macro Facility Tips and Techniques* assume that you know how to use base SAS software at your site. In addition, specific papers assume knowledge of various other areas, such as statistics.

This book is available to SAS software users as a service from SAS Institute. SAS Institute does not assume responsibility for the accuracy of any material presented in this book.

For a listing of other books that provide information about base SAS software and related topics, refer to "Additional Documentation," later in this section.

Conventions

The papers in *SAS Macro Facility Tips and Techniques* appear as they did in the SUGI *Proceedings.* There is no standard set of typographical or programming conventions.

Additional Documentation

SAS Institute provides many publications about software products of the SAS System and how to use them on specific hosts. For a complete list of SAS publications, refer to the current *Publications Catalog.* The catalog is produced twice a year. You can order a free copy of the catalog by writing, calling, or faxing the Institute:

SAS Institute Inc.
Book Sales Department
SAS Campus Drive
Cary, NC 27513
Telephone: 919-677-8000
Fax: 919-677-8166

In particular, the following titles provide useful reference information.

Base SAS Software

- *SAS Guide to Macro Processing, Version, 6, Second Edition* (order #A56041) provides a complete description of the SAS macro facility in Release 6.06.
- *SAS Language: Reference, Version 6, First Edition* (order #A56076) provides detailed reference information about the SAS language, the SAS Display Manager System, and the SAS Text Editor in Release 6.06.
- *SAS Procedures Guide, Version 6, Third Edition* (order #A56080) provides detailed reference information about the procedures in base SAS software in Release 6.06.
- *SAS Technical Report P-222, Changes and Enhancements to Base SAS Software, Release 6.07* (order #A59139) documents portable changes and enhancements to base SAS software from Release 6.06 to Release 6.07 of the SAS System.
- *SAS Technical Report P-242, SAS Software: Changes and Enhancements, Release 6.08* (order #A59159) documents changes and enhancements to the SAS System from Release 6.07 to Release 6.08.
- *SAS Technical Report P-252, SAS Software: Changes and Enhancements, Release 6.09* (order #A56169) documents changes and enhancements to the SAS System from Release 6.08 to Release 6.09.

Other Useful Reference Titles

- The *SAS Companion* for your operating system provides information about system specific features of the SAS System.
- *Syntax Guides* for many SAS products provide quick and complete references to the syntax for a particular product. (They document syntax for portable features, not for system-specific features.)
- *Master Index to SAS System Documentation, Version 6, Fourth Edition* (order #A56004) provides one comprehensive index of key terms that originally appeared in the indexes of SAS software documentation. This edition covers Release 6.06 and Release 6.07 documentation.

Chapter 1 Introducing the Macro Facility

An Introduction to the SAS Macro Language 3

Beginner

Tasks — Introduces the macro facility as a dynamic, generalized code generator.

Tools —
%DO, Iterative
%EVAL
%IF-%THEN / %ELSE
%LET
&& resolution
CALL SYMPUT
Macro debugging options
Macro parameters
Macro quoting
SYSPARM= system option / SYSPARM automatic macro variable
Simple substitution

The SAS Macro: An Aid to the User 10

Beginner

Tasks — Illustrates and explains macro programming basics.

Tools —
%DO, Iterative
%IF-%THEN / %ELSE
%INCLUDE
%LET
&& resolution
Autocall facility
CALL SYMPUT
Macro parameters
SYMGET
Simple substitution

SAS Macros - What's Really Happening? 17

Beginner

Tasks — Describes various components of the macro facility.

Tools —
Autocall facility
Command style macros
Macro debugging options
Macro quoting
Stored Compiled Macro Facility
Symbol tables / Referencing environments

The Mighty Macro versus the Lowly Link 22

Beginner

Tasks — Illustrates situations in which using ordinary code is more efficient than using the macro facility.

Tools — Simple substitution

Macros - A Few Uses to Get You Started 28

Beginner

Tasks — Demonstrates some simple macro programming to help new macro users get started.

Tools — %IF-%THEN / %ELSE
%LET
Macro parameters
SYMGET
Simple substitution

Make a Date with the SAS System 35

Beginner

Tasks — Demonstrates how to put user-formatted date values in titles.

Tools — CALL SYMPUT
Simple substitution

Building Macro-based Systems 37

Beginner

Tasks — Introduces users to the macro facility and suggests conventions for developing and organizing macro programs.

Tools — %IF-%THEN / %ELSE
%LENGTH
%LET
%SUBSTR
Autocall facility / SASAUTOS= / MAUTOSOURCE
CALL SYMPUT
Macro parameters
Simple substitution
Style suggestions
Symbol tables / Referencing environments

AN INTRODUCTION TO THE SAS® MACRO LANGUAGE

Gary L. Katsanis, Strong Memorial Hospital

This is an introduction to SAS macros, geared to the new macro programmer who may or may not be fluent in use of the SAS System. It will present general information and specific techniques for the novice to begin using macros in SAS applications. The following topics will be covered:

- a general introduction to the macro system and why it is useful;
- macros and macro variables: their similarities and differences, and when one or the other should be used;
- an introduction to macro expressions and functions;
- tips and techniques for using macros.

In each topic, real-world examples will be pro-vided to illustrate how SAS macros may be used to deal with difficult or awkward programming situations.

Introduction

In the language of the SAS Guide to Macro Processing, Version 6, Second Edition, the macro facility is "a tool for extending and customizing the SAS System and for reducing the amount of text you must enter to do common tasks." This is perfectly true, but it is so general that those who are not familiar with macro processing may not understand how macros can help them. This paper will provide an introduction to macro processing based on uses and real-world applications with the goal of demonstrating how macros can help you to produce better, more efficient, and more effective applications.

The macro facility can be thought of as a programming system. You are all familiar with the DATA Step: a tool for manipulating data files. In an analagous way, the macro facility is a tool for manipulating something: SAS source statements. The macro facility provides you with a flexible and powerful programming language for manipulating the text of your SAS programs - your SAS source statements. The macro facility allows you to work with two new objects: macro variables (identified by the ampersand &) and macros (identified by the percent sign %).

Macro Variables

A macro variable is a very simple thing. It is a string of text identified by a name. You create a macro variable by using a command and you use it by typing its name where you want the string of text to appear. The same macro variable can be used over and over again once it is defined.

For example, lets say you have a master file called MASTER containing information on clients that is updated periodically and that you keep a copy of the data prior to the last update in a file called OLDMSTR. You may want to run a report program against either the new file or the old file. You might approach this by creating a macro variable called *dset* and coding the following statement:

```
%let dset = MASTER ;
```

Now, you can refer to the macro variable in your code, instead of using the actual data set name; that is, you can code:

```
PROC PRINT DATA = &dset ;
```

The macro processor will substitute MASTER for *&dset* before it runs the source statement, so your program will behave as if you coded:

```
PROC PRINT DATA = MASTER ;
```

At this point, we don't have any significant savings. As a matter of fact, its taken MORE statements to perform a simple PROC PRINT. The efficiency of using macros in this sense is that you can use the macro variable *&dset* in many places, and you can change your source code in ALL of those places by changing the value of *&dset* in one place; see Figure 1. This is a very common use of macro variables by themselves: writing an extensive program and then customizing it for use on various data files by use of macro variables. Macro variables can be very long and are limited only by memory considerations. For a general discussion of these techniques, see Septoff, 88.

above. One way you could do this is as follows:

```
%macro dset ;
     MASTER
%mend ;
```

Figure 1 - Macro Variable Substitution

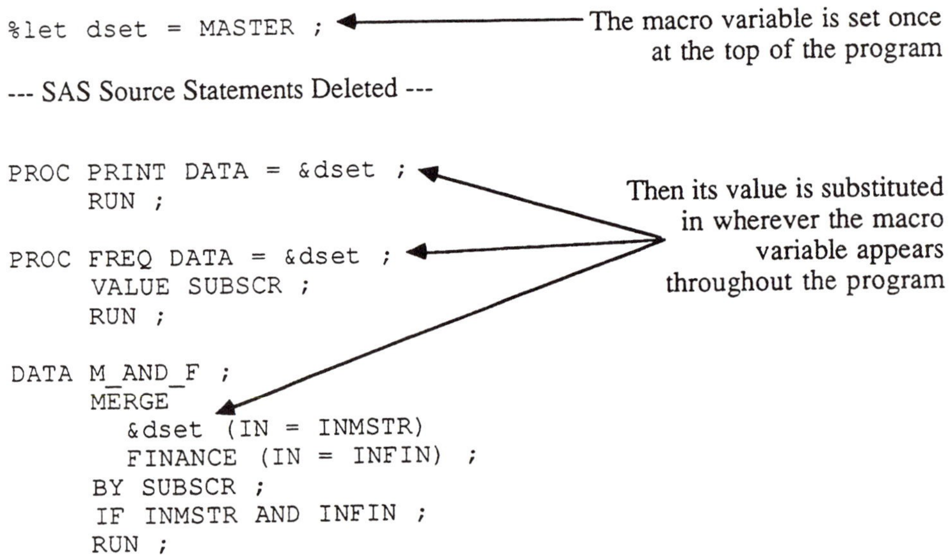

%let dset = MASTER ;
The macro variable is set once at the top of the program
--- SAS Source Statements Deleted ---
PROC PRINT DATA = &dset ;
RUN ;
Then its value is substituted in wherever the macro variable appears throughout the program
PROC FREQ DATA = &dset ;
VALUE SUBSCR ;
RUN ;
DATA M_AND_F ;
MERGE
&dset (IN = INMSTR)
FINANCE (IN = INFIN) ;
BY SUBSCR ;
IF INMSTR AND INFIN ;
RUN ;

Macros

A macro is a more complicated object than a macro variable. Like a macro variable, the end result of a macro is text that is included as a part of your SAS program, but unlike a macro variable, macros include executable statements that can manipulate information and perform logical control. Macros and executable statements that are a part of the macro processing language are all identified by the percent character %. The *%let* statement mentioned above is actually an executable macro statement that can appear any place in a SAS program, not just in a macro.

Defining and Calling Macros

You define a macro by coding *%macro* as the first statement and *%mend* as the last statement. You give the macro a name on the first statement, and call it later by using that name. For example, you could define a macro called *%dset* that does the same thing as the *&dset* variable mentioned

A statement using this macro to identify the file for a PROC PRINT could be:

```
PROC PRINT DATA = %dset ;
```

and the result would be the same as the previous example. You can add flexibility to this by defining macro parameters. Macro parameters are simply macro variables that are available within the macro and nowhere else. For instance, you could define *%dset* as follows:

```
%macro dset(file) ;
  &file
%mend ;
```

In this example, "file" on the command line is a macro parameter: a variable that exists inside the macro only and is deleted when the macro ends. To run this macro, you would code:

```
PROC PRINT DATA = %dset(MASTER);
```

The macro processor would call up the *%dset*

macro, define the *&file* parameter within it, and substitute the value MASTER. In this case, the *&dset* macro variable and the *%dset* macro give identical values when you use them. Moreover, the second example is much longer to type in than just typing "MASTER". Given this, you may ask why you should use macros rather than just macro variables.

Functions and Other Macro Statements

One thing that you can do in a macro that you cannot do with a macro variable is to perform character manipulation and calculation. For instance, titles are often centered on a page; while a TITLE statement will center text, a PUT statement will not. You can get around this by creating a macro. For example:

```
%macro center(text) ;
  %let space =
       %eval(132-%length(text));
  %let indent = %eval(&space/2);
  @&indent "&text"
%mend ;
```

This example does several things. First of all, the *%macro* statement creates a temporary macro variable called *&text* ; next it calculates values for *&space* using the *%eval* function (which treats its arguments as numbers - unless you use *%eval* , the macro processor will treat all information as character data). Finally, it calculates *&indent* and then uses *&indent* and *&text* to place the parameter in the center of a page using PUT statement syntax. If you called this by coding:

```
PUT %center(This is a Title) ;
```

the result would be:

```
PUT @58 "This is a Title" ;
```

which would be centered on a 132-column page. You could generalize this by using a second parameter for the page width as well.

Macro Processing

Macro processing is fairly involved; good references exist in the SAS Guide, and in such places as Hendren (89). Some aspects should receive special notice, though.

- Macro processing is triggered by the characters *&* and *%* .

- When a *&* is encountered, the macro processor will search its macro variable tables for the value of the variable in the string immediately following. That value is substituted for the reference to the macro variable.

- When a *%* is encountered, the macro processor will interpret the following characters as a macro you defined or as a macro function like *%let* or *%eval* . Don't name your macros with the same name as a macro function!! When a reference to a macro is found, the macro will be run and the result will be inserted in place of the reference. When a macro function is called, the function will be executed, and the result (if any) substituted for the original reference.

- After the macro processor has interpreted the value of a macro variable, a macro, or a macro function, the result will be scanned again until no more references with *&* or *%* exist. The final result is treated as if it were a part of your original SAS program.

Some macros and macro functions may leave code to be executed by the SAS compiler, others like *%let* leave nothing to be executed but rather perform some utility function. The only line in the *%center* macro that leaves anything for the SAS compiler is the fourth line, which uses *&indent* and *&text* to place the title you specified in the center of a page. For a detailed discussion , please refer to the references mentioned above.

Other Concepts

Two other major concepts in macro processing are use of the *%if* statement and the *%do* statement. These are often used together. The *%if* statement requires a condition and an action. If the condition is true, the action will be processed as macro code, otherwise the action will be skipped. An *%else* statement exists as well.

For example, you might create the following macro:

```
%macro varlist(oldnew) ;
  %if %upcase(&oldnew) = MASTER
      %then VAR1 - VAR3 ;
  %else OLDVAR1 - OLDVAR3 ;
%mend ;
```

Now, *%varlist(MASTER)* would resolve to "VAR1 - VAR3" and *%varlist* with any value other than *MASTER* would resolve to "OLDVAR1 - OLDVAR3".

Now, if you coded *%printn(MASTER)* , the macro would resolve to:

```
PROC PRINT DATA=MASTER ;
  VAR VAR1 - VAR3 ;
```

Note the reference to another macro, *%varlist* . When the macro processor reaches references like *%varlist* , it will put the first macro on hold, process the new macro in its entirety, and use the result as part of the original macro.

Figure 2 - Macro to List All Members in a Library

```
PROC CONTENTS DATA = INLIB._ALL_ OUT = MEMLIST ;        creates a file with the
  RUN ;                                                 names of all members
                                                        in the library "INLIB"

DATA _NULL_ ;
  LENGTH MVNAME $8 ;

  SET MEMLIST(KEEP=MEMNAME) END = LASTONE ;             pulls in the member list
  BY MEMNAME ;

  IF LAST.MEMNAME THEN DO ;
    I + 1 ;
    MVNAME =                                            MVNAME will be "ds1" for
      "ds" || LEFT(PUT(I),2.)) ;                        the first value of MEMNAME,
                                                        "ds2" for the second, etc.

    CALL SYMPUT(MVNAME,MEMNAME) ;                       saves the value of MEMNAME in macro
                                                        variable named by value of MVNAME
  END ;

  IF LASTONE THEN CALL SYMPUT("numds",_N_) ;            saves number of members
                                                        into macro variable &numds
  RUN ;

%macro memlist ;
  %do i = 1 to &numds ;                                 executes loop once for each member
    &&ds&i                                              value of &ds1 is the name of the first member,
  %end ;                                                value of &ds2 is the name of the second,
%mend ;                                                 and so forth
```

The *%do* statement is coupled with an *%end* statement, and when you use them in a macro, all lines between the two statements are treated as a unit. For example, you might code:

```
%macro printn(oldnew) ;
  %if &oldnew = MASTER %then %do;
      PROC PRINT DATA = &oldnew ;
          VAR %varlist(&oldnew) ;
  %end ;
%mend ;
```

Summary and Another Example

At this point, we've seen some information about macro variables, macros, and macro functions, as well as their uses and utility in some sections. These techniques can be used as a significant time saver during program development, can minimize the effort to support an application, and can provide a level of flexibility and control that is not available elsewhere in the SAS System.

Creating a List of All Files in a SAS Library

An illustration can be found in the following application. In this application, data sets are created interactively and saved in a permanent SAS Library called INLIB. On occasion, the data sets have to be concatenated through a SET statement, requiring a list of the files. For example, if there were 3 files called DATA1, DS2, and RECORD, we would need the SET statement: "SET DATA1 DS2 RECORD;".

To deal with this, we developed an application and a macro that ran PROC CONTENTS and saved the result in a SAS data set. A DATA step read the result, saving the member names in a series of macro variables. A macro, %memlist, was used to insert the macro variables into our SAS program. The program and macro are presented in Figure 2 on the previous page.

Note that this macro uses some techniques that we have not seen yet. In the DATA Step, you see a CALL SYMPUT statement. This statement creates a macro variable or sets the value of a macro variable based on the value of a variable in the SAS data set. You can find more about SYMPUT and SYMGET (which loads the value of a macro variable into a SAS data set variable) in Chapter 6 of the SAS Guide.

You also see an example of an iterative *%do* loop. In this case, we want to repeat a statement several times, as determined by the value of the macro variable *%numds* . As in the similar DATA Step statement, the counter (*%i*) is initialized to 1, then incremented automatically; and all statements between the *%do* and the *%end* statement are executed until the counter reaches the value *%numds* .

You also see an example of building the name of a macro variable by use of the values of another macro variable. Consider the string *&&ds&i* . A rule of macro processing states that two ampersands *&&* will always resolve to a single ampersand, *&* . When *&&ds&i* is seen in the first pass through the *%do* loop, *&i* will be 1. The two leading ampersands will resolve to a single ampersand; *ds* (which is not a macro variable) will be untouched, and *%i* will resolve to 1. The result is *&ds1* which itself is a macro variable. The macro processor will recognise this and resolve *&ds1* again, substituting its value, DATA1; see Figure 3.

Figure 3 - Resolution of %memlist Macro

The following macro variables exist in the macro variable table.

Macro Variable	Value
&ds1	DATA1
&ds2	DS2
&ds3	RECORD
&numds	3

&&ds&i is resolved inside the macro loop in two passes by the macro processor:

Value of %i	Value of &&ds&i after 1st pass	Value of &&ds&i after 2nd pass
1	&ds1	DATA1
2	&ds2	DS2
3	&ds3	RECORD

Each time the macro loop runs, the fully-resolved value of &&ds&i is left as a result, so %memlist will resolve to "DATA1 DS2 RECORD"

Some Other Issues

Semicolons present a problem in assigning macro variables: since a semicolon is treated as the end of a macro function line, you cannot just imbed a semicolon in the middle of a string you would like to define as a macro variable.

A way to deal with this situation is to use the quoting functions. These are documented in Chapter 10 of the SAS Guide; all quoting functions share a common attribute: they treat special characters like *&* , *%* and *;* as if they had no special meaning, or they restore the special meaning to those characters. For example, you might want to assign a macro variable to several lines of SAS code. The statement:

```
%let printn = PROC PRINT DATA =
  &dset;  VAR NAME VAR1-VAR3; ;
```

would create an error, since the semicolon after *&dset* would be considered as the end of the *%let* statement. The right way to do this is to code:

```
%let printn =
  %str(PROC PRINT DATA=&dset;
    VAR NAME VAR1 - VAR3;);
```

The *%str* function removes the special significance of the semicolons and the entire line, including semicolons, is stored in the variable called *&printn.*

There are a series of automatic macro variables that are created for your use. These are documented at the end of Chapter 2 in the SAS Guide. The automatic variables provide information about things like the date, time, environment (interactive or not), status after the most recent command, and so forth. One variable, &SYSPARM, can have its value set outside of SAS processing in an OPTIONS statement; useful for tailoring a noninteractive or batch program.

Several SAS options can be used with the macro facility (beyond SYSPARM mentioned above). The MACRO option turns macro processing on and off; make sure you specify "MACRO" before you try to use the macro facility! The options MPRINT (which prints the SAS code ultimately generated by a macro), MTRACE (which prints the macro statements as they execute), and SYMBOLGEN (which prints the resolved values of macro variables) are the Version 6 options for macro diagnostics. These are documented in the System Options section of the SAS Language Reference, Version 6, First Edition and also in Appendix 1 of the SAS Guide.to Macro Processing Version 6, Second Edition. See Figure 4 for the effect of these options on your macro execution. Note that messages in the log will be

Figure 4: SAS Log With and Without Macro Information Options

```
10          DATA _NULL_ ;
11             PUT %center(This is a Title) ;
12             STOP ;
13             RUN ;

                                               This is a Title
NOTE: The DATA statement used 0.03 CPU seconds and 3122K.

33          OPTIONS MPRINT SYMBOLGEN MLOGIC ;
34          DATA _NULL_ ;
35             PUT
MLOGIC(CENTER):  Beginning execution.
36                %center(This is a Title) ;
MLOGIC(CENTER):  Parameter TEXT has value This is a Title
MLOGIC(CENTER):  %LET (variable name is SPACE)
SYMBOLGEN:  Macro variable TEXT resolves to This is a Title
MLOGIC(CENTER):  %LET (variable name is INDENT)
SYMBOLGEN:  Macro variable SPACE resolves to 117
SYMBOLGEN:  Macro variable INDENT resolves to 58
SYMBOLGEN:  Macro variable TEXT resolves to This is a Title
MPRINT(CENTER):   @58 "This is a Title"
MLOGIC(CENTER):  Ending execution.
37             STOP ;
38             RUN ;
                                               This is a Title
NOTE: The DATA statement used 0.02 CPU seconds and 3122K.
```

marked on the left with the option that caused them to be generated.

Be careful about timing in macro applications. For example, a DATA Step is compiled before it executes. Macro variables created by SYMPUT are not available until after the DATA Step is executed, so you cannot use macro variables created in a DATA Step in the same DATA Step. Other timing issues exist as well; see Hendren (89) and Chapters 8 and 9 of the SAS Guide.

Bibliography

Note: this covers only a few of the many articles written about macros and presented in NESUG and SUGI over the years. I have limited this to references written in the last three years and referred to above or found to be particularly useful.

I would like to thank the management of the Office of Clinical Practice Evaluation for their unstinting support, and the staff, especially Daniel Gronell and Keith Skelton, for many valuable suggestions. An earlier version of this paper was presented at the NESUG '90 conference. I would like to thank those whose feedback (both positive and negative) have led to improvements in this version.

Jodie Gilmore and Linda Helwig, "Debugging Your SAS Macro Application Under VMS: A Practical Approach," *Proceedings of the 15th Annual SAS Users Group International Conference* , Cary, NC: SAS Institute, Inc. 1990, pp. 825-831.

Sandra Hendren, "Introduction to the Macro Language," *NorthEast SAS Users Group Proceedings of the Second Annual Conference* Cary, NC: SAS Institute, Inc. 1989, pp. 3-7.

Howard Levine, "Building Macro-based Systems," *Proceedings of the 14th Annual SAS Users Group International Conference* , Cary, NC: SAS Institute, Inc. 1989, pp 96-102.

Cynthia Miller, "Using Macros to Develop a Flexible End User System to Access, Edit, and Produce Reports from Any Permanent SAS Dataset," *Proceedings of the 14th Annual SAS Users Group International Conference* , Cary, NC: SAS Institute, Inc. 1989, pp. 1537-1541.

Maria Nicholson and Bob Pulgino, "The SAS Macro Facility," *Proceedings of the 13th Annual SAS Users Group International Conference* , Cary, NC: SAS Institute, Inc. 1988, pp. 1293-1299.

SAS Institute, Inc., *SAS Guide to Macro Processing, Version 6, Second Edition* , Cary, NC: SAS Institute, Inc., 1990. Referred to herein as "SAS Guide."

SAS Institute, Inc., *SAS Language Reference, Version 6, First Edition* , Cary, NC: SAS Institute, Inc., 1990.

Septoff, David, "Unlimiting a Limited Macro Environment," *Proceedings of the NorthEast SAS Users Group First Regional Conference,* Cary, NC: SAS Institute, Inc., 1988, pp. 125-132.

Earl Westerlund, " Common Misunderstandings About the SAS Macro Facility", *Proceedings of the 13th Annual SAS Users Group International Conference,* Cary, NC: SAS Institute, Inc. 1988, pp. 1288-1292.

H Ian Whitlock, "A Study in Repetition Resulting in a Utility Macro for Substitution," *Proceedings of the 15th Annual SAS Users Group International Conference* , Cary, NC: SAS Institute, Inc. 1990, pp. 25-31.

The SAS® Macro: An Aid to the User

Robert E. Johnson
Department of Mathematical Sciences, Virginia Commonwealth University, Richmond, VA 23284-2014

This paper is presented as a beginning tutorial on the SAS® macro facility. If you write your own code, either simple or complex then you may find the macro facility useful. The purpose here is to show you some of the fundamentals, share some examples, and start you on the path of learning more about the macro facility. It should be understood that this tutorial does not present an exhaustive coverage of macros. Indeed, to fully appreciate and utilize the power of macros, one should have mastered the art of structured programming. But the rest of us can still find useful applications.

Version 5, 5.16 or later, of the SAS® System allows full use of macros under the CMS, OS, VM/PC, and VSE operating systems. You will have limited use under the VMS operating system. Version 6.06 should bring VMS into the fold. The macros presented here were tested on version 5.18, version 6.03 (for the PC), and version 6.06 (beta).

• Applications

Several macro statements and their applications will be presented in this section. The examples are small so to keep them manageable, but you should *think big* - imagine them in larger applications.

The %LET Statement

The **%let** statement is a macro statement which assigns a character string to a macro variable. (This works under VMS.) Notice the "%" symbol. This distinguishes macro statements from the usual code. The **%let** statement has the form

%let *macrovariable = string* ;

The name of the macro variable must conform to the usual naming rules.

Here is an example:

```
* Use a Macro Variable;

%let procopt=          ;
data one;
  input x @@; cards;
  2 4 3 5 7 5 6 3 4 5 6 8 7 9
  proc means &procopt;
```

A macro variable **procopt** receives a null string via a **%let** statement. The macro variable is used by placing it in the code where you want the string to appear. In order to differentiate between regular variables and macro variables, a & symbol is placed before a macro variable. In this example, **procopt** is to contain the desired options for the means procedure.

A macro is resolved by substituting the string for the symbolic representation. For example, the above code is resolved to:

```
data one;
  input x @@; cards;
  2 4 3 5 7 5 6 3 4 5 6 8 7 9
  proc means;
```

RESOLVED

Here is the same example with a non-null string assigned:

```
* Use a Macro Variable;

%let procopt= n mean stderr t;
data one;
  input x @@; cards;
  2 4 3 5 7 5 6 3 4 5 6 8 7 9
  proc means &procopt;
```

```
data one;
  input x @@; cards;
  2 4 3 5 7 5 6 3 4 5 6 8 7 9
  proc means n mean stderr t;
```

RESOLVED

The MACRO Statement

The **macro** statement is used in conjunction with a **mend** statement to create a SAS macro. The form is:

```
%macro name-of-macro;

- SAS statements -

- Macro statements -

%mend name-of-macro;
```

The macro is placed in the code preceded by a % and the is then resolved. Here is an example:

```
* Create a Macro;

%macro means;

        proc means &procopt;

%mend means;
```

In order to use **%means** we must first assign a value to **procopt.** The following application will resolve to code similar to the previous examples:

```
data one;
  input x @@; cards;
  2 4 3 5 7 5 6 3 4 5 6 8 7 9
;

%let procopt=;
%means

%let procopt=n mean stderr t;
%means
```

Note that in the example above we must alter **procopt** with each application. This necessitates several **%let** statements. The next section describes a cleaner way to do this.

MACRO Parameters

Macro parameters provide a way to pass values to macros variables used within the macro. There are two kinds of parameters: positional and keyword. Keyword parameters will be demonstrated later.

Let's revisit one of the earlier examples and add a parameter to it.

```
* Create a Macro(parameters);

%macro means(procopt);

        proc means &procopt;

%mend means;
```

Suppose we invoke the macro with the command

%means(n mean stderr t)

The string ***n mean stderr t*** will be assigned to the macro variable **procopt** and the result will resolve as before. Invoking the command

%means

will replace **procopt** with a null string and **proc means** will display the default statistics.

How much can one parameter do? Consider the following example:

```
data one;
  input x @@; cards;
  2 4 3 5 7 5 6 3 4 5 6 8 7 9
;

data two;
  input y @@; cards;
  51 43 56 65 45 65 67
;

%means(data=one mean t prt)
```

The *desired* result is

proc means data=one mean t prt;

But you would see an error here:

keyword parameter DATA was not defined with the macro

Keyword parameters are those which start with the name of the macro variable followed by a = symbol and optionally followed by an initial value. The general form is

```
MACRO Parameters

%macro name-of-macro(positional...,
                     keyword=value);

- SAS Statements -

- Macro Statements -

%mend name-of-macro;
```

Positional parameters, if any, must appear first in the parameter list. Positional parameters receive their values in the order (position) in which they are specified in the macro invocation. Keyword parameters may appear in any order after positional parameters. Parameters are separated by commas.

Going back to our working example, here is an illustration of a positional and a keyword parameter used together:

```
* Create a Macro (parameters);

%macro means(procopt, dsn=_last_);

  proc means &procopt data=&dsn;

%mend means;
```

The parameter **dsn** will be equal to _**last**_, the symbolic name for the last SAS data set created, unless a different value is passed to it. The command

```
%means(mean t prt, dsn=one)
```

will yield

```
proc means mean t prt data=one;
```

and the command

```
%means(n mean var)
```

will yield

```
proc means n mean var data=_last_;
```

The last procedure will operate on the data set **two** since it was the last SAS data set created.

Using Macros in TITLE Statements

It is possible to customize title statements by placing macro variables within the text of the title. For a macro to be resolved within a quoted text, the double quotes (") must be used. Here is an example:

```
%macro means(procopt, dsn=_last_);

     proc means &procopt data=&dsn;

     title "Statistics for Dataset &dsn";

%mend means;
```

If the command

```
%means(mean t prt, data=one)
```

is submitted, the result will be

```
proc means mean t prt data=one;

title "Statistics for Dataset one";
```

RESOLVED

and the output will be similar to

```
  Statistics for Dataset one

Analysis Variable : X
N Obs     Mean        T   Prob>|T|
------------------------------------
   14    5.286     9.81    0.0001
```

If the command

```
%means(n mean var)
```

is submitted, then the result will be

```
proc means n mean var data=_last_;

title "Statistics for Dataset _last_";
```

RESOLVED

and the output will be similar to

```
Statistics for Dataset _last_

 Analysis Variable : Y
 N Obs   N  Mean  Variance
 -------------------------
     7   7  56.0     99.67
```

The parameter **dsn=_last_** may be replaced with **dsn=&syslast**, where **syslast** is an automatic macro variable supplied by SAS whose value is the two-level name of the last created SAS data set. For example, if **syslast** were used in the previous example, then the resolved title would read

Statistics for Dataset WORK.TWO

<u>%IF - %THEN - %ELSE Statement</u>

It is possible to execute macro statements conditionally or generate SAS code conditionally. One mechanism is the **%if-%then-%else** structure. Suppose that in our previous example we would like to use one title for specified data sets and another title for default data sets. Consider this macro:

```
%macro means(procopt,dsn=_last_);

proc means &procopt data=&dsn;
title
%if &dsn^=_last_ %then
"Statistics for Dataset &dsn";
%else
"Statistics for Last Created Dataset";
;
%mend means;
```

If the condition **&dsn^=_last_** is true, then a data set name must have been specified. In this case the title statement revealing the data set name is used. Otherwise, the generic title statement is used. Note again the % which precedes each macro statement. Were this left out, the data step if-then-else would be generated.

We have covered a few of the basic statements in the application section. There will more statements and applications presented in later sections as well.

- **Data Step Variables ↔ Macro Variables**

It is possible to assign values of data step variables to macros and values of macros to data step variables using the **symput** routine and the **symget** function. Both of these functions are available in the VMS operating system.

<u>SYMPUT Routine</u>

Consider the following data which is stored on an external file.

BOB	ANNE	RICHARD
41	30	42
36	45	37
40	38	40

File reference name: DATSET

The **symput** routine takes the value of a data step variable and assigns it to a macro variable. The macro variable can then be used in *subsequent* data or procedure steps. Consider this example.

```
data _null_;
infile datset obs=1;
input n1 $ n2 $ n3 $;
call symput('A',n1);
call symput('B',n2);
call symput('C',n3);

data hours;
infile datset firstobs=2;
input &a &b &c;

proc print data=hours;
var &a &b &c;
```

The three alpha-numeric fields on the first line of the data file are converted to values of the macro variables **A**, **B**, and **C** in the first data step via the

symput routine. In the second data step these macros are used to represent variable names in the input statement. The macros are used again in the procedure step.

SYMGET Function

The **symget** function may be used extract values from a macro variable which may in turn, for example, be assigned to a data step variable. The following example shows the usage.

```
data one; input a b c;
call symput('carry',sum(of a b c));
cards;
100 20 3
;
data two;
  thesum=symget('carry');
```

The summation of the values of variables A, B, and C is assigned to the macro variable **carry** in the first data step. In the second data step, the value of the macro variable is obtained and assigned to the data step variable **thesum**.

• %DO Loops

The macro statement %DO allows another way to conditionally execute macro statements or generate SAS code. The general form is:

```
%do macrovar = value %to value;

- SAS Statements -

- Macro Statements -

%end;
```

In the following example we wish to generate code which will read values from data lines, which follow a **cards** statement, in such a manner that the resulting data set is in a form needed for the **ANOVA** procedure. For instance, these data need to be analyzed.

	Gender 1	Gender 2
Treatment 1	2 3	1 4
2	4 6	4 3

We could write code specifically for this problem, but instead we will construct a macro which will have the flexibility to work with any number of factors, any number of levels for each factor, and any number of observations per cross-classification (same number for each cell - balanced ANOVA). Consider the following macro.

```
%macro anova;
 data tempaova;
%do i=1 %to &count;
 do &&fact&i = 1 to &&limit&i;
%end;
 do i=1 to &n;input y @@;
 output; end;
%do i=1 %to &count;
 end;
%end;
%mend anova;
```

This macro uses several macro variables:

count: The number of factors.
fact1: The name of the first factor.
⋮
fact*i*: The name of the *ith* factor.
limit1: The number of levels of the first factor.
⋮
limit*i*: The number of levels of the *ith* factor.
n: The number of observations in each cross-classification.
i: The index variable for the do loop.

Each of these variables, with the exception of **i**, will require the assignment of values prior to invoking the macro.

The first macro do loop will create as many SAS **do** statements are there values of the macro variable **count.** The second macro do loop will generate the corresponding **end** statements.

Here is how this macro may be used to read the data shown above.

```
%let count=2; %let n=2;
%let fact1=Treat; %let limit1=2;
%let fact2=Gender; %let limit2=2;
 %anova
 cards;
 2 3  1 4
 4 6  4 3
 proc print;
```

What does the **&&** symbol do? Take for example **&&fact&i**. When **&i**=1, **&&fact&i** is first resolved to **&fact1** and is then resolved to **Treat**.

The generated code is:

```
data tempaova;
do Treat= 1 to 2;
do Gender= 1 to 2;
 do i= 1 to 2;
   input y @@;
   output; end;
end;
end;
  cards;
  2 3 1 4
  4 6 4 3
  proc print;
```

RESOLVED

The resulting output is:

OBS	TREAT	GENDER	I	Y
1	1	1	1	2
2	1	1	2	3
3	1	2	1	1
4	1	2	2	4
5	2	1	1	4
6	2	1	2	6
7	2	2	1	4
8	2	2	2	3

• Storing and Calling Macros

For any of the aforementioned operating systems, a macro may be stored in a file and included as needed in the SAS code. A special macro, which you may have used under other circumstances, that brings a file into the SAS code is **%include**. Version 5 usage is

%include *file-reference*;

where the *file-reference* refers to the reference name assigned to the file containing the macro code. If the file is stored as a member of a partitioned file (as one might do with the OS operating system), the usage may be

%include *file-reference*(*membername*);

Version 6 usage may be as above or the actual file name may be used:

%include '*filename*';

The autocall facility is a convenient way to use stored macros. The OS operating system method will be illustrated here. Check your basics guide for the method pertaining to your operating system.

Macros should be stored in a partitioned file. The member name should coincide with the name of the macro stored under that member name. For batch use, add these lines to your JCL:

```
// EXEC SAS,OPTIONS='MAUTOSOURCE'
//SASLIB DD DSN=partitioned.file,DISP=SHR
```

For TSO under Version 5, invoke SAS with this command

SAS AUTOS(*partitioned.file*) +
OPTIONS(MAUTOSOURCE)

Under Version 6, invoke

SAS SASAUTOS(*partitioned.file*) +
OPTIONS(MAUTOSOURCE)

The stored macro is then used by simply placing it in the code. When it is first encountered, it will be compiled and executed. It is then available for further use in the remainder of the program.

• *Procedure-Like* Macros

Macros may be written and stored for later use. These macros may have been designed for small applications, but it is possible to design them with a considerable dose of flexibility for potentially large applications. These *procedure-like* macros can make your customized application programs available to other users without their understanding your code. They need only know how to access the macro and how to pass data and parameter values to it.

In the appendix is an extension of the ANOVA macro we saw earlier. It makes use of many of the statements and structures introduced in this tutorial, but, obviously, it makes use of more advanced aspects of the macro facility as well. You might take it as a challenge to learn about the statements, structures, and functions that appear in the macro.

Submitting the command

%anova(infile=DATIN,Treat 2 Gender 2);

where DATIN is the file reference name for the file containing the data to be analyzed, will yield the following SAS code:

```
data tempaova;
infile DATIN;
do Treat= 1 to 2;
do Gender= 1 to 2;
do until(y=.)'
  input y @;
  if y^=. then output;
  end;
end;
end;
proc anova data=tempaova;
class Treat Gender;
model y=Treat|Gender;
run;
```

RESOLVED

The **anova** macro has the flexibility of allowing any number of factors, any number of levels for a factor, any number of observations for a cross-classification, and external or internal data. Data is entered in a natural way, cell by cell. The observations within a cell are delimited by a ".".

• Summary

We have seen some of the basic uses of the SAS macro facility. In addition, we have seen a more complicated macro that can be added to a library of procedure-like macros. To learn more about how you might take advantage of this facility, consult your *SAS User's Guide: Basics, Version 5 Edition* (SAS Institute, 1985) or *SAS Guide to Macro Processing, Version 5 Edition* (SAS Institute, 1987), or *SAS Guide to Macro Processing, Version 6 Edition* (SAS Institute, 1987).

Appendix

```
%macro anova(infile=CARDS) / pbuff;
  %global count;
  %let count=1;
  %let add=;
  %let fact=%scan(&syspbuff,1);
  %do %while(&fact^=);
    %if %index(%upcase(&fact),INFILE)^=0 %then
      %let add=+1;
    %else %do;
      %global fact&count limit&count;
      %let fact&count =&fact;
      %let limit&count =%scan(&syspbuff,&count *2 &add);
      %let count=%eval(&count+1);
      %end;
    %let fact=%scan(&syspbuff,&count *2-1 &add);
  %end;
    data tempaova;
    infile &infile;
  %do i=1 %to &count;
    do &&fact&i = 1 to &&limit&i;
  %end;
    do until(y=.);
      input y @;
      if y^=. then output;
    end;
  %do i=1 %to &count;
    end;
  %end;
%if &infile=CARDS %then %do;
  %put ****************************************;
  %put Please submit the following statements.;
  %put ****************************************;
  %put %str(        CARDS;);
  %put %str(        -- data lines --);
  %put %str(        ;);
  %put %nrstr(        %anova2);
  %put ****************************************;
  %end;
%else %anova2;
%mend anova;

%macro anova2;
    proc anova data=tempaova;
    class
  %do i=1 %to &count;
    &&fact&i
  %end;
    ;
    model y=
  %do i=1 %to &count;
    %if &i>1 %then |;
    &&fact&i
  %end;
    ;
    run;
%mend anova2;
```

SAS® Macros - What's Really Happening?

Mark Bercov - Bercov Computer Consultants Ltd.

ABSTRACT

The SAS Macro Facility is an extremely powerful tool, which is often not utilized because it is not understood. This Hands-On PC Workshop is designed to build on the knowledge base established in previous introductory Macro Workshops and Courses. Presented in the form of an interactive tutorial, this workshop will delve deeper into the labyrinths of the Macro Processor to help the user understand what is really going on. However, the potential attendee can rest assured that the most innermost Macro secrets will not be revealed.

Some prior experience with SAS Data step programming and Display Manager are assumed. At least 6 months experience with the Macro Facility is highly desirable, and several unresolved Macro problems are absolutely mandatory.

INTRODUCTION

The SAS Macro Facility has now been available for almost 10 years. Unfortunately, the majority of SAS Users have yet to experience the benefits which accrue almost immediately from the utilization of this tool because they do not use it at all. Even more unfortunately, many who have attempted to use SAS Macros have become hopelessly confused by some of its more advanced constructs. In a paper presented at a previous SUGI conference, Kretzman [1] suggests that this is due to "a bewildering set of abstruse quoting functions, multiple ampersand constructions, and a syntax which is just similar enough to regular SAS programming to get you into trouble". Although I could not disagree with the preceding statement, I would suggest that much of the confusion relating to non-trivial aspects of the SAS Macro Facility is also directly related to the complexity and lack of clarity of the documentation presented and with the convoluted examples which are utilized to demonstrate advanced use of the SAS Macro Facility.

The benefits to be derived from the use of the SAS Macro Facility have been well documented in many previous SUGI tutorials and workshops, and need not be dwelt upon further. A basic familiarity with the SAS Macro Facility syntax and capabilities will be assumed. (A suggested reference for those just starting out with the Macro Facility is Tindall and O'Connor [2]). Those of you who are seeking a more complete understanding of the intricacies of input stack processing, the word scanner, the tokenizer, and the open code handler might wish to review Chapters 8 and 9 of the SAS Guide to Macro Processing [3] and O'Conner [4], because none of this information will be presented to confuse you at this workshop. It is the intention of this presentation to provide further insight into a few of the more confusing aspects of the Macro Facility, (hopefully) clarified by simple examples and interactive exercises.

SAS MACRO OPTIONS

Some of the SAS OPTIONS which are directly related to the use of the Macro Facility are described below.

1. MACRO
   Quite simply put, if OPTIONS MACRO is not set, the SAS Macro Facility may not be utilized. This option is normally set by the SAS Installation Representative, but can also be set by the user at SAS invocation {by specifying OPTIONS=(MACRO)}. This option may not be set once you have started your SAS Session.

2. MAUTOSOURCE and SASAUTOS
   If it is desired to utilize the Macro Autocall Facility, OPTIONS MAUTOSOURCE must be set. The SASAUTOS Option, which is of the form
   OPTIONS SASAUTOS = (lib1, lib2, ..., libn)
   allows the specification of the Autocall Library. Each of the lib_i parameters may be either a filename or a data set name. Both of these options may be set during your SAS Session.

   The objective of the Autocall Facility is to enable the automatic "inclusion" of the source code for a Macro Program at the first reference to that Macro Program name during the session. The net effect of the Autocall Facility is almost identical to that which would occur if the user %include'd the corresponding flat file at the first reference to the Macro Program name, but this process is performed automatically by SAS.

   Use of the Autocall Facility involves storing the source code for your SAS Macro Programs in flat files in one or more "aggregate storage locations". An "aggregate storage location" is just a fancy SAS multi-platform name for a computer file structure underneath which files are stored, for example, a partitioned dataset under MVS, a maclib under CMS, a directory or VMS text library under VMS, a library under VSE, and a directory under virtually all directory based systems. If your system supports file extensions, the file extension should be .SAS. The file name must be the same as the name of the Macro Program, with the following (poorly documented) exception. If ISPF is utilized as the text editor on your system, you may replace all _'s in the Macro Program Name with #'s in the file name.

   If the Autocall Facility is active, the first reference to a SAS Macro Program which has not previously been compiled (that is, which is not in Catalog SASMACR in the WORK Library) causes the (possibly concatenated) Autocall Library to be opened and searched for a member file of the same name as the SAS Macro Program. If such a member is found, the file is read in; otherwise an error message is output on the LOG.

Unfortunately, the Autocall Facility allows you the opportunity of copying the following two poor programming practices demonstrated by SAS in their distributed Autocall Libraries:

1. Inclusion of non-Macro code in the flat file, and
2. Inclusion of more than one Macro Program in a single flat file.

Since all of the code in the flat file which is "included" by the Autocall Facility is processed, the techniques above do work. However, the non-Macro code is only executed the very first time that the Macro Program is invoked, and the storage of several Macro Programs in one flat file contributes significantly to maintenance problems (who can remember where Macro M_WHERE is stored?). I would strongly urge you not to put any non-Macro code in any of the Autocall Library Files, and to store each Macro Program in a separate file in this library.

The Autocall Facility does provide the site with the capability of storing Macro Programs in several logical libraries, which might be categorized as SAS Institute Macro Programs, Site Macro Programs, Department Macro Programs, and Personal Macro Programs, and may therefore avoid many arguments relating to file access and security. It has been my experience that the advantages gained by such a structure far outweigh the execution time overhead of opening several libraries to resolve Macro Program references, particularly if statement style Macro Programs (which should be avoided like the plague) are not used.

3. MSTORED and SASMSTORE
   OPTIONS MSTORED must be set in order to utilize the Compiled Stored Macro Facility. The SASMSTORE Option, which is of the form
   OPTIONS SASMSTORE = libref
   allows the specification of the Compiled Stored Macro Library. At the present time, and for the foreseeable future, all compiled stored macro programs are stored as entries in the SASMACR catalog in only one library, that is, concatenation of libraries is not allowed. Both of these options may be set during your SAS Session.

   The objective of the Compiled Stored Macro Facility is the reduction of execution time by allowing previously compiled SAS Macro Programs to be accessed during the Session, thereby avoiding the overhead of compiling these Macro Programs. This technique is primarily applicable in a production environment, where it can yield impressive reductions in CPU time (particularly when large Macro Programs are involved).

   The Compiled Stored Macro Facility allows you to specify (as an option in the %MACRO statement) that the compiled Macro Program is to be stored in the Compiled Stored Macro Library. An example of such a %MACRO statement appears below.

   %MACRO M_MYMAC / STORE DES =
   'Sample Macro Program';

   Obviously, you will have to compile each SAS Macro Program once to cause it to be stored.

   CAUTION: If you decide to utilize the Compiled Stored Macro Facility, you are strongly urged to keep a copy (in a very very safe place) of the source code for each Macro Program stored in the Compiled Stored Macro Library. It is not possible to recreate the source code for the Macro Program from the compiled code. The compiled code is <u>not</u> platform independent, can <u>not</u> be ported from platform to platform, and is likely <u>not</u> to be version independent, that is, it is unlikely to work under SAS Release 7.xx.

   Assuming that all of the appropriate Macro Options have been set, SAS searches for Macro Programs in the following order:

   1. Session compiled Macro Programs,
   2. Compiled stored Macro Programs, and
   3. Autocall Macro Programs.

4. MPRINT, SYMBOLGEN and %PUT, and MLOGIC
   Debugging SAS Macro Programs is a complex and difficult task. The primary problem facing the user is determining whether the bug is in the macro code or the SAS code emitted by the Macro Program. Although none of the techniques are foolproof, the game plan below may prove helpful.

   1. Look at the error message(s) output on the LOG, and simply look at the source code for the Macro Program. It is truly amazing how many errors can be detected and resolved by this manual inspection technique.

   2. If the error message(s) on the LOG appear to be standard SAS messages (as opposed to macro error messages), setting OPTIONS MPRINT may be useful. MPRINT causes all of the SAS code emitted by the Macro Program to be listed on the LOG. Unfortunately, the error message numbers which appeared under SAS Version 5 (and which clearly separated macro errors from other SAS errors) have been eliminated under Version 6, so it is not always evident where the error message originated.

   3. If it appears that the problems are the result of incorrect branching in the Macro Program, it is likely that one or more symbolic macro variables contain a value other than that which was expected. Setting OPTIONS SYMBOLGEN will cause the resolved values of all symbolic macro variables to be output on the LOG. In addition, the judicious use of the %PUT statement to output text strings and/or symbolic macro variable values on the LOG often proves effective.

   4. If all else fails, and the execution of the Macro Program is not as expected, OPTIONS MLOGIC may be appropriate. This option will cause the flow of Macro Program execution, evaluation of parameters, the value of macro conditions being evaluated (%IF), the value of %DO loop counters, and the beginning and end of each Macro Program being executed to be noted on the LOG.

Further details relating to the SAS Options associated with the use of the Macro Facility may be obtained by perusing the SAS Language: Reference [5], the SAS Guide to Macro Processing [3], SAS Technical Report P-222 [6], and O'Connor [7].

ENVIRONMENTS

What is an environment, other than a forest in which the spotted owl lives? With respect to the SAS Macro Facility, an environment is an area of the program in which specific symbolic macro variables are defined or known. The easiest way to think of referencing environments is as a series of boxes, each of which contains one or more smaller boxes. The largest box, which portrays the *global referencing environment*, represents the entire SAS session, and contains symbolic macro variables which are created in open code (that is, outside of any Macro Program), symbolic macro variables created in %GLOBAL statements, all automatic macro variables, and possibly symbolic macro variables created by the DATA Step SYMPUT routine.

Every Macro Program creates its own *local referencing environment* (which is portrayed by an enclosed box). This environment is empty until the Macro Program creates a symbolic macro variable (other than with a %GLOBAL statement). Furthermore, each Macro Program which is invoked from another Macro Program creates a local environment which is contained in the environment of the invoking Macro Program. It is extremely important to understand that the local referencing environment created by any Macro Program (and all of the symbolic macro variables in it) exists only while the Macro Program is executing; when the Macro Program stops executing, the corresponding environment ceases to exist. The environment in which macro activity is currently occurring is the *current referencing environment*.

These concepts may be illustrated by some simple macro code and a related environment diagram [Figure 1].

```
%LET M_OPEN = open code;
%MACRO M_A;
   %LOCAL M_AVAR;
   %LET M_AVAR = local environment for m_a;
   %B
%MEND M_A;
%MACRO M_B;
   %LOCAL M_BVAR;
   %LET M_BVAR = local environment for m_b;
   %C (local environment for m_c)
%MEND M_B;
%MACRO M_C (M_CVAR);
%MEND M_C;
%M_A
```

Now that the concept of macro referencing environments has been introduced, we can begin to consider the relationship between these environments and the manner in which the macro processor creates symbolic macro variables and resolves references to these variables. Symbolic macro variables can be created by any of the following statements:

1. Iterative %DO statement,
2. %GOTO statement,
3. %GLOBAL statement,
4. %INPUT statement,
5. %LET statement,
6. %LOCAL statement,
7. %MACRO statement,
8. %WINDOW statement, or
9. SYMPUT routine (special case).

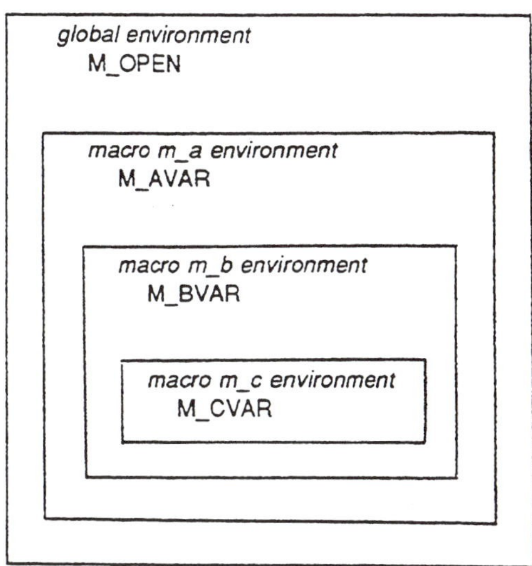

Figure 1: Macro Referencing Environments

The %GLOBAL statement always creates a variable in the global referencing environment. If a variable with the same name already exists in the global environment, the %GLOBAL statement has no effect.

The %LOCAL statement always creates a variable in the local referencing environment of the corresponding Macro Program. If a variable with the same name already exists in the local environment, the %LOCAL statement has no effect.

Parameters specified on the %MACRO statement always create variables in the local referencing environment of the corresponding Macro Program.

The macro processor will go to almost any lengths to avoid creating any new symbolic macro variables. Consequently, all other macro program statements (other than the SYMPUT routine) which can create symbolic macro variables are processed identically. The macro processor first searches the current (local) referencing environment for the existence of a symbolic macro variable of the appropriate name. If the macro processor finds such a variable, it assigns the new value to that variable. If the macro processor fails to find a symbolic macro variable of the appropriate name in the current (local) environment, it searches outward (one environment at a time) for the desired variable. If it finds such a variable, it assigns the new value to that variable. If it fails to find an existing symbolic macro variable of the appropriate name in any environment, it creates a new symbolic macro variable in the current (local) referencing environment, and assigns it the appropriate value.

Although it would be nice if the DATA Step SYMPUT Routine worked the same way, that would be too much to expect. The SYMPUT Routine searches all referencing environments for an existing symbolic macro variable of the appropriate name, and assigns the new value to any variable found just as indicated above. However, if it fails to find an existing symbolic macro variable of the appropriate name in any environment, the SYMPUT Routine does not automatically create such a variable in the current (local) referencing environment. It searches outward, starting from the current environment, looking for a referencing environment which is not empty, and creates the new symbolic macro variable in the first such non-empty environment which it encounters.

Resolution of symbolic macro variables proceeds in a manner which is analogous to that utilized for the creation of these variables. The macro processor first searches the current (local) referencing environment for the existence of a symbolic macro variable of the appropriate name. If the macro processor finds such a variable, it utilizes the contents of that variable to resolve the symbolic macro variable reference. If the macro processor fails to find a symbolic macro variable of the appropriate name in the current environment, it searches outward (one environment at a time) for the desired variable. If it finds such a variable, it utilizes the contents of that variable. If it fails to find a symbolic macro variable of the appropriate name after it has searched the global referencing environment, it outputs a message indicating that an unresolved symbolic macro variable has been detected (if OPTIONS SERROR is set).

MACRO QUOTING

The Macro Quoting Functions are the single area of the macro processor which cause the most user confusion and frustration. This is somewhat surprising, because the purpose of the quoting functions is quite similar to that of the single quote (') in standard SAS code.

The primary objective of the macro quoting functions is to hide something (normally containing one or more special characters or relational operators) from the macro processor.

There are basically only three situations which require the use of a macro quoting function.

1. It is desired to include one of the special characters quote ('), double quote ("), left parenthesis ((), right parenthesis ()), percent sign (%), blank ( ), or semi-colon (;) in a symbolic macro value which appears on the right hand side of a %LET statement.
2. It is desired to prevent one of the special characters, such as plus (+), (-), (*), from being treated as a numeric operator, or to prevent one of the special character strings, such as GT, LT, AND, NOT, <, from being treated as a relational condition by the nefarious %EVAL function.
   NOTE: Even though you may have not explicitly specified the use of the %EVAL function in your macro code, this function will be invoked automatically by the macro processor for the evaluation of *expression* in the constructs noted below.
   (a) %DO macro-variable = *expression* %TO *expression* <%BY *expression*>;
   (b) %DO %UNTIL(*expression*);
   (c) %DO %WHILE(*expression*);
   (d) %IF *expression* ...;
   (e) %QSCAN(argument,*expression*,<delimiter>)
   (f) %QSUBSTR(argument,*expression*,<*expression*>)
   (g) %SCAN(argument,*expression*,<delimiter>)
   (h) %SUBSTR(argument,*expression*,<*expression*>).
3. In addition to the conditions described in item 2 above, it is also desired to prevent the special characters & and % from causing symbolic macro variable resolution or Macro Program execution, respectively.

In general terms, the appropriate technique to address each of these situations is indicated below.

1. Use a compile time quoting function (either %STR or %NRSTR). If the value to be quoted contains a percent sign (%), or an unmatched single quote ('), double quote ("), left parenthesis ((), or right parenthesis ()), remember to precede each of these characters with an extra percent sign (%). The %NRSTR function is almost identical to the %STR function, but also quotes (prevents resolution of) & and %, and is therefore similar to the use of the single quotation mark in standard SAS code.
2. Use an execution time quoting function (either %BQUOTE or %NRBQUOTE). It should be noted that %NRBQUOTE quotes the result of resolving a symbolic macro variable reference or executing a Macro Program. Consequently, any & and/or % references in the value of the argument provided to this function will be resolved before the result is quoted.
3. Use the execution time quoting function %SUPERQ. This function quotes the value of the symbolic macro variable provided as the argument to the function without resolving any & and/or % references in the value of the argument.
   WARNING: The form of the argument to the %SUPERQ function differs from that of the arguments to all of the other quoting functions. The argument to %SUPERQ must be the name of a symbolic macro variable with no leading & (or a macro expression which produces the name of a symbolic macro variable with no leading &).

Two of the macro quoting functions (%STR and %NRSTR) are designed to take effect at Macro Program compilation time; all of the other quoting functions are effective at Macro Program execution time. A good rule of thumb for which of these two classes of quoting functions to use at any given time is "If the value to be quoted does not contain any symbolic macro variable names (&varname) or Macro Program names (%macname), use %STR; otherwise use %BQUOTE, %NRBQUOTE, or %SUPERQ".

The %QUOTE and %NRQUOTE macro quoting functions are now functionally obsolete. Consequently, use of these functions is not recommended.

The %QLOWCASE, %QSCAN, %QSUBSTR, and %QUPCASE macro quoting functions merely quote the result of the %LOWCASE, %SCAN, %SUBSTR, and %UPCASE macro functions, respectively, (utilizing the same rules as described above for the %NRBQUOTE function).

How does the macro processor actually quote the specified strings? Very simply. Under SAS Release 6.xx, it merely appends a single hexadecimal character to the start of the quoted string and another single hexadecimal character to the end of the quoted string. The starting hexadecimal character not only marks the beginning of a quoted string, but also denotes the type of quoting to be applied to the string. The ending hexadecimal character is currently always the same (irrespective of the quoting function used). Furthermore, the exact hexadecimal characters used to mark the start and end of the quoted string differ from platform to platform, and are not documented by the Institute. Consequently, as chronicled in several Usage Notes, it is possible for the user to inadvertently include these marker characters in the string to be quoted (particularly if the SYMPUT routine is used to create the symbolic macro variable). Finally, these marker characters are conceptually stripped off by all of the Macro Functions, so they do not affect comparisons (%EVAL) or string lengths (%LENGTH, %SUBSTR, etc).

All strings which have been quoted by a macro quoting function remain quoted as long as the string is being used by the macro processor, and therefore need not be quoted again.

When the macro processor generates text from a quoted string and passes this text to the SAS System, the marker characters are supposed to be removed automatically. However, due to bugs in some maintenance levels of several current releases of the SAS System on some platforms, the marker characters are not always correctly stripped. If this problem is encountered, the %UNQUOTE function can always be utilized in open code to correctly remove the quoting marker characters. (The %UNQUOTE function can also be used within a Macro Program, but this feature is seldom required).

COMMAND LINE MACRO PROGRAMS

A poorly documented feature of the SAS Macro Facility is the ability to develop a Macro Program which can be invoked on the Command Line of any screen. The Program Editor is the most likely candidate for this feature. Construction of a Command Line Macro Program is identical to the creation of any other Macro Program, as long as it is remembered that the code emitted from such a Macro Program must be processed by the Command Line interpreter, rather than the SAS System. In other words, the code emitted must consist of only valid Command Line commands.

The most useful feature of a Command Line Macro Program is the ability to emit to the Command Line interpreter more characters than could be typed on the Command Line itself (normally a maximum of 78 characters).

A Command Line Macro Program can be invoked in the normal manner by typing %macname on the desired Command Line. Alternatively, OPTIONS CMDMAC can be set, the Macro Program can be written with the CMD option specified, and the Macro Program can then be invoked by typing macname on the appropriate Command Line. However, if the latter approach is taken, the SAS session will incur (possibly non-trivial) additional CPU and I/O overhead to determine whether or not each word typed on any Command Line is in fact a valid Command Line Macro Program.

CONCLUSION

The SAS Macro Facility is indeed a powerful and robust tool. Not only does it allow the novice to utilize many of its capabilities, but it also contains many advanced features which can be used by the more sophisticated programmer. Hopefully, the information presented in this workshop will help explain some additional aspects of the macro processor, thereby enabling the attendees to make a more productive use of the capabilities of this tool.

REFERENCES

[1] Kretzman, P. (1992), "Ifs, Ands, and Buts: A Case Study in Advanced Macro Implementation", *Proceedings of the Seventeenth Annual SAS Users Group International Conference,* Cary, NC: SAS Institute Inc., pp. 176-182.

[2] Tindall, B. and O'Connor, S. (1991), "Macro Tricks to Astound the Folks on Thursday Morning: Ten Immediately Useful Macro Techniques", *Proceedings of the Sixteenth Annual SAS Users Group International Conference,* Cary, NC: SAS Institute Inc., pp. 189-195.

[3] SAS Institute Inc. (1990), *SAS Guide to Macro Processing, Version 6, Second Edition,* Cary, NC: SAS Institute Inc.

[4] O'Connor, S. (1991), "A Roadmap to Macro Facility Error Messages and Debugging", *Proceedings of the Sixteenth Annual SAS Users Group International Conference,* Cary, NC: SAS Institute Inc., pp. 215-222.

[5] SAS Institute Inc. (1990), *SAS Language: Reference Version 6 First Edition,* Cary, NC: SAS Institute Inc.

[6] SAS Institute Inc. (1991), *SAS Technical Report P-222, Changes and Enhancements to Base SAS Software,* Cary, NC: SAS Institute Inc.

[7] O'Connor, S. (1992), "Macros Invocation Hierarchy: Session-Compiled, Autocall, and Compiled-Stored Macros", *Proceedings of the Seventeenth Annual SAS Users Group International Conference,* Cary, NC: SAS Institute Inc., pp. 19-23.

Author Contact:

Mark Bercov
Bercov Computer Consultants Ltd.
3641 - 13 St. S. W.
Calgary, Alberta, Canada
T2T 3R2
(403) 243 - 0686

The Mighty Macro versus the Lowly Link

Barbara M. Ison and Dania P. Ferguson
National Agricultural Statistics Service
U. S. Department of Agriculture

ABSTRACT

With the advent of macros and the resulting publicity and interest in their use, the power and efficiency of the LINK may easily be overlooked for many appropriate applications. Efficiency needs to be a concern to us all, particularly those of us using mainframe time-sharing environments. The CPU/cost savings potential of techniques such as those described below are substantial, especially when developing SAS* systems to be used repetitively in a production mode. The efficiencies we found under MVS hold true for other operating systems running SAS.

This paper will describe when LINKs can, and probably should, be used instead of macros. We will present our real-life experiences as examples to demonstrate the power, similarities and differences in these two approaches as well as the relative efficiencies.

INTRODUCTION

Our continuous challenge is to develop flexible SAS systems, tailored to individual applications by screen-oriented expert user interfaces (we use SAS/AF* and SAS/FSP*). These systems must produce consistently accurate results within tight time frames and budget constraints. In order to meet these requirements, we rely heavily on the power of the SAS macro language, but have learned it pays to spend time analyzing and testing relative efficiencies of different coding techniques.

A CASE STUDY

A new procedure needed to be developed for analyzing selected survey data for outlier detection. Outliers are data values outside logical or normal limits (e.g. Hired Farm Worker Age < 12 or > 70). Records with especially high and/or low expanded values were to be printed with additional items for reference; and charts were to be produced showing the expanded and/or unexpanded variable value for all observations. Expanded data are data weighted by the sampling rate (number of units a sample represents). Our data covers the U.S. with differing sets of variables needing to be analyzed for each state. These variables often change from survey to survey.

Typically, we have 75 to 100 different variables to analyze for a single survey. A separate table was needed for each analysis variable. Each table had to have appropriate title information, supporting variables, tailored print formats and variable labels. The survey statisticians also wanted to designate for which states each different analysis table would be generated.

This seemed to be a natural for our generalized application approach, driven by parameters from which we generate tailored code (refer to our SUGI 16 paper)[1] Creating macros immediately came to mind and we generated code accordingly.

The examples presented here are simplified versions of the real thing but demonstrate the concepts and techniques used.

The macro approach:

First we designed FSEDIT procedure screens for the survey statisticians to use in defining analysis variables and all the accompanying information desired, including selecting the states for each table. Figure 1 shows a pair of FSEDIT screens used to define a table. The information entered on these two screens becomes one observation in the resulting parameter dataset. These observations are then read by a SAS program which creates the actual SAS statements shown in Figures 2, 3, 5 and 6. The two sets of SAS code were generated from one pass through the parameter SAS dataset.

Figure 2 shows the macro code generated to prepare the actual data for input into the outlier print and plot routines. Figure 3 shows the generated code to selectively invoke the macros. Figure 4 is the "base" SAS code designed to bring in and use the generated code.

What happened next

When we executed tests using the code in figures 2 through 4, the cost appeared to be extremely high -- 80 SRUs in this example to run through one state's data. SRUs are System Resource Units, the measure of cost by which we are charged for processing.

Analysis of the generated code

In looking at the actual SAS code generated for execution, we very quickly realized that, because the macro code was physically duplicated each time it was referenced, the executable code became VERY LONG! After exploring possible alternatives, we decided to try generating LINK routines the same way as the macros had been generated, and see if it helped.

The LINK approach

The code generating SAS program was modified to substitute LINKs and RETURNs in place of %MACROs and %MENDs -- See figures 5 and 6. The "base" code was re-ordered to place the LINKs at the end of the data step -- See Figure 7. A comparison of the code in figures 2 and 6 shows that very little has changed.

Results of the LINK approach (Are we having fun yet??)

When the revised code was executed for the same test data, the SRUs dropped from 80 to 30 -- a 62.5 percent saving! We tested both approaches with several sets of parameters and data, and found roughly the same savings. When you consider that this process will be used for all our major surveys (more than one per month) and for all states, the magnitude of savings is impressive. All this without changing the flexibility of the system or the accuracy of the results!

Subsequent elapsed time comparisons on the PC showed even more drastic differences, plus the macro code for this application caused "out-of-memory" problems when we ran more than 5 states!

The finished product

Figure 8 shows two of the output tables created from our case study code. The tables remained identical, only the method and cost changed!

ANALYSIS OF RESULTS

Because the link acts very much like a 2nd or 3rd generation subroutine, and is not physically reproduced in the executable code, the executable SAS code was much shorter. That and the elimination of the macro overhead for those calls resulted in much more efficient SAS code.

OTHER USES AND LIMITATIONS OF LINK

The main limiting factor of LINK is that it must be used within a data step but, as demonstrated in our case study, you can often design your application within this constraint. Keep in mind that LINK routines can be made flexible in many ways, such as setting certain variable values before calling LINK and having your LINK routine vary depending on the value passed to it. Also, macro variables can be used to vary the routine from run to run.

SUMMARY (The Moral Of The Story)

Macros are extremely powerful and versatile but they are not necessarily the best answer to every situation requiring flexibility. Faster, more efficient code can result from taking the time to analyze and test alternatives. The Lowly LINK has many useful places in your SAS code!

References

1. Ison, Barbara M. and Ferguson, Dania P.(1991), Using SAS Software as a Programming Language to Develop Generalized Systems, Proceedings of the Sixteenth Annual SAS Users Group International Conference, SAS Institute Inc., Cary, NC

* SAS, SAS/AF and SAS/FSP are the registered trademarks of SAS Institute Inc., Cary, NC

For further information contact:

Barbara Ison
USDA/SID,User Services Branch
Room 4808, South Building
Washington, D. C. 20250
(202) 720-3362

Dania Ferguson
USDA/SID, System Services Branch
Room 5862, South Building
Washington, D. C. 20250
(202) 720-9248

FIGURE 1. EXAMPLE OF FSEDIT SCREENS FOR PARAMETER INPUT:

```
                     EDIT SAS DATA SET: SASIN.QASINFO                SCREEN
COMMAND ===>                                                         OBS     1

     SETUP FOR CHARTS AND TABLES FOR POTENTIAL OUTLIER PRINTS       TABLE SEQ.
(Use '=n' to move to screen 'n' or use PF11 to shift to screen 2)   NUMBER  22

VARIABLE TO ANALYZE: D2        FORMAT: 10.0       LABEL ** EXPANDED*CHANGE

TITLE1: MINIMUM EXPANDED DIFFERENCE IN ACRES FOR CORN
TITLE2: MARCH VS. DECEMBER
TITLE3: DIFFERENCES THAT EXPAND TO ZERO HAVE BEEN EXCLUDED

   Extra       Print        Labels for extra                ** Use an asterisk
 Variables    Formats         Variables **                     (*) to split each
1. ________  ________  ____________________________________   label into max.
2. ________  ________  ____________________________________   of 3 print lines.
3. CROPLAND  9.0       CURRENT *CROPLAND*  ACRES               analysis variable
4. HCRNXXPL  9.0       DECEMBER*  CORN  *  ACRES               may have only 2
5. CCRNXXPL  9.0        CURRENT*  CORN  *  ACRES               print lines in
6. ED        9.1          ADJ *  EXP * FACTOR                  its label.)
7. ________  ________  ____________________________________

Expansion type: NONE   (NONE, XT, XF, XN, XW, XTC, XFC, XNC, XWC)
This will control minimum expansions using SPS Data Listings expansion macro.

   Additional sort variable for Hi-Lo print: ________
   Plot Character Variable Name: FRAME
   Hi-Lo Type: 1 (1=high 20; 2=10 high/10low; 3=10high/10 low positive) )
```

```
                     EDIT SAS DATA SET: SASIN.QASINFO                SCREEN  2
COMMAND ===>                                                         OBS    21

       (Use '=n' or PF10 for screen 1, PF11 for screen 3)

       Mark all types of analysis to perform for each state
'C' for CHART/HILO       'O' for OUTLIER EDIT       'S' for PRE-SUMMARY

AL(01) C       AK(02) ___     AZ(04) ___     AR(05) C       CA(06) C
CO(08) C       CT(09) C       DE(10) ___     FL(12) ___     GA(13) C
HI(15) ___     ID(16) C       IL(17) C       IN(18) C       IA(19) C
KS(20) C       KY(21) C       LA(22) C       ME(23) C       MD(24) C
MA(25) ___     MI(26) C       MN(27) C       MS(28) C       MO(29) C
MT(30) C       NE(31) C       NV(32) C       NH(33) ___     NJ(34) ___
NM(35) C       NY(36) ___     NC(37) C       ND(38) C       OH(39) C
OK(40) C       OR(41) C       PA(42) C       RI(44) ___     SC(45) C
SD(46) C       TN(47) C       TX(48) C       UT(49) C       VT(50) ___
VA(51) C       WA(53) C       WV(54) ___     WI(55) C       WY(56) ___

  Select criteria for commodity.  Data values of -1 are always excluded.

  Include records with 0 values (Y/N) N
  Include records for which frame(s): B  ('L'=List, 'A'=Area, 'B'=Both)
```

FIGURE 2

EXAMPLE OF GENERATED MACROS (CHMACS):

```
%MACRO CHL1; ** CHART/HILO %FOR CROPLAND ;
IF CROPLAND GT 0 THEN DO;
   IF FRAME = 'AREA' THEN PLOTCODE = 'AREA';
   ELSE PLOTCODE = 'LIST'; SORTVAL = 0;
   SEQ =1 ;VARNAME ='CROPLAND'; EFVALUE = XW ;
  XVAL1 =.; XAVAL1 ='';XVAL2 =HCROPLAN ; XAVAL2 ='';
  XVAL3 =.; XAVAL3 ='';XVAL4 =.; XAVAL4 ='';
  XVAL5 =.; XAVAL5 ='';XVAL6 =.; XAVAL6 ='';
  XVAL7 =.; XAVAL7 ='';
  SYSAHILO = 1 ; UNEXPNVL = CROPLAND ;
  VALUE = CROPLAND * EFVALUE;
  OUTPUT SASOUT.CALC2;
END;
%MEND CHL1;    ** END OF CHL1 ;
```

NOTE: Macros for tables 2 through 21 not shown

```
%MACRO CHL22; ** CHART/HILO %FOR D2 ;
IF D2 GT 0 THEN DO;
   IF FRAME = 'AREA' THEN PLOTCODE = 'AREA';
   ELSE PLOTCODE = 'LIST'; SORTVAL = 0;
   SEQ =22 ;VARNAME ='D2'; EFVALUE = 1;
  XVAL1 =.; XAVAL1 ='';XVAL2 =.; XAVAL2 ='';
  XVAL3 =CROPLAND ; XAVAL3 ='';XVAL4 =HCRNXXPL ;
  XAVAL4 ='';XVAL5 =CCRNXXPL ;
  XAVAL5 ='';XVAL6 =ED ; XAVAL6 ='';
  XVAL7 =.; XAVAL7 ='';
  SYSAHILO = 1 ; UNEXPNVL = D2 ; VALUE = D2 ;
  OUTPUT SASOUT.CALC2;
END;
%MEND CHL22;    ** END OF CHL22;
```

NOTE: Macros for tables 23 through 78 are not shown

FIGURE 3

EXAMPLE OF GENERATED CODE TO USE MACROS FROM FIGURE 2 (CHSELS):

```
LENGTH XAVAL1-XAVAL7 $  1;
SELECT (STATE) ;
WHEN (1) DO;
   %CHL1 ; ** CROPLAND ; %CHL2 ; ** CCRNXXPL ;
   %CHL3 ; ** CSOYXXPL ; %CHL4 ; ** CSRGXXPL ;
   %CHL22 ; ** D2 ; %CHL23 ; ** D3 ;
   %CHL24 ; ** D4 ; %CHL26 ; ** D6 ;
   %CHL74 ; ** L2 ; %CHL75 ; ** L3 ;
   %CHL76 ; ** L4 ; %CHL78 ; ** NHOGTOTL ;
  END;
```

Note: Generated code for states 2 through 55 not shown

```
WHEN (56) DO;
   %CHL1 ; ** CROPLAND ;
   %CHL2 ; ** CCRNXXPL ; %CHL9 ; ** CDEBXXPL ;
   %CHL76 ; ** L4 ; %CHL78 ; ** NHOGTOTL ;
  END;
   OTHERWISE ;
END;
RETURN;
```

FIGURE 4

EXAMPLE OF SAS CODE INCORPORATING FIGURES 2 & 3

```
%* BRING IN GENERATED MACROS;

   %INCLUDE CHMACS;        *** CODE FROM FIGURE 2 ;

RUN;

DATA SASOUT.CALC2(KEEP=&BREAKIDS &HILOEFS VARNAME
                  VALUE SORTVAL SYSAHILO EFVALUE
                  XAVAL1-XAVAL7 SEQ XVAL1-XVAL7
                  UNEXPNVL);
        LENGTH VARNAME $ 8;
        SET IN.SASMSTR;
        IF REPTIN GT 0 AND CRITERR LT 1;

        *** CALL IN MACRO TO CALCULATE EXPANSIONS ON
                DATA VALUES;

        %EXPAND;

        *** BRING IN GENERATED CODE TO CALL MACROS;

        %INCLUDE CHSELS;     *** CODE FROM FIGURE 3 ;
```

FIGURE 5

EXAMPLE OF GENERATED LINK CODE (CHLINKS):

```
CHL1 :; ** CHART/HILO LINK FOR CROPLAND ;
IF CROPLAND GT 0 THEN DO;
   IF FRAME = 'AREA' THEN PLOTCODE = 'AREA';
   ELSE PLOTCODE = 'LIST'; SORTVAL = 0;
   SEQ =1 ;VARNAME ='CROPLAND'; EFVALUE = XW ;
  XVAL1 =.; XAVAL1 ='';XVAL2 =HCROPLAN ; XAVAL2 ='';
  XVAL3 =.; XAVAL3 ='';XVAL4 =.; XAVAL4 ='';
  XVAL5 =.; XAVAL5 ='';XVAL6 =.; XAVAL6 ='';
  XVAL7 =.; XAVAL7 ='';
  SYSAHILO = 1 ; UNEXPNVL = CROPLAND ;
  VALUE = CROPLAND * EFVALUE;
  OUTPUT SASOUT.CALC2;
END;
RETURN;   ** END OF CHL1 ;
```

Note: Link code for tables 2 through 21 not shown

```
CHL22 :; ** CHART/HILO LINK FOR D2 ;
IF D2 GT 0 THEN DO;
   IF FRAME = 'AREA' THEN PLOTCODE = 'AREA';
   ELSE PLOTCODE = 'LIST'; SORTVAL = 0;
   SEQ =22 ;VARNAME ='D2'; EFVALUE = 1;
  XVAL1 =.; XAVAL1 ='';XVAL2 =.; XAVAL2 ='';
  XVAL3 =CROPLAND ; XAVAL3 ='';XVAL4 =HCRNXXPL ;
  XAVAL4 =''; XVAL5 =CCRNXXPL ;
  XAVAL5 ='';XVAL6 =ED ; XAVAL6 ='';
  XVAL7 =.; XAVAL7 ='';
  SYSAHILO = 1 ; UNEXPNVL = D2 ; VALUE = D2 ;
  OUTPUT SASOUT.CALC2;
END;
RETURN;   ** END OF CHL22 ;
```

Note: Link code for tables 23 through 78 not shown

NOTE: As you can see, the code remains very similar to that in Figures 2, 3, and 4. The links must be positioned physically within the data step instead of preceding it as the macros do.

FIGURE 6

EXAMPLE OF GENERATED CODE TO USE LINKS FROM FIGURE 5 (CHSELS):

```
LENGTH XAVAL1-XAVAL7 $  1;
SELECT (STATE) ;
WHEN (1) DO;
   LINK CHL1 ; ** CROPLAND ; LINK CHL2 ; ** CCRNXXPL;
   LINK CHL3 ; ** CSOYXXPL ; LINK CHL4 ; ** CSRGXXPL;
   LINK CHL22 ; ** D2 ; LINK CHL23 ; ** D3 ;
   LINK CHL24 ; ** D4 ; LINK CHL26 ; ** D6 ;
   LINK CHL74 ; ** L2 ; LINK CHL75 ; ** L3 ;
   LINK CHL76 ; ** L4 ; LINK CHL78 ; ** NHOGTOTL ;
  END;
```

Note: Generated code for states 2 through 55 not shown

```
WHEN (56) DO;
   LINK CHL1 ; ** CROPLAND ;
   LINK CHL2 ; ** CCRNXXPL ; LINK CHL9 ; ** CDEBXXPL;
   LINK CHL76 ; ** L4 ; LINK CHL78 ; ** NHOGTOTL ;
  END;
   OTHERWISE ;
END;
RETURN;
```

FIGURE 7

EXAMPLE OF SAS CODE INCORPORATING FIGURES 5 AND 6:

```
DATA SASOUT.CALC2(KEEP=&BREAKIDS &HILOEFS VARNAME
                  VALUE SORTVAL SYSAHILO EFVALUE
                  XAVAL1-SAVAL7 SEQ XVAL1-XVAL7
                  UNEXPNVL);
        LENGTH VARNAME $ 8;
        SET IN.SASMSTR;
        IF REPTIN GT 0 AND CRITERR LT 1;

        *** CALL IN MACRO TO CALCULATE EXPANSIONS ON
            DATA VALUES;

        %EXPAND;

        *** BRING IN GENERATED CODE TO CALL MACROS;

        %INCLUDE CHSELS;    *** CODE FROM FIGURE 7 ;

        RETURN;

        *** BRING IN GENERATED LINKS;

        %INCLUDE CHLINKS;  *** CODE FROM FIGURE 6 ;
```

FIGURE 8

EXAMPLE OF PRINT GENERATED USING LINK OR MACRO CODE

MARCH 1992 AG SURVEY -- POTENTIAL OUTLIER PRINTS
MINIMUM EXPANDED ACRES FOR CROPLAND
REPORTS THAT EXPAND TO ZERO HAVE BEEN EXCLUDED

ATLANTIS (01)

PLOT CODE	STRATA CODE	SEGMENT /LSF ID	EXPN FACT	OL/NOL CODE /LAF	JUNE TRACT ACRES	JUNE FARM ACRES	CURR FARM ACRES	DECEMBER CROPLAND ACRES	CROPLAND ACRES	EXPANDED CROPLAND ACRES
****************************** 20 LARGEST ******************************										
AREA	3103	250	714.3	1.00	25	25	145	0	145	103578
AREA	1304	9004	649.4	1.00	35	35	120	32	115	74677
AREA	2001	9181	1179.8	1.00	98	98	99	30	60	70789
AREA	1312	24	651.1	1.00	138	203	220	140	150	66631
AREA	1303	1027	126.5	1.00	389	490	500	400	470	47249
LIST	70	770294080	19.9	1.00	.	.	3000	.	2000	39859
LIST	70	790532510	19.9	1.00	.	.	1720	.	1645	32784
AREA	3104	1258	714.3	1.00	45	160	160	105	153	31080
AREA	1303	1027	126.5	1.00	30	30	275	250	240	30259
LIST	70	857513440	19.9	1.00	.	.	1600	.	1500	29894
AREA	1301	13	126.5	1.00	201	202	240	180	180	22646
AREA	2012	204	229.8	1.00	139	239	235	125	168	22456
AREA	1302	14	649.4	1.00	50	138	138	75	95	22351
AREA	2008	9188	229.8	1.00	139	163	170	90	110	21559
AREA	2012	204	229.8	1.00	150	160	160	100	100	21547
LIST	70	867674130	19.9	1.00	.	.	1103	.	1072	21365
AREA	2011	9131	229.8	1.00	177	460	450	240	240	21225
LIST	70	770060220	19.9	1.00	.	.	1100	.	900	17937
AREA	3105	9245	714.3	1.00	33	33	34	30	25	17858
AREA	1311	23	649.4	1.00	86	550	280	80	170	17261

MARCH 1992 AG SURVEY -- POTENTIAL OUTLIER PRINTS
MINIMUM EXPANDED DIFFERENCE IN ACRES FOR CORN
MARCH VS. DECEMBER
DIFFERENCES THAT EXPAND TO ZERO HAVE BEEN EXCLUDED

ATLANTIS (01)

PLOT CODE	STRATA CODE	SEGMENT /LSF ID	JUNE TRACT ACRES	JUNE FARM ACRES	CURR FARM ACRES	CURRENT CROPLAND ACRES	DECEMBER CORN ACRES	CURRENT CORN ACRES	ADJ EXP FACTOR	EXPANDED CHANGE
****************************** 20 LARGEST ******************************										
AREA	1312	24	138	203	220	150	20	50	651.1	13326
LIST	70	790529320	.	.	927	800	350	500	49.8	7474
AREA	1308	9008	20	20	0	0	18	0	392.8	7071
LIST	70	770139290	.	.	653	270	0	130	49.8	6477
LIST	70	790392320	.	.	447	380	60	190	49.8	6477
LIST	70	790484200	.	.	0	0	110	0	49.8	5481
LIST	66	857509450	.	.	0	0	62	0	87.9	5447
LIST	70	770334330	.	.	0	0	105	0	49.8	5232
AREA	1303	1027	30	30	275	240	80	120	126.5	5043
LIST	70	770302510	.	.	0	0	100	0	49.8	4982
LIST	66	770990860	.	.	197	140	75	20	87.9	4832
LIST	70	770157340	.	.	423	363	160	250	49.8	4484
AREA	2003	1147	147	276	218	50	50	20	229.8	3665
LIST	71	771598810	.	.	0	0	120	0	27.0	3246
AREA	1312	9072	10	10	40	38	7	15	393.9	3151
LIST	66	790155890	.	.	70	30	35	0	87.9	3075
LIST	66	790712950	.	.	130	128	65	100	87.9	3075
AREA	2008	9128	7	115	133	125	60	20	1179.8	3064
AREA	1311	23	86	550	280	170	20	50	649.4	3046
AREA	1303	1027	389	490	500	470	80	110	126.5	3016

MACROs - A FEW USES TO GET YOU STARTED

MICHAEL M. BROWN, SYNTEX RESEARCH

ABSTRACT

Due to the fact that MACROs are a large, complex, self-contained language, within an ever growing software system, figuring out where and how to use them can be difficult. Also, since there are always novice programmers appearing each year, reiterating MACRO uses becomes necessary. Therefore, this paper will present four ways to put the MACRO language to work. The first example shows how to create a block of statements for inclusion in other areas of the job. The second example, demonstrates a repetitive variable replacement within a block of statements. The third example shows how to use the %LET statement in the PROC step. Last, a use for the SYMGET statement will be demonstrated. The examples presented attempt to do so in a simple straightforward fashion; and when put to use they can become powerful.

INTRODUCTION

MACROs are very powerful and can be used in a very complicated manner, however, there are a few ways to use MACROs that are not so complicated. For instance, the same block of statements can be used over and over again. MACROS are good for simplifying this kind of problem. Instead of writing statements over and over, a programmer can write the statements once and embed them within a MACRO.

EXAMPLE 1, REPEATING BLOCKS OF CODE

This MACRO contains a DATA statement and a PROC PRINT statement which is executed before the data is statistically analyzed. The MACRO is named EX1, and will be stored temporarily in the program, by using the %MACRO EX1 and %MEND statements before and after the statements to be included in this particular MACRO. After creating this MACRO, it can be used later in the program by placing the statement %EX1 where this MACRO is to appear and be executed.

Figure 1 shows the DATA and MACRO EX1. Figure 2 shows program execution of this MACRO, and Figure 3 shows some of the output that was subsequently created.

EXAMPLE 2 USING MACROs WITH VARIABLE REPLACEMENT

MACRO usage is also very helpful when you have to run a PROC on one or two variables at a time, but you have quite a few variables to process. Instead of writing the same block of statements and changing the variable being processed, one block of MACRO statements is used to identify all my variables for replacement.

My second MACRO example does this. This MACRO contains a PROC TTEST and two MACRO variables in the VAR statement which will be used for replacement. The MACRO is named EX2 and the variables VAR1 and VAR2 are identified in parenthesis. After the MEND statement, the variables that are to be included in the PROC TTEST are identified with the MACRO replacement statement. This statement can be written as many times as one needs and will be executed that many times, so be careful.

Figure 4 shows the MACRO EX2 program statements, Figure 5 shows the program execution of this MACRO, and Figure 6 shows some of the output that was subsequently created.

EXAMPLE 3 USING THE %LET STATEMENT

Occasionally, a programmer may come upon a situation where it is necessary to pass a variable value to a group of MACRO statements. The %LET statement is good for this function.

In my third example of MACRO uses, the %LET statement is used to pass a value of a MACRO variable called CODE to the inside of a MACRO group. This MACRO group, CODCHART, uses the %IF, %THEN, and %DO statements to conditionally execute a PROC CHART, based on the value of the variable CODE. This example also shows how to use MACROs in a fashion that emulates DATA step programming.

Figure 7 shows the program statements using the %LET statement, Figure 8 shows the conditionally executed MACRO group, Figure 9 shows the output of the conditionally executed MACRO PROC group.

EXAMPLE 4 USING THE SYMGET STATEMENT

My final example shows one more way in which MACROs can be used without too much trouble. An occasion may arise where you want to assign a value of one MACRO variable to another variable. This can be done using the SYMGET statement.

In the final example, the SYMGET statement is used to retrieve the value of the variable CODE, which was used in the last DATA step. The SYMGET statement then passes the value of the MACRO variable CODE to the variable REPORT. This is used to execute a small report writer based on the value of the variable REPORT.

Figure 10 shows the statements used to pass the value of the MACRO variable CODE to the variable REPORT. Figure 11 shows the output produced by this sample used of SYMGET.

This MACRO program took some sales data and produced statistics, graphs and reports using some different MACRO statements. The way the MACROs were used was not too difficult to understand. Perhaps, you can use some of these examples or your own in a setting suitable for you.

I would like to acknowledge Marie Whalen and Kathy Jones for their valuable help in putting this poster/paper together.

wp/3443h

```
OPTIONS MACROGEN MPRINT SYMBOLGEN DQUOTE NONOTES;             ←OPTIONS THAT HELP DEBUG MACRO CODE

DATA EXAMPS;
  INPUT SUBJECT GROUP $ DM01 DM02 DM03 DM04 DM05
  DM06 DM07 DM08;
CARDS;
 1  A  76  87  90  12  45  54  75  27
 2  B  65  76  82  45  65  87  91  91
 3  B  32  45  12  73  64  62  65  87
 4  B  21  44  52  71  61  14  91  87                         ←DUMMY DATASET CREATION
 5  A  43  26  82  35  72  48  26  48
 6  A  25  36  47  58  40  58  48  95
 7  B  17  71  37  48  95  60  74  60
 8  B  52  47  26  69  85  85  73  59
 9  A  52  54  45  38  39  37  91  23
10  B  51  23  61  72  26  45  91  10
11  A  68  49  48  39  20  43  91  81
12  A  25  36  47  58  69  60  71  82

**EXAMPLE 1 BUILDING BLOCKS OF MACRO CODE;

%MACRO EX1;                                                   ←CREATION OF MACRO EX1
DATA EXMPS;                                                      [PROC PRINT TO BE USED AGAIN]
 SET EXAMPS;

 PROC PRINT;
  VAR DM01-DM08;
  ID SUBJECT;
  %MEND;

  **THE MACRO GROUP WILL BE INCLUDED HERE;

%EX1;                                                         ←INCLUDE THE DATASET
PROC FREQ;                                                       PRINT THE DATA BEFORE I DO A PROC FREQ
 TABLES DM01-DM08;

  **THE MACRO GROUP WILL BE INCLUDED HERE;

%EX1;                                                         ←INCLUDE THE DATASET
PROC MEANS;                                                      PRINT THE DATA BEFORE I DO A PROC MEANS
 VAR DM01-DM08;

  **THE MACRO GROUP WILL BE INCLUDED HERE;

%EX1;                                                         ←INCLUDE THE DATASET
PROC UNIVARIATE;                                                 PRINT THE DATA BEFORE I DO A PROC UNIVARIATE
 VAR DM01-DM08;

**EXAMPLE 2 MACROS USING VARIABLE REPLACEMENT;
```

FIGURE 1 (MACRO EX1 PROGRAM STATEMENTS)

```
OPTIONS MACROGEN MPRINT SYMBOLGEN DQUOTE NONOTES:

DATA EXAMPS;
  INPUT SUBJECT GROUP $ DM01 DM02 DM03 DM04 DM05
  DM06 DM07 DM08;
CARDS;
                                                      ←INPUT THE DATA                              FIRST PROC PRINT→
**EXAMPLE 1 BUILDING BLOCKS OF MACRO CODE;

%MACRO EX1;
DATA EXMPS;
 SET EXAMPS;
                                                      ←CREATED MACRO EX1
PROC PRINT;
 VAR DM01-DM08;
 ID SUBJECT;
 %MEND;

   **THE MACRO GROUP WILL BE INCLUDED HERE;

  %EX1                                                ←INCLUDED MACRO EX1→
+ DATA EXMPS;                                           BEFORE PROC FREQ             1-%EX1
+ SET EXAMPS;                                                                        1-%EX1
+ PROC PRINT;                                                                        1-%EX1
+ VAR DM01-DM08;                                                                     1-%EX1
+ ID SUBJECT;                                                                        1-%EX1

  PROC FREQ;
   TABLES DM01-DM08;

   **THE MACRO GROUP WILL BE INCLUDED HERE;

   %EX1
  + DATA EXMPS;
PAGE 2 FOR DM01
PAGE 2 FOR DM02
PAGE 2 FOR DM03
PAGE 3 FOR DM04                                       ←PROC FREQ PAGES
PAGE 3 FOR DM05
PAGE 3 FOR DM06
PAGE 4 FOR DM07                                                                                    PROC FREQ OUTPUT→
PAGE 4 FOR DM08                                       ←INCLUDED MACRO EX1→
  + SET EXAMPS;                                         BEFORE PROC FREQ             1-%EX1
  + PROC PRINT;                                                                      1-%EX1
  + VAR DM01-DM08;                                                                   1-%EX1
  + ID SUBJECT;                                                                      1-%EX1

    PROC MEANS;
     VAR DM01-DM08;
  + ID SUBJECT;

    PROC UNIVARIATE;
     VAR DM01-DM08;
     **THE MACRO GROUP WILL BE INCLUDED HERE;

   %EX1                                               ←INCLUDED MACRO EX1→
  + DATA EXAMPS;                                        BEFORE PROC UNIVARIATE       1-%EX1
  + SET EXAMPS;                                                                      1-%EX1
  + PROC PRINT;                                                                      1-%EX1
  + VAR DM01-DM08;                                                                   1-%EX1
  + ID SUBJECT;                                                                      1-%EX1

    PROC UNIVARIATE;
     VAR DM01 DM08
```

FIGURE 2 (MACRO EX1 EXECUTED PROGRAM STATEMENTS)

SAS

SUBJECT	DM01	DM02	DM03	DM04	DM05	DM06	DM07	DM08
1	76	87	90	12	45	54	75	27
2	65	76	82	45	65	87	91	91
3	32	45	12	73	64	62	65	87
4	21	44	52	71	61	14	91	87
5	43	26	82	35	72	48	26	48
6	25	36	47	58	40	58	48	95
7	17	71	37	48	95	60	74	95
8	52	47	26	69	85	85	73	59
9	52	54	45	38	39	37	91	23
10	51	23	61	72	26	45	91	10
11	68	49	48	39	20	43	91	81
12	25	36	47	58	69	60	71	82

SAS

DM01	FREQUENCY	PERCENT	CUMULATIVE FREQUENCY	CUMULATIVE PERCENT
17	1	8.3	1	8.3
21	1	8.3	2	16.7
25	2	16.7	4	33.3
32	1	8.3	5	41.7
43	1	8.3	6	50.0
51	1	8.3	7	58.3
52	2	16.7	9	75.0
65	1	8.3	10	83.3
68	1	8.3	11	91.7
76	1	8.3	12	100.0

DM02	FREQUENCY	PERCENT	CUMULATIVE FREQUENCY	CUMULATIVE PERCENT
23	1	8.3	1	8.3
26	1	8.3	2	16.7
36	2	16.7	4	33.3
44	1	8.3	5	41.7
45	1	8.3	6	50.0
47	1	8.3	7	58.3
49	1	8.3	8	66.7
54	1	8.3	9	75.0
71	1	8.3	10	83.3
76	1	8.3	11	91.7
87	1	8.3	12	100.0

DM03	FREQUENCY	PERCENT	CUMULATIVE FREQUENCY	CUMULATIVE PERCENT
12	1	8.3	1	8.3
26	1	8.3	2	16.7
37	1	8.3	3	25.0
45	1	8.3	4	33.3
47	2	16.7	6	50.0
48	1	8.3	7	58.3
52	1	8.3	8	66.7
61	1	8.3	9	75.0
82	2	16.7	11	91.7
90	1	8.3	12	100.0

FIGURE 3 (OUTPUT FROM MACRO EX1)

SAS

SECOND PROC PRINT→

SUBJECT	DM01	DM02	DM03	DM04	DM05	DM06	DM07	DM08
1	76	87	90	12	45	54	75	27
2	65	76	82	45	65	87	91	91
3	32	45	12	73	64	62	65	87
4	21	44	52	71	61	14	91	87
5	43	26	82	35	72	48	26	48
6	25	36	47	58	40	58	48	95
7	17	71	37	48	95	60	74	95
8	52	47	26	69	85	85	73	59
9	52	54	45	38	39	37	91	23
10	51	23	61	72	26	45	91	10
11	68	49	48	39	20	43	91	81
12	25	36	47	58	69	60	71	82

SAS

VARIABLE	N	MEAN	STANDARD DEVIATION	MINIMUM VALUE	MAXIMUM VALUE	STD ERROR OF MEAN	SUM	VARIANCE	CV
DM01	12	43.91666667	19.86984162	17.00000000	76.00000000	5.73592920	527.00000000	394.81060606	45.244
DM02	12	49.50000000	19.69540786	23.00000000	87.00000000	5.68557452	594.00000000	387.90909091	39.789
DM03	12	52.41666667	23.23578092	12.00000000	90.00000000	6.70759219	629.00000000	539.90151515	44.329
DM04	12	51.50000000	18.77861453	12.00000000	73.00000000	5.42091908	618.00000000	352.63636364	36.463
DM05	12	56.75000000	22.98665621	20.00000000	95.00000000	6.63567607	681.00000000	528.38636364	40.505
DM06	12	54.41666667	19.83320601	14.00000000	87.00000000	5.72535341	653.00000000	393.35606061	36.447
DM07	12	73.91666667	20.26397759	26.00000000	91.00000000	5.84970646	887.00000000	410.62878788	27.415
DM08	12	62.50000000	29.53734154	10.00000000	95.00000000	8.52669605	750.00000000	872.45454545	47.260

PROC MEANS OUTPUT____↑

FIGURE 3 (OUTPUT FROM MACRO EX1)

SAS

THIRD PROC PRINT→

SUBJECT	DM01	DM02	DM03	DM04	DM05	DM06	DM07	DM08
1	76	87	90	12	45	54	75	27
2	65	76	82	45	65	87	91	91
3	32	45	12	73	64	62	65	87
4	21	44	52	71	61	14	91	87
5	43	26	82	35	72	48	26	48
6	25	36	47	58	40	58	48	95
7	17	71	37	48	95	60	74	95
8	52	47	26	69	85	85	73	59
9	52	54	45	38	39	37	91	23
10	51	23	61	72	26	45	91	10
11	68	49	48	39	20	43	91	81
12	25	36	47	58	69	60	71	82

SAS
UNIVARIATE

VARIABLE-DM01

MOMENTS				QUANTILES(DEF=4)				EXTREMES	
N	12	SUM WGTS	12	100% MAX	76	99%	76	LOWEST	HIGHEST
MEAN	43.9167	SUM	527	75% Q3	61.75	95%	76	17	52
STD DEV	19.8698	VARIANCE	394.811	50% MED	47	90%	73.6	21	52
SKEWNESS	0.153089	KURTOSIS	-1.32251	25% Q1	25	10%	18.2	25	65
USS	27487	CSS	4342.92	0% MIN	17	5%	17	25	68
CV	45.2444	STD MEAN	5.73593			1%	17	32	76
T:MEAN=0	7.65642	PROB>|T|	0.0001	RANGE	59				
SGN RANK	39	PROB>|S|	0.00250684	Q3-Q1	36.75				
NUM = 0	12			MODE	25				

PROC UNIVARIATE OUTPUT_____↑

FIGURE 3 (OUTPUT FROM MACRO EX1)

```
%MACRO EX2 (VAR1, VAR2);

 PROC TTEST;
  CLASS GROUP;
  VAR &VAR1 $VAR2;

  %MEND;

%EX2 (DM01, DM02);
%EX2 (DM03, DM04);
%EX2 (DM05, DM06);
%EX2 (DM07, DM08);
```

←STATEMENTS CREATING MACRO EX2
(VAR1 & VAR2 ARE REPLACEMENT VARIABLES)

←STATEMENT IDENTIFYING VARIABLES THAT WILL BE USED FOR VAR1 AND VAR2. (THE BLOCK WILL BE EXECUTED 4 TIMES ONCE FOR EACH STATEMENT

FIGURE 4 (MACRO EX2 PROGRAM STATEMENTS)

```
**EXAMPLE 3 USING THE MACRO TO COMBINE DATA AND PROC STEPS;

 DATA EXAMPS3;
  SET EXAMPS;

%LET CODE=C;                          ←THIS STATEMENT GIVES A VALUE TO THE VARIABLE CODE

%MACRO CODCHART;                      ←A GROUP OF %IF STATEMENTS THAT WILL BE EXCUTED
%IF &CODE=A %THEN %DO;                  CONDITIONALLY
  PROC CHART;
  VBAR DMO1;
  %END;
%ELSE %IF &CODE=B %THEN %DO;
  PROC CHART;
  VBAR DMO2;
  %END;
%ELSE %IF &CODE=C %THEN %DO;
  PROC CHART;
  VBAR DMO3;
  %END;
%ELSE %IF &CODE=D %THEN %DO;
  PROC CHART;
  VBAR DMO4;
  %END;
%ELSE %IF &CODE=E %THEN %DO;
  PROC CHART;
  VBAR DMO5;
  %END;
%ELSE %IF &CODE=F %THEN %DO;
  PROC CHART;
  VBAR DMO6;
  %END;
%ELSE %IF &CODE=G %THEN %DO;
  PROC CHART;
  VBAR DMO7;
  %END;
%ELSE %IF &CODE=H %THEN %DO;
  PROC CHART;
  VBAR DMO8;
  %END;
%ELSE %IF &CODE=I %THEN %DO;
  PROC CHART;
  VBAR DMO9;
  %END;
%ELSE %IF &CODE=J %THEN %DO;
  PROC CHART;
  VBAR DMO10;
  %END;
%ELSE %IF &CODE=K %THEN %DO;
  PROC CHART;
  VBAR DMO11;
  %END;
%ELSE %IF &CODE=L %THEN %DO;
  PROC CHART;
  VBAR DMO12;
  %END;
%MEND CODCHART;

%CODCHART;
```

FIGURE 7 (MACRO CODCHART PROGRAM STATEMENTS)

```
  %MACRO EX2 (VAR1,VAR2);             ←MACRO BLOCK NAMED EX2

   PROC TTEST;
    CLASS GROUP;
    VAR &VAR1 &VAR2;

  %MEND;
                                      ←STATEMENTS CREATED FROM        1-%EX1
  %EX2 (DMO1,DMO2)                       THE REPLACEMENT VARIABLES    1-%EX1
+ PROC TTEST;                                                         1-%EX1
+ CLASS GROUP;
+ VAR DMO1 DMO2;
                                                                      1-%EX1
  %EX2 (DMO3,DMO4)                                                    1-%EX1
+ PROC TTEST;                                                         1-%EX1
+ CLASS GROUP;
+ VAR DMO3 DMO4
                                                                      1-%EX1
  %EX2 (DMO5,DMO6)                                                    1-%EX1
+ PROC TTEST;                                                         1-%EX1
+ CLASS GROUP;
+ VAR DMO5 DMO6;
                                                                      1-%EX1
  %EX2 (DMO7,DMO8)                                                    1-%EX1
+ PROC TTEST;                                                         1-%EX1
+ CLASS GROUP;
+ VAR DMO7 DMO8;
```

FIGURE 5 (MACRO EX2 EXECUTED PROGRAM STATEMENTS)

```
SAS (R) LOG  OS SAS 5.16              MVS/XA JOB

 DATA EXAMPS3;
  SET EXAMPS;

%LET CODE=C;

%MACRO CODCHART;
%IF &CODE=A %THEN %DO;
  PROC CHART;
  VBAR DMO1;
  %END;
%ELSE %IF &CODE=B %THEN %DO;
  PROC CHART;
  VBAR DMO2;
  %END;
%ELSE %IF &CODE=C %THEN %DO;
  PROC CHART;                    <-THIS IS THE CONDITION THAT GETS EXECUTED BASED ON THE
  VBAR DMO3;                      VALUE OF THE VARIABLE CODE
  %END;
%ELSE %IF &CODE=D %THEN %DO;
  PROC CHART;
  VBAR DMO4;
  %END;
%ELSE %IF &CODE=E %THEN %DO;
  PROC CHART;
  VBAR DMO5;
  %END;
%ELSE %IF &CODE=F %THEN %DO;
  PROC CHART;
  VBAR DMO6;
  %END;
%ELSE %IF &CODE=G %THEN %DO;
  PROC CHART;
  VBAR DMO7;
  %END;
%ELSE %IF &CODE=H %THEN %DO;
  PROC CHART;
  VBAR DMO8;
  %END;
%ELSE %IF &CODE=I %THEN %DO;
  PROC CHART;
  VBAR DMO9;
  %END;
%ELSE %IF &CODE=J %THEN %DO;
  PROC CHART;
  VBAR DMO10;
  %END;
%ELSE %IF &CODE=K %THEN %DO;
  PROC CHART;
  VBAR DMO11;
  %END;
%ELSE %IF &CODE=L %THEN %DO;
  PROC CHART;
  VBAR DMO12;
  %END;
%MEND CODCHART;

%CODCHART;
+ PROC CHART;
+ VBAR DMO3;
```

FIGURE 8 (MACRO CODCHART EXECUTED PROGRAM STATEMENTS)

SAS

TTEST PROCEDURE

VARIABLE: DMO1

GROUP	N	MEAN	STD DEV	STD ERROR	MINIMUM	MAXIMUM	VARIANCES	T	DF	PROB > |T|
A	6	48.16666667	21.36742068	8.72321297	25.00000000	76.00000000	UNEQUAL	0.7248	9.9	0.4854
B	6	39.66666667	19.20069443	7.83865068	17.00000000	65.00000000	EQUAL	0.7248	10.0	0.4852

FOR HO: VARIANCES ARE EQUAL, F'= 1.24 WITH 5 AND 5 DF PROB > F'= 0.8202

VARIABLE: DMO2

GROUP	N	MEAN	STD DEV	STD ERROR	MINIMUM	MAXIMUM	VARIANCES	T	DF	PROB > |T|
A	6	48.00000000	21.58703314	8.81286938	26.00000000	87.00000000	UNEQUAL	-0.2523	9.9	0.8059
B	6	51.00000000	19.54482029	7.97913947	23.00000000	76.00000000	EQUAL	-0.2523	10.0	0.8059

FOR HO: VARIANCES ARE EQUAL, F'= 1.22 WITH 5 AND 5 DF PROB > F'= 0.8327

TTEST OUTPUT FROM THE FIRST SET OF MACRO REPLACEMENT VARIABLES____↑

FIGURE 6 (OUTPUT FROM MACRO EX2)

```
                                   SAS

                           FREQUENCY BAR CHART

FREQUENCY

   5+                     *****
    |                     *****
    |                     *****
    |                     *****
    |                     *****
   4+                     *****
    |                     *****
    |                     *****
    |                     *****
    |                     *****
   3+                     *****                                 *****
    |                     *****                                 *****
    |                     *****                                 *****
    |                     *****                                 *****
    |                     *****                                 *****
   2+       *****         *****             ******              *****
    |       *****         *****             ******              *****
    |       *****         *****             ******              *****
    |       *****         *****             ******              *****
    |       *****         *****             ******              *****
   1+       *****         *****             ******              *****
    |       *****         *****             ******              *****
    |       *****         *****             ******              *****
    |       *****         *****             ******              *****
    |       *****         *****             ******              *****
    ----------------------------------------------------------------------
             20            40                60                  80

                              DMO3 MIDPOINT
```

↑THIS BAR CHART WAS DONE BECAUSE THE VALUE OF CODE WAS "C"

FIGURE 9 (OUTPUT FROM MACRO CODCHART)

```
**EXAMPLE 4 USING SYMGET;

  DATA EXAMPS4;
   SET EXAMPS3;

%LET CODE=C
REPORT=SYMGET ('CODE');                    ←THIS SYMGET PASSES THE VALUE OF THE MACRO VARIABLE CODE
IF REPORT='C' THEN GOTO QTR1;                TO THE VARIABLE REPORT

QTR1:

   DATA NULL_;
   SET EXAMPS;
   FILE PRINT NOTITLES HEADER=H;
   QTRSALES=DMO1+DMO2+DMO3;
   IF FIRST OBS THEN LINK H;

   PUT ////
     @1 SUBJECT @10 GROUP @15 DMO1 @20 DMO2 @25 DMO3
     @30 QTRSALES;
     RETURN;

   H:
      PUT @25 'QUARTERLY SALES REPORT';
RETURN;
RETURN;
```

FIGURE 10 (SYMGET PROGRAM STATEMENTS)

QUARTERLY SALES REPORT

1	A	76	87	90	235 ←THE SYMGET USED THE VALUE OF THE VARIABLE CODE PASSED IT TO THE VARIABLE REPORT, AND CREATED THIS OUTPUT.
2	B	65	76	82	223
3	B	32	45	12	89
4	B	21	44	52	117
5	A	43	26	82	151
6	A	25	36	47	108
7	B	17	71	37	125
8	B	52	47	26	125
9	A	52	54	45	151
10	B	51	23	61	135
11	A	68	49	48	165

FIGURE 11 (OUTPUT FROM THE USE OF THE SYMGET STATEMENT)

MAKE A DATE WITH THE SAS® SYSTEM

William R. MacHose
Pennsylvania Power & Light Co.

ABSTRACT

Dates in report titles can be generated automatically with SAS. This eliminates the need to modify programs each month or prompt for the appropriate date to be used. This poster demonstrates the use of the data step, the macro facility, date functions, and date formats to build dated report titles.

INTRODUCTION

The monthly report is probably the most common type of business report. In order to generate a dated title for the report it is necessary to:

1. Generate the Date Words
2. Put the Date Words in a Macro Variable
3. Use the Macro Variable in a TITLE

STEP 1 - GENERATE THE DATE WORDS

It takes several statements in a data step to generate date words. First the appropriate month and year must be calculated. Typically this is done by obtaining the current date and simply subtracting a month. The figure below shows two different ways of calculating a reference date for the prior month.

```
DATA _NULL_;

REFDATE=TODAY( )-31;
     or
REFDATE=TODAY( ) - DAY(TODAY( ));
```

Subtracting a number (like 31) has some advantages. It looks less complicated. You might even choose a larger number like 35 if you know that the input data is usually not ready until the fifth of each month. By subtracting 35 a report run on April 2 would assume that it was preparing a February report (March data not available until April 5). The disadvantage of subtracting a fixed number is that you could get the wrong reference month. Nevertheless, I find that the simple number subtraction is best.

Once the reference date is calculated it is a simple matter to extract the year with the YEAR date function.

```
YEAR =YEAR (REFDATE); /* YEAR =1989 */
```

Next we have to get the name of the month from REFDATE. This can be done with the PUT function and the WORDDATE9 format.

```
LENGTH MON_NAME $ 9;
MON_NAME=PUT(REFDATE,WORDDATE9.);
MON_NAME=LEFT(MON_NAME);
```

Now we have to add the year behind the month name. Use the TRIM function to remove trailing blanks on the month name and use the PUT function to convert the year to a five-letter character string (one blank and a 4-digit year).

```
LENGTH DATEWORD $ 14;
DATEWORD=TRIM(MON_NAME)||PUT(YEAR,5.);
```

STEP 2 - PUT THE DATE WORDS IN A MACRO VARIABLE

In order to make this character string available in a title we must first put the string into a macro variable. CALL SYMPUT is used in a data step to make a macro variable. A RUN statement completes the data step.

```
CALL SYMPUT('MAC_DATE',TRIM(DATEWORD));
RUN;
```

STEP 3 - USE THE MACRO VARIABLE IN A TITLE

After the above data step runs, the macro variable MAC_DATE will be available for substitution. A TITLE statement can now be written. It is important to make sure the step has completed before the TITLE statement is encountered. That is why it is important to finish the data step with a RUN statement. The TITLE statement should now be constructed with double quotes. Double quotes are used so that macro variables inside the quoted text can be resolved. (It may be necessary to specify OPTIONS DQUOTE; at your installation.)

```
TITLE1 "THE &MAC_DATE REPORT";
```

produces:

```
THE MARCH 1989 REPORT
```

PUTTING THE MONTHLY EXAMPLE TOGETHER

```
DATA _NULL_;
     REFDATE=TODAY( )-31;
     YEAR =YEAR (REFDATE);
     LENGTH MON_NAME $ 9;
     MON_NAME=PUT(REFDATE,WORDDATE9.);
     MON_NAME=LEFT(MON_NAME);
     LENGTH DATEWORD $ 14;
     DATEWORD=TRIM(MON_NAME)||PUT(YEAR,5.);
     CALL SYMPUT('MAC_DATE',TRIM(DATEWORD));
     RUN;

TITLE1 "THE &MAC_DATE REPORT";
```

```
THE MARCH 1989 REPORT
```

A QUARTERLY REPORT EXAMPLE

This data step demonstrates one way to build a quarterly title.

```
DATA _NULL_;
     REFDATE=TODAY( )-91;
     REFQTR =QTR(REFDATE);
     SELECT (REFQTR);
       WHEN (1) QWORD='FIRST ';
       WHEN (2) QWORD='SECOND';
       WHEN (3) QWORD='THIRD ';
       WHEN (4) QWORD='FOURTH';
       END;
     YEAR=YEAR(REFDATE);
     LENGTH DATEWORD $ 15;
     DATEWORD=TRIM(QWORD)||' QTR'||
              PUT(YEAR,5.);
     CALL SYMPUT('MAC_DATE',DATEWORD);
     RUN;

     TITLE1 'SALES REPORT';
     TITLE2 "&MAC_DATE";
```

```
SALES REPORT
FIRST QTR 1989
```

MORE EXAMPLES

To make each of the examples work, substitute the statements into the pattern data step below.

```
DATA _NULL_;
     TODAY=TODAY( );    (April 11, 1989)
     [ insert statements here ]
     CALL SYMPUT('DATEWORD',TRIM(DATEWORD));
     RUN;
TITLE1 "&DATEWORD";
```

Next 5 years: `1990-1994`

```
YEAR     =YEAR(TODAY);
NEXTYEAR=YEAR+1;
FIVEMORE=YEAR+5;
LENGTH    DATEWORD $ 9;
DATEWORD=PUT(NEXTYEAR,4.)||'-'||
          PUT(FIVEMORE,4.);
```

Last Saturday: `April 8, 1989`

```
LASTSAT =TODAY-WEEKDAY(TODAY);
LENGTH    DATEWORD $ 18;
DATEWORD=PUT(LASTSAT,WORDDATE18.);
DATEWORD=LEFT(DATEWORD);
```

End of prior quarter: `March 31, 1989`

```
QTRMONTH=QTR(TODAY)*3-2;
ENDDATE =MDY(QTRMONTH,1,YEAR)-1;
LENGTH    DATEWORD $ 18;
DATEWORD=PUT(ENDDATE,WORDDATE18.);
DATEWORD=LEFT(DATEWORD);
```


The author may be contacted at:
Pennsylvania Power & Light Co.
2 North Ninth Street   TW-5
Allentown, PA   18101
(215) 770-5278

Building Macro-based Systems

Howard Levine, Levine Software Systems

Introduction

SAS Macros give systems developers the ability to build easily maintained and sophisticated systems that can be built quickly and easily with the SAS® System. The key, of course, is to make extensive and thoughtful use of the macro language.

The macro language is well-suited for generating repetitive code and for conditionally executing code. In addition, the use of parameters allows even greater flexibility. Therefore, macros can generate standardized code that is made more flexible by using parameters. Flexible macros are useful as building blocks for systems. Such macros can be used in a variety of situations by changing parameters such as input and output data set names, variable names, date ranges, and various selection criteria. More simply, *well designed macros with parameters are good system building blocks.*

It is critical when building macro-based systems to build macros that are useful building blocks for writing other macros and SAS programs. There are essentially *two types of building blocks: Tools and Applications.*

A *tool* is a macro that can be used in any system because of its general usefulness. An example is an %OBS macro that determines how many observations are in a SAS data set.

An *application* is a macro that is useful only in a certain sub-system or project. An example of an application is a macro that prints out a report in a particular format. Such a macro might have to be used extensively for a particular project, but it unlikely to be of general use for all projects.

What is a Macro-based System

A macro-based system consists of application macros that may invoke other application and tool macros and generate SAS statements. All SAS statements are generated from macros. There is no "loose" SAS code which exists outside of a macro definition. The basic idea is that coding is changed from writing SAS statements to creating building blocks and then putting them together.

Why use them?

There are several advantages to using building blocks instead of having each programmer code everything himself every time he is building a system. Some of them are listed below.

- It is easier to simply invoke a macro rather than re-write the code every time it is needed.
- Expert coding that beginning SAS programmers could not understand can be used by everyone just by invoking the macro written by the expert.
- Changes to systems can be accomplished by making fewer coding changes - change one macro rather than all your programs.
- Programs are easier to read and understand because macros become a user defined language. It is a higher level language than the SAS program which is generated from the macros. This is true in the much same way that the SAS System is a higher level language than PL/I or C.

Some Examples

Some contrived, but useful, examples will illustrate these points.

The following three line program reads data, processes it, and then writes a report.

```
%READDATA(DDNAME=DATAIN,VAR= NAME $
DATE AMOUNT,OUT=DATA1)
%PROCESS(CLASS=DATE,VAR=AMOUNT,DATA=D
ATA1,OUT=DATA1)
%REPORT(DATA=DATA1,FILE=PRINT)
```

Just from looking at the macro names, it is obvious what each macro does in a general way. The keyword parameters provide much information about what the macro will be doing during that invocation of the macro. Once the macros are built, it is very easy to write programs that would have previously required much more coding. Also, the lack of clutter and good use of keyword parameters make the code easier to understand.

The next example shows how a macro can allow a change in one place (the macro) to affect every relevant program. Pretend that you are responsible for a reporting system that has many programs generating reports about snowfall and snow storms. You would want to be able to easily change the definition of a storm in all of your reports at once rather than change each one individually. Not only does this mean less work for you, but it also insures consistency among reports.

```
%macro
    snostorm(storm=snostorm,yes=1,no=0);

if (season="SUMMER" and snowfall gt 1)
    or (snowfall gt 12) then &storm = &yes
    ;
else &storm = &no;

%mend snostorm;
```

The snostorm macro, if used in all reports pertaining to snow storms, permits the definition of a storm to be changed for all programs in just one place.

The following example shows how macros with parameters can be very flexible building blocks for programs. The macro SALES creates a data set containing sales for the last N PERIODs. Since the period can be any of the periods used with the INTNX function, it is possible to create different data sets with the same macro. The macro enables a programmer or end user to easily specify the kind of data set desired. Another advantage is that all the data sets created with this macro should be consistent. That is, adding January, February, and March totals for a monthly data set will give you the first quarter total. If you write separate programs for each type of period, it is possible that there would be small differences in how the data sets are created.

```
DAY,WEEK,MONTH,   QUARTER,YEAR
    adaptable program

%macro sales(n=14,period=day);

data sales;
    set in.sales;
    saledate = intnx("&period",saledate,0);
    if saledate ge intnx("&period",today(), -
    &n);
run;
%mend sales;
```

Of course, this is a simple macro, but it demonstrates how macros can make building systems and writing applications much easier.

KEEPVAR Macro

The next example shows a macro tool that is used to keep variables in a data set only if they are also in another "base" data set. This can be useful when a data set is being prepared to replace a permanent data set. The new data set may have additional variables on it that were used to create the data set but are not required to be on the data set when it is stored. This macro is a tool because it performs a very general function and can be used in any system.

```
%MACRO KEEPVAR(DATA=, BASE=, OUT=,
  PREFIX=_);

 %LET LONG = %LENGTH(&PREFIX);
 %IF &LONG GT 5 %THEN %LET LONG = 5;

 %IF &LONG GT 0 %THEN
                        %LET   PREFIX   =
  %SUBSTR(&PREFIX,1,&LONG);

  PROC CONTENTS DATA = &BASE NOPRINT
  OUT=&PREFIX.VAR;
 RUN;

 DATA _NULL_;
   DO UNTIL (EOF);
     SET &PREFIX.VAR END=EOF ;
      COUNT + 1;
                              CALL   SYMPUT
 ('V'||LEFT(PUT(COUNT,5.)),NAME);
   END;
```

```
                    CALL    SYMPUT
 ('NUMVARS',LEFT(PUT(COUNT,5.)) );
 RUN;

 DATA &OUT;
     IF 0 THEN SET &BASE; /*GET VARIABLE
  LENGTHS*/
   SET &DATA;
   KEEP %DO I = 1 %TO &NUMVARS;
          &&V&I
       %END;
          ;
 RUN;

  PROC DATASETS NOFS;
    DELETE &PREFIX.VAR;
  RUN;
%MEND KEEPVAR;
%KEEPVAR(DATA=Y, BASE=X, OUT=Z,
   PREFIX=ABCDEFGH)
```

This macro shows that a piece of SAS code which is fairly complicated, but it performs a conceptually simple task. Because the code is part of an easy to use macro, inexperienced programmers can take advantage of programs written by someone else. Of course, even experienced programmers would want to use the macro because it is easier than rewriting the code and their application programs will be less cluttered.

The *advantages of macro-based systems* over standard SAS code are clear: systems are implemented more quickly, programs within a system are more consistent, and code can be executed conditionally depending upon input data, parameters, or global macro variables.

Standards

Once you have decided to build macro-based systems, you must resolve some issues with regard to your own organization in order to make your systems easy to build and maintain. In a word, you need *standards* .Standards are a set of rules, such as coding conventions, naming conventions, and documentation requirements, which help to make computerized systems easier to build and maintain. There is one key point that should be remembered when implementing standards: they should make your job easier - not harder.

Here are some characteristics of standards that you should keep in mind:

- Standards are *management tools* - not commandments meant to last forever.
- Standards should *help you* get systems built faster and help you to maintain them. They should not inhibit system construction needlessly or make system maintenance more difficult.
- *Automated techniques* should be employed whenever possible to help programmers follow standards and monitor their adherence to standards. This makes the programmer's job easier and allows management by exception to insure compliance with standards.
- Standards should be *useful for everyone* - from beginning programmers to experienced programmers familiar with your particular systems. This means that they will probably have to be able to bend to prevent them from breaking. They must be flexible and useful at the same time.
- A characteristic of bad standards is that they become more difficult to adhere to as your programming and system development skills improve. *Bad standards must be changed* , or they will degrade programmer efficiency.
- Since standards are management tools, it is usually a good idea to use characteristics of *your organization's management structure* as a basis for some of your standards.

Keeping those general characteristics of standards in mind, there are some issues that should be examined with regard to setting up macro-based systems.

Primary Concerns

The primary concerns are as follows:

- A central macro library versus decentralized macro libraries.
- Should naming conventions encourage descriptive names such as %LATE or non-descriptive names such as %L0001 or some combination of the two.

- Global macro variables - which ones should there be and what should their values mean.

- How are your macros and macro variables documented? How is this information disseminated throughout your organization?

A summary of the various trade-offs concerning standards you will have to consider is shown below. Some suggestions about the best approach to use are also provided.

Centralized Macro Libraries

Advantages:

- All macros are in one place

- No two macros can have the same name because a Partitioned Data Set (PDS) can only have one member with a particular name

- Macros can be centrally coordinated with standards centrally enforced

Disadvantages:

- More difficult to test macros. Temporary macro libraries must be used or macros must be explicitly included.

- Getting central approval for macros can delay project completion

- Sheer volume may be overwhelming for the person administering the central macro library. This can lead to either project delays or standards being poorly enforced or some combination of the two.

Decentralized Libraries

Advantages:

- Lets control of libraries be patterned after control of organization

- Smaller libraries are more manageable. You can have each of the following type of libraries so that the macros in them can be managed at the appropriate level:

  * Personal - Used for personal macros. Typically used by a programmer to set up a display manager environment, test new macros, and keep personal productivity macros.

  * Project - Used to store macros used for a particular project and to test macros being developed for that project. These are typically application macros for writing reports in particular formats, subsetting observations, and creating macro variables for that particular project.

  * Department - Used to store macros invoked in a variety of projects in a department. Such macros will mostly be application macros, but there will usually be some macro tools also. The line between application and tool macros sometimes gets blurred in these libraries. (One programmer's tool is another programmer's application.)

  * Company - Used primarily for storing macro tools and macros that initialize company level global macro variables. Also, any macros used by more than one department should be stored in this library.

- Allows easy testing of macros - macros can be easily put into personal or project libraries for testing and then moved up to a department or the company library if appropriate.

- Projects are not delayed because a central authority must approve every macro - macros can be put into project macro libraries immediately and be moved to the company library at a later time.

Disadvantages:

- Documentation and standardization might suffer - not requiring programmers to have their macros checked before having them put in a library permits them to ignore standards.

- Two macros with the same name could exist in two different macro libraries. In some situations, this could lead to confusion.

- There could be duplication of effort within a company. One project team could be working on a macro that another project team has already developed.

- There will be more data sets (libraries) to keep track of. Instead of one large, central PDS, there will be dozens or hundreds of smaller PDS's.

How MACRO LIBRARIES are accessed in an OS Batch Environment:

CENTRALIZED

```
//SASAUTOS DD DSN=MAINLIB,DISP=SHR
```

DECENTRALIZED

```
//   SASAUTOS DD DSN=MYLIB,DISP=SHR
//            DD DSN=PROJLIB,DISP=SHR
//            DD DSN=DEPTLIB,DISP=SHR
//            DD DSN=COMPLIB,DISP=SHR
```

The conclusion: Decentralized libraries are usually better because they allow for more flexibility, easier management of any one particular library, and they make it easier for people to share macros. Ironically, sharing macros is easier because people have less macros to look through in order to find existing macros that will serve their purposes. The company and department macro libraries will be smaller than one central company library would be. As an added bonus, the control of macro libraries can be patterned after the management structure of the company.

Using a Centralized macro library may be appropriate for installations concerned about the proliferation of partitioned data sets or for organizations that have relatively few people writing macros.

NAMING

Descriptive Names

Advantages:

- Easy to understand
- Simple

Disadvantages:

- 8 characters might not allow a good description

- Similar macros or variables will be hard to distinguish

Examples: REPORT, RPT, REPORTER
They all have something to do with reporting, but how are they different?

Non-Descriptive Names

Advantages:

- Names are not misleading.

- No imagination is needed for naming macros and variables. This can be a real advantage if you have to name dozens of macros and macro variables.

Disadvantages:

- Explicit documentation is absolutely essential. Since the name contains no information, the documentation must tell the programmer what the names mean.

- Less Intuitive - It is difficult to guess the purpose of a macro or variable from its name.

Examples: MAC001, MAC002, UTL101
Except possibly for three letters at the beginning of the name, these macro or variable names provide no clue as to their purpose.

The conclusion: A combination of the two methods should be used. Descriptive names should be used for high level activities such as certain global macro variables, macro tools, and certain application macros. Most application macros should have a prefix that identifies them as belonging to a particular phase of a system with a number or letter system for the rest of the name. Macro parameter names should, if possible, always be descriptive. Most macro variables should have descriptive names. A general rule of thumb is that descriptive names should be used up to the point when your systems become too cluttered to use them effectively.

GLOBAL VARIABLES

- For use in all Macros - any macro that does not refer a local variable of the same name can access the global macro variable.
- Good with SAS/AF® - Eliminates confusion caused by AF screens being invoked in different macro referencing environments.

GLOBAL VARIABLES vs. PARAMETERS

Global Variable:

- Any macro can change value
- Should be defined as GLOBAL in every macro
- Can require slightly less coding (for parameters).

Parameters:

- Individual macros can be tested
- Modularity

GLOBAL VARIABLE EXAMPLES

Variables You Might Want to use

ERRORMSG	An error message
ABORT	YES or NO
DEBUG	YES or NO
FIRSTOBS	a Number
OBS	MAX or a Number
TEST	YES or NO

The conclusion: Macro variables such as DEBUG and ABORT can be useful as global variables because you want them to affect every macro in your system.You may also want any of your macros to be able to change them in the event a processing problem occurs.

Parameters can often be very useful in situations where macros are transported from one library to another where they are exposed to different global macro variables. The modularity created by using parameters makes the macro more portable. They also enable the programmer to better control or eliminate side effects from macro invocations.

Advertising Macros

Like with many businesses, the most effective advertising for macros is word of mouth. One programmer tells another programmer about a macro that is useful. As effective as that is, it is a fairly hit and miss process. For macro-based systems to be fully taken advantage of, there has to be a more effective way of disseminating information about macro building blocks - applications and tools. Certain techniques tend to be fairly helpful.

First of all, each macro must have good documentation describing its purpose and its parameters. That makes it easier for someone to use an existing macro rather than build a new one because they are sure what the existing macro does. It is helpful to have documentation on-line as well as printed.

Next, it helps to have decentralized macro libraries. Smaller libraries make it possible for management at appropriate levels to direct the attention of their subordinates to particular macros that may be of interest. There is a better chance that someone in charge of a small library devoted to some particular area (such as a department or project) will know their macro library better than someone who administers an enormous, company macro library.

And it is also useful to have design meetings and code walk-throughs. There is a better chance that at least one member of a group of people knows more than one individual about a macro that can effectively perform a task.

GOOD TIPS for building Successful macro-based systems:

- Explicitly define every macro variable in a macro to be LOCAL or GLOBAL with a %LOCAL or %GLOBAL statement unless it is a parameter. Parameters are, by definition, LOCAL macro variables.

- Use Keyword parameters rather than positional parameters. They can be set with default values, the order they appear in does not affect how they work, and it is easier to understand what the program invoking the macro is doing.

- Use parameters as much as is practically possible - This keeps your macros more adaptable and easy to use when minor adjustments are needed. For example, input and output data set names should be able to be changed by using a keyword parameter.

- Incorporate error checking into macros - Give yourself or the maintenance programmer some helpful messages in case something goes wrong. Also, prevent disasters by cross checking parameter values, when appropriate, to see if they make sense in relation to one another.

- Use the RUN statement to end DATA and PROC steps.This will save you a lot of grief. Not using a RUN statement can cause a great deal of confusion about macro referencing environments and when data and proc steps get executed in relation to macro statements.

- Use common sense and expert advice when setting up standards. Remember that standards are supposed to help programmers, not decrease their efficiency. Also, if you do not know what your standards should be or are unsure of how they should change in the future, discuss your situation with a more experienced person who is able to give you sound advice.

Conclusion

The main points to consider about macro-based systems are they are more easily managed and maintained than "loose" SAS code. You are working with building blocks instead of SAS statements. The building blocks you construct provide for standardization among different application programs. They also enable you to build new systems quickly. Good standards and administration of your systems can help to make them more effective, but bad standards will damage productivity. ***Good management and administrative skills are just as important as technical skills when it comes to managing macro-based systems.***

References

From SAS Institute Inc.:

SAS Guide to Macro Processing
SAS Users Guide Basics
Technical Report P-146

SUGI 13 Proceedings:
Peter Kretzman,"Teflon and Tang: Forging Generic Macro Tools"

If you have any questions or comments, feel free to contact the author at

Levine Software Systems
1770 Bryant Avenue South #416
Minneapolis, MN 55403
(612) 377-5714

Chapter 2 Debugging Macro Programs

**WARNING: Apparent Macro Invocation Not Resolved . . .
Techniques for Debugging Macro Code 47**

Beginner

Tasks Describes how to debug macro problems.

Tools CALL SYMPUT
Macro debugging options
Macro quoting
SYMGET

A Debugging Facility for SAS Macro Systems 53

Intermediate

Tasks Discusses an approach to built-in macro debugging controls.

Tools %IF-%THEN / %ELSE
%LET
Macro debugging options
Macro parameters
Simple substitution

Conquering the Dreaded Macro Error 59

Intermediate

Tasks Discusses a logical, systematic approach to macro program development and debugging.

Tools %DO, Iterative
%IF-%THEN / %ELSE
%LET
%PUT
Macro parameters
Simple substitution

Debugging Your SAS Macro Application under VMS: A Practical Approach 66

Intermediate

Tasks Discusses various macro debugging techniques.

Tools

%DO, Iterative
%GLOBAL
%GOTO/Macro labels
%IF-%THEN / %ELSE
%LET
Autocall macros supplied by SAS Institute
Automatic macro variables
Macro debugging options
Macro functions
Macro parameters
Macro quoting
Simple substitution

A Roadmap to Macro Facility Error Messages and Debugging 73

Advanced

Tasks Discusses various error messages and macro debugging options.

Tools

%LET
Autocall facility
Command-style macros
Macro debugging options
Symbol tables / Referencing environments
Word scanner / Tokenizer

WARNING: APPARENT MACRO INVOCATION NOT RESOLVED . . . TECHNIQUES FOR DEBUGGING MACRO CODE

Jeff Phillips, ARC Professional Services Group
Veronica Walgamotte, ARC Professional Services Group
Derek Drummond, ARC Professional Services Group

INTRODUCTION

The macro facility is a powerful adjunct to The SAS® System. Macro allows SAS programmers to employ such techniques as symbolic substitution, conditional code generation, hierarchical application structure, and parameter-driven, reusable code. In spite of macro's power and usefulness, it often seems to generate fear and loathing rather than interest and excitement. There are two major barriers to wider use and acceptance of macro as a programming tool in the SAS world. New users are often unsure of exactly what it is that macro does, while beginning and even intermediate users find debugging macro errors to be baffling. Many papers and tutorials have ben written and presented describing just what macro can do. This workshop attempts to address the second problem: debugging. We will consider the most common macro problem types and illustrate their symptoms, causes, and corrections.

WHY MACRO DEBUGGING IS DIFFICULT

Problems occurring when using the macro facility are especially difficult to identify and correct because of the special role macro plays in SAS processing. Macro is a complete programming language, with its own variables, statements, functions, data structures, and syntax rules. However, macro is used primarily to generate and alter code in another programming language, SAS. Macro is in essence a language used to write another language. When a programmer makes a mistake using macro, that mistake can affect the macro code itself, the SAS code that is being generated, or, most often, both. An error that results from a macro mistake appears to be a SAS error. The programmer must distinguish between genuine SAS syntax errors and errors caused by incorrect macro code. The situation is made worse by the fact that macro and SAS have similar syntax. For example, the macro statement:

```
%IF &STATE = VA %THEN %PUT The State is
Virginia.;
```

is not very different from the SAS statement:

```
IF STATE = 'VA' THEN PUT 'The State is
Virginia.';
```

CLASSIFYING THE PROBLEM

The first step in debugging a macro problem is to figure out the type of problem. Typically, macro errors fall into one of the following categories:

- *Macro syntax errors* are caused by incorrect spelling, word order, or special character use in a macro statement.
- *Resolution errors* are caused when macro variables fail to resolve, or resolve to unexpected values.
- *SAS code construction errors* are caused when macro structures, especially macro variables, are improperly placed in SAS code.
- *SYMPUT and SYMGET errors* are caused by improper use of the two DATA step functions CALL SYMPUT and SYMGET to create and retrieve macro variables.
- *Quoting function errors* are caused when a particular special character (such as a semicolon) or a string has an ambiguous meaning to macro.

MACRO SYNTAX ERRORS

As in any programming language, the most basic type of error is incorrect syntax. Syntax errors are often caused by "typos," but the resulting error message may appear far more complex. Consider the following example:

```
        ERROR: Open code statement recursion
detected.
4      %PUT The following statement is a LET
statement:
5      %LET VAR = VALUE;
```

The error message "open code recursion" means that macro has detected a macro statement keyword, %LET, inside another macro statement, %PUT. The problem is caused by the accidental use of a colon instead of a semicolon at the end of the %PUT. The problem is a simple one; the identification is not.

Hints and rules: *In Version 6 of SAS, macro error messages have gotten much better than in "the old days". Since the context of the mistake determines the effect it will have on the code's interpretation, it is difficult to give rules of thumb for debugging. One rule, however, may prove helpful: in cases where the problem is not immediately apparent, the actual error may have occurred in the statement before the one flagged by the error message.*

RESOLUTION ERRORS

The second type of macro problem occurs when dealing with the most basic of macro functions: symbolic resolution. There are two "bad" things that can happen when macro attempts to resolve a macro variable reference: incorrect resolution and no resolution. The symptoms and treatments for each are quite different. In the following SAS log, the ERROR: message says that SAS is " expecting an relational or arithmetic operator."

```
99   %let state = VA;
100  data virginia;
101     length city $ 11;
102     set workshop.states;
103     if state = &stat;
                   -
                   390
WARNING: Apparent symbolic reference STAT not
resolved.
104  run;

ERROR 390-185: Expecting an relational or
arithmetic operator.

NOTE: The SAS System stopped processing this
step because of errors.
WARNING: The data set WORK.VIRGINIA may be
incomplete.  When this step was stopped there
were 0 observations and 4 variables.
NOTE: The DATA statement used 0.17 seconds.
```

The real problem is identified by the WARNING message above it, "apparent symbolic reference STAT not resolved." Many programmers ignore warnings because they do not stop the execution of the code. In this case, however, the warning showed that a macro variable, &STAT, could not be resolved. The unresolved string &STAT is passed to the SAS compiler, which evaluates the & as the symbol for logical "and." The unexpected operator message, caused by the misplaced "and," is only an indirect reference to the real problem, which was the misspelled macro variable name. There are two valuable lessons here: first, one should never ignore warnings in the SAS log, especially if a macro component is involved. Second, when dealing with SAS code containing macro, the programmer should be aware that any SAS error message may be a tipoff that macro has generated an incorrect string.

The following simple macro will illustrate a more subtle problem:

```
%macro subset (varname =,
                value = );
data &value;
   set workshop.states;
   if &varname = "&value";
run;
%mend subset;
```

The purpose of the macro is to allow the user to select both the variable name and value for a subsetting IF condition. A macro call of:

```
%SUBSET(VARNAME=STATE,VALUE=LA)
```

would yield the following DATA step:

```
DATA LA;
SET WORKSHOP.STATES;
IF STATE = "LA";
RUN;
```

However, it takes only a small error to create the following result:

```
132  %let varname = state;
133  %let value = LA;
134  %subset
135  proc print;

NOTE: The data set WORK.DATA1 has 4
observations and 4 variables.
NOTE: The DATA statement used 0.11 seconds.


136   title "Test of SUBSET Macro";
137  run;

NOTE: The PROCEDURE PRINT used 0.05 seconds.

Test of SUBSET Macro

OBS       NAME          STATE      FLOWER
 IF

 1      Louisiana        LA        MAGNOLIA
 2      Maryland         MD        BLACK-EYED SUSA
 3      New York         NY        ROSE
 4      Virginia         VA        DOGWOOD
```

What has happened to eliminate any subsetting criteria? How and why did SAS create a variable called "IF," whose value is missing? Why is the output data set called "DATA1"?

When the macro %SUBSET was called, the user failed to specify any value for either of the two parameters VARNAME and VALUE. Since these macro variables have been declared (they have been established during the macro's definition), but have not been given any explicit values, they will resolve to null. The DATA step then becomes:

```
MPRINT(SUBSET):    DATA ;
MPRINT(SUBSET):    SET WORKSHOP.STATES;
MPRINT(SUBSET):    IF = "";
MPRINT(SUBSET):    RUN;
```

These statements give us a data set called WORK.DATA1, no subsetting, and a new variable called "IF".

Such errors often occur when macro calls are involved, since macro parameters are *local*, or isolated within the macro that defines them. The example illustrates how the interaction between local parameters and variable created by %LET statements can cause a phenomenon known as *blocking*, when an executing macro cannot access variables assigned by %LET statements outside the macro. Blocking occurs because macro parameters are local and "get in the way" of the variables with the same name that are set outside the macro by %LET statements.

Hints and rules: (1) *Identify what happened: incorrect resolution or no resolution.* (2) *The warning message, "apparent symbolic reference not resolved" suggests that a macro variable cannot be resolved at all, as opposed to resolving incorrectly. Look first for misspellings and typographic errors.* (3) *Examine the generated SAS code and output carefully. In the previous examples, resolution errors were indicated by such clues as the presence of a variable called "IF" in a data set and the data set name "WORK.DATA1."* (4) *Use the SYMBOLGEN and MPRINT options when writing and debugging macro code. Otherwise, the log may not show enough information to help adequately in debugging.* (5) *Be especially careful when using macros. They may have local variables that interfere with access to* *variables set by %LET earlier in the program.*

SAS Code Construction Errors

One of the most basic errors in macro programming occurs when the programmer fails to pay proper attention to the way a code string generated by macro will appear to SAS itself. Consider the following SAS log:

```
%let flower = MAGNOLIA;
data flowers;
   set workshop.states;
   if flower = &flower;
run;

NOTE: Variable MAGNOLIA is uninitialized.
NOTE: The data set WORK.FLOWERS has 0
observations and 4 variables.
NOTE: The DATA statement used 0.11 seconds.


proc print data = flowers;
   title 'States With &flower as State
Flower';
run;

NOTE: No observations in data set WORK.FLOWERS.
NOTE: The PROCEDURE PRINT used 0.0 seconds.
```

There is nothing wrong with the *syntax* in either the macro or the SAS portions of the example (that is, no SAS syntax errors are generated). The incorrect results and the "UNINITIALIZED VARIABLE" message both indicate that there is something logically wrong. Here, the problem is the absence of quotation marks around the reference to &FLOWER in the DATA step. The SAS compiler interprets the resolved value of &FLOWER, which is MAGNOLIA, as if it were a variable name. Such an interpretation is correct in SAS terms because the string "MAGNOLIA" begins with a letter, contains only letters, has no blank spaces, and is less than eight characters long. In the SAS lexicon, that description fits what is called a "name token," and in the particular context of this DATA step, the name token MAGNOLIA looks like a variable name to SAS. Since the goal is to pass in a character constant to SAS, the programmer must add quotation marks:

```
%let flower = MAGNOLIA;
data flowers;
   set workshop.states;
   if flower = "&flower";
run;

NOTE: The data set WORK.FLOWERS has 1
observations and 3 variables.
NOTE: The DATA statement used 0.11 seconds.


proc print data = flowers;
   title 'States With &flower as State
Flower';
run;

NOTE: The PROCEDURE PRINT used 0.05 seconds.
```

A similar problem may arise if the wrong type of quotation marks are used:

```
States With &flower as State Flower

OBS     NAME        STATE     FLOWER

 1      Louisiana    LA       MAGNOLIA
```

Here, the single quotation marks prevent the resolution of the macro variable &FLOWER. The SAS compiler detects no syntax problems. However, when the PROC PRINT step executes, the title contains &FLOWER instead of MAGNOLIA. A debugging clue to the problem can be gained if SYMBOLGEN is invoked before the DATA step. If SYMBOLGEN is in effect, every appearance of &FLOWER in the DATA step should cause a message. Notice that no message is generated for the &FLOWER reference inside the TITLE statement:

```
%let flower = MAGNOLIA;
data flowers;
   set workshop.states;
   if flower = "&flower";
SYMBOLGEN:  Macro variable FLOWER resolves to
MAGNOLIA
run;

NOTE: The data set WORK.FLOWERS has 1
observations and 3 variables.
NOTE: The DATA statement used 0.16 seconds.


proc print data = flowers;
   title 'States With &flower as State
Flower';
run;

NOTE: The PROCEDURE PRINT used 0.0 seconds.
```

Changing the single quotes to double quotes will correct the problem, since double quotes are processed so they do not obscure the macro variable reference inside them.

Hints and rules: (1) *This is not a diagnosis rule, but it will eliminate many quote-mark related errors: always use double quotes when writing SAS code. If double quotes are the standard character literal symbols, then the chances of a macro variable being undetected are greatly reduced.* (2) *Pay attention to any "uninitialized variable" or similar messages. Each should be explainable; the cause could be a macro variable reference that should be inside quotes.*

SYMPUT and SYMGET Errors

The SYMPUT routine in the DATA step can lead to errors that are caused by the interaction of the macro facility and SAS. To understand these interaction errors, one must keep in mind that the DATA step has two distinct phases: compilation and execution. During compilation, SAS constructs its object code stream from the programmer's source code plus whatever additional information may come from the macro facility. The following code is an example:

```
%LET FLOWER = ROSE;
DATA &FLOWER;
  SET WORKSHOP.STATES;
  IF FLOWER = "&FLOWER";
RUN;
```

As the step compiles, the source code stream is examined, token by token, by a SAS system component called the wordscanner. Standard SAS code tokens are sent by the wordscanner to the SAS compiler to be checked for syntax and to construct the step's object code and data vectors. During the scanning and compilation process, any tokens containing macro triggers (& and %) are sent to the macro facility for processing. While the SAS compiler waits, macro examines the token(s) passed to it, executes whatever instructions are contained in them, and then sends the result back to the wordscanner. For example, in the previous code the token &FLOWER is sent to the macro facility and macro resolves it to ROSE. ROSE then replaces &FLOWER in the code stream so that the code reads:

```
DATA ROSE;
  SET WORKSHOP.STATES;
  IF FLOWER = "ROSE";
RUN;
```

The original source code (&FLOWER) has been changed or augmented (ROSE) by means of macro activity. A key to this process is that it happens during the scanning and compilation phase, while SAS is building the code that will be executed. The limitation on the process is that once the SAS code begins to execute, there is no way for macro activity to occur. For example, if a programmer wishes to assign or obtain the value of a macro variable based on a SAS data value, %LET and & are of no use. Another example will help illustrate the point:

```
190   data ivy;
191     set workshop.states;
192     if flower =  "IVY"  then
193     do;
194         %let found = YES;
195         output;
196     end;
197    run;

NOTE: The data set WORK.IVY has 0 observations
and 3 variables.
NOTE: The DATA statement used 0.05 seconds.

SYMBOLGEN:  Macro variable FOUND resolves to YES
198
199    %PUT FOUND = &FOUND;
FOUND = YES
```

This DATA step will *always* set the macro variable FOUND to YES, even if there are no observations containing "IVY" in the entire WORKSHOP.STATES data set. The %LET will be sent to macro to execute when the wordscanner detects it during compilation, despite the IF statement.

CALL SYMPUT allows the DATA step to communicate with macro during the execution phase. In effect, CALL SYMPUT is a %LET statement that operates under the control of DATA step logic. Thus, the following code would be appropriate, since CALL SYMPUT is a SAS routine, and executes under the control of DATA step program logic:

```
211   %let found = no;
212   data ivy;
213     set workshop.states;
214     if flower =  "IVY"  then
215     do;
216         call symput("found","YES");
217         stop;
218     end;
219   run;

NOTE: The data set WORK.IVY has 4 observations
and 3 variables.
NOTE: The DATA statement used 0.22 seconds.

SYMBOLGEN:  Macro variable FOUND resolves to
no
220
221   %put FOUND = &found;
FOUND = no
```

Problems occur when the programmer forgets the difference between macro statements and resolutions, which happen during compilation phase, and CALL SYMPUT, which happens *later*, during the execution phase. The following code is similar to the previous examples. Here, however, the programmer attempts to use the value of the macro variable &FOUND to write a message to the SAS log about the existence of roses in the data:

```
251   %let found = NO;
252   data roses;
253     set workshop.states;
254     if flower =  "ROSE"  then
255     do;
256         call symput("found","YES");
257         output;
258     end;
259     %PUT Are there roses? The answer is
&found.;
Are there roses? The answer is NO
260   run;

NOTE: The data set WORK.ROSES has 1
observations and 3 variables.
NOTE: The DATA statement used 0.16 seconds.

261
262   proc print data = roses;
263   title "ROSES Data Set";
264   run;

NOTE: The PROCEDURE PRINT used 0.05 seconds.
```

As the log shows, the answer is always "NO, " even when the log notes prove that there is at least one state with the rose as a state flower. The %PUT statement is executed by the macro processor while the DATA step code is still being compiled. The RUN; statement that trigger execution of the DATA step is not encountered until after the %PUT is finished.

The simplest solution to the problem is to make sure that the step containing a CALL SYMPUT has executed before attempting to use the macro variable the CALL SYMPUT assigns:

```
265   %let found = NO;
266   data roses;
267     set workshop.states;
268     if flower =  "ROSE"  then
269     do;
270         call symput("found","YES");
271         output;
272     end;
273   run;

NOTE: The data set WORK.ROSES has 1
observations and 3 variables.
NOTE: The DATA statement used 0.17 seconds.


274
275   %PUT Are there roses? The answer is
&found.;
```

```
Are there roses? The answer is YES
```

Hints and rules: (1) *Look for missing RUN; statements or other step boundaries.* (2) *Be suspicious of %LET, or any other macro statement, inside a DATA step. There are no situations in which %LET can be controlled by the DATA step; use CALL SYMPUT when the intent is to control the assignment of macro variables with DATA step logic.* (3) *Be equally suspicious of macro variables being both assigned and resolved in a single DATA step.*

QUOTING FUNCTION ERRORS

Normally, the macro facility interprets everything as a character string. There are no data types in macro; "1.25" is as much a character string as "ABC." There are situations, however, in which macro must attach special meaning to characters. For example, a semicolon ends a macro statement. Therefore, it is not just any character. Sometimes, though, a semicolon is part of SAS text, and is not meant to be of any special significance to macro. Consider the following code:

```
%let sasstep = proc print data=workshop.states;
&sasstep
title  This PRINT Was Generated By A Macro Variable ;
title  This PRINT Was Generated By A Macro Variable ;
       -----
       76
ERROR 76-322: Syntax error, statement will be ignored.

run;

NOTE: The SAS System stopped processing this step because of errors.
NOTE: The PROCEDURE PRINT used 0.11 seconds.
```

As the SAS log shows, there is a semicolon missing, which causes the TITLE statement to be looked at as part of the PROC PRINT statement. The error, however, is a macro error, not a SAS code error. The semicolon after "MYDATA" is meant to be part of the SAS code stream being stored as the value of the macro variable SASSTEP. Macro interprets the semicolon as signaling the end of the %LET statement, and so the semicolon does not get passed on to the compiler as was intended.

Problems such as the one just discussed arise when macro cannot accurately identify a given special character or character string. Such problems are generally called situations of *ambiguous meaning*. Ambiguous meaning often arises because SAS and macro share symbols such as the semicolon, or because a special character or character string within a piece of code could be taken two ways. Macro quoting functions, such as %STR, serve to eliminate the ambiguity by forcing macro to interpret the string being quoted as text and nothing more. Using %STR to the previous example eliminates any ambiguity caused by the presence of the semicolons:

```
%let sasstep = %str(proc print data=workshop.states;);
&sasstep
title  This PRINT Was Generated By A Macro Variable ;
run;

NOTE: The PROCEDURE PRINT used 18.55 seconds.
```

Another example of ambiguous meaning will serve to illustrate better the type of error caused by quoting problems:

```
%macro subset (state = );
data subset;
   set workshop.states;
   %if &state = NE or &state = OR %then
      %do;
         delete;
         %put No data for Nebraska or Oregon.;
      %end;
   %else
      %do;
   if state = "&state";
      %end;
run;
%mend subset;
%subset (state = VA);

ERROR: A character operand was found in the %EVAL function or %IF
       condition where a numeric operand is required. The condition was:
       &state = NE or &state = OR
ERROR: The macro will stop executing.
```

A problem results when the macro is compiled by the macro facility because there is obvious ambiguity in the phrase "&STATE = NE OR &STATE = OR. "NE" and "OR" can be seen as either state abbreviations or as logical operators. The log shows that macro is trying to evaluate an expression, in this case the expression in the %IF statement. As a rule, such an error message will occur when syntactical mistakes are made in macro %IF statements, %DO loops, or arithmetic expressions. However, there are times when the problem is an ambiguity rather than an outright error. The problem can be solved by using %STR:

```
%macro subset (state = );
data subset;
   set workshop.states;
   %if %str(&state) = %str(NE) or %str(&state) = %str(OR) %then
      %do;
         delete;
         %put No data for Nebraska or Oregon.;
      %end;
   %else
      %do;
   if state = "&state";
      %end;
run;
%mend subset;
%subset (state = OR);

NOTE: The data set WORK.SUBSET has 4 observations and 3 variables.
NOTE: The DATA statement used 1 minute 18.82 seconds.


No data for Nebraska or Oregon.

NOTE: The data set WORK.SUBSET has 0 observations and 3 variables.
NOTE: The DATA statement used 0.22 seconds.
```

The macro now works properly because macro has been "told" that NE and OR are to be treated as plain text, not as operators. Note that %STR must be used on both the constants NE and OR as well as the references to &STATE. When using quoting functions, the programmer must consider that macro variables may *resolve into* problems that are not immediately apparent. In this example, "&STATE" is not a problem as it stands, but when it resolves into "OR," it can cause an error if %STR is not in place.

Note: in SAS releases prior to 6.08, the %QUOTE function must be used in place of %STR to quote macro variable resolutions. In the example above, the code:

```
%str(&state)
```

is incorrect for releases 6.07 and prior (including 6.04 for DOS). The correct code would be:

```
%quote(&state)
```

In pre-6.08 SAS releases, The %STR function does not quote text resulting from either macro executions or macro variable resolutions. In 6.08, %STR has been enhanced.

Hints and rules: (1) *Examine macro syntax containing %IF, %DO, %SCAN (second function argument), %SUBSTR (second and third function arguments), or %EVAL. These macro activities involve logical and/or arithmetic evaluation, and are more "sensitive" to the meaning of symbols and character strings than statements such as %LET.* (2) *Examine areas in which macro statements are directly generating SAS code, such as the %LET SASSTEP ... &SASSTEP example above. SAS and macro share the semicolon, colon, period, comma and parenthesis, and these shared special characters may lead to ambiguous meaning.*

CONCLUSION

There is no question that macro adds a level of debugging complexity to SAS programs. However, macro problems are often caused by the same types of simple mistakes, such as typographical miscues, that cause SAS errors. When the causes of macro problems are not immediately obvious, they can be attacked by carefully observing the symptom and following the diagnosis hints and rules presented in this workshop.

The authors can be contacted at:

ARC Professional Services Group
Information Systems Division
1301 Piccard Drive
Rockville, MD 20850

(301) 258-5300
FAX: (301) 258-6878

A Debugging Facility for SAS* Macro Systems

David S. Frankel, Exxon Company, U.S.A.
Mark. A. Kochanski, Sierra Geophysics, Inc.

Abstract

This debugging facility makes it easy to trace the execution of one or more SAS macros within a SAS job. You can control printing start- and end-banners that identify macros, including revision date and support group; checking the values of macro parameters; printing notes following PROC and DATA steps; printing a simple or detailed source-code trace; and, deletion of temporary SAS data sets. Macros not to be traced execute "as is" with settings determined by their invocations and definitions.

The facility consists of two SAS macros -- %DEBUG and %_DEBUG. An end-user or developer calls %DEBUG from a SAS job to set the debugging options to be used for subsequent macro calls. Each SAS macro calls %_DEBUG to print banners, set status variables, delete temporary SAS data sets, and replace statements like OPTIONS NOTES. %_DEBUG determines the environment for each macro by arbitrating between "as is" settings and %DEBUG user requests.

Both end-users and developers have benefited from this facility--especially for highly nested systems. End-users control the SAS log file by printing only what they need to easily find where errors are occurring. Developers get a detailed trace of specific macros to pinpoint bugs without editing macro definitions, as well as simplified and standard debugging statements for developing macros.

Background

Developers who write macros have always had conflicting goals as to what the macros should write on the log file. The user typically is not concerned with the internal workings of the macro, and wants to see a minimum number of lines. However, if an execution problem is encountered, the developer needs to see the statements generated by macro execution.

The most primitive approach to this issue is coding an OPTIONS statement as the first and last executable statement in each macro definition. The production-level macro definition sets NOSOURCE NONOTES at entry and SOURCE NOTES at exit to avoid cluttering the log file. If an execution problem is encountered, the developer first edits the macro definition to set SOURCE NOTES at entry, then codes OPTIONS MPRINT ahead of the macro invocation.

A slightly more sophisticated approach is defining a macro parameter whose value controls the entry and exit OPTIONS statement. This lets the macro invocation control the "trace" environment for that macro and avoids the need to edit that macro definition.

Both approaches are adequate when a SAS job invokes a single macro. But when a system of nested macros is executing, these simple approaches are inadequate.

Consider a simple two-macro system comprising an outer macro that invokes an inner macro. Tracing the execution of the entire system forces you to edit both macro definitions. Even if your trace control is a macro parameter, you still must edit the outer macro definition to get at the trace control for the inner macro. Also the OPTIONS statement issued at the exit of the inner macro will control the trace environment of the outer macro. To re-assert control of its trace environment, the outer macro needs to issue an OPTIONS statement immediately after invoking the inner macro.

The situation grows more complex with deeper nesting. But nesting is the rule rather than the exception.

Our experience shows that macro systems provide an efficient way to deliver standardized, flexible, optimized, reliable, and user-friendly SAS applications to a large number of users. Within the system, each macro performs a single task. This may be data retrieval, validation, shaping, analysis, display, or reporting. When a user invokes a macro, he is normally executing a macro system that is often nested three levels deep and may be nested as much as six or seven levels deep.

The simple, intuitive approaches to managing the debug environment are grossly inadequate for nested macro systems. We developed a facility that manages the debug environment for each executing macro. You can control these individual environments without having to edit either the macro definitions or the macro invocations.

Debug-Facility Concepts

The facility consists of two macros stored in an autocall source library: %DEBUG and %_DEBUG. End-users only need to know about %DEBUG; developers need to know about both.

The end-user invokes the %DEBUG macro to specify any combination of five debug actions to apply to targeted macros. These actions are: writing entry/exit banners; verifying data; writing notes for DATA and PROC steps; writing a source-code trace; and, saving or deleting work data sets. If %DEBUG is not invoked or if a macro is not targeted by %DEBUG, the debug environment is said to be "as-is."

The developer invokes the %_DEBUG macro as the first and last executable statement in each macro definition. This delegates control of that macro's debug environment to the debug facility. In return the debug facility makes information available to that macro during execution.

Banners

A banner may be written to the log file when a macro starts executing (the entry banner) and again when it stops executing (the exit banner). The entry banner has two lines. The first gives the macro's name and version, which normally includes the date of last modification. The second line identifies the support staff. The exit banner is a single line that names the macro that is ending execution. All banner lines begin with 'NOTE:', which makes it possible to suppress them with a NONOTES system option.

You can locate an error within the macro system simply by turning on all banners so as to bracket the SAS error messages. The entry banners are essential to verify that you are executing the proper version of the macro. Quite often you get the wrong version if the SASAUTOS file reference is associated with a concatenation of several macro source libraries.

According to our macro-writing guidelines, every macro definition has a keyword parameter that lets you toggle the banners on or off. The normal default is on for "user-level" macros that are commonly invoked directly by end-users, and off for "utility" macros that are most often invoked from within other macros.

Verifying Data

Ironclad applications need to verify all input data. For macros this means checking the value of every macro parameter at execution time. Each of our macros contains a conditional block of code that invokes utility macros to verify:

- syntax (SAS names, host names, integers, date literals)
- existence (SAS data sets and variables, DB2 tables and columns)
- type (character or numeric)
- set functions (list, reserved, intersection, no intersection)
- range (floating point)

When a value fails a test, the verification macro writes an explanation on the log file, and the host macro sets a return code and exits without attempting execution.

Verification does trap most input-data errors and indicates how to correct them. However, it consumes time. The ability to toggle verification is helpful to speed execution when you are sure the input data are good or when you are invoking a macro within a loop.

Just as for banners, every macro definition has a keyword parameter that lets you toggle verification on or off. The normal default is on for user-level macros and off for utility macros.

The debug facility mediates between the user request (if any) and the as-is state to determine whether or not each macro should execute its internal verification code. The result of this determination is preserved as part of each macro's personal debug environment and is available to the executing macro as the value of a global macro variable.

Notes

The NOTES system option controls whether or not notes from DATA or PROC steps are written on the log file. The end-user only wants to see notes from the ultimate DATA or PROC step and from resource-intensive intermediate steps. The developer identifies these steps when coding the macro definition. However, the debug facility lets you suppress or activate <u>all</u> notes in targeted macros.

Source-Code Trace

The debug facility lets you select a simple or a detailed trace for targeted macros. A simple trace writes the text generated by macro execution to the log file. A detailed trace writes the macro code as it resolves during execution.

The default is no trace. The end-user does not want to see any code produced by the macro system. He is only interested in knowing that he got the correct version of the macro and that it produced the desired results. If the desired results are not produced, the developer will localize the problem and request a trace to see if the code is at fault. If so, the macro definition must be edited to correct the error.

Deleting Data Sets

Many macros create intermediate SAS data sets before completing their tasks. Some developers put these in the library associated with the WORK libref, using member names that begin with the underscore character to avoid interfering with the user's data. Other developers prefer to define a separate, temporary SAS library to ensure adequate space and to preclude interfering with the user. In both cases the work data sets should be cleared when the macro ends.

However, sometimes the developer needs to examine these work data sets. For example a macro may produce questionable results even though no syntax or execution errors are logged. You should check the intermediate data sets for unanticipated features such as duplicate observations. This check may reveal logic errors in the code.

In each macro definition the developer identifies the list of data sets to be deleted and libraries and files to be cleared when the macro finishes executing. The %_DEBUG macro does the actual deleting and clearing unless the user has requested otherwise with the %DEBUG macro.

The End-User's Perspective

The end-user invokes %DEBUG to change debug environments without editing macro definitions. Each invocation targets one or more macros for action, and specifies the settings for any combination of the five debug actions. Three of the five actions have on, off, and as-is modes: banner; verification; and notes. The trace action has off, simple, and detailed modes. The data-set option has delete and save modes.

You can invoke %DEBUG more than once in a job. These compound requests are stacked, with the most recent request taking precedence over earlier requests when the same macro is targeted more than once. Invoking %DEBUG with no parameter values clears all previous requests.

You are not required to invoke %DEBUG in each job. If you do not invoke %DEBUG, all macros execute with as-is debug environments. Likewise, when you do invoke %DEBUG, those macros not targeted execute as-is.

Targeting Macros

Targeting means identifying to the debug facility the group of macros whose debug environments you want to change. You can either list the macro names, or you select one of these categories: all; outer (one level removed from the base environment); inner (more than one level deep in the nest); user; or, utility.

Each macro identifies itself to the debug facility as a user, utility, or function macro. A user macro is commonly invoked directly by an end-user, and a utility macro is commonly invoked by a developer from within a higher-level macro. A function macro is a special kind of utility macro that generates text that is less than a complete statement. Usually it produces a single word that is interpreted as a value within an expression where it is invoked.

The As-Is Environment

As-is always means that work data sets are deleted when a macro ends, and that there is no source-code trace.

For the NOTES action, as-is reflects the way the developer coded the macro definition. If the developer did nothing, as-is means NONOTES. However, the developer normally will tell the debug facility to write notes for those DATA or PROC steps that the user may be concerned about. In such cases, as-is means NOTES for only those steps explicitly requested by the developer.

Each macro definition has keyword parameters to toggle banner and verification. The macro definition declares default settings, but these defaults may be overridden by the invoking statement. Consequently, as-is for these two actions reflects the settings declared in the invocation, superimposed on the default settings in the macro definition.

The Developer's Perspective

If you code macro definitions, you must invoke the %_DEBUG macro as the first and last executable statement within each macro definition. This allows the debug facility to manage each macro's debug environment.

The %_DEBUG invocation at the start of each macro specifies to the debug facility the macro name, category (user, utility, or function), version, and support string. The as-is values of banner and verification requests are also passed from the macro to the facility.

The %_DEBUG invocation at the end of each macro names the WORK data members to be deleted, and/or librefs and filerefs to be cleared.

You also request notes for DATA or PROC steps of interest to the user by invoking %_DEBUG before and after these steps to toggle notes on and off, respectively.

Feedback from the Debug Facility

%_DEBUG maintains global variables that can be used by the invoking macro.

The _CHECK_ variable indicates whether or not verification of parameter values should be done. If verification is on, the invoking macro (not %_DEBUG) must call the utility macros needed to check its input.

The _TRACE_ variable indicates whether the source-code trace is off, simple, or detailed. You may want to code customized debug actions in your macro that execute when a simple or detailed trace has been requested. These actions may be %PUT or PUT statements or descriptive PROC's like MEANS, FREQ, or UNIVARIATE.

The _NAMSTAK variable lists the names of macros in the invoking chain. The name of the immediate parent is separately assigned as the value of _MACNAM_.

Knowing the invoking chain is especially useful for the utility macros that handle verification functions. When these macros detect a fault, they must be able to write notes to the log file identifying the macro associated with the faulty data. Often the macro with a problem parameter is two or even three levels above the macro that detects the problem.

How the Facility Works

The debug facility has four tasks:

- communicating user requests into the executing environment, and imposing these requests on the as-is conditions;
- preserving each executing macro's debug environment;
- executing debug actions: %PUT banners; issue OPTIONS statements for notes and trace features; delete work members and clear work libraries;

- informing the executing macro about its debug environment to facilitate conditional debug actions handled by that macro, e.g. verification and custom trace actions.

These tasks are accomplished using 12, reserved, global, macro-variables that can be classified into three groups:

- seven variables used as stacks to communicate compound user-requests to the facility;
- two variables used as stacks for individual debug environments;
- three variables used to inform the executing macro about its debug environment.

Stack operations are emulated with macro character functions. New values are pushed onto the stacks by concatenation, with the new string on the left and the old string on the right. Old values are popped off the stack with the %SUBSTR function or the %SCAN function.

The debug environment for each macro is defined by single-character values for each of five macro variables corresponding to the five debug actions: banner; verify; notes; trace; and save/delete work data sets. Of these five macro variables, three are local to the %_DEBUG macro, and two are global.

The debug environment also has a macro variable whose value lists the chain of names for open (executing) macros.

Avoiding Interference with the Facility

Both the end-user and the developer can easily avoid interfering with the debug facility.

Do not set system options that are reserved for use by the debug facility. These are: SOURCE; SOURCE2; NOTES; MPRINT; MACROGEN; SYMBOLGEN; and MLOGIC. All toggling of these options is done by the %_DEBUG macro.

Do not assign values to any of these 12 reserved global macro variables: _BANNER; _CHECK; _CHECK_; _LEVEL; _MACNAM_; _MACROS; _NAMSTAK; _NOTES; _OPTSTAK; _SAVE; _TRACE; and _TRACE_. These variables provide communication among the user (%DEBUG), the debug facility (%_DEBUG), and the executing macro.

Version 5 Considerations

Version 5.18 trace options do not toggle on and off as they should. The debug facility emulates the desired toggling with the SOURCE option. The results are adequate but not as clean as in Version 6.

This flaw precludes compound user (%DEBUG) requests for a simple trace for one target group of macros and a detailed trace for a second target group.

Another problem stems from SAS procedures that write notes to the log file without beginning each line with 'NOTE:'. Version 5.18 DATASETS and GREPLAY do this when you ask to work with nonexistent members in the no-full-screen (NOFS) mode. If notes are turned off, the resulting log file contains orphan lines that bother end-users.

Function-Macro Considerations

Function macros respond differently than other macros. For function macros only the verification action works in the normal manner.

%_DEBUG cannot issue an OPTIONS statement while a function macro is executing. That means the banner and trace debug actions for function macros are controlled by the debug environment of the parent macro that invokes the function macro.

Since all banners are treated as notes (each line begins with NOTE:), notes must be turned on in the parent macro if you want function-macro banners to print on the log file.

The trace level for a function macro is the same as the trace level for the parent macro. This means a detailed trace for the parent macro automatically extends to any function macros invoked by the parent.

Fortunately, execution errors rarely occur in function macros.

Implementation Issues

Even if they don't know how to use %DEBUG, end-users benefit from the clean log file whenever they use the as-is environment of a macro system that has been written to work with the debug facility. Plus, it is easy to train users how to invoke %DEBUG to control the banner, verify, and trace actions so that they can find simple problems. Providing written documentation for the %DEBUG macro may be sufficient.

Developers need to retro-fit existing macros and code all new macros to use the debug facility. We are addressing this issue by providing a few model data sets that demonstrate how to call the %_DEBUG macro and how to include a conditional block of verification code in macro definitions. We also need to train these developers how to use %DEBUG to quickly find and correct more complex bugs. %DEBUG has proven invaluable to developers in cleaning up their own new macros.

Training developers how to use the library of verification utility macros is more difficult than teaching them to use the debug facility.

How To Find Bugs

The first step in dealing with execution problems in a macro system is locating the macro in which the problem occurs. You do this by calling %DEBUG to turn on all banners:

```
%DEBUG(level=all,banner=banner)
```

Any problem that previously was recorded on the log file will now be bracketed by banners, so you can pin down the problem macro.

Users often make syntax mistakes when they try to invoke a macro. For example, they misspell keywords, fail to separate keyword=value groups with a comma, or fail to properly quote values that contain special characters. Such mistakes produce "Error 1452: parameter not defined with macro" message. Since that macro never executes, the debug facility cannot help you with this problem.

After finding the problem macro (say its name is "problem"), you should verify its input data:

```
%DEBUG(macros=problem,banner=banner,check=check)
```

This should tell you if there are problems with that macro's input. If there are no input problems, you look for errors in the base SAS code produced by the macro by requesting a simple trace:

```
%DEBUG(macros=problem,banner=banner,trace=trace)
```

If this reveals no problems, look for errors in the macro code by requesting a detailed trace:

```
%DEBUG(macros=problem,banner=banner,trace=trace,
       detail=detail)
```

If your output looks wrong but no errors are logged, save the work data sets:

```
%DEBUG(macros=problem,datasets=save)
```

You would then need to examine the saved work data sets, which is most readily done in Display Manager.

Example Macro Definition

The following model for a macro definition shows how a developer might use the %_DEBUG macro.

```
%macro sorter(data=,by=,out=,banner=nobanner,check=check);

  /* header info */

%_debug(action  = start,
        name    = SORTER,type = utility,
        support = %str(Western Production Division, EUSA),
        version = %str(1.00.00 (1/10/91)),
        banner  = &banner,check=&check )

%local datalist;

%if &_check_=1 %then
%do;       /* validate data */
   %if %length(&data)  = 0  %then
     %let data      = _last_;
   %else %if %validation-function-macro = 0 %then %goto exit;

   ... etc., for all parameters

   %end;
%else %do; /* assign defaults when data are not validated */
   %if %length(&data)   = 0  %then %let data      = _last_;
   %if %length(&out)    = 0  %then %let out       = _data_;
   %end;

data _a_;
  set &data;
run;
%let dslist = &dslist _a_;

%_debug(action=notes)
proc sort data=_a_ out=&out;
  by &by;
run;
%_debug(action=nonotes)

%exit: %_debug(action=stop,banner=&banner,data=&datalist)
%mend sorter;
```

An entry call to %_DEBUG lets the %SORTER macro "check in" to the debug facility. The macro parameters BANNER and CHECK convey the as-is settings to the facility.

The global macro variable _CHECK_ has a value of 1 or 0 assigned by %_DEBUG to indicate whether verification is on or off. %SORTER has conditional code to actually check the values of its parameters. This checking is represented here by pseudo code to show that function macros are invoked to verify data. We have a complete library of these verification macros.

The body of the macro normally consists of a sequence of DATA and PROC steps. The names of intermediate work DATA members are collected in a list by appending to the local macro variable named DSLIST. DSLIST is referenced in the exit call to %_DEBUG so that the facility knows which members to delete.

The ultimate step in this model macro is PROC SORT. This step is bracketed by calls to %_DEBUG with ACTION=NOTES and NONOTES so the log file will normally capture the notes generated by PROC SORT.

The last executable statement is an exit call to %_DEBUG to close its debug environment and to restore the parent environment, which may be another executing macro or open code.

The following shows the log file after submitting:

```
%DEBUG(macros=sorter,banner=banner)
%SORTER(data=a,by=x,out=b)
```

```
NOTE: Starting execution of DEBUG    macro, version 3.02.00 (1/11/91)
NOTE:     supported by Western Production Division, EUSA.
NOTE: Ending   execution of DEBUG    macro
42          %DEBUG(MACROS=SORTER,BANNER=BANNER)
NOTE: Starting execution of SORTER   macro, version 1.00.00 (1/10/91)
NOTE:     supported by Western Production Division, EUSA.

NOTE: 4 CYLINDERS DYNAMICALLY ALLOCATED ON SYSDA FOR EACH OF 3 SORT
WORK DATA SETS.
NOTE: DATA SET WORK.B HAS 100 OBSERVATIONS AND 1 VARIABLES.
3912 OBS/TRK.
NOTE: THE PROCEDURE SORT USED 0.38 SECONDS AND 1800K.

NOTE: Ending   execution of SORTER   macro
423         %SORTER(DATA=A,BY=X,OUT=B)
```

Conclusions

We successfully implemented a debug facility for SAS macro systems that yields benefits to both end-users and developers.

End-users get a concise log file that contains only what they need to know about the execution of the macro system. This is normally entry and exit banners from the master macro and notes for the ultimate PROC or DATA step. If execution problems occur, an ambitious end-user can locate the error on his own. This saves time for the support staff.

Developers get the ability to carry out targeted debugging without editing macro definitions. Targeting minimizes the size of the log file. The ability to debug without editing lets you debug directly on the production macros and saves time.

* SAS is the registered trademark of SAS Institute Inc., Cary, NC, USA.

David S. Frankel**
Exxon Company, U.S.A.
P.O. Box 5025
Thousand Oaks, California 91359-5025
(805) 494-2300

Mark A. Kochanski
Sierra Geophysics, Inc.
11255 Kirkland Way
Kirkland, Washington 98033
(206) 822-5200

** Please address requests for user documentation and source code to Mr. Frankel.

CONQUERING THE DREADED MACRO ERROR

Katie A. Hubbell, Computer Data Systems, Inc.

ABSTRACT

The Macro facility is a very powerful tool in SAS* programming. By the same token, it can cause some powerful and, at times, intimidating errors. As macros become more complex with increased programmer skill, it becomes more and more important to form a system for writing macros that avoids as many pitfalls as possible. Debugging must become more systematic and orderly to avoid wasting time and computer costs.

This paper outlines some simple methods for ensuring that macro code is as clean as possible before testing, as well as methods for testing and debugging macros efficiently and quickly.

INTRODUCTION

Macro errors are a different species than SAS errors. There is a higher level of difficulty in resolving macro errors. In base SAS, error resolution is a two-step process: 1) find out why the error occurred, and 2) find out how to fix it. With the addition of macro, an extra step is needed first: find out *where* the error occurred. Also, when macro is involved there is more than one type of error. There can be:

1. Macro errors (for example, 1301, 1555);
2. SAS errors and program abends that are really caused by a macro (for example, 180 for an unresolved macro call, 405 for an invalid hex literal, S0C4 abend);
3. SAS errors caused by data, options, global macro variables, etc. that the macro inadvertently changed;
4. Not to mention logic errors, problems in output or data caused by something the macro did, which may not even cause error messages.

This difference in the complexity of errors makes sense when you realize that the macro language is in fact a completely different language than base SAS, though the syntax is similar. It operates on a lower level than base SAS and therefore requires more programmer intervention and control.

The following section will help you to avoid each of these types of errors by writing macros defensively, so to speak. The subsequent section will help you debug those problems that slip through anyway.

STARTING OFF RIGHT: WRITING BETTER MACROS

An idea for a useful Macro is born. The company Macro whiz (the one who was sent to the course) sketches it out on paper, then sits down and types in the code for the Macro. The next step should NOT be to test the Macro. There are a few steps which should be taken between writing and testing which can greatly increase testing efficiency and lower cost.

Modularity

First, consider how the Macro is to be stored. Modularity is a popular way to create order in program writing in general, and it can be applied to Macro writing as well.

Complex Macros should be stored as separate entities, since they may (and ideally should) be used by more than one program or even more than one programmer (see Figure 1). A good rule is one module per Macro, and only the Macro definition in the module.

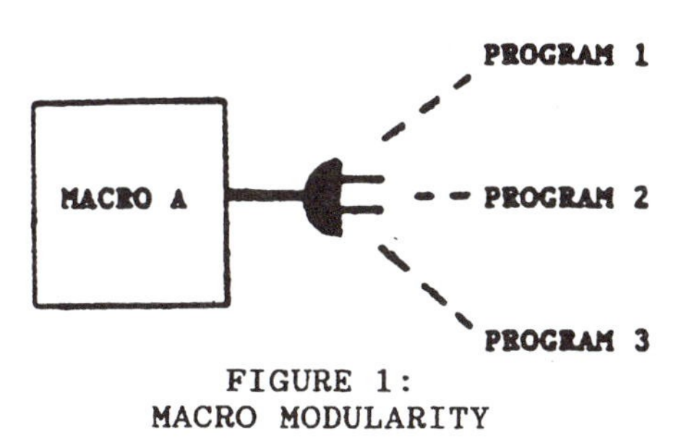

FIGURE 1:
MACRO MODULARITY

Even if a Macro is not to be used by others, another important reason for modularity is that it is much easier to test and debug a Macro as a separate entity. Rather than culling it out from your lengthy program for testing, or worse yet, running your entire program to test the Macro, it can be unit tested before it is put to use. In addition, code stored in this form is more easily reused and expanded as needs and programs change.

Know your environment

There is a lot of talk about "environments" when the subject of Macro comes up. This is not just another technical term used by Macro experts, but a vital aid to understanding how Macro works. One way to envision the concept is to think of a large program or system as a bunch of envelopes, some inside others, some just separate, in a large envelope which is the entire program (see Figure 2).

It is important to know what the total environment will look like during a given Macro's execution, because everything that is active in the "current processing environment" has the potential to affect the Macro's outcome. A good way to keep track of this is by knowing each Macro's inputs and outputs. Every Macro has obvious inputs, such as Macro parameters, and not-so-obvious ones, such as global Macro variables or Macro

---

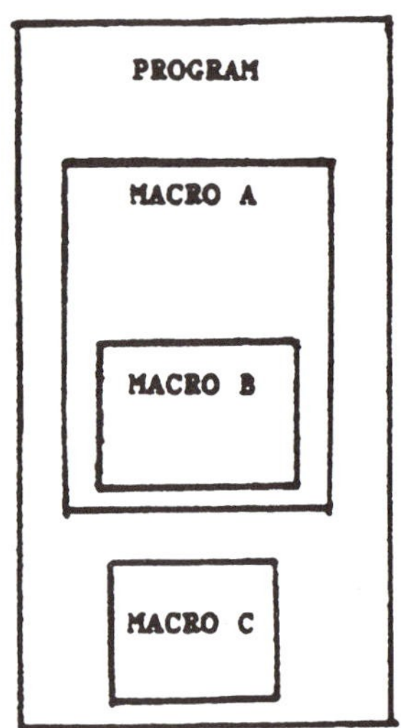

FIGURE 2:
MACRO ENVIRONMENTS

---

variables created in an environment which envelops the current Macro. Because the majority of Macros are created to be used in more than one program, it is important to note the variable names used in a Macro to avoid conflict with surrounding code.

It is also a good idea to use *meaningful* or *unique* names for variables which will only be used inside the Macro, or, better still, use the %LOCAL statement whenever possible to avoid ambiguity. %LOCAL is a very powerful means of avoiding logic problems. Using this statement, you can keep the variable names used in your Macro from affecting or being affected by the values of any global variables with the same name.

Macros have hidden outputs as well. A classic example is the %TESTPRNT Macro in Figure 3.

```
%macro testprnt
       (dsn=,
        nobs=100);
  %if &test=Y %then
  %do;  /* PRINT */
    PROC PRINT DATA=&DSN
               (OBS=&NOBS);
    TITLE "&DSN TEST PRINT";
    RUN;
  %end; /* PRINT */
%mend testprnt;
```

FIGURE 3:
%TESTPRNT MACRO

A hidden input to this Macro is the global variable &TEST. The Macro expects this variable to be available in the processing environment. A hidden output is the TITLE statement, which will wipe out any TITLE that may have been previously in effect. If this fact is not documented, it could lead to a nasty surprise for someone using the Macro.

Macros tend to grow and evolve as programmers find better ways to perform the task. For example, the Macro above could be improved by allowing the specification of title line to be used in the parameter list, so that in different programs only the parameter need be changed to avoid trashing TITLEs. Because of changes, the list of inputs and outputs to a Macro may change over time. It is a good idea, whenever possible, to keep track of the inputs and outputs, because they are an invaluable tool in testing. Knowing all of the inputs to a Macro allows you to completely separate the Macro unit and test by setting up all of the inputs and calling the Macro. For example, to test the %TESTPRNT Macro above a data set and a %LET TEST=Y or N are needed.

An organized list of inputs and outputs also makes the Macro more useful to others, because it will be a known quantity and will be "safe" to use. Researching the inputs and outputs should be a part of the analysis of any Macro. One way of listing the inputs and outputs to a Macro is shown in Figure 4.

After the %MACRO statement:

```
 /* MACRO TESTPRNT
    STORED IN [library]
    CREATED BY [name]
    CREATED ON [date]
    LAST MODIFIED [date]

    INPUTS:
     &TEST (=Y or N)
     &DSN
     &NOBS
    OUTPUTS:
     TITLE is changed */
```

FIGURE 4:
SAMPLE INPUT/OUTPUT LIST

Checklist

Before doing any testing, you can cut down on Macro syntax errors by going through a simple eye-check. Figure 5 shows a sample checklist. You may be surprised at how much this helps. Sometimes the simplest changes such as changing the name of the Macro can cause the most daunting errors (for example, if you forget to change the %MEND statement name); so don't forget to use it when modifying as well.

An additional aid in eye checking which some find useful is to separate Macro code from SAS code in some visual way such as using lower case for Macro code, as shown in Figure 3. One problem with eye checking is that a TO, for example, looks normal at a glance even when it should be a %TO. Identifying Macro code with lower case helps prevent confusion of the two.

Preparation for Testing and Debugging

When you have checked over the code and are ready to test, be sure the right options are in place to aid you. See Figure 6 for a complete set of options pertinent to Macro.

To see what your Macro actually does, you have two choices of Macro options: those that help you see the SAS code generated, and those that help you see the Macro code generated. If your Macro contains mostly SAS code, you will want to use the MPRINT option. If there are complicated

----

* Is the Macro the only thing in the module?
* Do the %MACRO and %MEND statements appear correctly and contain the same name?
* Do all %DOs and %ENDs have a match, and do they all start with %?
* What about %IFs, %THENs and %ELSEs? %TOs for %DO loops?
* Do you have an appropriate step break (PROC, DATA, or RUN) between the assigning of any Macro variable values using SYMPUT and their use?
* Do the variables used in your %IFs and Macro functions contain any "tricky" values and if so, have you used proper quoting functions?
* If you use any index Macro variables in loops, are they unique from any regular variable names you may be using inside the loop?
* Do all statements end with semicolons?
* If you use any double or multiple ampersands, do they plot out correctly?
* Are all comments ended correctly?
* Do all of the Macro variables used have meaningful names and %LOCAL or %GLOBAL statements as appropriate? (Note: Macro parameter variables do not need to be specified as %LOCAL; they automatically are.)
* Do you have any calls to other Macros inside this one? If so, have you checked out the inputs and outputs? What are the inputs to this Macro?

FIGURE 5:
MACRO SYNTAX CHECKLIST

Macro statements and functions, you will probably be better off with NOMPRINT MACROGEN SYMBOLGEN MLOGIC. (Note MPRINT must be explicitly turned off if it is the default or has been previously turned on.) The two types of options do not work together, so you will have to make a choice as to which will give you the most information. Routinely test with debugging options on, just in case of error. You can change from one type to the other in the middle if the situation warrants; however, remember to place a RUN; statement directly after the options statement to put it into effect immediately. In version 6, the MTRACE option is added and further clarifies Macro code. For the clearest picture, MPRINT should be paired with MTRACE. Figure 7 demonstrates the type of log output received using each option set.

---

* CMDMAC allows command style Macros; should be off unless needed
* DQUOTE allows Macro resolution inside double quotes; should be on
* IMPLMAC allows implied Macros; should be off unless needed
* MACRO must be on
* MAUTOSOURCE allows com- pilation of Macros from a specified library without %INCLUDEs; should be off until Macro is completely tested; use %INCLUDEs with SOURCE2 to check for syntax errors
* MCOMPILE, when off, introduces Macro compiler each time a Macro is referenced rather than only once for the entire job; should be on
* MERROR should be on
* MRECALL should be off
* SERROR should be on
* SOURCE and SOURCE2 are user's discretion, but for MPRINT to work, SOURCE must be on

* OBS=0 should be avoided if using CALL SYMPUT; it does not happen when OBS=0

FIGURE 6:
OPTIONS PERTINENT TO MACRO

An extra help in testing and debugging is the %PUT statement. A system of standard %PUT statements at the beginning and end of each Macro definition can be a great help in pinpointing problem location and determining whether a Macro executed in a given run. A sample is shown in Figure 8.

WHEN YOU DO GET AN ERROR: TESTING AND DEBUGGING TIPS

It is of course all well and good to plan the heavy analysis and preparation for Macro writing, but it doesn't always happen in practice. Even with the best of intentions, problems can slip through or develop later. In addition, at times programmers are left with predecessors' code which is already written and of course used none of these techniques. What is to be done when Macro code, especially in a large program, suddenly develops a strange bug?

```
%let test=Y;
OPTIONS SOURCE MPRINT;
%testprnt (dsn=cars)
PROC PRINT DATA=CARS
(OBS=100);
TITLE "CARS TEST PRINT";
RUN;

OPTIONS NOMPRINT MACROGEN SYMBOLGEN
MLOGIC;
>Y
     2-&SYMBOL
>&TEST=Y
     1-<MLOGIC>
 %testprnt (dsn=cars)
+PROC PRINT DATA=&DSN
     1-%TESTPRNT
+CARS
     2-&SYMBOL
+(NOBS=&NOBS)
     1-%TESTPRNT
+100
     2-&SYMBOL
+                            ;
     1-%TESTPRNT
+TITLE
     1-%TESTPRNT
>&DSN TEST PRINT
     2-<MLOGIC>
>CARS
     4-&SYMBOL
+         "&DSN TEST PRINT";
     1-%TESTPRNT
+RUN;
     1-%TESTPRNT

OPTIONS NOMLOGIC NOMACROGEN
NOSYMBOLGEN MTRACE MPRINT;
%testprnt (dsn=cars)
Beginning execution.
Parameter DSN has value CARS
%IF condition &TEST=Y is TRUE
 PROC PRINT DATA=CARS
 (NOBS=100);
 TITLE "CARS TEST PRINT";
 RUN;
```

FIGURE 7:
LOG RESULTS OF MACRO OPTIONS

```
%macro testprnt;
%put NOTE: *** MACRO TESTPRNT HAS
BEGUN;

     ... code ...

%put NOTE: *** MACRO TESTPRNT HAS
ENDED;
%mend testprnt;
```

FIGURE 8:
STANDARD %PUTS

The three main causes of Macro errors are:

1. Simple coding mistakes
2. Nonexistent or unexpected Macro variable values
3. Unforeseen changes to the processing environment caused by a Macro.

Coding mistakes

Always start with the obvious. The Appendix of this paper has hints on where to look for problems when you receive a Macro error message.

Unexpected values

Figure 9 shows two examples of unexpected values. Remember that Macro is a text processor, but unshielded keywords will always be seen as keywords. You might say that everything is out in the open in Macro, whereas you can shield values in SAS with quotes. The Macro quoting functions can solve these problems, as shown in Figure 10.

```
%let a=CARY,NC;
%let b=%scan(&a,1);
ERROR 1550: REQUIRED OPERATOR NOT
FOUND.

What Macro processor saw:
%let b=%scan(cary,nc,1);

%let instnm=SCHOOL OF SCIENCE AND
TECHNOLOGY;
%if &instnm ne %str( ) %then
  %put &instnm;
ERROR 1555: CHARACTER OPERAND FOUND
WHERE NUMERIC REQUIRED.

What Macro processor saw:
%if SCHOOL OF SCIENCE AND TECHNOLOGY
ne %str( ) %then
  %put &instnm;
```

FIGURE 9: UNEXPECTED VALUES

Unforeseen changes

A good example of this phenomenon is the "ubiquitous &I". Say that one Macro contains a large %DO loop with a lot of processing, inside of which a smaller Macro is executed. This Macro also contains a %DO loop. Both use &I as the counter. %LOCAL statements have not been used. Figure 11 shows the effect and results.

```
%let a=CARY,NC;
%let b=%scan(%quote(&a),1);
  OR
%let a=%quote(CARY,NC);
%let b=%scan(&a,1);

%let instnm=SCHOOL OF SCIENCE AND
TECHNOLOGY;
%if %quote(&instnm) ne %str( ) %then .
. .
  OR
%let instnm=%quote(SCHOOL OF SCIENCE
AND TECHNOLOGY);
%if &instnm ne %str( ) %then ...
```

FIGURE 10: SOLUTIONS

```
%do i=1 %to 3;
  < code >
  %do i=1 to 4;
    < code >
  %end;
%end;
```

The code in the outer loop will be executed only once, since the inner loop will increment and leave &I at 5.

Consider the opposite effect:

```
%do i=1 %to 4;
  %do i=1 %to 2;
  %end;
%end;
```

The loop is endless.

FIGURE 11: THE UBIQUITOUS &I

Debugging

If the problem is an obvious coding mistake, it can be fixed where it is. However, if it appears to be of the second or third variety, *do not* waste time and energy trying to debug the entire program. Instead, follow these steps:

1. Isolate
2. Replicate
3. Apply solution(s)
4. Reinstate

These steps are discussed in detail below.

Isolate

The first task is to pinpoint exactly where in the program the error is occurring. If the debugging options are not on, turn them on, or use %PUTs to track the statements. If you use standard %PUTs to signify the beginning and end of each Macro, you may be able to locate the offending Macro immediately. Note that as soon as an error is encountered in a given Macro, processing "skips" out to the next environment without executing any more statements in that Macro. Look for the last statement that was executed before the skip.

The idea is to find the smallest piece of code that will still trigger the error. Then you can remove that piece (a Macro module, or even part of one) and work on it separately. Interactive SAS is good for this.

Replicate

This is probably the most important step, and the one most often forgotten. If you forget this step, you may be running in circles without solving the real problem.

Using your input list and your knowledge of the program and data, manipulate the inputs to the Macro until you have replicated the error. If you can't replicate the error, you know it's either a bigger problem than just the portion you have isolated, and the real bug is probably prior to this part, and you need a larger chunk, or you have input values you don't know about.

Apply solution(s)

Once you've replicated the problem, congratulations -- the hard part is over. Ten to one you'll now know why the problem occurred, or if not why, at least what data value or statement caused it. Now all you have to do is fiddle with the quoting functions, syntax, values, or whatever needs to be changed. If the code worked with one input value and not with another, be sure to test both ways to make sure your fix hasn't merely created a new bug.

Reinstate

When you are satisfied that it works, reinstate the module and test the entire program. Note that sometimes the actual change to be made is elsewhere than the module that was tested.

CONCLUSION

Macro is a rewarding and powerful tool which provides users with a quantum leap in their ability to perform complex tasks using SAS. Macro errors encountered tend to grow in complexity as the user's ability grows, but the same rules apply no matter how complicated the code or obscure the error. Remember that the very characteristics which make Macro seem so daunting and hard to control are those which give it its amazing power. All it takes to tame the wild Macro is a little organization at the start and the right tools along the way.

APPENDIX:
MACRO ERROR REFERENCE

Common Macro Errors

1301: APPARENT SYMBOLIC REFERENCE NOT RESOLVED
Check Macro variables:
* Macro variable name misspelled
* Macro variable created in local environment and referenced outside that environment
* Macro variable created by CALL SYMPUT and referenced in same DATA step
* Variable created by CALL SYMPUT when OBS=0

1353: APPARENT MACRO INVOCATION NOT RESOLVED
Check Macro calls:
* Macro name misspelled
* Macro referenced before it is compiled

1550: REQUIRED OPERATOR NOT FOUND and 1555: CHARACTER OPERAND FOUND WHERE NUMERIC REQUIRED
Check %DO loops and %IF-%THEN statements:
* % signs missing on keywords
* Macro variable used in statement has character (or decimal) value
* Macro variable unresolved (or resolved incorrectly) inside statement

Macro Error Groupings

%DO loops: 1100, 1124, 1128, 1135, 1550, 1555
%IFs: 1115, 1116, 1120, 1404, 1405, 1550, 1552, 1555
%GOTOs: 1114, 1139, 1402, 1408
Parameters/Macro definitions: 1102, 1104, 1105, 1107, 1125, 1134, 1135, 1353, 1452, 1454, 1455, 1456
%LETs: 1302, 1350, 1500

Open error on Macro: 1101, 1354, 1355, 1400
%GLOBAL: 1501
%EVAL: 1555
MWORK option too small: 1300, 1600, 1603, 1653

SAS Error Messages That Can Be Caused By Macro

ERROR: UNEXPECTED END OF FILE
* %INCLUDEd code wrong LRECL
180: STATEMENT IS NOT VALID
* Unrecognized Macro variable or call
405: INVALID NUMERIC HEX LITERAL
* Macro variable whose value contains a valid hex literal is specified where a %EVAL or implied %EVAL is done
107: CHARACTER LITERAL IS TOO LONG
* A single quote appears in a Macro variable value

REFERENCES

1. SAS Institute, Inc., *SAS Views: SAS Macro Language*, Version 5 Edition, 1986.

2. SAS Institute, Inc., *SAS Guide to Macro Processing*, Version 6 Edition, 1987.

3. SAS Institute, Inc., *SAS Guide to Problem Solving and Error Messages*, Version 5 Edition, 1988.

* SAS is a registered trademark of SAS Institute, Inc., Cary, NC, USA.

The author may be contacted at:

Computer Data Systems, Inc.
20010 Century Boulevard
Germantown, MD 20874

Telephone: (301) 353-5729

Debugging Your SAS® Macro Application under VMS™: A Practical Approach

Jodie Gilmore, SAS Institute Inc., Cary, NC
Linda Helwig, SAS Institute Inc., Cary, NC

ABSTRACT

One of the most exciting features of Release 6.06 of the SAS® System under VMS™ is the full macro facility. As VMS users take full advantage of the macro facility, it is necessary for them to know how to efficiently debug their macro applications. This paper uses a hands-on approach to present debugging techniques and tools that are useful in macro applications running under VMS. The audience for this paper is programmers who are familiar with the SAS language and have a basic understanding of the SAS macro language.

INTRODUCTION

Debugging macro applications is often a frustrating, "guess and by golly" affair, full of trial and error. But it doesn't have to be that way.

One of the ways to decrease the time spent debugging a macro application is to develop it in such a way that problems are minimized. You can accomplish this by modular development and by adding problem-catching code. Then, when problems do arise, you can use several features of the SAS System to pinpoint the cause and location of the problem. This paper presents these and other techniques for debugging SAS macro applications to help you eliminate the guesswork when debugging your macro applications.

An example macro application is used throughout the following sections to illustrate the debugging techniques. This example is called GETINFO, an interactive macro application that allows you to display a list of directories or files, and the attributes, such as memory usage, file protection, and so on, for these files. You indicate which file you want information about by using a directory name (including the default, [ ]), a filename, or a VMS symbol. You can use this macro application, and the debugging techniques you learn as the application is developed, to develop and debug your own SAS macro applications.

Although the debugging techniques this paper presents are geared toward macro applications developed under VMS, many of the techniques can be adjusted for debugging macro applications developed under other host operating systems.

THE DEBUGGING PHILOSOPHY

Debugging macro applications is often difficult because the flow of control, resolution of variables, and so on are invariably more complex in a macro application. There are several basic debugging techniques that you can apply to your macro applications:

- Develop your macro application one module at a time.
- While working on each module, use SAS system options to monitor the macro's execution.
- Add your own debugging code to each module, using automatic macro variables, macro program statements, and macro functions to pinpoint or prevent problems.

Each of these techniques is discussed in this section.

Modularize Your Macro Application

One of the most common problems in debugging macro applications is caused by developing and executing the entire application at once, then being overwhelmed by the number of error messages and incorrect results. You don't know where to begin to fix the problems. You can avoid a lot of frustration by developing and debugging each module of your application separately.

Another good idea is to develop the open code first, then add the macro layer around it. (*Open code* is SAS programming statements that are outside a macro definition.) As you add the macro layer, add the simple macro code first, then the more complex macro code. This last technique is especially important for interactive macro applications such as GETINFO because debugging the use of the %WINDOW and %DISPLAY statements and macro variable resolution can be particularly complex.

This section provides examples of how we applied the techniques of developing each module separately and layering the code as we completed the GETINFO application.

Developing and debugging each module separately

There are 11 modules in the GETINFO application. Some are short, such as the CHK_SPEC macro shown below. This macro checks to see if the user invoked the GETINFO application using the default, a symbol, directory, or filename.

```
%macro chk_spec(filechk);
   %global type;

   %* If the user specified the default, [], goto ECHECK;
      %if %quote(&filechk)=%str([]) or %quote(&filechk)=%str(<>) or
          %quote(&filechk)= %then
         %do;
            %let type=dir;
            %goto ECHECK;
         %end;

   %CHK_SYM:
   %* First, see if the user specified a symbol;
      %let spec=%sysget(&filechk);
      %if &spec^= %then
         %do;
            %put The value of the symbol is:  &spec;
            %let filechk=&spec;
         %end;

   %DET_SYM:
   %* Now, determine if the user specified a file or a directory name;
      %let len=%length(&filechk);
      %let brkt=%substr(&filechk,&len,1);
      %put BRKT=&brkt;
      %if %quote(&brkt)=%str(]) or
          %quote(&brkt)=%str(>) %then %let type=dir;
      %else %let type=file;

   %ECHECK: %put type=&type;
%mend chk_spec;
```

When we first ran this module, we discovered two bugs: the %SUBSTR macro function was misspelled as %DINDYT; also, we didn't use the %QUOTE and %STR macro functions when checking the value of BRKT. This second error caused the SAS System to treat the character > as the greater than operator instead of just a character.

When we ran the whole application, including the erroneous CHK_SPEC macro, the log messages were obscure:

```
WARNING: Apparent invocation of macro GETINFO not resolved.
239  %getinfo(sugi$:<sasdemo.sas>)
      -
ERROR 180-322: Statement is not valid or it is used out of proper order.
```

These messages do not point to the problem; furthermore, they hide the source of the error.

In contrast to the obscure warning and error messages generated when we tried to run the whole application, the messages generated when we ran this module by itself made the errors easy to find. Below is an excerpt from the log messages generated when we executed the CHK_SPEC macro (with errors):

```
WARNING: The argument to macro function %SYSGET is not defined
         as a system variable.
WARNING: Apparent invocation of macro DINDYT not resolved.
WARNING: Apparent invocation of macro DINDYT not resolved.
ERROR: Required operator not found in expression: (&brkt = ])
       or (&brkt =>)
ERROR: The macro will stop executing.
```

The warning messages point directly to the misspelled macro function, and the error message about operators gives a clue to the other bug. It would have taken us much longer to find and fix the errors if we had not debugged the CHK_SPEC macro separately.

Developing each layer

Another way to modularize the development of your macro application is to add the macro layer at the very end. For example, while developing the GETINFO application, we concentrated first on simply getting the information generated by the DIR/FULL command into a SAS data set. When we could do that without errors, we then placed the code into a macro. Finally, we wrote another macro to create macro variables from the SAS data set variables. If we had tried to create a macro right away that performed all these tasks, the debugging time would have increased greatly.

Another advantage of creating the SAS data set first, and then the macro variables, is that the SAS data set variables provide material for many macro variables. For example, although the SAS data set has just one variable for file size, we created two macro variables from this one data set variable (number of blocks allocated and number of blocks used). This approach gives you more flexibility than creating only the macro variables.

Even adding the macro layer of code can be done in stages. For the GETINFO application, adding the %WINDOW and %DISPLAY code was the last thing we did. We wanted to be sure each task of the application worked correctly (tasks such as reading in the DIR/FULL command results, creating the SAS data set, and creating the macro variables) before we began to add the interactive portions of code. This cut down on our debugging time because debugging window macro application code can be time consuming: you have to consider window layout, the complexity of the macro variable resolution, and so on.

If you are writing a macro that has several logical divisions, code each piece separately, then combine them into the larger macro when each piece works by itself. For example, when we developed the CHK_SEL macro, which validates the user's selection of a file, we tested our use of the autocall macros %DATATYP and %VERIFY by creating a small macro named TEST. When the TEST macro ran without errors, we added that code to the original CHK_SEL macro.

The concept of modularization during development can be reversed and applied to debugging as well. If you have a fairly complex macro that contains an error, break that macro into several smaller pieces, and test each one. If you are creating a SAS data set with a macro and encounter errors, pare down the data set to just a few variables and observations. This approach helps you isolate problems and makes the debugging phase go much faster.

Each of these modularization techniques saved us a lot of time as we developed and debugged the GETINFO application. However, we occasionally ran across an error that was a mystery. In those cases, we used SAS system options to help us locate the problem. Some of these system options are discussed in the next section.

Use Debugging System Options to Your Advantage

The SAS language provides several system options to help you debug your SAS macro applications:

MACRO	controls whether the SAS macro facility is available.
MERROR	controls whether the SAS macro language compiler issues a warning message if the macro processor cannot match a macro-like name to an appropriate macro keyword.
SERROR	controls whether warning messages are issued when the SAS System encounters a macro variable reference that cannot be matched with an appropriate macro variable.
MLOGIC	displays information about the execution of a macro.
MPRINT	displays the statements the SAS compiler receives.
SYMBOLGEN	displays text resulting from macro variable resolution.

MACRO, MERROR, and SERROR should always be set. If they are not set, use the OPTIONS statement or OPTIONS window to turn on these options. The last three options, MLOGIC, MPRINT, and SYMBOLGEN, are useful tools during the debugging phase of a macro application. Knowing when and how to use each of these options can help you debug your macro application much faster.

MLOGIC, MPRINT, and SYMBOLGEN provide different results. Below are examples of using these system options with an error we found as we developed the GETINFO application. The macro GETINFO calls the macro CRT_DS, which creates a SAS data set from the text file containing the file attribute information returned from the DIR/FULL command. Initially, the CRT_DS macro contained some erroneous code.

```
options ls=80 ps=60;
filename fileinf '&&fileinfo';
filename filecvt '&&filecvt';

data convert;
   infile fileinf;
   file filecvt recfm=f lrecl=80;
   input;
   put _infile_;
run;
   .
   .
   .
```

Using no options

When we invoked GETINFO with all the macro debugging system options set to off, the log messages were as follows:

```
133  options nomlogic nomprint nosymbolgen;
134  %getinfo()
ERROR: Invalid physical name.
ERROR: Error in the LIBNAME or FILENAME statement.
ERROR: Invalid physical name.
ERROR: Error in the LIBNAME or FILENAME statement.

ERROR: No logical assign for filename FILEINF.
NOTE: The file FILECVT is:
      File=SUGI$:[SASDEMO.SAS]FILECVT.DAT
```

The log messages in this case are not all that helpful. You cannot even tell what macro was executing when the errors occurred.

Using the MLOGIC option

The MLOGIC option monitors macro execution, including information such as when the macro begins and ends, all results of conditional branching, whether a macro variable is local or global, and the values of parameters passed to a macro. When we invoked the GETINFO macro with the MLOGIC option, the log messages were as follows:

```
407  options mlogic nomprint nosymbolgen;
408  %getinfo()
MLOGIC(GETINFO):   %IF condition &sysrc ne 1 is FALSE
MLOGIC(CRT_DS):   Beginning execution.
ERROR: Invalid physical name.
ERROR: Error in the LIBNAME or FILENAME statement.
ERROR: Invalid physical name.
ERROR: Error in the LIBNAME or FILENAME statement.

ERROR: No logical assign for filename FILEINF.
NOTE: The file FILECVT is:
      File=SUGI$:[SASDEMO.SAS]FILECVT.DAT
```

From these log messages we could see that the problem occurred in the CRT_DS macro. But we still couldn't see which statements were causing the error. Because our error was not in the area of program logic, the MLOGIC option was not the best choice for discovering the problem.

Using the MPRINT option

Our next step was to try the MPRINT option. The MPRINT option displays the statements that the SAS compiler receives. When we invoked GETINFO again, we got the following log messages:

```
413  options nomlogic mprint nosymbolgen;
414  %getinfo()
MPRINT(CRT_DS):     OPTIONS LS=80 PS=60;
MPRINT(CRT_DS):     FILENAME FILEINF '&&fileinfo';
ERROR: Invalid physical name.
ERROR: Error in the LIBNAME or FILENAME statement.
MPRINT(CRT_DS):     FILENAME FILECVT '&&filecvt';
ERROR: Invalid physical name.
ERROR: Error in the LIBNAME or FILENAME statement.
MPRINT(CRT_DS):     DATA CONVERT;
MPRINT(CRT_DS):     INFILE FILEINF;
MPRINT(CRT_DS):     FILE FILECVT RECFM=F LRECL=80;
MPRINT(CRT_DS):     INPUT;
MPRINT(CRT_DS):     PUT _INFILE_;
MPRINT(CRT_DS):     RUN;

ERROR: No logical assign for filename FILEINF.
NOTE: The file FILECVT is:
      File=SUGI$:[SASDEMO.SAS]FILECVT.DAT
```

These messages point directly to the source of the problem: the physical file specifications in the FILENAME statements are incorrect. Macro variables won't resolve when they are enclosed in single quotes. With this information, we could fix the code. Here are the corrected statements:

```
filename fileinf "&fileinfo";
filename filecvt "&filecvt";
```

Another potential problem with the original FILENAME statements was our use of a double ampersand. Although in this case && was equivalent to &, confusion about how many ampersands are necessary is common. The general rule is that && resolves to &. You can avoid potential errors in macro variable resolution by familiarizing yourself with macro variable resolution rules before starting to develop your macro application.

Using the SYMBOLGEN option

The SYMBOLGEN option shows you what macro variables resolve to. This option is especially useful to check the value of a macro variable during macro execution. The log messages tell you what each macro variable's value is, and you can readily see if the value is not what you expected. When we invoked the GETINFO macro with the SYMBOLGEN option, the log messages were as follows:

```
250  options nomlogic nomprint symbolgen;
251  %getinfo()
SYMBOLGEN:  Macro variable FILECHK resolves to []
SYMBOLGEN:  Macro variable FILECHK resolves to []
SYMBOLGEN:  Macro variable FILECHK resolves to []
SYMBOLGEN:  Macro variable TYPE resolves to dir
type=dir
SYMBOLGEN:  Macro variable TYPE resolves to dir
type=dir
SYMBOLGEN:  Macro variable TYPE resolves to dir
SYMBOLGEN:  Macro variable FILEINFO resolves to
   sugi$:[sasdemo.dat]file.data
SYMBOLGEN:  Macro variable GETFILE resolves to []
SYMBOLGEN:  Macro variable SYSRC resolves to 1
ERROR: Invalid physical name.
ERROR: Error in the LIBNAME or FILENAME statement.
ERROR: Invalid physical name.
ERROR: Error in the LIBNAME or FILENAME statement.

ERROR: No logical assign for filename FILEINF.
NOTE: The file FILECVT is:
      File=SUGI$:[SASDEMO.SAS]FILECVT.DAT

NOTE: 0 records were written to the file FILECVT.
NOTE: The SAS System stopped processing this step because of errors.
WARNING: The data set WORK.CONVERT may be incomplete.  When this step
         was stopped there were 0 observations and 0 variables.

NOTE: The infile FILECVT is:
      File=SUGI$:[SASDEMO.SAS]FILECVT.DAT

NOTE: 0 records were read from the infile FILECVT.
NOTE: The data set SUGILIB.TEMP has 0 observations and 18 variables.
```

Because our error (using single quotes instead of double quotes) was not caused by an incorrect macro variable value, the SYMBOLGEN option did not provide too much more useful information. However, it does trace the resolution of all the variables in the macro, which could be valuable information at a later date in the debugging cycle.

Deciding which option to use

You should not use more options than you need; too much information may actually obscure the solution to the problem. Each option is useful for a particular type of error, at a particular place in macro execution, as shown in **Figure 1**.

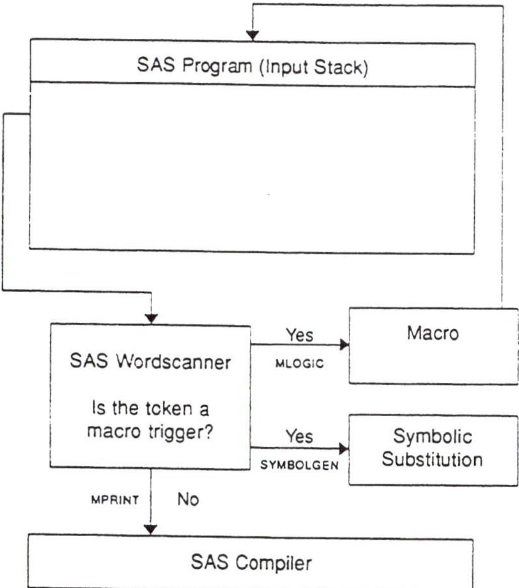

Figure 1 The Role of System Options during Macro Execution

Use MLOGIC to trace macro execution The MLOGIC option is especially useful for monitoring macro execution. The information generated by this option includes when a macro begins and ends and full tracing of branch execution (for example, %IF-%THEN-%ELSE code). It also tells you which macro variables are local and global, and displays the values of parameters passed to a macro. If you suspect your errors are caused by faulty logic or a section of code executing at the wrong time, use the MLOGIC option to trace what is really happening.

Use MPRINT to see generated statements The MPRINT option is especially useful for seeing the statements the SAS compiler receives. This option allows you to see in the SAS log the actual generated statements. If you suspect your errors are caused by incorrect SAS programming statements, use the MPRINT option.

Use SYMBOLGEN to see values of macro variables The SYMBOLGEN option is especially useful for seeing the resolved values of macro variables. If you suspect your errors are caused by a macro variable resolving to the wrong value, use the SYMBOLGEN option to display the values of the macro variables as your macro executes.

Add Your Own Error Diagnostics

There are many components of the macro facility you can use to add error diagnostic code to your macro application. This paper discusses only the most common components. Each macro application is different, and you may find other techniques that are useful as you develop your macro applications.

Some of the most common techniques for adding diagnostic code to a macro application include

- using automatic macro variables, such as SYSRC, with the %SYSEXEC and X statements
- using macro program statements, such as %PUT
- using macro functions, such as %SYSGET and the quoting functions
- using autocall macros supplied by SAS Institute, such as DATATYP and VERIFY.

Using automatic macro variables

Automatic macro variables are very useful in developing macro applications that perform error checking. The automatic macro variable we found most useful is SYSRC. This automatic macro variable contains the operating system return code for statements submitted to the operating system (with a %SYSEXEC or X statement or the X command, for example). We used this variable extensively throughout the GETINFO application. Here is an example of how we used the SYSRC automatic macro variable:

```
%sysexec dir/width=(display=80)/full/out=&fileinfo &getfile;
%if &sysrc ne 1 %then
   %do;
      %put SYSRC= &sysrc;
      %put %str();
      %put &getfile does not exist...;
      %put %str();
   %end;
```

In this code, we check the value of SYSRC. A successful DCL command sets SYSRC to 1. If SYSRC is not 1, then the command failed, and we print a message to that effect.

There are many automatic macro variables; some of the ones you may find most useful under VMS include

SYSDEVIC	gives the current graphics device. This macro variable is often used in macro applications requiring a specific graphics device.
SYSSCP	gives the current operating system. This macro variable is often used in macro applications running under several operating systems.

Using macro program statements

You may want to use macro program statements in your diagnostic code. One very useful statement is the %PUT statement. You can use this statement in combination with automatic macro variables and other macro variables to send diagnostic messages to the log. While we were developing the CHK_SPEC macro, we used the %PUT statement extensively to check the values of macro variables such as SPEC (the macro variable containing the resolved VMS symbol), FILECHK (to see what filename, symbol, or directory the user supplied), and BRKT (to see what the last character of &FILECHK was).

We also used the %PUT statement when we began to add the interactive layer to our macro application, as in this example:

```
%do i=1 %to &obs;
   %if %eval(&i)=1 %then
      %do;
         %put dir&i=&&dir&i;
      %end;
   %put file&i=&&file&i;
   %put actsz&i=&&actsz&i;
   %put allsz&i=&&allsz&i;
   %put ownr&i=&&ownr&i;
   %put rdat&i=&&rdat&i;
   %put rtim&i=&&rtim&i;
%end;
```

Using macro functions

Macro functions can also be useful tools. One such function, %SYSGET, is especially useful under VMS. This function returns the value of a VMS symbol. So, for example, if a user supplied the

VMS symbol MYSYM when invoking the GETINFO application, we could use the following code to catch undefined symbols:

```
%let symbol=%sysget(mysym);
%if &symbol= %then
   %do;
      %put There is no such symbol;
   %end;
%else
   %do;
      %put The value of symbol is &symbol;
   %end;
```

Another set of macro functions that are useful when you are debugging a macro application are the quoting functions, such as %QUOTE and %STR. (%QUOTE quotes the result of a macro variable resolution, and %STR removes the significance of special characters in a text string.) Errors or oversights in quoting strings and macro variable values are a common source of macro bugs. For example, the first time we tried our CHK_SPEC macro, discussed earlier in **Developing and debugging each module separately**, we forgot to quote the character >, so the SAS System treated it as a mathematical operator instead of plain text. We had to use the %QUOTE function on the macro variable value and the %STR function for the > character to get the text comparison to work correctly.

Another problem we had with quotes was using a single quote in a macro comment statement. This caused a "string greater than 200 characters" error. It is never a good idea to use contractions such as *didn't* in comment statements.

Review the macro quoting functions before you begin to develop your macro application, and watch out for the following:

- unbalanced quotes and characters that are also used as mathematical operators
- mnemonic operators such as NE, OR, and AND
- delimiters
- special macro characters such as % and &.

Errors in quoting can cause strange, misleading error messages, so avoiding such errors in the first place saves you time.

Using autocall macros supplied by SAS Institute

SAS Institute supplies several macros in the default autocall library that can help you write diagnostic code. Below are some of the most useful ones:

CMPRES	returns the unquoted argument after compressing multiple blanks to single blanks and deleting any leading blanks and trailing blanks.
DATATYP	tells you if the argument passed is numeric or character.
LEFT	returns the argument without any leading blanks.
QCMPRES	is the same as CMPRES, only it returns a quoted argument.
QLEFT	is the same as LEFT, only it returns a quoted argument.
QTRIM	is the same as TRIM (see below), only it returns a quoted argument.
TRIM	returns the unquoted argument without trailing blanks.
VERIFY	returns the position of the first character in the argument that is not in the target value.

These functions are available if the MAUTOSOURCE system option is set. Also, the SASAUTOS= system option must point to the location of the default autocall library. You can determine the default value of the SASAUTOS= option with the OPTIONS procedure. See your SAS Software Representative for more information on the location of the default autocall library.

We used the DATATYP and VERIFY autocall functions in the interactive layer of the GETINFO application to check the selection the user typed next to a file. Here is a portion of the code:

```
%do i=1 %to &obs;
   %if (&&s&i^= ) and (%datatyp(&&s&i)=CHAR) and
       (%verify(%upcase(&&s&i),X)=0 %then
      %do;
         data sugilib.tfile;
            set sugilib.temp;
            if filenm="&&file&i" then output;
         run;
      %end;
      .
      .
      .
```

This code uses the DATATYP autocall macro to check the user's selection to be sure it is a character. The VERIFY macro compares the entered selection to the character string X. If the entered selection passes these tests, the file attribute information is then output to the screen.

Under VMS, these autocall macros are stored in the autocall library referenced by the VMS logical name SASAUTOS. To see how an autocall macro is coded, you can type the following command at the VMS prompt:

```
$ TYPE SASAUTOS:macro-name.SAS
```

For more information on using these and other autocall macros supplied by SAS Institute, see the *SAS Guide to Macro Processing, Version 6, Second Edition*.

EFFICIENT MACRO APPLICATION DEVELOPMENT

Much of the frustration commonly involved in debugging macro applications can be avoided through an efficient development plan. Although everyone has his or her own way of organizing files and developing macro applications, there are several rules of thumb that you should follow to make your macro application development more efficient:

Use an appropriate compilation method Use the %INCLUDE statement to compile macros during the development and debugging phase of a macro application, not the autocall facility. The autocall facility (discussed in the next section) is not efficient in the debugging phase of macro application development. There are several reasons for this. One reason is that when you use the autocall facility with a "buggy" macro application, you constantly need to reset the MAUTOSOURCE and MRECALL system options. This can be tedious.

Also, the development phase focuses on separate modules of a macro application rather than having all utility macros available at once. If you use the %INCLUDE statement, you can selectively access and compile just those macros you need. If you use the autocall facility and have a long list of concatenated macro libraries, accessing all these libraries can be slower than accessing only a few macros from each library with the %INCLUDE statement.

The following suggestions are for the %INCLUDE method of compiling macros, not for the autocall facility.

Store source code separately from data files You should store all your source code in one place (or in a set number of places) and keep it separate from your data files. For example, for the GETINFO application, our source code is stored in SUGI$:[SASDEMO.SAS], while our data files are stored in SUGI$:[SASDEMO.DAT]. The advantage of this technique is that you always know where to find a file, and if you have several files of the same filename but different file types (such as FILEINFO.DAT and FILEINFO.SAS), you are less likely to delete, rename, or move the wrong file.

Store macro code separately from other SAS code You should store all your macro definitions in a separate place from your other SAS code. This helps reduce confusion over filenames, as both macro files and other SAS code files have a file type of .SAS. Also, when you migrate to using the autocall facility, there will be fewer files for the facility to keep track of.

Use the macro name as the filename This is not a requirement of the SAS language; you can name your files and macros anything you want. But your macro application should be as self documenting as possible. You will spend far less time thinking "Now what did I name that macro (or file)???" when you are finding and fixing bugs if you give the macros and files the same name. It also helps to give the macros and files informational names that remind you of their purpose.

If you later decide to use the autocall facility, the macro name must be the same as the filename, so it saves time if you plan for this at the start of your application development.

Store only one macro definition in each file As far as the SAS System is concerned, you can store all your macro definitions in one file. However, if you want to use one of the macros stored in the file, you must compile the entire file with the %INCLUDE statement. This compilation step can take a long time. It is more efficient to store only one macro definition in a file because you only have to compile the macros you want to use, and recompilation is faster when you correct a bug.

Autocall Facility

A final technique to modularize your macro application is to adjust how you tell the SAS System where to find the macros you are using. When you are first developing the application, it is best to use a %INCLUDE statement for each macro you want to compile. You could put all these statements in a start-up file. Below is an example of our initial start-up file:

```
libname  sugilib 'sugi$:[sasdemo.dat]';
filename sugi    'sugi$:[sasdemo.sas]';

%include sugi(windows);
%include sugi(welcome);
%include sugi(crt_spec);
%include sugi(getinfo);
%include sugi(chk_spec);
%include sugi(crt_ds);
%include sugi(crt_dvar);
%include sugi(dir_lis);
%include sugi(chk_sel);
%include sugi(crt_fvar);
```

As you can see, we used quite a few %INCLUDE statements, and the compilation step takes considerable time. However, this technique ensures each macro is compiled separately and makes error tracing much easier.

When your macro application is completely bug-free, however, it is more efficient to use the autocall facility to tell the SAS System where to find your macros. For example, when we were sure all our macros worked correctly, we simply invoked the SAS System with the following command:

```
$ SAS/SASAUTOS=("sugi$:[sasdemo.sas]",SASAUTOS)
```

This tells the SAS System that we have macros stored in SUGI$:[SASDEMO.SAS] and that we want to concatenate this library with the macro library supplied by SAS Institute, which is pointed to by the logical name SASAUTOS. Then, during our SAS session, we could simply invoke the GETINFO application; the autocall facility takes care of all compilation.

The techniques for efficient macro application development discussed previously also apply when you move into the production phase of the application and begin to use the autocall facility. Below are some other suggested efficiency considerations for using the autocall facility:

- Use filerefs to specify autocall libraries when possible because specifying physical file names as autocall libraries with the SASAUTOS= system option can result in repeated attempts at opening unavailable files with no error messages.

- Be aware of the efficiency trade-off between using many autocall libraries with fewer macros per library versus using fewer autocall libraries with more macros per library; having fewer libraries means less time is spent searching libraries, but you have less flexibility in storing logical groups of macros.

SUMMARY

One of the rewards of debugging is the great feeling of satisfaction when your macro applications run correctly--IT WORKS!! We hope the techniques this paper presents help you reach that satisfaction more quickly as you develop your macro applications under VMS. These techniques include

- modularizing your macro application and development process

- using SAS system options efficiently

- adding your own debugging code to pinpoint problems

- using the autocall facility to improve macro application efficiency only after the debugging phase of development is finished.

It may also be helpful to familiarize yourself with macro variable resolution rules and macro quoting functions before you begin to develop and debug a new macro application.

As you develop and debug your own macro applications, you can adjust and add to the debugging techniques presented in this paper, quickly and efficiently developing bug-free macros.

SOURCES OF MORE INFORMATION

- *SAS Guide to Macro Processing, Version 6, Second Edition*

- "SAS Macro for VMS Users: A Tutorial," by Ginny Dineley, SAS Institute Inc.

- *SAS Macro Language Course Notes* (for Version 6, available July 1, 1990)

- *SAS Companion to the VMS Environment, Version 6, First Edition*

- *SAS Views: SAS Macro Language, Version 5 Edition*

ACKNOWLEDGEMENTS

We would like to acknowledge Ginny Dineley and Yvonne Selby for their help in developing the GETINFO application. We would also like to thank Tom Cole, Anne Corrigan, Ginny Dineley, Darylene Hecht, Wayne Hester, Susan O'Connor, Dee Stribling, Jana Van Wyk, Keith Wagner, and Harriet Watts for their help in reviewing this paper.

SAS is a registered trademark of SAS Institute Inc., Cary, NC.

VMS is a trademark of Digital Equipment Corporation.

A Roadmap to Macro Facility Error Messages and Debugging

Susan M. O'Connor, SAS Institute Inc., Cary, NC

ABSTRACT

While the macro facility is a very powerful tool for SAS® application developers, most users of the SAS macro facility have at times experienced difficulty and frustration while debugging complex macros. A roadmap with a friendly legend would be helpful for even the most skilled macro programmer.

The purpose of this paper is to make suggestions for macro debugging options and for macro debugging techniques, which are available in the SAS macro facility. Version 6 macro error messages are enumerated and categorized. Some approaches are suggested to resolve the various errors.

The intended audience is applications developers who have a familiarity with the macro facility and who desire a closer understanding of macro error messages and macro debugging tools.

INTRODUCTION

While debugging is the complex problem of finding and correcting errors in program code, macro debugging is even more complex because the user must determine if the bug is in the macro code or in the code generated by the macro for the rest of the SAS System, such as the SAS programming language or display manager commands. Separating macro errors and SAS errors is easier if you understand a little of macro internals.

Understanding the timing and order in which the SAS macro facility resolves macro variables, compiles macro definitions, invokes a macro, and executes a macro is often useful in debugging macro errors. It is also believed that understanding when, where, and why a macro message is generated might help in tracking down the location and nature of your macro error. The types and lists of macro messages generated by the macro debugging options SYMBOLGEN, MLOGIC, and MPRINT might also suggest approaches to debugging your macro.

A macro error, for the purpose of this paper, is a condition in the macro language or the macro processor that generates a macro error message, warning, or note. There are also macro-generated errors, which are SAS errors caused by the SAS text generated by macro execution or macro variable resolution.

The first type of error, the macro error, might be traced by categorizing macro messages, which are written to the SAS log. In Release 6.06 of the SAS System, the almost 200 macro messages do not have prefix numbers written with the messages to the SAS log, but the messages are intended to be more explicit than they were in Version 5. Virtually all of the messages that could be generated by the macro facility to the SAS log in Release 6.06 will be listed in this paper. In most cases, if the message is listed here, the error message is generated by the macro facility. The second type of error, a SAS error generated by a macro, may have SAS messages. The problem may be an error in logic, output, or end results that do not generate an error message at all. Messages generated by this type of error may be in error messages to the SAS log. These messages may have a prefix message number or not. There may be messages from the command line generated by a macro.

OVERVIEW

Input to the SAS System can come from many sources, such as programming statements and display manager commands. This input is channeled to an input stack. The part of the SAS System called the word scanner reads the input stack and separates the input into words or tokens. These tokens are put into a word queue where they are requested by parts of the SAS System, such as the SAS compiler or display manager.

In the word scanner, the macro facility is triggered by an ampersand (&) or a percent sign (%) when either of these characters is followed immediately by a nonblank character. As the word scanner builds tokens (words) from the SAS input stack, an ampersand triggers an attempt at symbolic substitution, which is the resolution of a macro variable. Also in the word scanner, a percent sign triggers the macro facility's processor for some type of macro action to possibly occur. (See **Figure 1**.)

ROAD MAP TO MACRO ERROR MESSAGES

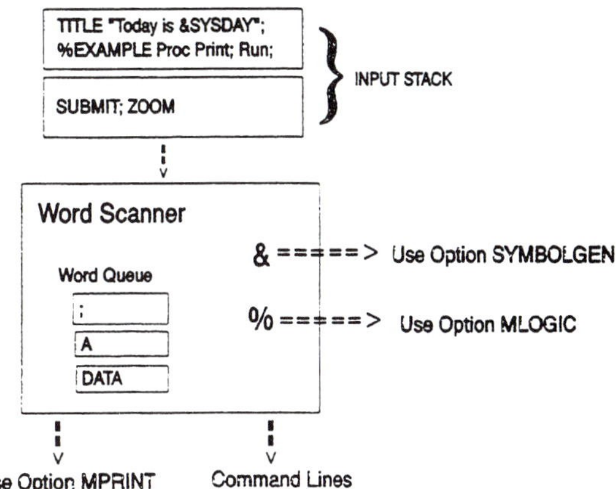

A percent sign might be triggering macro compilation with a %MACRO statement and the start of a definition of a macro. The percent sign could also be triggering macro invocation, the attempt to invoke a defined macro and to execute the macro. It could sometimes be triggering execution of macro programming statements or macro functions. In any case, the macro processor performs the activity indicated and returns any text generated to the input stack ahead of the remaining tokens. These tokens, when fully resolved, are passed on to the rest of the SAS System, which has been requesting tokens.

Macro programming statements beginning with a percent sign are handled by the open code handler inside the macro processor. The open code handler allows some macro programming statements to be valid anywhere in SAS code—either inside a macro definition, or in "open code," that is, outside the macro definition. These programming statements include: %DISPLAY, %GLOBAL, %INPUT, %KEYDEF, %LET, %MACRO, %PUT, %SYSEXEC, and %WINDOW. Other macro programming statements are valid only inside a macro definition. These macro programming statements being used inside a macro go through a compilation phase and an execution phase as does the macro itself. They include the following macro programming statements: %DO, iterative %DO, %DO %UNTIL, %DO %WHILE, %END, %GOTO, %IF-%THEN/%ELSE, %label:, %LOCAL, and %MEND.

The percent sign also signals macro string functions and macro quoting functions. There is also a function to evaluate macro expressions that can be handled either explicitly by %EVAL or implicitly. The macro processor could also be signaled by DATA step interfaces and not from the word scanner. DATA step interfaces are CALL SYMPUT and SYMGET and, in Release 6.07.03, CALL EXECUTE and the RESOLVE function.

For this roadmap, I have listed all the messages the SAS macro processor might generate and send to the SAS log. I describe a phase of the macro processor and list the potential messages generated by the code that might be executed by the macro processor in each process. It is hoped that a list of potential messages in categories by process might help the user more quickly discover the nature of a problem and more fully understand the phases of the macro facility. For some of the messages, I have added an explanation of the conditions that might generate an error in the general discussion or in the parentheses after the error. For other messages, it is hoped the message will be self-explanatory.

MESSAGES GENERATED BY MACRO VARIABLES AND THEIR RESOLUTION

There are two types of macro variables. Automatic macro variables are supplied by the SAS System and user-defined macro variables are created by macro programming statements, such as %LET. User-defined macro variables can be created by other macro features including: iterative %DO statement, %GLOBAL statement, %INPUT statement, %LOCAL statement, %MACRO statement, SYMPUT routine, and the %WINDOW statement. Generally speaking, user-defined macro variables are stored in macro symbol tables in memory or as entries in SAS catalogs in WORK which, by default, are deleted at termination of your SAS session.

It is possible for the same statement to issue different messages depending on where it is in your program. For example, in open code the following %LET macro statement prints a note to the SAS log but creates &OPEN, a valid macro variable:

```
%LET OPEN CODE = ERROR MESSAGE;
```

```
NOTE: A missing equals sign has been inserted after
the variable name OPEN.
```

and &OPEN resolves to:

```
%PUT &OPEN;
```

```
CODE = ERROR MESSAGE
```

However, if the same statement is inside a macro definition, no warning message is issued during macro compilation, but a different error condition occurs during the macro execution.

```
%MACRO TEST;
   %LET OPEN CODE = ERROR MESSAGE;   /* No warning message here.*/
%MEND;
%TEST /* Execution generates a different message execution stops.*/
```

```
ERROR: Symbolic variable name OPEN CODE must be 8
or fewer characters long.
```

```
ERROR: The macro will stop executing.
```

This happens because, in open code, the macro variable name should be one valid SAS name; in open code, the SAS System inserts an equal sign after the first word in the %LET statement, in this case, OPEN. However, in a macro definition, the SAS macro processor collects tokens until the equal sign. It is not until the macro executes that the error is detected and the macro variable name is determined to be OPEN CODE, clearly not a valid macro variable name. (This difference in behavior is fully compatible with the macro facility in Release 5.18 for the mainframes. It is assumed at compilation time that the user knows what he or she is doing and it is at macro execution time that the moment of truth occurs and the syntax must comform to SAS syntax rules.)

The following messages could be generated to the SAS log from the macro programming statements that create macro variables, such as %LET, %LOCAL, and %GLOBAL or from the attempt to resolve a macro variable (called symbolic substitution):

- Macro messages from %LET macro statement

```
ERROR: Expecting a variable name after %LET.
```

```
ERROR: Expected equals sign not found in %LET statement.
```

```
NOTE: A missing equals sign has been inserted after the
variable name ___.
```

- Macro message creating macro variables with %LOCAL and %GLOBAL

```
ERROR: Invalid symbolic variable name ___.
```

```
ERROR: Attempt to %GLOBAL a name (___) which exists in a
local environment.
```

- Macro messages for symbolic substitution

```
ERROR: The SAS System is unable to open a macro symbol
table.
```

(The local symbol table could not be opened in the WORK library. There may be a problem accessing your WORK library on your operating system. You may not have write access. Check the protection of your WORK library. You may be having network problems.)

```
ERROR: The SAS System is unable to write the macro
variable ___ to the macro symbol table.
```

(This could be a problem writing the macro variable to your symbol table, which is a SAS catalog in your WORK library.)

```
ERROR: Attempt to assign a value to a read-only symbolic
variable (___).
```

(An attempt to write a value to a read-only automatic SAS variable supplied by SAS Institute. The parentheses surround the SAS automatic variable name in this message. The read/write status of automatic macro variables are listed on p. 55 of the *SAS Guide to Macro Processing, Version 6, Second Edition*.)

```
ERROR: Symbolic variable SYSPBUFFR can not exist when
no macro is currently executing.
```

```
ERROR: Out of memory; unable to create &SYSPBUFF
macro variable.
```

```
ERROR: Not enough memory was available to resolve the
apparent symbolic (macro) variable reference.
```

```
ERROR: Not enough memory was available to create the
variable ___.
```

```
ERROR: Symbolic variable name ___ must be 8 or fewer
characters long.
```

```
ERROR: Symbolic variable name ___ must begin with a
letter or underscore.
```

```
ERROR: Symbolic variable name ___ must contain only
letters, digits, and underscores.

ERROR: Not enough memory was available to resolve the
apparent symbolic (macro) variable reference.

ERROR: Macro symbol table damaged.  Cannot resolve
macro variable ___.

ERROR: The reference to macro variable ___ is a recursive
reference.  This may cause the message "Apparent symbolic
reference not resolved".

ERROR: Invalid macro name ___.  It should be a valid SAS
identifier no longer than 8 characters.

ERROR: The macro variable name is either all blank or
missing.

WARNING: The argument to macro function %SYSGET is
not defined as a system variable.

WARNING: Apparent symbolic reference ___ not resolved.
```
(The macro variable &___ has not been created. The &___ is passed on by the word scanner to the SAS System probably causing a error. This warning is issued to the SAS log unless option NOSERROR is set. The default is SERROR.)

DEBUGGING MACRO VARIABLES WITH SYMBOLGEN

The best debugging tool to use when you are having trouble with macro variable resolution is the SAS option SYMBOLGEN. (See **Figure 2**.)

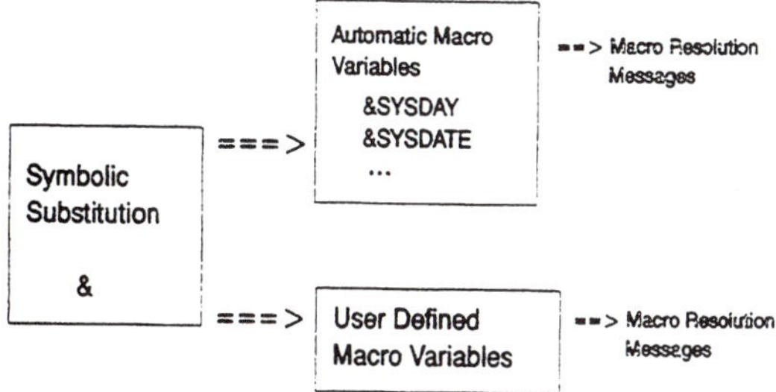

The default is NOSYMBOLGEN. SYMBOLGEN can generate the following three messages when the macro processor resolves macro symbols:

```
SYMBOLGEN:  Macro variable ___ resolves to ___

SYMBOLGEN:  Some characters in the above value which were
subject to macro quoting have been unquoted for printing.
```
(A macro variable's value contains characters that have been quoted by the macro quoting functions.)

```
SYMBOLGEN:  && resolves to &.
```
(A message whenever double ampersands resolve into a single ampersand.)

Another technique is to use the %PUT macro programming statement with the macro variable to write the macro variable's value to the SAS log in various environments in the program.

```
%LET MACNAME = THIS IS THE VALUE OF A MACRO VARIABLE;
%PUT ***&MACNAME***;

***THIS IS THE VALUE OF A MACRO VARIABLE***
```

Notice that putting the asterisks or other delimiters adjacent to the macro variable name helps to show leading or trailing blanks at resolution.

MACRO DEFINITION AND COMPILATION

When the word scanner triggers the macro processor with a percent sign and the macro processor detects the keyword MACRO, the open code handler begins to collect and examine tokens and proceeds to compile the macro. The %MACRO statement begins a macro definition, assigns the macro its name, may have a parameter list, and may have a macro option list. The macro definition ends with the %MEND macro statement. While the macro is compiling, all macro programming statements are compiled and stored as intermediate code and all noncompiled text is stored verbatim. Stored items that are not compiled include: macro variable references, macro functions except %STR and %NRSTR, nested macro definitions and invocations, names and values of local macro variables, and so on.

The macro, once defined and compiled, is stored as an entry in a SAS catalog, SASMACR, by default in a WORK library. This entry cannot be changed and the name of the catalog cannot be changed. The macro definition may contain macro programming statements, macro functions, and SAS text. By default, this catalog is deleted at the termination of your SAS session. (Using NOWORKTERM overrides this deletion, and NOWORKINIT reconnects to this catalog.) If the macro processor detects a syntax error during compilation, it continues to check the syntax in the rest of the macro definition and to issue messages for any errors it finds, but it does not store the macro as an entry of the SAS catalog in the WORK library. When the macro processor compiles, but does not store the macro, this macro is called a dummy macro and this message is generated:

```
ERROR: A dummy macro will be compiled.
```

Dummy macros are checked for syntax but never compiled and stored; therefore, a dummy macro cannot be accessed later in your session.

The following messages may be generated while compiling a macro definition:

```
ERROR: Macro ___ has been given a reserved name.
```
(The list of reserved words for the macro facility is listed in Appendix 2 of the *SAS Guide to Macro Processing*. Also note that the SAS System reserves the use of SYS for future use as macro names or macro variable names.)

```
ERROR: Invalid macro name ___.  It should be a valid SAS
identifier no longer than 8 characters.

ERROR: Invalid macro parameter name ___.  It should be a
valid SAS identifier no longer than 8 characters.

ERROR: The SAS System was unable to open the macro library.
```
(The macro catalog SASMACR in WORK is not accessible. You may not have access rights to the WORK catalog. This could be an operating system or a network problem.)

```
ERROR: All positional parameters must precede keyword parameters.
```
(You have your parameters in the wrong order.)

```
ERROR: Expecting comma (to separate macro parameters) or
close parenthesis (to end parameter list) but found: ___

ERROR: The SAS System is unable to write the macro ___
to the macro library.
```

(This may be a problem with write access to your SASMACR catalog in WORK.)

```
ERROR: Expected semicolon not found. The macro will not
be compiled.
```

```
ERROR: A dummy macro will be compiled.
```

```
ERROR: No matching %MACRO statement for this %MEND
statement.
```

(You must match %MACRO and %MEND.)

```
ERROR: The macro ___ contains a %GOTO statement with an
invalid statement label name. The macro will not be compiled.
```

```
ERROR: There were ___ unclosed %DO statements. The macro
___ will not be compiled.
```

(Match your %DO statements with %END statements.)

```
ERROR: There is no matching %IF statement for the %ELSE.
A dummy macro will be compiled.
```

```
ERROR: Macro library damaged. Cannot compile macro ___.
```

```
WARNING: Command-style macros are not supported.
To invoke macro ___ use name-style invocation.
```

(Release 6.07.03 will support command-style macros. Name-style invocation is invocation with the percent sign and the macro name.)

```
NOTE: Extraneous information on %MEND statement ignored.
```

(Usually this means you forgot the semicolon after %MEND macro name. It could mean that you spelled the macro name wrong.)

MACRO INVOCATION

When a macro is successfully compiled and stored as an entry in a SAS catalog it is ready to be executed when the macro is invoked. Name-style invocation is attempted when the word scanner encounters a percent sign followed by a nonblank character and triggers the macro processor. The macro processor attempts to locate the macro as an entry in the SAS macro catalog if the macro name is not a macro reserved keyword. If the macro is not located and the SAS option MERROR (the default) is on, the following warning message is issued to the SAS log:

```
WARNING: Apparent invocation of macro ___ not resolved.
```

Statement-style macro invocation is handled in the SAS tokenizer after the word scanner has returned a completed word or token to the SAS System. This is the situation if the SAS option IMPLMAC (implied macro) is on and the token starts a SAS statement, but there is no percent sign. The tokenizer checks with the macro processor to see if a macro is defined with the same name as the token. If no statement-style macro is located then no warning is issued to the SAS log.

In Release 6.07.03, command-style invocation is attempted if the SAS option CMDMAC is on and the token that has been passed by the word scanner to the SAS System is the start of a command line command. If no compiled command-style macro is located, no warning message is issued.

The autocall facility attempts to invoke a macro from macro definitions located as external files. These files are located in aggregate storage locations, usually on disk. An aggregate storage location is system dependent. It can be referred to by a FILENAME statement. On the MVS operating system it is a partitioned data set, on CMS it is a MACLIB, on VMS* it can be a VMS text library or a directory, and on directory-based systems, it is a directory. The autocall system is in effect when the SAS options SASAUTOS = and MAUTOSOURCE are set. When an autocall macro is invoked, all source code in the file containing the macro definition is included in the input stack, compiled, and then executed. The SAS option MRECALL determines if autocall libraries will be searched again for a member that was not found earlier in the same session. The following messages to the SAS log can be generated attempting to invoke an autocall macro:

```
ERROR: No file referenced by SASAUTOS OPTION can be opened.
```

```
NOTE: Autocall member, ___, has not been compiled by the macro
processor. It may contain a macro syntax error or not
define a macro with the same name as the member. To
autocall this member again, set OPTION MRECALL.
```

```
WARNING: Source level autocall is not found or cannot be opened.
Autocall has been suspended and OPTION NOMAUTSOURCE has
been set. To use the autocall facility again, set OPTION
MAUTOSOURCE.
```

While collecting parameters during macro invocation the following error messages could be written to the SAS log:

```
ERROR: All positional parameters must precede keyword parameters.
```

```
ERROR: Invalid macro parameter name ___. It should be a
valid SAS identifier no longer than 8 characters.
```

(A macro parameter variable name should be one to eight characters long, may contain only letters, numbers and underscores, and must begin with a letter or underscore.)

MACRO EXECUTION

After the macro is invoked, macro execution occurs. The macro processor executes compiled macro program statements and it places noncompiled code on the input stack as text. During macro execution, the macro processor may pause while text being put on the input stack is processed. The following messages are among the messages to the SAS log that can be generated by the macro facility during SAS macro execution.

```
ERROR: More positional parameters found than defined.
```

```
ERROR: The keyword parameter ___ was not defined with
the macro.
```

```
ERROR: The keyword parameter ___ was given a value twice.
```

```
ERROR: Macro library damaged. Cannot execute macro ___.
```

(The SAS catalog, by default SASMACR in WORK, in which the macro was stored has been damaged. It contains information the SAS System does not recognize and the macro cannot be executed. This can be an I/O error or it can indicate a bug in the SAS System.)

```
ERROR: The macro will stop executing.
```

(This is usually issued after some other error message.)

```
ERROR: Required operator not found in %EVAL or %IF
expression.
```

```
ERROR: %SYSRPUT statement is valid only when OPTION DMR is in
effect.
```

```
ERROR: A %WINDOW or %DISPLAY statement has occurred in the macro
___, which was invoked from a command line. In the current
release of the SAS System, such macros may be invoked only from
the primary source of input (the Program Editor).
```

```
ERROR: Literal contains unmatched quote.
```

```
ERROR: Out of memory.
```

(The SAS System has used all the computer memory available and cannot continue to execute.)

THE OPEN CODE HANDLER

Now that you have an idea of messages generated by the macro processor during the process of macro definition and compilation of macro invocation, and of macro execution, as well as messages generated during symbolic resolution of macro variable names, another part of the macro processor, the open code handler should be discussed. When the word scanner detects a percent sign followed by a nonblank character, the part of the macro processor that is called and decides what to do with the next token is the open code handler. The open code handler performs the following functions:

- has the table of reserved macro keywords
- decides if a macro is to be compiled or executed
- determines if a macro keyword is in SAS open code or in a macro definition
- if the macro programming statement is in open code, it determines if it is valid in open code
- calls macro functions
- inserts semicolons in text in some (but not all) situations.

One example of a message generated by the open code handler is when macro programming statements recursively invoke other macro programming statements in open code, usually when a semicolon is forgotten. For example,

```
%LET STRING  = THIS IS A MACRO VARIABLE VALUE
%PUT &STRING;

ERROR: Open code statement recursion detected.
```

This error would be corrected by a semicolon after the %LET statement. Messages to the SAS log from the open code handler include the following:

```
ERROR: Macro keyword ____ appears as text.  A semicolon or other
delimiter may be missing.

ERROR: %EVAL must be followed by a parenthesized
expression.

ERROR: Expected open parenthesis after macro function
name not found.

ERROR: There is no matching %IF statement for the %THEN.
The %THEN statement will be ignored.

ERROR: The %IF statement is not valid in open code.

ERROR: The %THEN statement is not valid in open code.

ERROR: The %ELSE statement is not valid in open code.

ERROR: The %DO statement is not valid in open code.

ERROR: The %END statement is not valid in open code.

ERROR: The %LOCAL statement is not valid in open code.

ERROR: The %GOTO statement is not valid in open code.

ERROR: Invalid symbolic variable name ____.

ERROR: Macro keyword ____ is not yet implemented.

ERROR: Open code statement recursion detected.

WARNING: Missing semicolon between %THEN clause and ____ has been
assumed.

WARNING: Apparent symbolic reference ____ not resolved.

NOTE: Extraneous text after %RUN will be ignored.
```

(The %RUN statement, while not technically part of macro syntax, is handled in the open code handler. %RUN ends input from the terminal following %INCLUDE * syntax. %RUN, %INCLUDE, and %LIST are SAS programming statements and not macro programming statements. They are documented in *SAS Language: Reference, Version 6, First Edition*.)

CERTAIN MESSAGES SPECIFIC TO MACRO PROGRAMMING STATEMENTS

For reference, I have included in categories below specific macro-generated messages for specific programming statements. Certain macro programming statements, by their nature, generate many specific messages. For convenience, the first three message groups are for macro programming statements that can be used anywhere in a SAS session, either inside or outside the macro definition in open code. These statements are %INPUT, %KEYDEF, %WINDOW, and %DISPLAY.

- Macro messages for %INPUT statement

```
ERROR: The %INPUT statement can be executed only in
an interactive SAS session.

ERROR: Cannot execute %INPUT statement while compiling an SCL
program.

ERROR: Expected closing quote for %INPUT item not found.
```

- Macro messages for %KEYDEF statement

```
ERROR: %KEYDEF expecting a keyname, either unquoted
or quoted, but found "____" instead.

NOTE: %____ set to "____".

NOTE: %KEYDEF macro statements are only valid in DMS mode.
```

- Macro messages for %WINDOW and %DISPLAY statements

```
ERROR: A WINDOW/WINDOW.GROUPNAME is required for the
%DISPLAY statement.

ERROR: The %WINDOW name NAME is not a valid SAS name.

ERROR: The %WINDOW GROUP= name NAME is not a valid SAS name.

ERROR: The %DISPLAY window/window.group name is not a
valid SAS name.

ERROR: Insufficient memory available to allocate %WINDOW field.

ERROR: Insufficient memory available to allocate %WINDOW field
data area.

ERROR: Invalid %DISPLAY option OPTION.
```

(%DISPLAY takes NOINPUT, BELL, or BLANK.)

```
ERROR: GROUP pane is not defined in window NAME.

ERROR: Insufficient memory to process the %DISPLAY statement.

ERROR: Required data needed at row ____ column ____.

WARNING: The field defined at ____:____ overlaps the
field defined at ____:____-____.
```

(New field overlaps the next field.)

```
ERROR: Unable to obtain window definition for the window NAME.

ERROR: Unable to load KEYS for the window NAME.

ERROR: Unable to open window macro file NAME.

ERROR: Cannot execute %WINDOW or %DISPLAY statement while
compiling an SCL program.
```

The following macro programming statements, valid only within macro definitions, issue specific messages either during compilation or execution.

- Macro messages while compiling %GOTO statement

```
ERROR: %GO not followed by TO.  A dummy macro will be compiled.

ERROR: The target of the %GOTO statement was a reserved macro
keyword, ___.  A dummy macro will be compiled.

ERROR: The %GOTO statement has no target.  The statement
will be ignored.
```

- Macro errors while compiling %DO statements

```
ERROR: Expected semicolon not found after %WHILE/%UNTIL clause.
A dummy macro will be be compiled.

ERROR: An unexpected semicolon occurred in the %DO
statement.  A dummy macro will be compiled.

ERROR: Expected %TO not found in %DO statement.  A dummy macro
will be compiled.

ERROR: Expected parenthesis not found after %WHILE/%UNTIL .
A dummy macro will be compiled.
```

(Expecting a '(' after a %DO %WHILE or %DO %UNTIL.)

- Macro messages while compiling the %END statement

```
ERROR: There is no matching %DO statement for the %END.
This statement will be ignored.

NOTE: Extraneous information on %END statement ignored.
```

- Macro messages while compiling the %IF statement

```
ERROR: Expected %THEN statement not found.  A dummy macro will
be compiled.
```

(A semicolon prematurely ended the %IF condition before the %THEN was found.

- Macro message while compiling a macro statement label %LABEL

```
NOTE: The label %___has already been defined.  Only the first
instance will be used.  Later instances will be considered to be
invocations of the macro %___.
```

- Macro message during %DO execution

```
ERROR: ___ is an invalid macro variable name for the
index variable of the %DO loop.

ERROR: The %BY value of the %DO ___loop is zero.

ERROR: Invalid branch into iterative %DO.

ERROR: Unable to assign value to macro variable ___
in %DO loop.

ERROR: Unable to read value of macro variable ___
in %DO loop.

ERROR: The index variable in the %DO %s loop has taken on
an invalid or missing value.  The macro will stop
executing.

ERROR: Overflow has occurred; evaluation is terminated.

ERROR: Unable to assign value to macro variable ___
in %DO loop.

ERROR: The ___ value of the %DO ___/%TO loop is invalid.

ERROR: The condition in the %DO %WHILE/%UNTIL loop,
___, yielded an invalid or missing value, ___. The macro
will stop executing.
```

- Macro message while executing %GOTO statement

```
ERROR: The target of the %GOTO statement, ___, resolved
into the label ___, which is not a valid statement label.

ERROR: The target of the %GOTO statement, ___, resolved
into the label ___, which was not found.
```

MACRO MESSAGES DURING MACRO EXPRESSION EVALUATION

A macro expression is a sequence of macro operators and operands. Any item stored as text can be an operand. The most common operands include macro variable references, macro invocations, macro functions, model text for the SAS System such as SAS statements and command line commands and integers in the case of the argument to the %EVAL function.

The evaluation of macro expressions resembles the way the DATA step handles expressions, except in the following ways:

- in the macro facility only integer arithmetic is performed.
- the range of the macro facility's integers is much smaller (±2,147,483,647) than the range of DATA step numbers because DATA step numbers are stored in floating-point form.
- the operators for MIN (><), MAX (<>), and concatenation (||) are not recognized as operators in the macro facility.

Also, be aware that depending on how macro variables in expressions are resolved, expressions in comparison operators that surround a macro expression may or may not be equal to DATA step compound expressions. For example, it may be safer to write the compound macro expression as

```
1 < &X AND &X < 20 /* safer to explicitly write*/
                   /* connecting operator*/
```

rather than

```
1 < &X < 20  /* evaluation depends on resolution*/
             /* of macro variable*/
```

Any macro language feature that requires a numeric value implicitly invokes the %EVAL function. The implicit evaluation occurs from expressions in the iterative %DO, %DO %UNTIL, %DO %WHILE, %IF/%THEN, %QSCAN, %QSUBSTR, %SCAN, and %SUBSTR. The following messages to the SAS log could be generated by explicit or implicit macro expression evaluation.

```
ERROR: Overflow has occurred; evaluation is terminated.
```

(The number is not within the range for integer arithmetic.)

```
ERROR: A character operand was found in the %EVAL function
or %IF condition where a numeric operand is required.
The condition was: ___.
```

(The macro facility treats a value containing a decimal as a string. Perhaps there is a decimal point in your value.)

```
ERROR: Division by zero in %EVAL is invalid.

ERROR: Error has occurred during exponentiation; evaluation is
terminated.

ERROR: Required operator not found in expression: ___

ERROR: Required operator not found in %EVAL or %IF
expression.

ERROR: %EVAL function has no expression to evaluate, or
%IF statement has no condition.

ERROR: Operand missing for ___ operator in argument to %EVAL
function.
```

MESSAGES GENERATED BY MACRO FUNCTIONS

The macro character string functions include %INDEX, %LENGTH, %SCAN, %SUBSTR, and %UPCASE, and their quoted analogues %QSCAN, %QSUBSTR, and %QUPCASE. These functions either change or provide information about the character strings used as their argument. The following error messages could be generated:

- Macro errors while collecting string to macro character functions

```
ERROR: Expected open parenthesis after macro function
name not found.

ERROR: Macro function %___ has too many arguments.  The
excess arguments will be ignored.

NOTE: One or more missing close parentheses have been
supplied for the %___ function.
```

- Macro errors while executing a macro character string function

```
ERROR: Macro function %___ has too few arguments.

ERROR: Argument ___ to macro function %___ is not
a number.

WARNING: Argument ___ to macro function %___ is missing
or out of range.

ERROR: Error occurred while executing macro function %___.

ERROR: The SAS System could not load the %___ macro function.
The system may be out of memory.  An error value (zero or null
string) will be supplied in lieu of the result of the function.
Results of this macro may be incorrect.
```

The macro quoting functions are used to prevent the macro processor from interpreting a special character or item as a symbol in the macro language instead of as text. For example, below, the macro quoting function %STR allows the first two semicolons to be treated as text and not as the end of the macro facility's %LET statement, while the last semicolon is treated as part of the macro facility at the end of the %LET statement.

```
%LET CONT = PROC CONTENTS %STR(;) RUN %STR(;);
```

or

```
%LET CONT = %STR(PROC CONTENTS; RUN;);
```

Macro quoting functions remove the significance of an item to the macro facility and treat the item as text. Macro quoting functions include %BQUOTE, %NRBQUOTE, %NRQUOTE, %NRSTR, %QUOTE, %STR, %SUPERQ, and %UNQUOTE. There are three types of macro quoting functions: compilation functions, execution functions, and functions to prevent resolution. %STR and %NRSTR are compilation macro quoting functions, which treat the items as text while compiling the macro or while compiling the macro programming statement in open code. Execution quoting functions cause the macro processor to treat as text items the result from resolving or executing a macro expression. They quote the results of resolving macro variables, macro invocation, or macro expression evaluation. During the execution of a macro or of a macro programming statement in open code with execution quoting functions the macro facility resolves the item as much as possible and then quotes the result. These execution macro quoting functions include %QUOTE, %NRQUOTE, %BQUOTE, and %NRBQUOTE. The %SUPERQ function prevents the resolution of the value of the macro variable named in its argument. For special cases the %UNQUOTE function undoes macro quoting.

The following errors could be issued to the log from macro quoting functions:

```
ERROR: Expected open parenthesis after macro function
name not found.
```

(Issued while collecting the string for a macro quoting function.)

```
ERROR: Maximum level of nesting of macro functions exceeded.
```

DEBUGGING MACRO EXECUTION WITH MLOGIC

The SAS option MLOGIC in Release 6.06 is the most useful macro facility debugging tool if the bug you have is probably caused by macro execution. If the behavior of the macro's execution is not what you anticipated use the MLOGIC option. (See **Figure 3.**)

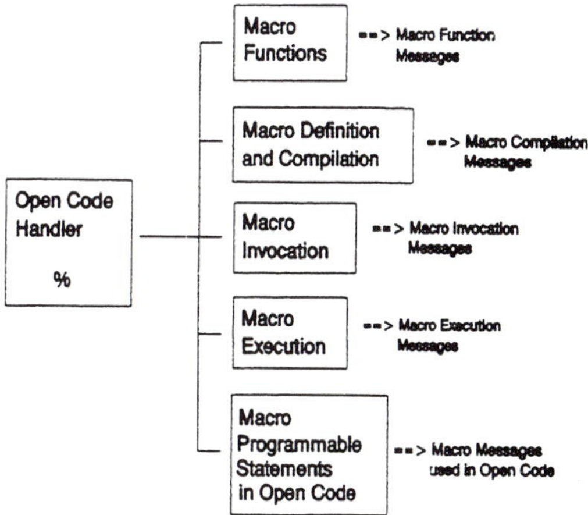

The default is NOMLOGIC. MLOGIC issues macro messages to the SAS log prefixed by MLOGIC and the name of each macro being executed. MLOGIC traces the flow of execution, the resolution of parameters, the condition of macro expressions being evaluated, the number of loop iterations, and the beginning and end of each macro execution. In Release 6.03 of the SAS System, this same function is performed by MTRACE and the default is NOMTRACE. The following debugging messages could be generated by the MLOGIC option:

```
MLOGIC(___):  Beginning execution.

MLOGIC(___):  Parameter ___ has value ___

MLOGIC(___):  ___ statement beginning.

MLOGIC(___):  %INCLUDE file is ___

MLOGIC(___):  %PUT ___

MLOGIC(___):  %LET (variable name is ___)

MLOGIC(___):  %SYSRPUT (variable name is ___)

MLOGIC(___):  %GLOBAL ___

MLOGIC(___):  %LOCAL ___

MLOGIC(___):  %INPUT ___

MLOGIC(___):  %GOTO ___ (label resolves to ___).

MLOGIC(___):  %DO loop beginning; index variable ___;
start value is ___; stop value is ___; by value is ___.

MLOGIC(___):  %DO loop index variable ___ is now ___; loop
will ___ iterate again.
```

```
MLOGIC(___):  %DO %WHILE(___) loop beginning; condition is
TRUE/FALSE.

MLOGIC(___):  %DO %WHILE(___) condition is ___; loop will ___
iterate again.

MLOGIC(___):  %DO %UNTIL(___) loop beginning.

MLOGIC(___):  %DO %UNTIL(___) condition is ___; loop will ___
iterate again.

MLOGIC(___):  %IF condition ___ is TRUE/FALSE

MLOGIC(___):  Ending execution.
```

The %PUT macro programming statement is useful also in verifying logic by writing text to the SAS log when certain conditions are met in macro execution. For example, a message you create could be

```
%PUT ***NONE OF THE CONDITIONS WERE MET***;
```

DEBUGGING MACRO-GENERATED CODE WITH MPRINT

If examining the macro execution does not help you find your macro bug, another debugging tool you can use is the MPRINT option. It may be that the problem is with the SAS source generated, rather than with the macro itself. (See **Figure 4.**)

Use Option MPRINT

SAS Statements	==> Messages from SAS source

The default is NOMPRINT. The MPRINT option displays SAS statements that have been generated by macro execution to the SAS log. The MPRINT option rebuilds the SAS statement token by token until it reaches the semicolon. It writes the prefix MPRINT, the name of the macro that generated the code, and the SAS statement generated. Each SAS statement is written as a separate line in the SAS log.

```
MPRINT(___):  separate_macro_generated_SAS_statements;
```

When you examine the SAS source generated to the log, you may quickly see your error. If the error is not obvious, write the log generated with MPRINT to an external file, edit it to remove the MPRINT debug prefixes, and submit the SAS statements to the SAS System for execution without the macro. If the error still occurs, debug your SAS statements first to find the error in your SAS statements. Then, debug your macro so it will not generate SAS code containing that error. In Release 6.07.03 there is an experimental version of the DATA step debugger that could be helpful in debugging your DATA step source code, which you have created in this manner.

ADDITIONAL MESSAGES IN RELEASE 6.07.03

The following messages have also been added to the macro facility for Release 6.07.03 to assist in detecting errors or to enhance new implementations, such as compiled stored macros.

```
WARNING: The RESOLVE function is disabled by the NOMACRO option.

ERROR: Invalid branch into %DO %WHILE.

ERROR: Invalid branch into %DO %UNTIL.

ERROR: Extraneous information on %MACRO statement ignored.

WARNING: Cannot execute %INPUT statement from the DMS command
line.

ERROR: The MSTORED option must be set to use the /STORE macro
statement option.

ERROR: The SASMSTORE = option libref is not set.

ERROR: The SAS System was unable to open the macro library
referenced by the SASMSTORE = libref ___.

ERROR: The syntax for this %MACRO statement option is /DES =
"description".

NOTE: The description for the macro parameter /DES = will be
truncated to 40 characters.

MLOGIC(___): Compiled stored macro in libref ___ compiled
on ___.

WARNING: The ___.SASMACR catalog is opened for read only.

ERROR: The WORK.SASMACR catalog is temporary and may not be used
for compiled stored macros.  Change OPTION SASMSTORE to a
different libref.

ERROR: The macro name ___ in the SASMACR catalog and the internal
macro name ___ differ.  Recompile this macro and try
again.
```

CONCLUSION

While, of course, sound programming techniques are the best way to prevent bugs in code, because of the complex nature of the macro facility, almost everyone needs debugging skills for it. It is important to remember when debugging that errors can be macro errors or errors in SAS code generated by macros. Understanding the internals of the macro facility and when a macro message might be generated to the SAS log can help detect an error. Looking for errors during symbolic substitution, macro definition and compilation, macro invocation, and macro execution might help isolate this type of error. Using the SAS options SYMBOLGEN, MLOGIC, and MPRINT in an informed fashion to print information about macro variable resolution, to trace macro execution, and produce macro-generated SAS programming statements, will certainly eliminate some frustration while debugging macros. It is hoped that grouping the macro facility's messages in logical categories will be helpful for macro debugging.

ACKNOWLEDGMENTS

I would like to thank my managers, Jeffrey A. Polzin and Bruce M. Tindall, and my other colleagues in the Core Shell Development Group for their support in the preparation of this paper.

REFERENCES

SAS Institute Inc. (1990), *SAS Guide to Macro Processing, Version 6, Second Edition*, Cary, NC: SAS Institute Inc.

SAS Institute Inc. (1990), *SAS Language: Reference, Version 6, First Edition*, Cary, NC: SAS Institute Inc.

Chapter 3 Efficient Macro Programming

Macros Invocation Hierarchy: Session Compiled, Autocall, and Compiled Stored Macros 101

Advanced

Tasks: Compares and contrasts three sources of macros in programs and their search order.

Tools:
Autocall macros
Efficiency and performance
Macro options
Session compiled macros
Stored compiled macros

Screen Control Language versus Macros in Batch Environments 106

Advanced

Tasks: Compares and contrasts the use of SCL and the macro facility in batch environments.

Tools:
%GLOBAL
%LET
&& resolution
Code portability
Macro parameters
Macro quoting
Program control
Symbolic substitution

A cross-reference listing program for SAS software® macros

Paul A. Thompson, Ph. D.

Introduction

One problem which I have consistently had in using **SAS** software macros lies in the documentation of said macros. Specifically, in setting up projects, I have often found myself with macro files of 1000, 2000 and up to 5000 lines long. Such files are difficult to work with, hard to conceptualize and onerous to list, because macro files have certain requirements not present in standard files.

Debugging macros. Debugging macros is generally difficult, even when **SYMBOLGEN** and **MPRINT** options are chosen. In fact, the use of **SYMBOLGEN** and **MPRINT** can make understanding macros more difficult. This is because these options print macro language after the macros have been interpreted. Some of the important execution code, involving "%IF", "%DO" and the other process control macro structures, is not printed in any case. When running macros, you do not want to see all of the possible branches for the code. When archiving code for printing and storage, and especially when debugging logical error, it is necessary to have a well-designed form for keeping track of the macro information. At this point, you wish to see all possible information about the macros.

Problems with macro files

Visual formatting of macro files. Macro files (simply put, a file containing **SAS** software macros) contain lots of peculiar characters and are (at least to me) inherently difficult to read. For simplicity, lists of such files should list each macro on a separate page, to allow the user to read them easily. At the very least, listing of macros should be done to enable the different macros to be visually distinguised easily. Invariably, persons who use macro files put more and more spaces between the macros, in an effort to visually distinguish them (see numerous examples in the *SAS BASICS Manual*). However, this is a very klugey solution. It is best to comment macros extensively, and then print them nicely for inspection purposes.

Macro variables. In debugging and cleaning large sets of macros, the programmer often finds him/herself trying to locate all occurrances of a certain macro variable. Finding the macro variables can be done using a search command on an editor, but it is difficult to understand an entire program when viewing macro files on terminals. In addition, we often wish to view several statements involving the same variable simultaeneously, in different parts of the file. For these reasons, we often wish to locate macro variables to understand the ways in which they are being used.

Other uses of macro variables are important to consider. It is sometimes useful to distinguish "%GLOBAL" macro variables from "%LOCAL" macro variables. It is certainly important to remember that a variable is "%GLOBAL" in scope, and identifying such variables is important in trying to understand a macro.

Finally, it is important to list macro variables in a way which allows the programmer to determine alternative spelling which must be corrected in order for the macro to perform correctly.

Initialization. Macro variable initialization can take place in several ways. Macros can be defined with parameter values. A "%LET" statement can be used to set up a macro variable with a certain value. "SYMPUT" and "SYMGET" statements can be used to transfer values in and out of macro variables. Initialization of macro variables can be a very useful technique, but it is sometimes difficult in large programs to determine if all macro variables have been initialized. When considering the listing of a macro file, it is important to determine if the variables have been initialized, and where this has been done.

Systems of macros

Locating macros One difficulty in large macro systems is merely locating the macros. In this regard, I refer to my personal experience. In some large simulation projects, I have created numerous (10 or 11) large files of macros. Needless to say, the few grains of wheat which are really of interest get considerably lost in all this chaff. One problem which continually comes up lies in merely finding the correct macro for a particular function. This can partially be overcome by note-taking, but hand-written notes are often overtaken by circumstances, and can't keep up with the process of creating files.

Cross-referencing programs

Cross-referencing programs. One approach to solving these problems lies in the use of a cross-referencing program. Such programs are common in third-generation language developement (**FORTRAN**, C, etc.). Basically, the cross-reference program lists occurrences of variables, in the context of macros and files of macros. The program also lists the different macros, indicates where variables are initialized and indicates variables which are uninitialized. A more advanced cross-reference listing program indicates macro calls in some fashion.

MLIST, a cross-reference program for macros. The program **MLIST** has been written to solve some of these problems. The program is really pretty simple in execution, and has only a very few options. The features of the program are as follows:

- Each macro is printed on a separate page, unless the user wishes a more compressed printing style used. In either case, the program visually distinguishes between macros.

- Macros are printed in a boxed style, to indicate active code. If lines are numbered, line numbers are excluded from the active area.

- A number indicating the depth of the code is printed. Lines not in macros are at depth 0, lines in a macro are at depth 1, and "%DO" loops and groups increase the depth by 1 for each "%DO" level that the code is found at.

- Macro variables found inside macro comments are ignored. Standard SAS language comments are processed for macro variables, but a variety of macro commands are designed to by-pass macro interpretation of the reserved characters "&" and "%". The program ignores code in these reserved sequences.

- All variable initialization is checked. If the initial value can be stated (not done on the fly in a SYMPUT statement, for instance), the initial value is indicated.

- No primitive error checking is done. However, error checking can be done using the listing.

- Macro calls are indicated. Each time a macro is used inside another macro, the call is indicated, and values which are substituted for parameters are also listed. This facilitates certain types of error checking.

- A directory of all macros defined in all programs processed by MLIST is maintained. This directory can be printed to serve as a central index of all macros.

Limitations of MLIST. In the SAS system, macros are a complex coding mechanism. Macro evaluation takes place at several points. MLIST is strictly an evaluation of name-style macros, and examines only the use of single-pass preprocessing for macros. Thus, the program does not correctly process:

- statement-style macros;

- multiple-pass macro evaluations (&& constructions);

- recursive evaluation of macros

- dynamic macro execution, involving the SYMPUT and SYMGET functions.

Most other constructions used with macros are processed correctly, however.

In addition, the program is not a formal SAS language macro debugger. MLIST will not catch many macro errors. Macro errors are a particularily nasty form of bug, as they are susceptible to both logical errors of the code itself, as well as errors of a dynamic nature (actual data failing to satisfy critical condition to initialize values, for instance). However, once a macro error has been encountered, MLIST will greatly facilitate the understanding and debugging of this error.

An example

As usual in these cases, I have concocted an example of macros, created by a "compleat idiot". However, the example does display the essential features of MLIST.

A "*.SAS" file, with macros. Here is an example of a macro file. The file contains five macros, one of which is a driver macro. Some of the macros invoke other macros. Some macro errors are included in the example. However, these errors are sometimes hard to find.

```
     * ************************************* ;
     * This macro file contains macros to
     * 1. Create random matrices, with
     *    certain covariance structures
     * 2. Running the matrices through
     *    the bootstrap replicator
     * 3. Using PROC STEPWISE to analyse
     * 4. Archiving results in a file
     * ************************************* ;
options dquote;

%macro _setup(_NO=40,
              _nl=5,
              _pctv=1.00,
              _errpct=.10,
              _ertype=1);

data start;
     * ************************************* ;
     * Begin by creating &_no.
     * observations
     * ************************************* ;
    %* ************************************* ;
    %* Each observation has &_ni.
    %* variables with random values
    %* ************************************* ;

     array vls vl1-vl&_nl.;
     do s=1 to &_NO.;
        do i=1 to &_nl.;
%IF &_ERTYPE. = 1 %then %do;
           vls{I}=normal(&_sd1.)*&pctv.;
%end;
%else do;
           vls{I}=uniform(&_sd1.)*&_pctv.;
%end;
        end;
        output;
 end;
run;
%_prnt(_ni=&_ni., _when=before, _ds=&_ds.);
%mend _setup;

%macro _prnt(_ni=25,
             _when=before,
             _ds=start);
     * ************************************* ;
     * Print the data
     * ************************************* ;
proc print data=&_ds.;
title2 "Listing of the original data, "
"&_when. transformation";
     var vl1-vl&_ni.;
run;
%mend _prnt;
```

```
%macro _corr(_ni=12.
          _type=pearson,
          _ds=start,
          _simp=nosimple);
     * ************************************ ;
     * Print the data
     * ************************************ ;
%_prnt(_ni=&_ni., _when=before, _ds=&_ds.);
proc corr data=&_ds.;
     var vl1-vl&_ni.;
title2 'correlations between variables';
run;
%mend _corr;

%macro _reg(_ni=12,
          _sls=.10,
          _type=1,
          _phrase=Stepwise regression);
     * ************************************ ;
     * Using regression methods for vars
     * ************************************ ;
%IF &_type. = 1 %then %do;
     * ************************************ ;
     * - stepwise regression here
     * ************************************ ;
proc stepwise
%else %do;
     * ************************************ ;
     * - standard regression here
     * ************************************ ;
proc reg
%end;
 data=&_ds.;
     * ************************************ ;
     * Here we actually state the model
     * ************************************ ;
     model dv=vl1-vl&_ni.
%if &_type. = 1 %then %do;
/ b sls=.05
%end;
;
run;
%mend _reg;

%macro _runreg(_no=15,
               _ni=10,
               _ds=start);

    * ************************************ ;
     * Driver macro file
     *
     * These macros control sessions
     * ************************************ ;
%_setup(_NO=&_no., _nl=&_ni., _ertype=1);
%_prnt(_ni=&_ni.);
%_corr(_ni=&_ni., _type=kendall, _ds=&_ds.);
%_reg(_ni=&_ni., _sls=.05);
%mend _runreg;
```

The errors include:

1. several variable errors, because "O" and "0" are interchanged, and because "i", "l" and "1" are interchanged, and because a "_" was left off;
2. a logical error, as "%" is left off a "DO";
3. a logical error, as a "%END" statement is excluded;
4. several possible logical errors, in which macro variables which are not defined in the macro statement are present in the macro body. These may be "%GLOBAL" variables, with the "%GLOBAL" specification contained in another file;
5. several questionable variables, which are defined in the macro statement, but not used in the macro itself.

In order to find these errors, we could carefully examine the code. However, the MLIST output shows some information which can be used to understand the errors.

The "*.OUT" file from MLIST. MLIST produces a listing file, the "*.OUT" file. This file is produced below for this example.

```
Page    1 --- c:\macset.sas

 1  0 !      * ***************************** ; !
 2  0 !      * This macro file contains macros!
 3  0 !      * 1. Create random matrices, with!
 4  0 !      *    certain covariance structure!
 5  0 !      * 2. Running the matrices through!
 6  0 !      *    the bootstrap replicator    !
 7  0 !      * 3. Using PROC STEPWISE to anal !
 8  0 !      * 4. Archiving results in a file !
 9  0 !      * ***************************** ; !
10  0 ! options dquote;                       !
11  0 !                                       !

*****************************************
 *     *    *      *****  *****   *****
 **   **   * *     *        *  *   *   *
 * * * *  *****    *      *****   *   *
 *  * **      *  *        *  *    *   *
 *     **      * *****    *   *   *****
*****************************************

12  1 ! %macro _setup(_NO=40,             !
13  1 !                _nl=5,             !
14  1 !                _pctv=1.00,        !
15  1 !                _errpct=.10,       !
16  1 !                _ertype=1);        !
17  1 !                                   !
18  1 ! data start;                       !
19  1 !      * **************************** ; !
20  1 !      * Begin by creating &_no.    !
21  1 !      * observations               !
22  1 !      * **************************** ; !
23  1 !     %* **************************** ; !
24  1 !     %* Each observation has &_ni.  !
25  1 !     %* variables with random values !
26  1 !     %* **************************** ; !
27  1 !                                   !
28  1 !      array vls vl1-vl&_n1.;       !
29  1 !      do s=1 to &_NO.;             !
```

```
30  1 !           do i=1 to &_nl.;                  !
31  2 ! %IF &_ERTYPE. = 1 %then %do;                 !
32  2 !           vls{I}=normal(&_sd1.)*&pcte.;      !
33  1 ! %end;                                       !
34  1 ! %else do;                                   !
35  1 !           vls{I}=uniform(&_sd1.)*&_pcte.;    !
36  0 ! %end;                                       !
37  0 !           end;                              !
38  0 !           output;                           !
39  0 !    end;                                     !
40  0 ! run;                                        !
41  0 ! %_prnt(_ni=&_ni., _when=before);            !
42 -1 ! %mend _setup;                               !
43 -1 !                                             !

*******************************************
 *    *    *     *****   *****   *****
 **   **   * *   *       *   *   *   *
 * * * *  *****  *       *****   *   *
 *  *  * *     * *       *  *    *   *
 *     **      * *****   *   *   *****
*******************************************

44  1 ! %macro _prnt(_ni=25,                        !
45  1 !                 _when=before,               !
46  1 !                 _ds=start);                 !
47  1 !       * ***************************** ;     !
48  1 !       * Print the data                      !
49  1 !       * ***************************** ;     !
50  1 ! proc print data=&_ds.;                      !
51  1 ! title2 "Listing of the original data,"!
52  1 ! "&_when. transformation";                   !
53  1 !       var vl1-vl&_ni.;                      !
54  1 ! run;                                        !
55  0 ! %mend _prnt;                                !
56  0 !                                             !

*******************************************
 *    *    *     *****   *****   *****
 **   **   * *   *       *   *   *   *
 * * * *  *****  *       *****   *   *
 *  *  * *     * *       *  *    *   *
 *     **      * *****   *   *   *****
*******************************************

57  1 ! %macro _corr(_ni=12,                        !
58  1 !                 _type=pearson,              !
59  1 !                 _ds=start,                  !
60  1 !                 _simp=nosimple);            !
61  1 !       * ***************************** ;     !
62  1 !       * Print the data                      !
63  1 !       * ***************************** ;     !
64  1 ! %_prnt(_ni=&_ni., _when=before);            !
65  1 ! proc corr data=&_ds.;                       !
66  1 !       var vl1-vl&_ni.;                      !
67  1 ! title2 'correlations between vars';         !
68  1 ! run;                                        !
69  0 ! %mend _corr;                                !
70  0 !                                             !

*******************************************
 *    *    *     *****   *****   *****
 **   **   * *   *       *   *   *   *
 * * * *  *****  *       *****   *   *
 *  *  * *     * *       *  *    *   *
 *     **      * *****   *   *   *****
*******************************************

71  1 ! %macro _reg(_ni=12,                         !
72  1 !                 _sls=.10,                   !
73  1 !                 _type=1,                    !
74  1 !                 _phrase=Stepwise regressi);!
75  1 !       * ***************************** ;     !
76  1 !       * Using regression methods for var!
77  1 !       * ***************************** ;     !
78  2 ! %IF &_type. = 1 %then %do;                  !
79  2 !       * ***************************** ;     !
80  2 !       * - stepwise regression here          !
81  2 !       * ***************************** ;     !
82  2 ! proc stepwise                               !
83  3 ! %else %do;                                  !
84  3 !       * ***************************** ;     !
85  3 !       * - standard regression here          !
86  3 !       * ***************************** ;     !
87  3 ! proc reg                                    !
88  2 ! %end;                                       !
89  2 !  data=&_ds.;                                !
90  2 !       * ***************************** ;     !
91  2 !       * Here we actually state the model!
92  2 !       * ***************************** ;     !
93  2 !       model dv=vl1-vl&_ni.                  !
94  3 ! %if &_type. = 1 %then %do;                  !
95  3 ! / b sls=.05                                 !
96  2 ! %end;                                       !
97  2 ! ;                                           !
98  2 ! run;                                        !
99  1 ! %mend _reg;                                 !
100 1 !                                             !

*******************************************
 *    *    *     *****   *****   *****
 **   **   * *   *       *   *   *   *
 * * * *  *****  *       *****   *   *
 *  *  * *     * *       *  *    *   *
 *     **      * *****   *   *   *****
*******************************************

101 1 ! %macro _runreg(_no=15,                      !
102 1 !                 _ni=10,                     !
103 1 !                 _ds=start);                 !
104 1 !                                             !
105 1 !       * ***************************** ;     !
106 1 !       * Driver macro file                   !
107 1 !       *                                     !
108 1 !       * These macros control sessions       !
109 1 !       * ***************************** ;     !
110 1 ! %_setup(_NO=&_no., _nl=&_ni.,_ertype=1);!
111 1 ! %_prnt(_ni=&_ni.);                          !
112 1 ! %_corr(_ni=&_ni., _type=kendall);           !
113 1 ! %_reg(_ni=&_ni., _sls=.05);                 !
114 0 ! %mend _runreg;                              !
```

Reading this output. The listing is rather straight-forward. Line numbers are shown. The level of the macro processing is also shown. Lines 44-45 shows a level of -1. This indicates an error of macro processing, originally produced on line 34 (no "%" sign for the "DO" statement). Lines 99-100 show a level of 1, which is another error. This error is produced by a missing "%END" statement, which should be after line 82. Macros are clearly distinguised.

The "*.XRF" file, the cross-reference listing. The cross-reference listing is also presented, to learn more about the macro file. This file is presented below.

```
e    1 --- Variable listing of c:\turboc\datafile\macset.sas

  Name  Print  File       MACRO Variable                         Occurrences
        Page   Line  Name      Initial    Type       Declared

_SETUP     1   12

                     _NO       40         MACRO          12   Macro variab
                     _NL       5          MACRO          13       30
                     _PCTV     1.00       MACRO          14       35
                     _ERRPCT   .10        MACRO          15   Macro variab
                     _ERTYPE   1          MACRO          16       31
                     _NI       --None--   --None--       28       28
                     _NO       --None--   --None--       29       29
                     _SD1      --None--   --None--       32       32
                                                                  35
                     PCTV      --None--   --None--       32       32
                     _NI       --None--   --None--       41       41
                     _DS       --None--   --None--       41       41

_PRNT      1   44

                     _NI       25         MACRO          44       53
                     _WHEN     BEFORE     MACRO          45       52
                     _DS       START      MACRO          46       50

_CORR      2   57

                     _NI       12         MACRO          57       64 66
                     _TYPE     PEARSON    MACRO          58   Macro variab
                     _DS       START      MACRO          59       64 65
                     _SIMP     NOSIMPLE   MACRO          60   Macro variab

_REG       2   71

                     _NI       12         MACRO          71       93
                     _SLS      .10        MACRO          72   Macro variab
                     _TYPE     1          MACRO          73       78 94
                     _PHRASE              MACRO          74   Macro variab
                          STEPWISE REGRESSION
                     _DS       --None--   --None--       89       89

_RUNREG    3  101

                     _NO       15         MACRO         101      110
                                                  111   112      113
                     _NI       10         MACRO         102      110
                     _DS       START      MACRO         103      112
```

This output can be read to determine several things. The different variables actually used are presented, and printed clearly. The name is presented, the line on which it first appears is shown, initial values are presented, and all occurrences are presented. Determining the cause of certain types of macro errors can be done very simply with this file.

Macro calls. In addition, macro calls are presented. Each time a macro is executed, the arguments for the calls have been presented, and the programmer can easily find all possible calls of the macro.

```
Page    2 -- Macro calls for c:\turboc\datafile\macset.sas

        Name    Initial      Calls

_SETUP                        110
      _NO            40       &_NO.
      _NL             5       &_NI.
    _PCTV          1.00     -Unused-
  _ERRPCT           .10     -Unused-
  _ERTYPE             1         1

_PRNT                         41          64        111
      _NI            25       &_NI.       &_NI.     &_NI.
    _WHEN        BEFORE      BEFORE      BEFORE   -Unused-
      _DS         START       &_DS.       &_DS.   -Unused-

_CORR                         112
      _NI            12       &_NI.
    _TYPE       PEARSON     KENDALL
      _DS         START       &_DS.
    _SIMP      NOSIMPLE    -Unused-

_REG                          113
      _NI            12       &_NI.
     _SLS           .10         .05
    _TYPE             1    -Unused-
  _PHRASE      STEPWI+     -Unused-
```

The "*.DIR" file, the macro directory. The macro directory is also presented. As this is a single file, the macro directory is of less interest. However, it acts as an index for the printed result from the file "*.OUT".

```
Page    1 -- Directory Listing for all MACRO files

 MACRO      File    Page             MACRO File
 Name       Line   Number

_CORR        57       2   c:\macset.sas
_PRNT        44       1   c:\macset.sas
_REG         71       2   c:\macset.sas
_RUNREG     101       3   c:\macset.sas
_SETUP       12       1   c:\macset.sas
```

Conclusions

MLIST is a simple program (to the user, that is) with only a few options. It is designed to list SAS language macro files in an organized fashion, so that archival and storage of SAS language macros can be done in a nice and organized way. While other simple ways are available for listing SAS language macro files, most do not take advantage of the salient and essential features of macros to make the listing clear and unambiguous. MLIST does do this. It facilitates the use of SAS language macros as a real programming language, and should facilitate their intelligent usage.

MLIST is written in Turbo C, and has been ported to the Lattice C compiler ®, with only minor modifications. It should compile and perform successfully on all systems which support the Lattice C compiler.

Contacting the author. If you are interested in this program, or wish to make suggestions to improve it, please contact the author at:

- Paul A. Thompson
- Departments of Psychiatry and Psychology
- Case Western Reserve University
- B-68 Hanna Pavilion
- University Hospitals of Cleveland
- Cleveland, OH 44106
- (216) 844-7463

SAS software ® is a registered trademark of SAS Institute, Inc., Cary, NC, USA. The Lattice C compiler ® is a registered trademark of Lattice Inc., Cary, NC, USA.

SAS® Macro Language Features for Application Development

Earl R. Westerlund, Eastman Kodak Company

ABSTRACT

The SAS® macro language has many uses. One use is to facilitate development of applications and systems. This talk will discuss some features of the SAS macro language that are useful to application developers. Topics to be discussed include:

- Application development features such as windows, statement style macros, and the autocall facility
- The hows, whys and whens of macro quoting
- Options and statements that aid in macro debugging.

This talk assumes a basic knowledge of SAS macros and macro variables.

INTRODUCTION

The SAS macro language is a very useful tool. Like all tools, however, they can be misused. Before we begin to discuss features of the macro language, it might be good to review what the macro language is good for, and other tools that are available to application developers.

WHEN TO USE MACROS

The *SAS Guide to Macro Processing, Version 6 Edition* defines the macro facility as a "tool for extending and customizing the SAS System and for reducing the amount of text you must enter to do common tasks."[1] The macro language is best used:

- For programs that perform repetitive tasks, such as processing a number of similar SAS data sets in the same way
- For conditional execution of SAS code; for example, executing particular procedures based on the type of data set or desires of the user
- For "packaging" blocks of reusable SAS code, for easy retrieval at a later time.

WHEN *NOT* TO USE MACROS

The macro language is so powerful and flexible that when people first learn it, they are sometimes impressed to the point that they overuse it. Do not use the macro language:

- "Because it's there." I have seen SAS programs which were one big macro definition, followed by the macro invocation, with no conditional or repetitive execution of code. Remember that the macro facility must compile the macro, then execute it *before* the SAS language processor even sees it. In other words, it adds overhead to your program.
- If the only time the macro would be used would be in a batch program and, again, there is no conditional or repetitive execution of code. The %INCLUDE statement uses less overhead because it reads in and immediately executes the code. It does not have to compile a macro first.
- Simply for interaction with the end user. There are times when it is appropriate, but there are a number of other ways to interact with the user.

Other application development tools are described at the end of this paper

APPLICATION DEVELOPMENT FEATURES

Here are some features that are useful for developing applications in the macro language.

For interaction with users

- **The %PUT and %INPUT statements** provide a quick, simple way to interact with the user in line mode. Here's an example of how they can be used:

```
%macro which;
  %put Which data set to print?;
  %input dsname;
  PROC PRINT DATA=&dsname;
  RUN;
%mend which;
```

  The big drawback is that the %PUT statement will only output to the SAS log. Your log must be directed to the terminal, which means that either your users will see lots of information they don't need, or you lose potentially valuable information about the execution of the job.

- **The %WINDOW and %DISPLAY statements** build and display windows for interaction. Here is the same example as above, using a window instead of line prompts:

```
%macro which;
  %window whichds
    #3 @5 'Which data set to print?'
    #5 @10 dsname 17 required=yes;
  %display whichds;
  PROC PRINT DATA=&dsname;
  RUN;
%mend which;
```

  Upon execution, a window opens with the displayed text, and waits for the required input. This is a simple process. The primary disadvantage is that there are few built-in functions for error checking. Such functions exist in SCL.

Statement-Style Macros

By using the STMT option in a macro definition, you can set up macros that look like SAS statements. Consider the following macro, which performs a standard analysis on a specified data set:

```
%macro analyze(dsname) / stmt;
  PROC MEANS DATA=&dsname;
  RUN;
```

[1]"SAS Guide to Macro Processing, Version 6 Edition," p.3

```
   PROC UNIVARIATE DATA=&dsname;
   RUN;
%mend analyze;
```

To run this macro, you simply invoke it as if it were a SAS statement:

```
ANALYZE MYLIB.MYDS;
```

With statement-style macros, you can integrate your macros into the SAS System. They look like other SAS statements; there is no apparently (to the user) artificial distinction between your macros and SAS commands. There are two disadvantages. First, the macro call must form a complete SAS statement; you cannot imbed a statement-style macro within another SAS statement. Second, the SAS system must do an extra check at the beginning of each statement to determine whether it is a statement-style macro. This adds to the overhead of running a program.

The Autocall Facility

The autocall facility is a way of making a library of commonly used SAS macros available without having to explicitly include them in each program in which they are used. When a macro is invoked and not yet defined, the autocall library is searched for the macro. If the macro is in the library, the SAS system reads the macro, compiles it and then runs it.

The form of the macro library depends on the operating system. On CMS, macros are stored as members of a CMS MACLIB. On MVS, they are members of a partitioned data set. The name of the member must be the same as the name of the macro.

Macro libraries that are to be available to the general public can be defined in the control program (EXEC, CLIST, etc.) that invokes SAS. They are defined by the SASAUTOS fileref.

You can add a macro library to the autocall list by using the SASAUTOS option. For example, to add the macro library MYMACS to the existing autocall library on CMS, use the statement:

```
OPTIONS SASAUTOS=(SASAUTOS 'MYMACS MACLIB *');
```

Data driven macros

The SAS System provides tools to facilitate data exchange between the macro facility and SAS data sets. It can be very useful to be able to run certain procedures based on the value of a variable in a SAS data set. You can use the `CALL SYMPUT` statement to accomplish this. For example, suppose you want to do different analyses depending on the value of the variable DATATYPE in a data set. You could accomplish it this way:

```
%macro analyze(dsname);
  DATA _NULL_;
    SET &dsname(OBS=1);
    CALL SYMPUT ("DTYPE",DATATYPE);
  RUN;
  %if &dtype = TYPEONE
    %then %analyz1;
    %else %if &dtype = TYPETWO
      %then %analyz2;
      %else %stananl;
%mend analyze;
```

When invoked, this macro will cause the macro variable &DTYPE to be assigned the value of the DATATYPE variable in the first observation of the data set. After the DATA step is done, the value has been assigned and is available for use. Based on the value of &DTYPE, one of three analysis macros is run. You can also use `CALL SYMPUT` to customize titles, select data set variables to be analyzed or, choose the type of analysis to be done based on a data value.

Transferring data from macro variables to SAS data set variables is easier. If the name of the macro variable is constant, you can simply issue an assignment statement in a SAS DATA step:

```
CHARVAR = "&macvar";        * Character variable;
NUMVAR = &macvar2;          * Numeric variable;
```

If the name of the macro can change based on data value, you can use the `SYMGET` function. The following example assumes there are three macro variables &X1-&X3, the values of which are to be assigned into SAS variables based on the value of the variable TYPE in SAS data set INFO, which has values 1 to 3:

```
DATA NEW;
   SET INFO;
   XX = SYMGET('X'||LEFT(TYPE));
RUN;
```

You can use these features to transfer information from one step to another. The following example generates a plot containing the mean as a reference line. The mean and standard deviation are listed in a footnote.

```
* Step 1: get the mean;
PROC MEANS NOPRINT DATA=MYDATA;
   VAR Y;
   OUTPUT OUT=STATS
          MEAN=YBAR
          STD=STD;
RUN;
* Step 2: create macro variables;
DATA _NULL_;
   SET STATS;
   CALL SYMPUT ('MEAN',PUT(YBAR,6.2));
   CALL SYMPUT ('STDEV',PUT(STD,6.3));
RUN;
* Step 3: generate the plot with mean as ref
line;
PROC GPLOT DATA=MYDATA;
   PLOT Y*TIME / VREF=&mean;
   TITLE 'Plot of Y Across Time';
   FOOTNOTE "MEAN=&mean;   ST.DEV.=&stdev";
RUN;
```

System Variables

There are a number of automatic macro variables that you can use to control macro execution or enhance output. Some of them are:

- **&SYSDATE** contains the date that the SAS job ran.
- **&SYSTIME** contains the time that the SAS job started.

- **&SYSDEVIC** contains the name of the graphics device specified by the DEVICE= option.
- **&SYSDSN** contains the name of the most recently created SAS data set.
- **&SYSMSG** contains a message that you want to display in the message area of a macro window. Use the %LET statement to set a value for &SYSMSG.
- **&SYSERR** contains the return code from the last DATA or PROC step.
- **&SYSRC** contains the return code from the last host system command issued from within a SAS session.

MACRO QUOTING

Macro quoting is one of the most difficult concepts to grasp - even for an experienced macro user. Understanding why it is necessary goes a long way toward using it effectively.

When it is necessary

The macro language is strictly a character-based language. Its sole purpose is to generate fragments of SAS code. Even "numeric" macro variables are actually character variables. The problem occurs when you need to use a character that has special meaning (such as & or %) in a character string in such a way that the macro language might interpret it as part of a macro statement. For example, the following macro prints data about a company from a data base. The company is identified by its stock ticker.

```
%macro company(ticker);
  %if &ticker eq EK   /* special for Kodak */
    %then PROC PRINT DATA=STATS.EK;
    %else %do;
      PROC PRINT DATA=STATS.OTHER;
        WHERE COMPANY="&ticker";
      RUN;
    %end;
%mend company;
```

There are two problems with the above macro. First, if we decide to get information on General Electric, we have a problem. General Electric's ticker symbol is "GE," which also happens to be SAS's comparison operator for "greater than or equal to." The %if statement becomes

```
%if ge eq ek ...
```

which the macro language does not know how to interpret. Adding the %BQUOTE function takes care of this. It hides the special meaning of "GE" from the macro processor so the comparison can be made.

The second problem occurs in the third line. The semicolon at the end of the line "%then PROC PRINT DATA=STATS.EK;" closes the %if statement, not the PROC PRINT statement. Consequently, there is no semicolon after the PROC PRINT statement, which will cause an error. Using a %STR statement ensures that a semicolon is passed to the SAS language.

The corrected macro becomes:

```
%macro company(ticker);
  %if %bquote(&ticker) eq EK
    %then %str(PROC PRINT DATA=STATS.EK;);
    %else %do;
      PROC PRINT DATA=STATS.OTHER;
        WHERE COMPANY="&ticker";
      RUN;
    %end;
%mend company;
```

Kinds of macro quoting

There are two basic kinds of quoting functions. %STR and %NRSTR quote strings at macro compilation time. They prevent the macro language from treating your string as part of the macro language while the macro is being compiled. The difference between %STR and %NRSTR is that %STR will resolve macros and macro variables, while %NRSTR will treat them as text and not resolve them.

The second kind of quoting functions take effect at macro execution time. %BQUOTE, %NRBQUOTE and %SUPERQ quote the resolution of a macro value, to prevent situations where special characters and mnemonic operators (like "GE") that happen to appear in a string are interpreted as macro code. The difference between %BQUOTE and %NRBQUOTE are similar to %STR and %NRSTR: %BQUOTE resolves macros and macro variables before quoting, and %NRBQUOTE does not. %SUPERQ only takes a macro variable as an argument; otherwise, its function it pretty much the same as %NRBQUOTE.

Refer to the *SAS Guide to Macro Processing* for more details on macro quoting. It contains some useful tables describing which functions quote which special symbols, and when they take effect.

OPTIONS AND STATEMENTS FOR DEBUGGING

Using any application development facility effectively requires effective debugging tools. Version 6 of the SAS System provides some useful options for tracing the execution of your macros. These are SAS system options, and can be invoked at startup in the configuration file or on the command line, or can be changed during execution through the OPTIONS statement or options window. Here are the available options:

- The **MPRINT** option displays in the SAS log all SAS code that has been generated by the macro facility. Use this to verify that the code that you want to generate is in fact being generated.
- The **SYMBOLGEN** option displays the resolution of all macro variables. Use this to verify that your variables are resolving correctly.
- The **MTRACE** option traces the execution of a macro. Messages are sent to the log indicating the beginning of a macro, statements that are executed, whether %IF conditions are true or false, and when a macro finishes execution.
- The **%PUT statement** is not a system option, but it can be very useful in determining the source of a problem. Use it to print macro variable values to the log, or to print messages indicating that you've reached a certain point in the macro.

OTHER DEVELOPMENT TOOLS

There are a number of other application development tools that are available with the SAS System. They can be used with the macro language when appropriate. The following chart describes the relationships between the tools that are described below.

For program control:

- SAS/AF® software is for development of windowed application systems. Its Screen Control Language was developed for user interaction, and works much better than the macro facility for that.
- SAS/ASSIST® software is a SAS program product, written in SAS/AF software, that allows users who don't know the SAS language to "point and click" their way through the system. The EIS (Executive Information System) option allows you to add applications to the ASSIST menus. If your users are going to use ASSIST software, consider adding your applications to its menus.

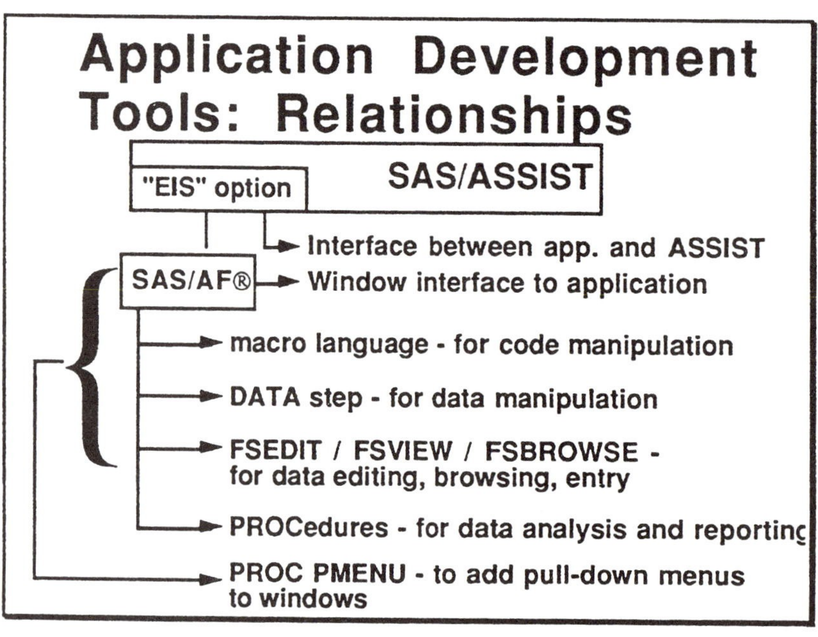

- The PMENU procedure in base SAS software allows you to build pull-down menus that can be added to any windows you build.

For data entry and manipulation:

- The SAS programming language (the DATA step) contains many tools for application development. For simple user interaction, the `PUT` and `INPUT` statements and `WINDOW` and `DISPLAY` statements are available. In release 6.03 and beyond, DATA steps can be stored in compiled form, saving some overhead. As of release 6.06, compiled macros still cannot be stored.
- PROC FSEDIT and PROC FSVIEW, in SAS/FSP® software, are procedures which allow data entry and editing. Screen Control Language (SCL) is available to customize screens.

CONCLUSION

While SAS Institute has provided a number of new features and products to facilitate application development, the SAS macro language remains a very useful and powerful facility. Knowing more about the tools available to you can make your system development task, and your users' lives, much easier.

ACKNOWLEDGMENTS

SAS, SAS/AF, SAS/ASSIST and SAS/FSP are registered trademarks of SAS Institute Inc. No endorsement of SAS software by Eastman Kodak Company is implied.

The opinions expressed in this paper are those of the author, and are not representative of Eastman Kodak Company.

REFERENCES

SAS Institute Inc. (1990), *SAS® Language: Reference, Version 6, First Edition,* Cary, NC: SAS Institute Inc.

SAS Institute Inc. (1987), *SAS® Guide to Macro Processing, Version 6, First Edition,* Cary, NC: SAS Institute Inc.

SAS Institute Inc. (1986), *SAS® Guide to Macro Processing, Version 5 Edition,* Cary, NC: SAS Institute Inc.

SAS Institute Inc. (1990), *SAS/ASSIST® Software: Your Interface to the SAS® System, Version 6, First Edition,* Cary, NC: SAS Institute Inc.

USING SAS MACROS WITH SAS/AF* AND SAS/FSP* SOFTWARE IN DEVELOPING USER-FRIENDLY APPLICATIONS

Jennifer C. Culp, GPU Service Corporation

ABSTRACT

SAS macros may be used with SAS/AF* and SAS/FSP* in developing solid, user-friendly applications. An application can be friendly in two ways, both to the user and to the maintenance programmer, each of which combine for an efficient, cohesive unit. Ways to develop an application which is friendly to the user include the use of SAS macros in displaying informative relevant messages on the screen and controlling code execution to perform only those tasks which are necessary to a function. Making changes and enhancements and performing testing should be as easy as possible for an application to be friendly to the maintenance programmer. To achieve this, SAS macros may be used to eliminate duplicate code by calling a section of code each time it is needed and to dynamically generate code when a number of different situations are possible. The methods of using SAS macros discussed in this paper will help assure that your application will be user-friendly, efficient, error-free, and successful.

INTRODUCTION

As the SAS family of software products becomes increasingly popular, more and more people, experienced programmers and novices, are developing custom applications which utilize SAS/AF and SAS/FSP. These applications may, in some cases, be hastily thrown-together conglomerations of menus and screens combined with an infinite number of SAS log messages which an inexperienced user cannot comprehend. Ideally, the flow of an application should be such that any unnecessary steps, messages, and keystrokes are eliminated, and those which are essential to the execution of the system should be easily followed and understood by all users of the system, experienced or otherwise. In addition, since the applications might be written by novice programmers, the code itself may be inefficient and difficult to modify. Another important facet of a user-friendly system is friendly to the maintenance programmer. The programming should be such that changes may be easily and quickly made. To achieve each of these goals, SAS macros may be used as the glue to tie the system together into a cohesive unit. The purpose of this paper is to show how SAS macros may be used with SAS/AF and SAS/FSP in developing solid, user-friendly applications in which processing is done behind the scenes efficiently, and users see only that which is necessary to performing a task.

(NOTE: All programming examples will use an employee application that provides browsing, editing, and reporting functions for employees and managers.)

MESSAGES

One of the simplest and most effective uses of SAS macros in developing user-friendly applications is that of messages to the user using %PUT. Messages on the screen are unfortunately ignored more often than not. For this reason, it is important that those which are shown to the user are relevant to the operation of the system or to the execution of a certain task. Messages of this nature serve to put the user at ease with the use of the computer and the application. No longer need one be afraid to press a key fearing that the program will go off to never-never land and do who knows what to the data. A truly user-friendly application will tell the user in terms he can understand what is occurring at the time.

Three examples of messages which convey relevant information to the user are those relating to the acknowledgement of an action taken by the user, the explanation of a blank screen or a long wait, and the result of a menu selection, criteria entry, or operation. These messages provide a medium between a system which displays the entire SAS log on the screen and one which displays nothing at all. The first overloads the user with information which, not understanding, he eventually entirely ignores. The other presents a black box into which the user inputs a selection and from which a result is produced which is assumed to be the correct one. Neither of these cases is user-friendly, because the user has no idea whether he performed the desired task.

The first example of a message is the acknowledgement of an action taken by the user. A situation where this message might be used is selecting an option from a menu.

```
                 REPORTS

1.  EMPLOYEE LISTING - ALPHA ORDER
2.  EMPLOYEE LISTING - SALARY ORDER
3.  EMPLOYEE LISTING - MANAGER ORDER
4.  EMPLOYEE LISTING - DEPT ORDER

5.  RETURN TO PRIMARY MENU
```

If a selection is made from the menu in this example, the simplest appropriate message would mimic the selection.

```
... EMPLOYEE LISTING - ALPHA ORDER
```

```
%PUT ... EMPLOYEE LISTING - ALPHA ORDER;
RUN;
```

This message will assure the user he actually selected the report he wished to produce.

Another use of messages is an explanation of a blank screen or a long wait. If processing is occurring behind the scenes which will not be displayed to the user and which may take some time to complete, inform him of this.

... PROCESSING OCCURRING. PLEASE BE PATIENT.

```
%PUT ... PROCESSING OCCURRING.
         PLEASE BE PATIENT.;
RUN;
```

In doing so, the user will know that there is not a problem with his computer or anything else. The longer the wait, the more important such messages become.

The final example of messages is displaying the result of a menu selection, criteria entry, or operation. When the user specifies that a task should be performed which may return a different result each time, tell the user how many records he is dealing with.

... 5 RECORDS SELECTED FOR BROWSE.

```
%PUT ... &COUNT RECORDS SELECTED FOR BROWSE.;
RUN;
```

... NO RECORDS MEETING YOUR SELECTION CRITERIA.

```
%PUT ... NO RECORDS MEETING YOUR SELECTION
         CRITERIA.;
RUN;
```

... 5000 RECORDS SORTED.

```
%PUT ... &COUNT RECORDS SORTED.;
RUN;
```

This is very useful in an interactive application, because it eliminates the "black box" effect and prepares the user for what lies ahead, whether it is returning to the selection screen or browsing a million records.

Again, these kinds of messages provide a link to the inner processes of the application without the user being overwhelmed or intimidated. A simple response using the %PUT statement can put the user at ease with the application and be helpful and informative at the same time.

CONTROLLING CODE EXECUTION

Another important use of SAS macros in developing user-friendly applications is that of controlling code execution. The % IF-%THEN-%ELSE structure allows certain procs, data steps, or even portions of them to be executed or not, depending on such factors as the number of observations in a dataset or the type of user who has logged on. Based on the amount of data available, a task may be performed in a different manner such as the use of PROC SORT or another sorting algorithm. Certain sections of code may be skipped if there is no data to process. The type of user can indicate that certain tasks should be executed or ignored. Thus the application is able to react to each situation in the most timely and efficient manner as possible.

The macro language in its simplest form is easy to program and understand. To determine if a block of code should be executed, a macro variable "flag" may be queried in a %IF statement within a macro. (The %IF-%THEN-%ELSE structure is available only in a macro.) The flag itself may contain the value of any data step variable, another macro variable, or a literal, and may be used anywhere throughout the application. Just remember that if the flag is assigned within a macro, a %GLOBAL statement must be specified to retain its value outside the macro. To assign the value of a data step variable to a macro variable, use the CALL SYMPUT statement.

```
DATA _NULL_;
     DATE  = TODAY();
     MONTH = MONTH(DATE);
     YEAR  = YEAR(DATE);
     YYMM  = (YEAR * 100) + MONTH;
     CALL SYMPUT('MDATE',LEFT(YYMM));
RUN;
```

If today's date is 08/13/90, the value of the macro variable is 9008. To assign the value of another macro variable or literal, use %LET.

```
%LET NEWDATE = &MDATE;
RUN;

%LET NEWFLAG = Y;
RUN;
```

The value of the macro variable NEWDATE is 9008, and the value of NEWFLAG is Y.

Each of the following examples demonstrate how SAS macro variables and the %IF-%THEN-%ELSE structure allow an application itself to determine, at run-time, how it will perform the task which was requested. The situations which will be discussed involve reducing response time, avoiding errors, and performing data initializations.

The response time of an application can be significantly improved by the use of SAS macros to avoid executing code which is not an integral part of performing the task in a particular situation. It is important to minimize the level of frustration on the part of the user as much as possible: the better the response time, the more willing the user is to utilize the application. If certain steps do not need to be executed as a result of a choice the user made or the outcome of an operation, the % IF-%THEN-%ELSE structure can be used to skip them and move on to the next menu or task. For example, say a user of the employee application wanted to modify the data for a single employee. Upon entry of the employee id to be modified, the following steps would be executed.

```
DATA EMPLOYEE;
     SET SASFILE.EMPLOYEE;
     IF EMPID EQ "&EMPID";
RUN;

<<DISPLAY RECORD>>
```

```
<<CHECK FOR ERRORS>>
<<REMOVE DUPLICATES, DO NOT ALLOW ADDITIONS OR
    DELETIONS>>
<<ASSIGN AUDIT TRAIL FIELDS - WHO CHANGED AND
    WHEN>>
<<REPLACE RECORD>>
<<REDISPLAY SELECTION PANEL>>
```

If the above steps were executed regardless of whether a corresponding record was found or not, the user would be displayed a blank data entry screen and would then have to wait while a number of operations were performed on an empty dataset. The friendliest system would give the user a message that no record was found and redisplay the selection panel for another try.

```
%LET NUM = 0;
DATA EMPLOYEE;
     DROP COUNT;
     SET SASFILE.EMPLOYEE;
     IF EMPID EQ "&EMPID" THEN
        DO;
             COUNT + 1;
             OUTPUT;
        END;
     CALL SYMPUT('NUM',LEFT(COUNT));
RUN;

%IF &NUM GT 0 %THEN        /* IF RECORD EXISTS */
    %DO;
       <<DISPLAY RECORD>>
       <<CHECK FOR ERRORS>>
       <<REMOVE DUPLICATES, DO NOT ALLOW
            ADDITIONS OR DELETIONS>>
       <<ASSIGN AUDIT TRAIL FIELDS - WHO CHANGED
            AND WHEN>>
       <<REPLACE RECORD>>
    %END;
%ELSE
    %DO;
       %PUT ... NO SUCH EMPLOYEE FOUND;
       RUN;
    %END;

<<REDISPLAY SELECTION PANEL>>
```

Controlling code execution in certain circumstances can serve to avoid errors for which vague messages may be displayed to the user and which could halt the execution of the application. When messages display on the screen, as mentioned before, they should be relevant to the operation of the system or to the execution of a certain task. They should not be caused by the program abending due to a processing error. If the user of the employee application wished to browse all the employees who report to a certain manager, he would enter the manager id, and the following would occur:

```
DATA MANAGER;
     SET SASFILE.EMPLOYEE;
     IF MGRID = "&MGRID";
RUN;

PROC FSBROWSE;
RUN;
```

An error message would be displayed if no employees existed for that manager or the manager id was not valid.

```
ERROR:  ERRORS DETECTED IN STATEMENTS.
        PROC EXECUTION TERMINATED.
```

With NONOTES in effect, no other explanation would be given to the user. The essential message is actually a log note and will not be displayed.

```
NOTE:  NO OBSERVATIONS IN DATA SET WORK.MANAGER.
```

An error such as this can cause the entire application to abend with the only alternative to start all over again. The user will have no idea what the problem is or what to do to resolve it. This entire situation could be avoided simply by counting the number of observations returned in the dataset and storing that value in a macro variable which can be queried in a %IF-%THEN-%ELSE structure.

```
%LET NUM = 0;
DATA MANAGER;
     DROP COUNT;
     SET SASFILE.EMPLOYEE;
     IF MGRID = "&MGRID" THEN
        DO;
          COUNT + 1;
          OUTPUT;
        END;
     CALL SYMPUT('NUM',LEFT(COUNT));
RUN;

%IF &NUM GT 0 %THEN        /* IF RECORDS EXIST */
    %DO;
       PROC FSBROWSE;
       RUN;
    %END;
```

Performing data initializations is yet another area where SAS macros may be used to control code execution. This case also serves to eliminate the need for user intervention in a process essential to the workings of the system. In the employee application, the audit trail dataset is updated each time a user modifies employee information. The statistics being kept on each user include the employee last changed, the date changed, and the total number of modifications performed. A new record must be created in this dataset for each new user of the application. In a system where SAS macros were not used, it might be required for a user to select an option from a menu to create this entry or to respond with a "yes" to a prompt. In either case there is no guarantee that the record would indeed be created, and if it were not, errors may result, and the proper data would not be gathered. With the use of SAS macros the user's logon id can be captured and checked for a corresponding entry in the audit trail dataset. If one is not found, the code to add a new record can be executed. If a record does exist for that user, this code would be skipped.

```
<<GET LOGGED ON USER'S ID>>
```

```
%LET NUM = 0;
DATA _NULL_;
     SET SASFILE.AUDIT;
     IF EMPID EQ "&USERID" THEN
        COUNT + 1;
     CALL SYMPUT('NUM',LEFT(COUNT));
RUN;

%IF &NUM EQ 0 %THEN
    %DO;
       <<ADD RECORD TO AUDIT DATASET>>
    %END;
```

One could go on and on with so many uses of SAS macros in this vein - using the % IF-%THEN-%ELSE structure to control code execution. You will find that this one statement can make the difference between an efficient successful application and a cumbersome one which no one wants to use.

ELIMINATING DUPLICATE CODE

An application should be easily understood not only by the users but the maintenance programmer as well. An application is only as good as the code that makes it up, and if changes or enhancements are not easy to make, the entire system becomes obsolete quickly. Another area in which SAS macros can benefit an application is the elimination of duplicate code. If several similar functions are to be performed in different parts of the system, the most efficient and easily modified solution is to have one instance of that code and utilize macro variables to handle each situation. This is similar to passing parameters to a subroutine in other programming languages - one set of code may be executed many ways. This is particularly advantageous regarding maintenance programming. Down the road someone will be maintaining your application who is not intimately familiar with its inner processes or your programming style. If several similar programs exist, they must all be located when a modification is to be made. If any one is missed, inconsistencies occur and possibly errors. The integrity of the entire system is degraded, along with the confidence of the user. There are several ways in which duplicate code may be avoided. The use of macro variables as parameters allow code to be generalized to handle any dataset, any screen, any other program. Within a program if a section of code will be utilized several times, that code can be placed in a macro and called each time it is needed. And the macro statement %INCLUDE provides the ability to call other programs that may contain data steps, procs or portions of them which are common to several different functions or programs.

A program may be generalized to process a number of different datasets of the same format, screens, or programs by assigning the name to a macro variable.

```
%LET DATASET = EMPLOYEE;
%LET SCREEN  = EMPLOYEE;
%LET PGM     = EMPLOYEE;
```

In each case the literal EMPLOYEE is assigned to a macro variable - DATASET, SCREEN, and PGM. The value EMPLOYEE will be substituted in the code when the program is executed.

```
DATA PERSONEL;
  SET SASFILE.&DATASET;     ==> SASFILE.EMPLOYEE
  IF ...
  .
  .
  .
RUN;

    or

PROC FSEDIT DATA=PERSONEL
  SCREEN=SASCREEN.&SCREEN; ==> SASCREEN.EMPLOYEE
RUN;

    or

%INCLUDE SASPROCS(&PGM);  ==> SASPROCS(EMPLOYEE)
RUN;
```

In this manner, these pieces of code can be used with any number of datasets, screens, or programs simply by changing the value of the literal assigned to the macro variables.

A second method of using SAS macros to eliminate duplicate code is using a macro itself. Any code in a program which is to be used more than once should not be appear in that program each place it is to be executed. This leads to difficulties in performing maintenance, since a single change may have to be made several times. The number of possibilities which must be tested increases dramatically along with the chances of an error occurring. This piece of code can be made to appear only once in a program by locating it within a macro. The code may then be called as often as needed, with macro variable parameters being used to generalize the code to fit each situation. A very simple example would be to place the code for browsing a dataset in a macro and call it each time it is to be used. The values of the dataset name and the screen name are assigned to macro variables which are used within the macro.

```
%MACRO DOBROWSE;
     PROC FSBROWSE DATA=&DATASET
        SCREEN=SASCREEN.SCREENS.&SCREEN..SCREEN;
     RUN;
%MEND DOBROWSE;

DATA EMPLOYEE;
     SET SASFILE.EMPLOYEE;
     KEEP ...;
     <<IF NOT A MANAGER THEN OUTPUT RECORD>>
RUN;

%LET DATASET = EMPLOYEE;
%LET SCREEN = EMPLOYEE;
%DOBROWSE;
RUN;

DATA MANAGER;
     SET SASFILE.EMPLOYEE;
     KEEP ...;
     <<IF MANAGER THEN OUTPUT RECORD>>
```

```
RUN;

%LET DATASET = MANAGER;
%LET SCREEN = MANAGER;
%DOBROWSE;
RUN;

DATA RICH;
     SET SASFILE.EMPLOYEE;
     KEEP ...;
     IF SALARY GE 50000;
RUN;

%LET DATASET = RICH;
%LET SCREEN = RICH;
%DOBROWSE;
RUN;
```

The code required to perform the browse function appears only once and is contained in the macro. Thus when a change is made such as changing from FSBROWSE to FSEDIT, it needs to be done only once, not three times. As a single program becomes more and more complex, this method of eliminating duplicate code becomes increasingly useful. (NOTE: The use of macros in this manner to eliminate code duplication is best done with entire data steps or procs due to the manner in which macros are executed.)

A third way duplicate code may be eliminated is using the %INCLUDE statement. Any portion of code which is common to a number of programs can be placed in a separate program and called any time it is needed. Like the use of a macro to execute common code, this method allows for easier maintenance of programs, since multiple changes are not necessary. And again, macro variable parameters may be used to generalize the code, so that it may be used in a variety of situations. Any data step, proc, or portion of these may be included in a program.

```
INCLUDED PROGRAM - SASPROCS(GETDATA)

    DATA GETDATA;
         SET SASFILE.EMPLOYEE;
         &IF;
    RUN;

PROGRAM 1 - REPORT OF ALL EMPLOYEES;

    %LET IF = ;
    %INCLUDE SASPROCS(GETDATA);
    RUN;

    PROC PRINT;
    RUN;

PROGRAM 2 - REPORT OF ALL EMPLOYEES FOR A SINGLE
            MANAGER

    <<USER ENTERS MANAGER ID>>

    %LET IF = IF MGRID EQ "&MGRID";
    %INCLUDE SASPROCS(GETDATA);
    RUN;

    PROC PRINT;
    RUN;

PROGRAM 3 - REPORT OF ALL EMPLOYEES WITH A
            CERTAIN SALARY OR MORE

    <<USER ENTERS SALARY>>

    %LET IF = IF SALARY GE "&SALARY";
    %INCLUDE SASPROCS(GETDATA);
    RUN;

    PROC PRINT;
    RUN;
```

This example shows how a single data step may be used to produce three different reports, simply by assigning to a macro variable the particular IF statement necessary to produce the desired report.

In the same manner a proc stored in a separate program may be used with a number of different datasets and specifications.

```
INCLUDED PROGRAM - SASPROCS(REPORT)

    OPTIONS DQUOTE DATE NUMBER;
    PROC PRINT DATA=&DATASET;
         TITLE "&TITLE1";
         TITLE "&TITLE2";
         VARS &VARS;
    RUN;

PROGRAM 1 - REPORT OF ALL EMPLOYEES

    %LET DATASET = SASFILE.EMPLOYEE;
    %LET TITLE1  = ALL EMPLOYEES;
    %LET TITLE2  =;
    %LET VARS = EMPID NAME  TITLE  SALARY
                DEPT  MGRID;
    %INCLUDE SASPROCS(REPORT);
    RUN;

PROGRAM 2 - REPORT OF TOTAL SALARY BY DEPARTMENT

    PROC SORT DATA=SASFILE.EMPLOYEE  OUT=SALARY;
        BY DEPT;
    RUN;

    DATA SALARY;
         KEEP DEPT TOTSAL TOTEMP;
         SET SALARY;
         BY DEPT;

         TOTSAL + SALARY;
         TOTEMP + 1;

         IF LAST.DEPT THEN
            DO;
              OUTPUT;
              TOTSAL = 0;
              TOTEMP = 0;
            END;
    RUN;

    %LET DATASET = SALARY;
    %LET TITLE1  = COMPANY ABC;
    %LET TITLE2  = TOTAL DEPARTMENT SALARIES;
    %LET VARS    = DEPT TOTSAL TOTEMP;
    RUN;

PROGRAM 3 - REPORT OF ALL ANALYSTS BY SALARY
```

```
DATA ANALYSTS;
     SET SASFILE.EMPLOYEE;
     IF TITLE = 'ANALYST';
RUN;

PROC SORT; BY SALARY;
RUN;

%LET DATASET = ANALYSTS;
%LET TITLE1  = ALL ANALYSTS;
%LET TITLE2  = BY SALARY;
%LET VARS    = EMPID NAME SALARY DEPT MGRID;
%INCLUDE SASPROCS(REPORT);
RUN;
```

The data for each of these reports is gathered in a different way and is in a different format, yet one PROC PRINT is able to accommodate them all.

The following is a simple example of how a portion of a proc or data step common to a number of programs may be stored separately and referenced as needed.

INCLUDED PROGRAM - SASPROCS(YEARS)

```
SET SASFILE.EMPLOYEE;
TODAY = TODAY();
DAYS  = TODAY - DATEMP;
YEARS = DAYS / 365;
```

PROGRAM 1 - FREQUENCY TABLE BY YEARS OF EMPLOYMENT

```
DATA EMPLOYEE;
     %INCLUDE SASPROCS(YEARS);
RUN;

PROC FREQ; TABLES YEARS;
RUN;
```

PROGRAM 2 - REPORT OF PROMOTION CANDIDATES

```
DATA PROMO;
     %INCLUDE SASPROCS(YEARS);
     IF TITLE = 'ANALYST';
     IF YEARS GE 3;
RUN;

PROC PRINT; TITLE 'PROMOTION CANDIDATES';
RUN;
```

PROGRAM 3 - BROWSE DATA FOR AN EMPLOYEE

```
<<USER ENTERS EMPLOYEE ID>>

DATA EMPLOYEE;
     %INCLUDE SASPROCS(YEARS);
     IF EMPID = "&EMPID";
RUN;

PROC FSBROWSE;
RUN;
```

Each of these sets of examples illustrate how valuable the use of SAS macros can be in eliminating duplicate code within a single program or an entire application. As you can see, maintenance of a portion of code which is used in a number of areas throughout a system is greatly simplified. If the calculation of the number of years an employee was with the company were to be changed, it only needs to be changed once, and the programmer does not have to waste valuable time locating other occurrences. Testing is greatly simplified as well, since a test in one program will produce the same results as anywhere else. These are all important, because enhancements and changes can be made to an application with far more ease and less impact than ever before.

DYNAMIC CODE GENERATION

Sometimes when there are a number of possible answers to a question or responses to a prompt, code is written to handle every possibility. If this happens, it is likely that a good deal of code duplication may occur which, as discussed at great length earlier, is not desirable from a maintenance programming perspective. SAS macros may be used in this situation to build the necessary code for each possibility as it occurs. Assigning a macro variable with a particular line, word, or group of words, which may be different in each case is the simplest method of building code. There are many ways of generating SAS code dynamically, some of which are too complex to discuss here. The examples which will be discussed are selecting data from a dataset based on a user entry on a SAS/AF panel, determining access to a menu selection, and controlling access to data on SAS/FSP screens.

A user-friendly application may give the user a number of choices for selecting data for functions such as browsing, editing, or reporting. A SAS/AF program screen is a useful tool for providing this capability quickly and efficiently. After the user enters his criteria on the panel, an IF statement is generated based on that selection.

SAS/AF PANEL

```
ENTER THE INFORMATION BY WHICH YOU WISH TO
SELECT DATA (IN ONE FIELD ONLY):

    EMPLOYEE ID:  &I___
           NAME:  &N_________________________
     DEPARTMENT:  &D_________________________
EMPLOYMENT DATE:  &M &D &Y  (MM DD YY)
-------------------------------------------
%LET EMPID = &I;
%LET NAME  = &N;
%LET DEPT  = &D;
%LET MM    = &M; %LET DD = &D; %LET YY = &Y;
%INCLUDE SASPROCS(DOIFSTMT);
RUN;
```

INCLUDED PROGRAM - SASPROCS(DOIFSTMT)

```
%MACRO DOIFSTMT;
  %IF %QUOTE(&EMPID) NE %THEN
      %LET IF = IF EMPID EQ "&EMPID";
  %ELSE
  %IF &MM NE %THEN
      %DO;
         DATA _NULL_;
           LENGTH DATEMP 8  MM DD YY $ 2;
```

```
            MM = "&MM";
            DD = "&DD";
            YY = "&YY";
            DATEMP = MDY(MM,DD,YY);
            CALL SYMPUT('DATEMP',LEFT(DATEMP));
         RUN;
         %LET IF = IF DATEMP EQ &DATEMP;
      %END;
   %ELSE
   %IF %QUOTE(&DEPT) NE %THEN
      %LET IF = IF DEPT EQ "&DEPT";
   %ELSE
   %IF &NAME NE %THEN
      %LET IF = IF INDEX(NAME,"&NAME") NE 0;
   %ELSE
      %LET ANYFLAG = NONE;

   %IF &ANYFLAG NE NONE %THEN
      %DO;
         DATA EMPLOYEE;
              SET SASFILE.EMPLOYEE;
              &IF;
         RUN;

         PROC FSBROWSE;
         RUN;
      %END;
 %MEND DOIFSTMT;

 %DOIFSTMT;
 RUN;
```

An IF statement is generated that reflects exactly what was entered on the panel and where. This line of code is then used in a data step to select the data to be browsed.

The second example of using SAS macros to dynamically generate code is that of determining access to a SAS/AF menu selection. Many applications have a different set of menus for each type of user who is logged on. In the employee application the types of users are EMPLOYEE and MANAGER. A manager may perform different functions than employees such as adding new employees or modifying salary information. SAS macros may be used to determine which type of employee is logged on and provide menu access accordingly. The user id and type code can be passed to SAS from the SYSIN statement used to call SAS, in a CLIST for example.

```
SET TYPE = M  or TYPE = E
SAS SYSIN(programname) +
    OPTIONS('SYSPARM=&SYSUID&TYPE,NONOTES)
```

The main program would be as follows:

```
DATA _NULL_;
     LENGTH USERID $ 5  TYPE $ 1;
     HOLD = SYSPARM();
     USERID  = SUBSTR(HOLD,1,5);
     TYPE = SUBSTR(HOLD,6,1);
     CALL SYMPUT('USERID',USERID);
     CALL SYMPUT('TYPE',TYPE);
RUN;

PROC DISPLAY CATALOG=SASMENU.MENU.PRIMARY.MENU;
RUN;
```

Once this data is captured, access to each selection on each menu may be controlled. Each SAS/AF menu selection to be checked should call a program which will accomplish that.

```
PRIMARY MENU

    1.  BROWSE MENU        ==>  CHKBRWS.PROGRAM

    2.  EDIT MENU          ==>  CHKEDIT.PROGRAM

    3.  REPORTS MENU       ==>  REPORTS.MENU

    4.  EXIT               ==>  ENDSAS.PROGRAM
```

Bear in mind that SAS does not permit a macro to be exited if it will not be returned to, so a program or menu cannot be displayed from within the macro.

```
CHKEDIT.PROGRAM

    %MACRO ACCESS;
       %IF &TYPE EQ M %THEN
           %LET MENUPROG = EDIT.MENU;
       %ELSE
           %LET MENUPROG = NOACCESS.PROGRAM;
    %MEND ACCESS;

    %GLOBAL MENUPROG;
    %ACCESS;
    RUN;

    PROC DISPLAY CATALOG=SASMENU.MENU.&MENUPROG;
    RUN;

NOACCESS.PROGRAM

    %PUT *** YOU DO NOT HAVE ACCESS TO THIS MENU
             SELECTION;
    RUN;

    PROC DISPLAY
         CATALOG=SASMENU.MENU.PRIMARY.MENU;
    RUN;
```

If an employee is logged on, access to editing data would be denied and the primary menu displayed. If a manager is logged on, the edit menu will be displayed. Thus the action taken is determined dynamically based on the type of user. Aside from eliminating duplicate code, another benefit of this type of programming is that duplicate sets of menus are not necessary. Two or more almost identical SAS/AF menus or programs unnecessarily increase the complexity of an application. One set will handle all the possibilities, so maintenance and testing are again simplified.

Lastly, access to the data to be modified can be controlled using SAS macros in much the same manner as the previous example; however, there is a need for duplicate screens. In version 5.18 there is no means of dynamically restricting data on a SAS/FSP screen. If the user logged on is a manager, the screen that allows him to change all data is displayed; otherwise, a screen which allows entry only in the name field will be displayed.

```
%MACRO GETSCRN;
    %IF &TYPE EQ M %THEN
        %LET SCREEN = MANAGER;
    %ELSE
        %LET SCREEN = EMPLOYEE;
%MEND GETSCRN;

%GETSCRN;
RUN;

PROC FSEDIT DATA=SASFILE.EMPLOYEE
            SCREEN=SASCREEN.&SCREEN;
RUN;
```

The screen to be displayed is dynamically selected depending on the type of user, so duplicate code to perform this is not necessary. Duplicate screens are needed, but there is no way around it at this time.

If SAS macros were not used in each of these examples, extensive IF-THEN-ELSE structures or %IF-%THEN-%ELSE structures with duplicate data steps or procs would have to be coded to handle each possibility, causing complex programs. Using SAS macros, maintenance and testing become much more easily accomplished, because code exists only once.

CONCLUSION

SAS macros may be used with SAS/AF and SAS/FSP in developing solid, user-friendly applications. An application can be friendly in two ways, both to the user and to the maintenance programmer, each of which combine for an efficient, cohesive unit. Ways to develop an application which is friendly to the user include the use of SAS macros in displaying informative relevant messages on the screen and controlling code execution to perform only those tasks which are necessary to a function. Making changes and enhancements and performing testing should be as easy as possible for an application to be friendly to the maintenance programmer. To achieve this, SAS macros may be used to eliminate duplicate code by calling a section of code each time it is needed and to dynamically generate code when a number of different situations are possible.

Several other techniques are also useful in developing applications. Use SAS/AF and SAS/FSP to prototype the way the application will look before any coding is done. A skeleton of just menus and screens enable the prospective users of the system to determine if that is what they really want. A lot of time can be saved making changes at this point in the design process rather than in the coding or testing phases. Be sure to use OPTIONS NONOTES to keep irrelevant messages from being displayed to the user. When actually writing the code for the application, follow the KISS principle - KEEP IT SIMPLE, STUPID! Provide the minimum functionality to satisfy the requirements of the system. Too many bells and whistles only clutter an application. And finally, be sure to test the application thoroughly. Nothing causes a system to fail in the eyes of its users faster than if it just does not work.

These development techniques combined with the methods of using SAS macros discussed in this paper will help assure that your application will be user-friendly, efficient, error-free, and successful.

* SAS, SAS/AF, and SAS/FSP are registered trademarks of SAS Institute Inc., Cary, NC, USA.

Macros Invocation Hierarchy: Session Compiled, Autocall, and Compiled Stored Macros

Susan M. O'Connor, SAS Institute Inc., Cary, NC

ABSTRACT

This paper describes the compiled stored macro facility's functionality and syntax. A comparison of positive and negative considerations in selecting the use of session compiled, autocall, and compiled stored macros is made. Such issues as maintenance, performance, and development environments are discussed.

Recommendations for macro-related considerations, such as autocall concatenation versus permanent macro catalogs and macro option defaults, are discussed. For a greater in-depth overview, related issues of hierarchy for these types of macros, of macro variable resolution, and of the interaction of compiled stored macros and the stored program facility are discussed.

The timing and resolution of CALL EXECUTE and the RESOLVE function with compiled stored macros and session stored programs are addressed. An overview of these facilities and the order and timing of them might be helpful for users.

SESSION COMPILED MACROS

The SAS® System historically has had macros which are compiled in a SAS session and can be executed many times in that same session. These macros, referred to as session compiled macros, are defined in a SAS job. A macro definition is everything contained between a %MACRO statement and a matching %MEND statement. A macro definition may contain both SAS text and SAS macro statements. The SAS macro facility compiles or translates the macro definition into intermediate code. The macro compiler has two passes; the first pass is completed when the %MEND statement is reached. The second pass is used to resolve such things as the %GOTO, %LABEL and %DO statements. The intermediate code consists of instructions such as "execute a %PUT statement" and "jump to another location to begin execution there". Intermediate code also may contain constant text to emit to the SAS System.

This intermediate code is stored in both pass one and pass two in a SAS catalog. A SAS catalog is a SAS file which is stored in a SAS data library and has the data type of CATALOG. SAS catalogs have two-level names like other SAS files; the first level name, a libref, refers to the SAS data library. In the session compiled macros, the first level name is WORK. The second-level name refers to the catalog itself, which for all macros is SASMACR. So for session compiled macros, the macro catalog is always WORK.SASMACR.

A SAS catalog contains entries which are referred to by two-level names also. The first-level name is the entry name, which for macros is the macro name from the macro definition. The second-level entry name is the entry type, MACRO. Actually, during the first pass the entry name is a temporary reserved macro name and it is at the completion of the second pass that the macro compiler renames the temporary entry name to the macro name. Of course, at the termination of the SAS session, SAS WORK files (such as data sets and catalogs) are erased from the current SAS work data library. Thus, by default, the WORK.SASMACR catalog containing the session compiled macros is deleted at the end of the SAS session.

After the macro has been compiled, whenever the macro is executed during the rest of the entire SAS session, the SAS System will locate the catalog entry for the macro, read the object record by record, and execute the interpreted code. If the macro is redefined again in the SAS session in open code, the macro object in WORK.SASMACR is deleted and the newly-compiled macro is written to the catalog object again. The next time the same SAS job is executed in a different SAS session, the macro is compiled again and is written to the WORK.SASMACR catalog again as an object. This object is then read when the macro is invoked during that session.

Rather than interpreting the macro statements' source code directly each time the macro itself is invoked, the macro facility uses intermediate code because it is faster. During compilation, for example, the macro compiler figures out where to jump to if the condition of a %IF statement is false, and it codes that information in an intermediate code instruction. It would be time consuming to figure out the macro source code each time you executed the macro. The macro interpreted code is very different from the interpreted code generated in the DATA step. In the SAS DATA step, the SAS System continues on with the machine-code generation because there are generally a lot of computations and other operations in the SAS DATA step that can be done very quickly if done directly by machine hardware. This is the part of the SAS System which can be accessed by the user with the stored program facility. The stored program facility stores and accesses machine code generated by the DATA step. In macro we stop at intermediate code rather than continuing on to machine-code manipulation because macro does very little numeric computation. While machine languages can quickly do string manipulations, macro string-handling is unusual and more complicated than most machine languages. Macro predominately does string manipulation which involves macro variable resolution and macro-quoting functions. But what gains a performance improvement in macro is eliminating the overhead of macro compilation each time a macro is executed.

To summarize then, for session compiled macros, each macro is compiled and written to a temporary catalog object during the first pass. The temporary object in the WORK.SASMACR catalog is closed and then reopened. During the processing of the second pass, the intermediate code in the temporary object is read, processed, and then written to a new object with the same macro name. So, there is a write-read-write scenario during the compilation phase before the macro itself is executed. During invocation of the macro, the catalog object is opened, and the intermediate instructions are read and executed. These instructions generate SAS session code which is passed to waiting parts of the SAS session, such as a procedure, DATA step, DMS, or SCL.

AUTOCALL MACRO FACILITY

If you have a macro which you like to use in several SAS jobs, you could always put the macro source definition code for that macro in an external flat file. This file could be shared by many SAS sessions, SAS jobs, and SAS users. One approach is to include a flat external file, using the %INCLUDE statement, containing a macro definition whenever you needed it in a SAS session. This way, you would always have access to the macro definition; it could be shared and easily maintained. However, you would have the overhead of reading an additional flat file from a disk as well as compiling the macro and storing it in a temporary SAS catalog, which will be deleted at the end of a SAS session. Another approach is to put the macro in an autoexec file and the macro would be compiled at the start of every SAS session. However, it would have the overhead of slowing down your session start-up unnecessarily if you were not going to invoke the macro in the current session.

The SAS autocall facility is another way of keeping macros as external files which can be accessed by the SAS System. The macros are stored in aggregate storage locations or autocall libraries: a partitioned data set under MVS, a maclib under CMS, a directory or VMS text library under VMS, a library under VSE, and a directory on most directory-based machines. The autocall facility is especially useful when you have a large number of macros you might need to execute, but you want to avoid having to compile all of them at the start of each SAS session.

The autocall facility allows you to store macros as members of an autocall library. The macro must have the same name as the member of an autocall library. (On some operating systems this may require a .SAS type extension.)

An autocall library is a storage location referenced by

OPTION SASAUTOS=*fileref* | *'physical_name'* |
(fileref 'physical_name' . . .);

OPTION SASAUTOS= may reference one autocall library or a concatenated list of autocall libraries.

To invoke an autocall macro, OPTION MAUTOSOURCE must be in effect. When you invoke a macro that has not been defined in the current session, the autocall facility searches the autocall library or libraries for a member with the same name as the macro being invoked. After finding a member in the autocall library, all the code in that file is included. The macro definition with the same name is compiled and any other contained macro definitions are compiled. Then the macro being invoked is executed automatically.

By default, OPTION NOMRECALL causes the autocall facility to search only once for an undefined autocall macro.

If you have a long list of concatenated autocall libraries, the SAS System will attempt to open the autocall libraries and then search them in order, looking for a file with the same name as the macro or, on some systems, for the same name with a .SAS extension. For example, in this hypothetical operating system, if you had:

```
filename a 'physical-name-of-directory';
filename b 'directory-across-inaccessible-network';
filename c 'physical-name-of-pds';
filename d 'physical-name-of-maclib';
options sasautos=(a b c d);
```

Here, A, B, C, and D are filerefs (or physical names in quotes) to aggregate storage locations. If B could not be opened, but at least one aggregate location did open, no message would be issued. However, the SAS System would try to open B for each attempted autocall macro invoked. The overhead of attempting to open a non-existing autocall library could be unnecessary overhead in a SAS session with a large concatenated list of autocall libraries.

An error and warning is only issued if no autocall library at all will open. This decision was made for such operating systems as OS/2* where the concatenated directories may be unavailable to be opened on the first attempt but available on subsequent attempts.

```
ERROR: No file referenced by SASAUTOS OPTION can be opened.
WARNING: Source level autocall is not found or cannot be opened.
Autocall has been suspended and OPTION NOMAUTOSOURCE has
been set.  To use the autocall facility again, set
autocall facility again, set OPTION MAUTOSOURCE.
```

The advantages of autocall macros are that they can be easily maintained in associated aggregate storage locations, accessed by differing applications and users, used to develop complicated macro systems, and concatenated between levels of macros from production to development.

But there are disadvantages also. When you execute an autocall macro, it is essentially including the flat file and executing anything in that file that could be open code as well as compiling the macro definition and executing the macro. You can have several macro definitons in the autocall member, and all macros will be compiled at once. But if you are only after the macro of the same name as the member, you have the overhead of compiling a lot of unused macros. Therefore, when using autocall macros, an important efficiency consideration is the organization of the autocall libraries and the contents of the autocall members. For the convenience of the autocall facility, you also have the risk of attempting to open unavailable autocall macro libraries with no warning or error.

COMPILED STORED MACRO FACILITY

The compiled stored macro facility allows you to compile and store SAS macros as objects in a permanent SASMACR catalog. Later, you can access the compiled stored macro code when you execute the macro in a different SAS program. This facility will save macro-compilation overhead in any SAS program which accesses the compiled stored macro.

When using the compiled stored macro facility, the macro code is compiled and then stored in a permanent catalog named SASMACR in an assigned SAS data library. This compilation will occur only once. The overhead of the attendant write-read-write of the two passes for the macro compilation will be gone. Later, when a different SAS session invokes that macro, the overhead of compilation will not be included in resource usage.

In order to use the compiled stored macro facility, macro code should be production macros, which will be accessed by user programs to eliminate macro compile-time overhead before macro invocation. The macro source code itself should be well-documented and saved, in addition to saving the compiled stored macro. This will be essential for maintenance.

COMPILED STORED MACRO SYNTAX

There are two SAS system options which must be set to use compiled stored macro:

MSTORED	allows the SAS System to use the compiled stored macro facility. The default is NOMSTORED.
SASMSTORE=	specifies libref for SAS data library containing the SAS compiled stored macro catalog SASMACR. The default is blank. This libref should be a valid libref.

There are also two new options in the %MACRO statement that relate to storing compiled stored macros. The expanded %MACRO statement options include:

%MACRO *name* <*parameters*> </<STMT>
<CMD> <PARMBUFF | PARM>
<STORE> <DES=*'text-string'*>>;

For stored compiled macros, the STORE option specifies that the compiled macro will be stored as an entry in a SAS macro catalog in a permanent SAS data library. The MSTORED system option must be in effect to use compiled-stored invocations.

You are not allowed to use the libref WORK for compiled stored macros. A dummy macro will be compiled if you use OPTIONS

SASMSTORE=WORK. A dummy macro is a macro that the macro processor compiles but does not store. It is recommended that compiled stored macros be name-style macros for the greatest performance gains. Both statement-style and command-style macros are a bit less efficient than name-style macros, and the purpose of using compiled stored macros is to increase performance by eliminating the overhead of macro compilations. When using compiled stored macros, as when using autocall macros, you should use %LOCAL for macro variables, which will be used only inside the compiled stored macro. Otherwise, a macro variable value in a different environment might be altered.

It will be essential that programmers using compiled stored macros maintain a copy of the macro source code used to compile and store the macro. One suggestion would be to maintain a copy of the macro source code in an autocall library.

The SAS System does not support the CPORT and CIMPORT procedures for macro catalogs because of the complicity of delta characters and upcoming KANJI development on your operating system. However, you could use the following to obtain the contents of a macro catalog containing compiled stored macros:

```
proc catalog catalog=libref.sasmacr <entrytype=macro>;
     contents;
run;
```

You will get the following headings:

```
# Name      Type      Date      Description
```

When OPTION MLOGIC is on to trace the execution of a macro for compiled stored macros, after the beginning execution message you will receive the following message indicating the libref and date of compilation:

```
MLOGIC(ONE):  Beginning execution.
MLOGIC(ONE):  Compiled stored macro in libref THERE compiled
              on 08/08/xx.
```

Also another new %MACRO statement option, the DES= option, is available to keep track of a macro description. The syntax for the DES= option is

DES=*'text-string'*

This option specifies a description or title for the macro entry in the macro catalog. The text string is limited to a length of 40 characters inside a quoted string. Strings longer than 40 characters will be truncated to 40 characters. The macro catalog-directory field will contain the description you provided with this %MACRO statement option for the macro entry. When you are in the DIRECTORY window, this description will appear when displaying the contents of the catalog containing the compiled stored macros. Since the WORK macro catalog is deleted for session compiled macros, there is no purpose for adding descriptions unless you are using the compiled stored macro facility.

COMPILED STORED MACRO CONSIDERATIONS

Compiled stored macros have been developed with the idea of performance, which means that design considerations were made for efficiency. For Release 6.07 of the SAS System, there is no concatenation of compiled stored macro DATA libraries. Compiled stored macros do not apply themselves to a macro development environment. The burden of maintaining the macro source code rests with the macro application developer. The macro performance gain is noticed especially for large macros, which would take a long time to compile. Since a macro is compiled once during a session, the overhead is only noticed the first time a compiled stored macro is executed and not for subsequent executions. Since autocall macros may contain several related macros, the additonal overhead of compiling several macros at once is eliminated.

WHICH COMES FIRST: SESSION COMPILED, COMPILED STORED, OR AUTOCALL MACROS

In the hierarchy of macro execution, assuming that all appropriate macro options have been set for the SAS session when a macro is invoked, the SAS System first looks for a session compiled macro, then for a compiled stored macro, and finally, for autocall macros. Of course, it would be less efficient to have this type of situation where every type of macro option is set and the search for the macro invoked is for all types of macros. If a macro is used only once by one user in one program, it might be just as well to have it session compiled. However, if it is a large macro, significant compilation time can be saved if it is compiled and stored. This compilation time would be reflected in CPU time, I/O, and elapsed time. Perhaps if the major consideration is for ease of maintenance and for organizing a lot of macros, the autocall facility is the best choice.

THE STORED PROGRAM FACILITY AND THE COMPILED STORED FACILITY

There are considerable differences between the compiled stored macro facility and the stored program facility. The stored program facility is for DATA step applications only, and only if those applications do not contain global statements (such as FILENAME, LIBNAME, FOOTNOTE, OPTION, and TITLE statements) or host-specific options for the data set (such as FILE or INFILE statements). Since the compiled stored macro facility is a text-generating facility, it has no program boundaries but can be used to generate SAS source code to execute across DATA steps, procedures, global SAS statements, and host interfaces. Both facilities store their code as intermediate code, but when the stored program facility executes, its unique intermediate code generates the executable machine code for the host environment. The macro intermediate code does not use a code generator to execute the macro statements. The compiled stored programs appear in a SAS data library with the member type of PROGRAM. The compiled macros are stored in SAS catalogs in a SAS data library. You cannot move stored programs to another host with incompatible machine architecture. You must compile and store macros on each host by porting the macro source code and compiling it on the target host.

Release 6.07 contains the CALL EXECUTE routine and the RESOLVE function. Both of these DATA step interface routines, as well as SYMGET and CALL SYMPUT, are routines which are called during execution of the DATA step. As with other DATA step functions, these macro interface routines are called when the SAS DATA step is executing. In the compiled stored macro code, they are just stored as part of constant text.

ONE CASE STUDY

At SAS Institute, the Quality Assurance department (QA) uses macros heavily to establish test environments across our operating systems and to have an organized macro system set up to test SAS code in all environments. This system has been in existence for several years. Originally, these start-up macros were in SAS autoexec files, which were executed every time a test was run. There was always a danger that a job might be using a different autoexec file in the user's environment which might override the official one being used.

Then QA began to use the autocall facility. This had the advantage of referencing a concatenated list of autocall libraries, which was established with the SASAUTOS= option at start-up with an autoexec or a SAS configuration file. These macros assured the testing level, the host machine, and autocall macro libraries. Any number of users could simultaneously use the same macros from one location. For efficiency, the autocall macros often contained several related macros, all of which would be compiled in one autocall macro when the invoked autocall macro was compiled and executed. The autocall macros could be shared and maintained in shared locations and ported to all hosts.

This year, with Release 6.07, these start-up macros were converted to compiled stored macros. The actual editing of the 14 flat autocall macro files and the contained 3 or 4 inner macros along with the port to three hosts took a half day of one programmer. These were established production macros which were rather large, but very well used and tested over the prior two-year period. The range in performance gain between using the autocall facility and the compiled stored facility for this test case was 10%-35%, depending on the host. The biggest difference was PC-related. However, significant differences are reported under MVS, CMS, VMS, and UNIX systems for this conversion to compiled stored macros. Losing source is not a problem at SAS Institute because of rigorous source management for the quality assurance test environment. This was an optimal conversion because the autocall macros had been production macros for over two years. Each macro was executed only once, and indeed, it is the first execution in which you would see the gain. The programmer doing the conversion reported ease of conversion, and he felt that the lack of concatenation for the compiled stored macro was not a problem for this application.

But this was an optimal example. The macros were large and had been autocall macros for several years. They were all start-up macros for a system and were used just once, which would be optimal in the performance statistics. Mileage varied in the performance statistics. This difference reflects file access on the individual operating system and the SAS System defaults on the operating system. They even reflect whether all of the autocall libraries were successfully opened in the concatenated autocall list.

RECOMMENDATIONS

It might be worth investing the time investigating whether a macro system used in your environment would be worth converting to compiled stored macros. A conversion would not show optimal results if the macros are small and used a lot. This compiled stored macro facility is not designed for security. It would not be recommended, either, if the macro source code is ever in danger of being lost in your environment because debugging a compiled stored macro would be impossible without the macro source code.

Catalogs are made up of a variety of components stored in logical units called pages. The host layer of each operating system maps units into physical units, blocks, on the disks. The physical transfer of data between disk and memory during a catalog read-or-write transfer of data can be a page, a section of pages, or a block of pages. Each host determines the optimal page size for a catalog, based on the characteristics of the mass storage on which the catalog will reside. The default SAS library block size and page size for catalogs will vary from host ot host. For catalog writes and reads performance is system-dependent. However, other conversion tests at the Institute by core testers indicate performance differences of 10%-45% using compiled stored macros versus autocall macros. These differences were reflected in CPU time, elapsed time, and I/O, and they are attributed to many factors. Measurement of performance gains are also difficult.

OTHER NEW MACRO OPTIONS

New to the SAS System in Release 6.07 are two options related to macro variables which can affect system performance. The MSYMTABMAX= system option specifies the maximum amount of memory available to the macro symbol table. The MVARSIZE= system option specifies the maximum size for in-memory macro variables. In both cases, once this value is reached, additional macro variables are written out to disk. The value specified can range from 0 to the largest nonnegative integer representable on your operating system. The default values for Release 6.07 are identical to the values used in Release 6.06 on your operating system. Since these options can affect SAS System performance, before you alter the defaults for production jobs, you should run tests to determine the optimum value. In general, the larger the amount of memory on a machine, the higher these values can be. For hosts such as the PC with little available memory, leave the defaults as they are. Adjusting the MSYMTABMAX and MVARSIZE values optimally could lead to a reduction of CPU and less I/O.

MACRO INVOCATION AND PERFORMANCE

Three SAS macro invocation types are now available in Release 6.07: name-style, statement-style, and command-style. Name-style invocation is the traditional way to call a macro to execute using a percent sign and the macro name. It is always the most efficient choice for performance of the macro.

Statement-style invocation allows you to call a macro which looks like SAS statements. When the macro is defined with the STMT option in the %MACRO statement and when the IMPLMAC system option is in effect, the first word of any SAS statement being processed by the tokenizer is considered a possible macro invocation. There is a search for the session compiled macro, which will take place always for start of statement tokens. This search would be less complex if only session compiled macros were available, increasing in depth as compiled stored and then autocall macros, were also available in the session.

Command-style invocation is now available compatibility with Version 5 of the SAS System. When a macro is defined with the CMD option in the %MACRO statement and when the CMDMAC system option is set, command-style macros are invoked as if they were display manager or full-screen procedure commands on the command line. If a session compiled macro is command-style or if compiled stored macros are available or if autocall macros are available, at each command-line command, a search will be made in respective locations for a command-style macro.

While statement-style and command-style macros may enhance an application, they will also impact performance slightly. If optimal perfomance is required of an application name-style invocation might be the first consideration.

CONCLUSION

There are many choices available in Release 6.07 for macro users which will affect the performance and ease of maintenance of macro applications. Macro developers may consider session compiled macros, the autocall macro facility, and compiled stored macros for their applications. Each choice has advantages. Performance improvements with compiled stored macros should be reflected in CPU time, I/O, and elapsed time, but results will vary with operating systems. The new SAS system options MSYMTABMAX= and MVARSIZE= may improve CPU and I/O performance. As with Version 5 of the SAS System, name-style invocations are more efficient than statement-style or command-style invocations. In an optimal situation, macro application developers would run tests to determine the best choices for their environment.

REFERENCES

SAS Institute Inc. (1990), *SAS Guide to Macro Processing, Version 6, Second Edition*, Cary, NC: SAS Institute Inc.

SAS Institute Inc. (1991), SAS Technical Report P-222, *Changes and Enhancements to Base SAS Software, Release 6.07*, Cary, NC: SAS Institute Inc.

Perry, Rebecca (1990), "Inside SAS Catalogs in Version 6 of the SAS System," *Proceedings* of the Fifteenth Annual SAS Users Group International Conference, Cary, NC: SAS Institute Inc.

ACKNOWLEDGEMENTS

I would like to thank my managers in the Core Shell Development Group, Jeff Polzin and Pat Herbert, for their support in the preparation of this paper. I would like to thank my colleague Bruce Tindall for his seminars and notes which led to issues addressed in this paper. I would especially like to thank Oita Coleman in the Core Testing Group for her performance statistics and Richard Ragland and David Horne, both of Quality Assurance, for information and discussions about their conversion experiences with compiled stored macros for their start-up testing environment.

Screen Control Language versus Macros in Batch Environments

Andrew A. Norton, Trilogy Consulting Corporation

Introduction

A. The SAS* Macro language

The SAS user community has had eight years of experience with the SAS Macro language. It was certainly a great step forward, but my developing understanding of the language has been leading to growing dissatisfaction. Like many others, I find many macros unreadable, even if I wrote them myself. I am also uneasy about the vulnerability of most macros to unexpected input.

I have come to conclude that much of the difficulty in writing and debugging macros is due to the syntax of the language. The Macro language provides some rarely used advanced features at the cost of increased complexity and decreased reliability in more common applications. In the words of one skilled macro programmer,

> "... I still wonder if the supreme power of the SAS macro facility may lead other users into the same Catch-22, where disaster is just another ampersand away."
> (Kretzman 1986, page 515)

B. The SAS Screen Control Language

Screen Control Language (SCL) has been available for three years. It is marketed as part of SAS/AF* software and SAS/FSP* software, which provide full-screen interactive capabilities. SCL also provides code-generation capabilities similar to those of the Macro language, and data manipulation capabilities similar to those of the DATA step and PROCs.

The design of SCL responds to lessons learned from experience with the Macro and Data Step languages. This paper contends that these improvements often justify the use of "Screen" Control Language in the development of large complex systems, even those with no interactive component.

This paper also provides instructions for executing SCL in batch environments, which to my knowledge have not previously been described.

The role of control languages in the SAS System

A. Control languages

In modern programming languages (such as PASCAL or C), programs are built from subroutines which may themselves be built from other subroutines. All subroutines are written using the same structure.

In contrast, the fundamental building blocks of the SAS System are invocations of procedures (including "PROC DATASTEP") which are not themselves built from similar procedures. A different language must be used to control execution of the procedures. Both SCL and the Macro language can fill this role.

I am using the term "control language" to refer to those components of the Macro language and SCL which provide overarching control of procedure steps, including:

- conditional execution of procedures,
- repeated execution of procedures,
- manipulation of global memory (macro variables),
- packaging of a series of procedure steps into a single unit, and
- dynamic generation of procedure code.

The particular importance of dynamic code generation within the SAS System stems from the run-time compilation of SAS procedure calls. In most programming languages, instructions and varying data are passed to subroutines via arguments which are evaluated during execution of the program. SAS uses much more complex syntax to provide specifications to its procedures, yielding increased power and clarity. In effect, the entire block of code for a procedure invocation provides its arguments. Dynamic code generation provides the means for the executing control language program to supply specifications for each procedure call.

B. Choosing between SCL and the Macro language

Although SCL is primarily marketed as a tool driven by user interaction, while the Macro language more typically obtains its parameters from other programs, the dividing line has increasingly begun to blur. Screen Control Language programs need not have associated screens or run in interactive environments, and the Macro language now provides a screen display facility of its own.

When selecting the software platform upon which to develop a system, two factors encourage a focus on one language, rather than a mix:

1) the difficulties and risks associated with interfacing different languages, and
2) the maintenance costs and potential inconsistencies from implementing the same shared modules in each language.

It is therefore a question of which language is best suited for a particular application. The obvious choice for full-screen interactive front-ends is SCL. Once this decision has been made, the factors above suggest using SCL for internal processing modules as well. Ideally, the same internal modules could be used in both interactive and batch environments.

C. Control languages for batch environments

In my opinion, SCL is sufficiently superior over the Macro Language to warrant consideration of SCL as the primary control language for large complex systems even if they have no interactive component at all.

The main drawback is that the specifications of SAS/AF and SAS/FSP do not provide for batch use of SCL. I have been very interested in finding ways around this limitation, and have met with some success.

There is, of course, a catch. The key to success is a procedure which is undocumented and not intended for this purpose.

Batch use of Screen Control Language

A. Invoking SAS/AF

There are three methods of invoking SAS/AF programs, each restricted to a particular environment.

A.1 AF Display Manager command

To invoke an AF system from Display Manager, use the command:

```
AF C=libref.catalog.entry.type
```

on any command line.

Arguments cannot be passed to the program. Information needed by the program may be obtained from a screen associated with the program, or read from macro variables or other data objects.

The AF command may be submitted to the Display Manager channel from Program channel code using the DM statement:

```
DM 'AF C=libref.catalog.entry.type' AF;
```

[I use the word "channel" to describe a route through which code may be executed. The most common channels are the Display Manager, Program (i.e. DATA step and PROCs), and SQL channels. Commands may be directed to any of these channels from SCL.]

Display Manager commands (including the AF command) cannot be executed in batch environments.

A.2 CALL DISPLAY and CALL GOTO

These two statements are used with SCL to transfer control to another SCL program. Parameters can be provided on the CALL DISPLAY statement to transfer data to the called program in accordance with the specifications of the ENTRY statement.

A.3 PROC DISPLAY

This undocumented procedure remains in version 6.06 to provide upward compatibility with version 5 SAS/AF. The primary documentation for version 5 PROC DISPLAY is of the SAS/AF User's Guide, Version 5 Edition (pages 69-74). The only reference I have found in version 6 documentation is a statement in the "Changes and Enhancements" section of the SAS/AF manual (page xxviii) that PROC DISPLAY is still honored with version 5 applications.

The syntax for using PROC DISPLAY in batch is simply:

```
PROC DISPLAY C=libref.catalog.entry.type;
RUN;
```

Note that if you are running SAS version 6, you must use version 6 AF catalogs.

The documentation does not discuss use of the procedure in batch environments (nor, of course, the execution of version 6 SCL programs). PROC DISPLAY will run such programs in batch provided that they:

1) Have blank screens, and
2) Do not use SUBMIT CONTINUE.

These conditions are further discussed below.

A.4 Limitations on invocations

Using PROC DISPLAY, AF can only be invoked from a program at a step boundary. The interactive AF command (submitted through the DM statement) is more flexible and can be invoked at a statement boundary.

Neither PROC DISPLAY nor the Display Manager AF command can run more than one AF application at a time, or have more than one window simultaneously active in that application. In general, it is not possible to invoke AF from code submitted using SUBMIT CONTINUE. A limited work-around is available based on the fact that two simultaneous AF applications may be invoked by invoking one application with the AF command and the other with PROC DISPLAY.

In contrast to AF, macros may be invoked in the middle of a statement or from code that is being generated by another macro. The ease and flexibility of macro invocations is the primary reason that I still prefer macro programs for simpler "quick and dirty" tasks.

SCL systems need to be designed differently from macro systems, separating the AF programs from the submitted code. This task is simplified by the version 6 SUBMIT CONTINUE feature, which permits the AF environment to be maintained while the submitted code executes.

B. SCL programs with blank screens

SCL programs may be written without an associated screen simply by leaving the screen definition blank. All of the code may be placed in the INIT section of the code, because the other sections relate to the display of screens. Empty MAIN: RETURN; and TERM: RETURN; sections may be included to avoid compilation warnings.

In Display Manager, a default "status window" is displayed if no screen has been associated with the program. This is somewhat unattractive, but I know of no way to suppress it.

C. Code submission using PROC DISPLAY

Because PROC DISPLAY executes as a procedure running in the Program channel, no other code submitted to the Program channel can be run until the current procedure is completed. As a result, PROC DISPLAY cannot process SUBMIT CONTINUE statements correctly.

Unfortunately, AF does not automatically recognize when this problem occurs. Instead, the submitted code accumulates in the PREVIEW buffer, and is executed all at once upon exiting PROC DISPLAY. The exception is that if the final SUBMIT block specifies the CONTINUE option, it is executed in the wrong order, prior to the contents of the PREVIEW buffer.

This is obviously undesirable. To avoid this problem, use the SCL function SASTASK to determine whether SCL has been invoked by a SAS procedure. If so, use the SUBMIT statement rather than SUBMIT CONTINUE. Generated code will be held in the Preview buffer and automatically executed when the application terminates.

A PROC DISPLAY reference can be included in the generated code to restart AF after execution. This method is awkward, but was standard practice before version 6 introduced the SUBMIT CONTINUE statement.

For the sake of consistency, SUBMIT commands can also be used when SAS/AF is invoked through the AF command of Display Manager. In this case, the Preview buffer can be executed prior to termination of the application by using the SUBMIT CONTINUE statement.

The limitations on the SUBMIT command using PROC DISPLAY are not as consequential as they might be because

1) SUBMIT CONTINUE works correctly when submitting code to the SQL* channel,

and 2) SCL has substantial data management capabilities of its own.

Because of these factors, it is often not necessary to submit code to the Program channel.

A comparative review of the SAS Macro Language and Screen Control Language

A. Advantages of SCL over the Macro Language

The most important advantage of SCL is that SCL avoids the unpredictability of SAS macros. Macros are difficult to write, debug, and maintain not only because of the complexities of the task they are undertaking, but also because the design of the language makes simple programs difficult.

SCL adheres to six principles that are frequently violated in the Macro Language:

1) Local actions have local consequences.
2) Programs treat all valid data values according to the same rules.
3) It is possible to review the data values entering a given module.
4) The algebraic properties of arithmetic are maintained.
5) Code generation can be avoided when it is more straightforward to manipulate data objects directly.
6) Code submission is under direct control control of the programmer.

These six principles make SCL programs more predictable, more reliable, and easier to understand than SAS macros.

A.1 Local actions should have local consequences

This makes it easier for the programmer to understand how a given block of code will function in a program.

A.1.a Context-sensitive defaults

The term "user-friendly" was coming into vogue while the Macro language was under development. One definition of this term is the provision of extensive defaults appropriate to the current context. This introduces interrelationships between the code and its context which are not problematic in ad hoc use but which complicate maintenance of complex systems with long lifespans.

The obvious solution is to specify defaults explicitly, so they do not depend upon the context in which the code is used. In some cases, this leads to inefficiencies, such as using the %EVAL function when it is already implied. In more serious cases, explicit specification of defaults causes errors.

One of these cases is the specification of empty parentheses when invoking a macro with no arguments. If a macro has been defined with no arguments, then any parentheses following its invocation are treated as open code. If arguments are later added to the macro definition, then the same parentheses are treated as part of the invocation. The correct syntax is dependent on the macro definition, and if it changes, the calls may need to be changed. To avoid this problem, you can quote parentheses intended as open code.

In Screen Control Language, program calls always specify the parentheses.

A.1.b Same code acting differently in different contexts

Code debugged in one context may not work correctly when transported to another context. For example, comment statements containing unmatched quotes work in SCL or open code but not within macros. CARDS statements also do not work within macros, but can be handled correctly in SCL by using the CONTROL ASIS statement.

Macro expressions are evaluated differently depending on the macro statement in which they are used. If the expression must have a numeric expression, then a %EVAL function is implied. If a character result is valid, then the expression will be evaluated as character unless a %EVAL function is specified explicitly. This requires the programmer and reader to be attentive to the rules of each macro statement. In SCL variables are defined as character or numeric and act accordingly.

Languages such as Screen Control Language and the DATA Step language allow individual terms of an expression to be freely substituted without disturbing other parts of the expression. In the Macro language, changing part of a word may alter the number of scans made of the entire word, thereby changing the number of ampersands and dot delimiters that are required. For example:

Macro	SCL
A.J	'A' || '.J'
&A2..J	A2 || '.J'
&&A&I...J	A{ I } || '.J'
&&&&A&&J&K....J	A{J{K}} || '.J'

These problems are derived from the design decision to have the dot following a macro variable reference be optional, so it could not be used to indicate nesting.

A.1.c Same code acting differently in different referencing environments

It is often not feasible to completely retest each module in each location. Problems that vary according to the environment in which the module is called can be difficult to detect and debug.

In the Macro language, all variables from the calling environment are accessible from the called subroutine unless superseded by a symbolic parameter or local variable. Experienced programmers know to explicitly declare local macro variables as such, in case the macro is ever called from an environment in which that variable exists. In SCL, no one makes this mistake, because all variables except for parameters are automatically local.

One use of external variables is to pass the name of an external variable to a macro rather than the value of the variable. The called macro can then update the external variable, as in:

```
%macro INIT (NAME);
   %let &NAME = 0;
%mend INIT;
```

This works fine as long as no one calls

```
%INIT(NAME)
```

in which case access to the external variable is blocked by the name of the local parameter. There is no warning, but the external variable remains unchanged. These limitations increase if the macro uses additional local variables.

A commonly used technique for creating a new macro variable employs the %GLOBAL statement:

```
%macro NEW (NAME);
   %global &NAME;
   %let &NAME = 0;
%mend NEW;
```

The problem is that this new variable is not defined at the level of the calling program, but at the outermost level. If a global variable of this name already exists, its value will be destroyed.

In Screen Control Language, program calls are transactions directly affecting only the parameters of the call, minimizing the risk of unintended side-effects.

A.2 Programs should treat all valid data values according to the same rules.

This assures the programmer that the program will operate correctly over the entire range of valid input.

In the Macro language, the programmer must anticipate every type of data that might cause trouble in that particular context. It is my impression that very few programmers consistently write bombproof macros that can deal with unexpected input.

In Screen Control Language (as in the DATA step) data values are isolated from program code. While some of the tricks of macro language are impossible, the quoting functions of SCL are trivial, and the programs consistently work.

A.2.a Numeric comparisons

The same macro expression will compare some values using numeric rules, and other values using character rules. Integer numbers are compared numerically. For example, 002=2. Decimal numbers are compared as characters. This will give the expected result only if both values have decimals and the number of leading zeros and trailing zeros are the same: 1.23 = 1.23, but 01.23<1.23 and 1.230>1.23.

SCL uses numeric comparisons for all numeric variables.

A.2.b Indirect macro variable references

The macro language allows data values to contain references to macro variables, which are then recursively resolved. This unusual capability can cause chaos because it introduces additional scans of the word. If an expression sometimes requires more scans than other times, it is impossible to use a consistently correct number of ampersands and dot delimiters in the program. The only solution is to resolve the variable value before using it in the complex expression. It is therefore unsafe to use this capability unless the procedure has been designed with this intention.

A.2.c Special symbols and reserved words

Macro calls, macro variable references, expressions, and label identifiers are all evaluated at execution time. This permits many tricks such as dynamic specification of varying numbers of arguments.

```
%if &CASE eq 1 %then
     %let ARG = %str(1,2,3,4);
%else
     %let ARG = %str(1,2);
%M (%unquote(&ARG))
```

The price of these features is the need for execution-time quoting functions. These are difficult to use and a common source of errors.

A.3 It should be possible to review the data values entering a given module.

When debugging is necessary, this aids in determining where the problem occurred.

A.3.a Quoted values

In order to deal with various problems, the Macro language provides quoting functions that work by recoding special characters to other unused codes. These recoded values can be safely manipulated without needing to use the quoting function again.

Both quoted and unquoted values print and compare identically, so you can't tell what is quoted when you are debugging.

In SCL, the characters printed are those used internally.

A.3.b Macro variable table contents

SCL provides a Debugger facility that allows executing a program one line at a time, pausing at a particular point in a program or when a specified condition is satisfied.

The Macro language has nothing like this. The most crucial gap is the absence of a command such as EXAMINE ALL, which dumps the value of all SCL variables in the current environment. This has been on the SASware Ballot* for years.

A.4 The algebraic properties of arithmetic should be maintained

This provides confidence that the implementation of an algorithm will not affect the outcome.

The Macro language only handles integer numbers. If an division operation produces a noninteger result, it is truncated to an integer:

```
%put %eval(7/3);  prints 2.
```

Because intermediate results are also truncated, fundamental algebraic laws such as commutativity may not hold even if the end result is an integer:

```
%put %eval ( (7*6)/3 );  prints 14.
%put %eval ( (7/3)*6 );  prints 12.
```

This is more difficult to debug if the arguments are macro variable references and the operations are divided into several steps.

SCL provides a real numeric variable type. Unlike the Macro language, missing values are supported.

A.5. Code generation should be avoided when it is more straightforward to manipulate data objects directly.

This reduces program complexity and is more computationally efficient. It also permits the program to determine the exact nature of errors and respond appropriately.

The Macro language cannot directly manipulate data objects other than macro variables. The appropriate Program channel code must be generated. Information is then transferred back to the macro level via CALL SYMPUT. The same technique is required to access functions other than the five (excluding quoting functions) that are supported at the macro level.

SCL can directly manipulate an even wider range of data objects than the Program channel, including SAS system options, host system options, titles, footnotes, external directories, SAS catalog directories, SAS catalog entries, and SAS datasets and indexes. Over 150 functions are available.

In many respects, SCL has capabilities superior to those of the program channel, including

- maintenance of open files (and associated locks) across steps,
- programmable response to many errors,
- execution-time specification of data objects (allowing more precompilation)
- linking of independently compiled programs at execution time,
- dynamic execution-time specification of WHERE clauses,
- programmable handling of input and output buffers.

A.6 Code submission should be under direct control of the programmer

In the Macro language, generated code is executed as soon as a complete unit is specified. This can cause confusion, because macro code and open code are interwoven and executed alternately.

SCL generates code into a PREVIEW buffer which can be edited, saved, or canceled prior to submission. The code is executed when the programmer specifies.

B. Advantages of the Macro Language over SCL

A primary advantage of the Macro language for batch use is that unlike SCL, it is designed and documented for these applications.

B.1 Named parameter syntax

Macros may be called using named parameters, which are easier to read, may be specified in any order, and will take the specified default value if omitted.

SCL only supports positional parameter syntax. Modifications of existing programs may require changing calls of those programs in existing code. The lack of support for named parameters is a serious limitation, but a useful work-around is to write macros that accept named-syntax calls and generate the corresponding SCL call. Macros may be used to generate SCL code at SCL compilation time.

B.2. Subroutine libraries

The SASAUTOS macro library facility allows searching a list of libraries in priority order. This makes it possible to have a set of standard macros which can be superseded by custom macros for specific projects: a limited form of the "inheritance" concept of object-oriented programming.

SCL does not provide such a capability.

B.3 Flexibility of macro invocations

This was discussed earlier.

B.4 Ease of program editing

SCL programs can only be edited using the full-screen interactive procedure PROC BUILD, even if there is no interactive component to the system.

Macro language programs can be edited using any text editor.

B.5 Automatic error handling

If a DATA step or PROC generated by a macro encounters an error, it is automatically handled by this system. While the method in which it is handled may not be the most desirable, it requires no attention on the part of the programmer.

Most error handling in SCL is the programmer's responsibility. This level of detail contributes to the typically messy appearance of SCL programs. A program may continue processing after an error has been encountered, unless instructed otherwise.

B.6 Lower-level programming

DATA steps and PROCs act at an abstract logical level. For example, the programmer need not be concerned with opening an input file, creating an output file, fetching the next case, transferring information to the program data vector, updating the output file, detecting the end of the input file, and closing the files.

In SCL, these operations are the programmer's responsibility and under his or her control. It is possible to accomplish tasks that cannot otherwise be done in the SAS System. On the other hand, if you want to do something routine, this level of detail is a nuisance. Of course, you could develop a set of standard SCL programs or SAS macros to generate commonly used code.

C. Summary

If you have large amounts of generated code with limited control code, macro is a good choice. It is also appropriate when building a set of tools for ad hoc use in developing other macros or Program channel code.

SCL is a good choice for the development of large complex systems that will require substantial maintenance. SCL programs intended for use in batch environments should avoid submitting code to the Program channel. SUBMIT SQL and the SCL data management facilities should be used instead.

Wish List for the future

The following enhancements to SAS would be extremely helpful for developing systems using Screen Control Language in batch environments.

- Document and support PROC DISPLAY, including its use in batch environments.
- Allow multiple AF sessions to be opened.
- Provide a %AF macro command which could be used to invoke an AF program from anywhere in open code or macro.
- Allow all methods of invoking SAS/AF to accept parameters. Support named-parameter syntax throughout, including specification of default values.
- Provide a CATSEARCH statement analogous to the version 5 LIBSEARCH statement, but using a specified list of catalogs.
- Support the SUBMIT CONTINUE statement in batch environments.
- Support ON units, which would define code to be executed whenever the indicated SAS return code occurred. For example,
  ON %SYSRC(_SENOLCK) DO; RETURN; END;
  This would simplify SCL error handling.

These enhancements would make "Screen" Control Language the preferred choice for systems control and code generation throughout all modes of SAS operation.

Acknowledgements

I would like to thank Grant Blank for his comments regarding an earlier draft of this paper.

References

Kretzman, Peter (1986), "Maintainable SAS-based systems and the SAS Macro Language: A Catch-22?", in SAS Users Group International Proceedings of the Eleventh Annual Conference, Cary, NC: SAS Institute Inc.

SAS Institute Inc. (1985), SAS/AF User's Guide, Version 5 Edition, Cary, NC: SAS Institute Inc.

SAS Institute Inc. (1989), SAS/AF Software: Usage and Reference, Version 6, First Edition, Cary, NC: SAS Institute Inc.

SAS Institute Inc. (1990), SAS Guide to Macro Processing, Version 6, Second Edition, Cary, NC: SAS Institute Inc.

SAS Institute Inc. (1990), SAS Language: Reference, Version 6, First Edition, Cary, NC: SAS Institute Inc.

SAS Institute Inc. (1990), SAS Screen Control Language: Reference, Version 6, First Edition, Cary, NC: SAS Institute Inc.

SAS Institute Inc. (1990), SAS Technical Report P-199, Using SAS Screen Control Language in Release 6.06, Cary, NC: SAS Institute Inc.

* SAS, SAS/AF, SAS/FSP, and SASware Ballot are registered trademarks of SAS Institute, Inc. SQL is a trademark of International Business Machines Corporation.

The author may be contacted at:

Andrew A. Norton
Trilogy Consulting Corporation
850 S. Greenbay Road
Waukegan, IL 60085-7076
(708) 244-9520

Chapter 4 Advanced Macro Programming

Intermediate

Tasks	Provides tips on macro programming.
Tools	%LET %KEYDEF %SYSEXEC Autocall facility Automatic macro variables CALL SYMPUT Command-style macros Macro debugging options Simulating arrays with && resolution Statement-style macros SYSSCP automatic macro variable

Intermediate

Tasks	Demonstrates and explains the use of the macro facility as a generalized, dynamic code generator.
Tools	%DO, Iterative %DO %WHILE %EVAL %IF-%THEN / %ELSE %LET && resolution CALL SYMPUT Simple substitution

Intermediate

Tasks	Offers tips and techniques for macro programming.
Tools	%EVAL Autocall facility Nested macro invocations PARMBUFF

Using SAS Macros to Generate Code (So Your Program Can Figure Out What to Do for Itself) 138

Intermediate

Tasks — Illustrates an application that uses the macro facility to change variable and data set names.

Tools — %IF-%THEN / %ELSE
Parameters
Simple substitution

Ifs, Ands, and Buts: A Case Study in Advanced Macro Implementation 143

Intermediate

Tasks — Offers tips and techniques for macro programming.

Tools — %DO, Iterative
&& resolution
CALL SYMPUT
Complex substitution
Macro parameters
Simulating arrays with macro variables
Style suggestions

Macro: Bells and Whistles for Version 6 150

Intermediate

Tasks — Introduces experienced macro users to new Version 6 macro features.

Tools — %DO, Iterative
%GLOBAL
%INPUT
%WINDOW / %DISPLAY
Autocall facility / SASAUTOS= / MAUTOSOURCE
CALL EXECUTE
Macro debugging options / MTRACE
Macro parameters
RESOLVE
Simple substitution

Using Macro Variable Lists 154

Intermediate

Tasks
Demonstrates and explains how to process lists with the macro facility.

Tools
%DO, Iterative
%DO %WHILE
%EVAL
%IF-%THEN / %ELSE
%INCLUDE
%LET
%LOCAL
%SCAN
CALL SYMPUT
Complex substitution
Macro parameters
Simple substitution

Generic Applications Development Using the SAS Macro Language 160

Advanced

Tasks
Defines and interprets dynamic parameter lists.
Uses the macro facility to generate DATA step array code.

Tools
%DO, Iterative
%DO %WHILE
&& and &&& macro variable references
CALL SYMPUT

Dynamic Code Replaces Itself Every 3,000 Executions or Less 166

Advanced

Tasks
Introduces the concept of generalized, dynamic programming with the macro facility.

Tools
%DO, Iterative
%DO %UNTIL
%EVAL
%IF-%THEN / %ELSE
%LET
%PUT
&&& resolution
CALL EXECUTE
CALL SYMPUT
Complex substitution
Macro parameters
Simple substitution

Macro Tricks to Astound the Folks on Thursday Morning: Ten Immediately Useful Macro Techniques

Bruce M. Tindall, SAS Institute Inc., Cary, NC
Susan M. O'Connor, SAS Institute Inc., Cary, NC

ABSTRACT

The SAS® macro language is useful as a tool for developing applications and for ensuring ease of maintenance. Frequently, however, SAS applications developers never get their feet wet with the macro language because the more bizarre features of the language have an intimidating reputation.

The purpose of this paper is to document ten tips that would be immediately useful to SUGI 16 attendees when they return to their sites on Thursday morning. This paper does not discuss the intricate and often difficult aspects of the macro facility, such as esoteric macro quoting functions and complex macro variable referencing environments. The goal is to offer suggestions for those users who are timid about approaching the macro facility.

The intended audience is applications developers with a need for immediately applicable macro skills that they could implement when returning to work after SUGI. Even those who do not know they need macro are invited.

INTRODUCTION

Here are ten simple, specific ways you can make more effective use of SAS software by using the SAS macro facility. You do not need any experience with the macro facility to get started, and you do not need access to any SAS software products other than base SAS software.

You learn how to

- create new SAS statements and SAS Display Manager System commands
- change and customize your SAS programs easily by using macro variables (including the "automatic" ones supplied as part of the SAS System and those you create yourself)
- make a SAS program change itself as it executes
- define function keys on your terminal and send commands to your computer's operating system
- create a library of useful SAS macro programs to share among SAS users at your organization
- create and use arrays of macro variables to simplify repetitive processes
- write SAS programs that can be used on different computer systems without changing a single line of code
- (when all else fails) debug a program that is not working the way you think it should.

MACRO TECHNIQUES

1. If This Is &SYSDAY It Must Be New Orleans (Automatic Macro Variables)

Suppose you want to put the current day's date into the title at the top of each page of output each time you run a particular SAS program. You could put the actual date into the title and change it by hand before running the program each day:

```
TITLE "REPORT FOR 20FEB91";
```

But you can also tell the SAS System to insert today's date automatically by putting a macro variable reference in the title:

```
TITLE "REPORT FOR &SYSDATE";
```

As soon as the SAS System reads this TITLE statement, it replaces the ampersand (&) and the name of the macro variable (SYSDATE) with the value of that macro variable (20FEB91 or whatever today's date is).

There are several macro variables that the SAS System creates and that you can use anywhere in a SAS program. They are all listed in Chapter 2, "Macro Variables," of the *SAS Guide to Macro Processing, Version 6, Second Edition.* They are called *automatic macro variables* because the SAS System sets them up automatically without the need to do anything. Some of them are

- SYSDATE (date on which SAS session began running)
- SYSDAY (day of the week on which SAS session began running)
- SYSTIME (the time at which the current SAS session began running)
- SYSERR (tells whether the previous PROC or DATA step ran successfully)
- SYSLAST (contains the name of the most recently created SAS data set).

To use any of them, place the name immediately preceded by an ampersand anywhere in a SAS program, and the SAS program will work as if you had placed the value of the variable, rather than the ampersand and the name, at that point in the SAS program.

Bonus tip The following two TITLE statements will cause today's date to appear in the title:

```
TITLE "REPORT FOR &SYSDATE";  /* Double quotes */
TITLE  REPORT FOR &SYSDATE ;  /* No quotes     */
```

but this one will not

```
TITLE 'REPORT FOR &SYSDATE';  /* Single quotes */
```

In this last case, the ampersand and the word SYSDATE will appear in the title on each page of output, instead of today's date. That is because the SAS macro facility ignores anything inside single quotes. This restriction is useful in cases where you really want the ampersand and variable name to be printed, not the variable's value. For instance, you might want to have this pair of titles on each page:

EXAMPLE USING THE &SYSDATE MACRO VARIABLE
REPORT FOR 20FEB91

You could put the first title in single quotes to prevent the SAS System from resolving the macro variable, but put the second title in double quotes to allow the resolution to happen.

2. You Say "&POTATO", I Say "TOMATO", %LET's Call the Whole Thing Off (%LET and Macro Variable References)

Suppose you have a SAS program that contains many DATA steps, procedures, and titles that refer to a single data set. Sometimes you want to process a data set named XYZ.A, sometimes XYZ.B, and sometimes XYZ.C. You could change each occurrence of the data set by hand each time you ran the program over a different data set, or you could get the same result much more easily by using the SAS macro facility as a simple text substitutor.

Instead of saying DATA XYZ.A, and PROC SORT DATA=XYZ.A, and TITLE "RESULTS OF PROCESSING DATA SET XYZ.A", and changing each A to a B or C when necessary, you could replace the changeable part of the data set name with a macro variable of your own creation, like this:

```
DATA XYZ.&MYNAME;
     ...
PROC SORT DATA=XYZ.&MYNAME;
     ...
TITLE "RESULTS OF PROCESSING DATA SET XYZ.&MYNAME";
```

To make the SAS System replace &MYNAME with A or B or C, you need only enter one statement, at the beginning of your SAS program:

```
%LET MYNAME = B ;
```

This creates a macro variable called MYNAME and gives it the value B. Then, after the %LET statement has occurred, whenever the SAS System sees an ampersand followed by MYNAME, it will replace that macro variable reference with the value of the macro variable — in this case, with a B.

To change every occurrence of &MYNAME in your program from a B to a C, all you have to do is make one change to the %LET statement, and the SAS System will do the rest:

```
%LET MYNAME = C ;
```

Note that you do not put an ampersand before MYNAME in the %LET statement. The ampersand means "put the value of the macro variable here." In the %LET statement you don't want the SAS System to see the value of the macro variable — it doesn't have a value yet anyway — you want it to see the variable's name, MYNAME.

Also note that you do not put the value of the macro variable in quotes (unless you want the quotation marks to become part of the value itself). This is different from how you assign a character string to a DATA step variable, where you do have to use quotation marks but the quotation marks do not become part of the string. In a macro %LET statement, everything after the equals sign and before the semicolon becomes part of the value of the macro variable.

It is even possible to have a macro variable whose value contains a semicolon, but to do that,you need to use the macro quoting functions, which we promised not to bring up in this paper!

You can create as many different macro variables as you want. You can give each variable any name that begins with a letter or underscore, contains nothing but letters, digits, and underscores, and is no more than eight characters long — but avoid names that begin with the letters SYS, because the SAS macro facility's automatic macro variables use that prefix, and you might inadvertently change one of them if you begin your names with SYS.

Once you have given a macro variable a value, you can change its value at any time by using another %LET statement.

Be aware that macro variables and DATA step variables are not the same, even though they may have the same name. You can use a %LET statement to create a macro variable named MYVAR, and you can use a DATA step assignment statement to create a DATA step variable named MYVAR with a different value. The macro variable will exist for the rest of the whole SAS program, and you reference it by putting an ampersand in front of its name. The DATA step variable exists only during that DATA step, and you reference it by using its name (without an ampersand). They have no more to do with each other than SAS Institute, SAS (the airline), and SAS (the British secret service) do, even though they have the same name.

3. Crossing the Great Divide (Call Symput)

It is all well and good to use the %LET statement when you know ahead of time what value you want to put into a macro variable, but what if the value is located in a file or a SAS data set?

Your first thought might be to try something like this:

```
DATA _NULL_;
  INFILE MYFILE;
  INPUT WHATZIS $;
  %LET MYNAME = WHATZIS ;     /* wrong-o! */
DATA XYZ.&MYNAME;
  ...
```

This will do something, but it will not be what you want. It will not put the value of the DATA step variable WHATZIS into the macro variable "MYNAME." Instead, it will put the seven letters W, H, A, T, Z, I, and S into the macro variable, and then the second DATA step will create a data set named XYZ.WHATZIS, not XYZ.A or XYZ.B or whatever you expected.

To get the value of a DATA step variable into a macro variable, you need to use the special DATA step statement, CALL SYMPUT. The name comes from SYM for symbolic variable (another term for macro variable) and PUT, meaning you are putting a value into the macro variable. Here is an example:

```
DATA _NULL_;
  INFILE MYFILE;
  INPUT WHATZIS $;
  CALL SYMPUT( "MYNAME", WHATZIS );  /* correct! */
DATA XYZ.&MYNAME;
  ...
```

You can use SYMPUT, for another example, to find out how many items there are in a list of Social Security Numbers, and, thus, how big an array to create in order to hold them all.

```
DATA _NULL_;
  SET LIST.OF_SSNS NOBS=N;
  CALL SYMPUT ( "HOWMANY", N );
  STOP;  /* Stop because you don't actually want  */
         /* to read the whole data set; you just  */
         /* want to use NOBS= to find out how     */
         /* many observations there are.          */
DATA;
```

```
ARRAY SSN SSN1-SSN&HOWMANY;
...
```

If there were 5,280 observations in the data set LIST.OF_SSNS, the second DATA step would create an array consisting of the variables SSN1 through SSN5280.

Bonus tips There are a couple of complications and potential pitfalls here, but don't worry; they're all for a good cause.

First, notice that "MYNAME" is in quotation marks, but WHATZIS is not. That is because the name of the macro variable you are creating is literally MYNAME, but the value you want to put into it is not literally WHATZIS — the value is the character string contained in the DATA step variable WHATZIS.

If you had wanted to put the actual seven letters WHATZIS into the macro variable, you would have put quotes around "WHATZIS."

```
DATA _NULL_;
  CALL SYMPUT("HOWMANY","WHATZIS");
```

Conversely, if you had wanted to create a macro variable named, not MYNAME, but some string contained in a DATA step variable, you would have put the name of that DATA step variable — without quotes around it — as the first argument to SYMPUT.

```
DATA;
  INFILE YOURFILE;
  INPUT ITSNAME $ ;
  CALL SYMPUT(ITSNAME,"THE VALUE");
```

This example puts the two words THE VALUE into a macro variable whose name is not ITSNAME, but rather, whatever string the INPUT statement read from the INFILE statement into the DATA step variable ITSNAME.

This technique makes SYMPUT very flexible; you can create a large number of macro variables whose names as well as values are derived from the contents of some SAS data set. (People really do this, and if you want to see why, there are some examples in the *SAS Guide to Macro Processing*.)

Also, be aware that SYMPUT does not create any macro variable until the DATA step actually *runs*, or *executes*. Therefore, you will not be able to use that macro variable while *compiling* the DATA step that creates it. For example, you cannot do this:

```
DATA _NULL_;
  INFILE MYFILE;
  INPUT WHATZIS $;
  CALL SYMPUT( "MYNAME", WHATZIS );
  PUT "WE JUST CREATED A MACRO
       VARIABLE WITH VALUE &MYNAME";
       /* wrong! */
```

This will result in a warning that the macro variable MYNAME does not exist — and it does not, yet, because when the SAS System reads the PUT statement, it has not yet executed the DATA step, and therefore it has not yet created the macro variable.

4. Yes, We Have No Macro Arrays (Indirect Macro Variable References)

The DATA step has a very convenient feature that lets you organize variables into arrays. There is nothing in the macro facility that is exactly parallel to DATA step arrays, but you can fake it with indirect macro variable references. (Here we begin to cross into the forbidden zone of scary and complicated macro features, but if you bear with us and master this one, you can really impress your buddies back home.)

In a typical DATA step array, you might have a series of variables named VAR1, VAR2, VAR3, up through VAR50, which you organize into an array named ABC with the statement

```
ARRAY ABC VAR1-VAR50;
```

You can reference an arbitrary member of this array by coding an array reference like ABC{12}, which refers to VAR12, or ABC{N}, which uses the value of the DATA step variable N to decide which element of the array to access.

Suppose, though, that you have a series of macro variables with names VAR1 through VAR50, as well as a macro variable N that contains some digits representing a number between 1 and 50. You want to use the value of the Nth one of those macro variables; if the value N is 35, you want to get the value of VAR35; if N is 2 you want to get the value of VAR2.

In general, you want the value of the macro variable whose name is generated by the expression VAR&N. So, to print the value of the Nth variable to the SAS log, you might try this:

```
%PUT &VAR&N;  /* wrong! */
```

Alas, if you try this you get a warning message saying that there is no macro variable named VAR. What has happened is that the SAS macro facility has tried to get the value of VAR and the value of N and then put them together, but there is no VAR, only VAR1, VAR2, and so on.

To get the result you want — to get the value of N appended to the prefix VAR, and then to reference the resulting variable name — you have to use an extra ampersand to create an indirect macro variable reference. Do this:

```
%PUT &&VAR&N;  /* right! */
```

and you will get the desired result.

Why? According to the rules of macro variable resolution (detailed in the *SAS Guide to Macro Processing*), the SAS macro facility takes the following steps.

1. It resolves && into &.
2. It resolves &N into 35.
3. The string now reads &VAR35.
4. It goes back to the beginning and sees that there is still an ampersand in the string, so it starts resolving from the beginning again.
5. It resolves &VAR35 into the value of VAR35.

(You can watch the SAS System take these steps one at a time by setting OPTION SYMBOLGEN and reading the diagnostic messages that appear on the SAS log.)

If you want to generate all the values of all the macro variables VAR1 through VAR50, you can use a macro %DO loop, just as you can use a DATA step DO statement to access each member of a DATA step array one at a time.

```
%MACRO EVERYONE;
   %DO N = 1 %TO 50;
       &&VAR&N
   %END;
   %MEND EVERYONE

%PUT %EVERYONE;
```

(Note that we have created a macro — that is, a macro program, not a macro variable — named EVERYONE. After the macro has been created, we can execute it by entering its name preceded by a % (percent sign).

The %PUT statement will print the result of the macro program EVERYONE; it will print the value of VAR1, then the value of VAR2, and so on through the value of VAR50. If, for example, the macro variables contain the names of SAS data sets, you could write a DATA step that creates all 50 of those data sets as follows:

```
DATA %EVERYONE;
   ...
```

5. The Key to %KEYDEF or for SAS Display Manager Only (The New %KEYDEF Macro Statement)

The %KEYDEF macro program statement was new in Release 6.06. It redefines function keys in an interactive SAS display manager session from within a macro or in open code. Open code is part of SAS code that is outside any macro definition. By default, the function key definitions remain in effect for the duration of your current SAS session or until you change them again in the session.

The syntax is

%KEYDEF *key-name* | *'key-name'* | *"key-name"* <*text*>;

The *key-name* is the name of any function key on your terminal. As you know, the names of function keys can vary by terminal and by operating system. If the *key-name* is more than one word or contains special characters, enclose it in quotes. There is a limit of eight characters for any function key and truncation will occur without a warning message being issued.

```
%KEYDEF  f1;
%KEYDEF  "SHF F4";
%KEYDEF  '^a';
```

To see how a key is set omit the text part of the %KEYDEF macro statement and a note will appear on the log.

```
%KEYDEF 'f3';
NOTE:  F3 set to "zoom off; submit".
%KEYDEF 'shf f4';
NOTE:  SHF F4 set to "".
```

The key F3 is set to "ZOOM OFF; SUBMIT" and shift F4 is a null setting.

The text can be display manager commands in an unquoted string up to the semicolon or in a quoted string that can include semicolons. The text can be up to 80 characters long. For example, set the function key, SHF F4, to execute a SAS statement or statements using text 80 characters long.

```
%KEYDEF 'shf f4' 'submit "proc print; run;";';
```

When you hit the SHIFT F4 key, the PRINT procedure will be executed. Of course, this macro statement could be executed inside a macro, executed conditionally, or invoked by an autoexec file. So, if you are lost and can't tell your function key setting from your Ferrari key you might use

```
%KEYDEF 'shf f4';
```

to give you the key to unlock your confusion.

```
NOTE: SHF F4 set to "submit "proc print; run;";".
```

Bonus tip Another useful text syntax is a string following a tilde.

```
%KEYDEF ~string;
```

This string does not have to be a display manager command; it can be a string to insert after the cursor in any window that accepts input. (Be aware that the tilde (~) is not in any way a part of the macro facility or a special macro character; it is valid here only as part of defining a key definition to cut and paste in a display manager input window.)

```
%KEYDEF 'shf f0'  ~OPTION MPRINT MLOGIC SYMBOLGEN SOURCE2;

NOTE:  SHF F0 set to "~OPTION MPRINT MLOGIC SYMBOLGEN SOURCE2".
```

The tilde and the semicolon will not be part of the text you paste in your window. This is a way you could conditionally cut and paste text into a window. In this example, hitting shift f0 in the program window would swiftly put "OPTION MPRINT MLOGIC SYMBOLGEN SOURCE2" at the cursor location in your window. To the folks at home it will appear as if you had studied speed typing while in New Orleans.

You can save function key definitions across SAS sessions and override the default if you invoke the KEYS window and issue the SAVE command. These key definitions will be stored in SASUSER.PROFILE. They will be accessed in subsequent sessions if you initialize your session in the same way, using the same directory or the same SASUSER.

6. You Say I'm on a PC? I Shouldn't Have Taken That Left Toin at Albuquoique! (Writing Portable Applications with &SYSSCP)

With Version 6 of the SAS System, you can write SAS applications that work identically on many different kinds of computers that use a variety of operating systems. The SAS System works the same on all machines, but if the names of external files, graphics devices, full-screen terminals, and function keys differ from machine to machine, how can you write a truly portable application that uses exactly the same SAS statements on all machines without change?

There is an automatic macro variable, SYSSCP, that tells you on which operating system your SAS application is running: OS, CMS, PC DOS, ULTRIX,* and so on. With that information, you can issue the appropriate commands to point the SAS System at the relevant local files, terminals, printers, and plotters.

Testers at SAS Institute use this technique extensively to write SAS programs that can be used, unchanged and unsupervised, to test the SAS System on all the different machines. It would be a nightmare to have to maintain a different copy of each of our thousands of test programs on each different machine. Using the SAS macro facility, though, we save immense amounts of time and trouble by writing each program only once, and then sending exact copies to all the different platforms.

For example, to issue a FILENAME statement that assigns the fileref ABCDE to the appropriate physical file name on the machine we're running on, you would code something like this in a macro program:

```
%MACRO PHYSICAL;
   %IF &SYSSCP = OS %THEN
         'TINDALL.MYSTUFF.CNTL';
   %ELSE %IF &SYSSCP = VMS %THEN
         'DISK5:[TINDALL]MYSTUFF.DAT';
   %ELSE %IF &SYSSCP = PC DOS %THEN
         'd:\tindall\pcfile.dat';
   %MEND PHYSICAL;

FILENAME ABCDE %PHYSICAL ;
```

When the macro PHYSICAL executes, the SAS macro facility will replace the percent sign and the macro's name with the appropriate physical file name. Thus, on different machines, the SAS System will see different FILENAME statements, but the code looks exactly the same.

7. How to Make Your Operating System Work for You without Leaving the SAS System (The %SYSEXEC Macro Statement)

Historically in the SAS macro facility, we had %TSO and %CMS, which executed operating system commands for the respective operating systems. You can see what a problem this could be in Release 6.06 and beyond! Now we have platforms from "a" with AOS/VS to "v" with VMS, not to mention all those other operating systems and letters we support. So to treat everyone fairly the Institute implemented a generic macro statement for operating system interfaces.

The macro language %SYSEXEC statement allows you to execute operating system commands immediately and places the operating system return code in the automatic macro variable &SYSRC. The default value for &SYSRC is 0. Thus, you can test for successful completion of the operating system command. You can use the %SYSEXEC statement inside or outside a macro.

The form of the statement is

%SYSEXEC [*command*];

where *command* can be any operating system command or any sequence of macro operations that generate an operating system command.

Omitting the command puts you into your operating system's command subset mode, which is an interactive operating system mode. To return to your SAS session, enter the command indicated by your operating system message; for example, "Enter 'EXIT' to return to the SAS System".

The following %SYSEXEC statements are examples:

```
%MACRO ASSIGN;
   %IF &SYSSCP = CMS %THEN
      %SYSEXEC FILEDEF IN DISK MYFILE DATA B;
   %ELSE %IF &SYSSCP =  OS %THEN
      %SYSEXEC ALLOCATE FILE(IN) DATASET('USERID.MY.SASDATA') OLD;
   %ELSE %IF &SYSSCP = VMS %THEN
      %SYSEXEC ASSIGN IN [USERID.MY]DATA.DAT;
   %PUT THE OPERATING SYSTEM COMMAND RETURN CODE IS &SYSRC.;
%MEND ASSIGN;
```

Since this interface is with operating systems, you might want to check in the SAS companion for your operating system if you have specific questions and to check for operating system dependencies such as batch restrictions. Think how %SYSEXEC could amaze the folks at home.

8. I'm So Tired of Those #@$! Percent Signs (Statement-style and Command-style Macros)

If you are the type of person who is exhausted at the keyboard with typing the percent sign and want to eliminate the hassle of hitting the shift key and the 5 key at any cost, then statement-style and command-style macros might be the ticket for you.

Name-style macros are macros that are invoked with the percent sign. For example, the macro definition

```
%MACRO MACNAME(DATASET,VAR);
   PROC DATASETS;
      MODIFY &DATASET;
         INDEX CREATE &VAR;
   RUN;
%MEND;
```

is invoked with the name-style macro invocation using the percent sign and the parameters in parentheses.

```
%MACNAME(A,X)
```

You can use the statement-style macro to create new, customized SAS statements and eliminate that nasty percent sign. Use the STMT option on the macro statement definition and set the SAS system option IMPLMAC, meaning "implied macro", to invoke statement-style macros.

```
%MACRO MACNAME(DATASET,VAR)/STMT;
   PROC DATASETS;
      MODIFY &DATASET;
         INDEX CREATE &VAR;
   RUN;
%MEND;
```

Of course, you could still invoke this macro in the name-style manner or you could use statement-style invocation to make this macro look like a SAS statement. Begin the statement with the macro name, separate the parameters with blanks, and end the statement-style macro invocation with a semicolon. It must be used as a complete statement and *not* within another SAS statement.

```
MACNAME A X;
```

It looks as if you have added a new SAS statement to the SAS language and you have eliminated the percent sign, the parentheses, and the comma, too.

You can also invoke name-style macros from the command line by using the percent sign, but in Release 6.07 on the non-UNIX* platforms, command-style macros have been implemented. With command-style macros, it can appear that you have created new display manager commands. Use the CMD option on the macro statement definition for the macros that you plan to use only from the command line and set option CMDMAC.

```
%MACRO MACCMD/CMD;
   SUBMIT "PROC PRINT DATA = &DSET; RUN;";
   OUTPUT;
   FILE "OUT.OUT";
   PGM;
%MEND;
```

Of course you can invoke this macro with name-style invocation from the command line with the percent sign and parentheses around the parameter.

```
Command ===> %MACCMD(_LAST_)
```

But when OPTION CMDMAC is set, command-style invocation looks like a new display manager command with the percent sign and the parentheses removed.

```
Command ===> MACCMD _LAST_
```

Everything has its price, however. When you use statement-style macros with option IMPLMAC, there is the overhead of the SAS System checking the first word of every SAS statement to see if it is a macro invocation. When you use command-style invocation with the option CMDMAC, the SAS System checks for command-style invocation whenever we process the start of a command-line command. With name-style invocation, the SAS System only attempts to invoke a macro when a percent sign is encountered. In other words, using statement-style or command-style macros may have a slight impact on performance, but then the danger of carpal tunnel syndrome from excessive percent sign usage may be significantly reduced.

9. Autocall Is Not a Car Phone (The Autocall Facility)

So you have a few favorite macros or you want to write a few or you really want it to appear as if you have mastered macros on Thursday morning. It is time to investigate the autocall facility. An autocall library contains files that define SAS macros. There are two types of autocall macros: those you write yourself and those provided by SAS Institute.

For macros you write yourself, the autocall facility offers you a way to access your macros without having to define the source code for the macro in every SAS job that uses it. You store your favorite macro by its name in an *aggregate storage location* on your system. An *aggregate storage location* is a fancy name on CMS for MACLIB, on MVS for PDS, or on directory-based systems for a directory. If you set option MAUTOSOURCE and option SASAUTOS= *aggregate-storage-location* before you invoke your macro, the SAS System locates the macro where it is in the autocall library, brings the source code into the SAS System, compiles the macro, and then executes the macro.

To create a macro, %MACNAME, to be autocalled use two steps.

1. Create the aggregate storage location to function as an autocall library.
   - On MVS create a partitioned data set.
   - On OS/2® create an OS/2 directory.
   - On VMS™ create either a directory or a VMS text library.
   - On CMS create a CMS MACLIB.
   - On PRIMOS® create a PRIMOS directory.
   - On AOS/VS create an AOS/VS directory.
2. Create a member in the autocall library containing the source statements defining the macro, %MACNAME.
   - On MVS use the name of the macro, MACNAME, as the member.
   - On OS/2 use the name of the macro with the file extension .SAS, MACNAME.SAS.
   - On VMS use the name of the macro with the file extension .SAS, MACNAME.SAS if the library is a directory or the name of the macro, MACNAME, if the library is a text library.
   - On CMS use the name of the macro, MACNAME, as the member.
   - On PRIMOS use the name of the macro with the file extension .SAS, MACNAME.SAS.
   - On AOS/VS use the name of the macro with the file extension .SAS, MACNAME.SAS.

The autocall macro facility is available on all operating systems with Release 6.06 and beyond. (It is also available in Version 5 on the mainframes, but concatenation of autocall libraries there is done with operating system commands.) Each SAS companion documents the type of aggregate storage location to create as an autocall library to hold members and tells you how to name the members you create in your storage locations. You can concatenate aggregate storage locations and they will be searched in order for the macro.

OPTIONS SASAUTOS=*library-specification*

| *(library-specification-1*, ..., library-specification);

Library-specifications can be quoted strings or filerefs to the aggregate storage locations.

If you are more timid, you might want to check out the autocall macros SAS Institute supplies. With base SAS software, SAS Institute ships a sample of macros to be working examples of macros, as extensions of the macro facility for immediate execution, and as models for developing your own macros. If you have other SAS software products, you may have other autocall libraries too. If your site has installed the autocall libraries using the standard configuration, you only have to set option MAUTOSOURCE to invoke your autocall macros. The autocall facility is documented in Chapter 7 of the *SAS Guide to Macro Processing.* That chapter includes explanations of the macros %CMPRES, %DATATYP, %LEFT, %QCMPRES, %QLEFT, %QTRIM, %TRIM, and %VERIFY. You should be able to study these sample macros on line to see how they are written, copy and cannibalize them, and make them role models for your macros. If your configuration is standard, they should be referenced by default by option SASAUTOS= , and each should be a member with the same name as the macro. If you can't locate these macros, ask your SAS Software Consultant for information on how to access them. These Institute-supplied macros are there for you, sort of as macro Cliff notes.

The autocall facility can save you time because it makes a whole lot of macros available to your SAS session, but it only compiles the macros you actually use. As your collection of macros grows, your autocall library will facilitate your program development. There are some more complex aspects of the autocall facility that are documented in the *SAS Guide to Macro Processing*, but there is no reason not to leap in and try the autocall facility. It is less expensive than a car phone.

10. C D BUG or I 1 2 B A MACRO D BUG R (Debugging a Macro)

When you start using macros you are eventually going to need to debug your macros. There are three SAS system options that will make this easier for you in Version 6: SYMBOLGEN, MLOGIC, and MPRINT.

If you are having a problem understanding how a macro variable is being resolved to a value, then the SYMBOLGEN option is what you need. The macro variable is the part of a macro that begins with the ampersand and has the name of the macro variable. Here is an example:

```
OPTION SYMBOLGEN;
TITLE "IF THIS IS &SYSDAY IT MUST BE NEW ORLEANS";
```

prints a line to the SAS log giving both the variable's name and its value.

```
SYMBOLGEN:  Macro variable SYSDAY resolves to Wednesday
```

SYMBOLGEN issues a message when double ampersands resolve into a single ampersand. SYMBOLGEN also issues a message when a macro variable's value contains characters that have been quoted by the macro quoting functions, but then we promised not to mention those macro quoting funtions.

When a macro is executing, if you need to debug, then MLOGIC will print messages to the SAS log. These messages trace the execution of every macro programming statement, as well as whenever the macro begins and ends.

For example, if we had a problem with the execution of the %PHYSICAL macro, which was used in tip 6, then we could run it with MLOGIC.

```
OPTION MLOGIC;
FILENAME ABCDE %PHYSICAL;

MLOGIC(PHYSICAL):  Beginning execution.
MLOGIC(PHYSICAL):  %IF condition &SYSSCP = OS is FALSE
MLOGIC(PHYSICAL):  %IF condition &SYSSCP = VMS is FALSE
MLOGIC(PHYSICAL):  %IF condition &SYSSCP = PC DOS is FALSE
MLOGIC(PHYSICAL):  Ending execution.
```

Clearly, our operating system is not OS or VMS or PC DOS! Each condition is false. To see which operating system we are running under, resolve the macro variable &SYSSCP BY turning on SYMBOLGEN.

```
OPTION NOMLOGIC SYMBOLGEN;
FILENAME ABCDE %PHYSICAL;

SYMBOLGEN:  Macro variable SYSSCP resolves to OS2
SYMBOLGEN:  Macro variable SYSSCP resolves to OS2
SYMBOLGEN:  Macro variable SYSSCP resolves to OS2
```

We get three messages because &SYSSCP is resolved three times when this macro executes. It looks as if our operating system is the OS/2 environment. What an easy way to figure that out!

To see what SAS statements a macro actually generates, use the MPRINT option, which prints each SAS statement as a separate line on the SAS log.

```
OPTION MPRINT;
%MACRO TTODAY;
   DATA A; X=1; RUN;
   TITLE "IF THIS IS &SYSDAY IT MUST BE NEW ORLEANS";
   PROC PRINT; RUN;
%MEND;

MPRINT(TTODAY):   DATA A;
MPRINT(TTODAY):   X=1;
MPRINT(TTODAY):   RUN;
NOTE: The data set WORK.A has 1 observations and 1 variables.
MPRINT(TTODAY):   TITLE "IF THIS IS Saturday IT MUST BE NEW ORLEANS";
MPRINT(TTODAY):   PROC PRINT;
MPRINT(TTODAY):   RUN;
```

CONCLUSION

Macros need not be intimidating. Using SYMBOLGEN to check macro variable resolution, MLOGIC to trace execution of macro programming statements, and MPRINT to show the actual SAS code the macro has generated should give you enough skills to give them a try.

SAS is a registered trademark of SAS Institute Inc., Cary, NC, USA.

UNIX is a registered trademark of AT&T. PRIMOS is a registered trademark of Prime Computer Inc. OS/2 is a registered trademark of International Business Machines Corporation. VMS and ULTRIX are trademarks of Digital Equipment Corporation.

A Macro Program for Generating Customized Reports from User-Specified Column Variables and Page-Sort Variables

Jim DeFoor, General Dynamics - Fort Worth

OUTLINE

Introduction
Actions Performed in Program
Macro Techniques Used
Description of Macro Code
Explanation of Macro Techniques
Three Reports Produced by Program

INTRODUCTION

The Macro techniques shown in this poster allow one program to generate many different reports, each with its own unique numeric columns and logical page sorts. That capability permits users to report or analyze many different 'cuts' of their data with one program. Having only one program perform a multitude of reporting tasks reduces the development and maintenance activities of the supporting programmer. The techniques are used in a program at General Dynamics - Fort Worth (GDFW) that generates cost estimate reports of F-16 aircraft. The program has been used for every major proposal at GDFW during the last five years.

Three reports generated by this program are shown in this poster. Each was created by the unique SAS code generated by one Macro program. That Macro code generated the SAS code according to the program-fixed row variable of the report and the user's selection of the report's column and page-sort variables. It created individual column variables from each data value of the column variable selected by the user. It then used those column variables and the page sorts selected by the user to create the specific SORT, SUM, TRANSPOSE, and PUT operations necessary to organize and report the data in the structure desired by the user.

The Macro code and SAS code sections are organized in parallel subsections. The reader will find the SAS code under the same subheading as the Macro code which generated it. This should aid the reader in understanding the form and purpose of the Macro code in that subsection by allowing line-by-line comparisons of the created code versus the generating code.

Only the significant Macro code in the program is shown in this poster. That code is shown in the order of its use in the actual program. The complete program reads an external data set, assigns the data to cost groups, sorts and sums the data, transposes the data to the structure needed for the report, and then reports the data. The comments embedded in the Macro code explain the purpose and function of the following or adjoining lines of Macro code. The comments in the SAS code explain only how the Macro code was resolved.

The section that explains the Macro techniques used in the program is meant as a brief reference of those techniques. Complete explanations may be found in the *SAS Guide to Macro Processing, Version 5.* Page citations are provided.

The last section provides three examples of the reports generated by the actual program. Those reports describe the estimated hours of effort for a proposed task at General Dynamics - Fort Worth. Note that all reports use the same variable, CEC (cost group), as the left-hand stub or row variable of the customized report, but that each has different numeric column variables and no sort variables.

ACTIONS PERFORMED IN PROGRAM

Each action listed here is fully described in the section describing the Macro code and the Macro-generated SAS code.

1. Collect the variables that will generate the columns and the logical page breaks of the report.
2. Sort and sum the data according to the column variable, the page-sort variables, and the program's fixed row variable.
3. Build Macro variables from the data values of the selected column variable.
4. Create a Data Step for transposing the data (one that is more efficient than PROC TRANSPOSE). Generate a SAS variable for each of the Macro variables that represent the new column variables.
5. Establish a report-writing Data _Null_ Step that
   A. Generates a new logical print page for each change in the data values of that last sort variable specified.
   B. Builds a TOTAL variable of the new SAS column variables.
   C. Writes the column data onto the report using PUT statements.
   D. Prints the values of the page-sort variables below the titles and above the column headings of the report using PUT statements in the HEADER area of the Data _Null_ step. Prints 'TOTAL' if no sort-variables were specified.
   E. Writes the column headings onto the report using PUT statements in the HEADER area of the Data _Null_ step.

MACRO TECHNIQUES USED IN PROGRAM

Several techniques are used in more than one section of the code. Accordingly, the numbers below do not correspond to the numbers of the subsections listed above. The techniques are, however, listed in their order of occurence in the section describing the Macro code.

1. Define a Macro variable with a %LET statement.
2. Simple Macro variable substitution.
3. Define a Macro variable with the CALL SYMPUT function.
4. Iterative %DO loops.
5. %IF-%THEN conditional execution.
6. %SUBSTR function.
7. %LENGTH function.
8. %EVAL function
9. Double resolution of Macro variables inside of %DO loops.
10. %DO %WHILE loops.

MACRO CODE USED IN PROGRAM

(See Section On Actions Performed In Program)

---------------------------- MACRO CODE ---------------------------- ---------------------- RESOLVED SAS CODE ----------------------

1. The user's selection of the column variable of his report is stored in the Macro variable &COLUMN using a %LET statement. A blank entry will cause the program to fail. In this example, the SAS variable YEAR is loaded into &COLUMNs.

```
%LET COLUMN = YEAR;
```

&COLUMN will resolve to YEAR.

The user's selection of the logical sort variables of his report are stored in the Macro variables &SORT1 - &SORT5. Blank entries are acceptable. They will resolve to blank during code generation. In this example, organization is loaded into the &SORT1 variable. Blanks are loaded into &SORT2 through &SORT5.

```
%LET SORT1 = ORG;
%LET SORT2 =  ;
%LET SORT3 =  ;
%LET SORT4 =  ;
%LET SORT5 =  ;
```

&SORT1 &SORT2 &SORT3 &SORT4 &SORT5 will resolve to ORG (blank) (blank) (blank) (blank).

2. The report's data is sorted and summed by the page-sorting variables, the fixed row variable of the report (CEC) and the column variable selected by the user. That summed data is placed in the data set SUMDATA. The order of that data corresponds to the order needed in the report to be generated by the program. SPECDATA is also created in the same Data Step. It contains only the data values of the selected column variable and will be used to create the MACRO variables that will generate the new SAS column variables of the report.

```
/* SORT DATA IN PREPARATION OF SUMMING*/
PROC SORT DATA = COSTDATA; /* INPUT DATA */
   BY &SORT1 &SORT2 &SORT3 &SORT4 &SORT5  /* PAGE SORTS */
     CEC                /* FIXED ROW VARIABLE OF REPORT */
     &COLUMN;           /* COLUMN VARIABLE OF REPORT */
RUN;

/* SUM DATA TO UNIQUE VALUES */
DATA SUMDATA(DROP=AMT)    /* DATA TO BE REPORTED */
   SPECDATA(KEEP=&COLUMN); /* DATA TO GENERATE COL VARS */
  SET COSTDATA;  /* SORTED INPUT DATA */
  BY &SORT1 &SORT2 &SORT3 &SORT4 &SORT5  /* PAGE SORTS */
    CEC                /* FIXED ROW VARIABLE OF REPORT */
    &COLUMN;           /* COLUMN VARIABLE OF REPORT */
  AMT + AMOUNT;
  IF LAST.&COLUMN THEN /* LAST OCCURENCE OF EACH DATA VALUE */
    DO;
      AMOUNT = AMT; /* MOVE SUMMED VALUE INTO AMOUNT */
      AMT    = 0;
      OUTPUT;          /* OUTPUT SUMMED VALUES */
    END;
RUN;
```

```
PROC SORT DATA = COSTDATA;
 BY ORG                    /* &SORT1 HAS RESOLVED TO ORG */
   CEC
   YEAR;          /* &COLUMN HAS RESOLVED TO YEAR */
RUN;

DATA NEWDATA(DROP=AMT)
     SPECDATA(KEEP=YEAR); /* &COLUMN RESOLVED TO YEAR */
  SET COSTDATA;
BY ORG                      /* &SORT1 RESOLVED TO ORG */
   CEC
   YEAR;        /* &COLUMN RESOLVED TO YEAR */
AMT + AMOUNT;
IF LAST.YEAR THEN /* &COLUMN RESOLVED TO YEAR */
  DO;
    AMOUNT = AMT;
    AMT    = 0;
    OUTPUT;
  END;
RUN;
```

3. SPECDATA, the data set containing only the data values of the selected column variable, is sorted by those data values. Then, in the subsequent Data Step, Macro variables of each of the data values of the column variable are created using CALL SYMPUT. Each Macro variable begins with the string 'VAR' and ends in an integer representing the sort order of the column attribute to be loaded into that variable. For example, if the column variable is YEAR and the data values of YEAR are 1990, 1991, 1992, 1993, 1994, and 1995, Macro variables VAR1 through VAR5 will be loaded with 1990 through 1995. An underscore (__) will be added to the beginning of each string, since SAS variable names cannot begin with integers. Also, using CALL SYMPUT, the total number of columns that will be printed will be loaded at the end-of-file to the Macro variable &TOT__COLS. The value of &TOT__COLS will be used to control the interative %DO loops that will generate the SAS code that sums all column variables into the TOTAL variable and that writes the column data and headings during the DATA __NULL__ print step;

```
/* SORT DATA VALUES OF COLUMN VARIABLE */
PROC SORT DATA = SPECDATA;
  BY &COLUMN;
RUN;

/* CREATE MACRO VARIABLES FOR COL VARIABLES OF REPORT */
 DATA __NULL__;
  SET SPECDATA END=EOF; /* DATA TO GENERATE COL VARIABLES */
  BY &COLUMN;
  IF FIRST.&COLUMN THEN /* FIRST OCCURENCE OF EACH VALUE */
    DO;
```

```
PROC SORT DATA = SPECDATA;
  BY YEAR;      /* &COLUMN HAS RESOLVED TO YEAR */
RUN;

DATA __NULL__;
  SET SPECDATA END=EOF;
  BY YEAR;      /* &COLUMN HAS RESOLVED TO YEAR */
  IF FIRST.YEAR THEN
    DO;
```

---------------------------- MACRO CODE ----------------------------

```
/* INCREMENT J BY ONE FOR EACH UNIQUE DATA VALUE */
J + 1;
/* CONVERT J TO AN ALPHANUMERIC. LOAD TO TOT_COLS. */
TOT_COLS = LEFT(PUT(J,2));
/* BUILD NAMES OF MACRO VARIABLES BY CONCATENATING */
/* TOT_COLS TO THE END OF THE STRING 'VAR' AND THEN */
/* LOADING THAT RESULTING STRING TO THE VARIABLE VAR. */
VAR = 'VAR' || TOT_COLS;
/* LOAD THE NEW SAS COL VARIABLE NAMES TO MACRO */
/* VARIABLES. PREFIX NUMERIC VALUES WITH AN '_' */
/* IN ORDER THAT THE VARIABLE NAME WILL BE LEGAL. */
/* THE RESULTING MACRO VARIABLES WILL BE &VAR1, &VAR2, */
/* &VAR3, ETC.                                      */
IF SUBSTR(&COLUMN,1,1) GE '0' AND
   SUBSTR(&COLUMN,1,1) LE '9' THEN
     CALL SYMPUT(VAR,('_' ||&COLUMN));
ELSE
     CALL SYMPUT(VAR,&COLUMN);
END;
/* LOAD TOTAL NUMBER OF COLUMN VARIABLES TO &TOT_COLS */
/* FOR USE IN CONTROLLING INTERATIVE %DO LOOPS.       */
IF EOF THEN
  CALL SYMPUT('TOT_COLS',TOT_COLS);
RUN;
```

---------------------- RESOLVED SAS CODE ----------------------

```
J + 1;

TOT_COLS = LEFT(PUT(J,2));

VAR ='VAR' || TOT_COLS;

/* &COLUMN HAS RESOLVED TO YEAR */
IF SUBSTR(YEAR,1,1) GE '0' AND
   SUBSTR(YEAR,1,1) LE '9' THEN
  CALL SYMPUT(VAR,('_' || YEAR));
ELSE
  CALL SYMPUT(VAR,YEAR);
END;

IF EOF THEN
  CALL SYUMPUT('TOT_COLS',TOT_COLS);
RUN;
```

4. The next Data Step transposes the data, creating numeric SAS column variables from the data values of the selected column variable. An iterative %DO loop generates IF-THEN-ELSE statements that assign the data values of the column variable to new variables having the same name as the data value. Beginning underscores (_) are excluded from the evaluation since they were added to the beginning of the Macro variable in order that the forthcoming SAS variable would have a legal SAS name.

```
/* TRANSPOSE DATA FOR REPORT */
DATA RPTDATA(DROP=AMOUNT &COLUMN); /* TRANSPOSED DATA SET */
 SET SUMDATA END=EOF;        /* SORTED AND SUMMED DATA */
 BY &SORT1 &SORT2 &SORT3 &SORT4 &SORT5 CEC;
 /*    CREATE A COLUMN VARIABLE FOR EACH DATA VALUE    */
 /* BY ASSIGNING THE NUMERIC TOTAL FOR THAT DATA VALUE TO */
 /* THE RELATED COL VARIABLE USING IF STATEMENTS JOINED */
 /* TO ASSIGNMENT STATEMENTS.                          */
 %DO J = 1 %TO &TOT_COL;
  /* GENERATE AN ELSE STATEMENT FOR EACH IF STATEMENT */
  /* EXCEPT THE FIRST.                                */
  %IF &J NE 1 %THEN
    %DO;
       ELSE
    %END;
     /* DROP BEGINNING UNDERSCORES (_) FOR THE          */
     /* EVALUATION USED TO CREATE NEW COLUMN VARIABLES.*/
     %IF %SUBSTR(&&VAR&J,1,1) = _ %THEN
       %DO;
         %LET DISTANCE = %EVAL(%LENGTH(&&VAR&J)-1);
         %LET READVAR = %SUBSTR(&&VAR&J,2,&DISTANCE);
       %END;
     %ELSE
         %LET READVAR = &&VAR&J;
     /*    GENERATE THE IF-STATEMENTS TO ASSIGN THE     */
     /* NUMERIC VALUES TO THE NEW COLUMN VARIABLES. */
     IF &COLUMN = "&READVAR" THEN
         &&VAR&J = AMOUNT;
%END;
/*  AT THE LAST OCCURRENCE OF EACH DATA VALUE OF THE  */
/* FIXED ROW VARIABLE, OUTPUT ALL COL VARIABLES TO THE */
/* TRANSPOSED DATA SET. THEN SET THEIR VALUES TO MISSING. */
```

```
DATA RPTDATA(DROP=AMOUNT YEAR); /* &COL RESOLVED TO YEAR */
  SET SUMDATA END=EOF;
  BY ORG CEC; /* &SORT1 RESOLVED TO ORG */

/*    IF-THEN-ELSE STATEMENTS TO CREATE SAS VARIABLES    */
/* FROM THE UNIQUE DATA VALUES OF THE SELECTED COLUMN */
/* VARIABLE HAVE BEEN GENERATED.                          */
IF      YEAR = "1990" THEN
  _1990 = AMOUNT;
ELSE IF YEAR = "1991" THEN
  _1991 = AMOUNT;
ELSE IF YEAR = "1992" THEN
  _1992 = AMOUNT;
ELSE IF YEAR = "1993" THEN
  _1993 = AMOUNT;
ELSE IF YEAR = "1994" THEN
  _1994 = AMOUNT;
ELSE IF YEAR = "1995" THEN
  _1995 = AMOUNT;
```

------------------------------ MACRO CODE ------------------------------

```
IF LAST.CEC THEN
  DO;
    OUTPUT;
    /* GENERATE SAS CODE TO SET VARIABLES TO MISSING. */
    %DO J = 1 %TO &TOT_COL;
      &&VAR&J = .;
    %END;
  END;
RUN;
```

------------------------ RESOLVED SAS CODE ------------------------

```
IF LAST.CEC THEN
  DO;
    OUTPUT;
    /* SAS CODE HAS BEEN GENERATED */
    /* TO SET THE NEW COLUMN VARIABLES TO */
    /* MISSING (.) AFTER OUTPUT. */
    _1990 = .;
    _1991 = .;
    _1992 = .;
    _1993 = .;
    _1994 = .;
    _1995 = .;
  END;
RUN;
```

5A. In the Data _Null_ Step that writes the report, a new logical page is printed each time there is a change in the data value of the last sort variable specified. The Macro code uses a %DO %WHILE loop to determine the last sort variable specified by the user.

```
DATA _NULL_; /* REPORT-WRITING STEP */
  SET RPTDATA;       /* TRANSPOSED REPORT DATA */
  FILE PRINT;
  BY &SORT1 &SORT2 &SORT3 &SORT4 &SORT5 CEC;
  %LET LASTSORT =   ; /* SET LASTSORT TO BLANK */
  %LET J = 1;         /* INITIALIZE J TO ONE (1) */
  /* DO WHILE SORT VARIABLES ARE NOT BLANK    */
  %DO %WHILE (&&SORT&J NE     );
    /* LOAD SORT VARIABLE INTO LASTSORT */
    %LET LASTSORT = &&SORT&J;
    %LET J = %EVAL(&J + 1); /* ADD ONE (1) TO J */
  %END;
  /* IF &LASTSORT IS NOT EQUAL TO BLANK, THEN ISSUE */
  /* THE SAS CODE TO PRINT A NEW LOGICAL PRINT PAGE. */
  %IF &LASTSORT NE %THEN
    %DO;
      IF FIRST.&LASTSORT THEN
        PUT _PAGE_;
    %END;
```

```
DATA _NULL_;
  SET RPTDATA;
  FILE PRINT;
  BY ORG CEC; /* &SORT1 RESOLVED TO ORG */

  /* &LASTSORT RESOLVED TO ORG */
  IF FIRST.ORG THEN
    PUT _PAGE_;
```

5B. In the Data _Null_ Step, a TOTAL variable is created by a SUM of the column variables generated by an iterative %DO loop. That loop is controlled by the &TOT_COL value that represents the number of column variables which were created in the TRANSPOSE step. The variables are generated using double resolution.

```
TOTAL = SUM(OF
  /* GENERATE SAS VARIABLES TO BE SUMMED INTO TOTAL */
  %DO J = 1 %TO &TOT_COL;
      &&VAR&J
    %END;
      );
```

```
TOTAL = SUM(OF _1991 _1991 _1992 _1993 _1994 _1995);
```

5C. In the Data _Null_ Step, the left-hand descriptive variable and the generated SAS column variables are written using an iterative %DO loop controlled by &TOT_COL. The pointer position for the PUT statements is controlled by &POSITION, which is initialized to 35 and advanced by 12 (the length of the numeric fields + 1) for each pass through the loop. The %EVAL function is used to add 12 to &POSITION.

```
%LET POSITION = 35;
PUT @ 3 CEC $CEC. /* LEFT-HAND DESCRIPTIVE VARIABLE */
  %DO J = 1 %TO &TOT_COL;
    /* PRINT LOCATION AND FORMAT OF EACH COLUMN */
    @&POSITION &&VAR&J COMMA11.
    /* CALCULATE NEXT PRINT POSITION */
    %LET POSITION = %EVAL(&POSITION + 12);
  %END;
    /* PRINT POSITION AND FORMAT OF TOTAL COLUMN */
    @&POSITION TOTAL COMMA13.;
```

```
PUT  @ 3 CEC $CEC30.
     @ 35 _1990 COMMA11. @ 47 _1991 COMMA11.
     @ 59 _1992 COMMA11. @ 71 _1993 COMMA11.
     @ 83 _1994 COMMA11. @ 95 _1995 COMMA11.
     @ 107 TOTAL COMMA13.;
```

------------------------------ MACRO CODE ------------------------------ ------------------------ RESOLVED SAS CODE ------------------------

5D. In the HEADER area of the Data _Null_ Step, the character string 'TOTAL' is printed just below the titles of the report if &LASTVAR is blank, which occurs when the user does not specify one or more sort variables. Otherwise, the values of the page-sort variables are printed just below the report's titles.

```
%IF &LASTVAR =   %THEN
  %DO;
        PUT     @18 'TOTAL';
  %END;
%ELSE
  %DO;                                                    /* ORG WAS SPECIFIED AS &SORT1 */
        PUT     @18 &SORT1  @50 &SORT2 /                  PUT @18 ORG //;
                @18 &SORT3  @50 &SORT4 /
                @18 &SORT5  ;
  %END;
```

5E. In the HEADER area of the Data _Null_ Step, the descriptive headings of each numeric column are generated using an iterative %DO loop controlled by &TOT_COLS. &POSITION is again used to control the pointer position for the PUT statement that writes the descriptive headings. Here, however, it is used with the %LENGTH value of the character string that is to be printed. The length of character string is subtracted from 11 (the numeric field width) and that difference is added to the &POSITION value using the %EVAL function. For example, if the string were '_1990', the %LENGTH value would be 5 and, thus, 6 (11-5) would be added to the value of &POSITION. Adding 6 to &POSITION places the '_1990' string at the right-most 5-character position of the numeric field.

```
%LET POSITION = 35;
PUT                                                       PUT @35 "_1990" @ 53 "_1991"
%DO J = 1 %TO &TOT_COL;                                       @ 66 "_1992" @ 78 "_1993"
  /* CALCULATE LENGTH OF HEADING STRING */                    @ 90 "_1994" @102 "_1995"
  %LET Y   = %LENGTH(&&VAR&J);                                @114 "TOTAL";
  /* CALCULATE STARTING LOCATION OF HEADING STRING */
  %LET START = %EVAL(&POSITION+(11-&Y));
  /* ISSUE HEADING STRING TO BE WRITTEN TO PRINT FILE */
  @&START "&VAR&J"
  /* DETERMINE LOCATION OF NEXT HEADING STRING */
  %LET POSITION = %EVAL(&POSITION + 12);
%END;
  /* LOAD LENGTH OF TOTAL STRING TO Y */
  %LET Y = 5;
  /* CALCULATE STARTING LOCATION OF TOTAL STRING */
  % LET Z = %EVAL(&POSITION+(13-&Y));
  /* ISSUE TOTAL STRING */
  @&Z "TOTAL";
```

EXPLANATION OF MACRO TECHNIQUES USED IN PROGRAM.

1. Define a Macro variable with a %LET statement.

   %LET COLUMNS = YEAR;

   A character string can be directly asigned to a Macro variable using the %LET statement. %LET statements can appear anywhere in a SAS program. See pages 72-73, *SAS Guide to Macro Processing, Version 5.*

2. Simple Macro variable substitution.

   &COLUMN

   Whenever the Macro processor sees an ampersand (&) joined immediately to a character string, it searches the appropriate symbol table for a Macro variable of that name and substitutes the character string stored there for the Macro variable. Macro Variables can be used anywhere in a SAS program. See pages 24-25, *SAS Guide to Macro Processing, Version 5.*

3. Define a Macro variable with the CALL SYMPUT function.

   CALL SYMPUT(VAR,YEAR) CALL SYMPUT('TOT__COLS',TOT__COLS)

   CALL SYMPUT(argument1,argument2) assigns the string value in argument2 to the Macro variable in argument1. Argument1 may be a quoted string, such as 'TOT__COLS', or it may be a SAS variable containing a character string, such as VAR, which contains the strings 'VAR1', 'VAR2', etc. Argument2 may be a quoted character string or a SAS variable. CALL SYMPUT can only be used in a Data Step. See pages 124-129, *SAS Guide to Macro Processing, Version 5.*

4. Iterative %DO loops.

   ```
   %DO J = 1 %TO &TOT__COL;
     &&VAR&J = .;
   %END;
   ```

   An iterative %DO loop repeats the actions inside the loop until the control variable of the loop equals the upper bound of the loop. It has a built-in counter that increments the value of the control loop after each pass through the loop. In this example where &TOT__COL = 6, the &&VAR&J will be resolved six times and the strings resulting from '&&VAR&J = .;' will be emitted six times. See pages, 54-55 *SAS Guide to Macro Processing, Version 5.*

5. %IF-%THEN conditional execution.

   ```
   %IF &J NE 1 %THEN
     %DO;
       ELSE
     %END;
   ```

   SAS statements located within an %IF-%THEN statement are emitted only when that statement evaluates to true. In this example, the ELSE statement will be released only when &J is not equal to 1. See pages 12 and 66, *SAS Guide to Macro Processing, Version 5.*

6. %SUBSTR function.

   %SUBSTR(&&VAR&J,2,4)

   The %SUBSTR(argument,starting position,length) function returns a substring of characters. It begins its substring operation at the starting position identified in the function and continues for a length specified in the function. If &&VAR&J resolves to __1990, the returned string would be 1990. See page 102-103, *SAS Guide to Macro Processing, Version 5.*

7. %LENGTH function.

   %LENGTH(&&VAR&J)

   The %LENGTH(argument) function returns the number of characters in the resolved value of the argument it is examining. If the resolved value is __1990, the length would be five (5). See page 96, *SAS Guide to Macro Processing, Version 5.*

8. %EVAL function.

   %EVAL(%LENGTH(&&VAR&J)-1)

   The %EVAL function performs simple integer arithmetic that does not involve integers greater than 2**32-1. In this example, it subtracts one (1) from the integer value returned from the %LENGTH function. Here, that would be 5, so the value returned by the %EVAL function would be 4 (5 - 1). See page 95, *SAS Guide to Macro Processing, Version 5.*

9. Double resolution of Macro variables inside of %DO loops.

   ```
   %DO J = 1 %TO &TOT__COL;
     &&VAR&J = .;
   %END;
   ```

   Double resolution results from the Macro processor's orientation to change double ampersands to a single ampersand (&) during each scanning of the tokens and then to rescan any strings resulting from a resolution. Thus, a resolved string is scanned at least twice.

   When J = 1, &&VAR&J resolves to &VAR1 after the first pass of tokenization. The && becomes a single &, the VAR remains as is, and the &J becomes a 1, creating &VAR1. Then, during the second pass, &VAR1 resolves to the string stored in the symbol table for that variable, which — in this example — is the SAS variable __1990. No further resolution occurs during the third pass, so the complete string emitted by this %DO loop would be '__1990 = .;'. %DO loops can occur only within the Macro code of a SAS program. See pages 6-8 and 28-31, *SAS Guide to Macro Processing, Version 5.*

10. %DO %WHILE loops.

    ```
    %LET J =1;
    %DO %WHILE(&&SORT&J NE   );
        %LET LASTSORT = &&SORT&J;
        %LET J = %EVAL(&J + 1);
    %END;
    ```

    A %DO %WHILE loop repeats the actions within the loop while a condition holds true. The evaluation occurs at the top of the loop, so the actions of the loop are never performed if the condition is untrue initially. Usually, %DO %WHILE loops are used with a counter that is explicitly initialized before the loop is started and explicitly incremented at the bottom of the loop before the control condition is evaluated. Like iterative %DO loops, %DO %WHILE loops can occur only within the Macro code of a SAS program. See page 59, *SAS Guide to Macro Processing, Version 5.*

THREE REPORT EXAMPLES

REPORT GENERATED FROM COLUMN = NRRC (NON-RECURRING/RECURRING).

08/27/90 15:07:49
General Dynamics
Fort Worth Division — Fort Worth, Texas

STANDARD FUNCTIONAL COST SUMMARY

TOTAL

	N_RECRNG	RECURRNG	TOTAL
HOURS			
Engineering			
Research & Engineering	0	44,239	44,239
Electronic Systems	0	3,422	3,422
Electronic Systems ICL	0	3,161	3,161
F-16 Program Mgmt.	0	9,741	9,741
F-16 Program Office	0	3,840	3,840
Logistics	659	29,941	30,600
Total Engr. Direct Hours	659	94,344	95,003
Manufacturing			
Tool Engineering	0	16,562	16,562
Tool Manufacturing Airframe	0	8,000	8,000
Tool Manufacturing Mse.	0	3,014	3,014
Plant Engineering	215	91	306
Factory Fabrication	0	39,116	39,116
Factory Assembly	0	86,155	86,155
Electronic Bench	0	33,232	33,232
Field Operations	0	24,370	24,370
Mod & Test Aircraft	0	307	307
Quality Assurance	0	725	725
Total Mfg. Direct Hours	215	211,572	211,787

REPORT GENERATED FROM COLUMN = PRRE (PRODUCTION/RETROFIT).

08/27/90 15:07:49
General Dynamics
Fort Worth Division — Fort Worth, Texas

STANDARD FUNCTIONAL COST SUMMARY

TOTAL

	PRDCTION	RETROFIT	TOTAL
HOURS			
Engineering			
Research & Engineering	44,139	100	44,239
Electronic Systems	3,422	0	3,422
Electronic Systems ICL	3,161	0	3,161
F-16 Program Mgmt.	9,741	0	9,741
F-16 Program Office	3,840	0	3,840
Logistics	30,600	0	30,600
Total Engr. Direct Hours	94,903	100	95,003
Manufacturing			
Tool Engineering	16,562	0	16,562
Tool Manufacturing Airframe	8,000	0	8,000
Tool Manufacturing Mse.	3,014	0	3,014
Plant Engineering	306	0	306
Factory Fabrication	39,116	0	39,116
Factory Assembly	86,155	0	86,155
Electronic Bench	33,232	0	33,232
Field Operations	24,370	0	24,370
Mod & Test Aircraft	307	0	307
Quality Assurance	725	0	725
Total Mfg. Direct Hours	211,787	0	211,787

REPORT GENERATED FROM COLUMN = YEAR (CALENDAR YEAR).

08/27/90 15:07:49
General Dynamics
Fort Worth Division — Fort Worth, Texas

STANDARD FUNCTIONAL COST SUMMARY

TOTAL

	_1988	_1989	_1990	_1991	_1992	TOTAL
HOURS						
Engineering						
Research & Engineering	0	337	4,669	23,819	15,414	44,239
Electronic Systems	0	0	0	379	3,043	3,422
Electronic Systems ICL	0	0	0	1,283	1,878	3,161
F-16 Program Mgmt	0	0	0	1,048	8,693	9,741
F-16 Program Office	0	0	0	413	3,427	3,840
Logistics	246	91	5,794	10,017	14,452	30,600
Total Engr. Direct Hours	246	428	10,463	36,959	46,907	95,003
Manufacturing						
Tool Engineering	0	0	212	14,319	2,031	16,562
Tool Manufacturing Airframe	0	0	102	6,910	988	8,000
Tool Manufacturing MSE	0	0	354	2,128	532	3,014
Plant Engineering	0	0	34	204	68	306
Factory Fabrication	0	0	1,855	37,033	228	39,116
Factory Assembly	0	0	1,716	74,149	10,297	86,155
Electronic Bench	0	0	229	32,609	394	33,232
Field Operations	0	0	996	11,540	11,864	24,370
Mod & Test Aircraft	0	0	1	203	103	307
Quality Assurance	0	0	0	78	647	7825
Total Mfg. Direct Hours	0	0	5,469	179,116	27,152	211,787

Putting the Pieces Together: Applying Advanced SAS® Macro Techniques to Everyday Problems

Jim C. Knoop, Aetna Life & Casualty, Hartford, CT

Abstract

This tutorial illustrates how SAS Macro features can drastically reduce the amount of maintenance needed by a macro-based reporting system. It also illustrates techniques which help prevent types of everyday problems encountered in a multi-programmer, shared-code environment. More emphasis is placed on the creative use of SAS macros than on their syntax.

Introduction

Over a dozen information specialists and SAS programmers were brought together to implement a reporting system with the following attributes:

- each report program was structured as a self-contained SAS macro, stored in an autocall library.
- code common to more than one report was defined as a macro, and referenced throughout multiple programs.
- explicit references to specific data sets, dates, etc. were eliminated.
- report titles, footnotes and cover pages were standardized, to promote a "common look".

As new ideas surfaced, and enhancements were proposed, we gained considerable experience modifying macros to provide new functionality, without having to convert existing programs which referenced them.

Although only a few examples are presented here, each represents a useful principle, and is well-suited for adaptation.

Overview

This tutorial is organized in the following sections:

- Symbolic Reference to SAS Data Sets
- A Few Macro Quoting Tips
- Undefined Macro Variables
- Minimizing Maintenance
- Upward Compatibility

Each section introduces a few examples and techniques which can be readily adapted to other uses. As you will see, however, none of the sections provide comprehensive or in-depth coverage of the subject matter.

SYMBOLIC REFERENCE TO SAS DATA SETS

SAS Data Sets on Disk

Our data sets are stored in the following SAS libraries on disk: DAILY, WEEKLY, MONTHEND and YEAREND.

Data sets stored in these libraries are named according to the date the data reflect (i.e., YEAREND.DEC92, MONTHEND.APR93, DAILY.MAY93, etc.).

Only one data set is stored in each of these disk libraries, reflecting the most recent year-end, month-end, weekly or daily file.

Macros were created for each library's data set to reflect their current names, and are stored in an autocall library.

For example:

```
%MACRO YEAREND;        %MACRO MONTHEND:
  DEC92                  APR93
%MEND YEAREND;         %MEND MONTHEND:
```

All SAS programs refer to these data sets symbolically:

```
DATA EXTRACT;                DATA TODAY;
SET MONTHEND.%MONTHEND;      SET DAILY.%DAILY;
etc.                         etc.
RUN;                         RUN;
```

Instead of *manually* changing the values of the MONTHEND, WEEKLY and DAILY macros in the autocall library whenever their contents change, these macros are instead updated by the same program that loads raw data into SAS data sets.

This is possible since each of our database extract files contains a field (Rundate) which reflects the "date-of-interest" of the raw data file.

Consider the following macro:

```
%MACRO _MACLOAD ( MACNAME );

DATA _NULL_;
INFILE RAWDATA;
INPUT @1705 RUNDATE $CHAR8.;    /*  yyyymmdd   */
LENGTH YY $ 2 MMM $ 3 ;
YY = SUBSTR(RUNDATE,3,2);
MMM = UPCASE(
   PUT(INPUT(RUNDATE,YYMMDD8.),MONNAME3.));
CALL SYMPUT("&MACNAME", MMM || YY);
STOP;
RUN;

DATA _NULL_;
FILE AHRLIB(&MACNAME);
PUT  @1      '%MACRO '  "&MACNAME;" /
     @1      "&MACNAME"             /
     @1      '%MEND '   "&MACNAME;" ;
STOP;
RUN;

%MEND _MACLOAD;
```

For example, the SAS program which loads raw data into the WEEKLY library contains the following macro call, which updates the contents of macro WEEKLY when the program is run:

```
%_MACLOAD (WEEKLY)
```

SAS Data Sets on Tape

All historical month-end data sets are stored on cartridge, using a naming convention of MMMYY (i.e., MAR92, OCT91, etc). Since these data sets are catalogued, they can be accessed via the following macro:

```
%MACRO HISTOPEN
       (DSN=,DATASET=,DDNAME=HISTORY,
       DISP=OLD,ENGINE=TAPE,UNIT=T3480,LABEL=);

OPTIONS FILEDEV=&UNIT;

%IF &DSN EQ AND &DATASET NE %THEN
       %LET DSN=F4WB.PB.SB.&DATASET;

%IF &DISP  NE %THEN %LET DISP = DISP=&DISP;

%IF &LABEL NE %THEN %LET LABEL = LABEL=&LABEL;

%IF &ENGINE EQ TAPE %THEN %LET ENGINE = ;

%IF &UNIT EQ T3480 %THEN %LET UNITX =;
%ELSE %LET UNITX = UNIT=&UNIT;

LIBNAME  &DDNAME  &ENGINE  "&DSN"  &DISP  &UNITX
  &LABEL;

%MEND HISTOPEN;
```

Sample Usage:

```
%HISTOPEN ( DATASET = MAR92 )
DATA EXTRACT;
SET HISTORY.MAR92;
etc.
RUN;
```

Examples

To access month-end data, as well as data for the same time a year ago:

```
DATA THISYEAR;
SET MONTHEND.%MONTHEND;
etc.
RUN;

%LET YEARAGO =
   %SUBSTR(%MONTHEND,1,3)%EVAL(%SUBSTR(
   %MONTHEND,4,2)-1);

%HISTOPEN (DATASET=&YEARAGO)

DATA LASTYEAR;
SET HISTORY.&YEARAGO;
etc.
RUN;
```

To load the formatted date of the last day of the month for data sets THISYEAR and LASTYEAR (for use in Titles, variable labels, etc.):

```
DATA _NULL_;
OLDDATE=PUT(INTNX('MONTH',"01%MONTHEND"D,1)
  -1,MMDDYY8.);
NEWDATE=PUT(INTNX('MONTH',"01&YEARAGO"D,1)
  -1,MMDDYY8.);
CALL SYMPUT('OLDDATE',OLDDATE);
CALL SYMPUT('NEWDATE',NEWDATE);
STOP;
RUN;
```

If %MONTHEND resolved to FEB93, this would produce **02/29/92** and **02/28/93** for &OLDDATE and &NEWDATE, respectively.

A FEW MACRO QUOTING TIPS

The Implicit %EVAL

SAS automatically invokes the %EVAL function with %DO (iterative), %DO %UNTIL, %DO WHILE, %SUBSTR, %QSUBSTR, %SCAN, %QSCAN and **%IF**.

%IF can be tricky when used within a macro to test macro arguments for specific values (including null), if the value assigned to the argument at macro invocation might contain SAS operators or other characters which require quoting.

For example, if a macro has a parameter (VARLIST=) which is supplied the value of VAR1-VAR10 when invoked, a statement such as **%IF &VARLIST EQ %THEN** ... will need to be quoted:

```
%IF %QUOTE(&VARLIST) EQ %THEN ...

        or

%IF %BQUOTE(&VARLIST) EQ %THEN ...
```

The %IF statement above (without quoting) may work fine for years without any problem, depending on what values are passed to the VARLIST parameter at macro invocation.

Then, seemingly out of nowhere, you might encounter an error (with a rather cryptic message), whose cause is far from obvious.

Using Macro Variables in Macro Calls

With 14 different SAS programmers producing thousands of reports each year, we like to include the name, phone number and internal mail code of the developer in a footnote to each report.

If any of this information changes, it is not feasible to change each individual report. Thus, each of our reports contains the following, at the very beginning of each program:

%LET INITIALS = xxx ;

where 'xxx' refers to the programmer's initials.

The following macros are stored in an autocall library for each programmer (we'll use myself as an example):

```
%MACRO NAMEJCK;
   JIM KNOOP
%MEND NAMEJCK;

%MACRO FONEJCK;
  (203) 636-3553
%MEND FONEJCK;

%MACRO MAILJCK;
   MC19
%MEND MAILJCK;
```

In a program, all I do is define **%LET INITIALS = JCK;** at the beginning, and call a macro which (among other things) does the following:

```
%LET NAME = %UNQUOTE(%NRSTR(%NAME)&INITIALS);
%LET FONE = %UNQUOTE(%NRSTR(%FONE)&INITIALS);
%LET MAIL = %UNQUOTE(%NRSTR(%MAIL)&INITIALS);

%LET F3A=NOTE: CONTACT &NAME AT &FONE/&MAIL FOR;
%LET F3B = QUESTIONS OR CHANGES TO THIS REPORT;

FOOTNOTE3 "&F3A  &F3B";
```

UNDEFINED MACRO VARIABLES

Our unit's SAS coding standards require that certain macro variables be defined at the beginning of each SAS program.

A few examples include:

```
%LET INITIALS=JCK;              /* programmer initials */
%LET PROGRAM=RPT6029;           /* report name         */

%LET RNAME=J. SMITH;            /* requestor name      */
%LET RMAIL=MB65;                /* requestor address   */

%LET MNAME=SUSAN WRIGHT;        /* mail-to name        */
%LET MMAIL=&RMAIL;              /* mail-to address     */
```

A variety of macros which produce consistent titles, footnotes and cover pages for our reports ***assume*** that these macro variables have been previously defined.

Therefore, these macros call a utility macro (stored in an autocall library) to test this assumption:

```
%MACRO _EXIST_ (NAME);
%IF %NRBQUOTE(&&&NAME) EQ %NRSTR(&)&NAME
   %THEN 0;
%ELSE 1;
%MEND _EXIST_;
```

Note that the argument to macro _EXIST_ is a macro variable's ***name***, and not its value. So, to test if macro variable INITIALS exists, use %_EXIST(INITIALS), and ***not*** %_EXIST(&INITIALS).

Unless, of course, &INITIALS resolves to the name of a macro variable (in this case, JCK) whose existence you wanted to verify.

At first glance, Macro _EXIST_ might appear to be bewildering.

However, given the statement **%IF %_EXIST_(INITIALS)** produces the following:

INITIALS	%IF Condition	%_EXIST_
Defined-(JCK)	JCK EQ &INITIALS	1
Undefined	&INITIALS EQ &INITIALS	0

To avoid a "Warning: Apparent Symbolic Reference Not Resolved" message, use OPTIONS NOSERROR; before calling %_EXIST_:

```
%MACRO COMPUTE;
OPTIONS NOSERROR;
%IF %_EXIST_(TOTAL) %THEN etc. ;
%ELSE etc. ;
OPTIONS SERROR;
%MEND COMPUTE;
```

PARMBUFF Option

Use of the PARMBUFF option on the %MACRO statement can be useful when you need to know if a macro was called without any parameters defined, or if a certain parameter was assigned a value at macro invocation:

%MACRO BANNER (COPIES=1,CENTRAL=YES) / PARMBUFF;

We have two types of reports (ad-hoc and scheduled/production). The type of report can be determined at runtime by a macro variable called _MODE_.

For scheduled/production reports (_MODE_=PROD), we want the name and phone number of a single person who is responsible for maintaining and distributing reports to print in the footnote at the bottom of each report page.

For ad-hoc reports (_MODE_=ADHOC), we want the programmer's name and phone number to appear, ***unless*** the default value of CENTRAL is explicitly overridden.

By itself, the value &CENTRAL can't be used, since a YES value could either reflect the default that was assigned when the macro was created, or an actual parameter value specified when the macro was called.

```
%IF &_MODE_ EQ ADHOC %THEN %DO;

   %IF %LENGTH(&SYSPBUFF) EQ 0
       %THEN %LET CENTRAL=NO;

   %ELSE %IF %INDEX(&SYSPBUFF,CENTRAL=) EQ 0
       %THEN %LET CENTRAL=NO;

%END;
```

If &SYSPBUFF has a length of 0, then the macro was called without any parameters.

If the parameter list supplied when the macro was called did **not** include CENTRAL=, then the value of CENTRAL is changed to NO.

MINIMIZING MAINTENANCE

Nested Definitions

When using macros to define groups, create separate macros for the lowest-level definitions, and then include these macros in any broader definitions you might need:

```
%MACRO SALESREP;
   (( ALLOC EQ '129' OR ALLOC EQ '132') AND
   (JOBNO EQ '014119' OR JOBNO EQ '023502'))
%MEND SALESREP;

%MACRO SALESMGT;
   (GRADE GE '15' AND (ALLOC EQ '054 OR ALLOC EQ '275')
   AND (JOBNO EQ '016836' OR JOBNO EQ '021366'))
%MEND SALESMGT;

%MACRO SALES;
   (%SALESREP OR %SALESMGT)
%MEND SALES;
```

This way, changes to any group can usually be applied to a single source (in an autocall library) in order to take effect in a number of programs.

In the examples above, the entire contents of each macro have been enclosed in parentheses, to prevent any ambiguity in the order of evaluation of logical operators in statements such as:

```
IF %SALES AND NOT %NEWHIRE;
```

KEEP= Data Set Option

Our unit's coding standards also require that programmers use a KEEP= data set option on their SET statements, to restrict the number of variables that are read by a Data step. This reflects the fact that our SAS data sets are extremely large, whereas a typical program will only need a very small subset of variables.

With so many autocall macros referenced by a program, it is difficult to remember which variables are used by the macros called in the program.

Also, when a macro changes (i.e., references a new variable), it can be cumbersome to identify reports which might be impacted.

Our solution is to create macros similar to the following:

```
%MACRO SALEKEEP;
        ALLOC JOBNO GRADE
%MEND SALEKEEP;

%MACRO STFFKEEP;
        BHSTATUS STATUS ALLOC ALOCLOC
%MEND STFFKEEP;
```

These are used as follows:

```
DATA EXTRACT;
SET WEEKLY.%WEEKLY
        (KEEP=ID NAME %SALEKEEP %STFFKEEP);
IF %STFF AND %SALES;
etc.
RUN;
```

Future Use Considerations

Our data sets contain 20 levels of organization structure information (OSKEY01-OSKEY20), even though we are only using the first 10 levels at present.

```
%MACRO OSKEYEQ ( VALUE );
      %LET MIN = 1;        %LET MAX = 10;
      %LET COND = OR; %LET ROOT = OSKEY0;
   (  %DO N = &MIN %TO &MAX;
           %IF &N EQ &MAX %THEN %LET COND = ;
           %IF &N GE 10 %THEN %LET ROOT = OSKEY;
           &ROOT.&N  EQ  &VALUE  &COND
      %END; )
%MEND OSKEYEQ;
```

The macro call **IF %OSKEYEQ('04232');** produces:

IF (OSKEY01 EQ '04232' OR OSKEY02 EQ '04232' OR OSKEY03 EQ '04232' OR ... OSKEY10 EQ '04232');

```
%MACRO OSKEEP;
      %LET MIN = 1;        %LET MAX = 10;
   ( %DO N = &MIN %TO &MAX;
           %IF &N LT 10 %THEN OSKEY0&N;
           %ELSE OSKEY&N;
      %END; )
%MEND OSKEEP;
```

%OSKEEP produces

(OSKEY01 OSKEY02 OSKEY03 ... OSKEY10).

By changing the value of MAX in OSKEYEQ and OSKEEP from 10 to 20, we can allow for the future use of these variables, without modifying existing reports.

Historical Considerations

We load our SAS data sets from raw data extracts from various databases. Additions, deletions or changes to data elements result in changes to the record layouts of our raw data extracts.

Our SAS data set nomenclature takes the form of MMMYY (i.e., NOV92). Thus, we can use a single macro to construct an INPUT statement that, depending on the date of the raw data file, can locate each element in its proper place:

```
%MACRO LOADFILE (LIBRARY=,DS=,DDNAME=RAWDATA);

   DATA _NULL_;
   IF   "01&DS"D GE '01JAN92'D      THEN
                  CALL SYMPUT('V','3');
   ELSE
   IF   "01&DS"D GE '01JUL91'D      THEN
                  CALL SYMPUT('V','2');
   ELSE
   IF   "01&DS"D GE '01APR89'D      THEN
                  CALL SYMPUT('V','1');
   ELSE           CALL SYMPUT('V','0');
   STOP;
   RUN;

   DATA &LIBRARY..&DS;
   INFILE &DDNAME;
   INPUT          @1       ID                  $CHAR7.
                  @8       NAME                $CHAR20.
   %IF &V LT 3 %THEN
                  @45      DEPTUSE  $CHAR10.;
   %ELSE          @90      DEPTUSE  $CHAR5.;
                  @30      YTDPAY   PD5.2
   etc.  ;
   RUN;

%MEND LOADFILE;

Sample call:

%LOADFILE (LIBRARY=YEAREND,DS=DEC90)
```

AUTOEXEC= System Option

We use the AUTOEXEC= system option to point to a file containing SAS statements which will be executed when SAS is invoked.

Some of the statements we include in our SAS autoexec file are:

```
%LET _MODE_ = TEST;
%LET _WARN_ = ;
%LET _EMPTY_ =       WARNING:  NO OBSERVATIONS
                     MET REPORT SELECTION CRITERIA;

LIBNAME XLOG DISK 'F4WB.PB.XLOG' UNIT=SYSDA,
DISP=(MOD,DELETE,DELETE),SPACE=etc.;

etc.
```

This allows us to initialize and define certain macro variables that might be referenced by any macro invoked in a given SAS session or job.

Since changes can be applied to a single source, future maintenance is simplified considerably.

UPWARD COMPATIBILITY

Avoiding Conversion

Efforts to improve existing macros (used by many programmers in numerous applications) are usually hampered by conversion considerations.

When a better mousetrap has been acquired, nobody likes to expend time and money fixing the older models—even though it can be argued that they do, in fact, still work.

To stick with the old results in considerable opportunity costs.

Dual maintenance (of old and new) can be tedious, expensive, confusing for programmer/users, and risky (from a quality perspective).

We have developed some useful strategies which, in many cases, allow us to continuously improve our macros, without jeopardizing our investment in their older counterparts.

Adding Parameters

Consider the following macro, which produces a standard report for any area of the Company, sorted in a standard order:

```
%MACRO ORGLIST (SELECT=,TITLE=);
```

Users supply selection criteria and a title, and the appropriate report is produced. Numerous programs referencing macro ORGLIST are run weekly.

After a recent reorganization, the standard sort order was not useful for a few departments. Rather than create a separate version of the macro for these customers, a new parameter SORTBY= was added, and assigned a default value which reflected the original sort order:

```
%MACRO ORGLIST (SELECT=,TITLE=,SORTBY=LEVEL1
     LEVEL2 LEVEL3 LEVEL4 LASTNAME);
```

The PROC SORT statement in the original version of ORGLIST was changed,

from:

```
PROC SORT DATA=EXTRACT;
BY LEVEL1 LEVEL2 LEVEL3 LEVEL4 LASTNAME;
RUN;
```

to:

```
PROC SORT DATA=EXTRACT;
BY &SORTBY;
RUN;
```

Existing programs which call macro ORGLIST continue to produce the same results as before. However, new programs can change the sort order of their reports by simply specifying an appropriate value for SORTBY=.

Old Macros Calling New Macros

Consider the following macro, which joins two tables, dropping observations not found on both tables:

```
%MACRO JOINK (MAINFILE=,TABNO=,DATEVAR=,KEEP=);
```

A more robust version, with a different name, was developed a year later by another unit, which was based on the original JOINK macro:

```
%MACRO JOIN (MAINFILE=,TABNO=,DATEVAR=,KEEP=,
             DROP=,DDNAME=AHRTAB,SORTBY=,
             OUTFILE=&MAINFILE);
```

The two units, along with their respective SAS programs, were consolidated into one area.

JOINK was then redefined, as follows:

```
%MACRO JOINK (MAINFILE=,TABNO=,DATEVAR=,KEEP=,
              DROP=,DDNAME=AHRTAB,SORTBY=,
              OUTFILE=&MAINFILE) / PARMBUFF;

%UNQUOTE(%NRSTR(%JOIN)&SYSPBUFF)

%MEND JOINK;
```

In other words, every time macro %JOINK is now called in existing programs, the parameter list specified in the %JOINK macro call is actually passed to the %JOIN macro, which subsequently executes.

Conclusion

The preceeding examples represent only a small sample of the many and various applications of SAS macro techniques to improve the management and reduce the maintenance requirements of reporting systems. Hopefully, they will stimulate your thinking, and lead to new and useful ideas on your part.

Although not directly addressed here, performance and efficiency concerns need to be factored into your own design criteria.

Comments, suggestions and questions are welcome. The author can be reached at the following address:

Jim C. Knoop
Aetna Life & Casualty
MC19
151 Farmington Avenue
Hartford, CT 06156

Voice: (203) 636-3553
FAX: (203) 636-3573

USING SAS MACROS TO GENERATE CODE (SO YOUR PROGRAM CAN FIGURE OUT WHAT TO DO FOR ITSELF)

Nancy K. Blood

Center for Medico-Actuarial Statistics
MIB, Inc., Westwood, MA

ABSTRACT

Ever find yourself trying to maintain multiple versions of essentially the same program? Each version may produce summary statistics for different variables (for example, HEIGHT and WEIGHT), or select different subsets of data for analysis (males, females, or age groups) but the numeric variables, the labels and format statements remain the same.

The techniques presented here use the SAS macro facility to demonstrate how designing your programs to be adaptable eliminates the need for multiple versions. You will structure your programs to use unique parameters you identify to generate the desired code.

INTRODUCTION

Breaking complex programs into simpler modules is readily achieved using the macro facility. The autocall facility further simplifies your programming when the macro source code is stored in an external file and invoked when you need it. When macro program statements are used within these macro definitions, you'll see your programs generating SAS code, eliminating repetitive code.

THE SITUATION

Among the projects done at the Center for Medico-Actuarial Statistics are studies of mortality of insured lives. Processing a typical study includes editing the data for syntax errors and feasibility checking. After verifying the accuracy of the syntax of the data submitted, we're left with a SAS dataset with at least 8 character and 8 numeric variables. The next step is to produce preliminary summary statistics and ratios to check the feasibility of the contributed data. Instead of writing separate programs for all the different combinations of character values in CLASS and BY statements, I used macro variables and macro program statements to generate the desired code.

THE SOURCE CODE

```
%FMTS;

   %* FMTS is a user defined MACRO in the
   user supplied autocall library containing a
   PROC FORMAT.;

%LET SET = DATA.COMPANYA ;
 TITLE1 "&SET";
 DATA TEST;
 SET &SET;

%TABULAR ;

   %* TABULAR is a user defined MACRO in
   the user supplied autocall library. This
   Macro is defined in the next section.;

%TABULAR (VAR2=YEAR, TABLE=TABLE2,
BYE=SEX) ;

%TABULAR (VAR2=AGE, TABLE=TABLE4 ) ;
```

THE MACRO CODE

```
%MACRO FMTS;

 PROC FORMAT;

VALUE $SEX 'U'='UNKNOWN' 'M'='MALE
'F'='FEMALE' ' '='ALL SEXES';

   %* A value statement exists for each variable
   which may exist in the CLASS or BY
   statements. ;

%MEND FMTS;
```

```
%MACRO TABULAR (VAR1=DISABIL,
VAR2=TYPEGRP, TABLE=TABLE1, BYE= ) ;

   %* The macro variables are defined as
   macro parameters with default values as part
   of the %MACRO statement. Notice the value
   of &BYE is null. ;

%IF %LENGTH(&BYE)>0 %THEN %DO;
  PROC SORT DATA=TEST;  BY &BYE;
  %END;

   %* Sort the data only when necessary.
   Since the default value of &BYE is null, this
   code will be generated only when &BYE is
   passed a value at invocation;

PROC SUMMARY DATA=TEST NWAY
MISSING;

%IF %LENGTH (&BYE) > 0 %THEN BY &BYE;;

   %*Use a BY statement only when the macro
   variable &BYE has a value;

CLASS &VAR1 &VAR2;
VAR
   AMT_ACC AMT_DIS AMT_DTH AMT_EXP
   LIV_ACC LIV_DIS LIV_DTH LIV_EXP ;
OUTPUT OUT=SUMM SUM=;

 DATA &TABLE ;
  SET SUMM ;

   %* Indexing over a list using %DO I=a,b,c
   etc. is currently unavailable, but the
   following macro code is a fine substitute.
   This technique is indispensable when
   dealing with large lists;

 %LET LIST = ACC.DTH.DIS;

   %* Define the elements of the list ;

 %LET N=3;

   %* number of items;

 %DO I=1 %TO &N;
   %LET THIS =%SCAN(&LIST,%EVAL(&I));

   %* Assign the value of the Ith element of the
   list to the macro variable &THIS;

 &THIS.RAT= 1000 * LIV_&THIS/AMT_&THIS;
  %END;
   %*end list processing;

   %* dataset &TABLE is ready to print ;

 %PRINT;

%MEND TABULAR ;


%MACRO PRINT ;

   %* Assign values for list processing ;

 %LET LIST=DTH.ACC.DIS;
 %LET N = 3;

TITLE2 "&TABLE";
TITLE3 'GROUP LIFE EXPERIENCE STUDY';

 %DO I=1 %TO &N ;
 %LET THIS =%SCAN(&LIST,%EVAL(&I));

   %* The print procedure will be executed &N
   times- once for each value in &LIST ;

TITLE5 "&THIS FILE";

PROC PRINT DATA=&TABLE SPLIT='*';
%IF %LENGTH(&BYE)>0 %THEN %DO;
      BY &BYE;
      ID &VAR1 &VAR2 ;
      %END;
%ELSE
%IF %LENGTH(&VAR2)>0 %THEN %DO;
      BY &VAR1;
      ID &VAR2 ;
      %END;
%ELSE %DO;
      ID &VAR1 ;
      %END;

 VAR
   LIV_EXP LIV_&THIS &THIS.RAT_L AMT_EXP
   AMT_&THIS &THIS.RAT_A ;
 SUM
   LIV_EXP LIV_&THIS AMT_EXP AMT_&THIS;
```

```
 FORMAT
%IF %LENGTH(&BYE)>0 %THEN
    &BYE $&BYE..;

   %* if &BYE has a value of VALUE, then
   $&BYE.. will resolve to $VALUE. (The
   semicolon ends the %IF statement so it
   doesn't contribute to generated code;

   LIV_EXP LIV_&THIS COMMA12.
   &THIS.RAT_L 7.2 AMT_EXP AMT_&THIS
   DOLLAR15. &THIS.RAT_A 7.2
%IF %LENGTH(&VAR1)>0 %THEN &VAR1
$&VAR1.. ;
%IF %LENGTH(&VAR2)>0 %THEN &VAR2
$&VAR2.. ;
           ;     %* This semicolon ends the
                 FORMAT Statement;

LABEL  LIV_EXP = 'LIVES*YEARS EXP'
    LIV_&THIS = 'LIVES*TOTAL CLMS'
    &THIS.RAT = 'RATIO*LIVES*PER $1,000'
      AMT_EXP = 'AMOUNT*YEARS EXP'
    AMT_&THIS = 'AMOUNT*TOTAL CLMS'
      ;
    RUN;
    %END;

%MEND PRINT ;
```

MACRO RESOLUTIONS

```
   %* The first resolution of the macro
   TABULAR uses the default values of the
   macro parameters. Since the value of &BYE
   is null, no SORT code is generated. ;

PROC SUMMARY DATA=TEST NWAY
MISSING;
CLASS DISABIL TYPEGRP;
VAR
   AMT_ACC AMT_DIS AMT_DTH AMT_EXP
   LIV_ACC LIV_DIS LIV_DTH LIV_EXP;
OUTPUT OUT=SUMM SUM= ;

DATA TABLE1;
SET SUMM;
ACCRAT= 1000 * LIV_ACC/AMT_ACC;
DTHRAT= 1000 * LIV_DTH/AMT_DTH;
DISRAT= 1000 * LIV_DIS/AMT_DIS;

TITLE2 'TABLE1';
TITLE3 'GROUP LIFE EXPERIENCE STUDY';


TITLE5 'DTH FILE';

PROC PRINT DATA=TABLE1 SPLIT='*';
BY DISABIL;
ID TYPEGRP;
VAR
   LIV_EXP LIV_DTH AMT_EXP AMT_DTH
   DTHRAT;
SUM
   LIV_EXP LIV_DTH AMT_EXP AMT_DTH;
FORMAT
   LIV_EXP LIV_DTH COMMA12. AMT_EXP
   AMT_DTH DOLLAR15. DTHRAT6.2 DISABIL
   $DISABIL. TYPEGRP $TYPEGRP. ;

LABEL LIV_EXP = 'LIVES*YEARS EXP'
     LIV_DTH = 'LIVES*TOTAL CLMS'
     DTHRAT  = 'RATIO*LIVES*PER $1,000'
     AMT_EXP = 'AMOUNT*YEARS EXP'
     AMT_DTH = 'AMOUNT*TOTAL CLMS'
      ;
    RUN;


TITLE5 'ACC FILE';

PROC PRINT DATA=TABLE1 SPLIT='*';
BY DISABIL;
ID TYPEGRP;
VAR
   LIV_EXP LIV_ACC AMT_EXP AMT_ACC
   ACCRAT;
SUM
   LIV_EXP LIV_ACC AMT_EXP AMT_ACC;
FORMAT
   LIV_EXP LIV_ACC COMMA12. AMT_EXP
   AMT_ACC DOLLAR15. ACCRAT6.2 DISABIL
   $DISABIL. TYPEGRP $TYPEGRP. ;

LABEL LIV_EXP = 'LIVES*YEARS EXP'
     LIV_ACC = 'LIVES*TOTAL CLMS'
     ACCRAT  = 'RATIO*LIVES*PER $1,000
     AMT_EXP = 'AMOUNT*YEARS EXP'
     AMT_ACC = 'AMOUNT*TOTAL CLMS'
      ;
    RUN;
```

```
TITLE5 'DIS FILE';

PROC PRINT DATA=TABLE1 SPLIT='*';
BY DISABIL;
ID TYPEGRP;
VAR
   LIV_EXP LIV_DIS AMT_EXP AMT_DIS
   DISRAT;
SUM
   LIV_EXP LIV_DIS AMT_EXP AMT_DIS;
FORMAT
   LIV_EXP LIV_DIS COMMA12. AMT_EXP
   AMT_DIS DOLLAR15. DISRAT6.2 DISABIL
   $DISABIL. TYPEGRP $TYPEGRP. ;

LABEL LIV_EXP = 'LIVES*YEARS EXP'
    LIV_DIS = 'LIVES*TOTAL CLMS'
    DISRAT = 'RATIO*LIVES*PER $1,000'
    AMT_EXP = 'AMOUNT*YEARS EXP'
    AMT_DIS = 'AMOUNT*TOTAL CLMS'
     ;
    RUN;



   %* The following resolution of the macro
   TABULAR is generated form the call:
   %TABULAR (VAR2=YEAR, TABLE=TABLE2,
   BYE=SEX) ;

PROC SORT DATA = TEST;
BY SEX;

PROC SUMMARY DATA=TEST NWAY
MISSING;
BY SEX;
CLASS DISABIL YEAR;
VAR
   AMT_ACC AMT_DIS AMT_DTH AMT_EXP
   LIV_ACC LIV_DIS LIV_DTH LIV_EXP;
OUTPUT OUT=SUMM SUM= ;

DATA TABLE2;
SET SUMM;
ACCRAT= 1000 * LIV_ACC/AMT_ACC;
DTHRAT= 1000 * LIV_DTH/AMT_DTH;
DISRAT= 1000 * LIV_DIS/AMT_DIS;

TITLE2 'TABLE2';
TITLE3 'GROUP LIFE EXPERIENCE STUDY';
```

```
TITLE5 'DTH FILE';

PROC PRINT DATA=TABLE2 SPLIT='*';
BY SEX;
ID DISABIL YEAR;
VAR
   LIV_EXP LIV_DTH AMT_EXP AMT_DTH
   DTHRAT;
SUM
   LIV_EXP LIV_DTH AMT_EXP AMT_DTH;
FORMAT SEX $SEX.
   LIV_EXP LIV_DTH COMMA12. AMT_EXP
   AMT_DTH DOLLAR15. DTHRAT6.2 DISABIL
   $DISABIL. YEAR $YEAR. ;

LABEL LIV_EXP = 'LIVES*YEARS EXP'
    LIV_DTH = 'LIVES*TOTAL CLMS'
    DTHRAT  = 'RATIO*LIVES*PER $1,000'
    AMT_EXP = 'AMOUNT*YEARS EXP'
    AMT_DTH = 'AMOUNT*TOTAL CLMS'
     ;
    RUN;


TITLE5 'ACC FILE';

PROC PRINT DATA=TABLE2 SPLIT='*';
BY SEX;
ID DISABIL YEAR;
VAR
   LIV_EXP LIV_ACC AMT_EXP AMT_ACC
   ACCRAT;
SUM
   LIV_EXP LIV_ACC AMT_EXP AMT_ACC;
FORMAT SEX $SEX.
   LIV_EXP LIV_ACC COMMA12. AMT_EXP
   AMT_ACC DOLLAR15. ACCRAT6.2 DISABIL
   $DISABIL. YEAR $YEAR. ;

LABEL LIV_EXP = 'LIVES*YEARS EXP'
    LIV_ACC = 'LIVES*TOTAL CLMS'
    ACCRAT  = 'RATIO*LIVES*PER $1,000'
    AMT_EXP = 'AMOUNT*YEARS EXP'
    AMT_ACC = 'AMOUNT*TOTAL CLMS'
     ;
    RUN;
```

```
TITLE5 'DIS FILE';

PROC PRINT DATA=TABLE2 SPLIT='*';
BY SEX;
ID DISABIL YEAR;
VAR
   LIV_EXP LIV_DIS AMT_EXP AMT_DIS
   DISRAT;
SUM
   LIV_EXP LIV_DIS AMT_EXP AMT_DIS;
FORMAT SEX $SEX.
   LIV_EXP LIV_DIS COMMA12. AMT_EXP
   AMT_DIS DOLLAR15. DISRAT6.2 DISABIL
   $DISABIL. YEAR $YEAR. ;

LABEL LIV_EXP = 'LIVES*YEARS EXP'
     LIV_DIS = 'LIVES*TOTAL CLMS'
     DISRAT  = 'RATIO*LIVES*PER $1,000'
     AMT_EXP = 'AMOUNT*YEARS EXP'
     AMT_DIS = 'AMOUNT*TOTAL CLMS'
      ;
    RUN;
```

CONCLUSION

Using the macro facility to generate code allows you to spend less time on programming and more time on analysis. I present these examples to demonstrate how you can simplify your own programs to make your job easier.

SAS Guide to Macro Processing, Second Edition, provides examples and detailed explanations of the autocall facility and macro program statements.

SAS is a registered trademark of SAS Institute Inc., Cary, NC, USA.

Ifs, Ands, and Buts:
A Case Study in Advanced Macro Implementation

Peter Kretzman, McCaw Cellular Communications, Inc.

ABSTRACT

If you have chosen to delve more deeply into the macro facility of the SAS® System, you probably started down the path by writing a few simple macros, and then noticing in the documentation that there are quite a few more capabilities than you are exercising. But, the intrepid journeyman macro programmer faces a variety of pitfalls: a bewildering set of abstruse quoting functions, multiple ampersand constructions, and a syntax which is just similar enough to regular SAS programming to get you into trouble.

This advanced tutorial will piggyback on (and assume prerequisite knowledge of syntax-oriented material contained in) other previous SUGI tutorials on the macro facility, but will focus on elucidating the specific macro constructs and techniques ("idioms of expression") used by guru-level macro programmers. Our major vehicle to impart these ideas will be to go through a case study in constructing a reasonably advanced macro, where we will broaden our scope to encompass implementation issues, including style, readability, and maintainability. These issues will focus the spotlight on some of the buts of advanced macro programming, discussing both the pros and the cons of certain techniques.

INTRODUCTION

A recent excellent and already influential book on the C++ language, *Advanced C++: Programming Styles and Idioms* [Coplien, 1992] makes the point that knowing the syntax of a programming language is not enough:

> Programming language syntax shapes our thinking to a degree, but what we learn in the "owner's manual" about syntax alone only gets us started. Most of what guides the structure of our programs, and therefore of the systems we build, is the *styles* and *idioms* we adopt to express design concepts.[1]

Coplien goes on to note that traditional ways of teaching programming languages tend to focus on syntax and basic semantics, neglecting for the most part what he calls "fundamental building blocks," or reusable "expressions" of programming semantics.

The same observation also pertains to most SAS System manuals as well as to most SUGI tutorials, of course: they tend to focus on the basic (or even advanced) *hows* of wrestling with this huge baggy monster that we call the SAS System. Meanwhile, the new user (or the user who is new to a particular appendage of that huge baggy monster), faced with an intimidating pile of SAS manuals, is largely left to figure out his or her own idioms, ways to put the syntax together to create useful work. As I have noted elsewhere, the manuals are intended more as a general reference than as a programming instruction tool. They tend not to discuss the issues involved in fitting procedure and data step chunks together into a viable program. I believe that the key to achieving fluency in the SAS System rests in learning how to do just that, how to piece together the mortar and the bricks.

The SAS macro facility represents one place in the SAS System where it is perhaps relatively easy to focus on syntax issues: the syntax is quite tricky, recondite, unforgiving, annoyingly similar to that of the base SAS System but just different enough to cause unexpected headaches. With all that required focus on syntax, it's hard to see your way to the kinds of building blocks that Coplien means. And without those building blocks, you have little more than a jumbled bag of quoting functions, ampersands, and percent signs, working in ways you can't really discern.

The primary purpose of this tutorial is to reveal several of the best-known macro facility "idioms of expression," building blocks which are intimately familiar to any expert macro programmer, but which tend to appear confusing or mysterious to the uninitiated. The idioms of expression we will focus on here are:

> inline macros
> Interstep communication using CALL SYMPUT
> macro variable "arrays"

At the same time, however, we will look at issues of style and structure when macro programming. I will attempt to point out wise and unwise methods of proceeding. And in fact, some of the unwise ways imply something quite drastic: I will argue that much of the macro facility, ingenious though it may be, should be avoided when other and better techniques exist, techniques that we will discuss.

As a vehicle for showing alternative techniques as well as sound structuring principles, we will focus in the latter half of the paper on two separate, yet functionally identical, versions of a utility macro, DSDUMP, designed to list the contents and sample observations of every data set within a given data library. Programming this relatively simple functionality, the purpose of which is understandable by all, will illustrate most of the basic building blocks with which most useful macro programming can be accomplished. At the same time, we will discuss reasons for choosing one version over another, reasons that in a larger, "real world" example would be all the stronger. So the secondary purpose of this tutorial, then, will be to propose some principles of good macro design, and to put forward the notion that you should choose *not* to use some of the macro facility's capabilities.

BASIC MACRO IDIOMS

Inline Macros

The following examples illustrate what can be done with what I call "inline macros," or macros that generate what amounts to a single SAS expression, suitable for direct inclusion in a calculation, function call, or whatever. These inline macros become almost like extensions to the language, serving in essence as reserved words. Like most macros, when used carefully and when well documented, they can make SAS code more readable and maintainable, in that they provide a "black

---

[1] Coplien, p. v.

box" solution to a simple, well-defined problem, meaning that neither the programmer nor the reader of the program needs to be concerned with exactly how the macro is achieving its results.

The pair of macros that follow are simple examples of inline macros; they provide tools, akin to system-provided functions, for calculating the beginning date of a particular month and the ending date. These might be used, then, in subsequent calculations, such as:

```
PAYDAY = %BEGMONTH() + 10;

PARTYDAY =
    %ENDMONTH(SASDATE = OLDDATE);
```

Here is the text of the two macros:

```
%macro begmonth
   (sasdate = date(),
    month = month(&sasdate)
   );

   mdy(&month,
       1,
       year(&sasdate)
       )
%mend begmonth;
```

```
%macro endmonth
   (sasdate = date(),
    month = month(&sasdate)
   );

   mdy((&month + 1) - (12*(&month=12)),
       1,
       year(&sasdate) + (&month = 12)
       ) - 1

%mend endmonth;
```

The simpler of these two macros, %begmonth, contains nothing more than a call to the SAS function MDY, with appropriate parameters. If the user supplies nothing as a parameter, the macro makes use of the current date. If we need to calculate the first day of the month in which a particular date falls, we supply the date (either via the name of a variable or via a SAS date literal, such as '05OCT56'D) in the date parameter; witness the second example above. The month parameter need never be specified at all, since it logically must correspond completely to the month of the specified date; it is provided for reasons of potential efficiency in both of the macros, so that if a variable already exists containing the appropriate value, it may be provided by the programmer so that the macro is not forced to spend the necessary CPU time to recalculate it.

The second macro, %endmonth, has identical parameter guidelines and is, in fact, used in exactly the same manner as **%begmonth.** But it uses a couple of tricks to adhere to the requirement that it be usable inline, within a SAS expression. Since that requirement means that it cannot make use of IF/THEN logic, for example, %endmonth has to come up with alternative ways of doing conditional calculation.

The basic technique used to calculate the last day of a given month, as anyone knows who has thought about this common problem, is to calculate the first day (as a SAS date, of course) of the subsequent month, and then simply subtract one. Of course, if the base month is December (or month number 12), the subsequent month is January, or month number 1. The macro makes use of the fact that a conditional statement (e.g., MONTH = 12) will, in an arithmetic expression, evaluate to either 0 or 1, based on whether it is false or true.. It uses the results of that evaluation as a multiplier by 12, to determine that we should subtract 12 from the result if we have come up with a 13 when we added 1 to the month. Of course, if we haven't come up with 13, we will multiply 12 by 0, and end up subtracting nothing. In the same manner, we will either add or fail to add 1 to the base year depending on whether the base month was December.

All of this somewhat contorted processing needs to take place within the bounds of a single SAS expression, so that we may adhere to the inline requirement and allow this macro to be used as a kind of SAS function. Admittedly, we may lose some efficiency (via possible double calculation of the month) if it turns out that we use the default MONTH parameter to the macro, rather than supplying the name of a variable that happens already to contain the month. However, it is quite possible that the SAS compilation process, now or in the future, will detect and optimize away that inefficiency, and in the meantime, we have won a great deal by simplifying the programming process through the construction of generic, reusable code.

Interstep Communication Using CALL SYMPUT

One of the chief powers granted through the macro facility is the ability to execute entire steps (DATA steps or PROCs) conditionally, by testing the value of macro variables. Those macro variables may be parameters to the macro, or they could be set via %LET, or they could be created in earlier steps through one of the chief "idioms of expression" available to the macro programmer: the use of CALL SYMPUT. This technique allows you to take information (data values) from within a DATA step and use those values actually to determine the flow of the rest of your overall SAS program, such as whether or not particular steps get executed at all, or what parameters are used within given PROCs. The macro facility would be considerably less useful if it lacked this ability to enable such *interstep communication.*

A simple example: if you maintain a counter within a DATA step (e.g., of all observations that meet a particular criterion), and then want to use that counter in subsequent steps, the typical idiom would look something like:

```
.
.
.
SET BLAHBLAH END=EOF;
.
.
.
IF EOF THEN
   CALL SYMPUT("COUNTER", COUNTER);
```

In all subsequent steps, the macro variable **&counter** will be available, containing the value that the COUNTER variable has accumulated by the end of the DATA step.

A typical mistake of new macro programmers, please note, is to forget that this macro variable is only available *after* the current step (the one containing the CALL SYMPUT) has executed.

We chose, in this case, to call that macro variable **&counter**, but we could have called it anything we wish, or we could have supplied, as the first parameter to CALL SYMPUT, the name of a data step variable that contained the name we wanted the macro variable to be. That means that we can build macro variable names on the fly, based on information in the DATA step. Our second, more complex example illustrates such a construction:

```
LENGTH VARNAME $8;

VARNAME = 'MEM' ||
          LEFT(PUT(COUNTER, 3.));

CALL SYMPUT(VARNAME, MEMNAME);
```

In this case, we are building a macro variable name of the form &MEMn, where n is determined by the value of the variable COUNTER at runtime. Note that you do need to perform a LEFT() function on the numeric variable COUNTER (and in this case, we also PUT it explicitly into character format), so that the "splicing" happens correctly and the result in VARNAME is the name of a legal SAS macro variable (i.e., no spaces!) Ability to do this on-the-fly construction anticipates our next major idiom, the concept of macro variable arrays.

Macro Variable "Arrays"

The principal piece of knowledge that separates the expert macro facility programmer from the novice is the ability to manipulate what I term macro variable "arrays." Of course, arrays do not exist in the macro language as a syntactical entity, hence groups of variables (e.g., &MEM1, &MEM2, &MEM3, and so on) must be dealt with via a common programming convention, which allows them to be thought of as logical arrays. Much of what is typically done, in fact, in complex macros that interface tightly with SAS data sets and DATA steps, consists of the programmer putting information from within the DATA step into such macro variable "arrays" and then making use of that information later on.

Let's go at this one backwards, first showing the idiom of expression, then explaining what it all means. Here's a typical construct using a macro variable array:

```
%do counter = 1 %to &total;
  PROC PRINT DATA = &&FILE&counter;
    TITLE "Contents of &&FILE&counter";
  RUN;
%end;
```

This code presupposes the existence of a set of macro variables, named &FILE1, &FILE2, &FILE3, etc., with the total count of such variables contained in the macro variable &TOTAL. Contained in each of these &FILEn variables, in this particular case, are the names of SAS data sets on which this code will run PROC PRINT.

How does the code work? The shell is obviously a simple macro %DO loop, which will generate however many PROC PRINTs are reflected in the value of the &TOTAL variable. When the SAS supervisor, parsing through the program code, reaches the DATA = **&&FILE&counter** statement, it will pass control to the appropriate routine to try to resolve the macro variable reference, using the standard algorithm: First, it resolves the && at the front of the reference to a single &. Then, it attaches the characters FILE to that, followed by the current value of the variable &COUNTER. The result, for the first pass through the loop, will be &FILE1, for the second pass, &FILE2, and so on. When it finishes the initial substitution in each case, it determines that it is not yet done, since the result still contains an ampersand, so it will resolve the &FILE1, for example, to get the value of that macro variable. Of course, the same thing happens in the TITLE statement, just as long as you remember to use double quotation marks, not single quotation marks.

MACRO STYLE GUIDELINES

As I have written elsewhere [Kretzman, 1988], style is surprisingly important in the design of macro tools, especially if they are intended to be widely used. In all but the rarest cases, all macro tool parameters should be coded as keyword parameters (e.g., **BLAHBLAH=YES**) rather than just plain positional parameters. This practice allows the ready use of defaults, permits the parameters to be used in any order in the calling program, and is considerably more readable both in the macro definition and in the macro call. It imparts a measure of self-documentation to the macro, especially if the parameter names are well chosen.

But how do you determine what should be a macro parameter? The purpose of a generalized macro tool is to serve as a black box, and preferably as a black box for all similar, yet not necessarily identical, needs. You want to be able to adjust the behavior of the black box in minor ways without having to alter (or even be aware of) the code within it. That means that one of your design tasks is to determine what kinds of things you would want to change in the code to make it behave in slightly different ways: a file name, a constant, a switch setting to turn certain behavior on or off. It is not necessary that the typical usage of the macro entail specifying each and every parameter; in fact, many parameters might rarely be used, and would be coded with suitable defaults, "just in case." A typical example is the DEBUG= parameter which is present in many or most of the macros I write. If that parameter is coded to anything other than an N (which is the default), then diagnostic messages are produced, along with test PROC PRINTs, etc.

In addition to having a meaningful, self-documenting name, of course, each macro parameter should be fully commented in the macro definition, describing its purpose and its typical and default values. In all but the rarest cases, macro parameters should be given reasonable default values, so that the user is never forced to specify a parameter unless the default behavior is to be changed.

If a macro is to be most useful, it is critical that it be documented rigorously, both internally (in the form of comments) and externally. I recommend especially the establishment of a generalized "header" block of comments, attached to the front of every macro, containing the name, author, revision dates, calling guidelines, and so on.

Every macro should take special care to "clean up" after itself, deleting any work data sets that it may have generated. In addition, these work data sets should be given names that are unlikely to conflict with those of the user's program: using the underscore as an initial character is a good convention to achieve this goal. One recommended macro parameter, typically coded as DELETE=Y, could be a switch that prevents this cleanup if the user (usually the macro developer) so desires, so that testing may take place.

THE DSDUMP MACRO: GENERAL APPROACH

Our major vehicle to illustrate some of the idioms of expression we have covered so far will be to go through a case study in constructing a reasonably advanced macro, where we will consider further implementation issues, including style, readability, and maintainability. We will do this by constructing two functionally identical versions of the case study macro, one which uses some of the idioms of expression discussed earlier, and one which avoids some of those idioms in favor of other techniques.

The simple objective of both versions of this illustrative macro will be to print the contents and selected number of observations for each of the data sets in a given SAS data set library. In both cases, we will use PROC CONTENTS, with an output data set, to generate an electronic list of the data sets in the specified data set library. Then, we will generate SAS code (either via the macro facility, as in Alternative A, or directly to a flat file, as in Alternative B) that performs the PROC PRINT and PROC CONTENTS on the individual data sets.

Although the second alternative avoids some of the macro techniques used in the first alternative, both versions *are* macros, using the "Teflon and Tang" kind of style that I have proposed here and elsewhere. For example, each alternative has a well-defined set of parameters, with appropriate defaults, meaning that the user could invoke the macro with no parameters specified at all, and, assuming that the libname DATA was defined, would get viable results rather than an error message.

Note that neither version happens to make use of inline macros; once such macros are established, of course, they may be used anywhere that SAS functions and other expressions may be called, so I saw no purpose in intentionally molding this case study just to make use of them.

THE DSDUMP MACRO: ALTERNATIVE A

The first version of the DSDUMP macro uses the macro facility to generate the SAS code that will actually perform the PROC CONTENTS and the PROC PRINT on each of the data sets that it finds. DSDUMP is defined with five keyword parameters, with the following defaults:

libname=DATA
numobs=10
format=Y
delete=Y
title='DSDUMP Macro'

These keywords, used throughout the macro in the form of macro variables, enable the user to achieve a great deal of flexibility from this black box: you can process any data library, print any number of observations, use or not use the internal data set formats, choose whether or not to "clean up" after the processing of the macro, and place any desired title on the contents and prints of the respective data sets. Any combination of these settings may be employed without having to touch the code within the black box.

Here is the text of the macro, with a detailed discussion following.

```
****************************************;
*                                      *;
*    ---- THE DSDUMP MACRO ----        *;
*                                      *;
* PROGRAM NAME: DSDUMP                 *;
*                                      *;
*  AUTHOR: Peter Kretzman              *;
*                                      *;
*                                      *;
* DATE CREATED:  3/15/88               *;
*                                      *;
* LAST REV      :          DESCRIPTION *;
*   DATE     BY             OF REVISION*;
*                                      *;
* -------------------------------------*;
*                                      *;
* -------------------------------------*;
*                                      *;
*  Purpose: Prints contents and        *;
*           selected obs of all data   *;
*           sets within a data base    *;
*                                      *;
*   This version uses pure macro       *;
*   concepts to achieve the goal.      *;
*                                      *;
****************************************;


%macro dsdump
   (libname=DATA,
      /*  LIBNAME of data base to
          print          */
    numobs=10,
      /*  # of obs to print for each
          data set       */
    format=Y,
     /*  Use the formats in
         data set?       */
    delete=Y,
     /*  Delete the work code
         when done?      */
    title='DSDUMP Macro'
     /*  Title for PROC PRINT
         (in tick marks) */
   );


%***************************************;
%*                                     *;
%*  Get a list of all members in       *;
%*  the referenced libref.             *;
%*                                     *;
%***************************************;

PROC CONTENTS DATA=&libname.._ALL_
              MEMTYPE=DATA
              OUT=_ALL(KEEP=MEMNAME)
              NOPRINT
              ;
RUN;

%***************************************;
%*                                     *;
%*  Now get the member names into      *;
%*  macro variables so that these      *;
%*  may be referenced later on.        *;
%*                                     *;
```

```
%*  When this step is complete, we    *;
%*  have a bunch of macro vars:       *;
%*                                    *;
%*    Macro var name   Data set name *;
%*                      (example)    *;
%*    --------------   ------------- *;
%*                                    *;
%*        MEM1            fred        *;
%*        MEM2            harry       *;
%*        MEM3            betty       *;
%*        MEM4            jane        *;
%*                                    *;
%*************************************;

DATA _NULL_;
   SET _ALL_ END=EOF;
   BY MEMNAME NOTSORTED;

   LENGTH VARNAME $8;  * This var will
      hold the current macro var name;

   IF LAST.MEMNAME;     * Get only one
      occurrence per member;

   RETAIN CTR 0;        * Counter for
     macro variables to be generated;

   CTR + 1;

   VARNAME = 'MEM' ||
             LEFT(PUT(CTR, 3.));

   * put member name into this
     macro var;
   CALL SYMPUT(VARNAME, MEMNAME);

   * preserve total # of members in
     a macro variable too;

   IF EOF THEN
      CALL SYMPUT("TOTALMEM",
                  LEFT(PUT(CTR,3.)));

RUN;


%do ctr = 1 %to &totalmem;

    PROC CONTENTS
         DATA=&libname..&&MEM&ctr;
       TITLE1 &title;
       TITLE2
    "Contents of &libname..&&MEM&ctr";
    RUN;

    PROC PRINT
DATA=&libname..&&MEM&ctr(OBS=&numobs);

    %if %upcase(&format) ne Y %then
       %do;
           FORMAT _NUMERIC_;
           FORMAT _CHARACTER_ ;
       %end;

       TITLE1 &title;
       TITLE2
     "Contents of &libname..&&MEM&ctr";
    RUN;

%end;

%if %upcase(&delete) eq Y %then
    %do;
       PROC DATASETS LIBRARY=WORK
                     NOLIST;
          DELETE _ALL;
       RUN;
    %end;

%mend dsdump2;
```

The first thing the macro needs to do is generate a SAS data set containing a list of members contained in the referenced libref, and it does so via a PROC CONTENTS with an output data set. The next task is to get all those members into an array of macro variables, which is done within a DATA step by using building macro variable names of the form MEMn and giving them the value of each member name by using SYMPUTs. The same counter that is used to compose the current macro variable name (of the form MEMn) is then written, at the last observation, into another macro variable called &TOTAL. When we exit this DATA step, then, we have a full symbol table, consisting of a set of member names in the variables &MEM1, &MEM2, &MEM3, etc., along with a variable called &TOTAL containing how many of those member variables there are. In short, we have performed some interstep communication. We can now use this information in subsequent steps.

Now that we have those macro variables, we can call PROC CONTENTS and PROC PRINT from within a macro %DO loop, counting from 1 to the value of &TOTAL. The only tricky part is telling the PROCs what member we're talking about. This requires dereferencing the macro variable array, as discussed earlier, using the construct &&MEM&ctr. Look again at one example of this:

```
    PROC CONTENTS
         DATA=&libname..&&MEM&ctr;
       TITLE1 &title;
       TITLE2
    "Contents of &libname..&&MEM&ctr";
    RUN;
```

Note that we also make use of several of the supplied keyword parameter variables, such as &libname and &title. The "extra" dot contained in the DATA=&libname..&&MEM&ctr reference is required, for the macro facility regards a dot at the end of a macro variable reference as a delimiter, and we ourselves need a dot in the generated SAS code data set reference, of the form DATA.MEMBER.

The rest of the %DO loop calls PROC PRINT, with some conditional processing depending on whether we have turned the "switch" on for using the data set formats (the default). After all the data sets are processed, then depending on the setting of the DELETE switch, the macro cleans up after itself, deleting the work data set it generating in the initial PROC CONTENTS on the referenced libname.

Now here's the style issue: as macros get more and more contorted and involved, they tend to make ever greater usage of constructs such as the example shown in the box above: DATA=&libname..&&MEM&ctr. The more complex the need, the more your code acquires triple ampersands, quoting functions, multiple dots, etc., all necessary to "get it to work." Readability and maintainability can become significant problems as complexity increases. Producing certain patterns of SAS code via the macro facility requires the use of arcane quoting functions, each designed to handle yet one more loophole that has emerged as people use the macro facility to its limit. Worst of all (and I have experienced this again and again, moving from Release 5 to Release 6.03, then to Release 6.06), macro functions and features can have subtly different behavior from release to release, meaning that the more complex a macro is, the more likely it is to break during a release upgrade.

For these reasons, I believe that one should Just Say No to overuse of the macro facility. If you can't tell the macro quoting functions apart without pages of explanation and examples, for example, maybe they should be avoided altogether. *The astonishing truth is that avoiding them is possible.* The next example illustrates that functional objectives can generally be met even if one is limited to the most basic macro coding techniques: simple interstep communications via SYMPUT, use of basic macro parameters, and the use of a simple key technique: write SAS code to a flat file and then %INCLUDE it.

THE DSDUMP MACRO: ALTERNATIVE B

This second version of the DSDUMP macro manages to avoid using any macro variables other than those defined as keyword parameters by the macro itself. Rather than going through a separate step of loading macro variables with the names of the members discovered in the referenced libref, this version deals with those names directly, writing out SAS code to a flat file. The key insight here is that any SAS program can write another SAS program, and it doesn't need to use the macro facility to do it. Here's the text of the macro:

```
**************************************;
*                                    *;
*    ---- THE DSDUMP MACRO ----      *;
*                                    *;
* PROGRAM NAME: DSDUMP               *;
*                                    *;
*  AUTHOR: Peter Kretzman            *;
*                                    *;
*                                    *;
* DATE CREATED:  3/15/88             *;
*                                    *;
* LAST REV       :       DESCRIPTION *;
*    DATE      BY         OF REVISION*;
*                                    *;
* -----------------------------------*;
*                                    *;
* -----------------------------------*;
*                                    *;
*  Purpose: Prints contents and      *;
*           selected obs of all data *;
*           sets within a data base  *;
*                                    *;
*   This version uses a flat         *;
*   file for output rather than      *;
*   pure macro concepts.             *;
**************************************;

%macro dsdump
   (libname=DATA,
      /*  LIBNAME of data base to
          print            */
    numobs=10,
      /*  # of obs to print for each
          data set         */
    format=Y,
     /*  Use the formats in
         data set?         */
    tempcode=_TMPCODE,
     /*  Data set name for temp.
         code              */
    delete=Y,
     /*  Delete the work code
         when done?        */
    title='DSDUMP Macro'
     /*  Title for PROC PRINT
         (in tick marks) */
   );

%************************************;
%*                                  *;
%*  Get a list of all members in    *;
%*  the referenced libref.          *;
%*                                  *;
%************************************;

PROC CONTENTS DATA=&libname.._ALL_
              MEMTYPE=DATA
              OUT=_ALL(KEEP=MEMNAME)
              NOPRINT
              ;
RUN;

%************************************;
%*                                  *;
%*  Now write out code to a flat    *;
%*  file.  Each data set in the     *;
%*  referenced libref.will get a    *;
%*  PROC CONTENTS and a PROC PRINT. *;
%*                                  *;
%************************************;

DATA _NULL_;
   FILE "&tempcode" NOTITLES;
   SET _ALL;
   BY MEMNAME NOTSORTED;

   IF LAST.MEMNAME;
* Get only one occurrence per member;

   PUT "PROC CONTENTS DATA=&libname.."
       MEMNAME " ;";
   PUT "title1 &title;";
   PUT "title2 'Contents of &libname.."
       MEMNAME "';";
   PUT "RUN;";

   PUT "PROC PRINT DATA=&libname.."
       MEMNAME " (OBS=&numobs);";
   %if %upcase(&format) ne Y %then
       %do;
           PUT "FORMAT _NUMERIC_;";
           PUT "FORMAT _CHARACTER_ ;";
       %end;

   PUT "title1 &title;";
   PUT "title2 'Contents of &libname.."
```

```
      MEMNAME "';";
   PUT "RUN;";

RUN;

%*************************************;
%*                                   *;
%*  Now run the code that was just   *;
%*  generated.                       *;
%*                                   *;
%*************************************;

%include "&tempcode";


%if %upcase(&delete) eq Y %then
    %do;
       x "erase &tempcode";
       PROC DATASETS LIBRARY=WORK
                     NOLIST;
          DELETE _ALL;
       RUN;
    %end;

%mend dsdump;
```

This version differs from the first version mostly in the middle area, where instead of creating SAS macro variables and then going through a %DO loop, we write out code to a flat file. You'll notice that another keyword parameter has been added to the macro, allowing the caller to specify, if so desired, exactly where the temporary flat file code will be placed. Again, this would be a parameter that would be used mostly for testing.

The chief advantage of operating in this manner is simplicity of approach. Although constructs such as PUT "PROC CONTENTS DATA=&libname.." MEMNAME " ;"; are not exactly unmuddy, they are still easier to code and understand, and significantly more robust to changes or release upgrades, than their pure macro equivalents. What's more, debugging the results will be considerably easier, since the generated code is *real* code, with associated line numbers at run time, and so on. If you have doubts as to what was generated in a particular instance, you can always go to the intermediate scratch flat file and peruse the code for yourself. With the macro facility, even given the excellent debugging enhancements and options that are now part of the SAS System, you're operating relatively blind.

CONCLUSION

Ever notice that "macro" and "macho" differ by only one letter? I once had a programmer proudly show me his intricate macro code, code that actually wrote macros conditionally and which was laden with triple ampersands and replete with quoting functions. Macro programming has almost become the macho side of SAS programming: the more complex, unreadable, and unmaintainable your macro code is, the more self-worth you feel as a programmer, having wrestled the bear down and then made him dance.

But like any powerful tool, macro programming requires steadfast discipline to use effectively. I believe that one should choose to exercise such discipline, avoiding in one's code the sublime and the ridiculous, in the interests of readability and maintainability. And in this case, that means gauging carefully just when, and to what extent, you will use the more abstruse areas of the macro facility.

Comments, suggestions, and questions are welcome. The author may be reached at the following address:

Peter Kretzman
McCaw Cellular Communications, Inc.
P.O. Box 97060
Kirkland, WA 98033-9760
Voice: (206)828-1344
FAX: (206)828-1300

In addition, the author may be contacted via Internet, using the address **mcgp1!peter@cs.washington.edu**

BIBLIOGRAPHY

1. Coplien, James O., *Advanced C++: Programming Styles and Idioms*, Reading, MA: Addison-Wesley, 1992, p. v.

2. Henderson, Donald J., "A Toolbox Approach to Networking SAS Experts, or, Reusing Instead of Reinventing the Wheel," *Proceedings of the Thirteenth Annual SAS Users Group International Conference,* Cary, NC: SAS Institute Inc., 1988, pp. 285-289.

3. Kretzman, Peter, "Lean and Mean: A Guide to Self-Discipline in Using the SAS System," *Proceedings of the Twelfth Annual SAS Users Group International Conference,* Cary, NC: SAS Institute Inc., 1987, pp. 144-146.

4. Kretzman, Peter, "Mortar and Bricks: Using Basic SAS System Procedures to Manipulate Your Data," *Proceedings of the Fifteenth Annual SAS Users Group International Conference,* Cary, NC: SAS Institute Inc., 1990, pp. 155-162.

5. Kretzman, Peter, "Teflon and Tang: Forging Generic Macro Tools," *Proceedings of the Thirteenth Annual SAS Users Group International Conference,* Cary, NC: SAS Institute Inc., 1988, pp. 34-41.

6. SAS Institute Inc., *SAS Guide to Macro Processing, Version 6, Second Edition,* Cary, NC: SAS Institute Inc., 1990.

Macro: Bells and Whistles for Version 6

Lynn Patrick, SAS Institute Inc.

ABSTRACT

As the SAS®System advances to meet user needs and future directions of the software industry, Version 6 of the macro facility makes user-oriented features and enhancements available to users of all operating system environments. Mainframe users will appreciate the new debugging features and macro windows. Microcomputer users will enjoy the autocall facility for establishing source level macro libraries. Minicomputer users will find applications much easier to develop with the full macro facility available to them.

Using specific examples, the paper illustrates the new features and functionality available on all operating systems. Users of the Version 5 System see a preview of what is ahead. Version 6 users see new features and learn new techniques for using the features already available.

INTRODUCTION

The macro facility first became available to SAS software users with Version 82.3. The components of the macro facility at that time are the foundation from which all subsequent versions have evolved. The 82.3 macro facility consisted of four components: name style and statement style macros, macro variables, macro functions, and macro statements.

Version 5 of SAS software included enhancements to the Version 82 macro facility. The most significant enhancement added was the autocall facility. Autocall makes it possible to compile macros only on an 'as needed' basis, eliminating the practice that all macros in an application must be compiled before any macro could be executed. The autocall facility also makes invoking macros which emulate SAS functions appear more sophisticated. SAS Institute Inc. began shipping autocall libraries containing utility macros to enhance the current functionality of the macro facility. Unfortunately, the full macro facility is available only to mainframe users under Version 5, only the limited availability of macro variables exists for minicomputer operating systems.

Version 6.03 of the SAS system for personal computers was the beginning of Version 6 macro. The intent of macro for Version 6.03 was that it contain all components of the macro facility available with Version 82.3. In addition to these components, some new features were added. Perhaps the most popular of these features was the improved diagnostic capabilies. MTRACE, a new option for tracing the logic of macro execution was added. With MTRACE in effect, the macro processor displays messages identifying the beginning and the end of macro execution, the values of macro parameters at invocation, the results of %IF conditions, and generally traces the logic a macro follows during execution. The output from the SYMBOLGEN option was also enhanced to display the results of symbolic substitution through all steps of resolution. Macro warnings and errors were enhanced to display more explicit information. Another significant enhancement to this version was the addition of macro windows. These windows can be used to prompt users for information or to display menus.

THE VERSION 6 MACRO FACILITY

With only a few exceptions, the Version 6.06 macro facility offers the full functionality of the Version 5 macro facility in addition to the enhancements of the Version 6.03 macro facility to users of all operating systems.

The Autocall Facility for Source Level Macro Libraries

The autocall facility allows you to store the source code for your macro definitions in a file, associate that file with the SAS session or job, and then execute macros on a 'demand' basis without having to include their source in your session or program. Consider that you may have an application, possibly menu driven, that may execute from one to twenty macros based on user input or other implicit information. Before the autocall facility was available, it was necessary to include the source for all these macros in your program. Using the autocall facility means that only macros that are actually invoked get compiled. This represents a tremendous overhead savings to applications containing macro systems.

Another feature of the autocall facility is that you can actually set up a system of macro libraries. It is common for a site to have its own set of autocall macros, the autocall library that is shipped with the SAS system, and unique macro libraries for individual users. The autocall facility allows you to concatenate these libraries to be seen as a single unit. Macros can be created to emulate functions not presently available with the SAS system. For example, suppose a macro programmer often uses the %GLOBAL statement to initialize a list of variables. Since it is not possible to use a variable list of the form SALES1-SALES10 on the %GLOBAL statement, the user always has to enter the name of each variable. The user can write a macro to generate a list of variables, place this macro in his autocall library, and then execute the macro whenever he needs to generate a variable list. The macro to generate this variable list is shown below.

```
%Macro varlist(prefix,start,stop);
  %Do I=&start %to &stop;
     &prefix&I
  %End;
%Mend varlist;
```

With the autocall facility in place, this macro can be executed on the %GLOBAL statement as shown.

```
%Global %varlist(SALES,1,10);
```

The first step in setting up an autocall library is to create a 'member' containing the source for the macro definition. On 'library oriented' systems (OS, CMS, VSE), an autocall library is a PDS or maclib containing members. On 'directory based' systems (PC, VMS, AOS, PRIMOS) an autocall library consists of a directory containing files that end in '.sas', and may also contain other files that are irrelevant to the autocall facility.

The 'member' must have the same name as the macro. On 'directory based' machines a 'member' is a file. The macro VARLIST should be put into the file VARLIST.SAS in the directory you are going to use as your autocall library. On 'library oriented' machines, a 'member' is a true member. The macro definition for VARLIST should be put into the member VARLIST of the library that is going to be your autocall library.

The autocall library must then be associated with your SAS session or SAS program. This is done by using the SASAUTOS—

ption to specify a single FILEREF, or a quoted string containing ne or more FILEREFs. If multiple FILEREFs are specified, they ill be searched in the order given. Each FILEREF used must be quated to an autocall library by using a FILENAME statement r system dependent command. The MAUTOSOURCE option ust be in effect in order for the autocall facility to be functional.

nprovements and Enhancements to Macro Diagnostics

he Version 6 SAS system has been enhanced to give clearer dication of errors and warnings that occur in macro processing. ne of the most common warnings encountered by macro pro- rammers is the famous

```
'ARNING 1301  APPARENT SYMBOLIC REFERENCE NOT RESOLVED
```

hich occurs whenever the macro facility attempts, unsuccess- lly, to resolve a pattern of the form &SASname. This warning as been enhanced so that it now gives the name of the macro ariable that could not be resolved. In the following example

```
Let code=1;
Put code is &code1;
```

e macro variable CODE1 has not been defined. The SAS sys- m issues the following

```
'ARNING:  APPARENT SYMBOLIC REFERENCE CODE1 NOT RESOLVED.
```

erhaps the second most common warning encountered is

```
'ARNING 1353  APPARENT MACRO INVOCATION NOT RESOLVED.
```

Version 6 this warning has also been expanded. In the follow- g example

```
Macro test1;
 %Put Beginning of macro Test1;
Mend;

Test
```

e following message is generated

```
'ARNING  APPARENT INVOCATION OF MACRO TEST NOT RESOLVED.
```

rrors occurring during the process of evaluation have also been nhanced. In Version 5 these errors were often the most difficult isolate. The errors that occurred when using the %EVAL func- on explicitly, or in places where an implied %EVAL was done, ere

```
RROR 1550:  REQUIRED OPERATOR NOT FOUND
```

nd

```
RROR 1555:  CHARACTER OPERAND FOUND WHERE NUMERIC REQUIRED.
```

hese errors have been replaced in Version 6 by a new error that veals the cause of the problem. In the following example

```
Let x=%eval(1+x);
```

e error message generated is

```
RROR:  A character operand was found in the %EVAL function
       or %IF condition where a numeric operand was required.
       The condition was: 1+x.
```

ikewise, a problem occurring in the %IF statement would also now the erroneous condition. In the following example

```
Macro check(state);
 %If &state=NC %then
   %Let st=North Carolina;
Mend;

Check(OR)
```

R, the abbreviation for Oregon, would be interpreted by the acro facility as an operator. The macro facility would generate e following

```
RROR:  A character operand was found in the %EVAL function
       or %IF condition where a numeric operand was required.
       The condition was &state=NC.
```

Improvements and Enhancements to Debugging Options

The SYMBOLGEN option has been enhanced in two ways. The first enhancement is that it now prints in a much more readable form. The second feature is that it now shows all steps of substitution encountered when performing resolution. Consider the following macro which writes the values of a list of symbolic variables.

```
%Macro chklist(prefix,start,stop);
  %Do I=&start %to &stop;
     &&&prefix&I
  %End;
%Mend

%Put %chklist(SALES,1,2);
```

The output generated by SYMBOLGEN for the above example is shown below.

```
SYMBOLGEN: Macro variable START resolves to 1

SYMBOLGEN: Macro variable STOP resolves to 2

SYMBOLGEN: && resolves to &

SYMBOLGEN: Macro variable PREFIX resolves to SALES

SYMBOLGEN: Macro variable I resolves to 1

SYMBOLGEN: Macro variable SALES1 resolves to 1000

SYMBOLGEN: && resolves to &

SYMBOLGEN: Macro variable PREFIX resolves to SALES

SYMBOLGEN: Macro variable I resolves to 2

SYMBOLGEN: Macro variable SALES2 resolves to 6000
```

A completely new debugging option for Version 6 is the MTRACE option. MTRACE 'traces' the execution of a macro. Output from MTRACE includes the invocation values of macro parameters, the beginning and ending points of the macro's execution, the results of %IF conditions, and the value of incrementation variables. Consider the following example.

```
%Macro Datalst(prefix,start,stop,lib=work);
  %If %upcase(&lib) ne WORK %then
    %Do i=&start %to &stop;
       &lib..&prefix&i
    %End;
  %Else
    %Do i=&start %to &stop;
       work.&prefix&i
    %End;
%Mend Datalst;

Data %datalst(Book,1,4);
```

With the MTRACE option in effect, the following is displayed on the SAS log.

```
MTRACE(DATALST): Beginning execution.

MTRACE(DATALST): Parameter PREFIX has value Book

MTRACE(DATALST): Parameter START has value 1

MTRACE(DATALST): Parameter STOP has value 4

MTRACE(DATALST): Parameter LIB has value work
```

MTRACE(DATALST): %IF condition %upcase(&lib) ne WORK is FALSE

MTRACE(DATALST): %DO loop beginning; index variable I; start value is 1; stop value is 4; by value is 1.

MTRACE(DATALST): %DO loop index variable I is now 2; loop will iterate again.

MTRACE(DATALST): %DO loop index variable I is now 3; loop will iterate again.

MTRACE(DATALST): %DO loop index variable I is now 4; loop will iterate again.

MTRACE(DATALST): %DO loop index variable I is now 5; loop will not iterate again.

MTRACE(DATALST): Ending execution.

Macro Windows

A new enhancement available with the Version 6 macro facility is the windowing capability. It is now possible to design and display customized windows from which macro variable values can be input. A macro window is created inside or outside a macro definition by using the %WINDOW statement. The syntax of this statement is

%WINDOW windowname{ *windowoptions* } { *field....* };

where

windowname

names the window. Windowname is required.

windowoptions

specify characteristics of the entire window. Options include COLOR=, IROW=, ICOLUMN=, ROWS=, COLUMNS=, and KEYS=.

field

identifies and describes a macro variable or string to be displayed in the window, its position in the window, and its attributes.

The form of a field definition is

{ *row column* } macrovariable { *fieldlength* }'text' { *options* }

where

row

column

controls the position of the text or macro variable. The following pointer controls are used to move the pointer to the desired position.

#expression

specifies the row within the window.

/

moves the pointer to the first column of the next line.

@expression

specifies the column within the window.

+expression

moves the pointer the number of columns given by the expression.

macrovariable

names a macro variable to receive a value when the screen is displayed.

fieldlength

is an integer defining how many positions in the current row are available for accepting input.

'text'

contains text to be displayed.

options

can include ATTR=, AUTOSKIP, COLOR=, DISPLAY=, PROTECT=, and REQUIRED=.

Once the window has been created using the %WINDOW statement, it can be displayed, either inside or outside a macro, by using the %DISPLAY statement. The syntax of this statement is

%DISPLAY window { **NOINPUT** }{ **BELL** };

where

window

names the window to be displayed.

NOINPUT

specifies that you cannot input values into fields.

BELL

rings the terminal's bell when the window is displayed.

The Macro Facility Beyond Version 6.06

The next Version 6 release will complete the conversion process and begin the addition of more features and enhancements. Items to be included in the next version will include command style macros, the RESOLVE function, and the CALL EXECUTE subroutine. Options for allowing explicit control over how memory is managed in the macro facilility will also be available. In Version 6.06, the macro facility performs optimal memory handling, that is it decides how memory would be used most appropriately based on the machine size available. The memory handling options would allow users to choose to reduce memory in exchange for higher execution time, or to reduce execution time and increase memory.

Items under consideration for a future version of SAS software include the ability to store compiled macros, a popular request from users over the past few years, and a window to 'pop up' when a %INPUT statement is executed. The window would allow the user to respond to the %INPUT and would then disappear. Others items include the ability to %DO over a list of values, the ability to read and write files, the ability to generate but not execute SAS source statements when a macro is executed, and a full screen debugger.

CONCLUSION

The macro facility did not undergo major changes from Version 5 to Verson 6.03. The development goal for Version 6.03 was to provide a macro facility containing all available features from the 82 version. The major development goal for Version 6.06 was to provide a macro facility that would be compatible to Version 5. With few exceptions, this has been accomplished. Macro programmers across all operating system environments will now have the added features and extensions to the SAS system provided by the macro facility.

The improvement in diagnostics and the windowing capabilites will be a major benefit to mainframe users. The addition of autocall and significant performace improvements over Version 6.03 will assist programmers on personal computer and UNIX® environments in developing more efficient and useful macro applications. Minicomputer users will have all these benefits as they begin to recognize the extended features and capablites now available to them. C goal for the future is to provide users in all environments with the tools they need in order to design and maintain systems that will be applicable to future demands.

For documentation on the Version 6 macro facility, refer to the *SAS®Guide to Macro Processing, Version 6 Edition.* Documentation for the Version 6 autocall facility will be provided in an update to this manual.

USING MACRO VARIABLE LISTS

Presented at the Pittsburgh SAS User's Group, November 19, 1987
Ken Whitaker
Duquesne Systems Inc.

ABSTRACT

A macro variable list is a SAS macro variable that contains a list of words. Although these lists are only a special use of SAS macro variables, they can be very powerful. Users can parameterize a system with them, and the system can drive itself by extracting the words from the lists, invoking macros using each word as a parameter, and by generating other lists for itself. This paper describes how macro variable lists can be used, and supplies several useful SAS macros that build and use lists.

INTRODUCTION

Duquesne Systems Inc. has developed a job accounting and chargeback system in SAS called the Billing Database Facility (BDBF). This is a very flexible and dynamic system that changes to accommodate the needs of the user.

For example, the starter set only processes SMF data (for jobs, TSO sessions, and started tasks). As the product is installed, the user adds other components as needed. If the user wants to bill for IMS, he copies three supplied members of a PDS into the base system, and BDBF starts processing IMS data, too. New data steps appear that process IMS data, new datasets are created, and all reporting and summarization processing automatically expand to include this new data source.

In fact, BDBF offers several different methods of processing IMS data:

* BDBF can read the IMS log tape with its own processor.
* BDBF can extract IMS data from the Performance Database Facility (another product of Duquesne Systems).
* BDBF can extract data from MXG (Merrill's Expanded Guide to CPE, a product of Merrill Consultants).
* Users can write their own BDBF components. Users have written components that use IMF (IMS Measurement Facility, by Boole and Babbage) their own IMS log tape processors, and can extract IMS data from MICS (a product of Morino Associates).

It makes no difference to BDBF, even though each approach produces different datasets in different formats with different dataset names and variable names. BDBF modifies itself automatically.

All reporting and summarization code is driven with macro variable lists. As the word IMS is added to the file list, new reports appear, new files are saved to tape, more files are summarized, etc. The system is fundamentally changed.

Many BDBF parameters are specified via macro variable lists. Some of these are used simply as variable keep lists. Others have a more profound effect. For example, users enter a list of summary variables in a macro variable. If a user adds a new variable (for instance, SHIFT), the summarization process is changed and new reports begin to appear showing how charges are distributed over the new summary variable.

This paper describes some of the inner workings of BDBF so these techniques may be applied to other systems. It will discuss how macro variable lists can be used to control the expansion of macros, how lists can be built dynamically from data encountered in SAS datasets, and how some fairly impressive special effects can be produced with surprisingly little effort. Code for some useful list manipulation macros and some examples of coding techniques are included.

COUNTING AND EXTRACTING WORDS

A macro variable list is a SAS macro variable that contains a list of words. If the list is only a list of variable names that are to be inserted into a keep list, then the entire macro variable can be routinely substituted into a keep statement. However, as they are used here, it is necessary to be able to extract individual words and count the number of words.

For example, if FILELIST is a list of data sources, such as:

```
%LET FILELIST=JOB TSO IMS;
```

and we must invoke a macro to calculate charges on each data source, then we want to generate calls such as these:

```
%BILL(JOB);
%BILL(TSO);
%BILL(IMS);
```

To accomplish this, we must be able to extract each word from the list.

As another example, suppose SUMLIST is a list of summary variables, such as:

```
%LET SUMLIST=SYSTEM SHIFT;
```

and we want to summarize a file by SYSTEM and SHIFT, then we may want to generate code like this:

```
BY SYSTEM SHIFT;
IF FIRST.SHIFT THEN DO;
     .
     .
     .
IF LAST.SHIFT THEN DO;
```

To accomplish this, we must be able to count the words in the list, and extract the last word in the list.

The SAS macro function SCAN is perfect for this job. It can return the first word, the second word, and so on, and it can be used repeatedly to count the number of words in the list.

Here is the macro function that BDBF uses to count words in a list:

```
%MACRO WORDCNT(LIST);
    %LOCAL COUNT;
    %LET COUNT = 0;
    %IF &LIST NE %THEN %DO;
        %LET WORD = %SCAN(&LIST,1);
        %DO %WHILE (&WORD NE);
            %LET COUNT = %EVAL(&COUNT+1);
            %LET WORD = %SCAN(&LIST,&COUNT+1);
            %END;
        %END;
    &COUNT
%MEND;
```

As you can see, this macro extracts each successive word in the list until it has extracted the last word, and counts the number of words it found.

A purist might call this macro inefficient. We are making SAS scan the list for the first word, then scan the list from the beginning to the second word, then scan the list again up to the third word, etc. However, remember that this work is done only during compilation, not during execution for each record read.

Note that this is a macro function. SAS offers many macro functions such as %SUBSTR and %SCAN. The above macro can also be used as a function. For example, it can be used like this:

```
%DO I=1 %TO %WORDCNT(&LIST);
```

It is easy to write a macro that behaves like a macro function. Most macros generate lines of SAS code. This macro generates only a number, and there is no semicolon generated. As SAS parses this %DO statement, it will expand the macro %WORDCNT with a parameter of &LIST and will replace %WORDCNT(&LIST) with the generated number.

So, to generate the three %BILL statements given in the above example, code the following:

```
%DO I=1 %TO %WORDCNT(&FILELIST);
    %BILL(%SCAN(&FILELIST, &I));
%END;
```

And, to generate FIRST.SHIFT and LAST.SHIFT as in the other example above, code:

```
BY &SUMLIST;
%LET WORD=%SCAN(&SUMLIST, %WORDCNT(&SUMLIST));
IF FIRST.&WORD THEN DO;
     .
     .
     .
IF LAST.&WORD THEN DO;
```

ELIMINATING DUPLICATE WORDS

Duplicates frequently arise from a variety of causes. Users may inadvertently enter the same word twice in a parameter list. Also, as the system is generating a list automatically, a list with duplicates can be the result.

For example, BDBF offers a different list of summary variables for each data source. A user may want to summarize job data by shift and project, but may only want to summarize DASD space usage by project (not by shift). When BDBF makes a list of all summary variables by concatenating lists from all data sources, project will appear twice.

Duplicates can be harmful for several reasons. If the same variable is listed twice in a keep statement, SAS flags one of them as never having been initialized. It is also inefficient to calculate charges for the same file twice, and incorrect to show job charges twice on each invoice.

The next example defines macro UNIQUE, which eliminates duplicate words from a list. This macro communicates with the rest of the system via global variables. Its input is passed in global macrovariable LIST. Macro UNIQUE builds a temporary list of unique words, then replaces the global variable LIST with this result. As a by-product, it also sets a global variable COUNT to the number of words in the new list.

```
%MACRO UNIQUE;
    %GLOBAL LIST COUNT;
    %LOCAL I;
    %LET UNIQUE=;
    %LET UCOUNT=0;
    %DO I=1 %TO %WORDCNT(&LIST);
         %LET VAR=%SCAN(&LIST,&I);
         %IF &UCOUNT=0 %THEN %DO;
              %LET UNIQUE=&VAR;
              %LET UCOUNT=1;
              %END;
         %ELSE %DO;
              %DO J=1 %TO &UCOUNT;
                   %IF &VAR=%SCAN(&UNIQUE,&J) %THEN %LET VAR=;
                   %END;
              %IF &VAR NE %THEN %DO;
                   %LET UNIQUE=&UNIQUE &VAR;
                   %LET UCOUNT=%EVAL(&UCOUNT+1);
                   %END;
              %END;
         %END;
    %LET LIST=&UNIQUE;
    %LET COUNT=&UCOUNT;
%MEND;
```

A fairly elegant special effect was produced with this macro. BDBF produces an invoice that shows charges by data source, that is, it shows job charges in one section, followed by TSO charges in another, etc. These sections are usually printed in alpha order, that is, if a user had only jobs, TSO, and CICS, CICS would appear first. Some users requested the ability to define the order of the sections.

We did not want to make the user have to supply a complete list of sections in the desired order. Some users do not care about this feature, and we did not want to make them enter a list. Also, if a user installed another component, the invoice program would not automatically pick it up. The user would have to remember to add new data sources to this invoice list.

The solution was to allow the interested user to specify the order of sections. BDBF appends to this list a list of all installed components (that appears in alpha order), then it eliminates duplicates. The results are:

* Uninterested users do not need to enter a list. They see all components in alpha order.
* Users can name one or two important data sources, and they appear first. Remaining sections appear next, in alpha order.
* Users can name a complete list of data sources in any order, but if they add a new component and forget to modify this list, the new data source will appear on the invoice, although at the end.

BUILDING LISTS

Many lists are automatically built. BDBF builds lists of installed components, lists of SAS datasets, lists of variables in a dataset, etc. These lists are built by scanning data files and calling SYMPUT from a data step. This means that lists vary according to the data encountered, which in turn means the system behaves differently from day to day and from user to user.

For example, BDBF stores the billing data for jobs from day 1 in a summary dataset called JOB001. Jobs from day 2 go into a dataset called JOB002. If a user adds the IMS component on day 3, then processing on day 3 will produce datasets JOB003 and IMS003. There will be no datasets called IMS001 and IMS002. BDBF keeps its own directory dataset containing the dataset names it builds, and can build a macro variable list containing each of these dataset names.

The next example is macro SETLIST. It does a SET against a BDBF directory dataset and builds a macro variable list. INPUT is the name of the directory dataset. VAR is the variable in the dataset to add to the list. The list might contain dataset names like JOB001, or only file names like JOB. TEST can restrict the contents by selecting certain files, such as only JOB files, or only files from day 3. The results are returned in global macro variables LIST and COUNT.

```
%MACRO SETLIST(INPUT,VAR,TEST=);
%GLOBAL LIST COUNT;
%LOCAL I;
DATA _NULL_;
    LENGTH STRING $200;
    RETAIN STRING ' ';
    RETAIN COUNT 0 I 1;
    SET &INPUT END=EOF;
    %IF %STR(&TEST) NE %STR() %THEN %DO;
         IF &TEST THEN DO;
         %END;
    COUNT=COUNT+1;
    IF LENGTH(STRING) + 1 + LENGTH(&VAR) > 200 THEN DO;
         CALL SYMPUT('L' °° TRIM(LEFT(PUT(I,3.))), TRIM(STRING));
         I=I+1;
         STRING=' ';
         END;
    IF STRING=' ' THEN STRING=&VAR;
                   ELSE STRING=TRIM(STRING) °° ' ' °° &VAR;
    %IF %STR(&TEST) NE %STR() %THEN %DO;
         END;
         %END;
    IF EOF THEN DO;
         CALL SYMPUT('COUNT',PUT(COUNT,3.));
         CALL SYMPUT('I',LEFT(PUT(I,3.)));
         CALL SYMPUT('L' °° TRIM(LEFT(PUT(I,3.))), TRIM(STRING));
         END;
RUN;
%LET LIST=;
%DO %WHILE(&I GT 0);
    %LET LIST = &&L&I &LIST;
    %LET I=%EVAL(&I-1);
    %END;
%MEND;
```

A complication is that SAS character variables have a maximum length of 200, while the resulting macro variables might have a length much longer than that. The solution was to generate smaller macro variables called L1, L2, etc, and then to combine these temporary macro variables into the final macro variable outside the data step.

For example, in order to construct a list containing all installed components, one might code this:

```
    %SETLIST(SUMMARY.DIR, FILE);
    %UNIQUE;
```

The %SETLIST macro might produce a list containing many duplicates. The %UNIQUE macro reduces this list to a list of installed components.

This macro would help if a list had to be saved in a SAS dataset for subsequent runs. This could become complicated if the list can be longer than 200 characters. The individual words can be saved in a SAS dataset with one word per observation. Then the list can easily be reconstructed using macro %SETLIST.

This code could save a list:

```
%MACRO LISTSAVE;
     DATA DD.LIST;
          KEEP WORD;
          %DO I=1 %TO %WORDCNT(&LIST);
               WORD="%SCAN(&LIST, &I)";
               OUTPUT;
          %END;
     RUN;
%MEND;
%LISTSAVE;
```

This code would restore the list in a later SAS job:

```
%SETLIST(DD.LIST, WORD);
```

BUILDING LISTS WITH %INCLUDE

Another method of building potentially large lists uses the %INCLUDE feature. This feature allows a SAS program to generate SAS code, then include and run that generated code. This feature has been available in SAS since its early releases. In fact, it was the only way to accomplish some of these tasks before the %MACRO feature was added. The %INCLUDE feature is not as widely used now, because the %MACRO feature is so much more powerful. However, it still has its place.

The next example is macro VARLIST. This macro generates several macro variable lists simultaneously. It is more efficient to use the %INCLUDE feature than to call macro SETLIST many times. The %INCLUDE feature also makes some tasks that could be done with the macro facility a little easier to accomplish.

The input is a BDBF parameter dataset that contains all the resources that the user has selected for each file. (Different users charge for different things.) Each observation has a FILE variable that contains a data source name, like CICS or JOB, and a four digit resource code that identifies a billable resource like CPU time.

For example, if the user is only billing for jobs and CICS, and is only charging three resources, the input dataset might look like this:

```
FILE   RESOURCE

JOB       1300
JOB       1600
CICS      2010
```

Then this macro creates these macro variables:

```
&NJOB=2
&QJOB=Q1300 Q1600
&CJOB=C1300 C1600
&NCICS=1
&QCICS=Q2010
&CCICS=C2010
```

&NJOB is the number of billable resources for jobs. This is used as a count variable with the next two macro variable lists. &QJOB is a list of BDBF quantity variables. For example, Q1300 is a variable containing the number of CPU seconds that were consumed. &CJOB is a list of BDBF cost variables. For example, C1300 contains the cost of the CPU time represented in Q1300. Similarly, these three macro variables are produced for each installed component.

```
%MACRO VARLIST(DD);
DATA _NULL_;
    ARRAY RCSAVE $4 RCSAV1-RCSAV99;
    RETAIN CTR RCSAV1-RCSAV99;
    LENGTH WORD $5;

    SET &DD..PARMS;
    BY FILE;

    IF FIRST.FILE THEN CTR=1;
                  ELSE CTR+1;
```

```
     _I_ = CTR;
     RCSAVE = RC;

     IF LAST.FILE THEN DO;
          FILE INCLUDE LINESIZE=72;
          PUT '%GLOBAL Q' FILE
                      'C' FILE
                      'N' FILE ';' ;
          PUT '%LET N' FILE '=' CTR ';' ;
          PUT '%LET Q' FILE '=' @;
          DO _I_ = 1 TO CTR;
               WORD='Q' °° RCSAVE;
               PUT WORD @;
               END;
          PUT ';' ;
          PUT '%LET C' FILE '=' @;
          DO _I_ = 1 TO CTR;
               WORD='C' °° RCSAVE;
               PUT WORD @;
               END;
          PUT ';' ;
          END;
RUN;
%INCLUDE INCLUDE;
%MEND;
```

The macro reads the dataset and retains the resource codes for a file in an array. At the end of a file, it generates some statements to the INCLUDE file. First, it generates %GLOBAL declarations. Then it generates %LET statements for each macro variable. There is no 200 byte limit here, because words are put to the INCLUDE dataset one by one, and statements can flow from one line to the next.

This could be accomplished without the %INCLUDE feature, but would be more difficult to code, and would require many more data steps and multiple passes of the input file.

A complication is that the macro variables are required to be globals, and there is no data step function like SYMPUT that can do this. It could be done without the %INCLUDE feature, however. If a macro variable called FILE had the value JOB (which could be done via SYMPUT), then this macro statement would define the global:

```
        %GLOBAL N&FILE;
```

But the variable must be defined as a global before it is filled in with a SYMPUT call. This means that two data steps are required. There must be a data step that can determine that the first file is JOB and call SYMPUT to define the variable FILE. Then the %GLOBAL statement can be executed. Only then can the other data step run that fills &JOBN with another SYMPUT. Allowing a single data step to write the %GLOBAL and %LET statements is much simpler.

Generic Applications Development Using the SAS® Macro Language

Christian M. Forster, DZS Computer Solutions, Inc.

ABSTRACT

The capabilities and innovative techniques of two generic, real-world, SAS® Macro Language reporting applications used internationally by a major pharmaceutical firm are presented. Together, these applications can handle the majority of listings and tables found in a typical clinical submission. Users of these applications find their report turnaround time reduced to a fraction of the time traditional methods used to take. The results they now achieve are more flexible, consistent, reproducible, aesthetically pleasing, and more accurate than results users accomplished using conventional SAS programming, or worse, hand-typing.

Generic reporting systems are emphasized, but the techniques presented have a wide variety of uses. Example calls to GENLIST, which is a generic listing system, and GENTABLE, a generic table-producing system (written by this paper's author and Amy Frueh, also from DZS) are presented along with some macro utilities. Using our approach, users need only to access their data and describe the contents of their reports. Attractive presentations are derived from end-user specifications without unnecessary user-overhead, or forcing static report layouts on the clinical department. This paper's goal is not to teach the SAS Macro Language, but to show powerful techniques and possibilities using it.

INTRODUCTION

Since the introduction of the first comprehensive release of the SAS system in 1976, programming departments in larger businesses have tried to automate and supplement SAS-supplied routines, particularly with regard to report presentation and production. This is especially true within the pharmaceutical industry, which places a high value on timely, accurate and aesthetically pleasing reports to submit to the FDA and foreign agencies. Delays due to the creation of individually prepared, time-consuming, faulty, or hard-to-read reports can be quite costly.

New releases of the SAS system have shown enhanced report creation capabilities, such as improvements in the PRINT and TABULATE procedures and the new REPORT procedure. However, the bulk of presentation and submission-ready reports are still not provided directly from SAS procedures. The personnel generating the reports often resort to tedious, complicated PUT statement programming or worse, to having the reports typed. The drawbacks to those methods include the excessive human intervention required and the increased risk of error. Many other drawbacks exist to those traditional methods, and have been discussed in papers such as "Simple Construction and Modification of Computer Generated Tables"[1]. Our solution to the problem of generic report production has been the use of the SAS Macro Language to create applications that marry the SAS Macro Language with SAS datastep and procedure output. GENLIST and GENTABLE are two such applications whose goals, benefits, and implementation will be discussed.

GOALS - GENERIC REPORTING APPLICATIONS

The basic goals of generic reporting applications such as GENLIST and GENTABLE include the following:

o **Ease of Use** - To create a system that is easy to use, the developers must have thorough knowledge of the background, needs, talents, and training of the target user community of the application. The resulting application should be one that the user community <u>wants</u> to use to expedite completion of their tasks.

o **Accuracy** - To achieve and maintain user confidence, the application must be written so that it is as "bullet-proof" as possible. This includes diagnosing user input errors and providing descriptive messages for special conditions or potential errors. Extensive quality assurance and validation should be done before each release of the application.

o **Flexibility** - The application must be flexible enough to meet the user's present and future needs. For report applications, this means simple alteration of titles, footnotes, display and content. Flexibility also refers to operating system and environment under which the application runs. Ties to particular features in the current operating environment should be avoided to allow future application porting.

o **Speed** - Time from the conception of the needed report to its actual production should be shorter than the current methods used.

o **Consistency** - Reports should present findings in a logical, predictable manner regardless of which particular clinical group generates them. This also aids in international reporting where tables and listings may be submitted from disparate clinical groups to various governing agencies. The generic application would have a "standardizing" effect on the way results are presented.

Discussed below are two examples of powerful systems written with these goals in mind.

GENLIST, A GENERIC LISTING SYSTEM

The user requirements for GENLIST included the goals listed above and the following criteria:

o A system that would provide a powerful, capable alternative to the PRINT and REPORT procedures for detailed demographic, laboratory, and other listings.

o Ability to print the value of more than one variable in a commonly-labeled column. Dynamic variable value displays in the column labels were also required.

o The maximum amount of information available in the SAS environment should be extracted, letting the caller use familiar SAS FORMAT and LABEL statements to pass information to the application.

o The burdens of exact column placement of values, balancing the multi-line column labels, calculating the lowest column width needed for a variable, and other tedious tasks should be removed from the user.

o Handling out-of-range and change-from-baseline flagging based on user requests was required.

o Many other bells and whistles such as left-justified or centered titles and footnotes with dynamic variable value substitution, the placement of text that spans several columns, solid line placement for subsequent inclusion in WordPerfect® documents, page-eject management based on user-defined groupings, and more would be necessary.

SAMPLE CALL

As the sample call to GENLIST in Appendix 1 shows, all the goals were attained. The input data, SAS program fragment, and output report are shown to illustrate the high degree of integration that can be achieved with the SAS system environment. The entire SAS job could not be shown due to limitations on the length of contributed SUGI papers. The section of code omitted simply merged demographic and vital signs data and assigned labels and formats. Please note that the solid lines on the report were not typed and not generated by the TABULATE procedure; they were applied by the macro (GENLIST does not use PROC TABULATE; it uses an actual datastep to have complete control of the presentation).

Please note that GENLIST presents the user with the following situation:

o The only "foreign" statements in a SAS job are the macro includer (%inc genlist;) and the actual macro call (%genlist(...)). Notice that there are not any %LETs and that intelligent parsing of the macro parameters avoids the tedium and limitations of repeated arguments (i.e. title1=, title2=, title3=, etc.)

o To associate custom column labels and formats, SAS FORMAT and LABEL statements are used instead of having the user specify them in the macro call. Since most of the GENLIST macro parameters have defaults, the only required parameters are COLVARS= (the column variables to print) and PGHEADS= (the title lines). The rest of the parameters are only needed for special features and custom presentation for that report.

o Delimiters and display flags have been chosen that mimic, as closely as possible, those used in base SAS software. In the COLVARS= parameter, for instance, the dot (.) prefix on a column variable means "print it on first occurrence" and the "@" suffix means "hold the pointer and pull the next column variable into this column."

o Column variables, title lines, and footnotes can be easily moved about, deleted, and added. The resulting report will always be of high quality, integrating the user's request for display variations as desired. The SOLIDLINES option can be used on listings that will be incorporated into WordPerfect documents, to facilitate correct centering and meet the desire for solid lines without human intervention.

<u>The process and techniques used are as follows:</u>

1. Parse and diagnose user input (parameters), sensing the presence of special feature requests (like normal range flagging) and options (like centering, solid lines). Extensive use of the BREAKUP macro is made (see its presentation later in this paper).

2. Execute a PROC CONTENTS with the OUT= specification and load needed information into macro variables for the user-referenced SAS variables. This is how the macro finds out about user-associated formats and labels. Please see the presentation of FINDTYPE below, a macro routine similar to the one used in GENLIST for this purpose.

3. Using any available information from the PROC CONTENTS, execute a datastep that discovers the widest column space each column variable needs. See the presentation of FINDFMT later in this paper for the method used. This method relieves the user of having to guess at the column width and number of decimal places needed for the printing of their variables, but allows them to specify labels and special formats. The end result is a listing that makes the best possible use of column space <u>for the particular data being reported</u> and maintains a uniform layout from page to page.

4. If special features were requested, perform them. For example, if the user requested that normal-range checking be done, a subprocess is performed that does the following:

<u>I.</u> Scans and set flags (loads global macro variables) for each column variable that is to be range-checked.

<u>II.</u> If the normal ranges are not on the report dataset, merge them to the report dataset based on user-supplied information (NRSOURCE and NRNORMBY parameters).

<u>III.</u> Create and set character-based flag SAS variables to print next to the range-checked column variables based on the normal range information. Insert these macro-generated SAS variable names into the user's COLVARS= parameter at proper locations.

<u>IV.</u> Append the categories and actual normal range values onto the column variable labels (already loaded into macro variables). Thus, the user has never typed in the normal range limits. Limits are displayed as they exist in the normal-range dataset the user has referenced (they have a single source where they can be changed). Please note in the example in Appendix 1 that the actual normal ranges appear in the column label without the user entering them (i.e. M:90-120).

5. Construct the page-header and footer routines from PGHEADS= and FOOTNOTE= parameter information. Begin to construct the sort order for the report by pulling out any SAS variables the user has included in the title lines. If there is an "@" prefix to the text, left-justify that title line, otherwise center it.

6. For every page necessary to display the column variables, construct the SAS column header routine looking at the width of the parsed SAS labels, and the width of the data printed in the column. In Appendix 1, the formatted data width of VISIT was wider than its label "VISIT". This causes the macro to use the data width for that column as the total column width. For "Diastolic BP" in the example, the label text was wider than the combined data widths of the BP value and High/Low flag, so use the label width in calculating the column layout.

7. If there are spanning headers (SPANHEAD=) or SOLIDLINES, make these adjustments to the column header routine. Note that information needed and stored during a GENLIST call is kept in macro variables. This prevents adding actual SAS variables to the report dataset that may clash with user variable names. These macro variables are kept local to particular routines whenever possible to avoid unnecessary filling the global macro variable table.

8. Construct the detail record SAS PUT statements. Since the column label and data widths are known, it is a straight forward matter to calculate the proper column placements.

9. Handle end-of-page control logic, integrating the observation count for sub-group data defined by the NOSPLIT= parameter (if one has been specified) and number of footnote lines. Allow constructed datastep to run.

While it is true that GENLIST is thousands of lines of macro code long, the actual building blocks were not that difficult to create. By breaking large system specifications into relatively small, manageable, well-defined pieces or modules, one can create powerful, reusable code. BREAKUP, FINDTYPE and FINDFMT presented later in this paper are good examples of these sorts of modules.

For now, I am trying to communicate the power that SAS offers to the applications developer and the level of integration the user should expect from a well-designed application.

GENTABLE, A GENERIC TABLE SYSTEM

GENTABLE is a more recently developed SAS macro application that builds on the goals set for GENLIST. Underscoring the power of generic, modular programming, GENTABLE actually uses GENLIST as its display formatter and output generator. Using GENLIST within GENTABLE dramatically reduced the development time needed for GENTABLE while enabling it to quickly show attractively presented results.

The theory and goals for GENTABLE included all those for GENLIST plus the following:

o Move to a more "English-like" user-interface than GENLIST. For example, if a user wants two or more variables printed in the same column, the "@" sign is used in GENLIST, the word "NEXTTO" is used in GENTABLE.

o Where GENLIST is excellent at producing detailed data listings, the purpose of GENTABLE would be to produce summary statistics tables based on user requests. The design of the system would allow the request of any combination of supported statistics for any number of variables printed to any precision. Any number of classification groupings would also be supported.

o Handle all necessary calls to SAS procedures, such as MEANS, FREQ, UNIVARIATE, GLM. Perform data transposing (NOT using the TRANSPOSE procedure!) where needed to combine all the information retrieved from the statistical procedures into a single dataset.

o Never perform any SAS procedure output-stripping (using PROC PRINTTO and then a datastep to read the output) to acquire statistics. Instead, the output data sets of the various statistical procedures should be read. This will dramatically improve the stability and dependability of the system.

o Continue the use of modular-programming techniques to facilitate easier quality assurance and the future inclusion of data from other statistical procedures.

o Provide the most efficient user-interface possible. This includes implementing "short-hand" methods of asking for repeated sets of statistics, and continuing to gather as much information as possible from the SAS environment.

o Begin with a X-by-Y or matrix style interface that would allow easy transposing of variables that lie across the page with those that run down the page.

Inspecting the user's calls to GENTABLE and subsequent output (Appendix 2) should show that these goals have been met. Even though GENTABLE development has spanned less than a year, impressive results are already being realized through its use. Very favorable comments have come from the user community, and the users are producing better looking and more accurate tables for submission faster than before. There are statistics needed that are not yet generated by GENTABLE, but due to its modular design, these will be fairly easy to integrate.

The basic process and techniques used in GENTABLE are as follows:

1. Parse user input parameters. Load requests for statistics (N, MEAN, MEDIAN, FREQ, etc.) for each variable into macro variables. Make a note (macro variable with a 0 or 1) of which SAS procedures will need to be run by GENTABLE based on the requested statistics.

DISPLAY is the key parameter in the call. The basic form of this parameter is:

DISPLAY = Statistic keywords optional rounding factors <variables>,

For example, if the user wanted to see the N, MEAN (to 2 decimal places), MINimum next to the MAXimum and the PVALUE (from GLM's lsmeans) next to the SIGnificance of the SAS variables SYSBP and DIABP:

```
DISPLAY = N MEAN .01 MIN NEXTTO MAX
        PVLSMEANS NEXTTO SIG <SYSBP DIABP>,
```

would be specified. Currently, over fifty statistic keywords are implemented.

2. Construct BY and TABLE statements from SAS variables in the TITLES= (page title lines), the DOWN= (the "Y" variables of the matrix), and the ACROSS= (the "X" variables of the matrix) parameters, if any.

3. Execute any necessary statistical procedures accumulating the results in a single dataset. For illustration I will show the basic process for the request DISPLAY= FREQ <DISC>. This is a request that GENTABLE look at the user's variable DISC in the user's dataset and print the counts of all values of DISC.

I. Perform a PROC FREQ for the variable based on any DOWN and ACROSS variables.

II. Using the FINDTYPE macro, find out if the user has associated a format with DISC. Load the discrete values for DISC from the PROC FREQ output dataset into macro variables. If there is a user format, execute a datastep using PUT(value,user-format.) to load the formatted values as potential column labels for the results. In the first GENTABLE example, note the placement of the formatted values for the SAS variable "DISC" as column labels for the cell counts.

4. Based on the DOWN= and ACROSS= parameters and the STATSACROSS (request for statistics to run across the page) and VARSDOWN (request for variables to run down the page) options, perform dataset transposing if needed.

5. Round the displayed statistics to default precision, if the user has not specified their own precision.

6. If the statistics are to run down the page, create a column labeled "Statistic" to display the types of statistics. Also, convert the statistic results to character equivalents (carefully, using the PUT function AFTER rounding the values) to allow them to display in a common column in the GENLIST call.

7. Setup and call GENLIST to produce the report, considering all other user parameters.

A more detailed explanation of how GENLIST and GENTABLE operate can be given at a later date, if user-group interest warrants it. This discussion of GENTABLE would not be complete without reference to the SUGI 12 paper by Bernard Costa entitled "TABLETS - A TABLE GENERATOR"[2]. The concept behind Bernard Costa's excellent TABLETS table macro has contributed to the theories used in GENTABLE.

A FEW UTILITY MACROS

Please see Appendix 3 for the source code and example calls to BREAKUP, FINDTYPE and FINDFMT. Macros similar to these are at the core of GENLIST and GENTABLE and should have equivalents in most major SAS macro applications. They comprise less than 200 lines of macro code, but illustrate the type of modular programming that lends itself to larger systems development. Their purposes are:

BREAKUP - Splits a macro variable value (BUTEXT) into as many macro variable pieces (NTEXT pieces will have names that begin with the &ROOT) as there are in the macro variable based on the specified delimiter (DELIM). See the BESTFMTS macro in Appendix 3 for an example call.

FINDTYPE - Loads the SAS variable types (into macro names prefixed with &TROOT and suffixed with numbers

1 - &N), any user-associated formats (prefix: &FROOT), and label (prefix: &LROOT) of &N macro variables that begin with &VAROOT that hold the SAS variable names. The PROC CONTENTS dataset name must be _CFCONT for this macro to run. See the BESTFMTS macro for an example call.

FINDFMT - Scans the report dataset (&DATA) for the best format and data width to use for those SAS variables (in &VAROOT1 - &VAROOTN) and that particular data. Loads the total length (&TLROOT1 - &TLROOTN), the number of decimal points needed (&DPROOT1 - &DPROOTN) and must be given the variable's type (&TYPRT1 - &TYPRTN) and any user-associated format (&FMTRT1 - &FMTRTN).

Appendix note: Most of the comments, spacing, and do-loop indentations have been removed from these macros due to space limitations. The appendices also had to be reduced to meet the six-page SUGI paper limit. The SAS Macro Language Developer, with proper training and manuals, should be able to figure out details of the macros' execution. I believe that applications departments that do not already have macros similar to these will appreciate the utility of these macros.

CONCLUSION

The payback for time and talents invested in well-designed, modular generic applications can be large. Making the best use of all the rudiments provided by the programming language and good end-user interaction is essential to the success of these applications. We approach our application system designs from the aspect of what would the users like the application to do for them, then work back to how we will accomplish the many small tasks that make up the goal.

By providing very functional, powerful, and flexible applications, end-users are finding they have more time to spend on tasks other than tedious manual report preparation. Now, users can quickly and easily try out different statistical report layouts, and their submissions are looking more consistent. By incorporating solid lines on the listings and tables, the outputs easily become centered WordPerfect sub-documents in clinical reports, and the human process of drawing lines on the output is eliminated.

CREDITS

Christian M. Forster from DZS Computer Solutions is the designer and developer of GENLIST.

Christian M. Forster and Amy Frueh from DZS Computer Solutions are the designers and developers of GENTABLE.

REFERENCES

[1]Litzsinger, Michael A. and Wright, Steven A. "Simple Construction and Modification of Computer Generated Tables", SUGI 16 Proceedings.

[2]Costa, Bernard "TABLETS - A Table Generator", SUGI 12 Proceedings.

SAS is a registered trademark of the SAS Institute, Cary, NC, USA in the USA and other countries. ® indicates USA registration.

WordPerfect is a registered trademark of WordPerfect Corporation, Orem, Utah, USA in the USA and other countries. ® indicates USA registration.

CONTACTS

Doron Z. Steger, President or
Christian M. Forster, Medical Systems Manager/Analyst
DZS Computer Solutions, Inc. (908) 356 - 6961
1661 Route 22 West
Bound Brook, NJ 08805

APPENDIX 1
GENLIST Sample Call

(Input Data)

Normal Range Dataset as sent to GENLIST:

```
OBS    SEX    DB_LOW    DB_HI    SB_LOW    SB_HI
 1      1       90       120      100       140
 2      2       80       110       90       130
```

Dataset fragment sent to GENLIST:

```
OBS  STUDY  SEX     INVEST  SUBJ   VISIT      DBP  SBP  AGE
 1    101   Male      1      1    Admission   80   120  (30)
 2    101   Female    1      2    Admission   80   120  (31)
 3    101   Male      1      3    Admission   80   120  (47)
```

(Program Fragment)

```
label subj='Subject¦(Age) Sex';
label dbp='Diastolic Blood Pressure (mmHg)';
label sbp='Systolic Blood Pressure (mmHg)';

/*   Call GENLIST to create the Vital Signs Lab Listing
   with normal range retrieval (from NR dataset).
 Special features:
  Paging by INVEST
  Skip a line between subjects
  Do not page-eject within subject
  Solidlined Report, RSUB character set for lines
  Report variables carry SUBJ AGE SEX VISIT to every page type
  Spanning headers based on start & stop SAS colvar names.
  Range check variables DBP and SBP
  Variables with low DBP and SBP are DB_LOW and SB_LOW
  Variables with hi DBP and SBP are DB_HI and SB_HI
  Normal Ranges may vary by SEX
  To get unique subject numbers look at INVEST and SUBJ
*/

%genlist(pgheads=@GENLIST will put this text at the Left Edge.
                 \@\Study (centered):!study\
                 Investigator (also centered):!invest,
        footnote=This is a sample footnote.,
        skipline=subj,
         nosplit=subj,
         options=solidlines rsub,
         colvars=<.subj@ .age@ .sex visit> dbp sbp,
        spanhead=dbp sbp Detail data\
                 subj visit This is over the¦Key Information\
                 subj sbp This Spans the Entire Report,
          nrvars=dbp sbp,
           nrlow=db_low sb_low,
            nrhi=db_hi  sb_hi,
        nrsource=nr,
        nrnormby=sex,
        nrsubjid=invest subj);
run;
```

(Output Listing)

GENLIST will put this text at the Left Edge.

Study (centered): 101
Investigator (also centered): 1

This Spans the Entire Report			
This is over the Key Information		Detail data	
Subject (Age) Sex	VISIT	Diastolic Blood Pressure (mmHg) M:90-120 F:80-110	Systolic Blood Pressure (mmHg) M:100-140 F:90-130
1 (30) Male	Admission Baseline Mid Point End Point	80 L 90 70 L 95	120 135 150 H 118
2 (31) Female	Admission Baseline Mid Point End Point	80 90 70 L 95	120 135 H 150 H 118
3 (47) Male	Admission Baseline Mid Point End Point	80 L 90 70 L 95	120 135 150 H 118

This is a sample footnote.

APPENDIX 2
GENTABLE Sample Calls

(Program [illegible])

```
proc format;
    value discf 1 = 'Adverse Reaction'
                2 = 'Uncooperative'
                3 = 'Completed';
    value tmtf  1 = 'Drug 1'  2 = 'Drug 2';

data demo;   /*     Construct Demo Data     */
week=1;tmt=1;pat=1;disc=1;sysbp=120;diabp=78;output;
week=1;tmt=2;pat=2;disc=2;sysbp=118;diabp=80;output;
week=1;tmt=2;pat=5;disc=2;sysbp=112;diabp=68;output;
week=1;tmt=1;pat=7;disc=1;sysbp=139;diabp=98;output;
week=1;tmt=2;pat=8;disc=3;sysbp=110;diabp=68;output;
week=1;tmt=1;pat=10;disc=3;sysbp=130;diabp=92;output;
week=1;tmt=1;pat=11;disc=3;sysbp=139;diabp=98;output;
week=1;tmt=2;pat=12;disc=2;sysbp=110;diabp=68;output;
week=1;tmt=1;pat=14;disc=3;sysbp=130;diabp=92;output;
format tmt tmtf. disc discf.;
label pat = 'No of¦Subj'
      tmt = 'Treatment'
    diabp = 'Diastolic BP'
    sysbp = 'Systolic BP';
proc print data=demo(obs=2);
title 'Input Dataset fragment to GENTABLE calls';

%inc gentable;  /*  Get GENTABLE system active */

/*  Call GENTABLE to display the Number of Patients (N),
  the FREQuency next to the PERCENT and the P-VALUE from
  Fishers Exact next to the SIGnificance of the SAS variable
  DISC which represents the patient disposition at Endpoint.
    Compare treatment group 1 to treatment group 2 and display
  treatment group running down the left.                    */

%gentable(titles=Example Table 1\@\Patient Status at Endpoint\@\,
   display = n <pat> freq nextto ppercentp
             pvexact_each nextto sig <disc>,
   compare = tmt 1 to 2,
      down = tmt,
      span = disc disc Patient Disposition at Endpoint,
   options = statsacross nostats solidlines rsub nodate nonumber);

/*  Call GENTABLE to display the N, the MEAN, MIN and MAX rounded
  to integers, the STandard Deviation to 1 decimal point and the
  MEDIAN of SYStolic and DIAstolic Blood Pressures.  Also present
  the LSMEANS P-value next to its SIGnificance from GLM comparing
  the 2 treatment groups.  Have treatment running across the page
  and week running down.                                     */

%gentable(Titles=Example Table 2\@\
          Vital Signs - Blood Pressure Statistics\@,
    Display = n mean 1. min 1. nextto max 1. std .1 median
              pvlsmean nextto sig <sysbp diabp>,
     Across = tmt,
       Down = week,
    compare = tmt 1 to 2,
       Span = all pgcells Treatment Group,
   Stattext = min BP\max Range,
    Options = varsdown solidlines rsub nodate nonumber);
```

(Input Dataset fragment to GENTABLE calls)

OBS	WEEK	TMT	PAT	DISC	SYSBP	DIABP
1	1	Drug 1	1	Adverse Reaction	120	78
2	1	Drug 2	2	Uncooperative	118	80

(Printout from GENTABLE)

Example Table 1
Patient Status at Endpoint

Treatment	No of Subj	Patient Disposition at Endpoint		
		Adverse Reaction	Uncooperative	Completed
Drug 1	5	2 (40%)	0 (0%)	3 (60%)
Drug 2	4	0 (0%)	3 (75%)	1 (25%)
P-values				
Drug 1 vs Drug 2		0.444	0.048 *	0.524

Example Table 2
Vital Signs - Blood Pressure Statistics

Variable	WEEK	Statistic	Treatment Group		Drug 1 vs Drug 2
			Drug 1	Drug 2	
Systolic BP	1	N	5	4	0.003 **
		Mean	132	113	
		BP Range	120 139	110 118	
		Std	7.9	3.8	
		Median	130	111	
Diastolic BP	1	N	5	4	0.004 **
		Mean	92	71	
		BP Range	78 98	68 80	
		Std	8.2	6.0	
		Median	92	68	

APPENDIX 3
BREAKUP, FINDTYPE, FINDFMT and BESTFMT Macros

```
*****************************************************************;
**   Macro Breakup - Splits up a parameter list and creates     *;
**  a global macro variable for each delimited string with the  *;
**  strings value.                                              *;
**  Parameters:                                                 *;
**       Butext  -  Text string to break up                     *;
**       Ntext   -  macro variable to assign the number of      *;
**                  strings parsed.                             *;
**       delim   -  String delimiter value (ex. \,¦,etc.        *;
**        root   -  String to use as root part of macro variable;
**                  created (ex. root of chris makes chris1,etc ;
** COPYRIGHT 1989, DZS Computer Solutions, Inc. By C.Forster    *;
** PUBLIC DOMAIN VERSION 1.0 - FREELY DISTRIBUTE AS LONG AS     *;
** CODE IS NOT MODIFIED AND ABOVE COPYRIGHT NOTICE IS RETAINED  *;
*****************************************************************;
%macro breakup(butext,ntext,root,delim);
 %**  Local variables: word - parsed piece of text                 ;
 %**                  count - no. of current piece of parsed text  ;
 %local word count;
 %* Create global var for # of parsed strings  ***;
 %global &ntext;
 %*  If they send me a null string, tell them there are no strings **;
 %if %length(&butext)=0 %then %let &ntext=0;
 %else %do;
    %let count=1;                              %**  Getting 1st word     **;
    %let word=%scan(&butext,&count,&delim);    %**  Put it in local word **;
    %do %while(%length(&word)>0);              %** While it exists, create *;
       %global &root&count;                    %** a global var from the root;
       %let &root&count=&word;                 %* passed appended with the # ;
       %let count=%eval(&count+1);             %* parsed string            *;
       %let word=%scan(&butext,&count,&delim);
    %end;
    %let &ntext=%eval(&count-1);          %* The # of pieces needs to be **;
 %end;                                    %* decremented                 **;
%mend breakup;

%Macro findtype(n,varoot,troot,froot,lroot);
%** FINDTYPE COPYRIGHT 1989, DZS Computer Solutions, Inc. By C.Forster ***;
%** Macro findtype(n,varoot,troot,froot,lroot) - Reads CONTENTS in _CFCONT *;
%**  Will load troot# with the type of SAS variable    **;
%** (blank for numeric, $ for character), and froot# with format length so *;
%** that on output, just need to concat troot# and froot# to produce fmt.  *;
%** also loads lroot# with the label text of the variable.                 *;
%* COPYRIGHT 1989, DZS Computer Solutions, Inc. By C.Forster   *;
%* PUBLIC DOMAIN VERSION 1.0 - FREELY DISTRIBUTE AS LONG AS    *;
%* CODE IS NOT MODIFIED AND ABOVE COPYRIGHT NOTICE IS RETAINED *;
 %local i j callstr;
 %**  Generate a Data Null to get more macro information of the dataset ***;
 %** Getting info from the _cfcont dataset created by the mandatory PROC  *;
 %** CONTENTS at the start of GENLIST.                                    *;
 data _null_; set _cfcont end=_cfeof;
 %if &n GT 0 %then %do;              %** As long as there are some...    **;
  retain _cft1-_cft&n _cff1-_cff&n _cfl1-_cfl&n;
  array _cftyps(&n) $ 1 _cft1 - _cft&n; ** Holds the variable type ($=char)*;
  array _cffmts(&n) $ 20 _cff1 - _cff&n;** Holds the format #s (width.dec) *;
  array _cflabs(&n) $ 40 _cfl1 - _cfl&n;** Holds the labels *;
  length fmt $ 20 _oldlab $ 40;
  if _n_=1 then do x=1 to dim(_cftyps);
                 _cftyps(x)=' ';
                 _cffmts(x)=' ';
                 _cflabs(x)=' ';
  end;
  if label=' ' or length(trim(label)) EQ 0 then label = name;
  %**  Clean out trouble characters in labels....    **;
  _oldlab=label;
  do while(index(label,',') GT 0 or (index(label,'&') GT 0 and
    index(label,' & ') EQ 0));
    if index(label,',') GT 0 then substr(label,index(label,','),1)=';';
    if index(label,'&') GT 0 and index(label,' & ') EQ 0 then
       substr(label,index(label,'&'),1)='+';
  end;
  if _oldlab NE label then
     put /'In label for ' name ' comma or ampersand was converted...'/;
  fmt=' ';
  if (formatl+formatd)>0 then do;     ** If user format present, grab it **;
    fmt=compress(format)¦¦compress(put(formatl,12.))¦¦'.';
    fmt=compress(fmt)¦¦compress(put(formatd,12.));
  end;
  else if length(format)>0 and format NE ' ' then
          fmt=compress(format)¦¦'.';
  select (upcase(name));          %** Branch on SAS variable name         **;
   %do i=1 %to &n;                %** Create WHEN clause based on SAS name **;
     %global &troot&i &froot&i &lroot&i;
     %let callstr=%upcase(%unquote(%bquote('&&&varoot&i')));
     when (&callstr) do;
      _cffmts(&i) = fmt;
      _cflabs(&i) = label;
      if type=2 then _cftyps(&i)='$';
     end;
   %end;
     otherwise;          **  Null otherwise clause for unused SAS names    **;
   end;
   if _cfeof then do x=1 to dim(_cftyps);
     xx=compress(put(x,12.));
     **  Symput the types **;
     %let callstr=%unquote(%bquote('&troot'¦¦xx));
     Call Symput(&callstr,trim(_cftyps(x)));
     **  Symput the formats *;
     %let callstr=%unquote(%bquote('&froot'¦¦xx));
     Call Symput(&callstr,trim(_cffmts(x)));
     **  Symput the labels *;
     %let callstr=%unquote(%bquote('&lroot'¦¦xx));
     Call Symput(&callstr,trim(_cflabs(x)));
   end;
 %end;
run;
%mend findtype;
```

```
%Macro findfmt(n,varoot,tlroot,dproot,typrt,fmtrt);
%** FINDFMT: COPYRIGHT 1989, DZS Computer Solutions, Inc. By C.Forster ***;
%***  Macro findfmt(n,varoot,tlroot,dproot,typrt,fmtrt);                 **;
%** Reads detail data in &data as  , will load tlroot# with total length *;
%** of the SAS variable in varoot#, dproot# with the # of dec. places,    *;
%** typrt is the type of the var, fmtrt will hold any assoc format      **;
%** typrt: $ for char, blank for numeric.                               **;
%* COPYRIGHT 1989, DZS Computer Solutions, Inc. By C.Forster   *;
%* PUBLIC DOMAIN VERSION 1.0 - FREELY DISTRIBUTE AS LONG AS    *;
%* CODE IS NOT MODIFIED AND ABOVE COPYRIGHT NOTICE IS RETAINED *;
  %local i j callstr;
  %**  Generate a Data Null to get macro information of the dataset ***;
  data _null_; set &data end=_cfeof;
  retain  _cfl1-_cfl&n 1 _cfd1-_cfd&n 0;
  array _cflens(&n) _cfl1-_cfl&n;  %**  To hold total lengths **;
  array _cfdecs(&n) _cfd1-_cfd&n;  %**             dec. places   **;
  array _cfvals(&n) $ 132 _cfv1-_cfv&n; %**         last values   **;
  array _cftyps(&n) _TEMPORARY_ (
   %do i=1 %to &n;
     %if &&&typrt&i NE $ and %length(&&&fmtrt&i)=0 %then 0;%** Set type num (0);
     %else 1;                                             %** Set type char(1);
   %end;     );
   %do i=1 %to &n;
     %global &dproot&i &tlroot&i;      %** Create global vars          ;
     %if &&&typrt&i NE $ %then %do;              %** If numeric          ;
       %if %length(&&&fmtrt&i) GT 1 %then %do;
         %** Raise min fmt width for date formats to 2;
         %if %index(%upcase(&&&fmtrt&i),DD) GT 0 %then
             if _cflens(&i) LT 2 then _cflens(&i) = 2 %str(;);
         _cfvals(&i) = put(&&&varoot&i,&&&fmtrt&i);
       %end;
       %else
        _cfvals(&i) = compress(&&&varoot&i||'') %str(;);
     %end;
     %else %do;                                  %** Else character  ;
       %if %length(&&&fmtrt&i) GT 1 %then
        _cfvals(&i) = put(&&&varoot&i,&&&fmtrt&i) %str(;);
       %else
        _cfvals(&i) = trim(&&&varoot&i||'') %str(;);
     %end;
   %end;
   do _cfx=1 to dim(_cflens);
      _cfl = length(_cfvals(_cfx));         %** Find total length          ;
     if _cfl GT 1 then do;
       if _cftyps(_cfx) EQ 0 then do;       %** If numeric  ;
         _cfd = index(_cfvals(_cfx),'.');  %** Find dec. pt. if any       ;
         if _cfd>0 then do;                %** If there are dec.s subtract that ;
            _cfd = _cfl - _cfd;            %** from the number of int numbers ;
            _cfl = _cfl - _cfd - 1;
         end;
       end;
       else _cfd = 0;                      %**  If char.  ***;
       %** Take the longest of all **;
       if _cfl > _cflens(_cfx) then _cflens(_cfx) = _cfl;
       if _cfd > _cfdecs(_cfx) then _cfdecs(_cfx) = _cfd;
     end;
   end;
if _cfeof then do _cfx=1 to dim(_cflens);
   _cfxx=compress(put(_cfx,12.));
   **  Symput the lengths **;
  if _cfdecs(_cfx)>0 then do;
       _cfd=_cflens(_cfx)+_cfdecs(_cfx)+1;
       %let callstr=%unquote(%bquote('&tlroot'||_cfxx));
       Call Symput(&callstr,compress(put(_cfd,12.)));
       **  done **;
  end;
  else do;
    %let callstr=%unquote(%bquote('&tlroot'||_cfxx));
    Call Symput(&callstr,compress(put(_cflens(_cfx),12.)));
  end;
  **  Symput the dec places ***;
  %let callstr=%unquote(%bquote('&dproot'||_cfxx));
  Call Symput(&callstr,compress(put(_cfdecs(_cfx),12.)));
  **  Symput the values ***;
end;
run;
%mend findfmt;
/*  Demonstrate reading of PROC CONTENTS and calculation of best
   format for the SAS variables.
*/
%macro bestfmts(data,varnames);
%local i temp;
  /*  Macro BESTFMTS scans the PROC CONTENTS of any dataset and
     then scans the actual data to construct the best format for
     any variable in any dataset.  Generic macros can use the
     data loaded to construct PUT statements for reports or
     data conversion.
     Parameters: DATA - Dataset name to analyze.
                 VARNAMES - Variable names to analyze separated
                            by blanks.
  */
  proc contents data=&data out=_cfcont noprint;
  run;
  %breakup(&varnames,nvars,var,%str( ));     /* Parse VARNAMES */
  %findtype(&nvars,var,type,fmt,label);    /* Read CONTENTS   */
  %findfmt(&nvars,var,nchar,ndecs,type,fmt);/* Calc FMTS      */
  %put .;
  %do i=1 %to &nvars;
    %if %length(&&fmt&i)>1 %then %do;/* If USER format...  */
      %let fmt&i = %substr(&&fmt&i,1,%length(&&fmt&i)-1);
      %put For variable &&var&i format is &&fmt&i, Total length: &&nchar&i,;
 %put
 Use &&type&i%str()&&fmt&i%str()&&nchar&i%str(.)&&ndecs&i for output format.;
      %put .;
    %end;
    %else %do;/* No user format assoc. */
      %put For variable &&var&i no format assoc., Total length: &&nchar&i,;
      %put Use &&type&i%str()&&nchar&i%str(.)&&ndecs&i for output format.;
      %put .;
    %end;
  %end;
 %mend bestfmts;
```

```
/*  Create formats to demonstrate decoded printing.
    Normally, the user relies on the LIBRARY libname reference
    that points to the common clinical format definitions.
*/
proc format;
     value sex 1='Male' 2='Female';
     value visit 1='Admission' 2='Baseline' 3='Mid Point'
               4='End Point';
     picture age other='009)' (prefix='(');

/* Construct dummy dataset with a couple of visits and values.
   Normally, the user would pull in production clinical data and
   handle the merging of demographic data (SEX, RACE, etc.) to the
   detail vital or lab dataset.
*/
data test;
study = 101;
sex = 1;
invest = 1;subj = 1;visit = 1; dbp = 80; sbp = 120; output;
                    visit = 2; dbp = 90; sbp = 135; output;
                    visit = 3; dbp = 70; sbp = 150; output;
                    visit = 4; dbp = 95; sbp = 118; output;
run;
** Create more dummy subjects by propagating the data;
data test; set test;
age = 30;         **  Fake age                            **;
wgt = 157.5;      **  Fake Weight ;
output;        **  Output Subj #1 data                  **;
do subj=2 to 3;** Create clone subjects altering SEX, AGE *;
  if subj=2 then sex=2; else sex=1; ** Fake SEX **;
  age = (subj * 15) + mod(11,subj);          ** Fake AGE **;
  wgt = (subj * 90.5) + mod(11,subj);        ** Fake WGT **;
  output;
end;
format sex sex. visit visit. age age.;  **   Do some formating   **;
run;

/*  Call BESTFMTS to find out the best formats for these variables */
%bestfmts(test,study invest subj visit sex dbp sbp wgt);
run;

.
For variable study no format assoc., Total length: 3,
Use  3.0 for output format.
.
For variable invest no format assoc., Total length: 1,
Use  1.0 for output format.
.
For variable subj no format assoc., Total length: 1,
Use  1.0 for output format.
.
For variable visit format is VISIT, Total length: 9,
Use  VISIT9.0 for output format.
.
For variable sex format is SEX, Total length: 6,
Use  SEX6.0 for output format.
.
For variable dbp no format assoc., Total length: 2,
Use  2.0 for output format.
.
For variable sbp no format assoc., Total length: 3,
Use  3.0 for output format.
.
For variable wgt no format assoc., Total length: 5,
Use  5.1 for output format.
.
```

Dynamic Code Replaces Itself Every 3,000 Executions Or Less

Kurt Luedke, Freddie Mac
Jeffrey Keene, Freddie Mac

The purpose of this paper is to explain what dynamic code is and what situations can benefit from it. It will then discuss what facilities are available in SAS® software versions 5 and 6 to create dynamic code. To conclude, the paper will illustrate two macros which significantly facilitate the writing of dynamic code in SAS software version 6.06.

What is dynamic code? Dynamic code is code which like the chameleon has the ability to alter itself in order to adapt to the current environment. That is, dynamic code has not only the ability to recognize the quarter in which it is running but also the ability to change titles and footnotes to reflect such. An investments program, for instance, would realize by a number of indicators that the market is beginning a new trend and then adjust its algorithms accordingly.

Typically when submitted, a dynamic program is incomplete. It does not have all of the code necessary to perform the intended task. It does contain code, though, which is designed to examine specified data and parameters and thereby make decisions. As the program makes these decisions, it generates the additional code required to complete the task.

Perhaps the easiest way to explain dynamic code is by example. Suppose you have four or five different programs. They are all identical except for the PROC PRINT at the conclusion. Which program is used is dependent upon which quarter of the year it is and what data need to be processed.

You could document which job to use under which scenario. An alternative would be to have one program which automatically handles any scenario correctly. In this method you would have a DATA step recognize what data need to be processed and in what quarter it is. The DATA step would then dynamically write the PROC PRINT to follow. A fairly easy method for accomplishing this end would be to have the cognitive DATA step write out to a flat file the code for the PROC PRINT. The next step would be to %INCLUDE the file back in at the end of the program, thus executing the PROC PRINT.

Another example of dynamic code would be the instream construction of a PROC FORMAT. Suppose you work for an insurance company. You have a list of one thousand specific policy numbers for which you need to pull data. The good news is that the file of policy information is sorted by policy number. The bad news is that it is a flat file with over thirty million records.

One way to approach this would be to read in the entire flat file. Merge that with your list, subsetting to those policies on your list. This method would require a large amount of work space and at least three I/O transactions for each of the thirty plus million policies in the flat file (see Figure 1).

Another approach would be to dynamically write a PROC FORMAT of your list (see Figure 2). Then, simply test each policy as you read it in from the flat file. This method saves considerable work space, time and I/O processing.

Now that we have established some understanding of both what dynamic code is and also what situations can benefit from it, we will look at two different methods of writing dynamic code in SAS software version 5.

```
data flatfile;
  infile flatfile;
  input @001 policy $char006.
        @024 premium 6.;                    30 million inputs
run;                                        30 million outputs

data subset;
  merge flatfile mylist(in=needed);
  by policy;                                30 million inputs
  if needed then output;                    1 thousand outputs
run;
```

Figure 1

```
data _null_;                                MYLIST
  set mylist end=eof;                         134215
  file tempform notitles;                     413505
  if _n_ = 1 then do;                         527355
    put 'proc format;';                          .
    put 'value $check "' policy '"';             .
  end;                                           .
  else put ',"' policy '"';
  if eof then do;
    put '= "yes"';
    put 'other = "no ";';
  end;
run;

%include tempform;

    proc format;
    value $check "134215"
    ,"413505"
    ,"527355"
       .
       .
    = "yes"
    other = "no ";

data subset;
  infile flatfile;
  input @001 policy $char006.
        @024 premium 6.;
  if put(policy,$check.) = 'yes' then output;
run;              30 million inputs
                  1 thousand outputs
```

Figure 2

The first method was demonstrated in the previous example. That is to write the needed code out to a flat file and %INCLUDE the file back into the job stream at the appropriate place.

The second method is to use the CALL EXECUTE macro facility. The syntax for CALL EXECUTE is

CALL EXECUTE(argument);

Just as with the PUT statements in the previous examples, text is passed through enclosed in single or double quotes.

CALL EXECUTE('proc format;');

In order to pass the value of a variable, one would not use quotes.

CALL EXECUTE(policy);

CALL EXECUTE writes out to the SYSIN whatever argument is passed to it. The SYSIN is the input stack of program statements to be executed. When the compile process is ready to accept more code, it reads the program statements from the SYSIN one at a time. Consequently, whatever code is placed on top of the SYSIN by CALL EXECUTE will automatically be submitted into the job stream following the completion of that DATA step's processing (see Figure 3).

```
data _null_;
  set mylist end=eof;
  if _n_ = 1 then do;
    call execute('proc format;');
    call execute('value $check "' policy '"');
  end;
  else call execute(',"' policy ');
  if eof then do;
    call execute('= "yes"');
    call execute('other = "no ";');
  end;
run;

  SYSIN

    proc format;
    value $check "134215"
    ,"413505"
    ,"527355"
      .
      .
    = "yes"
    other = "no ";
```

Figure 3

CALL EXECUTE is convenient since it relieves you from allocating a flat file of the correct size. From run to run the size requirements of the flat file will vary. One could continually adjust the allocation, except that the idea behind dynamic code is that we can leave the program unattended.

You must conclude any DATA step containing CALL EXECUTE statements with a RUN statement, or the dynamic code will be misplaced in the SYSIN. As long as you keep this in mind, though, CALL EXECUTE is very easy and very powerful. Now the bad news. CALL EXECUTE is not currently supported in SAS software version 6.

What to do? In our area of Freddie Mac we have a number of programs which use the CALL EXECUTE function. The only reasonable course of action that we saw available was to write our own facility. Now, we get to the heart of the paper, how to write macros to replace CALL EXECUTE.

We decided to use macro variables instead of writing to the SYSIN. What we would do is write one macro 'MSTACK' (see Figure 4) which would load an array of macro variables with the dynamic code and a second macro 'MDO' (see Figure 5) which would pull the dynamic code into the job stream at the desired point.

The intention is that MSTACK would be placed in a macro library available to the SAS Proc and CLIST. This would allow all users to reference it. There would be a problem though if one of the variables (data or macro variable) was of the same name as one the user had defined. This could cause some rather painful errors.

Macro To Create Array Of Macro Variables

```
%macro mstack(zqstring);
%global zqcount;
  do;
    zqcount = sum(symget('zqcount'),1);
    if zqcount le 9999 then do;
      call symput('zqcount',zqcount);
      call symput('zqln' || left(put(zqcount,4.)), &zqstring);
    end;
  end;
%mend mstack;
```

Figure 4

So, all of the variables used in MSTACK begin with 'ZQ'. This appears to be a very seldomly used combination of characters. Although, I have no doubt that some one will blunder into it.

MSTACK was written in SAS DATA step code as versus SAS Macro Language so that macro variables would not be resolved prior to execution. Any reference to a macro variable using an '&' would be resolved at compile time. This would hard code a value for every invocation of MSTACK. By using CALL SYMPUTs and SYMGETs with DATA step code, the user is able to retrieve and update the value of ZQCOUNT with each invocation.

The first line of MSTACK is simply the macro definition statement. The only argument to MSTACK will be the variable ZQSTRING. The second line declares ZQCOUNT to be a Global variable. This is necessary so that the symbolic variable ZQCOUNT exists when the SYMGET function first tries to retrieve it. If ZQCOUNT did not exist when SYMGET searched for it, you would see in your SAS log the message

NOTE: ILLEGAL ARGUMENT TO FUNCTION

A DO process is required to encase the code within MSTACK, since it consists of more than one statement. It is reasonable to assume that users will not set apart the MSTACK invocation with a DO process. Consequently, if MSTACK does not force the DO process the resulting logic paths could be severely radical to the user's intentions.

On the first invocation of the macro, MSTACK creates the variable ZQCOUNT in the global symbolic table with a missing value. Then, because ZQCOUNT is initially missing, the SUM function is necessary to increment ZQCOUNT. Any other method would simply perpetuate the missing value instead of incrementing it.

After incrementing ZQCOUNT, a CALL SYMPUT updates its value in the global table. Next a CALL SYMPUT creates an array variable in the global table with the value of ZQSTRING. The syntactic rules for the second argument of CALL SYMPUT are the same as those for CALL EXECUTE. By passing ZQSTRING straight through from macro argument to CALL SYMPUT argument, MSTACK has the same syntactic rules as CALL EXECUTE. Therefore, MSTACK can be easily substituted with a global change for CALL EXECUTE in extant programs without concern to the argument being passed.

It will be important to document that the user is limited to 9,999 invocations. The CALL SYMPUT which creates the macro array variable uses a PUT statement to compress the counter to a maximum of four digits. This is necessary so that the macro array variable names are limited to eight characters. Any invocations after 9,999 would start overwriting previous array members. Therefore, a conditional was placed inside of MSTACK to cause MSTACK to disregard any invocation when ZQCOUNT is equal to 9,999.

```
data _null_;
  set mylist end=eof;
  if _n_ = 1 then do;
    %mstack('proc format;')
    %mstack('value $check "' policy '"')
  end;
  else %mstack(',"' policy '"')
  if eof then do;
    %mstack('= "yes"')
    %mstack('other = "no ";')
  end;
run;

%mdo;
```

```
proc format;
value $check "134215"
,"413505"
,"527355"
  .
  .
= "yes"
other = "no ";
```

Note that a semicolon is not used when invoking MSTACK

Figure 5

Remember, though, that MSTACK does not write directly to the SYSIN as CALL EXECUTE does. When the current DATA step completes its processing, the statements given to MSTACK will not automatically run. Therefore, a mechanism is needed to pull these statements into the jobstream, the macro MDO (see Figure 6).

Macro To Execute Array Of Macro Variables

```
%macro mdo;
  %if &zqcount > 0 %then %do;
    %do i=1 %to &zqcount;
      &&zqlin&i
    %end;
  %end;
  %let zqcount = 0;
%mend mdo;
```

Figure 6

The first step is to make certain that there are indeed array elements to be processed. Should ZQCOUNT not be greater than zero, then there are two possibilities. The first possibility is that MSTACK has not yet been invoked and therefore ZQCOUNT does not yet exist. This will result in the following log messages.

> ERROR: A character operand was found in the %EVAL function or %IF condition where a numeric operand is required. The condition was: &zqcount > 0
> ERROR: The macro will stop executing.

This forces MDO to stop processing but does not cause an abend condition for the job, unless the ERRORABEND option has been specified.

The other possibility is that MDO has already been run and ZQCOUNT had been reset to zero. In this case, that macro will stop processing with no ERROR messages.

Had ZQCOUNT been greater than zero, the macro would loop from one to the value of ZQCOUNT writing to the jobstream the array of macro variables. Once this is done, MDO would reset ZQCOUNT to zero and stop processing. The code it generated would then be compiled and executed.

In conclusion, the major advantage of MSTACK is that the user has complete control over when the dynamic code is written and when it is executed. It may be the case that one DATA step does not have all of the information necessary to completely write the dynamic code. If you are using a flat file you would run into some problems with the file disposition. With MSTACK, there is no problem. Just resume invoking the macro in a later DATA step. You may continue adding to the dynamic code until you invoke MDO. At that point ZQCOUNT will be reset to zero.

Appendix:

On the following two pages is detailed a version of MSTACK which will allow up to twenty-six concurrent dynamic stacks of code. Each stack can hold up to 9,999 entries. Stacks are distinguished by labels 'A' through 'Z'. The user can bounce between stacks at will by specifying the stack label. Likewise MDO can reference specific stacks in any order. Additionally, MDO can be made to execute each extant stack in alphabetical order.

While it is not disastrous to skip a letter when adding a new stack, it is not advised. If MDO is told to execute all stacks, it will attempt to do them in alphabetical order. Had a letter been skipped, the non-extant counter would cause MDO to stop processing.

Syntax

Never use a semicolon when invoking MSTACK.

```
%MSTACK( argument )
```

will reference one of two stacks. If this is the first time MSTACK has been invoked, it will default to stack 'A'. Otherwise, it will default to the last specified stack.

```
%MSTACK( argument , MSTACK=B )
```

will add the argument as the next statement in stack 'B'.

```
%MDO;
```

will first try to execute the last specified stack. If it cannot execute this stack because the stack counter is not greater than zero, it will decrement through the alphabet until it finds a stack which has a counter greater than zero.

```
%MDO( MSTACK=D );
```

will execute stack 'D'.

```
%MDO( MSTACK=ALL );
```

will cause the sequential execution of each extant stack in alphabetical order.

MSTACK

```
%macro mstack(zqstring,mstack=);
do;
options nomacrogen nosymbolgen nomlogic nomprint;

%global azqcnt bzqcnt czqcnt dzqcnt ezqcnt fzqcnt gzqcnt
        hzqcnt izqcnt jzqcnt kzqcnt lzqcnt mzqcnt nzqcnt
        ozqcnt pzqcnt qzqcnt rzqcnt szqcnt tzqcnt uzqcnt
        vzqcnt wzqcnt xzqcnt yzqcnt zzqcnt zqhigh zqlast;
zqflag = 'yes';

zqstack = "&mstack";
if zqstack = ' ' then do;
  zqlast = symget('zqlast');
  if zqlast = ' ' then zqstack = 'A';
  else zqstack = zqlast;
end;

zqstack = upcase(zqstack);
if ('A' le zqstack le 'Z') and
     (zqstack ne '}') and
     (zqstack ne '\') and
     (length(zqstack) = 1) then do;
  call symput('zqlast',zqstack);
  if zqstack > symget('zqhigh')
     then call symput('zqhigh',zqstack);
end;
else zqflag = 'no';

if zqflag = 'yes' then do;
  zqtemp = trim(zqstack) || 'zqcnt';
  zqcnt = sum(symget(zqtemp),1);
  call symput(zqtemp,zqcnt);
  zqtemp = trim(zqstack) || 'lin' || left(put(zqcnt,4.));
  call symput(zqtemp,&zqstring);
end;
end;

%mend mstack;
```

Figure 7

MDO

```
%macro mdo(mstack=);
options nomacrogen nosymbolgen nomlogic mprint;

%let zqref = ABCDEFGHIJKLMNOPQRSTUVWXYZ;
%let mstack = %upcase(&mstack);

%if &zqhigh =    %then %put No Stacks Have Yet Been
Defined;

%else %if &mstack = ALL %then %do;
  %let endpoint = 0;
  %let stopthis = 0;

  %do %until(&stopthis ne 0);
    %let endpoint = (%eval(&endpoint + 1);
    %if %substr(&zqref,&endpoint,1) = &zqhigh
      %then %let stopthis = 1;
  %end;

  %let flag = no;
  %do i=1 %to &endpoint;
    %let mstack = %substr(&zqref,&i,1);
    %if &&&mstack.zqcnt > 0 %then %do;
      %let flag = yes;
      %do j=1 %to &&&mstack.zqcnt;

  &&&mstack.lin.&i

      %end;
      %let &mstack.zqcnt = 0;
    %end;
  %end;
  %if &flag = no %then %put All Stacks Have Already Been
Processed;
%end;

%else %if &mstack =  %then %do;

  %if &&&zqlast.zqcnt > 0 %then %let mstack = &zqlast;
  %else %if &&&zqhigh.zqcnt > 0 %then %let mstack =
&zqhigh;

  %else %do;
    %let endpoint = 0;
```

(continued on next page)

Figure 8

```
    %let stopthis = 0;
    %do %until(&stopthis ne 0);
      %let endpoint = %eval(&endpoint + 1);
      %let substrng = %substr(&zqref,&endpoint,1);
      %if &&&substrng.zqcnt > 0 %then %let mstack =
&substrng;
      %if &substrng = &zqhigh %then %let stopthis = 1;
    %end;
  %end;

  %if &mstack ne %then %do;
    %do i=1 %to &&&mstack.zqcnt;

  &&&mstack.lin&i

    %end;
    %let &mstack.zqcnt = 0;
  %end;
  %else %put All Stacks Have Already Been Processed;
%end;

%else %if (A le &mstack) and
        (&mstack le Z) and
        (&mstack le }) and
        (&mstack le \) and
        (%length(&mstack) = 1) %then %do;
  %if &&&mstack.zqcnt > 0 %then %do;
    %do i=1 %to &&&mstack.zqcnt;

  &&&mstack.lin&i

    %end;
  %end;
  %else %put Stack &mstack Has Not Yet Been Defined;
%end;

%else %put Stack &mstack Is An Invalid Stack Reference;

%mend mdo;
```

Figure 9

Contacting the authors

Kurt Luedke (703) 450-3050
Federal Home Loan Mortgage Corporation
1769 Business Center Drive
Reston, VA 22090

Jeffrey Keene (703) 450-3435
Federal Home Loan Mortgage Corporation
1769 Business Center Drive
Reston, VA 22090

Trademarks

SAS software is a registered trademark of SAS Institute Inc., Cary, NC, USA

A STUDY IN REPETITION
RESULTING IN
A UTILITY MACRO FOR SUBSTITUTION

H. Ian Whitlock, Westat

INTRODUCTION

A utility macro, REPLACE, is presented which can help avoid repetitious macro code. It will be discussed in the context of one of the programs which motivated its development. As a by-product of discussing the macro, various macro functions will be reviewed. In particular, the quoting functions %NRSTR and %UNQUOTE are demonstrated in a context which makes them a natural part of the macro facility.

The macro REPLACE is used to write a sequence of lines which are alike except for the occurrence of one sequence of characters. An important feature is that macro calls and macro variables are resolved after replacement when %NRSTR is used in the call. For example the call:

```
%REPLACE
    ( LIST= FIRST SECOND THIRD,
      TARGET= %NRSTR
       ( IF 0 < XXXX < 10 THEN %XXXX;)
    )
```

will produce the code:

```
IF 0 < FIRST < 10 THEN %FIRST ;
IF 0 < SECOND < 10 THEN %SECOND ;
IF 0 < THIRD < 10 THEN %THIRD ;
```

THE PROBLEM

Consider the following segment of code (taken from the motivating program shown in FIGURE 1 at the end of this paper):

```
ARRAY BN   (*) %ARRAYLST
   ( PREFIX=BN  , FROM=8808, TO=8907)
;
ARRAY CITP (*) %ARRAYLST
   ( PREFIX=CITP, FROM=8808, TO=8907)
;
ARRAY CMDT (*) %ARRAYLST
   ( PREFIX=CMDT, FROM=8808, TO=8907)
;
ARRAY DITP (*) %ARRAYLST
   ( PREFIX=DITP, FROM=8808, TO=8907)
;
ARRAY NOCT (*) %ARRAYLST
   ( PREFIX=NOCT, FROM=8808, TO=8907)
;
ARRAY OMSG (*) %ARRAYLST
   ( PREFIX=OMSG, FROM=8808, TO=8907)
;
ARRAY RPCD (*) %ARRAYLST
   ( PREFIX=RPCD, FROM=8808, TO=8907)
;
ARRAY STMN (*) %ARRAYLST
   ( PREFIX=STMN, FROM=8808, TO=8907)
;
```

This is one form of repetition. Each array statement is like the others; only the array name and the prefix change. Aha! It could be handled in a %DO - loop, i.e., it can be controlled by rewriting the offending code. (Note: %ARRAYLST generates a variable list in which each variable name consists of a prefix followed by a year/month in the given range. But what %ARRAYLST does or how it is coded is really irrelevant to the problem of interest: controlling repetition.)

FIRST ATTEMPT - AN INTERNAL SOLUTION

A first attempt might be to set up an array of macro variables V1 to V8 representing the changing part of the line. Remember the Ith element in the array is referenced by &&V&I. Thus we obtain:

```
%LOCAL I V1 V2 V3 V4 V5 V6 V7 V8
;
/* INITIALIZATION */
%LET V1 = BN   ;
%LET V2 = CITP ;
%LET V3 = CMDT ;
%LET V4 = DITP ;
%LET V5 = NOCT ;
%LET V6 = OMSG ;
%LET V7 = RPCD ;
%LET V8 = STMN ;

/* MAKE ARRAY STATEMENTS */

%DO I = 1 %TO 8 ;

   ARRAY &&V&I (*) %ARRAYLST (
         PREFIX=&&V&I,
         FROM=8808,
         TO =8907 ) ;

%END ;
```

It has the advantage of simplicity, but there is still an element of repetition in the initialization. Moreover, it would require modification to use in other contexts. Adding a little more complexity helps.

The macro function %SCAN can be used to generate the variable part of the above loop. But now the macro function %EVAL is needed to control the index of the loop. Now we have:

```
/* ------   SCANNING LOOP   ----- */

%LOCAL LIST WORD I ;
                  /* INITIALIZATION */
%LET LIST =
      BN    CITP CMDT DITP
      NOCT OMSG RPCD STMN ;
%LET I = 1 ;
%LET WORD =
      %SCAN ( &LIST , &I ) ;

%DO                    /* MAKE ARRAYS */
   %WHILE ( %LENGTH (&WORD) > 0 ) ;

      ARRAY &WORD (*) %ARRAYLST (
         PREFIX=&WORD,
         FROM=8808,
         TO =8907 )
      ;
      %LET I = %EVAL ( &I + 1 ) ;
      %LET WORD = %SCAN (&LIST, &I);

%END ;                 /* MAKE ARRAYS */
```

Has repetition been eliminated? Suppose the plan as suggested above were carried out for the program in FIGURE 1 at the end of this paper. There would be a lot of very similar %DO - %WHILE SCANNING loops - one for the %TIMESHFT calls, another for the array statements, and another for the array processing. Moreover, FIGURE 1 is only part of a larger program with several data steps similar to the one shown.

Each SCANNING loop has a core difference, but most of the code would be precisely the same because it has the same function. For example: in the SCANNING loop above, the core code is:

```
ARRAY &WORD (*) %ARRAYLST
   (PREFIX=&WORD, FROM=8808,TO=8907 )
;
```

How can the array statement be lifted out of the SCANNING loop? Now it is time to ask - "Can a macro handle the repetitious %DO - %WHILE loops?"

SECOND ATTEMPT - MOVE TOWARD AN EXTERNAL SOLUTION

It is difficult to remove the core code from the SCANNING LOOP because &WORD serves two masters:

- &WORD, an intimate part of the SCANNING LOOP, gives the value to be substituted.
- &WORD also indicates the code part to be replaced.

These functions must be separated before we can lift out the core code. This can be done by creating a new level of variable, known to the macro but not a macro variable. We will use XXXX for the new variable. Replace &WORD by XXXX in the core giving:

```
ARRAY XXXX (*) %ARRAYLST
   ( PREFIX=XXXX, FROM=8808, TO=8907)
;
```

The macro function %INDEX can be used to locate the first occurrence of XXXX, and %SUBSTR can be used to break up the line and piece it back together. For the first word scanned from the list of replacement values, this leads to the loop shown below.

```
%LOCAL
   X WORD TARGET FRSTPART LASTPART;

                 /* INITIALIZATION */
%LET WORD = BN ;
%LET TARGET =
   %STR ( ARRAY XXXX (*) %ARRAYLST
   (PREFIX=XXXX, FROM=8808, TO =8907)
   ; )
;

%LET X = %INDEX ( &TARGET , XXXX ) ;

%DO             /* DO REPLACEMENT   */
   %WHILE ( &X > 0 )
;
   %LET FRSTPART = %SUBSTR
      ( &TARGET , 1 , &X - 1 ) ;
   %LET LASTPART =
      %SUBSTR ( &TARGET , &X + 4 ) ;

   %LET TARGET =
      &FRSTPART.&WORD.&LASTPART ;
   %LET X = %INDEX ( &TARGET , XXXX )
   ;
%END ;          /* DO REPLACEMENT   */
```

Note that the core statement has been assigned to the macro variable, TARGET. This means that the core statement can be a parameter eventually. It is no longer a prisoner of the SCANNING LOOP.

There are, however, two things wrong with the above code.

1) %ARRAYLST will be executed when TARGET is defined. Hence &TARGET is really

   ARRAY XXXX (*) XXXX8808 XXXX8809
   XXXX8810 XXXX8811 XXXX8812
   XXXX8901 XXXX8902 XXXX8903
   XXXX8904 XXXX8905 XXXX8906
   XXXX8907 ;

2) There is no provision for XXXX occurring at the beginning or end of the target string.

The macro call to %ARRAYLST can be hidden by using the quoting function %NRSTR to hide both % and & signs. In this case we have:

```
%LET TARGET = %NRSTR
    ( ARRAY XXXX (*) %ARRAYLST
        (PREFIX=XXXX,FROM=8808,TO=8907)
      ;
    ) ;
```

%SUBSTR will reveal the macro call hidden by %NRSTR whenever the macro call is part of the returned substring. The macro function %QSUBSTR is needed. It leaves the created substring quoted.

Provision for XXXX at the beginning or end can be made by allowing FRSTPART and LASTPART to have either the NULL value or the result of applying %QSUBSTR.

When these features are added, the code is:

```
/* ---   REPLACEMENT LOOP   ---- */

%LOCAL
    X WORD TARGET FIRSTPART
    LASTPART     ;

              /* INITIALIZATION */
%LET WORD = BN ;
%LET TARGET = %NRSTR
    ( ARRAY XXXX (*) %ARRAYLST
        (PREFIX=XXXX,FROM=8808,TO=8907)
      ;
    ) ;
%LET X = %INDEX ( &TARGET , XXXX );

%DO             /* DO REPLACEMENT   */
    %WHILE ( &X > 0 )
;
    %IF &X > 1 %THEN
        %LET FIRSTPART = %QSUBSTR
            ( &TARGET, 1 , &X-1 );
    %ELSE
        %LET FIRSTPART = ;

    %IF &X+4<= %LENGTH (&TARGET) %THEN
        %LET LASTPART = %QSUBSTR
            (&TARGET, &X+4) ;
    %ELSE
        %LET LASTPART = ;

    %LET TARGET =
        &FRSTPART.&WORD.&LASTPART
    ;
    %LET X = %INDEX ( &TARGET, XXXX );

%END ;          /* DO REPLACEMENT   */
```

Finally the result of the loop should be sent to the input stack for macro execution. Now the macro function %UNQUOTE is needed to allow % and & signs to trigger macro activities. The extra line of code, placed after the replacement loop, is

```
%UNQUOTE ( &TARGET )
```

It only remains to specify what the macro will do and then to piece together the scanning loop and the replacement loop into coherent macro code.

THE MACRO SPECIFICATIONS FOR %REPLACE

Two parameters are required:

1) The source string of replacement values as given by LIST in the SCANNING LOOP above.

2) The target string where re-placement takes place as shown by TARGET in the REPLACEMENT LOOP above.

In addition, the choice of XXXX is clearly one that should belong to the calling macro, not %REPLACE. Hence a third parameter, VARIABLE, is added to allow the calling macro to assign any combination of letters in place of the default, VARIABLE = XXXX.

The following calls may now be used to replace the three blocks of repetitious code in FIGURE 1 at the end of this paper:

```
%LET LIST =
    BN   CITP CMDT DITP
    NOCT OMSG RPCD STMN ;

%REPLACE
    ( LIST = &LIST ,
      TARGET = %NRSTR
        (
            %TIMESHFT (
                PREFIX=XXXX, FROM=8703,
                TO=8808, LAST=8802 )
        )
    )

%REPLACE
    ( LIST = &LIST ,
      TARGET = %NRSTR
        ( ARRAY XXXX ( * ) %ARRAYLST
            ( PREFIX=XXXX,
              FROM=8808,
              TO=8907 )
            ;
        )
    )

%REPLACE
    ( LIST = &LIST ,
      TARGET =
            XXXX (I) = XXXX (I+1)
    )
```

To complete the macro it only remains to combine the SCANNING LOOP and the REPLACEMENT LOOP. The complete macro REPLACE is shown in FIGURE 2.

IMPROVEMENTS

The parameters LIST and TARGET can be quite long. Nothing above restricted TARGET to being one line of code. In the interest of readability, it is better to add one more level of indirection. Let the parameters LIST and TARGET name macro variables whose values hold the list and target strings.

This idea can be combined with the previous work by adding another parameter CALL, with the default CALL = DIRECT. When indirection is used then assign CALL = INDIRECT. For example the array call would be:

```
%LET VARS =
   BN   CITP CMDT DITP
   NOCT OMSG RPCD STMN ;

%LET TARG = %NRSTR
   ( ARRAY XXXX (*) %ARRAYLST
      (PREFIX=XXXX,FROM=8808,TO=8907)
      ;
   )
;

%REPLACE
   ( LIST = VARS ,
     TARGET = TARG ,
     CALL = INDIRECT
   )
```

To implement this improvement merely add the following lines at the beginning of the macro.

```
%IF &CALL NE DIRECT %THEN
%DO ;
   %LET LIST = &&&LIST ;
   %LET TARGET = &&&TARGET ;
%END ;
```

This implementation does not save the cost of passing large parameters, because the added %LET statements have the same cost. But this implementation is simple to execute and makes it possible to use %REPLACE in cases where the form in FIGURE 2 would not work because the parameters are too big. It is left to the interested reader to write the code making full use of indirection.

CONCLUSION

Using the suggested improvement, the code shown in FIGURE 1 may be rewritten as shown in FIGURE 3. Note that there is no duplication in this version. The most likely changes to the program are all at top housed in %LET statements, hence maintenance work has been simplified.

ACKNOWLEDGEMENTS

This paper was written while the author worked for the Atlantic Research Corporation Professional Services Group. FIGURE 1 is a simplified version of a program originally written under contract to the Bureau of Labor Statistics.

Comments are invited. A copy of the paper or a copy of the visuals shown at the SUGI conference may be from the author.

H. Ian Whitlock
Westat Inc.
1650 Research Boulevard
Rockville, MD 20850-3129

Phone: (301) 251-4347

FIGURE 1

```
/* SHIFT TIME SERIES AND */
/* COPY TO MAKE MONTHLY  */

DATA EVENOTLT ( DROP = I ) ;
   SET EVENOTLT ( RENAME =
         (
      %TIMESHFT ( PREFIX=BN,
                  FROM=8703,
                  TO=8808,
                  LAST=8802
                )
      %TIMESHFT ( PREFIX=CITP,
                  FROM=8703,
                  TO=8808,
                  LAST=8802
                )
      %TIMESHFT ( PREFIX=CMDT,
                  FROM=8703,
                  TO=8808,
                  LAST=8802
                )
      %TIMESHFT ( PREFIX=DITP,
                  FROM=8703,
                  TO=8808,
                  LAST=8802
                )
      %TIMESHFT ( PREFIX=NOCT,
                  FROM=8703,
                  TO=8808,
                  LAST=8802
                )
      %TIMESHFT ( PREFIX=OMSG,
                  FROM=8703,
                  TO=8808,
                  LAST=8802
                )
      %TIMESHFT ( PREFIX=RPCD,
                  FROM=8703,
                  TO=8808,
                  LAST=8802
                )
      %TIMESHFT ( PREFIX=STMN,
                  FROM=8703,
                  TO=8808,
                  LAST=8802
                )
         )
                )
   ;

   ARRAY BN   (*) %ARRAYLST
      (PREFIX=BN  ,FROM=8808,TO=8907)
   ;
   ARRAY CITP (*) %ARRAYLST
      (PREFIX=CITP,FROM=8808,TO=8907)
   ;
   ARRAY CMDT (*) %ARRAYLST
      (PREFIX=CMDT,FROM=8808,TO=8907)
   ;
   ARRAY DITP (*) %ARRAYLST
      (PREFIX=DITP,FROM=8808,TO=8907)
   ;
   ARRAY NOCT (*) %ARRAYLST
      (PREFIX=NOCT,FROM=8808,TO=8907)
   ;
   ARRAY OMSG (*) %ARRAYLST
      (PREFIX=OMSG,FROM=8808,TO=8907)
   ;
   ARRAY RPCD (*) %ARRAYLST
      (PREFIX=RPCD,FROM=8808,TO=8907)
   ;
   ARRAY STMN (*) %ARRAYLST
      (PREFIX=STMN,FROM=8808,TO=8907)
   ;

   DO    /* NO PRICE SENT MOVE INFO */
         /* FROM NEXT MONTH         */
      I = 1 TO DIM ( DITP ) BY 2
   ;
      IF DITP ( I ) = ' ' THEN
      DO ;         /* FILL IN GAPS */
         BN   (I) = BN   (I+1);
         CITP (I) = CITP (I+1);
         CMDT (I) = CMDT (I+1);
         DITP (I) = DITP (I+1);
         NOCT (I) = NOCT (I+1);
         OMSG (I) = OMSG (I+1);
         RPCD (I) = RPCD (I+1);
         STMN (I) = STMN (I+1);
      END ;        /* FILL IN GAPS */

   END; /* NO PRICE SENT MOVE INFO */
        /* FROM NEXT MONTH         */

RUN ;
```

FIGURE 2

```
%MACRO REPLACE ( LIST = ,
                 TARGET = ,
                 VARIABLE = XXXX
               ) ;

   %*---------------------------*;
   %* PURPOSE:                  *;
   %* REPLACE ALL OCCURRENCES OF *;
   %* &VARIABLE IN &TARGET WITH  *;
   %* EACH WORD IN &LIST.        *;
   %*                            *;
   %* USE %NRSTR() AROUND TARGET *;
   %* STRING TO HIDE MACRO CALLS *;
   %* AND RESOLUTION OF MACRO    *;
   %* VARIABLES UNTIL AFTER THE  *;
   %* REPLACEMENT IS FINISHED    *;
   %*                            *;
   %* EXAMPLE:                   *;
   %* %REPLACE                   *;
   %*  (LIST= FIRST SECOND ,     *;
   %*   TARGET= %NRSTR           *;
   %*    ( IF 0 < XXXX < 10 THEN *;
   %*        %XXXX;)             *;
   %*  )                         *;
   %* PRODUCES                   *;
   %*    IF 0 < FIRST < 10 THEN  *;
   %*        %FIRST ;            *;
   %*    IF 0 < SECOND < 10 THEN *;
   %*        %SECOND ;           *;
   %*                            *;
   %* AUTHOR: IAN WHITLOCK, ARC  *;
   %* DATE:   JUNE 20, 1989      *;
   %*---------------------------*;

   %LOCAL
      WKTARGET WORD FRSTPART
      LASTPART VARLEN X I ;

         /* INITIALIZE    */
         /* EXECUTE LOOP */
         /* VARIABLES    */
   %LET I = 1 ;
   %LET WORD =
      %QSCAN ( &LIST , &I ) ;
   %LET VARLEN =
      %LENGTH ( &VARIABLE ) ;

         /* SCANNING LOOP  */
   %DO %WHILE
      ( %LENGTH ( &WORD ) > 0 )
   ;

     /* INITIALIZE INNER LOOP */
     /*      VARS             */
      %LET WKTARGET = &TARGET ;
      %LET X = %INDEX (
         &WKTARGET,&VARIABLE
               );

      /* REPLACEMENT LOOP  */
        %DO %WHILE ( &X > 0 )
        ;
        %IF &X - 1 > 0 %THEN
           %LET FRSTPART =
             %QSUBSTR (
                &WKTARGET,
                1 ,
                %EVAL(&X-1)
                   ) ;
        %ELSE
           %LET FRSTPART =
           ;
        %LET X = %EVAL
             (&X+&VARLEN);
        %IF &X <=
          %LENGTH(&WKTARGET)
        %THEN
           %LET LASTPART =
             %QSUBSTR (
             &WKTARGET,
              &X      );
        %ELSE
           %LET LASTPART=;

        /* PREPARE FOR    */
        /* NEXT ITERATION */
        /* OF REPLACEMENT */
        /* LOOP           */

        %LET WKTARGET =
      &FRSTPART&WORD&LASTPART
        ;
        %LET X = %INDEX (
           &WKTARGET ,
           &VARIABLE  )
           ;
        %END ;
        /* REPLACEMENT LOOP */

     /*EXECUTE REPLACED CODE*/

        %UNQUOTE ( &WKTARGET )

        /* PREPARE FOR NEXT
           ITERATION OF
           OF SCANNING LOOP
        */
     %LET I = %EVAL (&I+1);
     %LET WORD =
        %QSCAN (&LIST, &I);

   %END ; /* SCANNING LOOP     */

%MEND REPLACE ;
```

FIGURE 3

```
   /* VARS FOR OTLT */
%LET PREFLIST =
   BN   CITP CMDT DITP
   NOCT OMSG RPCD STMN ;

   /* RENAMES FOR EVENOTLT */
%LET ETIMSHFT = %NRSTR
   ( %TIMESHFT ( PREFIX = XXXX ,
        FROM=8703,TO=8808,LAST=8802);
   )
;

   /* ARRAYS FOR EVENOTLT */
%LET EARRAYS = %NRSTR
   ( ARRAY XXXX (*) %ARRAYLST
      (PREFIX=XXXX,FROM=8808,TO=8907)
      ;
   )
;

   /* FILL IN GAPS FOR NO PRICE */
%LET MOVEVALS = %STR
   ( XXXX ( I ) = XXXX ( I + 1 ) ; )
;

DATA EVENOTLT ( DROP = I ) ;

   SET EVENOTLT ( RENAME = (
      %REPLACE ( LIST = PREFLIST ,
                 TARGET = ETIMSHFT )
      ) ) ;

   %REPLACE
      (LIST=PREFLIST, TARGET=EARRAYS)

   DO I = 1 TO DIM ( DITP ) ;
      IF DITP ( I ) = '' THEN
      DO ;
         %REPLACE ( LIST=PREFLIST,
                    TARGET=MOVEVALS )
      END ;
   END ;

RUN ;
```

"TWO OR THREE NEAT THINGS YOU CAN DO WITH SAS® SOFTWARE"

Frederick Pratter, Abt Associates Inc.

By almost any standards, the SAS® system can be considered a Fourth Generation Language. 4GLs, as they are usually termed, free the programmer from dependence on detailed procedural algorithms and from complex data typing and structures. Instead, they substitute modular building blocks and data dictionaries that allow for more straightforward and hopefully less error prone code.

One of the annoying requirements of third generation programming languages is the necessity to specify in advance, at compile time, the size of all the arrays or lists that will be used in the program. This is also true for the base version of SAS. This constraint places a very real limitation on the flexibility of the code developed. The difference between computers and living intelligences is that (ideally) the latter should be able to modify their behavior to accommodate changes in external circumstances, while the former are constrained to "Do What I Say" and "Not Do What I Mean." By using some of the features of SAS Macro language, one can enhance production code, giving it the capability to change depending on the requirements of the job. This paper will present a simple example of one way that this can done. I will start with a 3GL style program that contains absolutely no Macro code, and then illustrate, in successive steps, how the program can be made more flexible and more "artificially" intelligent. Figure 1 shows the initial code.

Figure 1

```
NOTE: SAS OPTIONS SPECIFIED ARE:
      NOOVP NOGRAPH NOINCLUDE NOCENTER SORT=4

1         DATA ONE;
2              INPUT VA VB VC VD VE VF VG VH VI VJ
3                    VK VL VM VN VO VP VQ VR VS VT
4                    VU VV VW VX VY VZ;
5         CARDS;

NOTE: DATA SET WORK.ONE HAS 6 OBSERVATIONS AND 26 VARIABLES. 220 OBS/TRK.
NOTE: THE DATA STATEMENT USED 0.02 SECONDS AND 148K.

12        PROC PRINT DATA=ONE;
13             TITLE 'INPUT DATA';
NOTE: THE PROCEDURE PRINT USED 0.03 SECONDS AND 236K AND PRINTED PAGE 1.

14        DATA TWO; **** THIS IS A SIMPLE PROGRAM TO COMPUTE % CHANGES;
15             SET ONE;
16             ARRAY V [*] VA VB VC VD VE VF VG VH VI VJ
17                         VK VL VM VN VO VP VQ VR VS VT
18                         VU VV VW VX VY VZ;
19             ARRAY L [26];
20             ARRAY P [26];
21             DO I=1 TO 26; /* COMPUTE PERCENTAGE CHANGES */
22                  P[I] = 100*(V[I]-L[I])/L[I];
23                  L[I] = V[I];
24             END;
25             RETAIN L1-L26;
26             KEEP P1-P26;

NOTE: MISSING VALUES WERE GENERATED AS A RESULT OF PERFORMING
      AN OPERATION ON MISSING VALUES.
      EACH PLACE IS GIVEN BY: (NUMBER OF TIMES) AT (LINE):(COLUMN).

      26 AT 22:19

NOTE: DATA SET WORK.TWO HAS 6 OBSERVATIONS AND 26 VARIABLES. 220 OBS/TRK.
NOTE: THE DATA STATEMENT USED 0.04 SECONDS AND 152K.

27        PROC PRINT DATA=TWO;
28             TITLE 'OUTPUT DATA';
29             FORMAT P1-P26 6.1;
NOTE: THE PROCEDURE PRINT USED 0.03 SECONDS AND 212K AND PRINTED PAGE 2.
NOTE: SAS USED 236K MEMORY.
```

This program was designed for test purposes, but it demonstrates a typical enough kind of application. The initial data step reads in a set of variables; for testing purposes, the program uses card input. Figures 2 and 3 show the input and output data sets. The body of the program takes place in Data step "TWO." The function of this program is simply to compute the percentage change between the current observation and the previous observation. The array "V" contains the 26 variables on which we wish to compute percentage changes. Array "L" holds the 26 values of previous observations; notice in statement 25 that the "L" array needs to be retained because otherwise it will be reset to missing each time the SET statement is executed. The "P" array at line 26 holds the computed percentage changes. The loop at statements 21 through 24 repeats the computation of the 26 percentage change variables, which are equal to 100 times the difference between the previous value and the current value over the previous value. The "L" value is set equal to the V_i value, so that on the next iteration of the data step, the value is lagged.

P1 through P26 now contain the 26 percentage changes. Figure 2 shows the 26 variables; there are six observations. I confess to a lack of imagination in giving the variables their values, but they will do for test purposes. The output data set shows the percentage changes. The values for observation 1 are always missing because there are no previous values. The value for observation 2 for P1 is the difference between 1 and 26, which is 2,500%. The difference between 26 and 1, P26, is -96.2%.

This program, while useful, is not very flexible; it has a number of disadvantages. For one thing, the list of the 26 input variables appears twice in the program, in both the first data step and in the second data step. Furthermore, the number 26 appears six times in the program. It appears in statement 19, statement 20, statement 21, statement 25, statement 26 and statement 29. Even if one only knows a little about the SAS Macro language, it should be fairly obvious that one can make some improvements in this program simply by defining a couple of substitutable strings. For example, the list of variables that appears twice in the program, as shown in lines 1 thru 5 of Figure 4, can be replaced with a macro called "VARS" naming the list of variables to be processed by the program. Now, VARS appears in line 8 of the initial step and in line 25 where we define the "V" array. In this particular program, VARS is going to be exactly the same in both places, so one can type it once and put the macro in in both places, thus avoiding typing those 26 names over again. At line 6, we have a %LET statement that creates a macro variable called "N." N's value is the character string "26." It doesn't have single quotes around it because all macro variables are character strings. But

Figure 2

INPUT DATA

OBS	VA	VB	VC	VD	VE	VF	VG	VH	VI	VJ	VK	VL	VM	VN	VO	VP	VQ	VR	VS	VT	VU	VV	VW	VX	VY	VZ
1	1	2	3	4	5	6	7	8	9	10	11	12	13	14	15	16	17	18	19	20	21	22	23	24	25	26
2	26	25	24	23	22	21	20	19	18	17	16	15	14	13	12	11	10	9	8	7	6	5	4	3	2	1
3	1	2	3	4	5	6	7	8	9	10	11	12	13	14	15	16	17	18	19	20	21	22	23	24	25	26
4	26	25	24	23	22	21	20	19	18	17	16	15	14	13	12	11	10	9	8	7	6	5	4	3	2	1
5	26	25	24	23	22	21	20	19	18	17	16	15	14	13	12	11	10	9	8	7	6	5	4	3	2	1
6	1	2	3	4	5	6	7	8	9	10	11	12	13	14	15	16	17	18	19	20	21	22	23	24	25	26

Figure 3

OUTPUT DATA

OBS	P1	P2	P3	P4	P5	P6	P7	P8	P9	P10	P11	P12	P13
1	.	.	.	.	.	.	.	.	.	.	.	.	.
2	2500.0	1150.0	700.0	475.0	340.0	250.0	185.7	137.5	100.0	70.0	45.5	25.0	7.7
3	-96.2	-92.0	-87.5	-82.6	-77.3	-71.4	-65.0	-57.9	-50.0	-41.2	-31.3	-20.0	-7.1
4	2500.0	1150.0	700.0	475.0	340.0	250.0	185.7	137.5	100.0	70.0	45.5	25.0	7.7
5	0.0	0.0	0.0	0.0	0.0	0.0	0.0	0.0	0.0	0.0	0.0	0.0	0.0
6	-96.2	-92.0	-87.5	-82.6	-77.3	-71.4	-65.0	-57.9	-50.0	-41.2	-31.3	-20.0	-7.1

OBS	P14	P15	P16	P17	P18	P19	P20	P21	P22	P23	P24	P25	P26
1	.	.	.	.	.	.	.	.	.	.	.	.	.
2	-7.1	-20.0	-31.3	-41.2	-50.0	-57.9	-65.0	-71.4	-77.3	-82.6	-87.5	-92.0	-96.2
3	7.7	25.0	45.5	70.0	100.0	137.5	185.7	250.0	340.0	475.0	700.0	1150.0	2500.0
4	-7.1	-20.0	-31.3	-41.2	-50.0	-57.9	-65.0	-71.4	-77.3	-82.6	-87.5	-92.0	-96.2
5	0.0	0.0	0.0	0.0	0.0	0.0	0.0	0.0	0.0	0.0	0.0	0.0	0.0
6	7.7	25.0	45.5	70.0	100.0	137.5	185.7	250.0	340.0	475.0	700.0	1150.0	2500.0

remember that it is not the number 26, it is the EBCDIC characters "two six." The macro variable is used at the 6 places in the program at which the number "26" appeared in the first example. At lines 31 and 33 the arrays are dimensioned &N rather than "26." We do "I" equals 1 to N in line 35, and in 40 and 42 we keep and retain L1 thru L&N. In the Print procedure, the format statement describes P1 thru P&N. The macro preprocessor simply goes through this program at the outset and every place it finds an &N it sticks in the characters "26."

One important question is the difference between "VARS" which is a macro and N which is a macro variable. For the purposes of this program, it would have been possible to "%LET VARS =" the list of variable names that you see at line 2 thru 4. However, there is a limit on how long a macro variable can be (it depends on the version of SAS used, but is usually 256 characters). In order to make this program more general purpose, VARS has been defined as a macro, rather than as a macro variable so that one can put in a longer list. For the purposes of this program, however, it could have been a macro variable rather than a macro. The point is that anything between the %MACRO statement and the %MEND statement is replaced with a character string. Anything that follows the "equal" sign in a %LET statement is also a character string that is substituted. But macro variables can only be character strings, while macros can be Macro programming language statements as well as character strings. So in a sense, the coded line 1 thru 5 is overkill. I don't need the macro here; it is including primarily to illustrate the difference between macros and macro variables.

The program is now (to all intents and purposes) pretty flexible, because all one has to do is change the first six lines and the rest of the program will work correctly no matter what variables are listed or how many of them there are. But there is something obscurely upsetting about this program; that is, the program ought to know there are 26 variables. Currently, it is necessary to count them up and specify their dimension in statement 6. What if you count them wrong? This paper started out by trying to illustrate less error prone code -- why doesn't the program count how many things there are in the variable list? The next version of the program (Figure 5) does precisely that. In lines 1 thru 6, the macro DIM, has been added to the previous version of the program. Comparing Figure 4 with Figure 5, it is evident that lines 7 thru 11 are still the macro VARS, unchanged from the previous example. This time, N is initialized to "0" as a global macro variable. (If N were initialized inside the macro, it would be a local variable, and would be undefined in the global context.) SAS skips a couple of lines in between lines 13 and 16 because it wrote some macro code in there that is invisible (with the Macrogen option turned off). By the time the program gets to line 16, it knows that N is equal to 26. That is, the purpose of the macro DIM is to assign to the macro variable N the character string 26. The entire function of the macro is to count the number of items in VARS and assign that value to N.

Figure 4

```
NOTE: SAS OPTIONS SPECIFIED ARE:
      NOOVP NOGRAPH NOINCLUDE NOCENTER SORT=4

1          %MACRO VARS; %* LIST OF VARIABLES TO BE PROCESSED;
2               VA VB VC VD VE VF VG VH VI VJ
3               VK VL VM VN VO VP VQ VR VS VT
4               VU VV VW VX VY VZ
5          %MEND VARS;
6          %LET N = 26; * NUMBER OF ITEMS IN LIST;
7          DATA ONE;
8               INPUT %VARS;
14         CARDS;

NOTE: DATA SET WORK.ONE HAS 6 OBSERVATIONS AND 26 VARIABLES. 220 OBS/TRK.
NOTE: THE DATA STATEMENT USED 0.03 SECONDS AND 148K.

21         PROC PRINT DATA=ONE;
22              TITLE 'INPUT DATA';
NOTE: THE PROCEDURE PRINT USED 0.03 SECONDS AND 236K AND PRINTED PAGE 1.

23         DATA TWO;
24              SET ONE;
25              ARRAY V [*] %VARS;
31              ARRAY L [&N];
33              ARRAY P [&N];
35              DO I=1 TO &N; /* COMPUTE PERCENTAGE CHANGES */
37                   P[I] = 100*(V[I]-L[I])/L[I];
38                   L[I] = V[I];
39              END;
40              RETAIN L1-L&N;
42              KEEP  P1-P&N;

NOTE: MISSING VALUES WERE GENERATED AS A RESULT OF PERFORMING
      AN OPERATION ON MISSING VALUES.
      EACH PLACE IS GIVEN BY: (NUMBER OF TIMES) AT (LINE):(COLUMN).
      26 AT 37:19
NOTE: DATA SET WORK.TWO HAS 6 OBSERVATIONS AND 26 VARIABLES. 220 OBS/TRK.
NOTE: THE DATA STATEMENT USED 0.04 SECONDS AND 152K.

44         PROC PRINT DATA=TWO;
45              TITLE 'OUTPUT DATA';
46              FORMAT P1-P&N 6.1;
NOTE: THE PROCEDURE PRINT USED 0.03 SECONDS AND 216K AND PRINTED PAGE 2.
NOTE: SAS USED 236K MEMORY.
```

Figure 5

```
NOTE: SAS OPTIONS SPECIFIED ARE:
      NOOVP NOGRAPH NOINCLUDE NOCENTER SORT=4

1          %MACRO DIM; %* MACRO FUNCTION FOR COUNTING LISTS;
2               %DO %WHILE(%SCAN(%VARS,%EVAL(&N+1))>'');
3                   %LET N = %EVAL(&N+1);
4               %END;
5               %PUT THE NUMBER OF ITEMS IN VARS IS &N.;
6          %MEND DIM;
7          %MACRO VARS; %* LIST OF VARIABLES TO BE COUNTED;
8               VA VB VC VD VE VF VG VH VI VJ
9               VK VL VM VN VO VP VQ VR VS VT
10              VU VV VW VX VY VZ
11         %MEND VARS;
THE NUMBER OF ITEMS IN VARS IS 26
12         %LET N = 0;
13         %DIM
16         DATA ONE;
17              INPUT %VARS;
23         CARDS;

NOTE: DATA SET WORK.ONE HAS 6 OBSERVATIONS AND 26 VARIABLES. 220 OBS/TRK.
NOTE: THE DATA STATEMENT USED 0.12 SECONDS AND 156K.

30         PROC PRINT DATA=ONE;
31              TITLE 'INPUT DATA';
NOTE: THE PROCEDURE PRINT USED 0.03 SECONDS AND 236K AND PRINTED PAGE 1.

32         DATA TWO;
33              SET ONE;
34              ARRAY V [*] %VARS;
40              ARRAY L [&N];
42              ARRAY P [&N];
44              DO I=1 TO &N; /* COMPUTE PERCENTAGE CHANGES */
46                   P[I] = 100*(V[I]-L[I])/L[I];
47                   L[I] = V[I];
48              END;
49              RETAIN L1-L&N;
51              KEEP  P1-P&N;

NOTE: MISSING VALUES WERE GENERATED AS A RESULT OF PERFORMING
      AN OPERATION ON MISSING VALUES.
      EACH PLACE IS GIVEN BY: (NUMBER OF TIMES) AT (LINE):(COLUMN).

      26 AT 46:19

NOTE: DATA SET WORK.TWO HAS 6 OBSERVATIONS AND 26 VARIABLES. 220 OBS/TRK.
NOTE: THE DATA STATEMENT USED 0.04 SECONDS AND 152K.

53         PROC PRINT DATA=TWO;
54              TITLE 'OUTPUT DATA';
55              FORMAT P1-P&N 6.1;
NOTE: THE PROCEDURE PRINT USED 0.03 SECONDS AND 216K AND PRINTED PAGE 2.
NOTE: SAS USED 236K MEMORY.
```

It works by executing the macro language code that you see at lines 2 thru 4. Line 3 shows how you increment a macro variable. (This is covered in the macro language reference section of the base **SAS** Reference Guide.) If you say "N = N+1," the value of N will be the character string "N+1." If you say "N = &N+1", the result of N will still be a character string "0+1." It is important to emphasize than using "%LET" to assign a value to a macro variable is only the way SAS assigns a character string to that variable. So in order to add 1 to N, you need to use a macro language function. There are a number of macro language functions described in the section on macro language function in the Base **SAS** Reference Guide. One of these is %EVAL, which returns the numeric value of a macro language expression. So "%EVAL (N+1)" is going to be evaluated by the macro execution phase into whatever the current value of N is plus 1. In line 12, N is set to be equal to 0; the first time the macro loop is executed, that will be translated into 0 plus 1, or 1. Thus, 1 is assigned as the value of N. The second time it is executed, N will be equal to 1. This parenthesis will evaluate to 1 + 1, that is 2, so 2 will be assigned to N. The %EVAL function is how you add to macro variables.

Statement 3 occurs inside a macro loop, that continues until the expression in parenthesis on line 2 results in an expression that is not true. In other words, it will continue as long as that expression is true, just like any other "DO WHILE" (except that this is a "%DO %WHILE"). This loop is only going to be executed at one place in the program no matter how many input observations there are in the input data set. The loop is going to count how many things there are in the list, and then it is going to rewrite the **SAS** code in the rest of the program. Every place it sees &N it is going to stick in 26.

Now to make some sense out of that expression in parentheses at line 2. Starting at the right hand end, whatever is to the left of that ">" sign has got to be some kind of character string. That character string is being tested to determine whether it is greater than a blank. If it is blank, then the test is false because blank is not greater than blank, since everything in the EDCDIC collating sequence is greater than blank. If it is blank, then the test is false because blank is the lowest character string. We know (from statement 3) that %EVAL(&N+1) returns a number that is greater than the current value of N by 1. Furthermore, we have seen that **%VARS** is our list of variables. That just leaves %SCAN, another of the **SAS** macro functions (documented in the same place as %EVAL). %SCAN takes two arguments. Argument 1 is a list of things and Argument 2 is a number. So **%VARS** is the list and N + 1 is the number; %SCAN returns the ith member of the list. It counts through the list by looking for delimiters, which are spaces or commas; you can even specify what kind of delimiters you want it to use. In the VARS macro (line 8 thru 10) each one of the items in the list is separated by a blank.

The first element that is returned by the %SCAN function from %VARS is "VA" and the last one it returns is "VZ." If N + 1 is equal to 27, the %SCAN function returns a blank, because there is not a 27th element in that list. That is how the loop is halted. If N is 0, the first time statement #2 is executed, the first item in the list IS "VA." When N is 26, N + 1 will be the 27th item (a blank) and so it will stop. N is 26 and that is how many items are on the list.

The rest of the program is identical to the one shown in Figure 4. In line 12, N is initialized as 0 (not 26). At line 13, DIM is called, returning a value of 26. In data step TWO, &N is substituted for all of those 26s in the former program. Line 34 is the array **%VARS**. The next line number is number 40 (because the macro language is putting some lines in there that are invisible). At 40 and 42, we dimension the arrays L and P with &N. The only difference between the program in Figure 4 and that shown in Figure 5 is that macro lets the program figure out how many items there are in the list. At line 5, we have a %PUT statement. The %PUT is inside the macro DIM, but is executed after the loop; its result appears following line 11. Interestingly enough, it appears in the log two lines ahead of where DIM is actually called. It always does that. That is to remind you, I suppose, that what you see is not necessarily what you get. The macro preprocessor is being executed prior to the data one step, but I think the SAS log does not get written until data one step executes it. Anyway you see that it is counted right. VARS is defined prior to the execution of dim. If I said **%DIM** and then %MACRO VARS, it would not work. The macro called DIM and the macro called VARS, do not happen until line 13. VARS has to be defined when I say **%DIM**, but DIM does not have to be defined prior to **%VARS**.

Figure 6

```
NOTE: SAS OPTIONS SPECIFIED ARE:
      NOOVP NOGRAPH NOINCLUDE NOCENTER SORT=4

1           %MACRO DIM(LIST,I); %* MACRO FUNCTION FOR COUNTING LISTS;
2                %DO %WHILE(%SCAN(%&LIST,%EVAL(&&&I+1))>'');
3                    %LET &&I = %EVAL(&&&I+1);
4                %END;
5                %PUT THE NUMBER OF ITEMS IN &LIST IS &&&I.;
6           %MEND DIM;
7           %MACRO VARS; %* LIST OF VARIABLES TO BE COUNTED;
8                VA VB VC VD VE VF VG VH VI VJ
9                VK VL VM VN VO VP VQ VR VS VT
10               VU VV VW VX VY VZ
11          %MEND VARS;
THE NUMBER OF ITEMS IN VARS IS 26
12          %LET N = 0;
13          %DIM(VARS,N)
16          DATA ONE;
17               INPUT %VARS;
23          CARDS;

NOTE: DATA SET WORK.ONE HAS 6 OBSERVATIONS AND 26 VARIABLES. 220 OBS/TRK.
NOTE: THE DATA STATEMENT USED 0.16 SECONDS AND 156K.

30          PROC PRINT DATA=ONE;
31               TITLE 'INPUT DATA';
NOTE: THE PROCEDURE PRINT USED 0.03 SECONDS AND 236K AND PRINTED PAGE 1.
```

Now we have a program that is pretty smart. You feed it VARS which is any arbitrary list and it will go ahead and run no matter how many items are in the list. I would argue that we have now made this program much smarter than it was before. As Figure 6 shows, however, this program can be made even smarter. The rest of the program following line 16 is exactly identical to the prior versions. Note the difference between the DIM macro in this program and that of the previous program (Figure 5). At line 13, the **%DIM** has been replaced by **%DIM** (VARS, N). The difference is that the new code is passing parameters to the macro. These parameters are themselves macro variables. The macro in Figure 5 required that the list be called VARS and that the macro variable be called N, because they were built into the macro. This new macro doesn't care what your list is called and it doesn't care what your macro variable list is called. It passes the names of the list and the names of the macro variables as parameters to the macro. It is now truly a general purpose macro; lines 1 thru 6 can now exist independently of any particular program. You have written a real function! The function takes two arguments: a list and a variable. Values of those macro variables are themselves macro statements; in the first case a macro name VARS, in the second case, a variable named N.

Each statement in Figure 6 corresponds to one in the Macro shown in Figure 5. Starting with line 5 for simplicity's sake, the number of items in &LIST is &&&I. &LIST evaluates to the first parameter, that is "VARS." &I is equal to "N." (Inside a Macro two ampersands always resolves to a single one, so &&&I is &N.)

The same principle applies to statement 3. &&&I is &N. In this case, &I is equivalent to N; you can use one ampersand or two, it works both ways (since two are always resolved to one). Using these substitution rules in statement 2 results in similar equivalences. %&List is **% vars,** while &&&I (as in statement 5) is &N.

Since this is now a universal function, it can be stored in a library of similar functions. Figure 7 replaces the macro with a %INCLUDE statement. "Macros" is a file name (or ddname in MVS) referencing a sequential file that contains the code that appeared in lines 1-6 of Figure 6. The library of Macro functions can be made available to all of the users at an installation, who need not be concerned with the details of the code. They do not even need to know that you, and not the SAS Institute, are the author of this clever code.

Figure 7 also includes, at lines 57 through 63, a macro that renames variables P1-P26 to VA--VZ. You should be able to see that the macro evaluates to the statements:

```
Rename
P1 = VA
P2 = VB
P3 = VC

P26 = VZ

;
```

Your homework assignment is to make %RENAME into a general purpose macro that can be used by passing the names of the two lists as parameters. (Hint: you can use %Dim inside of #Rename to determine the lengths of the lists.)

In conclusion, this example has been offered as an illustration of how you can use Macro code to make your programs more flexible and useful. With a little practice, the concepts demonstrated here should provide to be a framework on which you can construct user friendly and "intelligent" applications code.

Frederick Pratter
Abt Associates Inc.
55 Wheeler Street
Cambridge, MA 02138
617/492-7100

Figure 7

```
NOTE: SAS OPTIONS SPECIFIED ARE:
      NOOVP NOGRAPH NOCENTER SORT=4

1          %INCLUDE MACROS/NOSOURCE2;

9          %MACRO VARS; %* LIST OF VARIABLES TO BE COUNTED;
10              VA VB VC VD VE VF VG VH VI VJ
11              VK VL VM VN VO VP VQ VR VS VT
12              VU VV VW VX VY VZ
13         %MEND VARS;
THE NUMBER OF ITEMS IN VARS IS 26
14         %DIM(VARS,N)
17
18         DATA ONE;
19              INPUT %VARS;
25         CARDS;

NOTE: DATA SET WORK.ONE HAS 6 OBSERVATIONS AND 26 VARIABLES. 220 OBS/TRK.
NOTE: THE DATA STATEMENT USED 0.16 SECONDS AND 160K.

32         PROC PRINT DATA=ONE;
33              TITLE 'INPUT DATA';
NOTE: THE PROCEDURE PRINT USED 0.03 SECONDS AND 236K AND PRINTED PAGE 1.

34         DATA TWO;
35              SET ONE;
36              ARRAY V [*] %VARS;
42              ARRAY L [&N];
44              ARRAY P [&N];
46              DO I=1 TO &N; /* COMPUTE PERCENTAGE CHANGES */
48                   P[I] = 100*(V[I]-L[I])/L[I];
49                   L[I] = V[I];
50              END;
51              RETAIN L1-L&N;
53              KEEP  P1-P&N;
55              FORMAT P1-P&N 6.1;
57         %MACRO RENAME;
58              RENAME
59             %DO I=1 %TO &N;
60                 P&I = %SCAN(%VARS,&I)
61             %END;
62              ;
63         %MEND RENAME;
64         %RENAME

NOTE: MISSING VALUES WERE GENERATED AS A RESULT OF PERFORMING
      AN OPERATION ON MISSING VALUES.
      EACH PLACE IS GIVEN BY: (NUMBER OF TIMES) AT (LINE):(COLUMN).

      26 AT 48:19

NOTE: DATA SET WORK.TWO HAS 6 OBSERVATIONS AND 26 VARIABLES. 220 OBS/TRK.
NOTE: THE DATA STATEMENT USED 0.12 SECONDS AND 156K.
```

Chapter 5 Building User Interfaces

A Menu-driven Table Generator 209

Advanced

Tasks	Illustrates modular macro programming with a SAS/AF front end to implement a menu-driven application.
Tools	%DO, Iterative %DO %WHILE %IF-%THEN / %ELSE && and &&& resolution SAS/AF screen substitutions in a macro Complex substitution Macro parameters Macro quoting Simple substitution

WRITING SAS® CODE BEHIND THE SCENES: A CONVERSATIONAL MACRO EXAMPLE

Deb Cassidy, Trilogy Consulting Corporation

ABSTRACT

Conversational macros provide a way for a non-SAS user to "write" SAS code when only base SAS is available. This paper will give you some advantages/disadvantages of this method as well as how to write the code.

INTRODUCTION

The communications department of the company often sent mailings to selected customers. All too often, the mailing labels were needed immediately so the correct amount of materials could be ordered. Although creating the mailing labels using SAS was a relatively simple task, it did mean an analyst had to stop working on another project. The communications department staff not only did not know SAS, but some of them barely knew how to turn on a PC to use any computer software. Although SAS/AF® or SAS/ASSIST® were designed to create applications for such situations, these products weren't available at the company. The SAS macro course provided a solution which required only base SAS - conversational macros. In a conversational macro, the macro facility prompts you at the terminal and accepts you input. The input is stored in macro variables which are then used in writing the program.

The code was originally written in Version 5.18. Changes in the display manager in Version 6.07 make conversational macros awkward to use in some cases. The use of windows solves that problem and makes it easier for the user but the macro code does get more complicated. The concept is the same in both cases. This paper will show you both ways and you can decide which, if either, is right for your situation.

First, I want to go over some of the things to consider before you even write one line of code. Then I will cover how to write the code.

ADVANTAGES/DISADVANTAGES

Conversational macros have advantages and disadvantages. The main advantage for me was the ability to let non-SAS users "write" their own SAS code when only base SAS was available. Conversational macros also mean the user doesn't need to know such things as variable names, whether variables are character or numeric, if character variables are upper or lower cases, dataset names, and how to write the procedure. This can save time even for an experienced user. The user only needs minimal training.

Of course, there are disadvantages.

- Someone has to write the macro in the first place and know all the information just mentioned. This could take more time than it is worth.
- You probably won't be able to include all situations - either because you can't identify them in advance or it's not worth the effort for extremely complex or rarely used situations. I once had a request for all the customers who had purchased a certain product within the last year but had not purchased any of the related products within the last six months. These customers also had to be eligible for the discount rate which was determined by their purchase of another set of products. This request was complicated enough without trying to write it as part of a macro for someone else to use!
- Conversational macros are interactive. Some sites discourage interactive programs on mainframes because of the system resources required. If you have a very complex program or very large datasets to process, you might want to explore other alternatives. This is especially true if it's not practical to have the terminal locked up during processing.
- Different terminals will have different displays. Code must be written so it will work properly on any terminal that will be used.
- Conversational macros aren't very "pretty." Windows help the appearance.

- The use of the SUBMIT and ENTER keys can be confusing. All "answers" must be entered on line 1 of the Program Editor window and submitted. V6 windows do let you use the ENTER key instead.

QUESTIONS

How complex is the code even outside the macro? What parts of the code will change for each use?

- Complex code with only 1 line that changes may be easier to write as a conversational macro than simple code that permits a lot of changes to titles and labels.

Can you write questions clearly so the user will be able to give a valid and correct answer? How much "HELP" information will you need?

- "Enter state code" seems simple enough. You enter AL but do you get Alaska or Alabama? What about special codes used only in your dataset? Would everyone know that your company identifies customer type with 1 for Medical, 2 for Law, and 3 for Academic?

How often will the conversational macro be used?

- Several times a month or only a few times a year? Since you probably won't be able to write every possible choice, how often will you have to write new code - either as a modification to the macro or as a separate job?

How many different programs will the user need to run?

- The more programs needed, the more likely SAS/AF will be worth the cost.

If conversational macros are still an option for you, the following shows you how to write some of the code.

WRITING THE CODE

The basic code for the mailing label is:

```
OPTIONS LS=100 PS=75;
DATA CUST; SET CUST.INFO;
   IF STATE='NY';
POSITION='PRESIDENT';

PROC SORT; BY ZIP;
PROC FORMS DATA=CUST
  WIDTH=33 LINES=7 ACROSS=3;
  LINE 1 POSITION/REMOVE;
  LINE 2 NAME;
  LINE 3 ADDRESS;
  LINE 4 CITY STATE ZIP/PACK;
```

(You may need to modify the options depending on you label size and printer.)

Most of the code stays the same each time. You only need to change the IF statement and the value for POSITION.

How does the conversational macro work? When the macro is invoked, %PUT statements will place text in the log window. The user will read the text and respond by entering a value on line 1 of the program window and submitting it. The response will be stored in a macro variable for later user. This process will continue until the complete job is "written." The results will appear in the output window unless they have been directed elsewhere such as an output file for printing.

The "behind the scenes" code is shown here in all caps while macro code is lower case. The %PUT statements will show the line in upper and lower case as entered. % and & will identify macro statements and variables. Everything else will appear in the job.

If only STATE would change, the macro would read:

```
%macro mail;
  %put Enter a 2-character state code;
  %input state;
DATA CUST; SET CUST.INFO;
  IF STATE="%upcase(&state)";
  POSITION='PRESIDENT';

PROC SORT; BY ZIP;
PROC FORMS DATA=CUST
  WIDTH=33 LINES=7 ACROSS=3;
  LINE 1 POSITION/REMOVE;
  LINE 2 NAME;
  LINE 3 ADDRESS;
  LINE 4 CITY STATE ZIP/PACK;
%mend mail;
```

If you enter NY when asked, the macro variable state will have the value NY. The &state will resolve to NY and you will have the line:

```
IF STATE="NY";
```

You need to use double quotes to have macro variables resolved. The %UPCASE function is used so you can input NY or ny or Ny or nY). If your original data are also upper and lower case, you should use:

```
IF UPCASE(STATE)="%upcase(&state)";
```

The rest of the examples assume the data are already uppercase.

Now, what happens if you want to use:

```
IF STATE="NY" OR STATE="OH" OR
   STATE="MN";

%do i=1 %to 3;
   %put Enter a 2-character state code;
   %input state;
     %if &i=1 %then
       IF STATE="%upcase(&state)";
        /* semi-colon ends %if */
   %else
       OR STATE="%upcase(&state)";
          /* semi-colon ends %else */
    %end;  %* ends do i for state;
      ; /* end IF statement */
```

Notice I've also mixed the styles of comments to show that both work. Comments are extremely important. I did not have as many comments in the original code. When I started to write the paper, I could not remember why I had a semi-colon in a certain spot. Semi-colons can be tricky. You need semi-colons to end the macro statements just like you need them for regular SAS statements. The semi-colon after the %END is necessary to end the IF statement you are creating with the macro.

What happens if you want to vary the amount of states? How do you tell the system:

```
  %do i=1 %to some unknown value
```

There are actually several ways to accomplish this. I opted for the extra statements to ask how many states the user wanted. Although this option was easier for me, I selected it because it forced the user to think through the request before entering it. If they wanted 5 states but only entered 4, there will be an extra "Enter state" and (I hope), the user will realize a state was missed. To fix the problem, the user will need to run the macro again for that state. A blank entered by accident should also be noticed.

```
  %put Enter number of states;
  %input numstate;
  %do i=1 %to &numstate;
       (Same as above code)
```

Another option would be to have the user submit a blank line after the last state and use a %DO WHILE or %DO %UNTIL statement. In the macro language, there is no equivalent to the iterative DO with a while/until clause. I avoided this option because I felt it was more complicated to make sure I did not get a STATE=" " by accident since such a statement would retrieve some customers in foreign countries.

Believe it or not, that's really almost all you need to know. You would simply repeat the same code for other options.

What happens if the user wants to select by zip code instead of state. You don't want any SAS statements for state to appear in the final code. One way to solve this and add some error checking is to use macro label statements.

```
%statesel:
  %put Do you want to select by state?;
  %put Enter YES or NO.;
  %input states;

  %input %upcase(&states)=YES %then %do;
       (code for selecting state - can be
imbedded in this code or a separate
macro)
       %end;

%else %if  %upcase(&states) ^=YES and
       %upcase(&states)^=NO %then %do;
    %put ERROR: &states is an invalid
entry.;
    %put %str( ); /* blank line for
legibility */
    %put Enter any letter to continue.;
    %input cont; /* Keeps screen from
scrolling until you have read the
message.*/
    %goto statesel;
 %end; /* end invalid entry */

%else %if %upcase(&states)=NO %then %do;
     %put NO state restrictions
requested.;
     %put %str ( );
  %put Enter any letter to continue.;
  %input cont;
   %end;

%zipsel:
   (code for selecting zips)
/* You could have omitted the NO section
and the user would immediately jump to
the zipsel section after answering NO.
*/
```

V6 WINDOWS

What happens if a set of %PUT statements will need more that one screen? In V5.18 it was easy to create a macro that would split the screen so only 1 line appeared in the program editor and the rest of the screen could be devoted to the log. V6 dropped one command that was necessary. Changing window sizes in MVS is now rather awkward so I recommend taking advantage of the %WINDOW.

The %PUT statements wrote everything to the log window. %WINDOW lets you create your own windows which will be available for the session. A simple window is created by:

```
%window welcome
    #3 @15
'Welcome to the mailing label program'
    #6 @5
'Enter an X by the options to subset
your data'
    #10 @5  statex 1 @7 'STATE'
        @15 typex  1 @17 'TYPE'
    #14 @1
'Use TAB to move between options'
    #15 @1
'Use ENTER to move to the next screen';
```

Everything in quotes will appear in your window when you display it. This is the same as the %PUT statements except the entire screen will be used, previous statements will not appear and you can create several macro variables in one step. STATEX and TYPEX are 1-character macro variables which are used like the macro variables from %INPUT.

To display a window use:

%display window;

There are several options for %WINDOW statements such as color, underline, or reverse video. Some options do not work on all terminals - I couldn't use any options when I wrote this! Although it works without options, I strongly suggest you underline the spaces for the input, if possible.

Using %WINDOW will also require some additional code. You will need %LET statements to initialize macro variables to null if you want the ability to submit more that one job per session. Once a macro variable is assigned, that value stays until it is assigned again. With the %PUT/%INPUT method, you do not refer to any macro variable you did not reassign.

PUTTING IT ALL TOGETHER

You can write the code as one long macro or you can write several shorted macros which are called by another macro. You should use the latter method if you:
  have many options to process,
  may add options in the future,
  can use some options for multiple programs,
  or use %WINDOW.

You'll be able to work with each macro separately which will help with debugging. In the case of %WINDOW, you can create several sets of mailing lists in a session without having to recreate the windows each time. I originally wrote one long macro (never expecting it to end up as 25 pages of code including all the %PUT %STR() statements.) Having written the long version, I'd recommend doing several shorter macros.

In V6, I used:

```
%macro mail;
  %mailwin;/* Creates all windows */
  %mailsel;/* Displays the windows
             and write the code.
             Other macros are called
             from this macro*/
%mend mail;
```

The first step(s) to invoke the macro is site specific depending on the default options set for SAS and options for accessing stored code. You will need to have the proper library allocated. SAS will need to be invoked with the following options: MACRO, MAUTOSOURCE, and SASAUTOS=libref. You can have the user enter necessary statements, create a CLIST (SAS is actually invoked with a CLIST), or other methods available at your site. Macros must be stored in a member with the same name.

Once you are in SAS display manager, enter

%MAIL

on line 1 and submit the line. Your log screen or V6 windows will tell you want to do next - just follow the instructions you wrote.

By default, the mailing labels will appear in the OUTPUT window. How to print them on mailing labels will vary by site. I had to save the output to a file and use a batch job to print the file.

OTHER NOTES AND COMMENTS

Here is some other code which many users may want in V6 but may have trouble writing.

The following writes an IF statement with the IN operator.

```
%do i=1 %to &numstate;
  %if %i=1 %then
    IF STATE IN("&state" ;
  %else
      ,"&state" ;
%end;
      );
%* Notice the comma must precede the
next value or else you will have a
"dangling" comma.  The right parenthesis
is added at the end just like the semi-
colon to finish the statement;
```

%WINDOW also lets the user enter several values at once instead of a line at a time. In this window, the user could indicate one or more regions.

```
+ REGION----------------------------+
|                                   |
| Place an X by all regions you want |
|                                   |
| _ Northeast _ Southeast _ Midwest |
| _ Mountain  _ Pacific   _ Foreign |
|                                   |
+-----------------------------------+
```

How do you write the %DO loop when you don't know which region will be first or which will be last? Here is one method. Each choice of region has been assigned a different macro variable name matching the data values. These values are NE,SE,MW,MT,PC, and FO.

```
%macro asgnreg;
  /* %global enables the macro variables
to be used outside this macro.  Macro
variables are only available within this
macro if listed in %local */

%global kmax reg1 reg2 reg3 reg4 reg5
reg6;
%local k;
%let k=1;
%if &NE = X %then %do;
     %let reg&k=NE;
     %let k=%eval(&k+1);
     %end;
```

```
%if &SE = X %then %do;
    %let reg&k=SE;
    %let k=%eval(&k+1);
    %end;

(repeat for remaining regions)

%let kmax=%eval(&k-1);

%* If the region has been selected, a
new macro variable of the form reg&k
will be created. K will be increased by
1 for the next macro variable.  KMAX
will be the maximum number assigned.;
%mend asgnreg;

%if &regsel=X %then %do;
  %asgnreg;

  %do j=1 %to &kmax; /* 1 %to 1 works */
     %if &j=1 %then
    IF REGION="&&reg&j";
      %else
    OR REGION="&&reg&j";
  %end; %* ends do i for state;
     ; /* ends IF statement */
%end;  /* ends if &regsel=X */

/* &&reg&j must have the extra & to
resolve to the value of the macro
variable rather than the name of the
macro variable */
```

Another useful macro for mailing labels will determine the number of observations in the final dataset. This macro is explained in the writing utilities chapter of SAS Guide to Macro Processing.

Don't forget to include the option of repeating the processing without going all the way back to %MAIL. You may also need to include a way to name the output file. Another useful option for the user would be a verification screen. Whenever a macro variable has been assigned a value, that value will appear if you use the macro variable in a %WINDOW or %PUT statement. Verification is much easier to do with %WINDOW although it can be accomplished with %PUT.

While you are writing the macro, you may want to use options that show you what the macro facility is doing. MLOGIC will show you the logic of the code (ex. whether an %IF condition is true or false). SYMBOLGEN will show you how macro variables resolve. MPRINT will let you see the code that is actually written. These options add a lot to the log so you don't want to leave them on.

If you use V5.18 or V6 with windows, define the function key as SUBMIT. If you use V6 and the %PUT method, the function key should be SUBMIT;TOP.

OTHER OPTIONS

What about other options such as SAS/AF or CLISTs? A big advantage for both of these is the ability to create batch jobs which may be more desirable. SAS/AF can offer help screens along the way - for you to write the code as well as for the user. There is more flexibility in screen design. What' the catch - it also cost more! If you have only a couple jobs that users can run, then conversational macros will work. If there are many jobs, then contact the SAS Institute for details on SAS/AF.

The main disadvantage to CLIST is the limited flexibility. In general, the CLIST edits a job by issuing a series of FIND/CHANGE commands based on the information you entered. The edited version is submitted but the actual member isn't changed so you can reuse it. CLISTs are useful if the code never varies but the values do. For example, I had a set of related reports where the only thing that changed was the time period in the title and in the dataset names. Depending on the month, I might run one or as many as seven jobs. The jobs also required 2 or 3 tape mounts which prevented interactive jobs. With the CLIST, I could submit the appropriate jobs as batch jobs without editing each one. The "menu" also reminded me which ones were needed that month. I could also change the destination of the output because I could change the JCL.

CONCLUSION

Conversational macros offer one way of letting non-SAS users "write" code. There are advantages and disadvantages. This method is not useful for every situation, but now you know what is involved and how to write the code.

A copy of the complete code is available by contacting the author.

REFERENCES

SAS Institute Inc. (1990), SAS® Langruage: Reference, Version 6, First Edition Cary, NC: SAS Institute Inc.

SAS Institute Inc. (1990), SAS® Guide to Macro Processing, Version 6, Second Edition Cary, NC: SAS Institute Inc.

Deb Cassidy
3809 Secretariat Court
Columbus, OH 43221
(614) 771-7861 (messages only)

Macro Windows: Creating a User-Friendly Application

Tina Keene, SAS Institute Inc., Cary, NC

ABSTRACT

Macro windows allow you to create user-friendly applications requiring only base SAS® software. This paper presents a simple application that uses macro windows to interface with the user. It contains windows allowing user input for data set selection, data subsetting, and report generation. Techniques for validation of values are also shown.

INTRODUCTION

The addition of the %WINDOW and %DISPLAY statements to the Version 6 macro facility opens the door for enhanced, full-screen interaction between user and application. Using only base SAS software it is possible to prompt users for information, validate that information, then use it to substitute values in SAS programming statements or to selectively branch to other areas of the application. You can also enter data in a macro window and, through macro programming statements and macro variable substitution, store those data values in a SAS data set. This paper illustrates these capabilities by presenting portions of an application designed to maintain an imaginary catering business.

CREATING THE MAIN MENU WINDOW

The application produced for the catering company manages all aspects of the business. It maintains a recipe file, aids in employee and event scheduling, processes and stores sales information, and keeps track of client, vendor, and personnel data. Each of these tasks is presented as a separate choice in the MAIN window in the application, illustrated in **Display 1**.

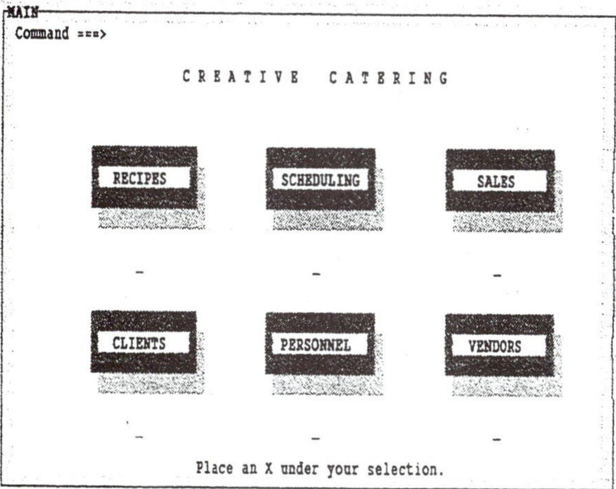

Display 1 MAIN Window

The MAIN window is defined by the %WINDOW statement in the code below. This %WINDOW statement gives a name to the window, MAIN, describes the text in the window, and provides a means for accepting user input.

```
   /*This code defines the MAIN window.*/
%window main color=black
   #1  @23 'C R E A T I V E    C A T E R I N G' color=white
   #5  @11 '              ' attr=rev_video color=magenta
       @34 '              ' attr=rev_video color=magenta
       @57 '              ' attr=rev_video color=magenta
   #6  @11 ' ' attr=rev_video color=magenta
       @14 'RECIPES' color=white
       @24 ' ' attr=rev_video color=magenta
       @25 ' ' attr=rev_video color=yellow
       @34 ' ' attr=rev_video color=magenta
       @36 'SCHEDULING' color=white
       @47 ' ' attr=rev_video color=magenta
       @48 ' ' attr=rev_video color=yellow
       @57 ' ' attr=rev_video color=magenta
       @61 'SALES' color=white
       @70 ' ' attr=rev_video color=magenta
       @71 ' ' attr=rev_video color=yellow
   #7  @11 '              ' attr=rev_video color=magenta
       @25 ' ' attr=rev_video color=yellow
       @34 '              ' attr=rev_video color=magenta
       @48 ' ' attr=rev_video color=yellow
       @57 '              ' attr=rev_video color=magenta
       @71 ' ' attr=rev_video color=yellow
   #8  @12 '              ' attr=rev_video color=yellow
       @35 '              ' attr=rev_video color=yellow
       @58 '              ' attr=rev_video color=yellow
   #10 @17 recipes 1 color=white  attr=underline
       @40 schedul 1 color=white attr=underline
       @63 sales   1 color=white attr=underline
   #13 @11 '              ' attr=rev_video color=magenta
       @34 '              ' attr=rev_video color=magenta
       @57 '              ' attr=rev_video color=magenta
   #14 @11 ' ' attr=rev_video color=magenta
       @14 'CLIENTS' color=white
       @24 ' ' attr=rev_video color=magenta
       @25 ' ' attr=rev_video color=yellow
       @34 ' ' attr=rev_video color=magenta
       @36 'PERSONNEL' color=white
       @47 ' ' attr=rev_video color=magenta
       @48 ' ' attr=rev_video color=yellow
       @57 ' ' attr=rev_video color=magenta
       @60 'VENDORS' color=white
       @70 ' ' attr=rev_video color=magenta
       @71 ' ' attr=rev_video color=yellow
   #15 @11 '              ' attr=rev_video color=magenta
       @25 ' ' attr=rev_video color=yellow
       @34 '              ' attr=rev_video color=magenta
       @48 ' ' attr=rev_video color=yellow
       @57 '              ' attr=rev_video color=magenta
       @71 ' ' attr=rev_video color=yellow
   #16 @12 '              ' attr=rev_video color=yellow
       @35 '              ' attr=rev_video color=yellow
       @58 '              ' attr=rev_video color=yellow
   #18 @17 clients 1 color=white attr=underline
       @40 prsonnl 1 color=white attr=underline
       @63 vendors 1 color=white attr=underline
   #20 @25 'Place an X under your selection.' color=white;
```

The text description not only consists of the literal string enclosed in quotes, but also the color, attributes, and position of that string in the window. Each piece of text is defined separately, beginning with its position. For example, the window heading **CREATIVE CATERING** begins at line 1 (#1) and column 23 (@23). The pound sign (#) and at sign (@) are pointer controls that indicate line number and column number, respectively. When you are designing a macro window, you need to keep in mind what type of terminal will be used to access the application. The size of the screen varies among terminals, and problems can occur when a window is displayed on a terminal that is smaller than the one used to design the window. When designing the window, make sure all line numbers fall within the range of the smallest terminal that will be used.

The color of the text in the window is determined by the value of the COLOR= option. In the MAIN window, all text is displayed as white. Finally, you can assign special attributes to a field using the ATTR= option. In the MAIN window, each of the task options is enclosed in a colored box. Each box is defined by specifying a string of blanks at the appropriate position and associating the reverse video attribute with it (ATTR=REV_VIDEO). Other attributes are available, though this availability is dependent on the type of monitor you use. For more specific details on the %WINDOW statement, consult the *SAS® Guide to Macro Processing, Version 6, First Edition* (for Release 6.03 and 6.04 users) or the *SAS® Guide to Macro Processing, Version 6, Second Edition* (for Release 6.06 and 6.07 users).

In addition to displaying text, macro windows provide the ability to accept input from the user. Refer to the %WINDOW statement shown earlier and note the following line:

```
#10 @17 recipes 1 color=white attr=underline
```

This line sets up a field containing a macro variable instead of text. The name of the macro variable is RECIPES (notice it is not enclosed in quotes). The variable is positioned at line 10, column 17 in the window. Its value is displayed in white and is underlined. Notice also the number 1 following the variable name. This number restricts the length of the macro variable RECIPES to 1 character. Also, all six of the macro variables defined in the MAIN window are blank because none of them has been given a value previously. The MAIN window accepts input in a simple block selection form. When you invoke the application, simply tab to the desired task and type an X in the field under that task. When you press the ENTER key, the value X is stored in the appropriate macro variable. Once a macro variable in the window has been assigned a value, that value is displayed in the window. Therefore, if you redisplay the MAIN window and the macro variables are globally defined, you must reset the values back to blank or null using a %LET statement before executing any subsequent %DISPLAY statements.

The catering application is designed as a hierarchical structure. The association between the different levels of this type of structure is often referred to as a parent-child association. In this application, the MAIN window is the parent window, and each task window that branches from it is a child window. When you select a task in the MAIN window, the value of that task's macro variable is used in conditional macro statements to control branching to a particular child window. It is also a good idea to include an option in each child window to return control to the parent window. In the example used here, a macro variable GOBACK is defined as a field in each task window. If you choose that option, all macro variables in the child window are reset to null and the MAIN window is redisplayed.

BRANCHING TO FIRST GENERATION CHILD WINDOWS

There are six first generation child windows that descend from the MAIN parent window. These six windows are shown in **Display 2** through **7**.

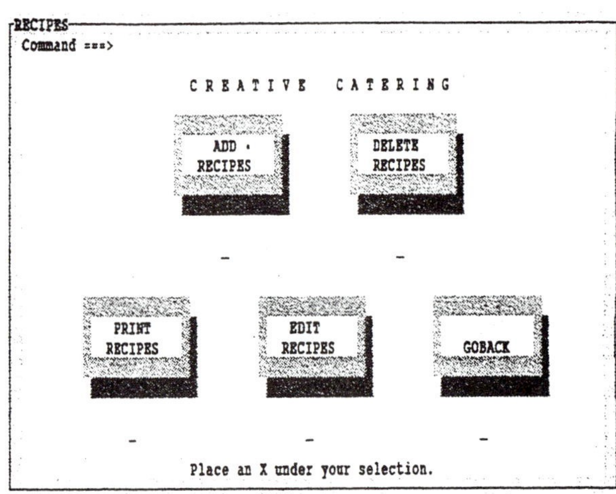

Display 2 RECIPES Window

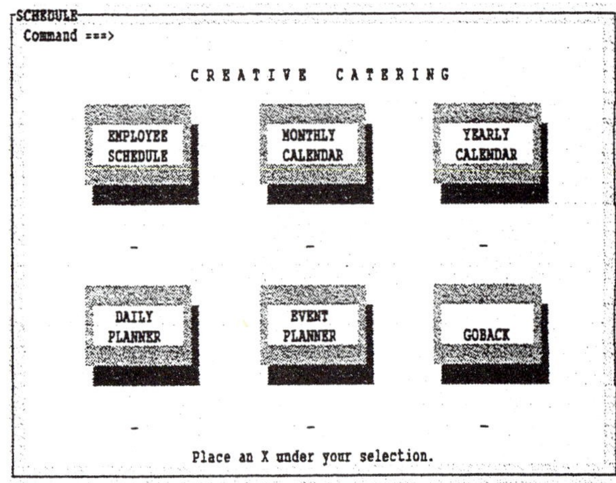

Display 3 SCHEDULE Window

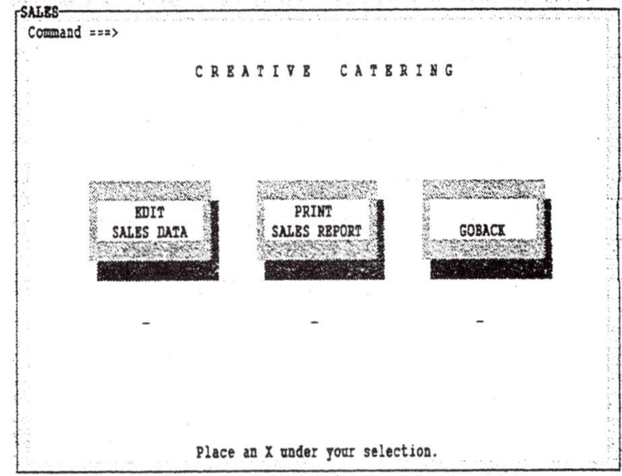

Display 4 SALES Window

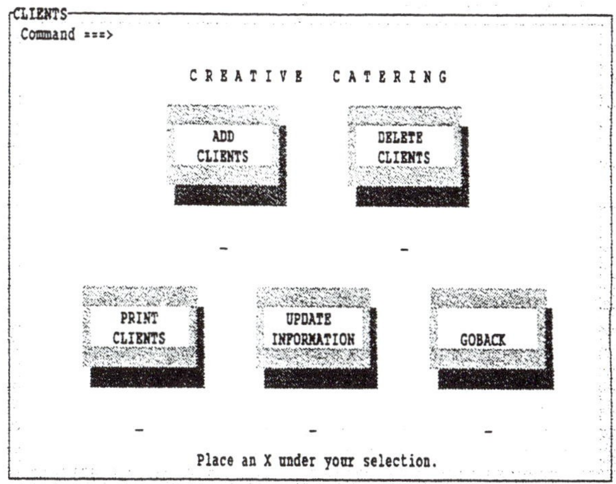

Display 5 CLIENTS Window

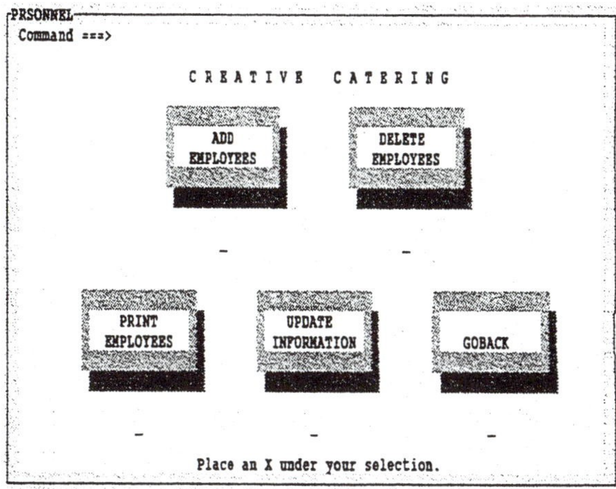

Display 6 PRSONNEL Window

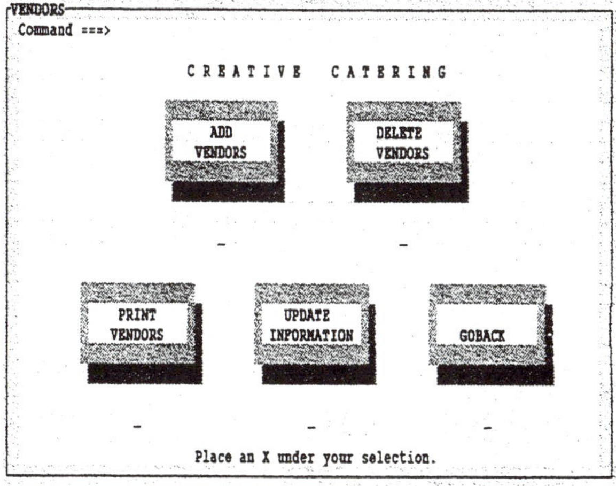

Display 7 VENDORS Window

You progress to a window at this level based on the choice you make in the MAIN window. As mentioned above, when you enter an x in the selected task field, the corresponding macro variable is assigned the value x. The application then uses conditional macro statements to branch to the appropriate point in the next level of processing. For example, the following macro provides a simple example of how the application might branch from the MAIN window to its child windows:

```
%macro mainsel;
   %if %upcase(&recipes) = X %then %display recipes;
   %else %if %upcase(&schedul) = X %then %display schedule;
   %else %if %upcase(&sales)   = X %then %display sales;
   %else %if %upcase(&clients) = X %then %display clients;
   %else %if %upcase(&prsonnl) = X %then %display prsonnel;
   %else %if %upcase(&vendors) = X %then %display vendors;
%mend mainsel;
```

The value of each macro variable defined in the MAIN window is checked to see if it equates to the value X. The %UPCASE function ensures that a match is recognized regardless of whether you enter a lower- or upper-case X. If a condition is met, the macro displays the window that corresponds to the task selected.

The code above checks these fields and performs an action when an X is entered into one of them. But what if you enter the wrong character, for example, an S instead of an X? It is possible for the application to check for this situation as well and either issue an error message or assume that you intended to select that particular task and continue. However, this application makes no assumptions, but, through the following statements, validates user input by first checking to see if the values of all macro variables are NOT null or X. If any of the variables contain an unexpected value, the application then issues an error message and redisplays the window with all fields reset to null, giving you the opportunity to try again.

```
%if (%upcase(&recipes) ne X or
     %upcase(&schedul) ne X or
     %upcase(&sales) ne X or
     %upcase(&clients) ne X or
     %upcase(&prsonnl) ne X or
     %upcase(&vendors) ne X) and
(&recipes ne or & &schedul ne
or &sales ne or &clients ne or
&prsonnl ne or &vendors ne)
%then %do;
       %display error;
       %let recipes=;
       %let schedul=;
       %let sales=;
       %let clients=;
       %let prsonnl=;
       %let vendors=;
       %display main;
%end;
```

The ERROR window is defined as a simple text window and appears in **Display 8**.

```
ERROR
Command ===>

        ERROR:  Incorrect value entered in task selection field

             You must place an X in the appropriate field.
                          Please try again.

                       Press ENTER to continue.
```

Display 8 ERROR Window

The MAINSEL macro also depends on having all the child windows defined at this point. In other words, the %WINDOW statements for all six child windows must be executed before the MAINSEL macro is invoked. If it is likely that only one or two selections will be made during a typical session, it would be more efficient to enclose the %WINDOW statement for each child window in a separate macro, then only invoke the macro (and define the window) for the tasks that are actually selected.

Each of these first generation child windows is in turn a parent to two or more subtask windows. You make selections in these six windows the same as in the MAIN window: tab to the desired task and enter an X.

The %WINDOW statement for the SALES window is shown below. While colors cannot be used in displaying the windows in the printed copy of this paper, they are used in the application to distinguish a change from one level of the hierarchy to another. Remember the %WINDOW statement that defined the MAIN window; the text is printed in white, and the boundaries surrounding the task choices are magenta shadowed by yellow. In the SALES window and the other first generation windows (the code for these windows is not shown here), the text is still white, but the boundaries have been reversed to yellow shadowed by magenta. It is a good idea to experiment with colors when defining windows. While there are no specific rules for color selection, the colors should be pleasant to look at and should complement one another. Color selection can also be used to help the user follow the flow of processing. The color change implemented in this example is a subtle way of letting you know that you have progressed (or regressed, if returning to a parent window) to a new level in the application.

```
   /*This code defines the SALES window.*/
%window sales color=black
   #1 @23 'C R E A T I V E   C A T E R I N G' color=white
   #7  @9  '                   ' attr=rev_video color=yellow
       @31 '                   ' attr=rev_video color=yellow
       @53 '                   ' attr=rev_video color=yellow
   #8  @9  ' ' attr=rev_video color=yellow
       @15 'EDIT' color=white
       @24 ' ' attr=rev_video color=yellow
       @25 ' ' attr=rev_video color=magenta
       @31 ' ' attr=rev_video color=yellow
       @36 'PRINT' color=white
       @46 ' ' attr=rev_video color=yellow
       @47 ' ' attr=rev_video color=magenta
       @53 ' ' attr=rev_video color=yellow
       @68 ' ' attr=rev_video color=yellow
       @69 ' ' attr=rev_video color=magenta
   #9  @9  ' ' attr=rev_video color=yellow
       @12 'SALES DATA' color=white
       @24 ' ' attr=rev_video color=yellow
       @25 ' ' attr=rev_video color=magenta
       @31 ' ' attr=rev_video color=yellow
       @33 'SALES REPORT' color=white
       @46 ' ' attr=rev_video color=yellow
       @47 ' ' attr=rev_video color=magenta
       @53 ' ' attr=rev_video color=yellow
       @58 'GOBACK' color=white
       @68 ' ' attr=rev_video color=yellow
       @69 ' ' attr=rev_video color=magenta
   #10 @9  '                   ' attr=rev_video color=yellow
       @25 ' ' attr=rev_video color=magenta
       @31 '                   ' attr=rev_video color=yellow
       @47 ' ' attr=rev_video color=magenta
       @53 '                   ' attr=rev_video color=yellow
       @69 ' ' attr=rev_video color=magenta
   #11 @10 '                   ' attr=rev_video color=magenta
       @32 '                   ' attr=rev_video color=magenta
       @54 '                   ' attr=rev_video color=magenta
   #13 @16 edsales  1 color=white attr=underline
       @38 prtsales 1 color=white attr=underline
       @60 goback   1 color=white attr=underline
   #20 @23 'Place an X under your selection.' color=white;
```

ACCEPTING AND APPLYING USER INPUT

In **Display 4**, notice that the SALES window provides two task options: **EDIT SALES DATA** and **PRINT SALES REPORT.** Each of these options brings up a window that prompts you to enter information.

Data Entry

The EDSALES window (see **Display 9**) prompts you to enter sales information. The values entered are initially written into the macro variables defined in the window. (The definition for this macro window is shown below). Then, assignment statements within a DATA step copy each of the values into corresponding variables in the NEWSALES data set. The application then clears the macro variable values and redisplays the editing window, ready for the next observation to be entered. Repetition of these steps is easily accomplished with the new %DO %WHILE statement. As the code below shows, these operations are performed until the value of the macro variable EXIT is X. The assignment to EXIT occurs when you place an X in the field at the bottom of the window.

```
EDSALES
Command ===>

                    C R E A T I V E   C A T E R I N G

                                SALES DATA


          Sale Date:        _____     (DDMMMYY)

          Client's Name:    ______________

          Sale Amount:      _______


     Enter values in all fields, then press ENTER


          Place an X here to exit  _
```

Display 9 EDSALES Window

```
   /* This code defines the EDSALES window.*/
%window edsales color=black
   #1  @23 'C R E A T I V E   C A T E R I N G' color=white
   #4  @32 'SALES DATA' color=magenta
   #8  @20 'Sale Date: '  color=yellow
       @36 tdate 7 attr=underline color=yellow
       @47 '(DDMMMYY)' color=magenta
   #10 @20 "Client's Name: " color=yellow
       @36 clname 20 attr=underline color=yellow
   #12 @20 'Sale Amount: ' color=yellow
       @36 saleamt 10 attr=underline color=yellow
   #16 @17 'Enter values in all fields, then press ' color=magenta
       @56 'ENTER' color=white
   #20 @20 'Place an ' color=magenta  'X' color=white
           ' here to exit' color=magenta
       @45 exit 1 attr=underline color=yellow;

   /* This code creates the observations in the data set NEWSALES.*/
%macro addsales;
   %global exit;
   %do %while(%upcase(&exit) ne X);
      trandate="&tdate"d;
      client="&clname";
      tranamt=&saleamt;
      output;
      %let tdate=;
      %let clname=;
      %let saleamt=;
```

```
      %display edsales;
   %end;
   %if &tdate ne or &clname ne or &saleamt ne %then %do;
      trandate="&tdate"d;
      client="&clname";
      tranamt=&saleamt;
      output;
      %let tdate=;
      %let clname=;
      %let saleamt=;
   %end;
   %let exit=;
%mend addsales;

data newsales;
   length client $ 20;
   %display edsales;
   %addsales
run;
```

Because you could choose to enter a new sales record and exit the editing process on the same iteration of the %DISPLAY statement, the %IF statement (following the %DO %WHILE loop) must be included. The %IF statement checks to see if any of the sales data macro variables currently have a value. If any of them do, the appropriate assignment statements are generated and the observation is included in the data set NEWSALES.

You could use the WINDOW and DISPLAY statements available in the DATA step to perform the data entry function. That way you could enter the values directly into the data set variables without going through the intermediate macro variables. This example is included here simply to illustrate that this capability exists and can be easily used.

Thus, using only a DATA step, several macro statements, and a single macro window, a full-screen data entry facility is created. While it is not as efficient or sophisticated as its SAS/FSP® PROC FSEDIT counterpart, it is still functional and can be achieved by implementing features found entirely in base SAS software.

Code Substitution

The SALERPT window (illustrated in **Display 10**) also prompts you for information. Instead of entering data for incorporation into a SAS data set, this window asks you to identify whether the report is to summarize the sales data by month or year and which years to include in the summary. Then it prompts you to choose between two report types: a simple plot of the sales data or a tabular summary report.

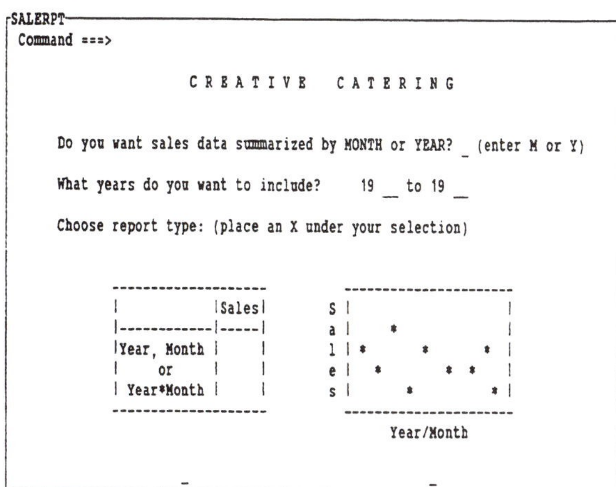

Display 10 SALERPT Window

If the plot is selected, the macro statements shown below are submitted. This segment of code generates a PROC PLOT step. First, a WHERE statement is used so only observations from the requested year range are included in the plot. Then, a PLOT statement requests a plot for SALES by DATE. The range of the horizontal axis is determined by the starting and ending years the user enters into the SALERPT window. The incrementation of these axis values and the format associated with the DATE variable depend on the summary type (monthly or yearly).

```
   /*This code generates a PROC PLOT step.*/
%if %upcase(&rpt2) = X %then %do;
   proc plot data=cater.sales;
      where trandate between "01JAN&year1"d and "31DEC&year2"d;
      plot tranamt*trandate /
         haxis="01JAN&year1"d to "31DEC&year2"d  by
            %if %upcase(&sumval)=M %then
               %str(month;  format trandate monyy5.;);
            %else %str(year;  format trandate year4.;);
      label tranamt='Sales'
            trandate='Transaction Date';
   run; quit;
%end;
```

The second report option requests a summary table. The application uses PROC TABULATE to create this report. However, as the code below shows, the DATE variable must first be split into two variables, MONTH and YEAR. Then the macro produces the PROC TABULATE step, with an appropriate WHERE statement to limit the data to the subset of years requested. The CLASS and VAR statements identify the variables in the table, and the TABLE statement sets up the structure of the table. This structure depends on three things:

- If you requested a summary by year in the SALERPT window, each row in the table represents a summarization for one year.
- If you requested a summary by month and that only one year's data be summarized, each row represents the sales for one month in that year.
- If you requested a summary by month and data for multiple years are included, each row contains data for a particular month/year combination.

The %IF-%THEN-%ELSE statements check for each of these scenarios and generate the appropriate row dimension expressions for the TABLE statement.

```
   /*This code generates a PROC TABULATE Step.*/
%if %upcase(&rpt1) = X %then %do;
   data tmpsales;
      set cater.sales;
      month=month(trandate);
      year=year(trandate);
   proc tabulate data=tmpsales;
      where trandate between "01JAN&year1"d and "31DEC&year2"d;
      class month year;
      var tranamt;
      table
         %if %upcase(&sumval) = Y %then %str(year,);
         %else %if %upcase(&sumval) = M %then %do;
            %if %eval(&year2-&year1) = 0 or &year2= %then
               %str(month,);
            %else %str(year*month,);
         %end;
         tranamt*sum=' ';
      label tranamt='Sales';
   run;
%end;
```

As these examples illustrate, values you enter in a macro window can be substituted in SAS statements to subset data and produce customized reports.

CONCLUSION

This paper presents examples of incorporating user feedback into an interactive application via macro windows. The application discussed here uses macro windows to guide users through its hierarchy of tasks, using simple color techniques to reflect changes to a new level in the hierarchy. It also prompts users for necessary information, validates that information, and uses it in SAS programming statements to perform requested operations. However, this paper has only scratched the surface of macro window capabilities. By implementing more advanced features such as groups and pmenus, you can produce even more sophisticated applications.

SAS and SAS/FSP are registered trademarks of SAS Institute Inc., Cary, NC, USA.

A MULTI-SITE DATA COLLECTION AND ANALYSIS SYSTEM BASED ON THE SAS* SYSTEM

Ray L. Ransom
Allen W. Hightower
Brian D. Plikaytis

Overview

In both industry and government, information systems that play strategic roles in virtually every aspect of program operations have become increasingly commonplace. At the Meningitis and Special Pathogens Branch (MSPB) of the Division of Bacterial Diseases at the National Centers for Disease Control (CDC), such systems have been in use since 1983, gradually replacing the function of more traditional systems of voluntary disease reporting. Prior to this time, voluntary reporting systems were used to monitor trends in mortality rates, resistance to antibiotics, and demographics of the cases of the diseases of interest to MSPB. Important studies often used cases reported in this way.

The new information systems are hospital-based since the diseases that MSPB has responsibility for (bacterial meningitis, Toxic Shock Syndrome, listeriosis) nearly always result in hospitalization. County or state health departments serve as "reporting area nodes" where information is aggregated and sent to CDC on a regular basis. CDC and MSPB contract the services of the health department staff of each reporting area for the duration of the study, usually one or two years, while hospitals graciously volunteer their services. Staff at the health department will make phone calls to infection control personnel at hospitals in their area searching for cases of the diseases of interest to MSPB. As a result, the case-seeking mechanism is much more active and less subject to the whims of the ill individual or the busy hospital. Once cases of disease are located, basic information and laboratory samples are forwarded to CDC. The laboratory samples are used to confirm diagnoses and in other MSPB lab studies and the cases are enrolled into various epidemiologic studies conducted by MSPB staff.

Since 1983, changing technology has had a substantial impact on the flow of information from the hospitals to CDC. Originally, all reporting was paper-based which required transcription by the health departments (to put the information on paper) and by CDC (to keypunch the data). Additional burdens of a paper-based system were: delay in keypunching, complexity in filing, storage, and Privacy Act considerations. Often, ten or more different types of forms would be managed simulataneously. Since the health departments did not have the ability to analyze their data for their own purposes, they were dependent upon MSPB for this function.

Personal computers have become widely available since the mid-1980's. As a result, data entry and analysis by the reporting areas is accomplished by the health departments using Epi Info, a CDC product for epidemiologic database management and analysis, along with DOS batch file menus and a BASIC label program, on their personal computers in the latest information system. Since the data are shipped to MSPB by diskette on a monthly basis, CDC is relieved of the coding and keypunching burden (reducing personnel needs), updates are available a month sooner, and storage considerations are greatly simplified. Epi Info is used by virtually every state and local health department, greatly simplifying training, and analyses formerly done by MSPB for the contractors are now done regionally. At every level, the latest system is easier to use, gives more useful and timely information, and requires less time and personnel to operate.

Counties from California (Los Angeles County and the San Francisco Bay Area), Tennessee, Georgia (Metro Atlanta), and the entire state of Oklahoma form the reporting areas of the latest system, begun in 1988, which has a population base of 19 million and covers areas served by 600 hospitals. Basic information on cases of Haemophilus influenzae (H flu), Neisseria meningitidis (N mening), Group B streptococcus (GBS), and Listeria monocytogenes (Listeria) are collected from each hospital and entered into a case report form file. A tracking system for laboratory isolates sent to CDC forms the lab isolate file.

Cases of H flu under five years of age are screened for enrollment into a study of the effectiveness of a new vaccine. Information needed to screen cases and to conduct the interview from CDC is entered into the H flu vaccine study case screening file. Information on potential control subjects for this study is entered into the H flu vaccine study control screening file. The study is conducted by phone from CDC, where the information is recorded on questionnaires that are keypunched.

Cases of listeria are asked to participate in a study of food preferences. A single screening file is used for both cases and controls. This study is conducted by phone from CDC, where information on the questionnaires is keypunched. Additionally, the contents of the refrigerator of consenting listeria cases are shipped to CDC laboratories to be checked for contamination. Each food item is entered into the laboratory isolate tracking system.

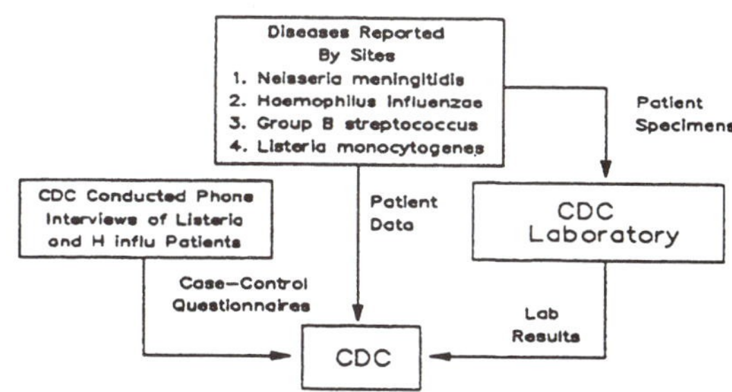

Information Flow

The diseases reported are bacterial meningitis and invasive disease resulting from the Haemophilus influenzae , Listeria monocytogenes, Neisseria meningitidis, and Group B streptococcus bacterial organisms. Data input screens were designed to record data pertaining to each of these illnesses. All patient demographic and hospital data are entered at the sites. Tissue and food specimens are sent to the CDC Division of Bacterial Diseases laboratories. An inventory of these specimens is also entered at the sites and sent to CDC. Other data that the sites collect include lists of potential controls for an H flu type B (HIB) vaccine efficacy study and a Listeria monocytogenes case control study. Results from laboratory testing of patient specimens and the phone interview questionnaires associated with the case-control studies are entered at CDC.

Data File Structure

The design of the flow of data resulted in a total of twelve mergeable files. The core file is the SURV file. This contains all of the demographic and disease type information on each patient. Each record in this file contains a unique value for the identification variable STATEID. All other files are linked to the SURV file by this variable.

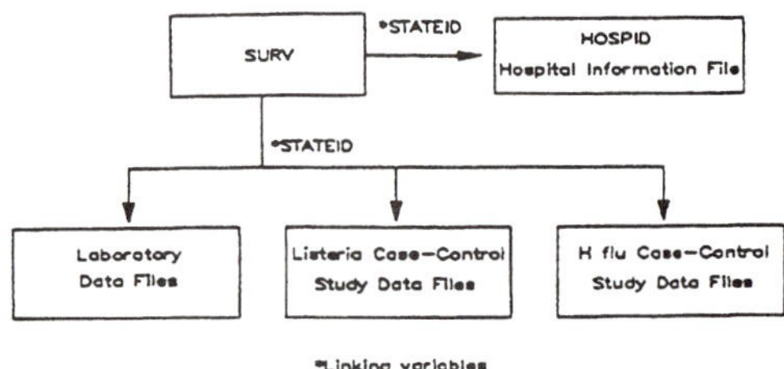

A HOSPID file was created at CDC for each site. This file contains names, addresses, and phone numbers of all hospitals located within each site. Each record in this file has a unique value for the variable HOSPID. The HOSPID of the hospital to which a patient was entered is recorded in that patient's record in the SURV file. This file plays a major role in that it permits the site coordinator to add, edit and delete hospitals and keeps CDC informed of the number and sizes of hospitals participating in the surveillance. In the 1986 study, a hospital identifier was assigned when the report form reached CDC. A Health Maintenance Organization (HMO) might have several locations at one site, but the names written on the forms would not distinguish the different locations. The HOSPID file allows the coordinator to specify precisely the source of data while the CDC epidemiologists can still monitor hospital participation.

The LISTER screening file contains the STATEID's of all Listeriosis cases, whether they are study participants, and if so, how to contact them for their interview. Each patient's record has a list of up to four enlisted controls. This file is linked to the SURV file by the STATEID variable. Each case-control set in this file is alphabetized by name and each member of a set is assigned a value for STUDY_ID. This produces a blinded list for the interviewer at CDC. It is blinded in that the interviewer does not know if he/she is speaking to a case or a control. Completed interviews are keypunched and stored on an IBM mainframe OS disk data set. This file can be downloaded using **PROC DOWNLOAD** and merged with the LISTER data set by the STUDY_ID variable.

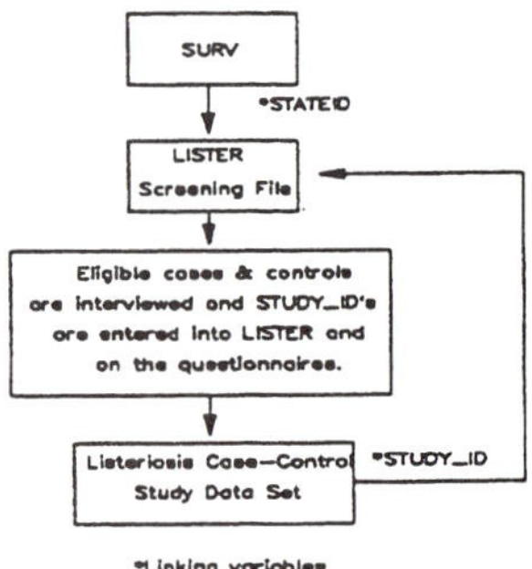

The cases and the controls for the HIB vaccine efficacy study are listed in separate files. The HIBSCR file is a screening file for potential HIB cases. This file contains one observation for each H flu patient eligible for the study and is linked to the SURV file by the STATEID variable. The controls are located in the HCONSCR file and are also linked to the SURV file by the STATEID variable, but will contain multiple records for each STATEID. Records in this file with the same STATEID can be distinguished using a CNTRLNUM variable which represents the control number. All members of these files are interviewed by CDC by phone and the resulting questionnaires are keypunched and stored on a mainframe disk data in the same manner as the Listeriosis interviews. This file can be downloaded and merged with the HIBSCR and HCONSCR data sets using the STATEID and CASECON variables. The CASECON variable tells whether a record is a case or a control and, if it is a control, its control number. This allows subsetting of this file by cases and controls and merging with the appropriate file.

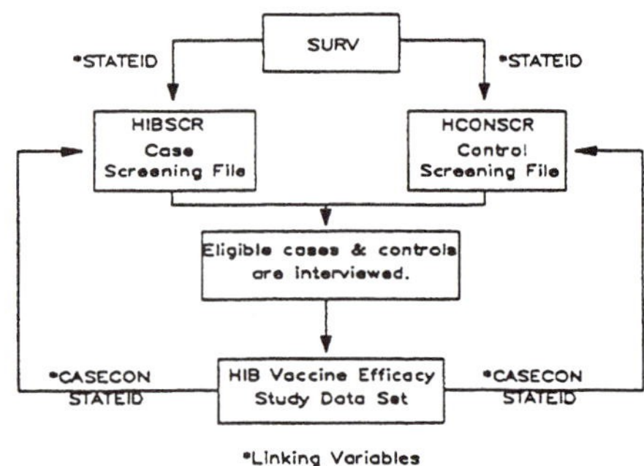

The ACT2LAB file is a laboratory specimen tracking system entered at each site. It contains one record on each specimen sent to the CDC laboratory by the site. The STATEID of the patient is also entered into each record, thus providing its link to the SURV file. Laboratory results are entered at CDC using SAS Full-Screen Product* (SAS/FSP) software customized data entry screens. There are three types of laboratory results (H flu, Listeria, and N mening). There are corresponding SAS data sets and screens for each of these three files. The NMENLAB and HFLULAB files can be merged directly with the ACT2LAB file using the STATEID and SOURCE variables. SOURCE is a variable identifying the source of the isolate (blood, spinal fluid, placenta, ..etc.).

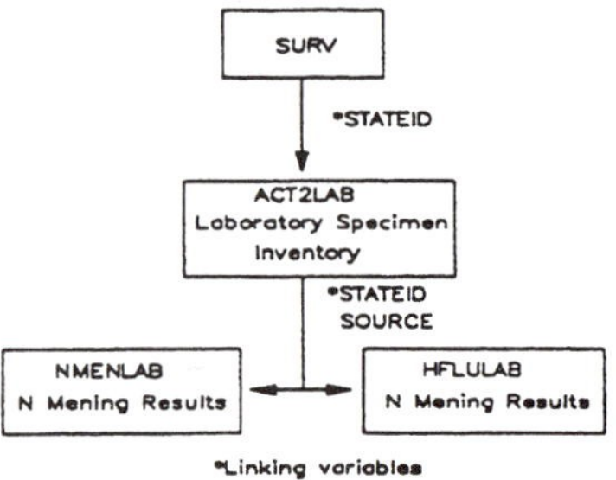

The LISTLAB file poses a different problem in that Listeria specimens might also include foods. When this happens, there may be several reports for one specimen because the food is divided into several sections and tested on a variety of culture media. This eliminates the one-to-one matching we enjoy with the other two laboratory result files. Each month the Listeria records are subsetted from the ACT2LAB file and stored in a new file LACT2LAB. This file has the same variable structure as ACT2LAB except it has an additional variable called ISOLATE. Every specimen for a given STATEID is given a unique isolate number. Each individual report from the laboratory on a food or isolate is given a unique laboratory number.

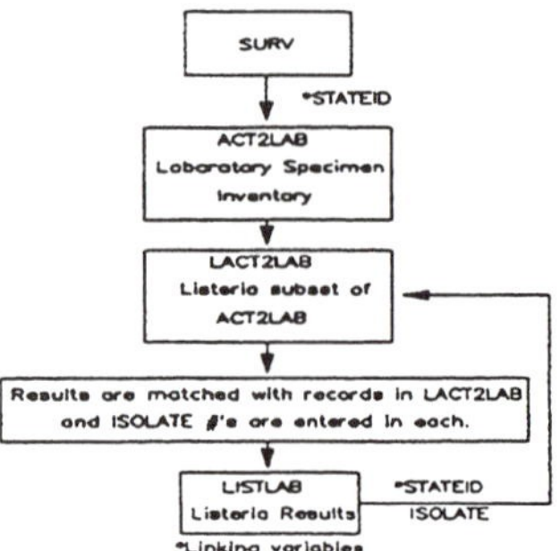

When these records are typed into the Listeria result file LISTLAB, the corresponding ISOLATE number for the specimen tested is also assigned. This allows for direct merging with the LACT2LAB records using the STATEID and ISOLATE variables. Tissue isolates for Listeria are assigned ISOLATE numbers 90 through 99 depending on the specific source. All ISOLATE values below 90 are reserved for foods. The LACT2LAB file must be compared directly to the LISTLAB reports for assignment of ISOLATE values, but once this is done, they can be linked easily.

The twelve files mentioned above contain all of the data entered into the system. The files SURV, HOSPID, LISTER, HIBSCR, HCONSCR, and ACT2LAB are Epi Info record (REC) files and are entered and edited at the sites. These files are copied to a floppy diskette and mailed to CDC every month. When these files reach CDC, they are converted into SAS data sets. All of the other files are created and entered at CDC.

Epi Info

Epi Info is a software package produced by the Epidemiology Program Office at CDC and is designed for quick, easy, and simple creation of data entry screens and limited data analysis. Epi Info data entry screens are easily constructed using the Epi Info menu and allow for extensive data integrity checks. "Check" files can also be created using selections from this menu. Epi Info builds a simple logic program in ASCII format that has the same name as the data file except for a "chk" extension.

```
STATE
 Legal
  GA
  LA
  OK
  SF
  TN
 END
END

SOURCE
 Range 1 9
 AutoJump SPECIES
 Jumps
  9 OTHSRCE
 END
END
```

This text file can be edited using the Epi Info editor or any of a variety of word processing programs. Data integrity checks can include variable types, ranges, repeated fields, lower to uppercase conversions, required entry, or even allowing only specific numeric or character strings to be entered. Also, "JUMP" statements can be specified to allow for skip patterns during study data entry. This prevents prompting for redundant or irrelevant data. Epi Info also allows for multi-colored entry screens which facilitate coordinating of text and allow for visual subsetting of data types. The final result is an extraordinarily user friendly data entry screen.

Epi Info also includes simple data handling, analysis , and graphics capabilities. This allows for further checks of the data for problems such as duplicates or ineligible records. All of these features can be run from DOS batch files. This allows the programmer to write editing programs that can be run from a menu system. An example is the DOS batch file line listing program used to check for duplicates.

```
CLS
ECHO
ECHO LISTS A MONTH OF SURVEILLANCE DATA TO
CHECK FOR DUPLICATES
ECHO
READ \ASURV\SURV
ROUTE ? ENTER SCREEN OR PRINTER OR DISK FILE
NAME FOR OUTPUT DEVICE:?
CLS
DEFINE STR1 STRING
LET STR1="? ENTER MONTH (AS A 2 DIGIT NUMBER
   WITH LEADING ZEROES):?"
DEFINE CMO STRING
LET CMO=CULT[1,2]
SELECT CMO=STR1
set memusage=off
set criteria=off
title 1 "\cSurveillance Record Listing"
SET BREAKCMD=TYPE "\n"
SORT species LNAME FNAME HOSPID CULT
break species
LIST STATEID SPECIES LNAME FNAME HOSPID CULT
   AGE UNIT
break
newpage
route screen
echo
? TASK COMPLETED. HIT ENTER TO RETURN TO
   MENU ?
QUIT
```

This program is a collection of Epi Info Analysis commands and DOS commands which are described in the documentation for the programs. This technique of combining Epi Info and DOS commands in a batch file allows the system designer to provide rather extensive data handling capabilities to users with limited computer knowledge.

The Information System at The Sites

The surveillance system is stored in the \ASURV directory at each site. It consists of 80 files and requires approximately 700,000 bytes of disk space. The files include the six data files entered at the sites and their associated check files and all Epi Info programs and DOS batch files. Epi info was stored in the \EPIINFO directory and requires approximately one megabyte of disk space. The surveillance system was designed to run completely from menus and requires no previous computer knowledge and little support. In addition, a user with computer experience can run his own Epi Info programs and write new programs to expand the existing menus.

A collection of additional programs were also incorporated into the menu. File handling DOS batch files were written to make back-ups of the system and create data diskettes for CDC. A BASIC program was written and compiled at CDC to print mailing labels for the frequent correspondence between the surveillance coordinator and the Infection Control Nurses (ICN), Medical Records Clerks (MRC), and microbiologists located at the hospitals. This program accessed the HOSPID file for addresses and names of contact personnel at each hospital. This REC file was converted to a BASIC data file using the Epi Info CONVERT function. The program also allowed for the printing of one label or a range of labels and the selection between the ICN, MCR, or microbiologist for the attention line of the address.

Data diskettes are created and mailed to the CDC by the 15th of each month. When all five diskettes have been received, back-up copies are made and the originals are stored in state specific diskette boxes by month. The back-ups are used for subsequent analyses.

From Epi Info to The SAS System at CDC

At CDC the data are stored and edited on a Compaq 386S with a 40 megabyte hard disk. Each month a DOS batch file, NEWDATA.BAT, is run when all 5 data diskettes have been received. This file calls a SAS program (CONCAT.SAS) which uses the SAS Macro Facility. This program prompts the user to enter the month and year of the data being entered using the %WINDOW function.

```
%MACRO MONYEAR;
 %GLOBAL MNYR OLDMNYR MNYR2 MN YR;
 %WINDOW DTE COLOR=BLUE
  #2 @17 "WELCOME TO THE DATA
CONCATENATION PROGRAM."
  #3 @21 "WHAT DATA ARE TO BE
CONCATENATED?."
  #4 @17 "******************************************"
  #6 @23 "ENTER THE MONTH AND YEAR."
  #8 @23 "THE MONTH MUST HAVE 3 LETTERS."
  #10 @23 "THE YEAR MUST HAVE TWO DIGITS."
 #13 @28 "MONTH:" @35 MN 3 REQUIRED=YES
 #15 @28 "YEAR:" @35 YR 2 REQUIRED=YES;
 %DISPLAY DTE;
 %LET MN=%UPCASE(&MN);
 %LET MNYR=%UPCASE(&MN&YR);
 %PUT MN=&MNYR;
%MEND MONYEAR;
%MONYEAR;
RUN;
```

Next, the macro OLDDATE takes the inputted data and creates the parameters to pass to the NEWDATA2.BAT file.

```
%MACRO OLDDATE;
%IF &MN=JAN %THEN %DO; %LET
OLDMN=NOV;%LET OLDYR=%EVAL(&YR-1);%LET
MN2=DEC;%LET YR2=%EVAL(&YR-1); %END;
%IF &MN=FEB %THEN %DO; %LET
OLDMN=DEC;%LET OLDYR=%EVAL(&YR-1);%LET
MN2=JAN;%LET YR2=&YR;   %END;
%IF &MN=MAR %THEN %DO; %LET
OLDMN=JAN;%LET OLDYR=&YR;   %LET
MN2=FEB;%LET YR2=&YR;   %END;
%IF &MN=APR %THEN %DO; %LET
OLDMN=FEB;%LET OLDYR=&YR;   %LET
MN2=MAR;%LET YR2=&YR;   %END;
%IF &MN=MAY %THEN %DO; %LET
OLDMN=MAR;%LET OLDYR=&YR;   %LET
MN2=APR;%LET YR2=&YR;   %END;
%IF &MN=JUN %THEN %DO; %LET
OLDMN=APR;%LET OLDYR=&YR;   %LET
MN2=MAY;%LET YR2=&YR;   %END;
%IF &MN=JUL %THEN %DO; %LET
OLDMN=MAY;%LET OLDYR=&YR;   %LET
MN2=JUN;%LET YR2=&YR;   %END;
%IF &MN=AUG %THEN %DO; %LET
OLDMN=JUN;%LET OLDYR=&YR;   %LET
MN2=JUL;%LET YR2=&YR;   %END;
%IF &MN=SEP %THEN %DO; %LET
OLDMN=JUL;%LET OLDYR=&YR;   %LET
MN2=AUG;%LET YR2=&YR;   %END;
%IF &MN=OCT %THEN %DO; %LET
OLDMN=AUG;%LET OLDYR=&YR;   %LET
MN2=SEP;%LET YR2=&YR;   %END;
%IF &MN=NOV %THEN %DO; %LET
OLDMN=SEP;%LET OLDYR=&YR;   %LET
MN2=OCT;%LET YR2=&YR;   %END;
%IF &MN=DEC %THEN %DO; %LET
OLDMN=OCT;%LET OLDYR=&YR;   %LET
MN2=NOV;%LET YR2=&YR;   %END;
%LET MNYR2=%UPCASE(&MN2&YR2);
%LET OLDMNYR=%UPCASE(&OLDMN&OLDYR);
%PUT MNYR=&MNYR;
%PUT OLDMNYR=&OLDMNYR;
%PUT MNYR2=&MNYR2;
%MEND OLDDATE;
```

NEWDATA2.BAT uses the passed parameters to create subdirectories for the new data and remove the old data. Some of the code in this file consists of Norton Utilities$_{TM}$ commands to set screen attributes and create and remove directories. Regular DOS commands can be substituted for these. The file then prompts the user to insert the diskettes and copies the new data to the appropriate subdirectories.

```
SA WHITE ON WHITE
SA BRIGHT YELLOW ON BLACK /N
@ECHO OFF
CLS
CD \ATL\A%2
DEL *.REC
CD \LA\L%2
DEL *.REC
CD \OK\O%2
DEL *.REC
CD \SF\S%2
DEL *.REC
CD \TN\T%2
DEL *.REC
CD \ASURV\%2
DEL *.REC
CD \ESURV\E%2
DEL *.REC
CD \
CLS
NCD MD \ATL\A%1
NCD MD \LA\L%1
NCD MD \OK\O%1
NCD MD \SF\S%1
NCD MD \TN\T%1
NCD MD \SURV89\%1
NCD MD \ESURV89\E%1
COPY \ATL\A%3\*.rec \ATL\A%1
COPY \LA\L%3\*.rec \LA\L%1
COPY \OK\O%3\*.rec \OK\O%1
COPY \SF\S%3\*.rec \SF\S%1
COPY \TN\T%3\*.rec \TN\T%1
CLS
@ECHO ON
@ECHO Insert the ATLANTA diskette in DRIVE A: !
@ECHO OFF
PAUSE
COPY A:*.rec \ATL\A%1
CLS
@ECHO ON
@ECHO Insert the LOS ANGELES diskette in DRIVE A: !
@ECHO OFF
PAUSE
COPY A:*.rec \LA\L%1
CLS
@ECHO ON
@ECHO Insert the OKLAHOMA diskette in DRIVE A: !
@ECHO OFF
PAUSE
COPY A:*.rec \OK\O%1
CLS
@ECHO ON
@ECHO Insert the SAN FRANCISCO diskette in DRIVE A:!
@ECHO OFF
```

```
PAUSE
COPY A:*.rec \SF\S%1
CLS
@ECHO ON
@ECHO Insert the TENNESSEE diskette in DRIVE A: !
@ECHO OFF
PAUSE
COPY A:*.rec \TN\T%1
CLS
@ECHO CONCATENATION PROGRAM HAS STARTED!
@ECHO OFF
CD \MYSASDIR
```

After all diskettes have been copied, CONCAT.SAS continues to execute. The remainder of the program reads in all six REC files from each of the five sites and concatenates them creating six different SAS data sets containing all five sites' data. These files are stored in the \SURV89 directory under a subdirectory named after the month corresponding to the data. For instance, March's unedited data for 1990 was stored in the \SURV89\MAR90 directory. An example of the tree structure for one month's data is shown below. Notice that a copy of each individual site's data is also kept on the hard disk. Since every month is backed up on floppy, only one month's data are stored on the hard disk.

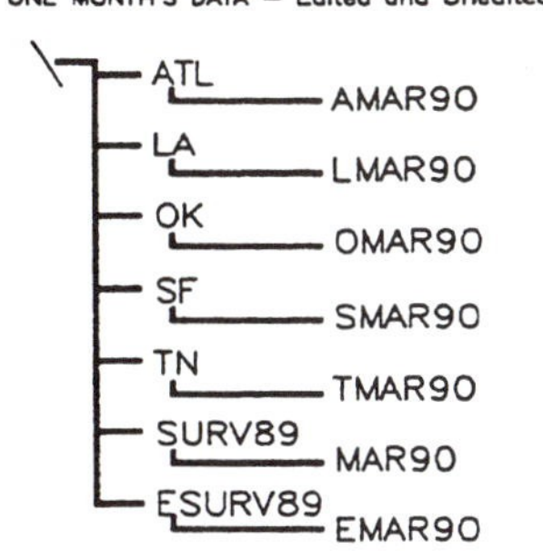

A REC file is an ASCII file made up of three basic parts. They are the header length, the header record, and the data lines.

```
17
_HOSPITALIN  27  2 12 54  2  9  0 15 HOSPITAL INFORMATION
RECORD
#DUMMY0      1  3 15 80  3  0  0 15
=========================================
_HOSPID   2  5 11 15  5  3  5  14    HOSPITAL ID:
_AHAID   37  5 11 45  5  3  7  14    AHA ID:
_NAME     2  7 11 20  7  3 30  14    NAME OF HOSPITAL:
_STREET   2  9 11 20  9  3 30  14    STREET ADDRESS:
_CITY     2 10 11  8 10  3 20  14    CITY:
_STATE    2 11 11  9 11  3  2  14    STATE:#
ZIP      27 11 11 37 11  6  5  14    ZIP CODE:
#BEDS     2 13 11 18 13  0  4  14    NUMBER OF BEDS:
_PHONE   32 13 11 46 13  3 13  14    PHONE NUMBER:
_ICP      2 14 11  7 14  3 30  14    ICP:
_ICPEXT   2 15 11 23 15  3 20  14    EXTENSION OR BEEPER:
_MICRO    2 16 11 18 16  3 30  14    MICROBIOLOGIST:
_MICEXT   2 17 11 23 17  3 20  14    EXTENSION OR BEEPER:
_MEDREC   2 18 11 18 18  3 30  14    MEDICAL RECORDS:
_MEDEXT   2 19 11 23 19  3 20  14    EXTENSION OR BEEPER:

GA0011232211VETERANS ADMINISTRATION HOSP  2020 CLAIRMONT
ROAD  ATLANT!
A        GA303281233(404)629-9299MOLLY ICP PERSON       1212    !
    MANNY AMOEBA          1234         GARY GUINESS     !
    1235        !
GA0021234567NORTHSIDE GENERAL          1221 HAPPY LANE
ATLANT!
A        GA30321 234(404)633-5999                          !
                                     MIKE MEDICALREC  !
    1221        ?
GA0051332211DEKALB COUNTY MEMORIAL     3333 NORTH DECATUR
ROAD     ATLANT!
A        GA33033 453(404)633-9999                          !
                                     MARY M. RECORDS  !
    5999        !
```

On the first line is a number telling how many lines make up the header record (17 in this example). Starting on the second line is the header record that defines the location, color, and content of the text for the entry screen and the names and types of the variables. Immediately following the header record is the data. This structure allows you to use the SAS system to read the header and use this information to read past the header record to the data. The macro STRIP in CONCAT.SAS does just this.

```
%MACRO STRIP(DTA1,DTA2,DTA3);
DATA &DTA1;
INFILE &DTA2;
FLAG+1;
*** READ IN NUMBER OF HEADER LINES AND SAVE
HEADER, DEL OBS ***;
IF FLAG=1 THEN DO;
INPUT HEADER;
RETAIN HEADER;
IF HEADER^=. THEN DELETE;
END;
*** DELETE THE NEXT HEADER LINES ***;
IF 1<FLAG<=HEADER+1 THEN DO;
 INPUT DUMMY$;
 IF DUMMY^='' THEN DELETE;
END;
IF FLAG>HEADER+1 THEN DO;**** NOW INPUT
DATA ***;
%&DTA3;
%MEND STRIP;
```

Once you have read past the header record, you are now ready to input the data.

Writing the **INPUT** statements is the most tedious part of the program, but fortunately, it only has to be done once. Epi Info stores data in fixed lines of 78 columns, so if you know the order and lengths of your variables then the **INPUT** statement can be written easily. The 79th column contains "!" for an end-of-line marker, except in the last line of records that have been marked for deletion in Epi Info and then you will find "?". This allows for easy permanent deletion of these records. Another situation that might arise is when a variable is split between two lines. To solve this problem you can read in the two parts as two separate variables and then combine them using the concatenation operator(| |). At present, the entire **DATA** step for a file is divided into two macros. First is the shell of the **DATA** step and second is the variable list.

```
%MACRO HCNR;
INPUT
%HCNVAR;
IF DUMMY2='?' THEN DELETE;
LENGTH CLNAME $ 20;
CLNAME=CLNAMEA || CLNAMEB;
SUBSTR(CLNAME,16,5)=CLNAMEB;
END;
RUN;
PROC SORT; BY STATEID; RUN;
%MEND HCNR;
```

```
%MACRO HCNVAR;
FNAME $1-10 LNAME $11-30 STATEID $31-36
INTDATE $37-44 ADMIT $45-52 CASETYPE 53
CFNAME $54-63 CLNAMEA $64-78 DUMMY1 $79  /
CLNAMEB $1-5 CPHONE $6-18 CBIRTH $19-26
CATTEND $27 CHOURS 28-29 CRESIDE $30
ENROLLED 31 CNTRLNUM 32 TIME $33-52
RELATION 53 DUMMY2 $54 ;
%MEND HCNVAR;
```

The variable list is separate so we can later use it in a **PUT** statement to create REC files of the concatenated data sets. These files allow for quick searches for certain records. Plans for the future include the development of screens using SAS/FSP software for all files so we will not need two copies of the data. The macro SETALL concatenates the SAS data sets. It also reads in a header record for the REC file creation.

```
%MACRO SETALL(VAR1,VAR2);
DATA KEEP.&VAR1; SET ONE TWO THREE FOUR
FIVE;
RUN;
*******   BEGIN CREATION OF EPI INFO HEADER
RECORD *****;
DATA HEAD;
INFILE EMP;
FLAG+1;
*** READ IN NUMBER OF HEADER LINES AND
OUTPUT ***;
IF FLAG=1 THEN DO;
INPUT HEADER ;
RETAIN HEADER;
OUTPUT;
END;
*** WRITE THE NEXT HEADER LINES ***;
IF 1<=FLAG<=HEADER THEN DO;
 INPUT DUMMY $CHAR126.;
NEWDUMMY=TRIM(DUMMY);
DROP DUMMY;
OUTPUT;
END;
ELSE
INPUT;
RUN;
PROC PRINT; RUN;
*** HEADER RECORD SHOULD BE COMPLETE ***;
*** NOW ADD CONCATENATED DATA ***;
***IN THIS DATA SET FLAG=1 FOR THE HEADER
***NUMBER LINE AND THE FIRST LINE
***OF THE HEADER RECORD. THAT IS WHY WE
***MUST USE THE DUMMY='' IN THE IF
***STATEMENTS.;
DATA TOTAL;SET HEAD KEEP.&VAR1;
IF FLAG=1 & NEWDUMMY='' THEN DO;*** OUTPUT
HEADER LENGTH ****;
FILE &VAR1;
PUT HEADER;
END;
*** OUTPUT HEADER RECORD ***;
IF 1<=FLAG<=HEADER & NEWDUMMY^='' THEN
DO;
FILE &VAR1;
PUT NEWDUMMY;
END;
IF FLAG>HEADER+1 THEN DO;
FILE &VAR1;
PUT
%&VAR2;
END;
RUN;
RUN;
%MEND SETALL;
```

The macro ALLSTATE calls the macro STRIP for files from all sites.

```
%MACRO ALLSTATE(FILEN);
**PROCESSING ATL DATA;
%STRIP(ONE,ATL,&FILEN);
**PROCESSING LA DATA;
%STRIP(TWO,LA,&FILEN);
**PROCESSING OK DATA;
%STRIP(THREE,OK,&FILEN);
**PROCESSING SF DATA;
%STRIP(FOUR,SF,&FILEN);
**PROCESSING TN DATA;
%STRIP(FIVE,TN,&FILEN);
%MEND ALLSTATE;
```

All macros for a given file are ran in the macro FINAL.

```
%MACRO FINAL(CON1,CON2,CON3);
%STATUS(&CON2,&CON3);
LIBNAME KEEP "C:\SURV89\&MNYR";
FILENAME EMP "C:\ASURV\EMPTYFIL\&CON2..REC";
FILENAME ATL "C:\ATL\A&MNYR.\&CON2..REC";
FILENAME LA  "C:\LA\L&MNYR.\&CON2..REC";
FILENAME OK  "C:\OK\O&MNYR.\&CON2..REC";
FILENAME SF  "C:\SF\S&MNYR.\&CON2..REC";
FILENAME TN  "C:\TN\T&MNYR.\&CON2..REC";
FILENAME &CON2.
"C:\SURV89\&MNYR.\&CON2..REC";
%ALLSTATE(&CON1.R);
%SETALL(&CON2,&CON1&VAR);
%MEND FINAL;
```

The macro STATUS called by the macro FINAL displays a message on the screen to keep the user informed of the progress of the program. Once all of the macros have been read, the remaining program is quite simple.

```
%FINAL(LST,LISTER,RED);
%FINAL(HIB,HIBSCR,WHITE);
%FINAL(SRV,SURV,BLUE);
%FINAL(LAB,ACT2LAB,MAGENTA);
%FINAL(HCN,HCONSCR,GREEN);
%FINAL(HSP,HOSPID,CYAN);
DATA ONE;
X=1;
OUTPUT;
X "CLS";
X "ECHO OFF";
X "CD \UPDATE";
X "BORDER";
X "ECHO *";
X "ECHO *";
X "ECHO *";
X "ECHO *          FINISHED!!!!";
X "ECHO *";
X "ECHO *";
X "ECHO *";
RUN;
```

The resulting data sets are saved in the appropriate subdirectory of the SURV89 directory. The data is now ready for editing.

Data Editing

The SAS datasets are uploaded to an IBM mainframe using **PROC UPLOAD**. This allows for quicker printing. SURV8901, a SAS program written with Version 5 of the SAS system for mainframes, prints frequencies and line listings for checking for entry errors in the data not caught by built in checks. Editing corrections are then typed into one of six programs written with the SAS software for personal computers depending on which file they are to correct. These corrections, in the form of **IF** statements, are added to an ongoing program each month, resulting in a complete documentation of changes to the data at CDC. These programs are stored in the \MYSASDIR\SURV89\EDIT directory. A list of these changes are mailed to the sites each month and they are asked to implement these changes. This keeps track of differences between the datasets at CDC and the ones at the sites. The edited SAS datasets are stored in the \ESURV89 directory.

The test results of the specimens sent to the CDC laboratories are typed into data entry screens created with SAS/FSP software. There are results on all bacterial organisms reported except Group B Streptococcus, therefore, there are three corresponding entry screens. These screens, data sets, and programs are all accessed from a DOS batch file menu. All files associated with these screens are stored in the \MYSASDIR\SURV89\FSP directory.

Cases and controls that are entered into the Listeria and H flu case-control studies are interviewed by phone for additional information. This information is written on questionnaires which are keypunched onto magnetic tape. These tapes are read using SAS programs on the mainframe and the data sets are edited and stored on the mainframe. The datasets are downloaded using the micro-to-mainframe link once again and PROC DOWNLOAD. This will allow them to be merged with other datasets on the PC.

All of the data sets in this surveillance project contain the variable STATEID. This is an identifier that is unique to each case report for each patient. All data sets can, and will be, merged together when the analyses begin.

Data Analyses

The goal of the H flu vaccine study is to monitor the effectiveness of the new vaccines for this disease in children between 18 and 59 months of age. Since daycare attendance and age are both important risk factors for disease and are related to the likelihood of vaccination, control subjects are chosen that are similar to the cases with respect to these factors. This study uses information from the SURV, ACT2LAB, HFLULAB, HIBSCR, HCONSCR, and the study interview files. Demographic information on the case of disease is obtained from the SURV file, hospital laboratory diagnosis from the ACT2LAB file, CDC laboratory confirmation and more extensive information from the HFLULAB file, eligibility and telephone contact information for the case and the matched controls from the HIBSCR and HCONSCR files, and finally, vaccination and daycare attendance information from the study questionnaire. PROC MCSTRAT, a user contributed SAS system procedure for conditional logistic regression, is used to examine the association between multiple risk factors and the risk of disease. Since this procedure for analysing matched case-control data is available only on the the mainframe, the PC-based data is uploaded and matched with the mainframe-based study questionnaires whenever updated analyses are desired. PROC FREQ and PROC UNIVARIATE are used for descriptive analysis.

The goal of the listeria food preference study is to identify foods associated with the acquisition of this disease, and using the contents of the cases' refrigerators, to see if these foods are contaminated with this bacteria. This study has a structure that is only slightly different from the H flu vaccine study in that a single screening file is used for both cases and controls (LISTER). A matched study design is used here, too. As a result, the same SAS system procedures are used for statistical analyses as before. Comparison of the listeria isolated from cases and whatever is isolated from the refrigerator contents serves as another component of this study.

This system is also being used to monitor trends of MSPB program interest, such as antibiotic resistance, mortality, and overall incidence for each of these diseases. The tissue samples serve as a basis for many laboratory studies, such as the comparison and development of new bacterial isolation techniques, strain matching methodology, and development of other tools potentially useful to epidemiologists.

Conclusion

This surveillance system is only limited by the amount of additions you wish to make. Being run from DOS batch file menus, the system is easy to operate and modify. As a result, plans for modification are encouraged and eagerly accepted by the programmers. We are currently working on SAS/FSP software entry screens for all files. Since a Local Area Network(LAN) has been recently established in the Division of Bacterial Diseases(DBD) at CDC, share space will be allocated on the file server where screen programs and their associated data sets can be stored and updated each month with the most recently edited files. All eligible users will be allowed read-only access to these files. After all of these programs are written, they too will be incorporated into the DOS batch file menus. Following this, the laboratories have expressed an interest in entering their data straight into the system instead of onto laboratory forms and into laboratory books. This task will be addressed with the LAN environment in mind also. Our LAN support is already working on a means of automatic daily back-up of certain files.

As you can see, this system's structure promotes flexibility while maintaining simplicity. It is easily adapted to other types of studies. One of the reporting areas has already adapted this system for use on a different group of studies. All that was necessary was altering the data entry screens and databases.

*SAS and SAS/FSP are registered trademarks of SAS Institute Inc., Cary, NC, USA.

Norton Utilities is a trademark of Peter Norton Computing.

Ray L. Ransom
CID, DBD, SSA mailstop C-09
Centers for Disease Conrol
Atlanta, GA 30333
(404) 639-3907

Menu-Driven Interfaces Using SAS/FSP* Software and the SAS* Macro Language

Michael F. Perry, New York State Department of Transportation

SUMMARY

Problem Discussed: Interfacing main frame SAS applications at sites without SAS/AF* or SAS/ASSIST* applications development software.

Intended Audience: Beginning to intermediate SAS programmers who must develop applications without SAS/AF or SAS/ASSIST software.

Suggested Solution: Interfacing SAS applications using SAS/FSP data entry software in combination with the SAS macro language.

Benefits: Allows users to customize program/menu variables in a format that conceals application code, displays detailed user instructions and provides basic input error trapping capabilities.

Outline:

I. INTRODUCTION
II. TWO SIMPLE EXAMPLES
III. CUSTOMIZING SAS/FSP ENTRY SCREENS
IV. ADDING OPTIONAL TESTS AND FEATURES
V. CREATING MENU DRIVEN SYSTEMS
VI. CONCLUSION

I. INTRODUCTION

SAS programmers at sites without SAS/AF or SAS/ASSIST software must either learn third-party application development packages such as ISPF** or physically change "hard coded" statements with new variables each time an application is run. The New York State Department of Transportation (NYSDOT) has licensed SAS, SAS/FSP and SAS/GRAPH* software since 1986 but has been unable to license SAS/AF software due to budgetary constraints. The interface described presents an alternative to learning ISPF or "hard coding" applications by:

1. Establishing a temporary (work) data set of initial program variables or menu choices;
2. Displaying the data set of initial program variables for user modification with PROC FSEDIT and a customized SAS/FSP data entry screen;
3. Converting the user modified initial program variables to SAS macro variables using simple data step "CALL" statements and "SYMPUT" functions, and;
4. Customizing the application with the converted macro variables as necessary.

NYSDOT has successfully used this technique to interface single screen applications as well as small menu driven systems. While no substitute for SAS/AF software, a SAS/FSP interface employs portions of the same SAS Screen Control Language used to drive SAS/AF and SAS/ASSIST software and is far superior to "hard coding" an application. The application programmer may display detailed on-screen instructions, create menus, and establish basic input error trapping capabilities without learning ISPF or exposing program code or macro invocations for user modification.

II. TWO SIMPLE EXAMPLES

Example 1: The first example customizes an application used to browse an existing data set. The code begins by establishing a temporary data set of initial program values to ensure that PROC FSEDIT presents the user with an existing record that is ready to edit. The "SCREEN=" option of the "PROC FSEDIT" statement references a SAS/FSP data entry screen that the application programmer may customize with detailed instructions and basic input error trapping routines. Figures 1 and 2 are fully customized SAS/FSP data entry screens for Examples 1 and 2.*** The macro variable to be created appears first in the SYMPUT function and may duplicate the name of the input data set variable:

Ex. 1 Code: Browsing a Specified Data Set

```
/* Create an initial variable value.   */

DATA TEMP;
  DATASET='        ';
```

```
/* Display the initial value on-screen */
/* with SAS/FSP for user modification. */

PROC FSEDIT DATA=TEMP SCREEN=SCRN.BROWSE;
```

Figure 1: Entry Screen for Example One

```
=====================================
Command ===> _

   Data Set Browse Selection Screen
   ****************************************

Directions: Tab to the entry area below,
type the name of the data set to browse
from the list below and then press PF3:

        Data Set: ________

Data set names/content:
  CONTRACT - Contract Level Data.
  PROJECT  - Fiscal Share Data.
  ESTAMT   - Engineer Estimate Data.
  ITEMPEST - Eng. Est. Item Price Data.
=====================================
```

```
/* Convert input to a macro variable. */

DATA TEMP; SET TEMP;
  CALL SYMPUT('DATASET',DATASET);

/* Customize code with macro variable. */

PROC FSBROWSE DATA=DB.&DATASET; RUN;
```

Example 2: The second example customizes an application used to print all NYSDOT contracts with specified minimum values for date of award, awarded dollar amount and number of bidders. SAS system option DQUOTE allows referencing a macro variable (a variable preceded by an "&" symbol) from within quotes. Input data set variables MINAMT and MINDATE create a second set of formatted macro variables for use in customizing the TITLE statement. The code formats MINBIDS as a two position character variable to avoid leading blank spaces caused by converting a numeric data step variable with a default length of eight to a macro variable:

Ex. 2 Code: Printing User Specified Data

```
/* Create a data set of initial values.*/

OPTIONS DQUOTE;

DATA TEMP;
  MINDATE= . ; MINBIDS='  '; MINAMT= . ;

/* Display initial values on-screen    */
/* with SAS/FSP for user modification. */

PROC FSEDIT DATA=TEMP SCREEN=SCRN.AWDBID;
  INFORMAT MINDATE YYMMDD.;
```

Figure 2: Entry Screen for Example Two

```
=====================================
Command ===> _

   Award Report Modification Screen
   ****************************************

Directions: Tab to the entry areas below
and type a minimum award date, number of
bidders and awarded dollar amount for
contracts to be included in the report.
Press PF3 when done.

     Min. Award Date: ______
              (E.G.: YYMMDD)
    Min. No. Bidders: __
              (E.G.:  3)
    Min. Award $ Amt: ________
              (E.G.:  5000000)
=====================================
```

```
/* Convert input to macro variables.   */

DATA TEMP; SET TEMP;
  CALL SYMPUT('MINDATE',MINDATE);
  CALL SYMPUT('FMTDATE',PUT(MINDATE,
    WORDDATE12.));
  CALL SYMPUT('MINBIDS',MINBIDS);
  CALL SYMPUT('MINAMT',MINAMT);
  CALL SYMPUT('FMTAMT',PUT(MINAMT,
    DOLLAR12.0));

/* Customize code with macro variables.*/
/* File TEMP has served its purpose    */
/* and may be overwritten.             */

DATA TEMP; SET DB.CONTRACT(READ=XXX);
  IF DATE_AWD >= &MINDATE AND
     CONTAAMT >= &MINAMT AND
     NUMBIDS  >= &MINBIDS;

PROC PRINT N DATA=TEMP;
  VAR CONTRACT DATE_AWD CONTAAMT NUMBIDS;
TITLE "CONTRACTS AWARDED ON OR AFTER
&FMTDATE WITH A MINIMUM DOLLAR VALUE OF
&FMTAMT AND &MINBIDS OR MORE BIDDERS";
RUN;
```

The next section discusses modification of SAS/FSP data entry screens with detailed user instructions and basic on-screen input error trapping capabilities.

III. CUSTOMIZING SAS/FSP ENTRY SCREENS

Customizing starts at a default screen the programmer may modify with titles, instructions, examples and basic input error trapping capabilities. For instance, the second example described above would produce the default screen shown in Figure 3 the first time "PROC FSEDIT" displayed the initial program variables for user modification:

Figure 3: Default Screen for Example Two

```
=====================================
Command ===> _

        MINDATE: __________

        MINBIDS: __

        MINAMT: ________
=====================================
```

To begin customizing, type MODIFY on the command line of the default screen and press the enter key. The "FSEDIT Screen Modification Menu" shown in Figure 4 will appear after a few seconds:

Figure 4: SAS/FSP Modification Menu

```
=====================================
Select Option ===> _

1  Information about screen modification
2  Screen Modification
3  Field Identification
4  Field Attributes
5  Parameter Modification
=====================================
```

Option two allows the programmer to customize the basic screen using line editing commands similar to those used during SAS Display Manager sessions. The programmer may completely rearrange the location of input variables, type detailed instructions or even replace the basic variable name prompts with longer and more descriptive prompts. Option three, or pressing PF3 after completing screen modification, allows identification of the area on the modified screen where a user will input a variable. Options four and five manage screen colors and basic error trapping capabilities to verify minimum, maximum, required, capitalized or initial input values. Pressing PF1 after selecting any option provides excellent on-screen help facilities. To revise a previously modified screen, retype MODIFY on the command line of the screen to be revised and press enter.

Since most users assume SAS/FSP screens are normal menus driven by the enter and arrow keys, SAS/FSP interface screens should include instructions reminding the user to tab to the entry areas and press PF3 to submit their choices. There is also a slight chance the user could become confused by accidentally issuing a SAS/FSP command to add or repeat a record. So far, NYSDOT has experienced a few instances of users forgetting to tab and press PF3 and no instances of users accidentally creating additional records.

The fully modified SAS/FSP screen file must be stored in a manner accessible to the application code it interfaces. While the SAS system usually handles such tasks automatically, problems may result if the programmer allows access to the application code without also allowing access to its modified SAS/FSP screen files. An application which loses access to its modified screen will produce a default screen once again. Restoring access to the appropriate screen file corrects the situation the next time the application is run.

IV. ADDING OPTIONAL TESTS AND FEATURES

Formatting a SAS/FSP interfaced application as a simple SAS macro allows testing and supplementing user input with the SAS macro language. For instance, browse Example 1 could supplement a data set read password based on user input as shown below in Modification (Mod.) 1:

Mod. 1: Optional Macro Tests & Features

```
/* %MACRO begins macro compilation.   */
/* Establish/edit variable as before. */

%MACRO BROWSE;
DATA TEMP;
  DATASET='        ';

PROC FSEDIT DATA=TEMP SCREEN=SCRN.BROWSE;

/* The RUN statement completes the     */
/* SYMPUT function prior to execution  */
/* of the macro %IF test.              */

DATA TEMP; SET TEMP;
  CALL SYMPUT('DATASET',DATASET);
  RUN;

/* Test and supplement user input.     */

%IF &DATASET = ESTAMT   OR
    &DATASET = ITEMPEST
    %THEN %LET PW=YYY;
  %ELSE %LET PW=XXX;

/* Customize code with macro variables */
/* and close and call the macro.       */

PROC FSBROWSE DATA=DB.&DATASET(READ=&PW);
RUN; %MEND BROWSE; %BROWSE
```

V. CREATING MENU DRIVEN SYSTEMS

A macro format also allows interfacing applications with a common menu. The following code establishes the menu shown in Figure 5 to determine which example the user wishes to execute:

Mod. 2: Menu for Examples 1 and 2

```
/* Execute the %DO-%UNTIL loop until a */
/* blank entry is detected from a      */
/* previous loop execution.            */
```

```
%MACRO MENU;
%DO %UNTIL(&OPTION=  );

/* Create a data with an initial menu  */
/* choice.                             */

DATA TEMP;
  OPTION=' ';

/* Display the initial menu choice for */
/* user modification with SAS/FSP and  */
/* the customized screen shown below.  */

PROC FSEDIT DATA=TEMP SCREEN=SCRN.MENU;
```

Figure 5: Example SAS/FSP Menu

```
=====================================
Command ===> _

          Example Application Menu
          ********************************

Directions:  Tab to the entry area below,
type the one letter code of the task you
wish to perform and then press PF3:

            Task to Perform: _

 Valid Letter Codes: B = Screen Browse.
                     A = Award Report.
                       = (blank) Exit.
=====================================
```

```
/* Convert input to macro variables.   */

DATA TEMP; SET TEMP;
  CALL SYMPUT('OPTION',OPTION);
  RUN;

/**********************************************/
/* If user input is "B," execute the         */
/* following browse example code.            */
/* Otherwise, skip to the next %END.         */
/* (Note:  For full commenting of the        */
/* example code, refer to the previous       */
/* discussions of the examples.              */

%IF &OPTION = B %THEN %DO;

DATA TEMP;
  DATASET='        ';

PROC FSEDIT DATA=TEMP SCREEN=SCRN.BROWSE;

DATA TEMP; SET TEMP;
  CALL SYMPUT('DATASET',DATASET);
  RUN;

%IF &DATASET = ESTAMT   OR
    &DATASET = ITEMPEST
    %THEN %LET PW=YYY;
  %ELSE %LET PW=XXX;

PROC FSBROWSE DATA=DB.&DATASET(READ=&PW);
RUN;

%END;  * Close the option B %DO group.;

/**********************************************/
/* If user input is "A," execute the         */
/* the following browse example code.        */
/* Otherwise, skip to the next %END         */

%ELSE %IF &OPTION = A %THEN %DO;

OPTIONS DQUOTE;

DATA TEMP;
  MINDATE= . ; MINBIDS='   '; MINAMT= . ;

PROC FSEDIT DATA=TEMP SCREEN=SCRN.AWDBID;
  INFORMAT MINDATE YYMMDD.;

DATA TEMP; SET TEMP;
  CALL SYMPUT('MINDATE',MINDATE);
  CALL SYMPUT('FMTDATE',PUT(MINDATE,
    WORDDATE12.));
  CALL SYMPUT('MINBIDS',MINBIDS);
  CALL SYMPUT('MINAMT',MINAMT);
  CALL SYMPUT('FMTAMT',PUT(MINAMT,
    DOLLAR12.0));

DATA TEMP; SET DB.CONTRACT(READ=XXX);
  IF DATE_AWD >= &MINDATE AND
     CONTAAMT >= &MINAMT AND
     NUMBIDS  >= &MINBIDS;

PROC PRINT N DATA=TEMP;
  VAR CONTRACT DATE_AWD CONTAAMT NUMBIDS;
TITLE "CONTRACTS AWARDED ON OR AFTER
&FMTDATE WITH A MINIMUM DOLLAR VALUE OF
&FMTAMT AND &MINBIDS OR MORE BIDDERS";
RUN;

%END;  * Close the option A %DO group.;
%END;  * Close/loop the %DO-%UNTIL group.;
%MEND MENU;  * Close macro MENU.;
%MENU  * Call macro MENU.;
```

More complex menu driven systems are possible and best designed using an autocall SAS macro library and SAS system option MAUTOSOURCE. For instance, Mod. 3 demonstrates how the MAUTOSOURCE option could streamline the above menu code by storing the example code as individual members (subroutines) entitled BROWSE and AWDPRIN in an autocall (MACLIB) library and referencing them as %BROWSE and %AWDPRIN when and if necessary:

Mod. 3: Using an Autocall Macro Library

```
%MACRO MENU;
%DO %UNTIL(&OPTION=  );

DATA TEMP;
  OPTION=' ';

PROC FSEDIT DATA=TEMP SCREEN=SCRN.MENU;

DATA TEMP; SET TEMP;
  CALL SYMPUT('OPTION',OPTION);  RUN;

/* Test user input and call the macro  */
/* chosen from the autocall library.   */
```

```
%IF &OPTION = B %THEN %BROWSE;
%ELSE %IF &OPTION = A %THEN %AWDPRIN;
%END; * CLOSE THE INITIAL DO-UNTIL GROUP;
%MEND MENU;
%MENU
```

Contact the SAS Software Consultant at your site if you are uncertain whether or not your site has an existing autocall macro library to which you may add SAS macros.

VI. CONCLUSION

Programmers at sites without SAS/AF or SAS/ASSIST applications development software may create single and multiple screen user interfaces using SAS/FSP data entry software in combination with the SAS macro language. Specifically, the technique establishes a temporary SAS data set of initial program variables, displays the initial values for user modification with SAS/FSP data entry software and retrieves user choices from the modified data set as macro variables used to customize the application.

The technique works best with single screen applications or small menu driven systems progressing no more than two to three screens beyond an opening menu. Specific limitations include:

1. A few seconds delay each time PROC FSEDIT displays an input screen;

2. A slight chance users may become confused by accidentally issuing a SAS/FSP software command to create an additional entry record, and;

3. A data entry screen format which requires users to Tab to the designated entry area and press PF3 when done.

However, for sites without SAS/AF or SAS/ASSIST applications development software, the technique is preferable to exposing actual program code for user modification and accesses many otherwise unavailable capabilities of the SAS Screen Control Language. NYSDOT has successfully expanded the basic concepts of this presentation to interface relatively complex single and multiple screen applications.

For Additional Information Contact:

Michael F. Perry
NYS Department of Transportation
Computer Services Bureau
1220 Washington Ave.
Albany, NY 12223
Telephone (518) 457-5575

* SAS, SAS/FSP, SAS/AF, SAS/ASSIST and SAS/GRAPH are registered trademarks of SAS Institute Inc., Cary, NC, USA.

** ISPF is a trademark of International Business Machines Corporation.

*** Please note that this presentation purposely limits all SAS/FSP screen examples to forty columns to match the forty column format of the SUGI-15 Proceedings. Actual SAS/FSP data entry screens are eighty columns wide and much neater than the manually retyped examples of this presentation.

Acknowledgements: Thanks to Carol Fryc and Ted Mulberry for proofreading, Bob Holland and Ken Harper for paper layout.

A MENU-DRIVEN TABLE GENERATOR

Joy Y. S. Jair, Kaohsiung Refinery, CPC
Rex C. T. Wu, Kaohsiung Refinery, CPC

Abstract

Instead of coding a SAS program each time when a demand is requested, a user firendly, menu-driven table generator is introduced. In the generator, users can define their tables by just selecting some conditions and interested items he needed in the menu. The desired tables are produced to a great degree of flexibility according to the variate selections. SAS/AF ® and SAS ® macro facilities incorporated with PROC TABULATE are fully utilized to meet the versatile requirements. A personnel system is used as an example and is under normal operation now. The results show great success.

Preface

SAS PROC TABULATE constructs table of descriptive statistics from class variables, analysis variables and keywords for statistics. It is not uncommon that the demands to produce different kinds of tables from the end users have become the major loads of an application programmer. Instead of coding program for each demand, a menu-driven table generator is needed for most of the cases. We can display the most frequently used items on the menu by using SAS/AF. After the user selects the desired conditions and classes, we will use SAS macros to convert them into a complete SAS program which will then generate the desired tables. In this way, we only have to write one program to meet variate kinds of demands. As a result, the end users not only get their wanted tables ahead of schedule, but the Information Systems Department personnel also be free from constant interruptions for adhoc demands . Thus the overall productivity is increased.

System Structure

The system structure of the table generator is shown below.

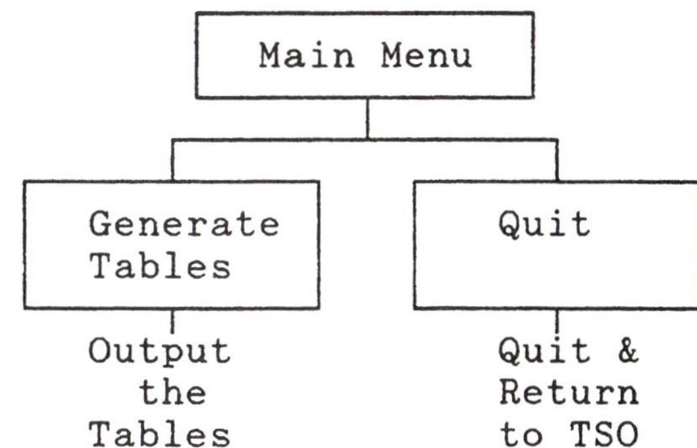

When the "Generate Tables" option is selected, the system will show the selection menu which will guide the user to select the conditions and interesting items he needed. After the completion of the selection, the required tables will be generated automatically . When the "Quit" option is selected, the system will quit and return to TSO.

System Description

An existing personnel system is selected as our example. Since our personnel system is in Chinese System and the SAS System also supports DBCS (Double Bytes Character Set)

, so we use Chinese to design the menu. Thus all the tables generated are in Chinese , too. In this article, we translated the menu into English for explanation purpose, but the sample output is in Chinese to show the originality.

In the menu, there are four selection items divided into five maps as can be seen from Fig. 1 to Fig. 5. The four items are Column Selection, Row Selection, Condition Selection and Output Selection. In the Column/Row Selection, the user can select Column/Row classes he wanted in the table.

Within the Column/Row Selection , the selection items are classified into several groups in vertical direction (e.g. Employee Status, Sex,..., etc.) which will be treated as cancatenation elements. Within each group, there are up to ten selectable items which will be treated as cross elements when selected. In order to handle the Column/Row Selection, there are four macros which will be described briefly as follows:

(1)%TABLE : will generate the TABLE statement of PROC TABULATE. The sequence of the cross elements of each group can be specified by user using the digits from 0 to 9. It also generates the CLASS variables and VAR variables.

(2)%INTERVAL : will calculate and genrate the class range of class variables for those numerical items which the user specifies the starting, ending and interval information (e.g. Age).

(3)%RANGE : will classify those non-numerical variables which are specified by High-Low limits to the appropriate classes (e.g. Salary Rate).

(4)%FORMAT : will generate PROC FORMAT which will show the range type class variables described above in Chinese specified by the user.

In the Condition Selection, one can make the single condition selection or a From-To type selection. Two macros have been designed :

(1)%CONM : will handle the single condition selection (e.g Department : L100).

(2)%CONNECT : will handle the From-To type selection (e.g. from Department L100 to L600) and connect to the other conditions.

In the Output Selection, one can select output to the desired printer or save as a file. Macro %PRINT will handle this.

After all the selections have been made, the user then press <PF3> to execute. The desired tables will be generated automatically.

Conclusion

The idea of designing a menu-driven table generator comes from the needs to solve the great demands from the end users. Through this system, many versatile forms of tables selected by users can be generated automatically. After the implementation of this system, the responses of the end users show great favorable. The benefits we expected are realized gradually. Not only the users feel easy and friendly,but also the number of requests dropped dramatically as much as 85%.

Major Macro Programs

There are six major macros in the following :
(1)%INTERVAL(BEGN,END,RANGE,VAR);
(2)%RANGE(START,STOP,LOW,UP,VAR);
(3)%FORMAT(START,STOP,LOW,UP,VAR,SPEC);
(4)%TABLE(BG,START,STOP,V0,V1,V2,V3,V4,V5,V6,V7,V8,V9,V10);
(5)%CONM(START,STOP,VAR,OP,PN,QT);
(6)%CONNECT(A,B,C,D,E,F,G,H);

```
%MACRO INTERVAL(BEGN,END,RANGE,VAR);
 %LET I=1;
 %IF &&&BEGN¬=0 & &&&END¬=0 & &&&RANGE¬= %THEN %DO;
  %LET INTL=%EVAL((&&&END-&&&BEGN)/&&&RANGE);
  %LET L=%EVAL(&&&BEGN+1); %LET U=%EVAL(&&&BEGN+&&&RANGE);
  %DO %WHILE(&I<=&INTL);
    %IF &I=1 %THEN PUT "IF &VAR<=&&&BEGN THEN &VAR.1='<=&&&BEGN ';";;
    PUT "ELSE IF &L<=&VAR<=&U THEN &VAR.1='&L-&U';";
    %LET L=%EVAL(&L+&&&RANGE); %LET U=%EVAL(&U+&&&RANGE);
    %LET I=%EVAL(&I+1);
  %END; %LET U=%EVAL(&U-&&&RANGE+1); PUT "ELSE &VAR.1='&U-99';";
 %END;
%MEND INTERVAL;

%MACRO RANGE(START,STOP,LOW,UP,VAR);
 %LET SW=Y; %LET I=&START;
 %DO %WHILE(&I<=&STOP);
   %IF &&&LOW&I¬= 0 & &&&UP&I¬=0 %THEN %DO;
    %IF &SW=Y %THEN %DO; %LET SW=N;
        PUT "IF &VAR<:'&&&LOW&I' THEN &VAR.1='<&&&LOW&I**';"; %END;
    PUT  "ELSE IF &VAR<=:'&&&UP&I' THEN &VAR.1='&&&LOW&I-&&&UP&I';";
    %IF &&&UP&I¬= %THEN %LET SS=&&&UP&I; %END; %LET I=%EVAL(&I+1);
 %END;
 %IF &SW¬=Y %THEN PUT "  ELSE &VAR.1='&SS>**';";;
%MEND RANGE;

%MACRO FORMAT(START,STOP,LOW,UP,VAR,SPEC);
  %LET SW=Y; %LET BL=%STR( ); %LET I=&START;
  %DO %WHILE(&I<=&STOP);
    %IF %LENGTH(&&&LOW&I)¬=0 & %LENGTH(&&&UP&I)¬=0 %THEN %DO;
      %IF &SW=Y %THEN %DO; %LET SW=N; PUT "PROC FORMAT;"
          PUT "  VALUE $&VAR" /"   '<&&&LOW&I****'='<=&&&LOW&I'";
      %END; PUT @1 "   '&&&LOW&I-&&&UP&I'=" @16
      "'&&&SPEC&I.1&BL&&&SPEC&I.2&BL&&&SPEC&I.3&BL&&&SPEC&I.4'";
    %END; %LET I=%EVAL(&I+1);
  %END;
  %IF &SW¬=Y %THEN %DO;
    %LET FORMAT=%STR( &VAR.1 $&VAR..);PUT "   OTHER='Other';"; %END;
%MEND FORMAT;

%MACRO TABLE(BG,START,STOP,V0,V1,V2,V3,V4,V5,V6,V7,V8,V9,V10);
 %LET J=1; %LET I=&STOP; %LET TABLE=; %LET RS=;
 %IF &&FIELD&BG¬= %THEN %DO;
   %DO %WHILE(&I>=&START);
    %LET K=&&FIELD&I;
    %IF &&FIELD&I¬= %THEN %DO;
```

```
      %IF %INDEX(&CLS,%STR(&&V&J))=0 %THEN %LET CLS=%STR(&&V&J )&CLS;
      %LET TAB&K=%STR(*%(&&V&J); %LET RS=%EVAL(&RS+13);
    %END; %LET I=%EVAL(&I-1); %LET J=%EVAL(&J+1);
   %END;
   %DO K=9 %TO 0 %BY -1;
     %IF &&TAB&K¬= %THEN %DO;
       %LET TABLE=%STR(&&TAB&K&TABLE&SUB%)); %LET TAB&K=; %END;
   %END;
   %LET RS=%EVAL(&RS+13); %LET TABLE=%STR((&V0&TABLE&TOT)&NN);
   %IF %INDEX(&CLS,%STR(&V0))=0 %THEN %LET CLS=%STR(&V0 )&CLS;
 %END;
%MEND TABLE;

%MACRO CONM(START,STOP,VAR,OP,PN,QT);
  %LET I=&START; %LET CONL=;
  %DO %WHILE(&I<=&STOP);
    %IF %LENGTH(&&&VAR&I) ¬= 0 %THEN %DO;
     %IF %LENGTH(&CONL)¬= 0 %THEN %LET CONL=&CONL&OP&PN&&&VAR&I&&QT;
     %ELSE %LET CONL=&PN&&&VAR&I&&QT;
    %END;  %LET I=%EVAL(&I+1);
  %END;
%MEND CONM;

%MACRO CONNECT(A,B,C,D,E,F,G,H);
  %IF %LENGTH(&&&A) ¬= 0 %THEN %DO;
    %IF %LENGTH(&&&B) ¬= 0 %THEN %DO;
     %LET &C=&F&G&H%STR(')&&&A%STR('<=)&D%STR(<=:')&&&B%STR(');
     %IF %LENGTH(&CONL) ¬= 0 %THEN %LET &C=&CONL&E&&&C;
    %END; %ELSE %LET &C=&CONL;
  %END; %ELSE %LET &C=&CONL;
%MEND CONNECT;
```

Illustrations and Sample Run

```
 1.Column Selection:  X Subtotal  X Total

   _ Employee : _ Work   _ Job   _ Rate   _ Sex     _ Age
     Status     _ Wkyear _ Educ  _ Exam   _ Native  _ Merit

   _ Sex      : _ Work   _ Job   _ Rate   _ Status  _ Age
                _ Wkyear _ Educ  _ Exam   _ Native  _ Merit

   _ Native   : _ Work   _ Job   _ Rate   _ Status  _ Age
                _ Wkyear _ Educ  _ Exam   _ Sex     _ Merit

   _ Education: _ Work   _ Job   _ Rate   _ Status  _ Age
                _ Wkyear _ Sex   _ Exam   _ Native  _ Merit

   X Age      : From 20 to 50, Interval: 10.  _ Average Age
                _ Work   _ Job   _ Rate   _ Status  1 Sex
                _ Wkyear _ Educ  _ Exam   _ Native  _ Merit
```

Fig. 1 Table Generator —— Map 1

```
_ Work Year: From ___ to ___, Interval: ___.   _ Average Wkyr
             _ Work    _ Job     _ Rate    _ Status _ Age
             _ Sex     _ Educ    _ Exam    _ Native _ Merit

_ Salary   : _ Work    _ Job     _ Sex     _ Status _ Age
  Rate       _ Wkyear  _ Educ    _ Exam    _ Native _ Merit
             -Low-     High    ----Chinese Specification----
              ___      ___     _____ _____ _____ _____ _____
              ___      ___     _____ _____ _____ _____ _____
              ___      ___     _____ _____ _____ _____ _____
              ___      ___     _____ _____ _____ _____ _____

_ Exami-   : _ Work    _ Job     _ Rate    _ Status _ Age
  nation     _ Wkyear  _ Educ    _ Sex     _ Native _ Merit
              ___      ___     _____ _____ _____ _____ _____
              ___      ___     _____ _____ _____ _____ _____
              ___      ___     _____ _____ _____ _____ _____
              ___      ___     _____ _____ _____ _____ _____

_ Job Code : _ Work    _ Sex     _ Rate    _ Status _ Age
             _ Wkyear  _ Educ    _ Exam    _ Native _ Merit
              ___      ___     _____ _____ _____ _____ _____
              ___      ___     _____ _____ _____ _____ _____
              ___      ___     _____ _____ _____ _____ _____
              ___      ___     _____ _____ _____ _____ _____
```

Fig. 2 Table Generator —— Map 2

```
_ Work     : _ Job     _ Rate    _ Status _ Sex     _ Age
  Class      _ Wkyear  _ Educ    _ Exam   _ Native  _ Merit

_ Merit    : _ Merit Code  _ Times

2.Row Selection   :  _ Subtotal  X Total

X Employee : _ Work    _ Job     _ Rate    _ Sex     _ Age
  Status     _ Wkyear  _ Educ    _ Exam    _ Native  _ Merit

_ Sex      : _ Work    _ Job     _ Rate    _ Status _ Age
             _ Wkyear  _ Educ    _ Exam    _ Native _ Merit

_ Native   : _ Work    _ Job     _ Rate    _ Status _ Age
             _ Wkyear  _ Educ    _ Exam    _ Sex    _ Merit

_ Education: _ Work    _ Job     _ Rate    _ Status _ Age
             _ Wkyear  _ Sex     _ Exam    _ Native _ Merit

_ Age      : _ Work    _ Job     _ Rate    _ Status _ Sex
             _ Wkyear  _ Educ    _ Exam    _ Native _ Merit

_ Work Year: _ Work    _ Job     _ Rate    _ Status _ Age
             _ Sex     _ Educ    _ Exam    _ Native _ Merit
```

Fig. 3 Table Generator —— Map 3

```
 _ Salary     : _ Work    _ Job     _ Sex     _ Status _ Age
   Rate         _ Wkyear  _ Educ    _ Exam    _ Native _ Merit

 _ Exami-     : _ Work    _ Job     _ Rate    _ Status _ Age
   nation       _ Wkyear  _ Educ    _ Sex     _ Native _ Merit

 _ Job Code   : _ Work    _ Sex     _ Rate    _ Status _ Age
                _ Wkyear  _ Educ    _ Exam    _ Native _ Merit

 _ Work       : _ Job     _ Rate    _ Status _ Sex     _ Age
   Class        _ Wkyear  _ Educ    _ Exam    _ Native _ Merit

 _ Merit      : _ Merit Code  _ Times

3.Condition Selection :

  a.Depart-   : ____ ____ ____ ____ ____ ____ ____ ____
    ment        Form A000 To R900,  From 1A00 To 9R00
                Form ____ To ____,  From ____ To ____

  b.Employee  : _ Staff        _ (E) Worker    _ (C) Worker
    Status      _ Temp-Staff   _ Other

  c.Course    : ___ ___ ___ ___ ___ ___ ___ ___ ___ ___
```

Fig. 4 Table Generator —— Map 4

```
  d.Chief     : From ___ To ___,  From ___ To ___
    Rank        From ___ To ___,  _ Non-Chief Rank

  e.Start-    : From (YYMMDD) 500101 To (YYMMDD) 801231
    Date        From (YYMMDD) ______ To (YYMMDD) ______

  f.Transfer-: From (YYMMDD) ______ To (YYMMDD) ______
    Date        From (YYMMDD) ______ To (YYMMDD) ______

  g.Service-  : From (YYMMDD) ______ To (YYMMDD) ______
    Date        From (YYMMDD) ______ To (YYMMDD) ______

 4.Output Selection :
  a.Printer :
    _ 3820 B4 Form     _ 3820 A4 Form(V)   X 3820 A4 Form(H)
    _ 3835 B4 Form     _ 3835 A4 Form(V)   _ 3835 A4 Form(H)
    _ 3835 B4 (W:200, H:62)

  b.File     : (Data Set Name : PA.PXXX.SASOUT.SAM)
    _ B4 ( W:160, H:60)    _ A4 (88,62)     _ A4 (128,48)

 5.Title    : ______________________________________________
 6.Footnote: ______________________________________________

          After Selection press <PF3> to submit
```

Fig. 5 Table Generator —— Map 5

(Kao-hsiung Refinery ---- Statistics of Employee's Age)
高雄煉油總廠 ---- 工作人員年齡統計表

	年齡 (Age)														Total 合計
	<=20		21-30			31-40			41-50			51-99			
	性別 (Sex)	Sub-total 小計	性別 (Sex)		Sub-total 小計	性別 (Sex)		Sub-total 小計	性別 (Sex)		Sub-total 小計	性別 (Sex)		Sub-total 小計	
員別 Employee Status	男 (M)		男 (M)	女 (F)		男 (M)	女 (F)		男 (M)	女 (F)		男 (M)	女 (F)		
派用人員 Staff			132	56	188	532	44	576	408	15	423	277	2	279	1,466
評價僱用 (E) Worker	4	4	830	11	841	2,353	25	2,378	1,075	13	1,088	704	34	738	5,049
聘用人員 Temp-Staff			1	10	11	4	12	16	17	44	61	48	19	67	155
分類僱用 (C) Worker			20	28	48	161	155	316	107	66	173	60	48	108	645
合計 (Total)	4	4	983	105	1,088	3,050	236	3,286	1,607	138	1,745	1,089	103	1,192	7,315

Note: The handwriting English Part is translated from Chinese for reading purpose.

System design: Information Systems Department　　Data from: Personnel Department
系統設計：資訊室　　使用軟體：ＳＡＳ／ＡＦ　　資料提供：人事室

Chapter 6 Writing Macro Utility Programs

MACPAGE - A SAS Macro for Enhancing Reports 240

Intermediate

Tasks	Uses the macro facility as a front end to a report post-processing application.
Tools	%EVAL %GLOBAL %IF-%THEN %DO %LET %QUOTE %QUPCASE %STR %SUBSTR Complex substitution Macro parameters Simple substitution

Macro-based Report Generator 244

Advanced

Tasks	Uses the macro facility as a modularized, generic report generator.
Tools	%DO, Iterative %EVAL %INDEX %LENGTH %LET %PUT %SCAN %STR && and &&& resolution CALL SYMPUT Complex substitution Simple substitution

A SAS Macro Procedure to Summarize the Output of Logistic Regression Models 250

Advanced

Tasks	Defines and interprets dynamic parameter lists. Creates a list of variable names with a given prefix and a numeric suffix.
Tools	%DO, Iterative Macro quoting PARMBUFF

A Macro to Separate Records Into Output Datasets By Date And Create Dataset Names With Date As A Part

Michael J. Schilling, Burlington Northern Railroad

ABSTRACT

Provides a Macro to solve the dilemma of how to find data in SAS* GDG's like history files. With file names like XXXXXX01-XXXXXX99, how do users find records with dates in the range of January 1 - January 30, 1988?

In the Capacity Management Group, we work with the output records generated by computer software monitors. The monitors are continuously producing records that contain date and time stamps. Each day we run extract programs that gather up the monitor records that have been accumulated and create a series of SAS datasets that have a name in the format XXXXXX99, where XXXXXX is some unique name and 99 is a numeric value that represents one generation of the dataset name. Each day history maintenance routines roll the generation numbers such that 01 represents the most current generation, 02 the next oldest, etc.. This is common practice and from a maintenance standpoint, works wonderfully well.

This is where the issue addressed by the subject Macro arrives on the scene. Let's look at this situation from a "User's" perspective. I would like you to meet our user, Tip E. Call. Tip would like to access some of the records in our database for the period January 15-January 30, 1988. Tip, being an astute as well as atypical user, actually knows the SAS dataset name of the files where the data he wishes is stored. Tip executes a **PROC CONTENTS** and discovers the following datasets are contained in the SAS library:

TIP_01
TIP_02
:
TIP_99

How would Tip find the records of interest? There are many ways Tip could choose for the solution, none of which is of the slightest interest to the subject at hand. Suffice it to say, none is straightforward. The proposed solution creates a SAS dataset that contains only the records for a specific period of time and that the SAS dataset name identify the period. For example, instead of creating the dataset with the name of TIP_01 let's append the records into a dataset with the name such as TIPJAN88. Now, if the input data contains records for more than one period, say January as well as February (as will happen at the end of a period as well as at the beginning of a period), let's append the January records to TIPJAN88 and the February records to TIPFEB88.

Now, let's revisit Tip and his request. Any question where the records are in which Tip is interested?

TIPJAN88
TIPFEB88

The following SAS Macro will provide a solution for this problem. Remember, the object of this exercise is to create an output SAS dataset(s) with the date(s) of the input data.

The following explanation applies to the Macro "**FILENAME**". The code for the macro definition is attached.

On the **%MACRO** statement the input macro variables are defined.

DATE_FMT	=	Date format to be used as part of the output dataset name, i.e., .MONYY5. yields JAN88
IN_DD	=	The input SAS datasets ddname.
IN_FILE	=	The input SAS filename.
OUT_DD	=	Prefix to be appended to the date to create the output SAS dataset name.
BY_LIST	=	The variables in the output SAS dataset that will be used in the PROC SORT to eliminate duplicate records.

The SAS procedure **PROC FREQ** solves the problem of getting unique dates. **DATE** is a SAS variable in the input dataset. The variable **DATE** must be a SAS date value. The **PROC FREQ** has been set up to create an output SAS dataset and no print. The output dataset will contain one record for each unique date value. The FORMAT statement insures the unique date value.

The **DATA** routine will read the dataset created by the **PROC FREQ** and create a non SAS output dataset **(SASCMDS)** that contains the SAS statements to create the output SAS datasets. The **PUT** statements are creating the SAS commands that will be input and executed by the **%INCLUDE.** We use this method because we cannot resolve the value of DATE or the number of unique datasets to be accessed until after the data in the source file has been examined.

There are three **DO** loops in this routine each reading the SAS dataset created by the **PROC FREQ**. The first **DO** loop creates a unique output SAS dataset name for each value of date. The second loop creates the unique **IF** and **OUTPUT** statements to create the output SAS datasets. Each **IF** statement must refer to a unique combination of YEAR and MONTH needed to create the proper output SAS dataset. The third **DO** loop creates a **PROC APPEND** and **PROC SORT** for each output SAS dataset. the **PROC APPEND** was chosen because we didn't want to concern ourselves with whether the output SAS dataset exists or not. With **PROC APPEND**, if the dataset does exist, the data is appended to it and if the dataset does not exist, it will be created new.

The **PROC SORT** is an optional feature. We included it to prevent duplicate data from being appended to the output SAS dataset. It is also the only reason for the **"BYLIST"** macro variable. If you choose to drop the sort code from the macro, be sure to also take the **"BYLIST"** variable off the **%MACRO** statement variable list.

The **%INCLUDE SASCMDS** statement brings the records created in the **DATA** routine execution as if they were part of the original stream of SAS code.

Let's see this macro in action. On the page headed "**MACRO EXECUTION EXAMPLE**" is a simple example of the macro. The **OPTION** statement will cause the expanded macro statements and the resolved macro variables to appear on the **SAS** log. The **DATA** routine creates a **SAS** dataset with record with dates that span three months. The **%FILENAME...**is the macro with all input parameters included. The **PROC FREQ's** are included to show the results of the macro execution. The **PROC FREQ** listing follows the execution for the input and each output **SAS** dataset. Next, we will take a look at the **SAS** log. Beginning with line 290 through line 305 we see the **PROC FREQ** statements. The **SAS** note following line 305 explains that 3 records were included in the output **SAS** dataset. Each record in the output corresponds to a unique date. The date format included on the **&DATE FMT** macro variable was **MONY5**. The unique date then is month and year. Lines 308 through 386 is the **DATA** routine that creates the **SAS** code that will create the **SAS** datasets with date in their name. Following line 386 the message, **"NOTE: 36 LINES WERE WRITTEN TO FILE SASCMDS"** is the point where **SAS** notified us that the records were written to the non-**SAS** file **SASCMDS**. The statements following the **%INCLUDE SASCMDS** statement at line 389 show the commands that are executed.

Author:

Michael J. Schilling
Information Systems Services
Burlington Northern Railroad Company
176 East Fifth Street
St. Paul, MN 55101

(612) 298-2633

*Trademarks:

SAS is a registered trademark of SAS Institute, Inc., Cary, NC, USA.

******* MACRO DEFINITION *******

```
%MACRO FILENAME(DATE_FMT,IN_DD,
   IN_FILE,OUT_DD,PREFIX,BYLIST);


PROC FREQ DATA = &IN_DD..&IN_FILE;
  TABLE DATE / OUT = D
     NOROW NOPERCENT NOCOL NOCUM
     NOPRINT NOFREQ;
  FORMAT DATE &DATE_FMT.;
RUN;

DATA _NULL_;
  FORMAT DATE &DATE_FMT;
  FILE SASCMDS;
  PUT @1 'DATA';

  DO UNTIL(EOF_D1);
   SET D END = EOF_D1;
   PUT @1 "&OUT_DD..&PREFIX."
     DATE;
  END;

  PUT @1 ';';
  PUT @1 'SET' + 1 "&IN_DD..&IN_FILE"
    ';' ;
   PUT @1 'MONTH = MONTH(DATE);';
   PUT @1 'YEAR = YEAR(DATE);';

  DO UNTIL(EOF_D2);
   SET D END = EOF_D2;
   YEAR = YEAR(DATE);
   MONTH = MONTH(DATE);
   PUT @1 'IF YEAR = ' YEAR ' AND
     MONTH = ' MONTH;
   PUT @1 ' THEN OUTPUT '
     "&OUT_DD..&PREFIX" DATE
     ';' ;
  END;
  PUT 'RUN;' ;

  DO UNTIL(EOF_D3);
   SET D END = EOF_D3;
   PUT @1 'PROC APPEND BASE = '
     "&IN_DD..&PREFIX." DATE;
   PUT @1 ' DATA = '
     "&OUT_DD..&PREFIX."
     DATE ';' ;
   PUT @1 'RUN;';
   PUT @1 'PROC SORT DATA = '
     "&IN_DD..&PREFIX." DATE
     ' NODUP;' ;
   PUT @1 'BY ' "&BYLIST" ';' ;
   PUT @1 'RUN;' ;
  END;

  STOP;
RUN;

%INCLUDE SASCMDS;

%MEND FILENAME;
```

***** MACRO EXECUTION EXAMPLE *****

```
OPTION SOURCE SOURCE2 MACROGEN
    SYMBOLGEN;

X ALLOC FI(SASCMDS) DA(SASCMDS) NEW
    DELETE SP(1,1) CYL;
X ALLOC FI(HISTORY)
    DA('TSU509.MXG.HISTORY');

OPTION OBS = 501;

DATA WORK.RECS_IN;
 SET HISTORY.C_JAN89;
 OUTPUT;
 DATE = DATE + 30;
 OUTPUT;
 DATE = DATE + 30;
 OUTPUT;
 RETURN;
RUN;

%FILENAME(MONYY5.,WORK,RECS_IN,
  WORK,X_,SYSTEM DATETIME PERFGRP);

PROC FREQ DATA = WORK.RECS_IN;
  TABLE DATE /
  NOROW NOCOL NOCUM NOPERCENT;

 DATE    FREQUENCY  PERCENT
------------------------------
02JAN89      20    4.0
03JAN89     147   29.3
01FEB89      20    4.0
02FEB89     147   29.3
03MAR89      20    4.0
04MAR89     147   29.3

PROC FREQ DATA = WORK.X_JAN89;
  TABLE DATE /
  NOROW NOCOL NOCUM NOPERCENT;

 DATE    FREQUENCY  PERCENT
------------------------------
02JAN89      20   12.0
03JAN89     147   88.0

PROC FREQ DATA = WORK.X_FEB89;
  TABLE DATE /
  NOROW NOCOL NOCUM NOPERCENT;

 DATE    FREQUENCY  PERCENT
------------------------------
01FEB89      20   12.0
02FEB89     147   88.0

PROC FREQ DATA = WORK.X_MAR89;
  TABLE DATE /
  NOROW NOCOL NOCUM NOPERCENT;

 DATE    FREQUENCY  PERCENT
------------------------------
03MAR89      20   12.0
04MAR89     147   88.0

RUN;

X FREE FI(SASCMDS);
X FREE FI(HISTORY);
```

***** SAS LOG *****

```
%MACRO FILENAME(DATE_FMT,IN_DD,
   IN_FILE,OUT_DD,PREFIX,BYLIST);


PROC FREQ DATA = &IN_DD..&IN_FILE;
  TABLE DATE / OUT = D
     NOROW NOPERCENT NOCOL NOCUM
     NOPRINT NOFREQ;
  FORMAT DATE &DATE_FMT.;
RUN;

DATA _NULL_;
  FORMAT DATE &DATE_FMT;
  FILE SASCMDS;
  PUT @1 'DATA';

  DO UNTIL(EOF_D1);
   SET D END = EOF_D1;
   PUT @1 "&OUT_DD..&PREFIX."
      DATE;
  END;

  PUT @1 ';';
  PUT @1 'SET' + 1 "&IN_DD..&IN_FILE"
   ';' ;
   PUT @1 'MONTH = MONTH(DATE);';
   PUT @1 'YEAR = YEAR(DATE);';

  DO UNTIL(EOF_D2);
   SET D END = EOF_D2;
   YEAR = YEAR(DATE);
   MONTH = MONTH(DATE);
   PUT @1 'IF YEAR = ' YEAR ' AND
      MONTH = ' MONTH;
   PUT @1 ' THEN OUTPUT '
      "&OUT_DD..&PREFIX" DATE
      ';' ;
  END;

  PUT 'RUN;' ;

  DO UNTIL(EOF_D3);
   SET D END = EOF_D3;
   PUT @1 'PROC APPEND BASE = '
      "&IN_DD..&PREFIX." DATE;
   PUT @1 ' DATA = '
      "&OUT_DD..&PREFIX."
      DATE ';';
   PUT @1 'RUN;';
   PUT @1 'PROC SORT DATA = '
      "&IN_DD..&PREFIX." DATE
      ' NODUP;' ;
   PUT @1 'BY ' "&BYLIST" ';' ;
   PUT @1 'RUN;' ;
  END;

  STOP;
RUN;

%INCLUDE SASCMDS;

%MEND FILENAME;

OPTION SOURCE SOURCE2 MACROGEN
    SYMBOLGEN;

X ALLOC FI(SASCMDS) DA(SASCMDS) NEW
    DELETE SP(1,1) CYL;
X ALLOC FI(HISTORY)
```

```
277     DA('TSU509.MXG.HISTORY');
278
279 OPTION OBS = 501;
280
281 DATA WORK.RECS_IN;
282   SET HISTORY.C_JAN89;
283   OUTPUT;
284   DATE = DATE + 30;
285   OUTPUT;
286   DATE = DATE + 30;
287   OUTPUT;
288   RETURN;
289 RUN;

NOTE:    DATA SET WORK.RECS_IN HAS 1503
         OBSERVATIONS AND 18 VARIABLES.
            316 OBS/TRK.

290
291 %FILENAME(MONYY5.,WORK,RECS_IN,
292   WORK,X_,SYSTEM DATETIME PERFGRP)
295 + PROC FREQ DATA = &IN_DD..&IN_FILE                      1-%filename
296 + WORK.RECS_IN                                           2-&SYMBOL
295 +                  ;                                     1-%filename
298 + TABLE DATE / OUT = D                                   1-%filename
299 +     NOROW NOPERCENT NOCOL NOCUM                        1-%filename
300 +     NOPRINT NOFREQ;                                    1-%filename
302 + FORMAT DATE &DATE_FMT.                                 1-%filename
303 + MONYY5.                                                2-&SYMBOL
302 +             ;                                          1-%filename
305 + RUN;                                                   1-%filename

NOTE:    THE DATA SET WORK.D HAS 3 OBSERVATIONS
         AND 3 VARIABLES.
            1676 OBS/TRK
308 + DATA _NULL_;                                           1-%filename
310 + FORMAT DATE &DATE_FMT                                  1-%filename
311 + MONYY5                                                 2-&SYMBOL
310 +             ;                                          1-%filename
313 + FILE SASCMDS;                                          1-%filename
313 + FILE SASCMDS;                                          1-%filename
315 + PUT @1 'DATA';                                         1-%filename
318 + DO UNTIL(EOF_D1);                                      1-%filename
320 + SET D END = EOF_D1;                                    1-%filename
322 + PUT @1 "&OUT_DD..&PREFIX."                             1-%filename
323 +    DATE;                                               1-%filename
325 + END;                                                   1-%filename
328 + PUT @1 ';';                                            1-%filename
330 + PUT @1 'SET' + 1 "&IN_DD..&IN_FILE"                    1-%filename
331 +    ';' ;                                               1-%filename
333 + PUT @1 'MONTH = MONTH(DATE);';                         1-%filename
335 + PUT @1 'YEAR = YEAR(DATE);';                           1-%filename
338 + DO UNTIL(EOF_D2);                                      1-%filename
340 + SET D END = EOF_D2;                                    1-%filename
342 + YEAR = YEAR(DATE);                                     1-%filename
344 + MONTH = MONTH(DATE);                                   1-%filename
346 + PUT @1 'IF YEAR = ' YEAR ' AND                         1-%filename
347 +    MONTH = ' MONTH;                                    1-%filename
349 + PUT @1 ' THEN OUTPUT '                                 1-%filename
350 +    "&OUT_DD..&PREFIX" DATE                             1-%filename
351 +    ';' ;                                               1-%filename
353 + END;                                                   1-%filename
356 + PUT 'RUN;' ;                                           1-%filename
359 + DO UNTIL(EOF_D3);                                      1-%filename
361 + SET D END = EOF_D3;                                    1-%filename
363 + PUT @1 'PROC APPEND BASE = '                           1-%filename
365 + "&IN_DD..&PREFIX." DATE;                               1-%filename
367 + PUT @1 ' DATA = '                                      1-%filename
368 +    "&OUT_DD..&PREFIX."                                 1-%filename
369 +    DATE ';' ;                                          1-%filename
```

```
371 + PUT @1 'RUN;';                                         1-%filename
373 + PUT @1 'PROC SORT DATA = '                             1-%filename
374 +     "&IN_DD..&PREFIX." DATE                            1-%filename
375 +     ' NODUP;' ;                                        1-%filename
377 + PUT @1 'BY ' "&BYLIST" ';' ;                           1-%filename
379 + PUT @1 'RUN;' ;                                        1-%filename
381 + END;                                                   1-%filename
384 + STOP;                                                  1-%filename
386 + RUN;                                                   1-%filename

NOTE:   FILE SASCMDS IS:
        DSNAME = TSU509.SASCMDS,
   UNIT = SYSALLDA,VOL = SER = WKB444,DISP = NEW,
   DCB = (BLKSIZE = 6400,LRECL = 80,RECFM = FB)

NOTE:   36 LINES WERE WRITTEN TO FILE SASCMDS.

389 + %INCLUDE SASCMDS;                                      1-%filename
390 + DATA                                                   2-//SASCMDS
391 + WORK.X_JAN89                                           2-//SASCMDS
392 + WORK.X_FEB89                                           2-//SASCMDS
393 + WORK.X_MAR89                                           2-//SASCMDS
394 + ;                                                      2-//SASCMDS
395 + SET WORK.RECS_IN;                                      2-//SASCMDS
396 + MONTH = MONTH(DATE);                                   2-//SASCMDS
397 + YEAR = YEAR(DATE);                                     2-//SASCMDS
398 + IF YEAR = 1989                                         2-//SASCMDS
399 +  AND               MONTH = 1                           2-//SASCMDS
400 +  THEN OUTPUT WORK.X_JAN89 ;                            2-//SASCMDS
401 + IF YEAR = 1989                                         2-//SASCMDS
402 +  AND               MONTH = 2                           2-//SASCMDS
403 +  THEN OUTPUT WORK.X_FEB89 ;                            2-//SASCMDS
404 + IF YEAR = 1989                                         2-//SASCMDS
405 +  AND               MONTH = 3                           2-//SASCMDS
406 +  THEN OUTPUT WORK.X_MAR89 ;                            2-//SASCMDS
407 + RUN;                                                   2-//SASCMDS

NOTE:   DATA SET WORK.X_JAN89 HAS 167
        OBSERVATIONS AND 18 VARIABLES.
           316 OBS/TRK.

NOTE:   DATA SET WORK.X_FEB89 HAS 167
        OBSERVATIONS AND 18 VARIABLES.
           316 OBS/TRK.

NOTE:   DATA SET WORK.X_MAR89 HAS 167
        OBSERVATIONS AND 18 VARIABLES.
           316 OBS/TRK.

408 + PROC APPEND BASE = WORK.X_JAN89                        2-//SASCMDS
409 +  DATA = WORK.X_JAN89 ;                                 2-//SASCMDS
410 + RUN;                                                   2-//SASCMDS

NOTE:   WORK.X_JAN89 HAS 167 OBSERVATION(S)
        BEFORE APPENDING.

NOTE:   167 OBSERVATION(S) ADDED.

411 + PROC SORT DATA = WORK.X_JAN89  NODUP;                  2-//SASCMDS
412 + BY SYSTEM DATETIME PERFGRP;                            2-//SASCMDS
413 + RUN;                                                   2-//SASCMDS

NOTE:   1 CYLINDER DYNAMICALLY ALLOCATED ON
        WORK FOR EACH OF 3 SORT WORK DATA SETS.

NOTE:   DATA SET WORK.X_JAN89 HAS 167
        OBSERVATIONS AND 18 VARIABLES.
        316 OBS/TRK.
```

```
NOTE:    167 DUPLICATE OBSERVATIONS WERE
         DELETED.

414 + PROC APPEND BASE = WORK.X_FEB89                  2-//SASCMDS
415 +  DATA = WORK.X_FEB89 ;                            2-//SASCMDS
416 + RUN;                                              2-//SASCMDS

NOTE:    WORK.X_FEB89 HAS 167 OBSERVATION(S)
         BEFORE APPENDING.

NOTE:    167 OBSERVATION(S) ADDED.

417 + PROC SORT DATA = WORK.X_FEB89  NODUP;            2-//SASCMDS
418 + BY SYSTEM DATETIME PERFGRP;                       2-//SASCMDS
419 + RUN;                                              2-//SASCMDS

NOTE:    DATA SET WORK.X_FEB89 HAS 167
         OBSERVATIONS AND 18 VARIABLES.
             316 OBS/TRK.

NOTE:    167 DUPLICATE OBSERVATIONS WERE
         DELETED.

420 + PROC APPEND BASE = WORK.X_MAR89                  2-//SASCMDS
421 +  DATA = WORK.X_MAR89 ;                            2-//SASCMDS
422 + RUN;                                              2-//SASCMDS

NOTE:    WORK.X_MAR89 HAS 167 OBSERVATION(S)
         BEFORE APPENDING.

NOTE:    167 OBSERVATION(S) ADDED.

423 + PROC SORT DATA = WORK.X_MAR89  NODUP;            2-//SASCMDS
424 + BY SYSTEM DATETIME PERFGRP;                       2-//SASCMDS
425 + RUN;                                              2-//SASCMDS

NOTE:    DATA SET WORK.X_MAR89 HAS 167
         OBSERVATIONS AND 18 VARIABLES.
             316 OBS/TRK.

NOTE:    167 DUPLICATE OBSERVATIONS WERE
         DELETED.

292                    ;
427
428 OPTION PS = 37 TPS = 37;
429 PROC FREQ DATA = WORK.RECS_IN;
430    TABLE DATE /
431    NOROW NOCOL NOCUM NOPERCENT;
432

433 PROC FREQ DATA = WORK.X_JAN89;
434    TABLE DATE /
435    NOROW NOCOL NOCUM NOPERCENT;
436

437 PROC FREQ DATA = WORK.X_FEB89;
438    TABLE DATE /
439    NOROW NOCOL NOCUM NOPERCENT;
440

441 PROC FREQ DATA = WORK.X_MAR89;
442    TABLE DATE /
443    NOROW NOCOL NOCUM NOPERCENT;
444
445 RUN;
446
447 X FREE FI(SASCMDS);
448 X FREE FI(HISTORY);
449
```

A Macro to Make External Flat Files

H. Ian Whitlock, Westat Inc.

Abstract

A SAS® macro to construct external flat files from SAS data sets is considered from the view point of the user interface.

The central issue is - How do you give the user as much control as he wants without requiring more work than it takes to write out the whole program?

The universality of the problem and the simplicity of the "PUT" statement DATA step program make it a classic macro problem. The topic is presented as an example for teaching how to develop a SAS macro. A plan is laid out, the parameter interface as a system of defaults is discussed, and then the macro code is presented. With the exception of using arrays of macro variables and some optional %UNQUOTEs, only basic macro techniques are used in the code.

Introduction

Many SAS users have to make external flat files from SAS data sets when delivering data to non-SAS clients. In each case, the "PUT" statement DATA step to do this is very simple, but writing the program and file documentation can be both tedious and boring, when many variables are involved. Remember statements like,

```
PUT
    @1      LNAME       $CHAR20.
    @21     FNAME       $CHAR15.
    @36     BIRTHDAT    MMDDYY8.
    .........
    @832    QUEST_1     2.
    .........
```

that seem to go on endlessly? A general solution to the production of external files corresponding to SAS data sets is presented in the form of a SAS macro, FLATFILE. Now the DATA step indicated can be replaced by a macro invocation. For example:

```
%FLATFILE ( DATA = MYDATA, OUT = 'FLATFILE.DAT' )
```

Basic Questions

We begin the task of design by asking the basic questions, "What does the macro need to know?", and "How should the macro know it?". These questions break down into the simpler questions:

- What data SAS set?
- What variables?
- In what order?
- How are they to be formatted?
- What descriptive names for documentation?
- Where does the external file go?

The Basic User Interface - Parameters

The first and last questions are simple. The answers can only be known by the user, hence the answers must be given as parameters to the macro. I chose the parameters:

```
DATA = _LAST_
OUT = null-value
```

Both the parameter name, DATA, and the default value, _LAST_, are chosen to be consistent with procedure parameters for easy use.

OUT gives a FILEREF; thus the user is responsible for making the FILENAME statement and seeing that it does not conflict with other FILEREFs in his program. (The macro invocation in the introduction uses a physical name. Since SAS will accept a physical name in quotes in place of a FILEREF, the choice is up to you.) The default, null-value, is used to say do not make an external file. It will become clear later why you do not always want the macro to produce an external file.

If the requirements for the external file are sufficiently flexible, all of the remaining questions *might* be answered by looking at the data set output by the CONTENTS procedure for the given SAS data set.

This data set can give a complete list of the variables, but what about order? For simplicity, I assume there is something good about alpha-numeric order (eg. x before y2 before y10) and nothing particularly bad about it. In this case the output data set of PROC CONTENTS is adequate.

This data set can also supply labels for documenting variables with descriptive names. This assumes that variables have already been assigned labels, but the user who does not use labels probably does not want complete documentation for this data set. In any case labels can be supplied with the DATASETS procedure before applying the macro.

The question of formatting variables is more complex. PROC CONTENTS can give format information, but it is likely to be missing or inappropriate. Hence we might reject the direct format information from PROC CONTENTS. Yet formats can be so handy and variable specific that I did not want to rule out their use entirely. I added the parameter switch, USEFMTS, with the default value, NO. Now if the formats associated with the data set are appropriate whenever they exist, they can be used to override the system described below by simply calling the macro with USEFMTS=YES.

PROC CONTENTS also provides the SAS storage size of variables. For character variables this should be their length in a flat file, but what about numeric variables? Each length has an associated inherent number of significant digits. For example, on a VAX or IBM mainframe, no more than 5 significant digits can be stored in 3 bytes. Hence BEST7. (allowing for a decimal point and a minus sign), is a good format for preserving information stored in length 3 numeric variables. Instead, I chose BEST5., as a better default format because proper decimal data should not be assigned to length 3 variables and in my firm, negative numbers requiring the extreme number of digits are rare. (In any case, the choices are only default parameter values which can be easily changed.) I assumed only length 8 variables might be proper decimals; then for each length I chose the shortest BEST format which would guarantee no loss of significant digits for positive numbers.

These formats are in keeping with the general SAS philosophy: don't allow a default to lose data; but they may strike you as ridiculously wide. For example, BEST19., is the corresponding format for 8 byte numeric variables. The solution is to let the user decide. Parameters L2, L3, ... L8 have the default widths given above with no loss of significant digits for positive integers. But they can be shortened in the macro call whenever appropriate. For example, if you know that only two digit numbers are stored in numeric variables of length 3, then you can override the default, L3=5, using L3=2. In practice, SAS data sets contain only one or two numeric lengths less than 8, and then only for special purposes. Thus this system of length parameters is simple and adequate in many cases.

Note that the default values above were chosen for the VAX and IBM mainframes. For PC's the values can be slightly smaller but the ones chosen will work. (SAS does not allow 2 byte numerics on the PC, but this simply means the value of L2 will be irrelevant when the macro is used on a PC.)

Here a macro call might look like

```
%FLATFILE ( DATA=MYDATA, OUT=OUT, L2=1, L8=5 )
```

Adding More Control To The User Interface

Using only the ideas presented above, we could write a macro that would be applicable to many problems for the user with flexibility in his external file specifications. But, of course, a user written "PUT" program could be much better. The question is - how can we let the user give better control than can be provided by PROC CONTENTS without requiring an effort comparable to writing the "PUT" program.

There are two ways to proceed. First, simply give the user the "PUT" statement program that can be written as specified above. He is then left to modify and run it. (In this case the modified program must serve to document what was done.) Second, allow the macro to work with a control file which specifies the order of variables, their formats, and their labels. Any SAS data set can serve as a control file as long as it has the required variables:

```
NAME      $ 8,
OUTFMT    $ 15, and
LABEL     $ 40.
```

The order of variables for the flat file is indicated by the observation order of the control data set. Building this file may look like as much work as writing "PUT" statement program, but the macro already generates a control file, __CNTL, with all the NAME and LABEL values, and many of the OUTFMT values as desired. Now the strategy for detailed control is:

- execute macro FLATFILE to make __CNTL,
- modify __CNTL, and
- execute macro FLATFILE to make the external data set.

__CNTL also has the variables OUTPOS and OUTLEN giving the field position and length on the external file. In addition, when created from the output of PROC CONTENTS, it has NPOS and APOS giving the order of variables stored on the SAS data set and the alpha-numeric order of the variables.

Usually only minor changes to __CNTL are required. For example, suppose you want the variables to appear in the order that they are stored on the SAS data set, with the format for several 8 byte numeric variables shortened to 1.

To make the new control file interactively, simply sort by NPOS, and then use the FSEDIT procedure to make the required changes to OUTFMT. In batch mode, a simple DATA step can replace the use of FSEDIT. Code for this example is given at the end of the next section.

If many standardized changes are required, you can easily add macros as tools to aid in handling the control information.

I added two more parameters to control the new possibilities:

```
CNTLIN = null-value
PGM = null-value
```

CNTLIN names the control file when one is used. The default, null-value, indicates that the default control file built from PROC CONTENTS is used. No corresponding CNTLOUT is needed, since the macro always produces a temporary control file __CNTL. If you want a permanent control file, add a simple data step or use the COPY procedure after your macro invocation.

PGM names the FILEREF for the "PUT" statement DATA step. If none is named then this program is not written out.

The External File Documentation

Documentation consists of printing the variables

NAME, OUTPOS, OUTLEN, OUTFMT, and LABEL

on __CNTL using the PRINT procedure. Two parameters control this operation.

```
REPORT = YES
TL = 3
```

The switch, REPORT, is used to indicate that the documentation is wanted.

The parameter TL allows you to control the heading for the documentation. By default you can supply two title lines, then the macro supplies

"Flat file layout made from DATA = &DATA"

for the third (&TL) title line. If a separator (discussed in the next section) is given, the phrase

using separator &SEP

is appended. When TL = 0 or TL = null-value, only your title lines are used.

Code for the example in the prvious section follows.

```
FILENAME OUT 'FLATFILE.DAT' ;
TITLE "BIG PROJECT" ;
TITLE2 "DOCUMENTATION" ;

%FLATFILE ( DATA=MYDATA, REPORT=NO )

PROC SORT DATA = __CNTL ;
    BY NPOS ;
RUN ;

DATA MYCNTL ;
    SET __CNTL ;
    IF NAME IN ( 'A' 'B' 'C' ) THEN OUTFMT = 'BEST1.' ;
RUN ;

%FLATFILE
    ( DATA=MYDATA, OUT=OUT, CNTLIN=MYCNTL, TL= )
```

Extra Parameters For Ease of Use

Since complete control can be obtained by using a control file and then possibly modifying the "PUT" statement DATA step generated, no more parameters are required. But three problems are so common that their solutions should be provided by the macro. They are:

- only a subset of the data set is wanted,
- only a subset of the variables is wanted, and
- a separator is required between each field.

These problems are solved with the three corresponding parameters:

```
COND = null-value,
VCOND = null-value, and
SEP = null-value
```

Subsetting the data requires adding a subsetting statement in the "PUT" statement DATA step which writes out the external file. The COND parameter allows you to directly specify this subsetting code. To simplify code specification for a single statement, the semi-colon is assumed. For example, to delete all records where the variable STATUS has a missing value, use

```
COND = IF STATUS = . THEN DELETE
```

Since the code specified is simply executed by the macro at the appropriate point, it can be used for other purposes as well. When more than one SAS statement is needed, the semi-colons must be hidden by a quoting function, say %STR. Suppose that in addition to the above subsetting condition you want to blank out the last four digits of the eight digit variable ID. Then use

```
COND = %STR (IF STATUS = . THEN DELETE;
             SUBSTR(ID, 5, 4) = '    '; )
```

For still more complex coding you can set

```
COND = %NRSTR ( %TEMPMAC )
```

and compile a macro TEMPMAC with whatever code is required.

Unwanted variables can be removed when processing either the SAS data set output from PROC CONTENTS or the control file when one is specified. I used the same method as above. The parameter, VCOND, specifies SAS code for the subsetting the list of names with the final semi-colon is assumed. For example, to eliminate the extraneous variables, X, Y, and Z you might specify

```
VCOND = IF NAME IN ('X' 'Y' 'Z') THEN DELETE
```

The VCOND parameter is provided for simple deletions. When the required changes are complex or numerous, it is clearer to build and then modify __CNTL before invoking %FLATFILE to make the external file.

The SEP parameter gives a one byte SAS character literal used to separate fields. By default there is no separator. Typical values might be ' ', ',', '#', or '09'X. (Where '09'X is the ASCII control character for TAB.)

To illustrate the techniques suggested in this section suppose

- X, Y, and Z are unwanted variables,
- W1-W50 require 12 bytes, 6 after the decimal point,
- other 8 byte numeric variables need only 6 digits, and
- TELEPHONE should be replaced by AREACODE.

For this problem you might have the following code.

```
%MACRO VARCHNG ;
    IF NAME IN ( 'X' 'Y' 'Z' ) THEN DELETE ;
    IF NAME = 'TELEPHONE' THEN
    DO ;
        NAME = 'AREACODE' ;
        LABEL = 'AREA CODE' ;
    END ;
    IF NAME =: 'W' AND LENGTH ( NAME ) <= 3 THEN
    DO ;
        IF 1 <= INPUT ( SUBSTR ( NAME, 2 ), 2. ) <= 50
            THEN OUTFMT = 'F12.6' ;
    END ;
%MEND VARCHNG ;

%FLATFILE ( DATA=MYDATA, REPORT=NO, L8=6 )

%FLATFILE ( DATA = MYDATA, CNTL = __CNTL,
    VCOND = %NRSTR ( %VARCHNG ),
    COND = AREACODE = SUBSTR(TLEPHONE,2,3) )
```

The Macro Code

The macro (see appendix) can be broken up into two blocks; the first converts SAS data control information into macro variables using CALL SYMPUT and produces a new control file, __CNTL; the second uses these variables to produce results.

The first block requires a decision. If CNTLIN = null-value, then PROC CONTENTS and a DATA step to process the output is needed; otherwise a DATA step to process the control file is needed. Separate DATA steps are used because the processing is different for the two cases.

The second block is a sequence of three decisions. If a report is wanted, then print __CNTL. If a program is wanted, then run the DATA step to write it out. If an external file is wanted, then execute the DATA step to make it.

Conclusion

Try using %FLATFILE the next time you need to make an external flat file with many variables. Let me know how it works.

I can be contacted by mail at:

Westat Inc.
1650 Research Boulevard
Rockville, MD. 20850-3129

or by E-mail at:

WHITLOI1%WESTAT@MCIMAIL.COM

Appendix

```
%macro flatfile (
    data = _LAST_ ,          /* SAS input data                 */
    cntlin = ,               /* SAS control file               */
    out = ,                  /* filename for flat file output  */
    pgm = ,                  /* filename for flat file program */
    report = YES ,           /* YES produce print file report  */
    usefmts = NO ,           /* YES get format from contents   */
    sep = ,                  /* separator: null, ' ', '09'x, etc. */
    l2 = 3 , l3 = 5 , l4 = 8 , /* dflt out len as function of */
    l5 = 10 , l6 = 13 , l7 = 15 , /* stored length for VAX     */
    l8 = 19 ,                /* decimal point assumed for l8   */
    vcond = ,                /* variable subsetting condition  */
    cond = ,                 /* data subsetting condition      */
    tl = 3                   /* available title line number    */
) ;

%*-------------------------------------------------------------*;
%* FLATFILE -                                                  *;
%* Purpose: Create one or more of the following                *;
%* Flat file corresponding to SAS data set &data               *;
%* Documentation layout for the flat file                      *;
%* Data step "PUT" program to create the flat file             *;
%* Control file __CNTL for controlling another execution       *;
%*                                                             *;
%* Side effects:                                               *;
%*   work data sets __contnt & __cntl may be generated         *;
%*   title line &tl (when > 0) used and cleared                *;
%*                                                             *;
%* Examples:                                                   *;
%*   %flatfile (out=out)       report and file                 *;
```

```
%*   %flatfile(data=mydat,pgm=pgm) reprt & program   *;
%*   %flatfile(data=mydat,out=out,l3=2,l8=6,usefmts=yes)*;
%*   %flatfile (cntlin=mycntl,out=out)  use control file   *;
%*                                                      *;
%* Reference: Ian Whitlock RE302 x4347          20mar92 *;
%* ---------------------------------------------------- *;

%local nv i tlsep lrecl pgm_file ;
%let data = %upcase ( &data ) ;
%let report = %upcase ( &report ) ;
%let usefmts = %upcase ( &usefmts ) ;
%let pgm_file = %length ( &pgm&out ) ;

%if &data = _LAST_ %then %let data = &syslast ;

%if %length ( &cntlin ) = 0 %then %goto getcntl ;

data __cntl ( keep = name outpos outlen outfmt label ) ;
  length outlen $ 3 name $ 8 outfmt __revout $ 15 label $ 40
        outpos 8 ;
  retain
    __pos 1
    __xcl 'ABCDEFGHIJKLMNOPQRSTUVWXYZ$_'
  ;
  %if &pgm_file %then
  %do ;
    if __eof then
    do ;
      __pos = __pos - 1 ;
      call symput ( 'lrecl' , left ( put ( __pos , 5. ) ) ) ;
      call symput ( 'nv' , left ( put ( __nv , 4. ) ) ) ;
    end ;
  %end ;
  set &cntlin end = __eof ;
  %unquote ( &vcond ) ;
  __nv + 1 ;
  %if &pgm_file %then
  %do ;
    call symput ( 'v'||left(put(__nv,4.)) , name ) ;
    call symput ( 'f'||left(put(__nv,4.)) , trim ( outfmt ) ) ;
    %if %length ( &pgm ) > 0 %then %str (

      call symput ( 'lab'||left(put(__nv,4.)) , label ) ;
    ) ;
  %end ;
  outpos = __pos ;
  __revout = reverse ( upcase ( outfmt ) ) ;
  __x1 = index ( __revout , '.' ) ;
  __x2 = indexc ( __revout , __xcl ) ;
  if __x2 > 0 then outlen =
    reverse(substr(__revout, __x1 + 1 , __x2 - __x1 - 1 ));
  else
    outlen = reverse(substr(__revout, __x1 + 1 ) ) ;
  output __cntl ;
  __pos + input ( outlen , 3. )
        %if &sep ^= %then + 1 ;
  ;
  run ;

  %goto results ;

%getcntl:

  proc contents
    data = &data noprint
    out = __contnt ( keep = name type length label npos
                           format formatl formatd ) ;
  run ;

  data
    __cntl ( keep = name outpos outlen outfmt label npos __nv
            rename = ( __nv = apos )
    ) ;
    retain outpos 1 ;
    length outlen $ 3 outfmt $ 15 ;
    array __lens ( 0:6 ) _temporary_
        ( &l2 &l3 &l4 &l5 &l6 &l7 &l8 ) ;
    %if &pgm_file %then
    %do ;
      if __eof then
      do ;
        outpos = outpos - 1 ;
        call symput ( 'lrecl' , left ( put ( outpos , 5. ) ) ) ;
        call symput ( 'nv' , left ( put ( __nv , 4. ) ) ) ;
      end ;
    %end ;
    set __contnt end = __eof ;
    %unquote ( &vcond ) ;
    __nv + 1 ;
    %if &pgm_file %then
      %str ( call symput ( 'v'||left(put(__nv,4.)) , name ) ; ) ;
    %if %length ( &pgm ) > 0 %then
      %str ( call symput ( 'lab'||left(put(__nv,4.)) , label ) ; ) ;
    if type = 2 then
    do ;                  /* --- character format --- */
      %if %substr ( &usefmts , 1 , 1 ) = N %then
      %do ;               /* do not use format info    */
        outlen = put ( length , 3. ) ;
        outfmt = '$char' || trim ( left ( outlen ) ) || '.' ;
      %end ;
      %else
      %do ;                          /* try format info   */
        if format ^= ' ' and formatl ^= 0 then
        do ;              /* enough format info        */
          outlen = put ( formatl , 3. ) ;
          outfmt = trim ( format ) || trim ( left ( outlen ) ) || '.' ;
        end ;
        else
        do ;              /* not enough format info    */
          outlen = put ( length , 3. ) ;
          outfmt = '$char' || trim ( left ( outlen ) ) || '.' ;
        end ;
```

```
    %end ;
  end;                        /* —— character format —— */
  else
  do ;                        /* —— numeric format —— */
    %if %substr ( &usefmts , 1 , 1 ) = N %then
    %do ;                     /* do not use format info       */
      outlen = put ( __lens ( length - 2 ) , 3. ) ;
      outfmt = 'best' || trim ( left ( outlen ) ) || '.' ;
    %end ;
    %else
    %do ;                                   /* try format info    */
      if format ^= ' ' and formatl ^= 0 then
      do ;          /* enough format info with name          */
        outlen = put ( formatl , 3. ) ;
        outfmt =
            left ( trim ( format ) ) || left ( trim ( outlen ) ) || '.' ;
        if formatd ^= 0 then
          outfmt = trim ( outfmt ) || left ( put ( formatd , 2. ) ) ;
      end ;
      else
      if formatl ^= 0 and formatd ^= 0 then
      do ;          /* enough format info with out name      */
        outlen = put ( formatl , 3. ) ;
        outfmt = left ( trim ( outlen ) ) || '.' ||
                 left ( put ( formatd , 2. ) ) ;
      end ;
      else
      if formatl ^= 0 then
      do ;          /* enough format info for best.          */
        outlen = put ( formatl , 3. ) ;
        outfmt = 'best' || trim ( left ( outlen ) ) || '.' ;
      end ;
      else
      do ;                    /* not enough format info       */
        outlen = put ( __lens ( length - 2 ) , 3. ) ;
        outfmt = 'best' || trim ( left ( outlen ) ) || '.' ;
      end ;
    %end ;
  end ;                       /* —— numeric format —— */

  %if &pgm_file %then
    %str ( call symput ('f' || left(put(__nv,4.)),trim(outfmt)); ) ;
  output __cntl ;
  outpos + input ( outlen , 3. )
    %if &sep ^= %then + 1 ;
  ;
run ;

%results:

  %if &sep = %then %let tlsep = ;
  %else
  %let tlsep = using separator &sep ;

  %if %substr ( &report , 1 , 1 ) = Y %then
  %do ;
    %if ( &tl ^= ) and ( &tl ^= 0 ) %then
      %str
      (title&tl "Flat file layout made from DATA = &data &tlsep";)
    ;
    proc print data = __cntl ;
      var name outpos outlen outfmt label ;
    run ;
    %if ( &tl ^= ) and ( &tl ^= 0 ) %then %str ( title&tl ; ) ;
  %end ;

  %if %length ( &pgm ) > 0 %then
  %do ;
    data _null_ ;
      now = today ( ) ;
      file &pgm ;
      put "/* flatfile program for &data " now date7. " */"     //
        "data _null_ ;"                               /
        "   set &data ;"                              /
        "   %unquote ( &cond ) ;"                     /
        "   file out lrecl = &lrecl ;"                /
        "   put"                                      /
            %do i = 1 %to &nv - 1 ;
              @5 "&&v&i" @15 "&&f&i &sep"
              @33 "/* &&lab&i */"     /
            %end ;
            @5 "&&v&nv" @15 "&&f&nv"
            @33 "/* &&lab&nv */"                      /
        "   ;"                                        /
        "run ;"
      ;
    run ;
  %end ;

  %if %length ( &out ) > 0 %then
  %do ;
    data _null_ ;
      set &data ;
      %unquote ( &cond ) ;
      file &out lrecl = &lrecl ;
      put
        %do i = 1 %to &nv - 1 ;
          &&v&i &&f&i &sep
        %end ;
        &&v&nv &&f&nv
      ;
    run ;
  %end ;

%mend flatfile ;


/*
   Note: most of the complexity in the data step to process the
      output of proc contents is due to the support of the
      parameter, USEFMTS.
*/
```

A Macro for a Multiple Stars Plot

Andy Mauromoustakos, University of Arkansas
Kevin Thompson, University of Arkansas

ABSTRACT

The usual methods of statistical analysis of data from experiments in which the objective is to compare treatment means for each one of several response variables involve analysis of variance followed by some technique for means separation. Usually in most experiments the investigator measures treatment performance on several response variables. Research scientists are familiar with the process of making interpretations, and subsequently presenting the results from these methods in multiple figures, one for each response, with an error bar on the side as a guide for comparing treatments. But occasionally the researcher may be interested in presenting treatment differences for all responses in a single graph so that he can gain some additional information on the relationships among the responses in addition to the treatment performance. A need for graphs of this sort arises in many fields, but it is most commonly used for presenting the results in sensory evaluations studies. A macro written for SAS/GRAPH® software referred to as the MSTARS macro is developed to accomplish this goal. Examples of the use of the macro and the output produced to represent the results presented.

INTRODUCTION

Graphs are inherently two dimensional. Some ingenuity is therefore required to display the relationships of several variables in addition to differences in the average performance of different "treatments" in each of the response variables on a flat piece of paper. Star plots (Friedman et. al. 1972; Chambers et. al. 1983) are useful ways to display multivariate observations with an arbitrary number of variables. A star plot represents multivariate data as a set of stars, with each star representing one case or row, and each point (or radial) of a star representing a particular variable or column. The length of each radial is proportional to the data values of the corresponding variable. Thus both the size and the shape of the stars have meaning: size reflects the overall magnitude of the data, and shape reveals the relationships between variables. Comparing two stars gives a quick exploratory graphical picture on similarities and differences between two cases. Similarly shaped stars indicate similar cases.

The usual (univariate) methods of statistical analysis of data from experiments in which the objective is to compare "treatment" means for each one of several response variables. It involves analysis of variance followed by some technique for mean separation. A typical example of such experiments arises in sensory evaluation studies where each panelist is asked to evaluate several characteristics of multiple replications on each "treatment" in some kind of an artificial scale.

A general SAS macro, MSTARS, is written that creates a multiple (overlaid) star plot which can be used to display the treatments means for each response with an optional error bar next to each radial. The macro operates on a data set with several rows representing the class identifier ("treatment") and multiple columns representing each one of the responses to be represented by a radial in the plot. This SAS macro is based upon the STAR Macro found in Friendly (1991). The macro code and examples of its usage is presented below.

PROGRAM EXAMPLES AND OUTPUT

Examples that demonstrate how to use the macro and the kinds of output produced are below. The first is from a panel evaluation study at the Food Science Department of the University of Arkansas. The data for the Example 1. describe an experiment where eight trained panelists evaluated each of four replications of peach puree, prepared from peaches directly following harvest, of three different maturities (2, 4 and 6). The maturity stages of fruits were determined by using ground color chips in which 1 corresponds to a green color and 6 to a full ripeness. The objective of this portion of the experiment was to evaluate the effect of fruit maturity on eleven chosen sensory quality parameters shown in Figure 1. As always variables variables were ordered according to similarity, for example, flavor responses followed othed flavor variables and before the aroma variables. The intensity of these variables was rated by using a straight line with a 1 to 9 grading scale with anchor words on each end. Panelists were asked to place a mark to indicate their quality rating for each sample. Each ray in the star plot represent one attribute with the lower intensity (1) towards the center point and maximum intensity (9) farthest from the center. The researcher in this case was interested in presenting the average ratings of the three maturities in the original scale. In addition error bars at the side of each ray indicate the magnitude of the Least Significant Difference (LSD), for comparing differences among the mean maturity rating for each variable. These bars are calculated based on a two-way random model with four replications that treats the panelist and the panelistxmaturity interaction as random effects. The multiple star of Figure 1. is very helpful in identifying significant differences among puree made from maturity 6 from the others for virtually every subjective sensory parameter. In addition relationships among parameters as expected are evident in Figure 1.

Another set of data from the same research project is used to illustrate the second example. The same panelists evaluated for replications of puree made from maturity 4 peaches stored at a cold storage 0 °C, for various storage times (0, 10, 20, 30, and 40 days). the investigator in this instance was interested in average performance of the various storage times versus their control. Thus the end of each ray in Figure 2. has been rescaled by the MSTARS macro to correspond to the maximum and minimum average ratings over the 4 replications.

The last example treats a multivariate data set of 12 numeric variables in the automobiles data from Chambers et al. (1983), and Friendly (1991, p.415, and p.595). The same 35 observations (cars) display by Friendly's star macro in p. 415 of his text are display by the MSTARS macro in Figure 3. It is evident that the presence of color could help identify relationships, influential observations, or potential outlier in the data when used properly.

CONCLUSION

Statistical graphs are a powerful form of visual communication, but in order to achieve their full potential it is essential that the highest standards of quality be observed and rigorously maintained. In the construction and utilization of statistical graphs, emphasis is based both in presentation and analysis. To imply that the ancient

Chinese proverb "One picture is worth a thousand words" is generally applicable to statistical graphs produced a decade ago. However K. W. Heamer suggests that, providing the chart is accurate, relatively simple, easily interpretable, forceful, convincing, revealing and attractive, the proverb is relevant and meaningful when applied to star plots: "One MSTARS plot could be worth a thousand words or figures."

TRADEMARKS

SAS and SAS/GRAPH are registered trademarks or trademarks os SAS Institute Inc. in the USA and other countries. ® indicates USA registration.

REFERENCES

Chambers, J. M., Clevelend, W. S., Kleiner, B., and Tukey, P. A., (1983), *Graphical Methods For Data Analysis*, Belmont, CA: Wadsworth Publishing Company, 158-162.

Friedman, H. P., Farrell, E. S., Goldwyn, R. M., Miller, M., and Sigel, J. (1972), "A Graphic Way of Describing Changing Multivariate Patterns," *Proceedings of the Sixth Interface Symposium on Computer Science and Statistics*, Berkeley, CA: University of California Press, 56-69.

Friendly, M., (1991), *SAS System for Statistical Graphics, First Edition*, Gary, NC:SAS Institute Inc., 414-420.

CONTACT INFORMATION

Kevin Thompson
AGRI STAT LAB
AGRX 101
University of Arkansas
Fayetteville, AR 72703

Phone: (503) 575-2448

BITNET: KT27032@UAFSYSB
INTERNET: KT27032@UAFSYSB.UARK.EDU

ACKNOWLEDGMENTS

Dr. Alfredo Gonzalez of the Department of Food Science in the University of Arkansas, provided the sensory evaluation data and encouraged us to write the program.

The MSTARS macro

```
%macro MSTARS( /* Star plot of Multivariate data                             */
/** Param     Default      Req Description ***********************************/
    Data     =_LAST_  . /* N  Input SAS Data Set                              */
    Class    =        . /* N  Observation identifier (Must uniquely id obs)  */
    Var      =        . /* Y  List of (numeric) variables                     */
    ErrorBar=         . /* N  List of error bar lengths                       */
/***********************      Tuning Parameters ******************************/
    Minimum =DATA     . /* N  Minimum data value ('DATA' or number)           */
    Maximum =DATA     . /* N  Maximum data value ('DATA' or number)           */
    MinRay  =.1       . /* N  Offset of minimum data value from origin (>=0) */
    NTicks  =2        . /* N  Number of tick marks (0=none. >=2)              */
    Circle  =Yes      . /* N  Draw a circle around the plot                   */
    Symbols =Yes      . /* N  Generate SYMBOL statements                      */
    Symbol_C=COLOR1   . /* N   Colors on generated SYMBOL statements          */
    Symbol_V=DOT      . /* N   Symbols on generated SYMBOL statements         */
    Symbol_F=NONE     . /* N   Symbol fonts on generated SYMBOL statements    */
    Symbol_H=1        . /* N   Symbol sizes on generated SYMBOL statements    */
    Symbol_L=1        . /* N   Line types on generated SYMBOL statements      */
    AdjHoriz=1.6      . /* N  Adjustment of horizontal plot width (>=1)       */
    AdjVert =1.1      . /* N  Adjustment of vertical plot width (>=1)         */
    AdjLabel=1.02     . /* N  Closeness of label to ray endpoints (>=1)       */
    AdjEBar =4        . /* N  Closeness of error bar to ray (in degrees)      */
    AdjTick =1        . /* N  Width of Tick mark (in degrees)                 */
    );
/*****************************************************************************
/* Create a star plot of multivariate data.                                  *
/* Each observation is represented by a separate star figure with one       *
/*   ray for each variable.  An observations position along a ray (obs) is *
/*   proportional to the value of the observation.                          *
/* You may need the GOPTIONS  HSIZE= VSIZE= HORIGIN= VORIGIN= to modify      *
/*    the aspect of the plot.                                                *
/* Description of the paramerers                                             *
/* DATA      specifies the SAS Data Set containing the data.                 *
/* CLASS     specifies a single variable that uniquely determines the        *
/*           observation.  The variable's label and formatted values         *
/*           are printed below the plot as the plot legend. If omitted the   *
/*           observation number is used.                                     *
/* VAR       specifies a list of numeric variables representing the rays     *
/*           of the star plot.  The variables are spaced equi-angularly      *
/*           in order around the unit circle, counter-clockwise from the     *
/*           horizontal (3 o'clock) position.  The variables' labels are     *
/*           printed next to each ray.                                       *
/* ERRORBAR specifies a numeric list of error bar lengths (one per VAR       *
/*           variable.  You may optionally specify a 1 observation SAS Data *
/*           Set containing the error bar lengths.  This SAS Data Set must   *
/*           have the same variable names as those listed on the VAR         *
/*           statement.  If omitted, no error bars are produced.             *
/* MINUMUM   specifies a minimum and maximum value for the length of a ray.  *
/* MAXIMUM   If omitted,the minimum and maximum observed values are are used*
/*           These values will be listed in the SASLOG but not indicated     *
/*           on the plot itself.                                             *
/* MINRAY    specifies the offset from the origin for the MINIMUM= value.    *
/*           A value of 0 specifies that each ray starts at the origin.      *
/*           A small positive value (default=0.1) displaces this minimum     *
/*           from the origin.                                                *
/* NTICKS    specifies whether tick marks are placed on the rays.  The       *
/*           value may be either 0 (for no tick marks) or an integer larger *
/*           than 1.                                                         *
/* CIRCLE    specifies whether the unit circle is plotted.                   *
/* SYMBOLS   specifies whether the macro generates the SYMBOL statements     *
/*           used to draw the lines of the plot.  If NO is coded, the user  *
/*           should provide one SYMBOL statement for each observation.       *
/*           If YES is coded. The user may modify the color, line type       *
/*           and plotting symbol of the generated SYMBOL statements with     *
/*           the SYMBOL_X parameters.  If fewer than NOBS values are         *
/*           coded in a SYMBOL_X parameter, the last value is repeated       *
/*           for all remaining SYMBOL statements.                            *
/* SYMBOL_C specifies the colors.                                            *
/* SYMBOL_V specifies the plotting symbols.  A value of NONE specifies       *
/*           that only lines are used.                                       *
/* SYMBOL_F specifies the font of the plotting symbol (eg. XMARKER.          *
/*           SPECIAL).  A value of NONE allows for the use of the            *
/*           standard SYMBOL statement symbols (eg. DOT, PLUS. etc.).        *
/* SYMBOL_H specifies the size of the plotting symbol.                       *
/* SYMBOL_L specifies the line type of the lines joining the star vertices.*
/*           A value of 0 specifies that no lines be drawn.  If fewer than  *
/*           NOBS values are coded. the line type values are incremented     *
/*           by 1.                                                           *
/* ADJHORIZ is an adjustment of the horizontal plot width (>=1). This        *
/*           value may need to be increased for long labels                  *
/* ADJVERT   is an adjustment of the vertical plot width (>=1).              *
/* ADJLABEL is an adjustment of the closeness of label to ray                *
/*           endpoints (>=1)                                                 *
/* ADJEBAR   is an adjustment of the closeness of error bar to ray           *
/*           (in degrees)                                                    *
/* ADJTICK   is an adjustment of the width of each tick mark (in degrees)    *
/*****************************************************************************
/* Contact:  Kevin Thompson      <KT27032@UAFSYSB.UARK.EDU>                  *
/* Created:  24AUG1992                                                       *
/* Requires: BASE SAS  (TRANSPOSE. SORT. SUMMARY. FORMAT)                    *
/*           SAS/Graph (GPLOT)                                               *
/* Based on the program STARS.SAS by Michael Friendly.  From                 *
/*   ''SAS System for Statistical Graphics, First Edition''                  *
/*     Copyright(c) 1991 by SAS Institute Inc., Cary, NC, USA                *
/* Reference: Chambers, Cleveland, Kleiner & Tukey, Graphical methods        *
/*              for data analysis. Wadsworth, 1983. pp158-162.               *
/*****************************************************************************/

*Error Checking;
%Local NV NOBS CERROR DLM EB I T C L V H F;
%if %UPCase(&DATA)=_LAST_ %then %let DATA=&SYSLast;
%if %UPCase(&DATA)=_NULL_ %then %do;
    %put ERROR: Data Set &DATA not found.;
    %goto EXIT;
    %end;
%if %scan(&CLASS XXXXXXXX XXXXXXXX,2)^=XXXXXXXX %then %do;
    %put ERROR: Only one CLASS variable is allowed;
    %goto EXIT;
    %end;
%if &VAR=   %then %do;
    %put ERROR: No list of VAR variables were provided.;
    %goto EXIT;
    %end;

*Use Observation number if CLASS= is omitted;
data s_scaled;
     set &DATA;
     length s_obs 3;
     s_obs + 1;
     label s_obs='Observation';
     keep s_obs &CLASS &VAR;
run;
%if &CLASS= %then %let CLASS=s_obs;


* Restructure the data;
proc transpose data=s_scaled out=s_scaled(rename=(col1=s_value))
                name=s_name label=s_label;
     by s_obs &CLASS;
     var &var;
quit;
data s_scaled;
     length s_obs s_var 3 s_name $8 s_label $40;
```

```
     set s_scaled end=s_end;
     by s_obs &CLASS;
     if s_label=' ' then s_label=s_name;
     if first.s_obs then  s_var=0;
     s_var+1;
     if s_end then do;
        call symput('NV'   , left(put(s_var, 2.)));
        call symput('NOBS', put(s_obs,5.));
        end;
run;
proc sort data=s_scaled;
     by s_var s_obs;
quit;

*Rescale the data;
proc summary data=s_scaled;
     by s_var;
     var s_value;
     output out=s_minmax(drop=_type_ _freq_) min=s_min max=s_max;
quit;
data s_scaled;
     merge s_scaled s_minmax;
     by s_var;
     %if %upcase(&MINIMUM)=DATA | &MINIMUM=
        %then %do;
              call symput('MINIMUM', left(put(s_min,best5.)));
              %end;
        %else %do;
              s_min=&MINIMUM;
              %end;
     %if %upcase(&MAXIMUM)=DATA | &MAXIMUM=
        %then %do;
              call symput('MAXIMUM', left(put(s_max,best5.)));
              %end;
        %else %do;
              s_max=&MAXIMUM;
              %end;

     select;
        when (          s_value <  s_min) do
             s_scaled = &MINRAY ;
             put 'WARNING: Var ' s_name 'has been reset from ' s_value 'to '
s_min
                 'for &CLASS=' &CLASS;
             end;
        when (s_min <= s_value <= s_max) do;
             s_scaled = &MINRAY + ( 1 - &MINRAY ) * ( s_value - s_min ) /
                                                    ( s_max   - s_min ) ;
             end;
        when (s_max <  s_value            ) do
             s_scaled = 1;
             put 'WARNING: Var ' s_name 'has been reset from ' s_value 'to '
s_max
                 'for &CLASS=' &CLASS;
             end;
        otherwise;
        end;

     s_angle = 2 * 3.1415926 * (s_var-1) / &NV;
     s_degree = 180 * s_angle / 3.1415926;
     s_x = s_scaled * cos(s_angle);
     s_y = s_scaled * sin(s_angle);
run;
proc sort data=s_scaled;
     by s_obs s_var;
quit;

*Close the star polygon;
data s_scaled;
     set s_scaled s_scaled(where=(s_var=1) in=s_closed);
     by s_obs;
     if s_closed then s_var = -1;
run;

*Create the Annotate SAS Data Set;
proc format;
   value posn
              22.5-67.5 = 'C'  /* left, above      */
             292.5-337.5= 'F'  /* left, below      */
                 0-22.5 = '6'  /* left, centered   */
             337.5-360  = '6'  /* left, centered   */
             112.5-157.5= 'A'  /* right, above     */
             202.5-247.5= '7'  /* right, below     */
             157.5-202.5= '4'  /* right, centered  */
              67.5-112.5= 'B'  /* centered, above  */
             247.5-292.5= 'E'  /* centered, below  */
                 other  = '6'
                 ;
run;
data s_anno;
   set s_scaled(where=((s_obs=1) & (s_var>0)));

   LENGTH X Y SIZE                 LINE      8;
   LENGTH TEXT                             $200;
   LENGTH FUNCTION COLOR STYLE              $ 8;
   LENGTH XSYS YSYS HSYS                    $ 1;
   LENGTH WHEN POSITION                     $ 1;

   WHEN='B';
   XSYS = '2';  YSYS  = '2' ;
   COLOR='        ';
   LINE=1;                                 *Line type of rays;
   SIZE=1 ; HSYS='4';                      *Size of text;
   STYLE    = '        ';                  *Font of text;
   ANGLE=0; ROTATE=0;                      *Orientation of text;
   position=put(s_degree, posnl.);
   Text=s_label;                           *Text;

   %if %substr(%upcase(&CIRCLE),1,1)=Y |
       %substr(%upcase(&CIRCLE),1,1)=B %then %do;
       if _N_=1 then do;
          Function='Move'  :    x=1;        y=0;        output;
          do i = 0 to 2*3.1415926 by 0.01;
             Function='Draw' ; x=cos(i);  y=sin(i);  output;
             end;
          end;
       %end;
   %if %substr(%upcase(&CIRCLE),1,1)=B %then %do;
       if _N_=1 then do;
          Function='Move'  ;    x=&MINRAY; y=0;        output;
          do i = 0 to 2*3.1415926 by 0.01;
             Function='Draw' ; x=cos(i);  y=sin(i);  output;
             end;
          end;
       %end;

   Function='Move'  ; x=cos(s_angle)*(&MINRAY)   ;
                      y=sin(s_angle)*(&MINRAY)   ;   output;
   Function='Draw'  ; x=cos(s_angle)             ;
                      y=sin(s_angle)             ;  output;
   Function='Label'; x=cos(s_angle)*(&ADJLABEL);
                      y=sin(s_angle)*(&ADJLABEL);   output;

   s_tickw = 3.1415926 * (&ADJTICK) / 180;
   if &NTICKS > 1 then do s_tickn = (0+(&MINRAY=0)) to (&NTICKS-1);
      s_tick = &MINRAY + s_tickn * (1-&MINRAY)/(&NTICKS-1);
      Function='Move'; x=s_tick*cos(s_angle-s_tickw/(2*s_tick));
                       y=s_tick*sin(s_angle-s_tickw/(2*s_tick)); output;
      Function='Draw'; x=s_tick*cos(s_angle                     );
                       y=s_tick*sin(s_angle                     ); output;
      Function='Draw'; x=s_tick*cos(s_angle+s_tickw/(2*s_tick));
                       y=s_tick*sin(s_angle+s_tickw/(2*s_tick)); output;

      end;

run;

%if &ERRORBAR^= %then %do;
    %let EB = %substr(&ERRORBAR,1,1);
    %if ((0<=&EB) & (&EB<=9)) %then %do;
         data s_errbar;
              %do I = 1 %to &NV;
              %scan(&NV,&I) = %scan(&ERRORBAR,&I);
              %end;
          run;
          %let ERRORBAR=s_errbar;
          %end;
    proc transpose data=&ERRORBAR out=s_errbar(rename=(col1=s_errbar))
                   name=s_name;
          var &VAR;
    quit;
    data s_errbar;
          set s_errbar;
          length s_var 3;
          s_var+1;
          keep s_var s_errbar;
    run;
    data s_errbar;
          merge s_scaled(in=in_sc where=((s_obs = 1) & (s_var > 0)))
                s_errbar(in=in_eb);
          by s_var;

          s_diff = s_max - s_min;
          if s_errbar > ( s_max - s_min ) then do;
             put 'WARNING: Var ' s_name 'Errorbar has been reset from '
                 s_errbar 'to ' s_diff;
             s_errbar = s_diff;
             end;
          s_errbar = ( 1 - &MINRAY ) * ( s_errbar ) / ( s_max - s_min );

          LENGTH X Y SIZE                 LINE      8;
          LENGTH TEXT                             $200;
          LENGTH FUNCTION COLOR STYLE              $ 8;
          LENGTH XSYS YSYS HSYS                    $ 1;
          LENGTH WHEN POSITION                     $ 1;

          WHEN='B';
          XSYS = '2';  YSYS  = '2' ;
          COLOR='        ';
          LINE=1;                                 *Line type of error bars;

          s_adjeb = 3.1415926 * (&ADJEBAR) / 180;
          s_angle = s_angle - s_adjeb;

          Function='Move' : x=cos(s_angle);    y=sin(s_angle);    output;
          Function='Draw' : x=(1-s_errbar)*x;  y=(1-s_errbar)*y;  output;

          s_tickw = 3.1415926 * (&ADJTICK) / 180;
          do s_tick = (1-s_errbar), 1 ;
             Function='Move': x=s_tick*cos(s_angle-s_tickw/(2*s_tick));
                              y=s_tick*sin(s_angle-s_tickw/(2*s_tick)); output;
             Function='Draw': x=s_tick*cos(s_angle                     );
                              y=s_tick*sin(s_angle                     ); output;
             Function='Draw': x=s_tick*cos(s_angle+s_tickw/(2*s_tick));
                              y=s_tick*sin(s_angle+s_tickw/(2*s_tick)); output;
             end;
     run;
     data s_anno;
          set s_anno s_errbar;
     run;
     %end;

%put Note: MSTARS plots for data set &DATA ;
%put       Variables are scaled to range &MINRAY(&MINIMUM) to 1(&MAXIMUM) ;
%put       Number of variables    = &NV ;
%put       Number of observations = &NOBS ;

*Create plot;
proc gplot data=s_scaled annotate=s_anno;
     plot s_y*s_x=&CLASS  /haxis=axis1 vaxis=axis2;
     axis1 order=(-&ADJHORIZ to &ADJHORIZ by &ADJHORIZ) style=0
           label=none value=none major=none minor=none;
     axis2 order=(-&ADJVERT  to &ADJVERT  by &ADJVERT ) style=0
           label=none value=none major=none minor=none;

     %if %substr(%upcase(&SYMBOLS),1,1)=Y %then %do;
         %let dlm=' ';
         %do i = 1 %to &NOBS;
             %let T=%scan(&Symbol_C,&I,&DLM);  %if &T^= %then %let C=&T;
             %let T=%scan(&Symbol_L,&I,&DLM);  %if &T^= %then %let L=&T;
             %let T=%scan(&Symbol_V,&I,&DLM);  %if &T^= %then %let V=&T;
             %let T=%scan(&Symbol_H,&I,&DLM);  %if &T^= %then %let H=&T;
             %let T=%scan(&Symbol_F,&I,&DLM);  %if &T^= %then %let F=&T;
             %if %upcase(&F)=NONE %then %let F=;
             %if &L=0
                 %then %do; symbol&I C=&C F=&F H=&H V=&V I=NONE     ;  %end;
                 %else %do; symbol&I C=&C F=&F H=&H V=&V I=JOIN L=&L;  %end;
             %if &L ^= 0 %then %let L=%eval(&L+1);
         %end;
     %end;
quit;

%Exit:
%Mend MStars;
```

Example 1: Sensory Evaluation data (Absolute scaling).

```
title 'Sensory Evaluation Data for Peach Puree';
goptions device=hplj3 rotate=portrait ftext=swiss
         vsize=5 in  vorigin=0.9 in   hsize=6 in  horigin=1.0 in;
options nosource2 nomprint;  %include 'MStars.MAC';

data means lsd; input type$ mat fa fu fb fso fs fp con ap ac cob cg;
  if type='MEAN' then output means;  else output lsd;
  label mat='Maturity'       ap ='Aroma Peach'        ac ='Aroma Cook'
        con='Consistency'    cob='Color Orange-Brown' cg ='Color Green'
        fp ='Flavor Peach'   fs ='Flavor Sweet'       fso='Flavor Sour'
        fb ='Flavor Bitter'  fu ='Flavor Unripe'      fa ='Flavor Astringent' ;
cards;
MEAN    2   4.1  6.3  3.2  6.0  2.3  2.8  3.0  3.4  2.7  2.6  5.0
MEAN    4   4.3  5.4  3.1  6.0  2.3  3.2  2.5  4.3  2.8  2.2  4.3
MEAN    6   2.0  2.2  1.6  2.8  5.4  6.3  2.2  6.2  3.5  3.1  2.1
LSD     .   1.5  1.7  1.4  1.1  0.9  1.1  0.7  1.2  1.1  1.3  0.9
run;

symbol1 c=yellow i=join l=1 f=xmarker v='W' w=5;
symbol2 c=yellow i=join l=2 f=xmarker v='C' w=5;
symbol3 c=yellow i=join l=3 f=xmarker v='V' w=5;
symbol4 c=yellow i=join l=4 f=xmarker v='P' w=5;
symbol5 c=yellow i=join l=5 f=xmarker v='U' w=5;
%MStars(data=means,errorbar=lsd,
        class=mat, var=fa fu fb fso fs fp con ap ac cob cg,
        minimum=1, maximum=9, minray=.1, nticks=9,
        symbols=No, circle=No);
```

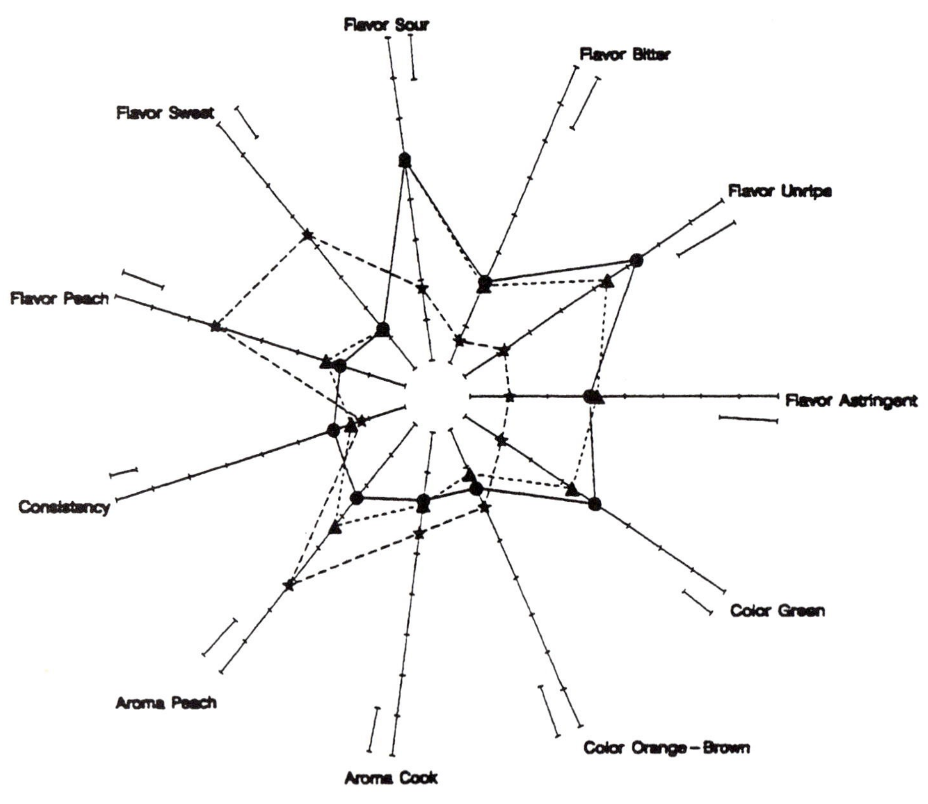

Figure 1.

Example 2: Sensory Evaluation data (Relative scaling).

```
title h=2 'Maturity 4'; title2 h=1.5 'Cold Storage';
 goptions device=hplj3 rotate=portrait ftext=swiss
         vsize=5 in  vorigin=2.5 in   hsize=6 in  horigin=1.0 in;

options nosource2 nomprint;
%include 'MStars.MAC';
%let VAR=fa fu fb fso fs fp con ap ac cob cg;
symbol1 c=yellow i=join l=1 f=xmarker v='W' w=5;
symbol2 c=yellow i=join l=2 f=xmarker v='C' w=5;
symbol3 c=yellow i=join l=3 f=xmarker v='V' w=5;
symbol4 c=yellow i=join l=4 f=xmarker v='P' w=5;
symbol5 c=yellow i=join l=5 f=xmarker v='U' w=5;

data sensmns lsd;
  input type$ slength  &VAR;
  if type='MEAN' then output sensmns;  else output lsd;
  label mat='Maturity'      ap ='Aroma Peach'         ac ='Aroma Cook'
        con='Consistency'   cob='Color Orange-Brown'  cg ='Color Green'
        fp ='Flavor Peach'  fs ='Flavor Sweet'        fso='Flavor Sour'
        fb ='Flavor Bitter' fu ='Flavor Unripe'       fa ='Flavor Astringent'
        slength ='Storage time (days)';
cards;
MEAN    0   4.33  5.42  3.14  6.02  2.33  3.23  2.46  4.33  2.77  2.21  4.27
MEAN   10   3.13  4.69  2.76  4.00  4.23  4.65  4.19  3.65  3.38  4.04  3.85
MEAN   20   2.77  3.73  2.36  3.58  4.38  4.90  6.81  4.63  3.96  5.02  2.94
MEAN   30   1.96  2.94  2.27  3.02  5.00  5.38  5.52  4.88  4.44  4.33  2.29
MEAN   40   1.54  1.96  2.14  1.94  5.79  5.40  6.41  5.04  6.25  6.77  1.54
LSD     .   1.17  1.26  0.90  1.14  1.17  1.32  1.00  1.07  0.99  1.15  0.67
run;

%MStars(data=sensmns, class=slength, var=&VAR, errorbar=lsd, symbols=No, circle=No);
```

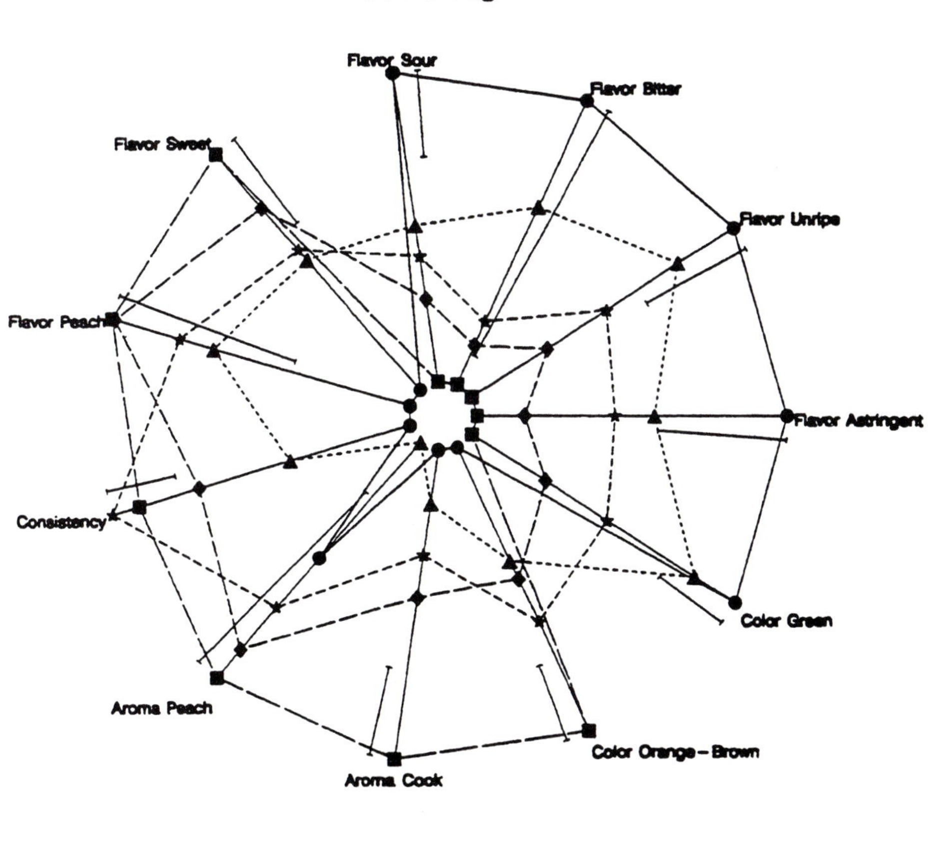

Example 3: Multivariate data exploration (Relative scaling).

```
title 'Automobile data from the 1979 model year';
goptions device=hplj3 rotate=portrait  hpos=120 vpos=75 ftext=swiss
         vsize=5.5 in  vorigin=0.9 in   hsize=7 in  horigin=0.5 in ;
options nosource2 nomprint;   %include 'MStars.MAC';


data auto;  infile 'auto.dat';
  input model $1-15  origin $17 price mpg rep78 rep77 hroom rseat trunk
        weight length turn displa gratio;
  if rep78=. or rep77=. then delete;
run;
proc sort data=auto; by weight; quit;
data auto; set auto; if _n_ <=15 or _n_ > 66-15 ;
  price =-price; turn  =-turn ; gratio=-gratio;
  label model  = 'Make & model '
        price  = 'Price'
        mpg    = 'Mileage'
        rep78  = 'Repair record 1978'
        rep77  = 'Repair record 1977'
        hroom  = 'Headroom (in.)'
        rseat  = 'Rear seat (in.)'
        trunk  = 'Trunk space (cu ft)'
        weight = 'Weight (lbs)'
        length = 'Length (in.)'
        turn   = 'Turn circle (ft)'
        displa = 'Displacement (cu in)'
        gratio = 'Gear ratio';
run;
  %MStars(data=auto, class=model, symbol_v=none, circle=no,
 var=gratio turn rep77 rep78 price mpg hroom rseat trunk weight length displa);
```

Automobile data from the 1979 model year

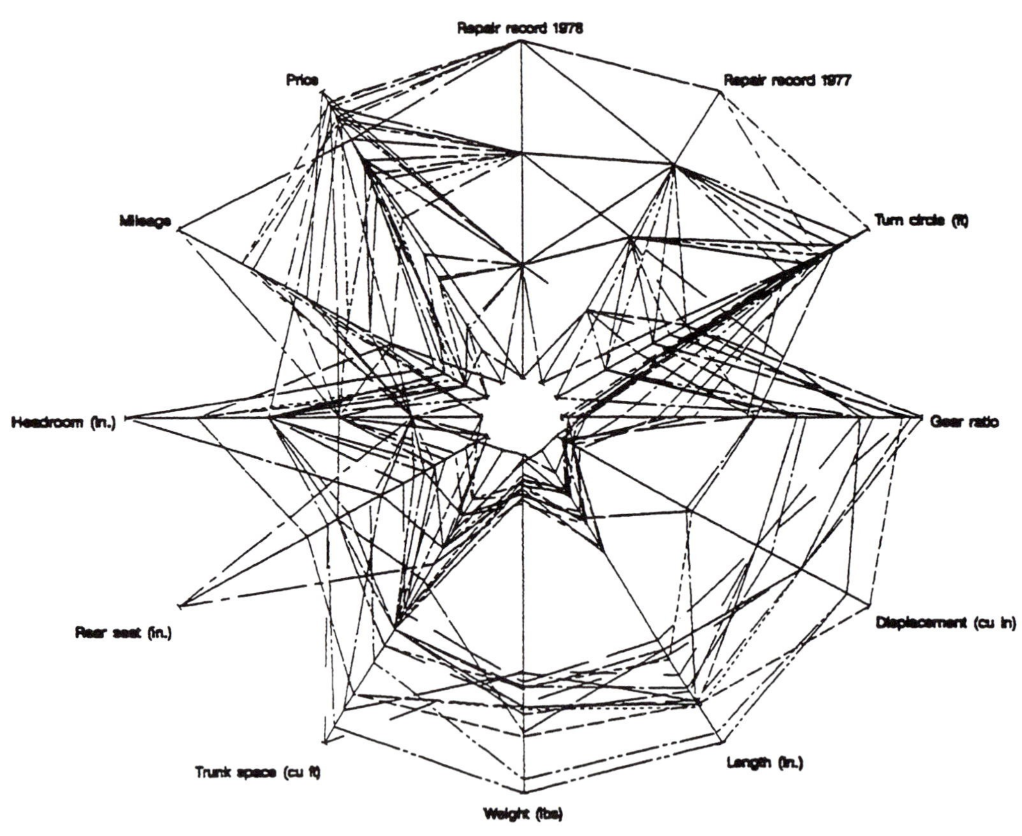

Figure 3.

A Supplemental SAS® Function for Computing Moving Average

Shi-Tao Yeh, Environmental Resources Management, Inc.

I. Introduction

Many real world variables are in the form of time series. A time series data consists of several observations of a value at different points in time. When analyzing time series data, researchers often have two goals: to describe the patterns of the series in the past and to predict values of a particular quantity. The major components of the time series data are: the trend component, the cyclical component, and the irregular component.

The moving average is the average value of the observations in a time series that are closest to one particular value. The moving average method is one of techniques for determining the trend of a set of time series. This method can smooth the variation of a time series data due to seasonal, mean quarterly, or monthly values influences. In some cases, the trend component of a time series can be identified by the moving average method easily.

This paper provides a SAS® macro routine for calculating the moving average and illustrates how to use it.

II. Computation of the Moving Averages

If the observations in a time series are denoted by $Y_1, Y_2, \ldots, Y_n$, then a moving average of length k is the series of successive means of k consecutive observations. The computations of the series of moving averages are

$$\bar{Y}_1 = \frac{Y_1 + Y_2 + \cdots + Y_k}{k},$$

$$\bar{Y}_2 = \frac{Y_2 + Y_3 + \cdots + Y_{k+1}}{k},$$

$$\bar{Y}_3 = \frac{Y_3 + Y_4 + \cdots + Y_{k+2}}{k}, \cdots$$

Since the values of these means, $\bar{Y}_1$, $\bar{Y}_2, \ldots$, are based upon k observations, they are centered in a graph at the midpoint of the set of obervations for which the mean has been calculated.

2.1 Length k is an Odd Number

If user assigns an odd number of length k, the computation is straightforward. For example, if k = 5, then $\bar{Y}_1$ is centered at Y_3 ; similarly, $\bar{Y}_2$ is centered at Y_4, and so on. Note that the routine cannot calculate the moving averages for the first two observations and the last two observations. A missing value will be assigned to each of these four moving averages.

2.2 Length k is an Even Number

In this case, the calculation of the midpoint means will be performed first. For example, if k = 6, then $\bar{Y}_1$ is centered at the midpoint between Y_3 and Y_4 ; similarly, $\bar{Y}_2$ is centered at the midpoint between Y_4 and Y_5 , and so on.

In order to obtain a moving average centered at each observation, we calculate the mean of $\bar{Y}_i$ and $\bar{Y}_{i+1}$, and assign this mean value to Y_i . These means are called the 'centered moving averages'.

The routine sets the first (k/2) centered moving averages and the last (k/2) centered moving averages to missing values.

III. SAS Macro Codes

The complete SAS macro codes are shown in Figure 1.

The macro module accepts user supplied arguments of

- **f:** data set name which contains the variable to be performed the moving average calculation,
- **v:** variable name in f data set for which the calculation of the moving average is to be performed,
- **k:** the length of the moving average, and
- **mv:** the variable name for newly computed moving average.

To invoke this function, write its macro function name **%mavg** and then the

```
%macro mavg(f,v,k,mv);
   %let  ck = mod(&k,2);
   %let  m = &k - 1;
   %if ck = 1  %then %do;
      %let m2=%eval((&k - 1)/2);
      %end;
   %else %do;
      %let  m2 = %eval(&k / 2);
         %end;
data ma(keep=&mv);
   set &f;
   &mv = &v;
   %do b = 1 %to  &m;
      &v&b = lag&b(&v);
      &mv = &mv + &v&b;
   %end;
   &mv = &mv / &k;
   if &ck = 0 then do;
      mv1 = lag(&mv);
      &mv = (&mv + mv1)/2;
      end;
   if &mv = . then delete;
run;


data mg;
   &mv = .;
run;
%if &m2 > 1 %then %do;
   %do b = 2 %to &m2;
   data mg&b;
      &mv = .;
   data mg;
      set mg mg&b;
      %end;
   %end;
data ma;
   set mg ma mg;
data &f;
   set &f ; set ma;
%mend mavg;
```

Figure 1. A Complete Set of Macro Codes

arguments of data set name **f**, variable name **v**, length of moving average **k**, and new variable name for computed moving average **mv**, enclosed in parentheses.

IV. Illustration of How to Invoke this Function

Figure 2 shows a sample input data set **f1** which contains one variable **x**.

```
data f1;
   input x;
   cards;
156
156
158
198
205
237
260
317
380
255
210
165
146
157
159
202
227
232
283
260
345
340
195
151
;
```

Figure 2. Sample Input Data Set

This macro function **%mavg** is used in DATA step programming statements. It might be used as follows:

```
data f1;
   set f1;
   %mavg(f1,x,12,xmavg)
run;
```

This example selects variable **x** in data set **f1** for performing the moving average calculation with length of 12 and assigns a new variable name **xmavg** to the result of computation.

The sample output is shown in Figure 3.

Sample Output

X	XMAVG
156	.
156	.
158	.
198	.
205	.
237	.
260	224.333
317	223.958
380	224.042
255	224.250
210	225.333
165	226.042
146	226.792
157	225.375
159	221.542
202	223.625
227	226.542
232	225.333
283	.
260	.
345	.
340	.
195	.
151	.

Figure 3. Sample Output

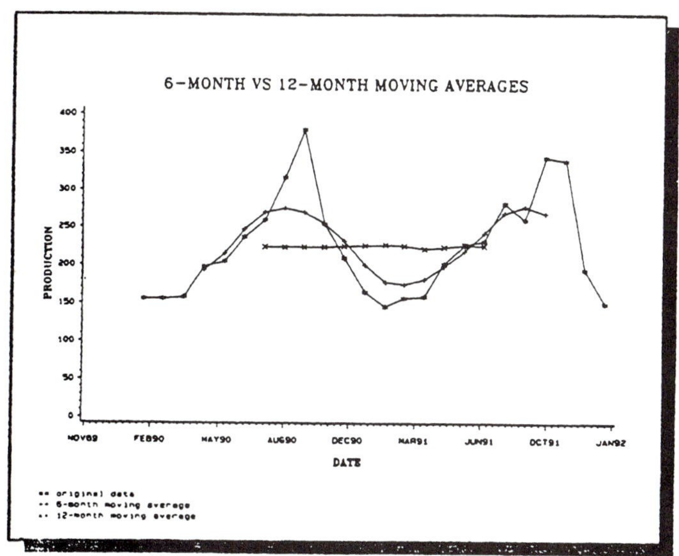

Figure 4. Comparison of 6-month vs. 12-month Moving Averages

If user assigns a larger length, the cyclical component of the time series will disappear. Figure 4 shows a comparison of 6-month vs. 12-month moving averages.

SAS is a trademark of SAS Institute Inc.

MACPAGE - A SAS® MACRO FOR ENHANCING REPORTS

Kathleen D. Edwards, Burroughs Wellcome Co.
John Henry King, Trilogy Consulting Corporation

This paper describes a macro which allows the user to enhance the presentation quality of SAS reports. Specifically, the macro generates page numbers in a variety of styles, it differentiates zeros from the letter "O" by overstriking the zeros with a "/", it hikes up the underscore to mimic the appearance of an overstrike, and it allows for the adjustment of the top and left margins. The top margin adjustment is similar to the SAS SKIP option. The macro uses PROC PRINTTO and a data step to accomplish these enhancements.

The reports which use the page numbering feature can be generated by PUT statements, from procedure calls or by a combination of these methods. The placement of the numbers can be right, left, or center justified and can appear on any line of the page. The user can also define the starting page number. Some of the styles available include:

page *p*
page *p* of *n*
p of *n*
a·*p* (where *a* is an appendix number)

The macro uses PROC PRINTTO and is called twice by the user. In the first call, the user sets up the "unit" where the SAS output file is captured. In the second call, the user passes parameters into the macro call.

Specifications for defining these parameters are listed below:

SPECIFICATIONS:

UNIT = *nn*

The user is strongly encouraged to read the PROC PRINTTO section of the SAS User's Guide before defining the UNIT parameter. To use MACPAGE, you must actually supply 2 filerefs that reference the same file, this is so that the file can be read twice in the same data step: once to count the pages and again to print the file with the enhancements. The UNIT parameter defines the unit number of the Fortran style fileref that references the output file in the control language for your job or session. Use UNIT = *nn* as the only parameter in the first call of %MACPAGE to initiate redirection of the SAS system printed output. If any other parameters are specified in a call to %MACPAGE that includes the UNIT = nn, the other parameters will be ignored.

Following are examples of filerefs that you would use in CMS and OS. In CMS it would be convenient to add these 2 filerefs to the SAS exec.

In CMS use:

```
FILEDEF FT23F001 DISK PRINTTO LISTING A3
(BLKSIZE 2604 LRECL 260 RECFM VBA DISP MOD)

FILEDEF FT24F001 DISK PRINTTO LISTING A3
(BLKSIZE 2604 LRECL 260 RECFM VBA DISP MOD)
```

In OS use:

```
//FT23F001 DD DSN = &&PRINTTO, UNIT = SYSDA,
//             DCB = (RECFM = VBA, LRECL = 260,
//             BLKSIZE = 2604),
//             SPACE = (TRK, (10, 10)),
//             DISP = (MOD, PASS)
//FT24F001 DD VOL = REF = *.FT23F001,
//             DSN = *.FT23F001,
//             DISP = (OLD, PASS)
```

In these example filerefs, UNIT = 23 would be specified in the call to %MACPAGE. The important thing here is that UNIT = 24 must also be defined to reference the same file.

TARGET =

specifies a character string target which %MACPAGE will look for when positioning the numbers on the output pages. The target should be unique and must appear on each page in the line where the numbering text is to be placed. The special target **CC** can be specified to cause %MACPAGE to look for the carriage control character '1' in the print file. Otherwise, the target must be specified in either double or single quotes. If target is not specified, then page numbers will not appear on the output.

JUSTIFY =

specifies whether the page number text will be **R**, **L**, or **C** (right, left, or center) justified. The default is **R**.

LS =

specifies the linesize used in determining the placement of the page numbers for right justified and centered page numbers. The default is 132.

STYLE =

specifies the style used for page numbering. The following options are available:

OPTION	RESULTING STYLE
Page	Page n (default)
SAS	*n*
Pageof	Page *n* of *p*
Brief	n of p
string format	where string can be any character string and format is a valid SAS format. *e.g.*, Appendix 1.z3 produces Appendix 1.00n

FPAGE =

specifies the starting page number. The default is 1.

ADJUST =

specifies the number of columns to skip on the left margin before printing out each line in the report. The default is 0.

SKIP =

specifies the number of lines to skip on the top margin before printing each page. This works like the SAS SKIP= option. The default is 0.

ZEROS =

causes zeros to be slashed in order to distinguish them from the letter "O". The default is NO (for noslash). To slash the zeros, the user must specify ZEROS = S (for slash).

UNDER =

output will be searched for underscores. %MACPAGE will place a '+' in the carriage control column of those lines which contain the number of contiguous underscores specified in the UNDERLEN parameter (below). This causes the underscores to appear as overstrikes on the output. The default is **Y** (Yes). To suppress this feature specify **N** (No).

UNDERLEN =

specifies the number of contiguous underscores which must be found before the underscore is hiked up. The default is 8.

Example:

```
%MACPAGE(UNIT = 23)              * sets up the unit;

        PROC PRINT DATA = SOMENAME;
        RUN;

%MACPAGE(TARGET = CC, STYLE = 1. Z3, ADJUST = 2,
              SKIP = 3,ZEROS = S)
```

In the example above, the parameters take on the following values:

TARGET = CC	the carriage control character "1" is the target line for writing the page numbers.
STYLE = 1.Z3	the page numbers will print as 1.001 - 1.00n.
ADJUST = 2	shifts the entire report over by 2 columns.
SKIP = 3	the report will begin 3 lines down from the printer default.
ZEROS = S	all of the zeros in the report will be slashed.

Contact author:

John Henry King
Burroughs Wellcome Co.
3030 Cornwallis Rd.
RTP, NC 27709
(919)248-4723


```
%macro MacPage(unit = ,
             target = ,
                 ls = 132,
            justify = Right,
              style = Page,
              fpage = 1,
             adjust = 0,
               skip = 0,
              under = Y,
           underlen = 8,
              zeros = NOSlash);
   %if %quote(&unit)¬= %then %do;
      %global __unit__;
      %let __unit__ = &unit;
      PROC PRINTTO UNIT=&unit NEW;
         RUN;
      %end;
   %else %do;
      %let justify = %substr(%upcase(&justify),1,1);
      %if ¬%index(%quote(&style),%str(.))
         %then %let style = %upcase(&style);
      %let under    = %substr(%upcase(&under),1,1);
      %if        %quote(&justify)=L %then %let at=1;
      %else %if %quote(&justify)=C %then %let at=ROUND((LS2-LEN)/2);
      %else                            %let at=(LS2 - LEN);
      %let zeros    = %substr(%upcase(&zeros),1,1);
      %local tof count txt format chapter;
      %if %quote(%qupcase(&target))=CC
         %then %let tof = SUBSTR(LINE,1,1)='1';
      %else %if %quote(&target)= %then %let tof = 0;
```

```
%else %let tof = INDEX(LINE,&TARGET);
%if %quote(&style) = PAGE %then %do;
   %let txt=%str('Page '||COMPRESS(PUT(PAGE,8.)));
   %let count = 0;
   %end;
%else %if %index(%quote(&style),%str(.)) %then %do;
   %let chapter = %scan(&style,1,%str(.));
   %let format  = %scan(&style,2,%str(.));
   %let txt=%str("&chapter"||'.'||LEFT(PUT(PAGE,&format..)));
   %let count = 0;
   %end;
%else %if %quote(&style) = SAS %then %do;
   %let txt=%str(left(PUT(PAGE,8.)));
   %let count = 0;
   %end;
%else %if %quote(&style) = PAGEOF %then %do;
   %let txt=%str('Page '||COMPRESS(PUT(PAGE,8.))||' of '||
        COMPRESS(PUT(PAGES,8.)));
   %let count = 1;
   %end;
%else %if %quote(&style) = BRIEF %then %do;
   %let txt=%str(compress(PUT(PAGE,8.))||' of '||
        COMPRESS(PUT(PAGES,8.)));
   %let count = 1;
   %end;
PROC PRINTTO;
   RUN;
DATA _NULL_;
   LS2    = &LS + 1;
   PAGES  = MAX(&fpage  + 0 - 1 , 0);
   PAGE   = MAX(&fpage  + 0 - 1 , 0);
   ADJUST = MAX(&adjust + 0 , 0);
   SKIP   = MAX(&skip   + 0 , 0);
   MINUS  = -1;
   LENGTH CC $1 SUBLINE $200 TXT $200;
%if %quote(&target)¬=  & &count %then %do;
   INFILE FT&__unit__.F001 EOF=EOF1 LENGTH=LENGTH1;
   DO WHILE(1);
      INPUT @1 LINE $VARYING200. LENGTH1;
      IF &tof THEN PAGES + 1;
      END;
 EOF1:
   %end;
   INFILE FT%eval(&__unit__+1)F001 EOF=EOF2 LENGTH=LENGTH2;
   FILE PRINT NOPRINT;
   DO WHILE(1);
      INPUT @1 LINE $VARYING200. LENGTH2;
      CC = SUBSTR(LINE,1,1);
      SUBLINE = SUBSTR(LINE,2);
      LENGTH3 = LENGTH(SUBLINE);
   %if %quote(&under) = Y %then %do;
      IF INDEX(SUBLINE,REPEAT('_',&underlen-1)) THEN CC = '+';
      %end;
      PUT @1 CC $CHAR1. @;
      IF CC='1' THEN DO I = 1 TO SKIP;
         PUT / @1 ' ' @;
         END;
      IF &tof THEN DO;
         PAGE + 1;
         TXT = &txt;
         LEN = LENGTH(TXT);
         SUBSTR( SUBLINE , &at , LEN ) = TXT;
         LENGTH3 = LENGTH(SUBLINE);
         END;
      PUT @2 +ADJUST SUBLINE $VARYING200. LENGTH3;
```

```
      %if %quote(&zeros) = S %then %do;
         IF INDEX(SUBLINE,'0') THEN DO;
            SUBLINE = TRANSLATE(SUBLINE,' ',COLLATE(0,199),
                   ' ',COLLATE(200,239),' ',COLLATE(241,255));
            SUBLINE = TRANSLATE(SUBLINE,'/','0');
            PUT '+' @2 + ADJUST SUBLINE $VARYING200. LENGTH3;
            END;
         %end;
         END;
       EOF2:
         FILE LOG;
         PUT / "NOTE: MACPAGE numbered pages &fpage to " PAGES
             / 'NOTE- ' skip= adjust=;
         STOP;
      RUN;
   %end;
%mend MacPage;
```

MACRO-BASED REPORT GENERATOR
by ANTHONY B. KREAMER

ABSTRACT

The macro presented in this paper is intended for end-users who wish to use "PUT" statements to generate reports, but do not want to spend a lot of time counting columns to make sure everything fits nicely within the available space. The macro takes the variables that the user supplies for the report and calculates the BESTFIT within the 132 available columns, henceforth; macro %BESTFIT was created.

Macro BESTFIT calls several other macros in determining the appropriate column locations of each variable. This paper will discuss each of the sub-macros and how they interrelate to produce a nice formatted report.

INTRODUCTION

Generating reports using PUT statements can be very tedious and time consuming. Often users plan what their reports look like on some kind of spread sheet that contains 132 columns so as to be sure everything fits within the available space. If a user has a report encompassing many variables, more than one page may be necessary. If more than one page is generated, ID variables are a good idea so each observation may be easily identified on each page.

Macro **%BESTFIT** solves all these problems. It calculates the number of pages depending on how many variables are in the report and in what order they are to appear. Moreover, it enables the user to specify which variables are ID variables and on which page thay are to be placed.

SUB-MACROS

%BESTFIT consists of several sub-macros that determine the page on which to put the variables, what columns to put them in, and how much extra space is available.

%INITLZE initializes the following macro variables:

DSN	Data Set Name
SEARCH	Upper bound LINESIZE
STRTID **ENDID**	Start - End of ID Variables
STRT **END**	Start - End of other Variables
VARLIST	List of the SAS® variables that are to be in the report
TITLES	Labels associated with each sas® variable in VARLIST above.

Below is an example of the values each of the above macro variables may hold :

```
%LET DSN=GRADES;
%LET SEARCH=132;

%LET STRTID=1;
%LET ENDID=2;
%LET STRT=3;
%LET END=5;

%LET VARLIST=SOCNUM/NAME/GRADE/COURSE/AVG;
%LET TITLES=SOCIAL SECURITY*NUMBER/
         STUDENT*NAME/
         GRADE*LEVEL/
         COURSE*NAME/
         AVERAGE;
```

Notice that the value of VARLIST contains 5 SAS® variables from the GRADE data set. Consequently, TITLES contains labels for each variable. Each label spans 2 rows with an asterisk (*) denoting the split much like a split character of PROC PRINT.

The variables in VARLIST appear in the order in which they will appear in the report. The values of STRTID and ENDID indicate that there are two ID variables; in this case, SOCNUM and NAME respectively. STRT and END refers to the remaining variables.

The value of SEARCH informs BESTFIT of the number of columns in which the variables in VARLIST must fit. In this case, 132 columns.

MACRO-BASED REPORT GENERATOR
by ANTHONY B. KREAMER

%SETUP takes the values of **VARLIST** and TITLES and scans them to create macro variables **VAR1**, **VAR2**, ..., **VAR&N** and TITLE1, TITLE2, ..., **TITLE&N** respectively. In the aforementioned example, **VAR1=SOCNUM** and **TITLE1=SOCIAL SECURITY*NUMBER**. Thus far the variables in the report have been defined as have the order in which they will appear and their labels.

%HEADINGS takes the values of TITLE1, TITLE2, ..., **TITLE&N** and scans for the asterisk which serves as a split character. Thus, two labels can be generated for a given variable. For example, **HEADINGS** takes the value of TITLE1 above and creates macro variables TITLE11 and TITLE12 which have the value of **SOCIAL SECURITY** and **NUMBER**, respectively. If no split character is found, then **TITLE&N**.1 is blank and **TITLE&N**.2 has the value.

Below is a layout of what has been defined thus far.

```
SEARCH
1                                              132
•---------------------------------------------•
•                                              •
•   TITLE11   TITLE21   . . .   TITLE&N.1      •
•   TITLE12   TITLE22   . . .   TITLE&N.2      •
•                                              •
•    VAR1      VAR2     . . .    VAR&N         •
•                                              •
•                                              •
```

%MAXTITLE calculates how much space is required for **TITLE&N**.1 and **TITLE&N**.2 and places that with the most characters in macro variables **MAXTITLE&N**.

%MAXVALUE calculates the maximum space required for SAS® variable **VAR&N** and places the result in macro variable **MAXVAL&N**.

%MAX compares the length of **MAXTITLE&N** and **MAXVAL&N** and places the larger in **MAX&N**. **MAX&N**; therefore, determines which takes up more space, the label for a given sas variable or the value of the variable.

At this point, all the necessary macro variables for BESTFIT are created. Pagination, as well as column locations, are determined by **%EXTRA**. Also, if the maximum space that is used on a particular page is less than **&SEARCH** (132), **%EXTRA** will attempt to use all of **&SEARCH** spaces by inserting "extra" spaces between variables. Let us take a closer look at **%EXTRA**.

%EXTRA assumes one page will be generated. If more are needed, the macro increments the macro variable &PAGE. The order of **&VARLIST** is crucial in determining the order of the variables on the report and in turn what page they appear on. For example, let us assume that the maximum space required to fit all five variables is 150. **%EXTRA** will know that **&SEARCH** is less than 150 and tell us two pages are required. Here is where the use of ID variables come into play. Two variables had been previously designated as ID variables (**SOCNUM** and **NAME**). They will appear on both pages so as to easily identified each observation. The remaining three variables will be placed in the appropriate columns of their respective pages.

If the variables **SOCNUM**, **NAME**, and **GRADE** take up a total of 120 spaces and the next variable (**COURSE** in our case) takes up 20 spaces, **%EXTRA** will put **COURSE** on the next page along with **SOCNUM** and **NAME**. Since the first three variables take up 120 spaces and there are **&SEARCH** (132) available spaces as defined by **&SEARCH**, twelve spaces are left to be dispersed within the columns of the report.

```
          3 SPACES     3 SPACES
1            •            •            120        132
•-----------------------------------------------------•
•                                        •            •
•TITLE11      TITLE21      TITLE31•  12 SPACES•
•TITLE12      TITLE22      TITLE32•  LEFT OVER•
•                                        •  TO BE     •
•                                        •  DISPERSED•
• VAR1         VAR2         VAR3     •  IN REPORT•
•                                        •            •
•SOCNUM       NAME         GRADE     •            •
•                                        •            •
•----------------------------------------•-----------•

             •            •
          9 Total      9 Total
           Spaces       Spaces
```

%EXTRA allocated the 12 extra spaces evenly between the columns; ie, it added 6 extra spaces between columns 1 & 2 and 6 spaces between 2 & 3.

MACRO-BASED REPORT GENERATOR
by ANTHONY B. KREAMER

We now know that there are 12 spaces left over, 3 variables on page one of the report which means 2 columns we can add these extra spaces to. This means that we can add an additional 6 spaces to the already 3 spaces that we originally accounted for. This will evenly spaces out the final report by using all the available space.

Once **%EXTRA** determines how much extra space to add, it will then call macro **%STRTEND** which calculates the starting and ending columns for every variable. If we know where a variable will start and end, we can calculate the center point between the two. At this time, we already know what the maximum space for the labels and values of a particular variable, so we can now calculate the centers for the titles and values. **%STRTEND** will create the following macro variables:

S&PAGE&N	Start position of variable **&N** on **&PAGE**.
E&PAGE&N	End position of variable **&N** on **&PAGE**.
CNTR&PAGE&N	Center location between **S&PAGE&N** and **E&PAGE&N**.
CVAL&PAGE&N	Center location for variable **&N**. This is calculated based on the variables maximum space. ie. **MAXVAL&N**
CTL&PAGE&N.1	Center location of label one for variable **&N**.
CTL&PAGE&N.2	Center location of label two for variable **&N**.

%BESTFIT now has what it needs to produce the report. It knows the number of pages it needs to generate the report, what sas® variables go on a particular page, the column locations of each variable and of each heading for a given variable. All **%BESTFIT** does is produce the "PUT" statements for each variable and each heading.

The nice thing about this application is that all a user needs to do to generate a report is change the macro **%INITLZE** to their specific needs.

SAS is a registered trademark of the SAS Institute., Cary, NC, USA.

AUTHOR'S ADDRESS:

Anthony B. Kreamer
Roy F. Weston, Inc.
Weston Way
West Chester, PA 19380

MACRO-BASED REPORT GENERATOR
by ANTHONY B. KREAMER

```
%MACRO INITLZE;
  OPTIONS MPRINT LINESIZE=132;
  LIBNAME IN 'C:\SAS\SUGI';
  DM 'LOG;ZOOM;'LOG;
  %LET DSN=IN.GRADE;
  %LET SEARCH=132;

  %LET STRTID=1;
  %LET ENDID=2;
  %LET STRT=3;
  %LET END=16;

  %LET VARLIST=SOCNUM/NAME/GRADE/COURSE/TEST1/TEST2/TEST3/TEST4/TEST5/
              TEST6/TEST7/TEST8/TEST9/TEST10/AVG/FINALGRD;

  %LET TITLE=SOCIAL SECURITY*NUMBER/STUDENT*NAME/GRADE*LEVEL/COURSE*NAME/
            TEST SCORE*#1/SCORE*#2/EXAMINATION*#3/TEST*NUMBER 4/
            MIDTERM*TEST #5/TEST*SIX/SCORE*NUMBER SEVEN/TEST*#8/
            TEST*SCORE #9/TEST*#10/AVERAGE/FINAL*GRADE;
  %SETUP;
%MEND INITLZE;
```

```
%MACRO SETUP;
  %DO I=&STRTID %TO &END;
    %LET VAR&I=%SCAN(&VARLIST,&I,/);
    %LET TITLE&I=%SCAN(&TITLE,&I,/);
  %END;
  %HEADINGS
%MEND SETUP;
```

```
%MACRO HEADINGS;
  %DO I=&END %TO &STRTID %BY -1;
    %LET POS=%INDEX(&&TITLE&I,*);
    %IF &POS NE 0
    %THEN %DO;
            %DO J=1 %TO 2;
              %LET TITLE&I&J=%SCAN(&&TITLE&I,&J,*);
            %END;
          %END;
    %ELSE %DO;
            .LET TITLE&I.1=%STR( );
            %LET TITLE&I.2=&&TITLE&I;
          %END;
  %END;
  %MAXTITLE
%MEND HEADINGS;
```

```
%MACRO MAXTITLE;
  %DO I=&STRTID %TO &END;
    %LET MAXTITLE=0;
    %DO J=1 %TO 2;
      %LET LEN=%LENGTH(&&TITLE&I&J);
      %IF &LEN GT &MAXTITLE
      %THEN %LET MAXTITLE=&LEN;;
    %END;
    %LET MAXTTL&I=&MAXTITLE;
  %END;
  %MAXVALUE
%MEND MAXTITLE;
```

```
%MACRO MAXVALUE;
  %DO I=&STRTID %TO &END;
    %PUT %STR(      ) I = &I;
    DATA TEMP; SET &DSN;
      KEEP &&VAR&I LEN;
      LEN=LENGTH(TRIM(LEFT(&&VAR&I)));
    PROC MEANS NOPRINT;
      VAR LEN;
      OUTPUT OUT=TEMP MAX=MAXVAL;
    DATA TEMP; SET TEMP;
      CALL SYMPUT("MAXVAL&I",(TRIM(LEFT(MAXVAL))));
    RUN;
  %END;
  %MAX
%MEND MAXVALUE;
```

```
%MACRO MAX;
  %DO I=&STRTID %TO &END;
    %IF &&MAXTTL&I GE &&MAXVAL&I
    %THEN %LET MAX&I=&&MAXTTL&I;
    %ELSE %LET MAX&I=&&MAXVAL&I;;
  %END;
  %RESULTS(VAR/TITLE/MAXTTL/MAXVAL/MAX)
%MEND MAX;
```

MACRO-BASED REPORT GENERATOR
by ANTHONY B. KREAMER

```
%MACRO RESULTS(PAR);
  %LET LIST=&PAR;
  %DO K=1 %TO 5;
    %LINES(2)
    %LET L=%SCAN(&LIST,&K,/);
    %DO I=&STRTID %TO &END;
      %IF &L=TITLE OR &L=CTITL OR &L=CTTL
      %THEN %DO;
              %DO J=1 %TO 2;
                %PUT %STR(      )&L&I&J = &&&L&I&J;
              %END;
            %END;
      %ELSE %DO;
              %PUT %STR(      )&L&I = &&&L&I;
            %END;
    %END;
  %END;
  %LINES(2)
  %EXTRA
%MEND RESULTS;
```

```
%MACRO LINES(NL);
  %DO W=1 %TO &NL;
    %PUT %STR(      );
  %END;
%MEND LINES;
```

```
%MACRO EXTRA;
  %LET PAGE=1;
  %LET J=0;
  %LET SPACES=3;
  %LET T=1/;
  %LET SUM=&MAX1;
  %IF &ENDID EQ &STRTID
  %THEN %LET IDMAX=&SUM;
  %DO I=%EVAL(&STRTID+1) %TO &END;
    %LET J=%EVAL(&J+1);
    %LET TSUM=&SUM;
    %PUT %STR(      )SUM = &SUM;
    %LET SUM=%EVAL(&SUM + &&MAX&I + &SPACES);
    %IF &I EQ &ENDID
    %THEN %LET IDMAX=&SUM;
    %IF (&SUM GT &SEARCH)
    %THEN %DO;
            %LET F=&J;
            %LET EXTRA=%EVAL((&SEARCH - &TSUM) / (&J - 1));
            %PUT %STR(      )F = &F;
            %PUT %STR(      )PAGE = &PAGE;
            %PUT %STR(      )EXTRA = &EXTRA;
            %PUT %STR(      )T = &T;
            %STRTEND
            %LET T=;
            %DO R=&STRTID %TO &ENDID;
              %LET T=&T%STR(&R/);
            %END;
            %LET J=&ENDID;
            %LET PAGE=%EVAL(&PAGE + 1);
            %LET SUM=%EVAL(&IDMAX + &&MAX&I + &SPACES);
          %END;
    %IF &I EQ &END
    %THEN %DO;
            %LET EXTRA=%EVAL((&SEARCH - &SUM) / (&J));
            %LET J=%EVAL(&J+1);
            %LET F=&J;
            %LET T=&T%STR(&I/);
            %PUT %STR(      )SUM = &SUM;
            %PUT %STR(      )F = &F;
            %PUT %STR(      )PAGE = &PAGE;
            %PUT %STR(      )EXTRA = &EXTRA;
            %PUT %STR(      )T = &T;
            %STRTEND
          %END;
    %ELSE %LET T=&T%STR(&I/);
  %END;
%MEND EXTRA;
```

```
%MACRO STRTEND;
  %LET S&PAGE.1=1;
  %DO K=2 %TO &F;
    %LET N=%SCAN(&T,%EVAL(&K-1),/);
    %LET L=%EVAL(&K-1);
    %LET S&PAGE&K=%EVAL(&&S&PAGE&L + &&MAX&N + &SPACES + &EXTRA);
    %LET E&PAGE&L=%EVAL(&&S&PAGE&K - (&SPACES + 1) - &EXTRA);
    %LET CNTR&PAGE&L=%EVAL((&&S&PAGE&L + &&E&PAGE&L)/2);
    %LET CVAL&PAGE&L=%EVAL(&&CNTR&PAGE&L - (&&MAXVAL&N / 2) + %ADD);
    %DO A=1 %TO 2;
      %LET LEN=%LENGTH(&&TITLE&N&A);
      %LET CTL&PAGE&L&A=%EVAL(&&CNTR&PAGE&L - (&LEN/2) + %ADD);
    %END;
  %END;
  %LET NEW=%SCAN(&T,&F,/);
  %LET E&PAGE&F=%EVAL(&&S&PAGE&F + &&MAX&NEW -1);
  %LET CNTR&PAGE&F=%EVAL((&&S&PAGE&F + &&E&PAGE&F)/2);
  %LET CVAL&PAGE&F=%EVAL(&&CNTR&PAGE&F - (&&MAXVAL&NEW / 2) + %ADD);
  %DO A=1 %TO 2;
    %LET LEN=%LENGTH(&&TITLE&NEW&A);
    %LET CTL&PAGE&F&A=%EVAL(&&CNTR&PAGE&F - (&LEN/2) + %ADD);
  %END;

  %LINES(3)
  %PUT %STR(     )START POSITIONS AND ENDING POSITIONS;
  %PUT %STR(     )-----------------------------------;
  %LINES(1)
  %DO K=1 %TO &F;
    %PUT %STR(     )S&PAGE&K = &&S&PAGE&K                E&PAGE&K = &&E&PAGE&K;
    %LINES(1)
    %PUT %STR(                )CNTR&PAGE&K = &&CNTR&PAGE&K;
    %PUT %STR(                )CVAL&PAGE&K = &&CVAL&PAGE&K;
    %DO A=1 %TO 2;
      %PUT %STR(                )CTL&PAGE&K&A = &&CTL&PAGE&K&A;
    %END;
  %LINES(3)
  %END;
  %PUT %STR(     )-----------------------------------;
  %LINES(2)
  %BESTFIT
%MEND STRTEND;
```

```
%MACRO BESTFIT;
  DATA _NULL_; SET &DSN;
    FILE PRINT HEADER=H NOTITLES N=1;
    %PUT %STR(     )PAGE = &PAGE  T = &T  F = &F;
    PUT
    %DO C=1 %TO &F;
      %LET TT=%SCAN(&T,&C,/);
      %PUT %STR(     )C = &C   TT = &TT  CVAL&PAGE&C = &&CVAL&PAGE&C  VAR&TT = &&VAR&TT;
      %STR( )@&&CVAL&PAGE&C  &&VAR&TT
    %END;;
  RETURN;
  H: PUT /
     %PUT %STR(     )PAGE = &PAGE  T = &T  F = &F;
     %DO R=1 %TO 2;
       %DO C=1 %TO &F;
         %LET TT=%SCAN(&T,&C,/);
         %PUT %STR(     )R = &R  C = &C   TT = &TT  CTL&PAGE&C&R = &&CTL&PAGE&C&R  TITLE&TT&R = &&TITLE&TT&R;
         %STR( )@&&CTL&PAGE&C&R  "&&TITLE&TT&R"%STR( )
       %END;
       /
     %END;;
  RETURN;
  RUN;
%MEND BESTFIT;
```

A SAS® Macro Procedure To Summarize the Output of Logistic Regression Models

Benjamin I. Broder, University of Southern California School of Medicine
Chih-Ping Chou, University of Southern California School of Medicine

Abstract

A SAS program, LOGRPT, has been developed to summarize the results obtained from logistic regression. The summary presents the results from several logistic regression models, all with the same set of covariates, but with differing dependent variables. For each covariate the following information is provided: regression weights, their standard errors, odds ratios, and a one character indication of the significance level of each regression weight. To assess the fit of the entire model, the -2 Log Likelihood statistic and its p-value are also presented. This statistic has a chi-square distribution under the null hypothesis that all of the explanatory variables (covariates) in the model are zero. The LOGRPT program also allows users to specify a subset of covariates to be reported for comparison between models. The program uses the LOGISTIC procedure as well as SAS/IML and SAS macros to summarize the results. Making comparisons between several regression models is more efficient and error free when they are all presented on a single page, rather than scattered throughout many pages of SAS output.

Introduction

Binary and ordinal response categories arise in many fields of study. For example, presence or absence of disease in an epidemiologic study or severity of symptoms (mild, moderate, or severe) in a drug efficacy trial. Unlike standard linear regression, where we predict the level of the dependent variable given a set of independent variables, in studies such as these we often are interested in predicting the probability that the dependent variable has a certain value. Furthermore, the relationship of the covariates to this probability is in general multiplicative, rather than linear. We therefore use a logit transform of the risk of disease. In the following equation, P denotes the risk of disease, and y denotes the dependent variable for analysis:

$$Y=logit(P)=\log(\frac{P}{1-P}) \quad (1)$$

Equation 1 allows us to use linear regression by transforming a multiplicative relationship between the covariates into a linear one. Because P/(1-P) is known as the odds of disease, the logit transform is also known as the log odds transform. Finally, we have a standard linear regression equation:

$$Y=\alpha+\beta_1X_1+\beta_2X_2+...+\beta_pX_p+\epsilon \quad (2)$$

which can be solved using standard methods of linear regression.

Method

In epidemiologic research we often assess the effects of a given set of covariates on various outcome variables using equation (2). To assess the appropriateness of the entire model we can evaluate the -2 Log Likelihood statistic, which has a chi-square distribution under the null hypothesis that all the regression weights are zero. To investigate the impact specific covariates have on the model we evaluate the relative magnitude of the regression weights (parameter estimates) and their standard errors. These values are all presented in the LOGISTIC procedure's printed output, but this output can span 3 pages per model and therefore it is difficult to compare several models with each other. Creating summaries from the output datasets from the LOGISTIC procedure is insufficient, because although the maximum likelihood estimates of the parameters are present in the OUTEST output dataset, the standard errors are not, making interpretation difficult. In addition, no statistics assessing overall model fit exist in the OUTEST output dataset.

When comparing different models by examining many pages of output, the possibility for error is great. By using the LOGRPT program to summarize the results of the logistic regression, comparisons between models can be made in a more error-free manner. LOGRPT uses SAS macros and SAS/IML to produce the summaries. The OUTEST option in the LOGISTIC procedure yields the regression weights. The COVOUT option causes the covariance matrix of parameter estimates to be output. The diagonal of this matrix contains the variances (or square of the standard errors) of the parameter estimates. The -2 Log Likelihood statistic may be obtained by comparing the null model in which no covariates are included with the current model. The OUTPUT option provides the information necessary for the computation of this statistic.

The LOGRPT program allows users to include a large set of covariates in the models, but only to summarize statistics on a subset of these covariates. The summarized results are placed in a permanent file and are available to be included in a report.

Input Required for LOGRPT:

The LOGRPT program can be used on any system that supports SAS/IML and the SAS MACRO facility. The program will be attached, in Appendix 1. The following information must be provided by the user:

1. Input Data Set - including any necessary data transformations.
2. Output Destination - location of summarized output.
3. Model Specification - Separate lists of covariates (both reported and unreported) and dependent variables for the models. Details are given in Appendix 1.

Example

An example will be provided in Appendix 1 analyzing the effects of program vs control group on weekly alcohol use at two follow-up times (FALC_WK1 and GALC_WK1) while controlling for baseline use (AALC_WK1).cents. Two logistic regression models, one for each dependent variable, are assessed, each with the same set of independent variables. The covariates included demographic variables such as race, sex, and grade as well as baseline use of alcohol (AALC_WK1). Only the covariates {group, grade, sex, and baseline use} were compared in the summary. The summary output will also be demonstrated in Appendix 2.

Discussion

The advantages of the LOGRPT program are that several logistic models can be compared on a single page of output. Previously this would have required retyping to summarize the results, an often error-prone step. Furthermore, as the names of the dependent variables are included in the summary, the summary output can be included as a table in a report for publication with only minor modifications.

The authors may be contacted at:

University of Southern California School of Medicine
Department of Preventive Medicine
Institute for Health Promotion and Disease Prevention Research
1000 S. Fremont Ave. Suite 641
Alhambra, CA 91803-1358
(818) 457-4029 (Broder), (818) 457-4100 FAX

Appendix 1

```
%**************************************************
*                PROGRAM : LOGRPT.SAS              *
* PURPOSE: This program summarizes the results from logistic  *
*          regression models for several dependent variables with  *
*          the same set of covariates.              *
* USAGE:   Users must modify the lines at the end of this program  *
*          to specify (1) the dependent variables,   *
*          (2) covariates to be used in the regressions,  *
*          (3) the dataset to be used in the regression   *
*          (4) location of output file for summary output.  *
* PROGRAMMER:                                       *
*    Benjamin I. Broder                             *
*    created by modifying REGRPT which was written by   *
*    CHIH-PING CHOU & ERIC WANG                     *
* DATE CREATED: MAY 7, 1992.                        *
* DATE OF LAST REVISION: APRIL 19,1993.             *
**************************************************;
OPTIONS PS=58 LS=132;
*OPTIONS MLOGIC SYMBOLGEN MPRINT;
OPTIONS MPRINT;

%**-----------------------------------------------**
* The following LET and GLOBAL declaration macro statements are  *
* required input information, the values are passed from the   *
* user-modified section at the end of this file.    *
* 1. DEPVAR: Names of dependent variables.          *
* 2. NDEP:   Number of depvar.                      *
* 3. COVRPT: Names of independent variables to be reported.   *
* 4. NRPT:   Number of covrpt.                      *
* 5. COVNRP: Names of independent variables not to be reported. *
* 6. NNRP:   Number of covnrp.                      *
* 7. OSET:   Output sas datasets for each dependent variable.  *
*            These files are named from o1 to o&ndep, i.e.   *
*            01, 02, etc.                           *
**-----------------------------------------------**;
%global depvar covrpt covnrp ndep nrpt nnrp debug printsum;

%**-----------------------------------------------**
* Set DEBUG to be non-zero for debug information to be printed.  *
* Set PRINTSUM to be non-zero for the summary dataset to be     *
*   printed in the listing file in addition to the summary output  *
*   file being created. This can be useful because the summary   *
*   dataset has values, including Odds Ratios, Parameter Estimates,*
*   and P-values, to a greater precision than the summary output  *
*   file.                                           *
**-----------------------------------------------**;
%let debug=0;
%let printsum=0;

%**++++++++++++++++++++++++++++++++++++++++++++++++
* This macro will expand to nothing if the DEBUGVAR is equal to 0, *
* otherwise it will expand to its argument TXT. An explicit     *
* DEBUGVAR argument can be given if you want it only to expand  *
* to TXT under certain conditions.                  *
**++++++++++++++++++++++++++++++++++++++++++++++**;
%macro dbug(txt, debugvar=&debug);
  %if (&debugvar NE 0) %then %str(&txt);
%mend dbug;

%**++++++++++++++++++++++++++++++++++++++++++++++++
*  INIT   - Macro to do the needed initializations prior to running  *
*           running the regressions or reporting the results.   *
*  Arguments                                        *
*    DEPVARS  Used for the list of dependent variables. One regression *
*             will be run (and reported) for each dependent variable.  *
*    COVRPTS  Used for the list of independent variables (i.e.   *
*             covariates) that will be reported.    *
*    COVNRPS  Used for the list of independent variables (i.e    *
*             covariates) that will NOT BE REPORTED in the summary   *
*             output.                               *
**++++++++++++++++++++++++++++++++++++++++++++++**;
%macro
init(depvars=,covrpts=,covnrps=,debug=&debug,printsum=&printsum);

  %let DEPVAR = &depvars;
  %let COVRPT = &covrpts;
  %let COVNRP = &covnrps;

%**++++++++++++++++++++++**
*  INIT_ARR -- IML module to initialize some datasets  *
*              using arrays to set up the datasets.   *
**++++++++++++++++++++++**;
PROC IML;
%dbug(reset print;);
START INIT_ARR;

%**++++++++++++++++++++++++++++++++++++++++++**
*  V1 = array of dependent variable names           *
*  V2 = array of reported covariate variable names   *
*  V3 = array of not reported covariate variable names   *
**++++++++++++++++++++++++++++++++++++++++++**;
V1={&DEPVAR};
V2={&COVRPT};
V3={&COVNRP};

%**++++++++++++++++++++++++++++++++++++++++++**
*  NDEP = 1x1 Array containing Number of Dependent Variables   *
*  NDEP = 1x1 Array containing Number of Reported Covariates   *
*  NDEP = 1x1 Array containing Number of Not Reported Covariates *
*  NV = 1x3 array of all of the above 3 scalars.    *
**++++++++++++++++++++++++++++++++++++++++++**;
NDEP=NCOL(V1);
NRPT=NCOL(V2);
NNRP=NCOL(V3);
NV=NDEP||NRPT||NNRP;
CNAME={'NDEP' 'NRPT' 'NNRP'};

%dbug(PRINT NV [COLNAME=CNAME];);

%**+++++++++++++++++++++**
* Create an empty SAS dataset INF1 from the Array NV, with variable names
*   given in the array CNAME: i.e., variables named NDEP, NRPT, and NNRP.
* Then add a single observation to INF1 with values of the three variables *
*   equal to the values of NDEP, NRPT, and NNRP.    *
**+++++++++++++++++++++**;
CREATE INF1 FROM NV [COLNAME=CNAME];
APPEND FROM NV [COLNAME=CNAME];

FINISH INIT_ARR;
RUN INIT_ARR;
%dbug(proc contents data=inf1;);

%**++++++++++++++++++++++++++++++++++++++++++++**
*  Uses the values of the NDEP, NRPT, and NNRP variables in the INF1  *
*    dataset to assign values to the global macro variables with the  *
*    same names.                                    *
**++++++++++++++++++++++++++++++++++++++++++++**;
DATA INFO;
```

```
SET INF1;
CALL SYMPUT('NDEP',left(NDEP));
CALL SYMPUT('NRPT',left(NRPT));
CALL SYMPUT('NNRP',left(NNRP));
RUN;

%mend init;

%**+++++++++++++++++++++++++++++++++**
* OSET   -- Creates a series of names, all beginning with the same  *
*           substring and all ending in numbers ranging from 1 to the *
*           number passed as an argument.                             *
* ARGUMENTS-                                                          *
*   PREFIX - The prefix substring, remains the same for all generated *
*           strings.                                                  *
*   NUMBER - The number of generated strings to create.               *
* Sample Output -- %OSET(prefix=Z,number=3) yields the text: Z1 Z2 Z3
**+++++++++++++++++++++++++++++++++**;
%MACRO OSET(prefix=O,NUMBER=);
  %DO I = 1 %TO &NUMBER; &prefix&I %END;
%MEND OSET;

%**+++++++++++++++++++++++++++++++**
* Utility function used by the COLNAMES macro.                        *
**+++++++++++++++++++++++++++++++**;
%macro colname_(names) / parmbuff;
  %local i;
  %let first=1;
  %let stop = %length(&syspbuff);
  %do i = 1 %to &stop;
    %let colname = %scan(&syspbuff, &i);
    %if (%quote(&colname) NE) %then &colname&NUM;
    %else %let i = &stop;
  %end;
%mend colname_;

%**++++++++++++++++++++++++++++++**
* COLNAMES -- Creates a series of column names, each set of names ends
*           with the same number, and the number of sets to generate  *
*           is passed as an argument.                                 *
* ARGUMENTS -                                                         *
*   COLROOTS - The prefix roots for the column headings.              *
*   NUMBER   - The number of generated sets of strings to create.     *
* Sample Output -- %COLNAMES(colroots=EST OR,number=3) yields the
*               text:
*                 EST1 OR1 EST2 OR2 EST3 OR3                          *
**++++++++++++++++++++++++++++++++**;
%MACRO COLNAMES(COLROOTS=EST STE TRATIO P,N=);
  %DO NUM = 1 %TO &N; %COLNAME_(&COLROOTS) %END;
%MEND COLNAMES;

%**+++++++++++++++++++++++++++++++++
* REG    -- The macro that actually performs each logistic regression. *
*           This is called once for each regression to be performed.  *
*           After all of the calls on %REG are done, call %REPORT.    *
* ARGUMENTS -                                                         *
*   DVAR    - Dependent variable for this regression.                 *
*   MODELN  - Should be an unique integer for each regression, the first*
*           regression should have MODELN=1, the second would have    *
*            MODELN=2, and so on.                                     *
* Sample Calling Sequence --                                          *
*   %REG(DVAR=falc_wk1, MODELN=1)                                     *
*   %REG(DVAR=galc_wk1, MODELN=2)                                     *
*   %REPORT(OUTPUT=OUT1)                                              *
**++++++++++++++++++++++++++++++++**;
%MACRO REG(DVAR=,MODELN=);

%**++++++++++++++++++++++++++++++++**
* MNOUT dataset contains 1 observation, with the variable MDVAR
*   containing the mean of the dependent variable DVAR.
**++++++++++++++++++++++++++++++++**;
proc means mean data=DATA1 noprint %dbug(print);
  var &dvar;
  output out=mnout mean=mdvar;
%dbug(proc print data=mnout;)

%**++++++++++++++++++++++++++++++**
* The actual call on PROC LOGISTIC to perform the regressions, REGOUT
*   dataset, created by the OUTTEST statement, contains parameter     *
*   estimates as well as the estimated covariance matrix of the parameter*
*   estimates (because of the COVOUT option to PROC LOGISTIC). The
*   covariance matrix contains the variances, which are used to generate *
*   standard errors for the parameter estimates.                      *
* REGOUT2 dataset, created by the output statement, is used to calculate *
*   a Chi-Square value for model fit, i.e. how much the addition of the *
*   covariates improves the predictive power of the model.            *
**++++++++++++++++++++++++++++++**;
PROC LOGIST COVOUT DATA=DATA1 OUTEST=REGOUT
        %if (&debug = 0) %then noprint; ;
  MODEL &DVAR = %STR(&COVRPT)
          %STR(&COVNRP) / MAXITER = 100;
  output out=regout2 prob=phat;
%dbug(proc print data=regout;
    title "OUTTEST from &dvar= &covrpt &covnrp";);

%**++++++++++++++++++++++++++++++**
* THIS IS ONE OF THE DEPENDENCIES ON BINARY DEPENDENT
*   VARIABLES -- WE ASSUME ONLY 1 INTERCEPT VARIABLE
*   AND OBSERVATION (so we only keep 1 obs for the                    *
*   parameter estimates and NRPT+1 observations for the est. cov.     *
*   matrix). The part of the covariance matrix that represents        *
*   covariates that have been specified to be UNREPORTED is deleted.  *
**+++++++++++++++++++++++++++++**;
DATA O&MODELN;
SET REGOUT;
IF _N_ LE (&NRPT+2);
KEEP INTERCEP %STR(&COVRPT);

%**+++++++++++++++++++++++++++++++++
* The following calculations are used to calculate the equivalent of  *
*   the -2 Log L statistic in the PROC LOGISTIC output. Unfortunately *
*   PROC LOGISTIC does not allow this statistic to be output in an    *
*   output data set.                                                  *
+++++++++++++++++++++++++++++++**;
DATA LOGRPT;
SET REGOUT2 (KEEP = &DVAR PHAT);
IF _N_ = 1 THEN SET MNOUT;

Q=1-MDVAR;
T=1/Q-1;
ALPHA=-LOG(T);
IF &DVAR=. OR PHAT=. THEN DELETE;
PNHAT=1/(1+EXP(-ALPHA));
IF &DVAR=1 THEN PHAT=1-PHAT;
IF &DVAR=1 THEN PNHAT=1-PNHAT;
TPH=LOG(PHAT);
TPH=-2*TPH;
TNPH=LOG(PNHAT);
TNPH=-2*TNPH;
%dbug(proc print data=mnout; title "mnout - used to calculate -2 Log L";);

PROC MEANS SUM NOPRINT %dbug(PRINT);
  var tph tnph;
  output out=chisq sum=;
%dbug(proc print data=chisq; title "CHISQUARE";);

%**+++++++++++++++++++++++++++++++++
* Each CHISQR1, CHISQR2, etc. data set contains the -2 Log L value in *
*   the variable CHISQ, and the associated p-value in the variable P. *
**++++++++++++++++++++++++++++++**;
data chisqr&modeln;
  set chisq (keep = tph tnph);
  chisq = tnph - tph;
  p = 1 - probchi(chisq, &NRPT+&NNRP);
```

```
 drop tph tnph;
%dbug(proc print data=chisqr&modeln; title "CHISQUARE&modeln";);

%MEND REG;

%**+++++++++++++++++++++++++++++++++
* Create the first two lines of the output summary, they show what     *
*   dependent variables are being evaluated and what the columns mean. *
* Local variable WIDTH is dependent on what statistics are being printed*
*   and should be equal to the sum of the lengths of the format       *
*   specification in the PUT statement at the very end of the %REPORT  *
*   macro.                                                           *
* WIDTH    -- Width of one set of summary statistics for one regression.*
* OFFSET1  -- Offset from left margin of first dependent variable      *
*            name to be used as a label for one set of summary stats.  *
* OFFSET2  -- Offset from left margin of first set of column headings  *
*            (these will be repeated for each set of summary stats).   *
* Ex:      %header(&depvar)                                          *
* Used by %REPORT.                                                   *
**+++++++++++++++++++++++++++++++**;
%macro header(dvs=,width=20,offset1=15,offset2=8,
        hdr_str='    beta    SE    OR ');
 %header_(&dvs);
%mend header;

%macro header_(dvs) / parmbuff;
 %local i;
 %let first=1;
 %let stop = %length(&syspbuff);
 %do i = 1 %to &stop;
  %let fromvar = %scan(&syspbuff, &i);
  %if (&fromvar NE) %then
   put @(&offset1+((&i-1)*&width)) %str("&fromvar" @;);
  %else %let i = &stop;
 %end;
 %str(put;);
 %str(put @&offset2 &NDEP*&hdr_str);
%mend header_;

%**********************************************
* REPORT -- This is the macro that actually formats and outputs the    *
*         summary of the regressions.                                *
* Arguments -- The only argument is OUTPUT, which specifies an output
*         file by giving a file specifier. The OUTPUT argument should  *
*         correspond to a FILENAME statement (see below in the LOG1    *
*         macro).                                                    *
* Sample Calling Sequence:   %REPORT(OUTPUT=OUT1)
*
*******************;
%MACRO REPORT(OUTPUT=);

%* Data Set DATA1 (and DATA2) contain the data to be analyzed -- DATA1
 * is created in the LOG1 macro below.                           *;
DATA DATA2;
SET DATA1;

%**+++++++++++++++++++++++++++++++**
* ARRAYs and variables used in the creation of the summary report.     *
*   COVS     - Array of variables, each named after one of the         *
*            covariates.                                   *;
%*    DEPS   - Array of variables, each named after one of the         *
*            dependent variables.                          *;
%*   VARNCES - Array of variables, named VAR1, VAR2, etc., one for each
*            dependent variable, used to hold the values of the        *
*            variances of each of the dependent variables.        *;
%*   N_DVS   - Array of variables, named N_DV1, N_DV2, etc. one for each
*            dependent variable, used to hold the values of the        *
*            Ns for each logistic regression.                    *
**+++++++++++++++++++++++++++++++**;
ARRAY COVS %STR(&COVRPT) %STR(&COVNRP);
ARRAY DEPS %STR(&DEPVAR);
ARRAY VARNCES VAR1-VAR&NDEP;
ARRAY N_DVS N_DV1-N_DV&NDEP;

%**++++++++++++++++++++++++++++**
* The mean of the dependent variables calculated below must be on the  *
*   same set of observations as the logistic regressions, so all       *
*   observations with missing values for the covariates must be removed. *
**++++++++++++++++++++++++++++**;
DO OVER COVS; IF COVS=. THEN DELETE; END;

PROC MEANS N VAR NOPRINT %dbug(PRINT);
 VAR %STR(&DEPVAR);
 OUTPUT OUT=MEANOUT
  N=N_DV1-N_DV&NDEP VAR=VAR1-VAR&NDEP;
%dbug(proc print data=meanout;);

%**++++++++++++++++++++++++++++++**
* Data Set DATASUM contains all of the O1, O2, etc. datasets
   concatenated together. Each O1, ..., O&NDEP dataset contains the
   parameter estimates and estimated covariance matrix of the parameter
   estimates for reported covariates for each of the logistic regressions that
   run.                                                            *
**++++++++++++**;
DATA DATASUM;
SET %OSET(NUMBER=&NDEP);

%**+++++++++++**
* Data Set CHISQR contains all of the CHISQR1, CHISQR2, etc. datasets
*   concatenated together. Each CHISQR1, ..., CHISQR&NDEP dataset
*   the -2 Log L Chi-square statistic for one logistic model as well as *
*   the associated p-value.                                        *
**+++++++++++++++++++++++++++++**;
DATA CHISQR;
SET %OSET(prefix=CHISQR,NUMBER=&NDEP);

PROC IML;
START IML_RPT;
%dbug(reset print;);

%**++++++++++++++++++++++++++++++++++
* This is one of the dependencies on binary dependent              *
*   variables -- we assume only 1 intercept variable              *
*   so only add 1 to NRPT.                                    *
**++++++++++++++++++++++++++++++++**;
NDEP={&NDEP};
NRPT1={&NRPT} + 1;
NNRP={&NNRP};
NCOV=NRPT1+NNRP;

%**++++++++++++**
* Matrix REG contains all of dataset DATASUM, i.e. alternating 1 row of  *
*   parameter estimates from one regression, then the estimated covariance
*
*   matrix of the parameter estimates for the same regression, then the  *
*   parameter estimates for the next regression, followed by the cov.   *
*   matrix for the next regression, etc.                            *
* The size of the REG matrix is therefore                            *
*   # ROWS    = (# reported covs + 2) * (# DVs)                       *
*   # COLUMNS = (# reported covs + 1)                                *
**+++++++++++++**;
USE DATASUM;
READ ALL INTO REG;
 *
%**++++++++++++++++++++++**
* Matrix TVN contains values for the variances and total N for each    *
*   dependent variable. It is a column vector, where the first NDEP rows *
*   (i.e. elements 1 through NDEP) contain the Ns for each regression and *
*   the next NDEP rows (i.e. elements NDEP+1 through 2*NDEP) contain the
*   variances for each dependent variable.                          *
* Where NDEP = # of DVs = Number of dependent variables.               *
* The size of the TVN matrix is therefore (2 * NDEP) x 1              *
**+++++++++++++++**;
USE MEANOUT var { %oset(prefix=N_DV,number=&ndep)
```

```
             %oset(prefix=VAR,number=&ndep) };
READ ALL INTO TVN;

%**+++++++++++++++**
* Matrix CHISQRS contains values for the model fit statistic -2 Log L and *
*   the associated P-value for each regression. The first column contains *
*   the chi-square (-2 Log L) value and the second the p-value.           *
* The size of the CHISQRS matrix is therefore NDEP x 2                    *
**++++++++++++++++**;
USE CHISQR;
READ ALL INTO CHISQRS;

%**++++++++++++++**
* Matrices:                                                               *
*   RNAME   - Row vector containing labels for each of the summary rows.
*   N       - Column vector containing the Ns for each regression on each *
*             dependent variable.                                         *
*   V       - Column vector containing the variances for each dependent   *
*             variable.                                                   *
*   Colname - Specifies the summary variable names to be printed in the   *
*             summary report.                                             *
*             EST   - Parameter Estimates.                                *
*             STE   - Standard errors of parameter estimates.             *
*             OR    - Odds Ratio = Odds of dependent variable equal to 1  *
*                     if the parameter is = 1 (and all others are equal   *
*                     to 0) divided by odds if parameter=0.               *
*             LCI   - Lower limit of 95% confidence interval of OR.       *
*             UCI   - Upper limit of 95% confidence interval of OR.       *
*             TRATIO - T-ratio for parameter estimate.                    *
*             P     - P-value for the parameter estimate.                 *
**++++++++++++++++++++++++++++++++++**;
RNAME='INTERCEP'||{&COVRPT}||'NCOV/DF'||'N'||'-2LogL/P';
N=TVN[,1:NDEP];
V=TVN[,NDEP+1:(2*NDEP)];
COLNAME={ %COLNAMES(COLROOTS=EST STE OR LCI UCI TRATIO P,
N=&NDEP) };

%**+++++++++++++++**
` Scalars:                                                                *
'   I        - Specifies which dependent variable and regression we are   *
*              calculating summary statistics for (i.e. ranges from 1 to  *
*              NDEP -- the number of dependent variables.)                *
*   Est_Row  - Start row in REG matrix for parameter estimates of the     *
*              regression results currenltly being summarized.            *
*   Cov_Row  - Start row in REG matrix for estimated covariance matrix    *
*              of the reported covariates for the regression currently    *
*              being summarized.                                          *
*   End_Row  - End row in REG matrix for estimated covariance matrix      *
*              of the reported covariates for the regression currently    *
*              being summarized.                                          *
*   P        - Probability that a particular parameter estimate is actually*
*              zero and the estimated value has occurred by chance.       *
*                                                                         *
* Matrices:                                                               *
*   E        - Vector containing parameter estimates from a single        *
*              regression (i.e. for a single dependent variable.)         *
*   T        - Matrix containing estimated covarianc matrix for the       *
*              parameter estimates from a single regression (i.e. for a   *
*              single dependent variable.)                                *
*   S        - Vector from the diagonal of the T matrix above -- first it *
*              contains the variances of the parameter estimates, then    *
*              after taking the square root of each element it contains   *
*              standard errors of the parameter estimates.                *
*   T1       - Matrix of values to put in the summary table -- it         *
*              initially contains just the estimates, standard errors     *
*              of the estimates, t-ratios, and probabilities for a single *
*              regression, but then the summary values for the Total N for *
*              this regression, the number of covariates, and the -2 Log L *
*              statistic for the model are added as new rows.             *
*   TT       - Matrix of values to put in the summary table -- it         *
*              contains the values for Total N, number of covariates, and *
*              the -2 Log L model fit statistic.                          *
*   RST      - Matrix of values to put in the summary table -- made up of *
*              successive versions of T1 (one for each regression)        *
*              concatenated together horizontally.                        *
**++++++++++++++**;
DO I = 1 TO NDEP;
  Est_Row=(I-1)*(NRPT1+1)+1;
  Cov_Row=Est_Row+1;
  E=REG[Est_Row,];
  E=E';
  E=E*(-1);
  End_Row=Est_Row+NRPT1;
  T=REG[Cov_Row:End_Row,];
  S=VECDIAG(T);
  S=SQRT(S);
  OR=EXP(E);
  LCI=EXP((E-(1.96*S)));
  UCI=EXP((E+(1.96*S)));

%**+++++++++++++**
* By dividing the parameter estimates by their standard errors we get     *
*   a new vector T with (Number of reported covariates + 1) elements whose
*   elements have a T-distribution.                                       *
* The number of degrees of freedom for each of these elements is equal to
*   the total N for the regression minus the total number of covariates  *
*   minus 1 for the intercept (i.e. DF = TotalN - NRPT - NNRP - 1)        *
%**+++++++++++++++**;
  T=E/S;
  NN=N[1,I];
  DF=NN-NRPT1-NNRP;
  P=PROBT(T,DF);
  T1=(E||S||OR||LCI||UCI||T||P);
  VY=V[1,I];

%** TT IS USED FOR N and N_COV and the -2 Log L model fit statistic. *;
  TT=J(3,7,-99);
  TT[1,1]= (NCOV-1);
  TT[2,1]=NN;
  TT[3,1]=CHISQRS[I,1];
  TT[3,2]=CHISQRS[I,2];
  T1=T1//TT;
  RST=RST||T1;
END;

%**++++++++++++++++++++++++++++++++**
*  Dataset SUMMARY contains the data for the summary table from the       
*    matrix RST. The variable names are given by the COLNAME vector and   
*    each observation (row) has a label given by the RNAME vector.        *
**+++++++++++**;
CREATE SUMMARY FROM RST [ROWNAME=RNAME
COLNAME=COLNAME];
APPEND FROM RST [ROWNAME=RNAME];

FINISH;
RUN IML_RPT;

%**+++++++++++**
*  This is where the actual summary report gets output.                   *
* Because we have converted the matrix RST to the SAS Data set SUMMARY
* and REPORT the summary data is now stored 1 observation per line of the*
*  summary. Each column of the summary represents a different summary
* parameter and the columns are grouped by dependent variable. This means*
*  that there are different variables in the dataset for each dependent   *
*  variable: EST1 for the parameter estimates of the first DV, EST2 for   *
*  the parameter estimates of the second DV and so on.                    *
*  Several arrays of variable names are used, the variable names within   *
*    each of these arrays all take the form VARNAME1, VARNAME2, etc. up
*    through the number of dependent variables:                           *
*    EST     - Parameter estimates.                                       *
*    STE     - Standard errors of parameter estimates.                    *
*    OR      - Odds Ratio = Odds of dependent variable equal to 1 if the *
*              parameter is = 1 (and all others are equal to 0) divided   *
*              by the odds of DV=1 if parameter=0.                        *
```

```
*    LCI     - Lower limit of 95% confidence interval of Odds Ratio.    *
*    UCI     - Upper limit of 95% confidence interval of Odds Ratio.    *
*    TRATIO  - T-ratios for the parameter estimates.                    *
*    P       - P-values for the parameter estimates.                    *
*    SG      - Single character signifying the significance level of the *
*              parameter estimate: + p<.10, * p<.05, $ p<.01, ! p<.001   *
**+++++++**;
DATA REPORT;
SET SUMMARY;
FILE &OUTPUT;
ARRAY EST    %OSET(prefix=EST,NUMBER=&NDEP);
ARRAY STE    %OSET(prefix=STE,NUMBER=&NDEP);
ARRAY OR     %OSET(prefix=OR ,NUMBER=&NDEP);
ARRAY LCI    %OSET(prefix=LCI,NUMBER=&NDEP);
ARRAY UCI    %OSET(prefix=UCI,NUMBER=&NDEP);
ARRAY TRATIO %OSET(prefix=TRATIO,NUMBER=&NDEP);
ARRAY P      %OSET(prefix=P,NUMBER=&NDEP);
ARRAY SG  $  %OSET(prefix=SG,NUMBER=&NDEP);

format %do i=1 %to &NDEP; STE&I E10. P&I E10. %END; ;

label
 RNAME = "Row labels for summary output"
  %do i=1 %to &NDEP; EST&I = "Parameter Estimates of
%QSCAN(&COVRPT,&I)" %END;
  %do i=1 %to &NDEP; STE&I = "Standard Errors EST&I" %END;
  %do i=1 %to &NDEP; OR&I = "Odds Ratio from EST&I" %END;
  %do i=1 %to &NDEP; LCI&I = "Lower 95% confidence interval of OR&I"
%END;
  %do i=1 %to &NDEP; UCI&I = "Upper 95% confidence interval of OR&I"
%END;
  %do i=1 %to &NDEP; TRATIO&I = "T-ratios for significance of EST&I"
%END;
  %do i=1 %to &NDEP; P&I = "P-values for EST&I" %END;
    %do i=1 %to &NDEP; SG&I =
"1char-EST&I-+p<.10,*p<.05,$p<.01,!p<.001" %END;
;

%** Convert -99 (place-holders) in the summary data to missing values. *
*  Convert P-values from one-tailed to two-tailed tests.              *
*  Calculate values for the SG character indication significance level. *;
DO OVER STE;
IF TRATIO=-99 THEN TRATIO=.;
IF STE   =-99 THEN STE   =.;
IF OR    =-99 THEN OR    =.;
IF LCI   =-99 THEN LCI   =.;
IF UCI   =-99 THEN UCI   =.;
IF P  =-99 THEN P  =.;
SG=' ';
IF P>0.5 THEN P=1-P;
P=2*P;
IF P<0.10  THEN SG='+';
IF P<0.05  THEN SG='*';
IF P<0.01  THEN SG='$';
IF P<0.001 THEN SG='!';
IF P=.     THEN SG=' ';
END;

%** The PUT Statements can be modified as needed to provide identifying
** information. *;
KEEP RNAME EST1-EST&NDEP STE1-STE&NDEP OR1-OR&NDEP
    LCI1-LCI&NDEP UCI1-UCI&NDEP P1-P&NDEP SG1-SG&NDEP;
if (_N_ = 1) then do;
  now = datetime(); put "      LOGRPT1.OUT  at " now datetime18.;
  put "Logistic Regression of Drug Use adjusting for Standard Covariates";
  put "+ == p<.10, * == p<.05, $ == p<.01, ! == p<.001 Only for
parameter estimates";
  put "OR=Odds Ratio, beta=Parameter Estimate, SE=Standard Error of beta";
  put "-2LogL/P = Chi-Square model fit stat. (DF deg. of freedom)/P-value for
-2 Log L"; put ;
  %header(dvs=&depvar,width=20,offset1=15,offset2=8,
       hdr_str='    beta   SE    OR ');
end;
if RNAME='-2LogL/P'
then PUT (RNAME %COLNAMES(COLROOTS=EST STE OR SG, N=&NDEP))
   ($CHAR8. %do i=1 %to &NDEP; 7.2 E8. 4.0 $CHAR1. %END;);
else PUT (RNAME %COLNAMES(COLROOTS=EST STE OR SG, N=&NDEP))
   ($CHAR8. %do i=1 %to &NDEP; 7.2 6.2 6.2 $CHAR1. %END;);
%dbug(proc contents; PROC PRINT;,
    debugvar=%if ((&printsum ne 0) or (&debug ne 0)) %then 1;
          %else 0;);
%MEND REPORT;

%** THE FOLLOWING SECTIONS NEEDS TO BE REVISED BY USERS: *
*     The section labelled "DATA SET TRANSFORMATION"     *
*     and the arguments to the call on %LOG1 below.  +++++**;
%macro log1(lib=,outfile=,data=,depvars=,covrpts=,covnrps=,n=1,
            debug=,printsum=);
 LIBNAME in "&lib";
 FILENAME OUT&n "&outfile&n..out";

 %init(depvars = &depvars, covrpts = &covrpts, covnrps = &covnrps,
     debug = &debug, printsum = &printsum);
 data DATA1;
 set in.&data;

 %* PROVIDE THE DATA SET TRANSFORMATION SECTION HERE **;

 %* Macro LOG1_ is used by LOG1 to create the necessary calls on *
 *  the %REG macro, one for each dependent variable (i.e. once  *
 *  for each variable named in DEPVARS.)                    *****;
 %log1_(&depvars);
 %REPORT(OUTPUT=OUT&n);
%mend log1;

%macro log1_(dvs) / parmbuff;
 %local i; %let first=1;
 %let stop = %length(&syspbuff);
 %do i = 1 %to &stop;
  %let dv = %scan(&syspbuff, &i);
  %if (&dv NE) %then %REG(DVAR=&dv, modeln=&i);
  %else %let i = &stop;
 %end;
%mend log1_;

%** Specify the variables used in the regressions, as well as dataset *
*    used, library name, and output file. Do not quote the library   *
*    and output file names.                                          *
*   Specify DEBUG and/or PRINTSUM to print debugging information     *
*    and/or a printout of the summary dataset in the LISTING file.   *;
%LOG1(DEPVARS  = falc_wk1 galc_wk1 falc_wk2,
    COVRPTS  = group grade aalc_wk1 sex1,
    LIB      = /c/bbroder/sugi93/,
    OUTFILE  = /c/bbroder/sugi93/logrpt,
    DATA     = tst, debug = 1, printsum = 1);
RUN;
```

Appendix 2

```
      LOGRPT1.OUT  at   16APR93:10:17:58
Logistic Regression of Drug Use adjusting for Standard Covariates
+ == p<.10, * == p<.05, $ == p<.01, ! == p<.001 Only for betas
OR=Odds Ratio, beta=Parameter Estimate, SE=Standard Error of beta
-2LogL/P = Chi-Square model fit stat. (DF deg. of freedom)/P-val for -2 Log L

               falc_wk1          galc_wk1          falc_wk2
            beta  SE   OR     beta  SE   OR     beta  SE   OR
INTERCEP -1.93 0.23 0.15!  -1.77 0.22 0.17!  -1.93 0.23 0.15!
GROUP    -0.25 0.18 0.78   -0.20 0.17 0.82   -0.25 0.18 0.78
GRADE     0.25 0.18 1.28    0.16 0.18 1.18    0.25 0.18 1.28
AALC_WK1  1.58 0.60 4.84$   0.62 0.68 1.85    1.58 0.60 4.84$
SEX1      0.41 0.15 1.51$   0.59 0.15 1.81!   0.41 0.15 1.51$
NCOV/DF   5.00  .    .      5.00  .    .      5.00  .    .
N      1105.00  .    .   1007.00  .    .   1105.00  .    .
-2LogL/P 39.59 1.8E-07     36.42 7.8E-07.    39.59 1.8E-07.
```

Chapter 7 A Gallery of Macro Applications

A Program to Compute Odds Ratios and Confidence Intervals from LOGISTIC Output 278

Intermediate

Tasks: Illustrates an application that uses modular and generalized macro programming techniques.

Tools:
%DO, Iterative
%EVAL
%GLOBAL
%IF-%THEN / %ELSE
%LET
&& and &&& resolution
CALL SYMPUT
Macro parameters
Simple substitution

Automated Generation of Statistical Tables: Integration of Structured Programming and SAS Macros 282

Intermediate

Tasks: Illustrates an application that uses modular, generalized, and dynamic macro programming techniques.

Tools:
%GLOBAL
%LET
CALL SYMPUT
Macro parameters
Simple substitution

PLOTCORR: A SAS Macro for Appending Correlation and Regression Statistics to the PLOT or GPLOT Procedures 287

Intermediate

Tasks: Illustrates an application that uses generalized and dynamic macro programming techniques.

Tools:
CALL SYMPUT
Macro parameters
Simple substitution

Using the SAS System in the Pharmaceutical Industry: Project Setup and Standardization for the Analysis of Clinical Trial Data 291

Advanced

Tasks: Uses the macro facility to retrieve values from the operating system. Uses macro quoting functions to ensure accurate text comparisons in the macro facility.

Tools:
%SYSGET
&& macro variable references
CALL SYMPUT
Macro quoting
Nested macro function calls

SAS Macros for Converting between ARC/INFO Import/Export Files and SAS Data Sets 296

Advanced

Tasks — Illustrates an application that uses modular, generalized, and dynamic macro programming techniques.

Tools — %DO, Iterative
%EVAL
%LET
%LOCAL / %GLOBAL
%PUT
&& resolution
CALL SYMPUT
Complex substitution
Macro parameters
Macro quoting
Simple substitution

SAS Macros for Source Program Tracking 302

Advanced

Tasks — Illustrates an application that uses generalized and dynamic macro programming techniques.

Tools — %CMS
%IF-%THEN / %ELSE
%INDEX
%INPUT
%LENGTH
%LET
%LOCAL
%STR
%SUBSTR
%UPCASE
Macro parameters
Macro quoting
Simple substitution

SHORTCUTS TO CUSTOMIZE CLINICAL TRIAL REPORTS

Aileen L. Tsien, Carter-Wallace Inc.

ABSTRACT

Accuracy, efficiency and flexibility are essential to research in all fields. This paper illustrates ways to customize clinical trial reports with little programming or editing efforts as well as to automate the production of a series of reports. Although written in the context of clinical research, the general approach to tailoring and mechanizing report production described in this paper is applicable also to other research disciplines.

INTRODUCTION

Usually in clinical research, many studies are performed on a single product and there is a need to generate a series of similar reports for the product. These reports generally have a similar format, with certain relevant pieces of information extracted from statistical procedure output. Producing such customized reports can be a labor intensive task because such information cannot easily be output from procedure statements or DATA _NULL_ statements. Sometimes, one has to type in the relevant information in a specified format, and a second person has to read and verify it. Still the end result does not look aesthetically coherent, because some results are typed in while others are directly output from SAS® listings. At other times, DATA steps are used to design the final output, but this approach requires counting and hardcoding columns, and the questions of efficiency and flexibility arise. The goals of data processing in clinical research or in any other research settings is to maintain data integrity and yet retain efficiency and flexibility.

PROGRAMMING TECHNIQUES

This paper covers the following approaches to generate customized reports:

1. Extracting certain information from statistical procedures for restructuring the output,
2. Avoiding the need to edit SAS® listings,
3. Avoiding the need to count and hardcode columns,
4. Using macros and format libraries to produce a series of reports of the same analysis with one program,
5. Producing all title pages at once.

1. EXTRACTING CERTAIN INFORMATION FROM SAS® PROCEDURES FOR RESTRUCTURING THE OUTPUT

Statistical procedure statements generally output listings in a pre-defined format. In addition, some statistical procedures do not output all the statistics into a file. To obtain those statistics for customized report writing, one can use PROC PRINTTO to route the output of a SAS® job into a different file and then read from the file the necessary information for producing reports in a specific format. Since PROC GLM is one of the most frequently used procedures to analyze clinical research data, it is used here to illustrate a way of obtaining statistics that cannot be directly output into a file.

```
FILENAME SASLIST 'sasout.lst';
     /* The FILENAME statement associates the name 'SASLIST'
        with an external file named 'sasout.lst'. */

PROC PRINTTO NEW PRINT=SASLIST;
     /* The PRINTTO procedure routes the output of the
        following GLM procedure to a file reference named
        'SASLIST'. The option NEW is used to clear any
        information in a file if the file already exists, rather than
        appending to the output in an existing file. */
RUN;
PROC GLM DATA=A;
     CLASS FYSICIAN TRT;
     MODEL TEST=FYSICIAN TRT
              FYSICIAN*TRT/SS3;
     LSMEANS TRT/STDERR PDIFF;
RUN;
PROC PRINTTO;
     /* Ends the routing of output to the file named 'sasout.lst'
        and routes the output back to a standard SAS® print file.
        */
RUN;
```

Suppose the desired information is the p-values of the contrast between two treatment groups and placebo. These values cannot be obtained directly from an OUTPUT statement, but are available from the PROC GLM listing of Least Squares Means table:

```
          SAS  14:47 MONDAY, SEPTEMBER 18, 1989
         GENERAL LINEAR MODELS PROCEDURE
              LEAST SQUARES MEANS

TRT          TEST      STD ERR     PR> |T|        LSMEAN
            LSMEAN     LSMEAN    HO:LSMEAN=0     NUMBER

TRT1      3.78901234  0.07896543   0.0001           1
TRT2      2.93456789  0.08765234   0.0001           2
PLACEBO   2.87654321  0.08123456   0.0001           3

          PR > |T|  HO: LSMEAN(i)=LSMEAN(j)

          i/j         1          2          3
          1           .        0.1234     0.5678
          2         0.1234       .        0.2345
          3         0.5678     0.2345       .
```

The following data step illustrates how to extract the necessary information from the SAS® listing that has already been routed to and saved in the output file named 'sasout.lst'.

```
DATA X;
     INFILE 'sasout.lst';
          /* The INFILE statement identifies the file
             'sasout.lst' to be read by the INPUT statement. */
     INPUT ANYNAME $ @;
          /* The trailing @ holds the line pointer on the current
             input line when the data line is read by the next
             INPUT statement. */
     IF ANYNAME='i/j' THEN DO;
          /* Search for the string 'i/j' because 'i/j' is a unique
             identifier appearing shortly before the probability
             values. */
          INPUT /// DUMMY PROB1 PROB2
PROB3;
               /* Skip the current line and the next two
                  lines, as indicated by the three slashes,
                  and then read in the first value (i.e. 3) as
                  DUMMY, the second value (0.5678) as
                  PROB1, the third value (0.2345) as
                  PROB2, and the fourth value (.) as
                  PROB3. */
          KEEP PROB1 PROB2 PROB3;
               /* Keep only the probability values that
                  are a contrast between the first
                  treatment and placebo (PROB1), a
                  contrast between the second treatment
                  and placebo (PROB2), and a contrast of
                  the placebo by itself (PROB3). */
     OUTPUT;
          /* Output the probability values into a file created in
             the DATA statement named X. */
     END;
```

The file X contains the desired information. It can be merged with any data file to produce a customized report.

2. AVOIDING THE NEED TO EDIT SAS® LISTINGS

Once the analysis is output, it is time consuming to locate the probability levels that are significant, for example, at the .05 level, and to manually put an asterisk after them. But such process can be automated with PROC FORMAT.

```
PROC FORMAT;
     PICTURE PROB    LOW-0.05    ='9.9999*'
          /* For any value equal to or below 0.05, literally
             write out those numbers and put an asterisk after
             them. */
                     0.05<-HIGH  ='9.9999 '
                         /* Any value greater than
                            0.05 will be written literally
                            without an asterisk. */
          .                      ='   .    ';
                         /* Missing values are
                            represented by a dot. */
RUN;
```

To try out the above format statement, associate the variable that contains probability values with the above format by means of the FORMAT statement (e.g. FORMAT VARNAME PROB.;). The following is an example:

```
DATA X;
     INPUT VARNAME;
VARNAME=ROUND(VARNAME,.0001);
     /* Round off the probability values to 4 decimal places. When
        probability values are output into a file with PROC
        PRINTTO, they generally have more than 4 decimal
        places. In order to be consistent with pre-defined SAS®
        statistical procedure listings, which generally have
        probability values carried out to 4 decimal places, the
        ROUND function is illustrated here. */
CARDS;
0.234531
0.057892
.
0.622035
0.770087
0.020000
0.022342
;
PROC PRINT;
FORMAT VARNAME PROB.;
RUN;
```

The SAS® listing varies depending on the type of computer used, but the listing will appear similar to the following:

```
OBS        PROB
1          0.2345
2          0.0579
3            .
4          0.6220
5          0.7701
6          0.0200*
7          0.0223*
```

3. AVOIDING THE NEED TO COUNT AND HARDCODE COLUMNS

Frequently, there is a need to prepare summary tables with a lengthy list of data that include visit numbers, medication names, physicians' center identification, subjects' identification, subjects' personal data, and test results at different time periods. For the sake of readability and parsimony, it would be best to include all variables for each observation in a wrap-around fashion rather than separating the data into several listings. For example, the following is the desired output format to list all the data:

```
FIRST DOSE, MAXPOWER
Physician=98765 Subject=1 Age=17 Sex=Female Weight=120
         HR 0   HR 3   HR 4   HR 5   HR 6   HR 7
 TEST1   2.45   2.60   2.39   2.98   3.20   3.66
 TEST2   2.67   2.82   2.96   2.66   3.06   3.21
 TEST3   2.87   2.95   2.99   3.22   3.56   3.64
 TEST4   1.98   2.70   2.69   3.01   3.08   3.07

2 WEEKS, MAXPOWER
Physician=98765 Subject=1 Age=17 Sex=Female Weight=120
         HR 0   HR 3   HR 4   HR 5   HR 6   HR 7
 TEST1   2.12   2.73   2.56   2.78   3.11   3.23
 TEST2   2.34   2.37   2.69   2.82   3.33   3.61
 TEST3   2.37   2.86   2.32   3.20   3.29   3.56
 TEST4   2.28   2.98   2.72   3.21   3.12   3.51

and so on
      .
      .
      .
```

PROC PRINT has limitations for producing such reports because it can fit observations on a single line only, it provides little control over where variables are placed on an output page, and it cannot print constant texts in a certain line of output if the texts are not labels. On the other hand, to customize the listings with DATA _NULL_ steps requires intricate work when the report is prepared, and also when minor modifications are necessary. Mainframe users are blessed with PROC QPRINT. However, PROC QPRINT is not available to PC or HP workstation users. One other option is to use PROC FORMS, which is available to users of all operating systems. Although often treated as a procedure for printing mail labels, PROC FORMS provides fast and flexible ways to write customized reports. The following example shows the display layout capabilities of PROC FORMS. A major problem of PROC FORMS is that it does not display variable names or labels, but this problem can be counteracted by creatively using the PUT function and PROC FORMAT to provide variable names, labels, or explanatory text.

```
PROC FORMAT;
    VALUE  TRT 1='MAXPOWER'
               2='MAXSTREN'
               3='PLACEBO';
    VALUE  $SEX    'M'='MALE'
                   'F'='FEMALE';
    VALUE   VISIT   1='FIRST DOSE,'
                    2='2 WEEKS,'
                    3='4 WEEKS,';
    VALUE   HOURS   1='HR 0'
                    2='HR 3'
                    3='HR 4'
                    4='HR 5'
                    5='HR 6'
                    6='HR 7';
RUN;

DATA A;
    SET DAT.PERM;
NEWFYSI='Physician='||PUT(FYSICIAN,5.);
    /* Create a new variable, NEWFYSI, by concatenating (||)
       the string 'Physician=' with the values of the variable
       FYSICIAN. The variable FYSICIAN is defined as a
       numeric variable that has 5 digits. */
NEWSUBJ='Subject='||PUT(SUBJ,3.);
NEWAGE='Age='||PUT(AGE,3.);
NEWSEX='Sex='||PUT(SEX,$SEX.);
    /* The variable SEX is a character variable ($), and its format
       is defined above in the PROC FORMAT. */
NEWWT='Weight='||PUT(WEIGHT,3.);
H1=1; H2=2; H3=3; H4=4; H5=5; H6=6;
    /* Create the values for hours so that each test is labelled
       with the corresponding hours. */

PROC FORMS DATA=A SKIP=2 WIDTH=80;
    /* The option SKIP=2 skips two lines between each form unit.
       Each form unit consists of the lines specified below. The
       width=80 option specifies the page width to be 80. */
LINE 1 VISIT TRT/PACK;
    /* The pack option removes extra blanks so that each value is
       separated by one space. */
LINE 2  NEWFYSI NEWSUBJ NEWAGE
        NEWSEX NEWWT/PACK;
LINE 3 H1-H6/I=14;
    /* The option i=14 indents the line by 14 spaces. */
LINE 4 TST1 TA0 TA3-TA7/I=3;
    /* The option i=3 indents the line by 3 spaces. */
LINE 5 TST2 TB0 TB3-TB7/I=3;
LINE 6 TST3 TC0 TC3-TC7/I=3;
LINE 7 TST4 TD0 TD3-TD7/I=3;
FORMAT TRT TRT. VISIT VISIT. H1-H6 HOURS.;
TITLE2 'DEMOGRAPHIC INFORMATION AND
TEST RESULTS';
TITLE3 'BY VISIT, TREATMENT, PHYSICIAN AND
SUBJECT';
RUN;
```

4. USING MACROS AND FORMAT LIBRARIES TO PRODUCE A SERIES OF REPORTS OF THE SAME ANALYSIS WITH ONE PROGRAM

A major goal in using the SAS® System to analyze clinical trials is to attain flexibility. Since clinical studies generally vary in terms of the number of treatments, the number of visits, and/or the number of hours, it is necessary to accommodate variations in study design and, at the same time, maintain consistency in the reports.

Instead of writing one program for each study protocol, macros and external format libraries are used to write one program for all studies.

a. One Program for Each Study:

```
DATA STEP STATEMENTS..........

PROC TRANSPOSE DATA=A OUT=B
       NAME=VISIT;
       BY FYSICIAN TRT PAT;
       VAR VISIT2 VISIT4 VISIT6 VISIT9;
              /* Change the number of visits for each protocol. */
       ID TESTS;
RUN;

PROC SORT  DATA=B;
       BY VISIT TRT;
RUN;

PROC SUMMARY DATA=B;
       BY VISIT TRT;
       VAR TEST0 TEST3-TEST7;
              /* Change the number of tests for each protocol. */
       OUTPUT OUT=C MEAN=HR0 HR3-HR7
              /* Change the number of hours for each protocol. */
                                   N=N0 N3-N7;
RUN;

OTHER PROC STATEMENTS..........
```

For each study, there will be a slightly different program with the correct number of visits, treatments, or hours entered, and with label formats changed. Therefore, for each kind of analysis, there will be several programs differing only in the number and labels of treatments, visits and hours. In order to save space and time and to make programming jobs more manageable, one program can be written for all studies by means of SAS® macros and format libraries.

b. One Program for All Studies:

First, store macro and format statements peculiar to a protocol in an external format library.

```
LIBNAME S1234 'ssd1234';
     /* The LIBNAME statement locates the directory where the
        permanent SAS® data sets are stored. */
%LET NV=4;       /* Let the number of visits equal to 4. */
%LET NH=6;       /* Let the number of hours equal to 6. */

     /* Because the number of visits and the number of hours are not
        consecutive, the following is a way to get around the problem.
        */

%LET VS1=2;  %LET VS2=4;  %LET VS3=6;
%LET VS4=9;
     /* Let the first visit be visit 2, the second visit be visit 4, the
        third visit be visit 6, and the fourth visit be visit 9. */
%MACRO VISIT(NAME1);
     /* The macro VISIT can be invoked with any parameter
        assigned as NAME1. */
     %DO V=1 %TO &NV;
          /* The iterative %DO statement generates visit
             values from 1 to 4, because NV is given the
             value of 4 in the previous LET statement. */
          &NAME1&&VS&V
               /* The value assigned as NAME1 will be
                  a prefix.  The second macro variable
                  reference &V will be resolved before
                  the first macro variable reference &VS
                  is resolved.  For example, if NAME1 is
                  assigned to be VIS, the first iteration
                  of the DO loop will resolve V as 1, and
                  VS1 as 2, because VS1 is assigned to be
                  2 in the LET statement.  The constant
                  text produced is a combination of the
                  prefix VIS and the macro variable
                  reference 2, thus VIS2.  As the DO loop
                  continues to execute, the texts VIS4,
                  VIS6 and VIS9 will be generated. */
     %END;
%MEND VISIT;

%LET HR1=0;  %LET HR2=3;  %LET HR3=4;
%LET HR4=5;  %LET HR5=6;  %LET HR6=7;
%MACRO HOUR(NAME2);
     %DO H=1 %TO &NH;
          &NAME2&&HR&H
     %END;
%MEND HOUR;

PROC FORMAT;
     VALUE VIS      2='FIRST DOSE'
                    4='2 WEEKS'
                    6='4 WEEKS'
                    9='7 WEEKS';
     VALUE $HOURS        'TEST0'='HR 0'
                         'TEST3'='HR 3'
                         'TEST4'='HR 4'
                         'TEST5'='HR 5'
                         'TEST6'='HR 6'
                         'TEST7'='HR 7';
RUN;
```

These macros and formats need to be created once for each protocol. They can later be included in one common program for all protocols with the statement:

```
%INC 'm1234.fmt';
     /* The above macros and formats are stored in a file named
        m1234.fmt and are included.  For PC users, any name can
        be used, as long as the filename is not more than 8
        characters and the file extension is not more than 3
        characters.  For mainframe users, the macros and formats
        would be stored in a file with the file extension MACLIB.
        */
```

The common programming statements for all protocols would be as follows:

```
%MACRO ALL;

DATA STEP STATEMENTS..........

PROC TRANSPOSE DATA=A OUT=B
       NAME=VISIT;
       BY FYSICIAN TRT PAT;
       VAR %VISIT(VIS);
            /* The resolution of the macro VISIT varies
               according to the external format library
               included below. */
       ID HOURS;
RUN;

PROC SORT DATA=B; BY VISIT TRT;
RUN;

PROC SUMMARY DATA=B;
       BY VISIT TRT;
       VAR %HOUR(TEST);
OUTPUT OUT=C MEAN=%HOUR(HR)
                    N=%HOUR(N);
RUN;

OTHER PROC STATEMENTS..........

%MEND ALL;

%INC 'm1234.fmt';
     /* Each external file included contains the macros and
        formats for a protocol. One can include as many external
        files as necessary to run the same program. The program
        needs to be run only once to obtain the results of all the
        protocols included. */
%ALL;
     /* Invoke the macro ALL to execute the above program. */

%INC 'm2345.fmt';
%ALL;

%INC 'm3456.fmt';
%ALL;

etc.
   .
   .
   .
```

The same analysis with the correct labels and number of treatments, visits and hours will automatically be produced for each study, without the need to create, edit and store many programs.

5. PRODUCING ALL TITLE PAGES AT ONCE

Once all the reports have been produced, there is usually a need to insert a title page in front of each report. One can prepare the title pages with a typewriter or a word processor. However, to simplify the task, the SAS® System can handle all title pages in one program through the use of macros.

```
%MACRO TITLES;

TITLE ' ';
     /* The TITLE statement suppresses the SAS® System from
        automatically outputting the word SAS® on the first title
        line. */
TITLE7 "STUDY NO. &SNUM/PROTOCOL NO.
&PNUM              &SYSDATE
";
     /* The quote ends on a different line in order to left justify the
        title. Double quotes are used for the macros to resolve.
        Current system date (SYSDATE) is used. The titles start at
        line 7. */
TITLE8 'TABLE 1';
TITLE9 'DEMOGRAPHIC INFORMATION AND
TEST RESULTS';
TITLE10 'BY VISIT, TREATMENT, PHYSICIAN
AND SUBJECT';
DATA _NULL_;
     /* This step will put the title on a new page. */
FILE PRINT;
PUT ' ';
RUN;

TITLE7 "STUDY NO. &SNUM/PROTOCOL NO.
&PNUM              &SYSDATE
";
TITLE8 'TABLE 2';
TITLE9 'PULMONARY FUNCTION TESTS';
TITLE10 'PERCENT CHANGE FROM PREDOSE
BASELINE';
DATA _NULL_;
FILE PRINT;
PUT ' ';
RUN;

TITLE7 "STUDY NO. &SNUM/PROTOCOL NO.
&PNUM              &SYSDATE
";
TITLE8 'TABLE 3';
TITLE9 'BACKUP MEDICATION USAGE';
TITLE10 'BY VISIT AND TREATMENT';
DATA _NULL_;
FILE PRINT;
PUT ' ';
RUN;

%MEND TITLES;
```

```
OPTIONS NONUMBER NODATE PS=50 LS=74;
    /* Title pages do not need to be numbered or dated, thus the
       options NONUMBER and NODATE are used.  The
       pagesize(PS) and linesize(LS) options used here assume
       that the printing is portrait; they can be modified to fit
       individual needs. */

/* The above three title pages will be created for each of the three
   study protocols designated below. */

%LET SNUM=1234;     %LET PNUM=789;
    /* Specify the study number to be 1234 and the protocol
       number to be 789. */
%TITLES;
    /* Invoke the macro named TITLES. */

%LET SNUM=2345;     %LET PNUM=678;
%TITLES;

%LET SNUM=3456;     %LET PNUM=567;
%TITLES;
```

APPLICATIONS TO THE PHARMACEUTICAL INDUSTRY AND BEYOND

The SAS® System can be quite versatile for outputting results in user-defined formats. This paper demonstrates three main ideas for producing customized reports. These ideas deal with shortcuts in:

1. retrieving a certain piece of information from pre-defined output of SAS® statistical procedures without having to manually leaf through several pages of the output,
2. avoiding the need to edit SAS® listings, or the need to count and hardcode columns,
3. generating a series of reports for all studies with one program while accommodating for differences in the design of each study.

The techniques described above not only deal with some common problems in writing customized reports for clinical research, but also serve as a stimulus for readers to come up with similar techniques. Such techniques are very helpful in mechanizing the production of research results in a variety of industries. Examples are: in the automobile industry where similar reports are to be generated for different carlines; and in major business corporations where similar sales and expense reports are to be produced regularly for various products.

Acknowledgment:

Special thanks to John F. Pauls, director of Statistical Services at Carter-Wallace Inc., for editing this paper.

For additional information, contact:

Aileen L. Tsien
Carter-Wallace Inc.
Half Acre Road
Cranbury, NJ 08512

Producing Multiple Graphs Using Macros
60% Code Reduction

Madelyn A. Remsburg
U.S. Army Medical Research Institute of Infectious Diseases

SAS/GRAPH® used with macros improves efficiency and reduces code in the production of multiple graphs. This technique allows the creation of template programs that become dynamic with the use of macros. The parts of the program that change most frequently are represented as macro reference variables and modified, as needed, in one convenient place. An excellent data source to display and utilize this technique is in the research and development area. Typical research and development data have several variables measured at specified time points. Normally, means and standard errors of all variables of comparison groups are displayed graphically against each time point -- generally as a simple plot: X*Y=Z. This is done at the onset of analysis so that the researcher and statistician may have a quick "look see" at which variables should be examined more closely. "Quick" is the operative word. By use of macros, these graphs can be produced, revised, and reproduced quickly and easily either on hardcopy or screen display.

HOW? Using PC SAS® and PC SAS/GRAPH® , this technique can be submitted interactively or batch. A source code template program and a macro code file must be developed and saved. The source code template program contains all of the SAS® code used to produce one graph, including titles, footnotes, goptions, and libnames. The template program must begin with "%MACRO XX" and end with "%MEND XX" (XX being an optional name). Also included in the program are macro reference variables, standard variable names proceeded by an ampersand (&), which are placed at strategic points. These variables will be replaced with actual values referenced in the macro code file. The macro code file assigns values by use of the keyword "%LET" for each macro reference variable in the source code program. Each macro reference variable in the template program must be listed in the macro code file with an appropriate value. If the value is hard code, be sure that the code is syntactically correct. At the end of each sequence of values, "%MM" (with NO ";") is entered. This executes the macro. After the source code template program and the macro code file is complete, submit the source code, then the macro code. The source code submission will simply check code for syntax errors and set in the macro XX. The source code template program only needs to submitted once per SAS® session. The macro code submission will execute the code program for the number of sequences that are included in the macro code. Revisions are easily made by editing the macro code file, then resubmitting only the macro code file. This technique is more easily understood by actual example on the following pages.

CAUTION: When a macro reference variable is included in a title or name statement, DOUBLE QUOTES must be used.

The views of the author does not purport to reflect the positions of the Department of the Army or the Department of Defense.

Madelyn A. Remsburg
Armed Forces Medical Intelligence Center
Automation Management Division
Fort Detrick
Frederick, MD 21701-5004
(301) 663-7581

SOURCE CODE PROGRAM

```
%MACRO MM;
GOPTIONS DEVICE=EGAL COLORS=(BLACK RED GREEN
      BLUE) ;
LIBNAME YY 'C:\MYLIB\DATA';
LIBNAME ZZ 'C:\MYLIB\GH';
TITLE1 'SAMPLE STUDY OF DRUG XX';
FOOTNOTE1 J=L "&SET";
SYMBOL1 C=BLUE V=NONE I=STD1MJT L=1
      MODE=INCLUDE;
SYMBOL2 C=RED V=NONE I=STD1MJT L=3 MODE=INCLUDE;

PROC GPLOT GOUT=ZZ.&SET DATA=YY.TEST;
      AXIS1 LABEL=(A=90 R=0 "&VAR DEPARTURE FROM
               BASELINE &PAREN") &ORDER MINOR=(N=1);
      AXIS2 LABEL=(H=1 'DAYS POST TREATMENT')
               MINOR=(N=1);
PLOT &VAR*DAY=GROUP/HAXIS=AXIS2 VAXIS=AXIS1
               NAME="&VAR";
RUN;
%MEND MM;
```

MACRO CODE FILE (4 sequences)

```
%LET VAR=RBC;
%LET ORDER=ORDER=(-2 TO 1 BY 1);
%LET PAREN=(X10 );
%LET SET=SET1;
%MM
%LET VAR=WBC;
%LET ORDER=ORDER=(-8 TO 4 BY 2);
%LET PAREN=(X10 );
%LET SET=SET1;
%MM
%LET VAR=HCT;
%LET ORDER=ORDER=(-10 TO 4 BY 2);
%LET PAREN=(%);
%LET SET=SET1;
%MM
%LET VAR=PLT;
%LET ORDER=ORDER=(-100 TO 400 BY 100);
%LET PAREN=(X10 );
%LET SET=SET1;
%MM
```

** See next page for actual graph output.

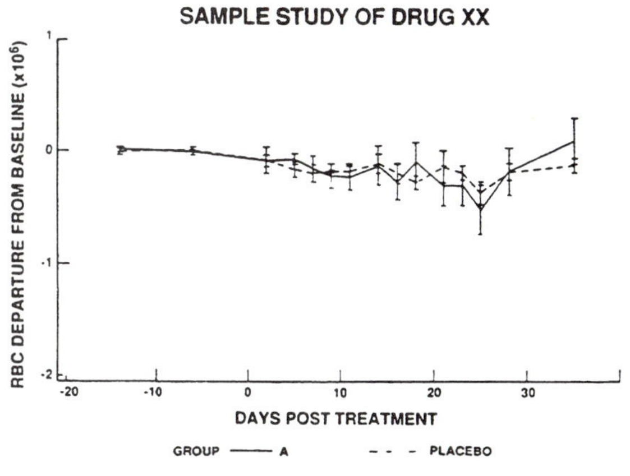
SAMPLE STUDY OF DRUG XX
RBC DEPARTURE FROM BASELINE (x10⁶)
DAYS POST TREATMENT
GROUP —— A
- - - PLACEBO
Set 1

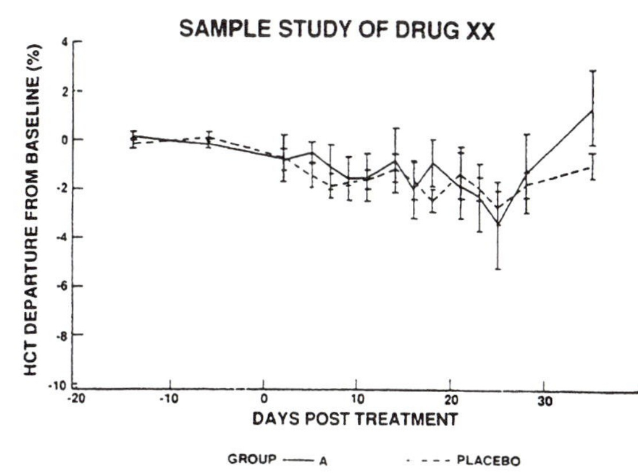
SAMPLE STUDY OF DRUG XX
HCT DEPARTURE FROM BASELINE (%)
DAYS POST TREATMENT
GROUP —— A
- - - PLACEBO
Set 1

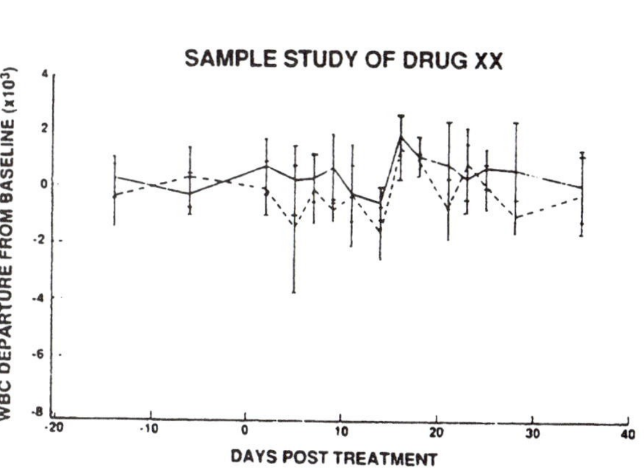
SAMPLE STUDY OF DRUG XX
WBC DEPARTURE FROM BASELINE (x10³)
DAYS POST TREATMENT
GROUP —— A
- - - PLACEBO
Set 1

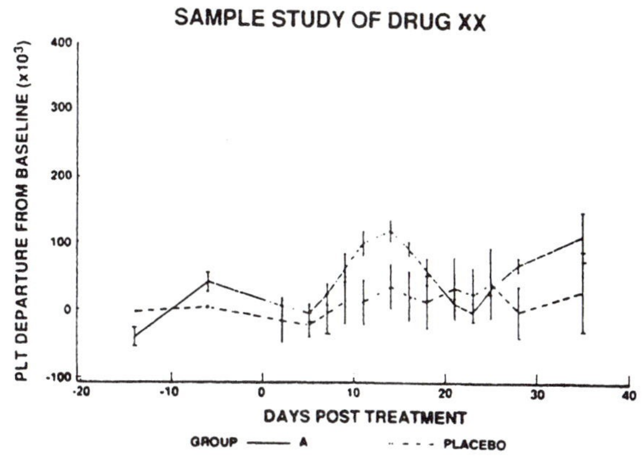
SAMPLE STUDY OF DRUG XX
PLT DEPARTURE FROM BASELINE (x10³)
DAYS POST TREATMENT
GROUP —— A
- - - PLACEBO
Set 1

The Generation of a Series of Annotated and Templated Statistical Graphs Using SAS® Macros

Susan J. Kenny Ph.D., Centers for Disease Control and Prevention, Atlanta, GA 30341

ABSTRACT

This paper describes the strategy used to automate the production of a series of annotated and templated statistical graphs. Seven macros, written with the SAS® software, are used in this approach. The first macro, %MINMAX, determines the minimum and maximum values for the X and Y axes over the range of plot coordinates. Using these values, appropriate sizes for the axes increments are determined. These macro variables are passed to two macros, %PLOT1 and %PLOT2, that produce X-Y plots for the macro specified variables of &X and &Y. The %ANNO macro utilizes an output data set from PROC MEANS to place descriptive statistics within a template to the side of the graphic display. Two additional macros, %TITLE and %DESCR are used to produce the graph title and additional annotated descriptive text. The %TREPLAY macro places the graphic streams into the appropriate template panels and produces the hard copy output. The procedures described here can be easily modified to a variety of research and business situations.

INTRODUCTION

Serial graphs are frequently required to present scientific and business data analysis reports. When a series of related graphic output is produced, several considerations must be made. If the axes are to be uniform throughout the series then the maximum and minimum x and y values must be determined over the entire range of values. When each single output consists of several templated graphs that display different variables, proper labelling of subtitles and axes must occur. Titles need to contain the proper figure number and specific conditions for the display. When faced with the production of a large number of individualized graphs, it becomes tedious to do each one separately. Such a situation is ideal for the use of the MACRO facility available in the SAS system software.

This paper presents a strategy for producing a series of templated and annotated statistical graphs which are used to summarize the results of statistical research. In brief, the focus of the research was to describe the distribution of a parameter in a statistical model under a combination of five conditions. Each condition has several values under investigation: three sample sizes, two event probabilities, two true parameter values, two types of independent variable, and three method of utilizing an independent variable. Since the focus of the research is to compare the three methods of utilizing the independent variable, it is desirable to have all of these graphs on one page. Each of the three graphs, however, require individual annotation and subtitles. A main title that describes the simulation conditions is needed for the entire page. Thus, for any one series of graphical displays, there are 24 (3*2*2*2) composite graphs to be produced, each with at least three templated graphs containing unique annotation and labelling.

The SAS macros and the general approach used to produce the graphical display shown in Figure 1 are presented. Since the top half of the figure is similar in form to the bottom half, the set of macros is used twice to produce the entire page. Each half of the page is a composite of five templates; three for graphical displays and two for annotated text. After both halves are produced, one additional template is defined as the entire page to allow placement of the figure title at the top of the page. Thus, the entire figure is a composite of 11 templates. The salient features of the macros used to produce the display are presented.

METHODS

In order for the X and Y axes of the graphs to be uniform, the macro, %MINMAX, was developed (see appendix). This macro uses the output from PROC MEANS and the CEIL and FLOOR functions to determine the integer values for the minimum and maximum values of X and Y for each of the three methods under investigation. An appropriate axis increment is determined by first considering the difference between the maximum and minimum values. When an axis increment is too small relative to this difference, the SAS system will stop processing and report an error message that 'the axis could not be fit as specified'. To avoid this error, an appropriate increment value is computed based upon the size of the MAX-MIN difference. The minimum and maximum values are then adjusted to be multiples of this increment. Using the call SYMPUT function, the maximum, minimum, and increment values, &XMAX, &XMIN, &INCR, are made available for use in subsequent plotting macros.

To create the three statistical graphics, the %PLOT1 and %PLOT2 macros are used. The %PLOT1 macro produces the square scatter plot and two calls of the %PLOT2 macro produce the marginal frequency distribution graphs that share an axes with the scatter plot. These two macros are similar in their approach since the plot statement in the GPLOT procedure in SAS/GRAPH utilizes macro variables to specify the desired X and Y variables. The axes statements in both macros use the previously determined minimum, maximum, and increment values. During production of the graphic streams, a description of each graph is created using a combination of the specified macro variables. This description references each graph when the GREPLAY window is opened.

Within the %PLOT2 macro, the labelling and increment values of the axes is suppressed. This is done because distortion or illegibility of text can occur when graphic output is placed in an irregularly sized template. As a solution to this problem, a template panel is defined that overlays the three statistical graphs produced by the %PLOT1 and %PLOT2 macros. The macro, %DESCR, is then used to place the text '%', '3', and the two titles of the frequency distribution graphs at the appropriate location on the graphic display. The text strings used for the graph titles are macro variables. Since the template is of a uniform size, minimal distortion of this text occurs.

To the right side of three statistical graphs in Figure 1, descriptive text is generated using the macro %ANNO. The descriptive statistics are obtained, in part, from the output data set of the MEANS procedure (not shown). An annotate data set is created which places macro defined headings and appropriate statistics in column form. The entire macro %ANNO is not given in the appendix due to its length and relative simplicity.

Since each composite graph is one figure in a manuscript, it is necessary for the figure heading to contain both a unique figure number and the specific simulation conditions being displayed. To automate the production of the figure heading, the macro %TITLE is used. The variables for this macro includes the figure_number and simulation conditions. This graphic stream is replayed through a template that encompasses the entire page, thus minimizing any distortion and producing text that is similar to typed text.

To facilitate the production of the set of graphics for one half of a page, all of the above macros were rolled into one comprehensive macro, %GPH, as follows:

```
%MACRO GPH(lib,dsn,cat,vert,catlabel);
   %MINMAX(lib=&LIB,dsn=&DSN);
   %PLOT2(lib=&LIB,dsn=&DSN,wald=w1_x1);
   %PLOT2(lib=&LIB,dsn=&DSN,wald=w1_&CAT);
   %PLOT1(lib=&LIB,dsn=&DSN,cat=&CAT);
   %DESCR(vert=&VERT);
   %ANNO(lib=&LIB,dsn=&DSN,cat=&CAT,
         catlabel=&CATLABEL);
%MEND GPH;
```

This macro initializes the values of the macro variables that reference the SAS data library, the data set name, the variables to be plotted and summarized, and the appropriate labels for the graphs. To produce the entire one page figure, two calls of the %GPH macro, followed by the %TITLE macro, are necessary. For example, the macro submission to produce Figure 1 is as follows:

```
%GPH(N2,N50_3_0,A1,
      WALD FOR MEAN CUTPOINT,MEAN);
%GPH(N2,N50_3_0,F1,
      WALD FOR FIXED CUTPOINT,FIXED);
%TITLE(50,0.03,0,55);
```

The individual macros are ordered within %GPH so that the graphic streams are generated in an order which correspondes to the template panel number in which they will appear. Since each graphic stream has associated descriptive text which describes the simulation conditions, browsing through the catalog or replaying individual graphs of interest is facilitated.

To create the final composite graph, the macro %TREPLAY is used. Since the graphs are placed within the SAS graphic catalog in an order that corresponds to the template panel number in which they will appear, this replaying is done with a simple %DO loop. Macro variables are used to specify the first and last stream to be selected for replaying. This allows for any one or several composite graphs to be generated with a specific call to the macro.

CONCLUSION

The production of serial graphs is not a new problem and has been discussed by other authors. The use of SAS macros for axes determination were addressed by Joseph and Horman (1988), Lovell (1989) and Murto-(1990). Remsburg (1989), Lovell (1989), and Joseph and Horman (1988) discuss approaches for production of annotated serial graphs. The use of the SAS macros, coupled with the annotate and template facilitiies, undoubtedly will continue to provide powerful tools for producing complex statistical and business graphics.

REFERENCES

Joseph, J. and Horman, T. (1988), "Generation of Serial Reports and Graphs in a Production Environment," *Proceedings of the Thirteenth Annual SAS Users Group International Conference,* 13, 401-403.

Lovell, R. (1989), "You Too Can Produce and Customize Complex Graphs Using the Annotate Facility and the GSLIDE Procedure with Release 6.03 of SAS/GRAPH Software," *Proceedings of the Fourteenth Annual SAS Users Group International Conference,* 14, 629-634.

Murto, M. S. (1990), "An Automated, Intelligent Algorithm for GPLOT Procedure and PLOT Procedure Graphics Axis Scaling," *Proceedings of the Fifteenth Annual SAS Users Groups International Conference,* 15, 1150-1154.

Remsburg, M. A. (1989), "Producing Multiple Graphs Using Macros 60 Percent Code Reduction," *Proceedings of the Fourteenth Annual SAS Users Group International Conference,* 14, 1166-1167.

ACKNOWLEDGMENTS

I would like to thank Andrew J. Cucchiara and Scott R. Pitts for their invaluable expertise and suggestions in the development of this application.

AUTHOR CONTACT

The author may be contacted for questions or comments:

Susan J. Kenny, PhD
Division of Diabetes Translation
Centers for Disease Control and Prevention
4770 Buford Highway NE, MS K-10
Atlanta, GA 30341
(404)-488-5042

email: sjk3@ccdddt1.em.cdc.gov

APPENDIX

```
/*************************************************************************/
%MINMAX: This macro determines the minimum, maximum, and
axis increment values across a range of data sets. Declaring these
variables as global macro variables allows them to be referenced
in subsequent plot macros. The macro variables, lib and dsn,
reference the SAS library and the data set name to use.
/*************************************************************************/

%MACRO MINMAX(lib,dsn);
%global xmin xmax ymax incr;
proc means data=&lib..&dsn noprint;
var w1_x1 w1_a1 w1_f1;
output out=minmax min=minx1 mina1 minf1
      max=maxx1 maxa1 maxf1;
run;
data _null_; set minmax;
maxx=ceil(max(maxx1,maxa1,maxf1));
minx=floor(min(minx1,mina1,minf1));
if maxx-minx>10 then do;
  if mod((maxx-minx),2) ne 0 then maxx=maxx+1; inc=2;
end;
else if maxx-minx>5 then do;
  if mod((maxx-minx),1) ne 0 then maxx=maxx+0.5; inc=1;
end;
else inc=0.5;
call symput ('xmax',left(put(maxx,5.1)));
call symput ('xmin',left(put(minx,5.1)));
call symput ('incr',left(put(inc,3.1)));
run;
%MEND MINMAX;

/*************************************************************************/
%PLOT1 and %PLOT2: These 2 macros use the values
determined by %MINMAX to define the axes. They are used to
produce the 3 statistical graphs of Figure 1. %PLOT1 produces the
larger scatter plot and %PLOT2 produces the 2 side frequency
plots.
/*************************************************************************/

%MACRO PLOT1(lib,dsn,cat);
axis4 label=none value=(h=3) minor=none
      order=(&xmin to &xmax by &incr) length=2.1 in;
axis5 label=none value=(h=3 r=0 a=90) minor=none
      order=(&xmin to &xmax by &incr) length=2.1 in;
symbol1 v=plus h=1 c=red;
proc gplot data=&lib..&dsn gout=&lib..waldn1;
plot w1_&cat*w1_x1/haxis=axis4 vaxis=axis5
              des="w1_&cat*w1_x1";
title;
run; quit;
%MEND PLOT1;

%MACRO PLOT2(lib,dsn,wald);
data frq; set &lib..&dsn(keep=&wald);
 &wald=round(&wald,0.05 );
run;
proc freq data=frq; where &wald>.;
table &wald/out=counts noprint; run; quit;
data counts; set counts;
if percent>3 then percent=3; run;

symbol i=needle c=black value=dot;
axis3 label=none value=none
       order=(&xmin to &xmax by &incr) length=2.1 in;
```

```
axis1 label=none order=(0 to 3 by 0.5)
      length=.9 in value=none;
proc gplot data=counts gout=&lib..waldn1;
plot percent*&wald/vaxis=axis1 haxis=axis3
              des="dist-&wald";
title;
run;quit;
%MEND PLOT2;

/**************************************************************************/
%DESCR MACRO: This macro places descriptive text over the 3
statistical graphs. This text consists of the subtitles and the axes
labelling of the small side graphs. This approach avoids distortion
of text that occurs when replaying graphs through small templates.
The macro variable, &vert, provides the text to use for the vertical
graph.
/**************************************************************************/

%MACRO DESCR(vert);
data anno;
length text $ 25 style $ 8 function $ 8;
retain style 'swissl' xsys '3' ysys '3'
     position '6' function 'label';
x=2; y=30; angle=90; size=2.5; text='3'; output;
x=10; y=30; angle=90; size=3; text='%'; output;
x=28; y=2; angle=0; size=2.5; text='3'; output;
x=28; y=15; size=3; text='%'; output;
x=45; y=2; size=3; text='WALD FOR CONTINUOUS'; output;
x=2; y=50; angle=90; size=3; text="&vert"; output;
run;
proc gslide annotate=anno des='labelling'
    gout=&lib..waldn1;
run; quit;
%MEND DESCR;

/**************************************************************************/
%ANNO: This macro uses data obtained from the output data set
from PROC MEANS (not shown) for annotation to the right of the
graphs. The macro variables &CAT and &CATLABEL reference the
data set variable name and a descriptive label, respectively, for use
in the side table annotation. Since the entire annotation of the
table is lengthly, only a portion of the macro is illustrated here.
/**************************************************************************/

%MACRO ANNO(lib,dsn,cat,catlabel)
data anno; set error;
length function $8 style $8 text $25;
retain position '6' function 'label';
xsys='3'; ysys='3'; style='swissl';
size=4.5; x=20; y=98; text='TYPE ! ERROR RATES'; output;
size=3.5; x=33; y=92; text='MISSING INCLUDED'; output;
x=33; y=87; text='CONTIN'; output;
x=73; text="&catlabel"; output;
x=33; y=83; size=4; style='swisslu'; text='2000'; output;
x=73; text='2000'; output;
x=5; y=80; size=6; style='math'; text='N'; output;
x=3; y=76; size=4; style='swisslu'; text='0.01'; output;
x=30; text=left(put(bt01_x1,6.4)); output;

. . . etc . . .

proc gslide annotate=anno des="type1-&cat"
    gout=&lib..waldn1;
run; quit;
%MEND ANNO;

/**************************************************************************/
%TITLE: This macro produces the composite title that is placed at
the top of the page. The macro variables,n, p, and b, specify the
particular simulation conditions being presented. These values are
used in the stream description and are placed in the graphics
catalog.
/**************************************************************************/

%MACRO TITLE (n,p,b,figno);
proc gslide des="&n-&p-&b" gout=&lib..waldn1;
title h=1.5 f=triplex j=left
  "Figure &figno.. Comparison of the    Distribution of the Wald"
f=cgreek 'X' move=(-0.0,+1.0) h=1
f=triplex '2' h=1.5 move=(+0.8,-1.0)
' and Type I Error Rates';
title2 h=1.5 f=triplex j=left
'           for parameters'
" N = &n, " f=cgreek 'p' f=triplex " = &p, and "
f=cgreek 'b' move=(-0.1,-0.6) f=triplex h=1 '1' h=1.5
move=(+0.1,+0.6) f=triplex
" = &b with the Standard Normal.";
run; quit;
%MEND TITLE;

/**************************************************************************/
%TREPLAY MACRO: This macro specifies the first and last
graphic stream to use in the production of one composite figure.
This process is factilitated by the fact that the graphs are
ordered in the graphics catalog according to their appropriate
template number. The format of the filename statement is
specific to the UNIX versions of the SAS softare and produces
hardcopy output to a postscript printer.
/**************************************************************************/

%MACRO TREPLAY(begin,end);
filename gsasfile pipe 'lp -dps';
goptions device=ps1200 gaccess=gsasfile
       gsfmode=replace;
%do g=&begin %to &end %by 11;
   %let p1=%eval(&g);   %let p2=%eval(&g+1);
   %let p3=%eval(&g+2);  %let p4=%eval(&g+3);
   %let p5=%eval(&g+4);  %let p6=%eval(&g+5);
   %let p7=%eval(&g+6);  %let p8=%eval(&g+7);
   %let p9=%eval(&g+8);  %let p10=%eval(&g+9);
   %let p11=%eval(&g+10);
   proc greplay igout=&lib..waldln2 tc=&lib..plates
              template=rotate3 nofs gout=c.twaldln2;
   treplay 1:&p1 2:&p2 3:&p3 4:&p4 5:&p5 6:&p6
          7:&p7 8:&p8 9:&p9 10:&p10 11:&p11;
   run;
%end;
quit;
%MEND TREPLAY;
```

Figure 1. An example of one annotated and templated composite graph from a serial production.

Figure 55. Comparison of the Distribution of the Wald X^2 and Type I Error Rates for parameters N = 50, π = 0.3, and β_1 = 0 with the Standard Normal.

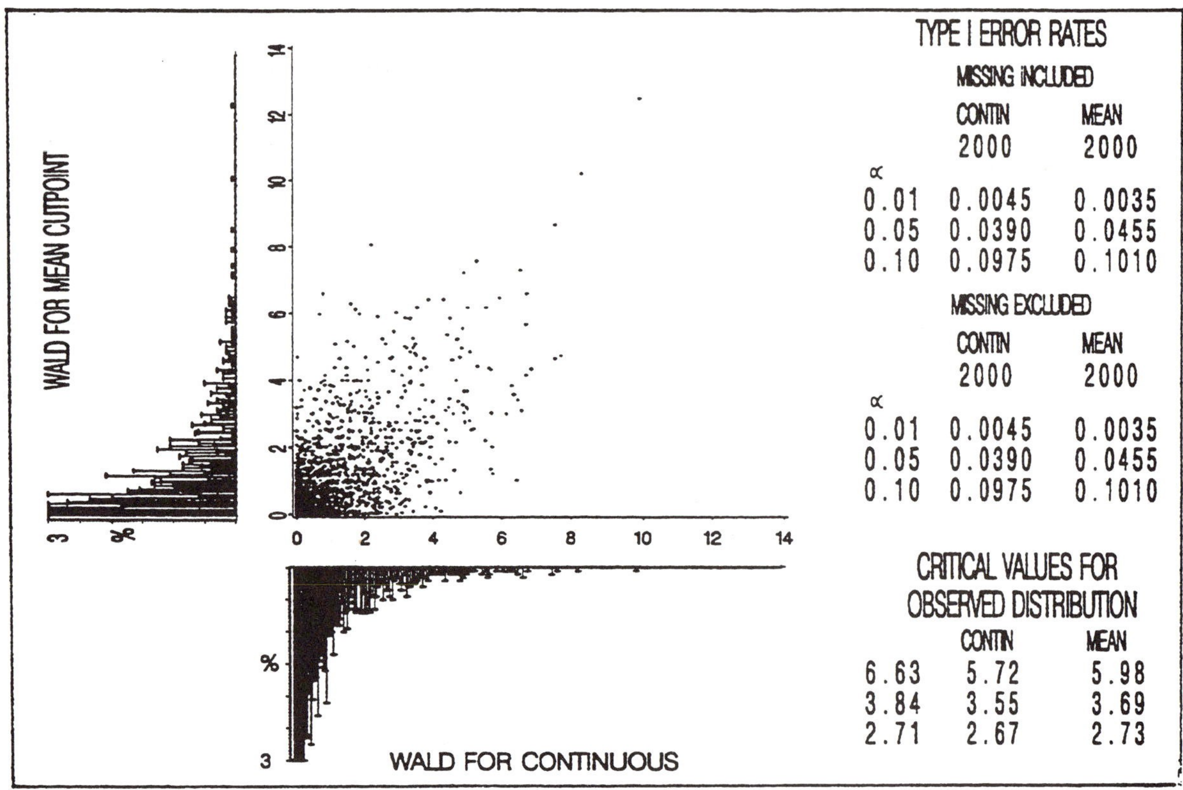

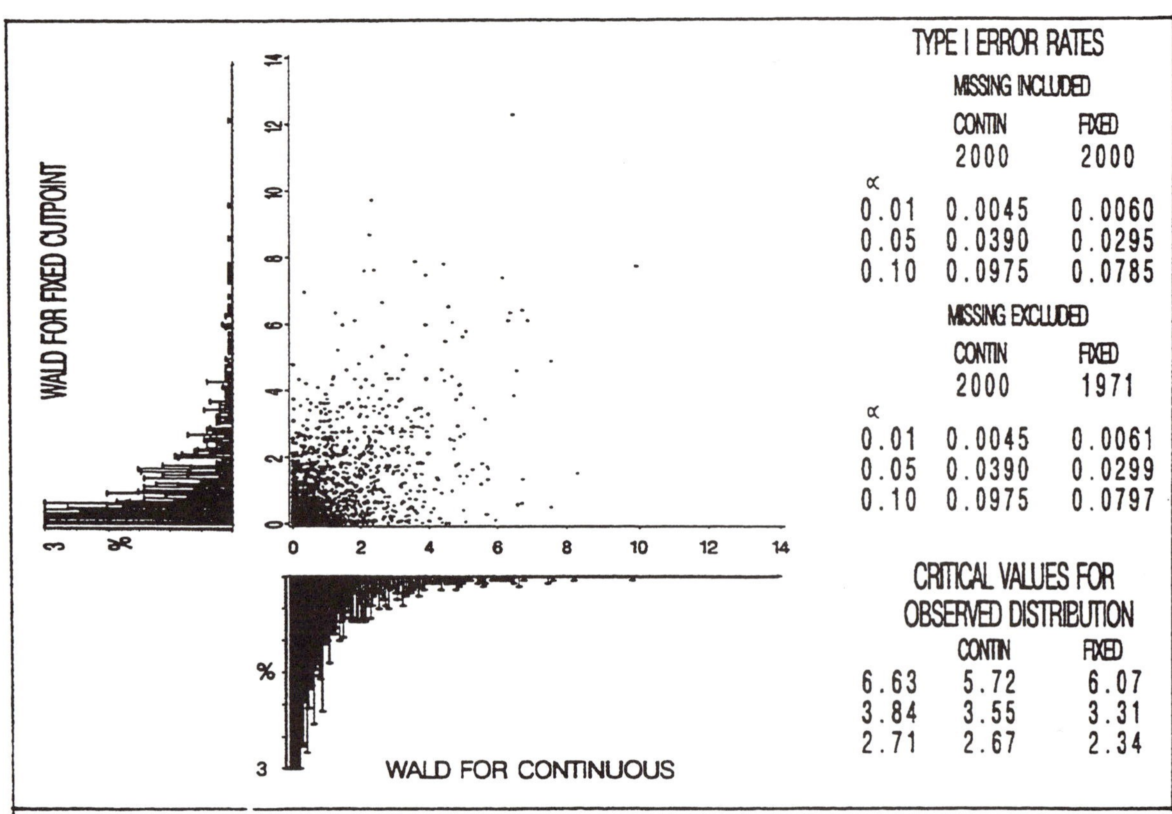

TRAVERSE: The Macros' Macro

Edmond Williams, Wyeth-Ayerst Research

Abstract

Manipulation with multiple tables within a SAS data base can become a data processing nightmare. Nevertheless such tasks as consolidation, data analysis, updating, and validation are frequently required to be performed across the entire SAS data base. This paper presents a set of macro routines TRAVERSE which relieves programmers from the painful "hard-code" repetitive programming. It offers a powerful programming tool which simplifies data manipulation.

Introduction

In the course of manipulating SAS tables in a SAS database, there may arise the belaboring task of performing some operations, functions, or procedures upon all tables found in a SAS DB. An example would be to perform cascading updates on a key field found in all the tables of the DB, for example:

> PROTOCOL and PATIENT_ID keys in a Pharmaceutical data base;
> EMPLOYEE_NO in a Personnel or Payroll data bases

Each of the above-mentioned fields may be a primary or foreign key, a part of a composite key, or a non-key field. A solution to such a problem may vary widely.

1) Quit your job, let others worry about the problem.
2) Put your head in a hole hoping that no one notices the sweeping error in the DB

.
.
.

n-h) Quickly fix the DB by writing many SAS data steps utilizing the unique name of all the SAS tables contained in the SAS DB.

.
.
.

n-1) Develop your own set of macros to automate the process of traversing a SAS DB.
n) Easily use an existing SAS macro pack, which contains the proper tools for accomplishing an automated traverse on any SAS DB.

After contemplating all solution options, we, at Wyeth-Ayerst wisely chose solution **n-1** which eventually led us to **n**. You may discover that using the latter solution appears particularly attractive, since it is now available. You will also be able to write your own TRAVERSEE-compatible macros, since this paper explains the macro pack, contains the macro code, and instructions for its usage. In addition, we will explore how TRAVERSE addresses various real programming problems.

Environment

A macro pack is a set of related macros in the same INCLUDE module; this concept is frequently used in the design of modular systems and programs. In languages, such as ADA we have packages; in Turbo Pascal we have units; in C we have object function modules, INCLUDE files (header and definition), and libraries. Therefore, why can't we have logical SAS macro packs!

The macro pack, TRAVERSE, was developed on an IBM 3084 under MVS XA system using SAS 5.18. This macro will be revised to work under SAS version 6.06. Even though I demonstrate TRAVERSE's particular uses in the field of pharmaceuticals, it is a generic macro pack, independent of the application environment. The examples may be adapted for your industry-specific macro library. Additionally, I recommend installing TRAVERSE not in your AUTOMACro library, but in your standard macro library.

Basic Algorithm

The TRAVERSE macro pack contains two macros which are the anchors of the pack, TRAVERSE and BI_LIB. TRAVERSE traverses one SAS DB, and BI_LIB compares and traverses two SAS DBs concurrently. The remainder are the companion macros, which would be commonly used with TRAVERSE or BI_LIB. The programming techniques in TRAVERSE are as follows:

1. The macro first obtains the SAS DB table of contents and saves the table names.

2. Then it dynamically creates the local SAS macro variables and stores the names of the SAS DB tables in each of the variables. It also obtains the number of SAS DB tables.

3. Loops through the local SAS macro variables containing the SAS DB table names, passing them to your (the user) macro routines.

Thus, TRAVERSE and BI_LIB are the macros that call and manage user macros allowing the user macros to operate on every table given SAS DB(s). *You can* handle more than two databases by utilizing TRAVERSE on two databases, then using the resulting DB with the third one, etc.

But, how do we use this technique?

How To Use TRAVERSE

Include the TRAVERSE macro pack before defining or including *your* macros (those that are managed by TRAVERSE or BI-LIB). TRAVERSE will set up the environment for proper execution.

I. **Using TRAVERSE macro.**

The user macro must be declared as a statement macro with the following parameters as shown below.

```
%MACRO User_Macro_Name( TABNAME = ,
                        LIBNAME = ,
              < Parameter_Name = Parameter > )
                        / STMT;
  .
  .
Macro statements
  .
  .
%MEND User_Macro_Name;
```

Please note that here and further in this paper, any parameter surrounded by < > symbols defines an optional parameter.

User_Macro_Name can be any variable name. TABNAME (for Table Name) must be specified along with Library Name, LIBNAME. Additionally, TRAVERSE, the host macro, will allow the user macro to specify one additional parameter, which may or may not have a default. Please note, however, that the additional parameter is optional.

The syntax for calling the TRAVERSE macro is as follows:

```
TRAVERSE USING = User_Macro_Name
   < LIBNAME = DB_Library_Name ( WORK ) >
   < TYPES = Content_Member_Type ( DATA ) >
   < PARMS       = Simple=Parameter > ;
```

USING is the only mandatory TRAVERSE parameter, calling for the user-defined macro name. LIBNAME is the SAS DB target library name or DDname; the default is the WORK library. TYPES is the SAS library member type specification (refer to MEMTYPE parameter of PROC CONTENT in SAS User's Guide: Basics) with the default of DATA. The PARMS parameter allows the user to pass a parameter to the user-defined macro. Spaces are not allowed between the user-defined macro parameter name, equal sign, and the user-defined parameter. Only one parameter may be specified.

II. **Using BI-LIB macro.**

Macros slated to be managed by the BI_LIB macro should be established in the following way:

```
%MACRO User_Macro_Name ( TABNAME = ,
                 LIB1NAM = ,
                 < LIB2NAM = ,>
                 < LIB3NAM = ,>
                 < WHICH = , >
                 < Parameter_Name = Parameter > )
               / STMT;
  .
  .
Macro statements
  .
  .
%MEND User_Macro_Name;
```

User_Macro_Name can be any SAS name. TABNAME must be specified along with the first Library Name, LIB1NAM. The second and third library names are optional; the second denotes the name of second library to be compared to the first. The third library is the destination library where the resultant from the user macro operation is placed. Keyword WHICH is an indicator showing which library(s), i.e. FIRST, SECOND, or BOTH, are contributing information. Additionally, BI_LIB gives an option to specify one additional parameter.

The syntax for calling the BI_LIB macro is as follows:

```
BI_LIB USING = User_Macro_Name
    LIB_1 = first Library_Name
  < LIB_2 = second Library_Name ( WORK ) >
  < LIB_3 = destination Library_Name ( WORK ) >
  < TYPES = Content_Member_Type >
  < PARMS = Simple=Parameter > ;
```

USING and LIB_1 are mandatory BI_LIB parameters. USING calls for the user-defined macro name, while LIB_1 needs the first library name. LIB_1 is the DB target library name. LIB_2 is the comparison db library; the default is the WORK library. The third parameter, LIB_3, is the destination library for the resultant macro operation. For explanations on parameters TYPES and PARMS see definitions above (in TRAVERSE).

Examples

Problem 1

Consider an example from a pharmaceutical application. Assume that in every table of a DB, variable PATNUM contains patient numbers. The task is to change the name PATNUM to PAT_NO. Assume also that library name is NDA and the user macro name is Cor_Nam (for Correct Name). Utilizing TRAVERSE the solution code is as follows:

```
%INCLUDE Macro(TRAVERSE);
%MACRO Cor_Nam( TABNAME = ,
        LIBNAME = WORK ) / STMT;
   PROC DATASETS
      LIBRARY = &LIBNAME
      NOFS
      ;
      MODIFY &TABNAME
         ;
         RENAME PATNUM = PAT_NO
            ;
      RUN;
 %MEND Cor_Nam;
 .
 .
 .
TRAVERSE USING   = Cor_Nam
     LIBNAME = NDA
     ;
```

TRAVERSE passes through every table in the NDA data base, transferring control to Cor_Nam which changes the name PATNUM to PAT_NO.

Problem 2

Let there exist two SAS DBs where the definitions of some tables are the same in both databases, and some are different. The task is to consolidate these databases. Let the tables come from the libraries SASDB1 and SASDB2, and the user macro name is CC_TABLE. Utilizing BI_LIB, the solution code is as follows:

```
%INCLUDE Macro(TRAVERSE);
%MACRO CC_TABLE( TABNAME = ,
           LIB1NAM = ,
           LIB2NAM = ,
           LIB3NAM = ,
           WHICH   = BOTH ) / STMT;
    %IF  &WHICH EQ FIRST
    %THEN %DO;
        PROC COPY IN = &LIB1NAM OUT = &LIB3NAM;
SELECT &TABNAME;
            RUN;
        %END;
    %ELSE %IF  &WHICH EQ BOTH
        %THEN %DO;
            DATA &LIB3NAME..&TABNAME;
                SET &LIB1NAM..&TABNAME
                    &LIB2NAM..&TABNAME;
                RUN;
            %END;
%MEND CC_TABLE;
 .
 .
 .
BI_LIB USING = CC_TABLE
       LIB_1 = SASDB1
       LIB_2 = SASDB2
       LIB_3 = SASDB2;
```

BI_LIB steps through every table in both the DBs passing control to CC_TABLE macro, which concatenates the DB tables, mapping the resultant table back into the second library. If SASDB1 appears to have a table that is not present in SASDB2, then this table is simply copied into the second library. Understandably, the second library table need only to stay put if the first library is absent from that table. When both tables are present in each DB, they are concatenated. Note that PROC APPEND is not used; this allows one table to be concatenated to the other even if it contains more or less columns than the other table.

In addition to the TRAVERSE and BI_LIB macros, the TRAVERSE macro pack contains several general purpose user macros to solve common-place problems.

<u>More Protocols For Subsequent Macros</u>

Besides TRAVERSE and BI_LIB, the TRAVERSE macro pack possess seven general purpose TRAVERSE and BI_LIB compatible macros. In fact, we will revisit problem 1 and 2 using some of these macros (see the Section entitled Examples):

1. ORDER . . . . . Sorts a SAS DB, given a common table key.
2. RNAME . . . . . Renames a table column-name.
3. EXAMINE . . . .Performs a frequency on all table columns.
4. DROP_EM . . . Drop variables from a DB, given a list.
5. DUMP_EM . . .Dumps records of all tables.
6. CC_TAB . . . . Concatenates DBs.
7. VM_LIST . . . . Converts a list of column-names in a macro variate into a table/dataset.
8. D_LIST . . . . Creates an alternate drop list based on the columns present in the target table.

VM_LIST is perhaps the only macro that can be used efficiently apart from TRAVERSE and BI_LIB.The user macro ORDER, RNAME, EXAMINE, DROP_EM, and DUMP_EM work in conjunction with the TRAVERSE macro; while, CC_TAB is slated for BI_LIB. The macros VM_LIST and D_LIST are primitive macros utilized by the previously mentioned five macros.

TABNAME, (TABle NAME) is a required macro TRAVERSE and BI_LIB parameter. TRAVERSE and BI_LIB will pass the table name through TABNAME. LIBNAME (LIBrary NAME) is utilized by TRAVERSE and has a default of the WORK library. For further information on the TRAVERSE syntax see section entitled Using the TRAVERSE Macro.

The ORDER macro sorts a DB using the sort list of table columns. The variates mentioned in the sort list need not be present in every table; however, they should be listed in respective sort order. The syntax for he ORDER macro is as follows:

```
%LET Ord_By = Sort_Presidents_Variates;
ORDER TABNAME = Table_Name
    < LIBNAME = Library_Name (WORK) >
    < NODUP > ;
```

NODUP (NO DUPlicates) is a conditional parameters which defaults to duplicates. The Ord_By macro variable must contain a BY list of common table variates. The syntax for using ORDER in conjunction with TRAVERSE is shown below:

```
%LET Ord_By = Sort_Presidents_Variates;
TRAVERSE USING = ORDER
      < LIBNAME = SAS_db_library_Name (WORK) >
      < PARMS = NODUP > ;
```

RNAME ReNAMEs table column-names. These variates need not be found in every table of a given target DB. The syntax is shown below:

```
%LET OLD_NAM = Present_name_of_table_column;
%LET NEW_NAM = New_name_of_table_column;
RNAME TABNAME = SAS_TABle_NAME
    < LIBNAME = LIBrary_NAME (WORK) >;
```

OLD_NAM and NEW_NAM must be specified with only one variate. When using RNAME in proper conjunction with TRAVERSE, the syntax is as follows:

```
TRAVERSE USING = RNAME
      < LIBNAME = SAS_db_library_Name (WORK) > ;
```

EXAMINE performs a frequency on all table columns. The syntax is shown below:

```
%LET Droplst = Variable_Drop_List;
EXAMINE TABNAME = SAS_TABle_NAME
      < LIBNAME = LIBrary_NAME (WORK) >;
```

The Droplst macro variable must be specified; this macro variable contains the list of table column to be omitted from the table column examination. If there are no table columns to be omitted Droplst should be specified as blank (i.e. %LET Droplst =;). When using EXAMINE in proper conjunction with TRAVERSE, the syntax is as follows:

```
%LET Droplst = Variable_Drop_List;
TRAVERSE USING = EXAMINE
      < LIBNAME = SAS_db_library_Name (WORK) >;
```

The DROP_EM macro deletes columns from DB tables via a drop list. The variables mentioned in the drop list need not be present in every table. The syntax for the DROP_EM macro is demonstrated below:

```
%LET Droplst = Drop_Variable_List;
DROP_EM TABNAME = Table_Name
     < LIBNAME = Library_Name (WORK) >;
```

The Droplst macro variable is required, and must contain a drop list of table variates. The syntax for using DROP_EM in TRAVERSE is shown below:

```
%LET Droplst = Drop_Variable_List;
TRAVERSE USING = DROP_EM
     < LIBNAME = DB_library_Name (WORK) >;
```

The DUMP_EM macro prints a given number of table rows from a DB. The syntax for the DROP_EM macro is demonstrated below:

```
%LET Droplst = Drop_Variable_List;
DUMP_EM TABNAME = Some_SAS_Table_Name
     < LIBNAME = Library_Name (WORK) >
     < ROWS = #_of_rows ( MAX ) >;
```

ROWS is a conditional parameter, here the user specifies how many rows on each table he/she wishes to dump. The entire DB is dumped when no ROWS specification is made. The utilization of DUMP_EM in connection with TRAVERSE is shown below:

```
%LET Droplst = Drop_Variable_List;
TRAVERSE USING = DUMP_EM
     < LIBNAME = SAS_db_library_Name (WORK) >
     < PARMS = ROWS=#_of_rows (MAX) > ;
```

Note: There are no spaces between ROWS and *#_of_rows*.

The CC_TAB macro concatenate any two SAS DBs. The syntax for the CC_TAB macro is as follows:

```
CC_TAB TABNAME = Table_Name
      LIB1NAM = First_Library_Name
    < LIB2NAM = Second_Library_Name (WORK) >
    < LIB3NAM = Destination_Library_Name (WORK) >
    < WHICH   = Which_Lib._Contributed{ FIRST,
                SECOND,(BOTH)} >;
```

LIB1NAM must be specified (first LIBrary NAME). The second, LIB2NAM, and destination, LIB3NAM, have the default of the WORK library. WHICH, denotes which library is contributing table data (i.e. If both tables are present then both will be contributing data; BOTH, is the default for parameter WHICH. If, however, only the first or the second table is present, then FIRST or SECOND should be specified respectively). The call utilizing BI_LIB is as follows:

```
BI_LIB USING = CC_TAB
      LIB_1  = The_first_db_library_Name
    < LIB_2  = The_second_db_library_Name (WORK) >
    < LIB_3  = The_destination_db_library_Name (WORK) >;
```

The D_LIST macro, given a drop list, returns an alternate variable drop list in respect to the table contents. The protocol for D_LIST is as follows:

```
D_LIST TABNAME = Table_Name
    < LIBNAME = Library_Name (WORK) >
    < D_NAME = Drop_list_macro_NAME_variable (DROPLST) >
    < OPTN = Alternate_table_variable_list_OPTioN {(D),O} >;
```

The D_NAME parameter for the Drop list macro NAME variable houses the name of the macro variable which contains the drop list; this parameter is optional, the default is the macro variable name DROPLST, for DROP LiST. The OPTN parameter, for OPTioN, may be set to D or O.

1. D - This is the default option specifying that the drop list is to be altered with respect to the column contents of a table. Allow *A, B, C, L, P, and Q* to be column table names. Thus, a drop list with {*A B C*} in it and a table with {*A C Q P L*}, will produce an alternate drop list of {A C}.
2. O - option produces a set of column variates name such that if {*A B C*} is the drop list and {*A C Q P L*} is the current table column content, then the resultant set is {*Q P L*}. In effect, the drop list has be subtracted from the current table column list.

The resultant drop list is returned in ALTDROP, the alternate drop list. _N_OBS, Number of OBservationS, is also returned holding the number of column-name contained in the alternate drop list. The user will need to check _N_OBS to avoid errors in processing the alternate drop list when it is empty, i.e. when _N_OBS will be zero. The D_LIST macro utilizes VM_LIST.

The VM_LIST macro takes a macro variable containing a table column list, and place the list in a table. For example let's take the macro variable, Ord_By, where:

```
%LET Ord_By = Pat_No Lab_Test;
```

VM_LIST would create a table such that the observations would be:

```
PROC PRINT DATA=Ord_By;

obs  Name      Sc_idx
 1   Pat_No      1
 2   Lab_Test    2
```

The protocol for VM_LIST is as follows:

```
VM_LIST < VM_NAME =
The_Name_of_the_macro_variable_and_resultant_table > ;
```

The default for VM_NAME is MV_LIST, Member name and macro Variable LIST name. VM_NAME should be set to the macro name that contains the table column list. The macro, VM_LIST will return a SAS table column-name containing a row-wise list of the names in the macro variable list; it will return this table as the same name of the macro variable list name. The table will be in the WORK library. The user of this macro is responsible for managing these newly-created tables (i.e. deleting them when they are no longer needed during a process).

A complete macro listing of the TRAVERSE macro pack is available in the appendix.

More Examples

Problem 3

First, let's revisit both problem one and two (see the section entitled 'Examples' for the statement of problem one and two). Utilizing the macro packs' user macros, the solution SAS code for problem one and two respectively should appear as follows:

Solution to Problem 1 Revisited

```
%INCLUDE Macro(TRAVERSE);
  .
  .
%LET OLD_NAM  = Patnum;
%LET NEW_NAM = Pat_No;
TRAVERSE_USING    = RNAME
         LIBNAME = NDA;
```

Solution to Problem 2 Revisited

```
%INCLUDE Macro(TRAVERSE);
  .
  .
BI_LIB USING = CC_TAB
      LIB_1 = SASDB1
      LIB_2 = SASDB2
      LIB_3 = SASDB2;
```

Problem 4

The TRAVERSE macro pack has great difficulty in operating on a library where there are varied passwords set on the tables with varied access levels. However, if the password is constant among the tables of a particular library one can strip the passwords off of the tables, do the traversing operation, and place the passwords back on the tables. Let there exist a SAS library associated with the name NDA, which has a write protect password, Gazel, on the tables within the library. I will call the macro for stripping and setting passwords, SOS_PW (Strip Or Set PassWords). The solution code should be similar to the following:

```
%INCLUDE Macro(TRAVERSE);
  .
  .
%MACRO SOS_PW( TABNAME = ,
               LIBNAME = WORK ,
               PASSWORD =  ) / STMT;
    PROC DATASETS
         NOLIST
         NOFS
         LIBRARY = &LIBNANE
         ;
         MODIFY &TABNAME
               ( PROTECT = &PASSWORD %IF  &SOS_KY
                 EQ STRIP %THEN /; );
         RUN;
 %MEND SOS_PW;
  .
* Let's strip the passwords off.
  .
%LET SOS_KY = STRIP;
TRAVERSE_USING    = SOS_PW
         LIBNAME  = NDA
         PARMS    = PASSWORD=Gazel;
  .
* Let's do some other traverse operation on the library.
  .
  .
* Now let's place the passwords back on.
  .
%LET SOS_KY = SET;
TRAVERSE_USING    = SOS_PW
         LIBNAME  = NDA
         PARMS    = PASSWORD=Gazel;
```

Problem 5

The client wishes to visually examine the data by using a PROC FREQUENCY on all columns, except the key relation columns, in every table of the DB. Let's say that the name of the key relation fields are Pat_no (patient number), Study, and Trt_drug (treatment drug). Let's call the library, NDA, which contains our SAS DB. Using the macro called EXAMINE, the solution code should be similar to the following:

```
%INCLUDE Macro(TRAVERSE);
  .
  .
%LET Droplst = study pat_no trt_drug;
TRAVERSE USING     = EXAMINE
         LIBNAME = NDA;
```

Conclusion

In this paper I introduced the concept of SAS macro packs, along with the subject macro pack, TRAVERSE. I have explained the conceptual algorithm of TRAVERSE. I showed the potential user the protocols for the set of macros contained in TRAVERSE, and I have included the macro pack in the appendix. Together, we explored only a minute set of problems that the TRAVERSE macro pack, addresses. I lightly exploited TRAVERSE in terms of consolidation of databases (problems 2, 3), validation (problem 5), and DB updating (problems 1, 4). And I have shown the overall effectiveness of TRAVERSE on SAS DBs. I challenge you to discover your industry-specific utilization of TRAVERSE--The Macros' Macro.

Acknowledgements

Dr. Joseph Uhimov, Mr. Suresh Patel, Dr. Richard Entsuah, Lurleen Bontigao.

SAS is a registered Trademark of SAS Institute, Inc., Carey, NC, USA.

IBM is a registered trademark of International Business Machines Corporation, Armonk, NY, USA.

Wyeth-Ayerst is a registered trademark of American Home Products Corporation, New York, NY, USA.

References

1. (1985) SAS User's Guide: Basics Version 5 Edition, Carey, North Carolina: SAS Institute Inc.
2. (1985) SAS User's Guide: Basics Version 5 Edition, Carey, North Carolina: SAS Institute Inc.

Contact Information

Edmond Williams
Wyeth-Ayerst Laboratories
145 King of Prussia Road
B-1 Building
Radnor, PA

If one desires a magnetic copy of the macro pack, TRAVERSE, simply send a scratch IBM compatible cartridge, nine-track tape, 5.25", or 3.5" floppy disk. Please include a self-addressed stamped envelope and specify that you desire a copy of this macro pack by name. We will copy it onto your magnetic medium and return it as soon as possible. If you have a medium that is not mentioned, please call the number below before sending it.

Telephone (215) 341-5720

A Program to Compute Odds Ratios and

Confidence Intervals from LOGISTIC Output

Eric Yu I Wang, Aili Gong

University of Southern California

Department of Preventive Medicine

and David P. MacKinnon

Arizona State University

Department of Psychology

Abstract:

The odds ratio and its 95% Confidence Interval are widely used in epidemiology and clinical trial research. The purpose of this paper is to describe a program to automatically compute these statistics with the SAS/STAT LOGISTIC procedure and the SAS MACRO product. The program can be used for both binary and ordinal response measures with one or many independent variables. The use of the program is demonstrated in two examples from prevention research.

Introduction:

The odds ratio was originally proposed by Cornfield (1951) as measure of the degree of association between an antecedent factor and an outcome. It widely used in clinical trial and epidemiology research particularly because of its simple interpretation as the odds of the outcome occurring given the antecedent factor. Despite the importance of odds ratio, SAS/STAT procedures do not provide the odds ratio in the output of the CATMOD, LOGIST, or LOGISTIC regression programs. The simple 2 by 2 odds ratio is presented when the MEASURES option is requested in the PROC FREQ procedure. The purpose of this paper is to describe the use of the PROC LOGISTIC procedure and the SAS MACRO language to compute and display the odds ratio and its 95% confidence interval, standardized parameter estimates, along with the parameter estimates and standard errors generated from PROC LOGISTIC. The standardized parameter estimates, odds ratio and its confidence limits should make it easier to interpret the results of PROC LOGISTIC. The standardized parameter estimates are used to judge the effects of the predictors on a uniform scale. And in the case of large models with many predictors, hand computation of these measures is cumbersome. This program greatly reduces the time to compute and double check these values.

Statistical Background:

The logistic density function is defined as follows:

$$\pi(X) = \exp(\beta_0 + \beta_1 X)/1 + \exp(\beta_0 + \beta_1 X)$$

where x is the covariate vector, and β_1 is the parameter of estimates. The logit transformation of (x) yields the LOGISTic regression equation as follows:

$$g(X) = \mathrm{Ln}\{\pi(X)/1 - \pi(X)\} = \beta_0 + \beta_1 X$$

The odds ratio and its 95% confidence interval is usually the parameter of interest in a LOGISTic regression due to its relatively straightforward interpretation. It is written as the following:

odds ratio of β = $\exp(\beta_1)$
confidence interval = $\exp\{\beta_1 + Z_{.05} * se(\beta_1)\}$

The variance of the Logistic distribution is approximately $\pi^2/3$. The standardized estimate for the slope parameter is computed by dividing the slope parameter estimate by the ratio of the standard deviation of the underlying distribution, (inverse of the link function) to sample standard deviation of the explanatory variable. (SAS Technical Report P-200 SAS/STAT Software: Callis and Logistic Procedures, 1990, Page 201) For example, if we have age as independent variable in the model the standardized estimate of
age = β_{age}*std(age)/sqrt(π**2/3)

We use,

```
PROC means mean std n noprint;
var %set_var;
output out=std_out (keep=&keep)
std=%set_var;
PROC transpose data=std_out
                    prefix=sd

out=s_std(keep=NAME_sd1);
```

to get standard deviation of the independent variable
We use:

```
PROC LOGIST data=log_data covout
outest=new;
model &dev = %set_var;
```

to get parameter estimate and estimated covariance matrix to calculate standard deviation of the intercept and parameter estimate.

Macro Logit description and use:

Attached is a listing of the SAS MACRO logit program to compute odds ratios, confidence limits and standardized parameter estimates from the output of the LOGISTIC program. First, logistic regression parameter estimates are computed in the LOGISTIC program and stored in an output file. Second the LOGISTIC output data set then serves as input to the section of the program that computes the odds ratio, confidence limits, and standardized parameter estimates. Finally, the odds ratio, confidence limits, and standardized parameter estimates are printed along with the usual PROC LOGISTIC output. The program is written for use with PC SAS.

The program requires the user to input:

1) dataset name

2) dependent variable (binary or ordinal)

3) sets of independent variables, now there is a limit of 10 independent variables but it is relatively easy to expand to more independent variables.

4) index k is the number of independent variables.

5) since PROC LOGISTic output is different for binary and ordinal response measures. The binary only case has an intercept, and ordinal case has j-1 intercepts (j is the response levels). The macro variable ordinal = 1 indicates that the dependent variables is ordinal, and ordinal = 0 indicates that the dependent variable is binary. The program could be easily extended for the LOGISTic regression output in CATMOD or LOGIST. The most important difference is the manner in which output files are written and organized in these two programs.

Examples:

Two examples are used to illustrate the logit program. The first example comes from a logistic regression in the study of the predictors of drug use and the second example is from an ordinal logistic regression in the study of the impact of the alcohol warning label.

Drug use. Cigarette use in the last month is the dependent measure in the first example, with predictors of grade, socioeconomic status, and monthly cigarette use one year before. The data is from a large community drug prevention program (Pentz et al., 1989). A person who reported smoking in the last month on year earlier was 9.7 (UCL=12.9, LCL=7.2) times more likely to be a smoker a year later. The standardized estimate for prior smoking status was substantial (.38). Students in the ninth grade were 2.2 (UCL=3.3, LCL 1.5) times more likely to be smokers than eighth graders.

Beliefs about Fetal Alcohol Syndrome. The second example comes from a study of the impact of the new alcohol warning label (MacKinnon, Pentz, and Stacy, 1990). Ordinal logistic regression was used to determine whether gender, alcohol use, race, party attendance, beliefs about the positive consequences about alcohol and the number of friends who use alcohol predict whether the respondent believes that alcohol can harm an unborn baby if the mother consumes alcohol while she is pregnant. The dependent measure was a four point scale ranging from yes definitely, probably, I don't think so, and no. The odds in this case reflect the average odds across the 4-1=3 logits corresponding to the j-1 transitions across the scale of the dependent measure. Females were 3 (UCL=4.1, LCL=2.2) times more likely to believe that alcohol can harm an unborn baby. Non-whites were .8 (UCL=.9, LCL=.7) as likely as Whites. Non-whites and males were less likely to believe that maternal alcohol consumption can harm an unborn baby.

Summary:

The macro logit program generates the usual LOGISTIC output along with odds ratios, 95% confidence intervals, and standardized estimates. The program is very useful in our data analysis because it automatically computes these statistics which often make more practical sense that the parameter estimate alone. The program is especially useful when there are many predictor variables as shown in the example of the predictors of beliefs about drinking while pregnant.

PROGRAM LISTING:

```
****** 1 *****;
%MACRO KEEPVAR;
 %LET KEEP= ;
 %DO N=1 %to &I;
  %LET KEEP = &KEEP %UPCASE(&&V&N) ;
 %END;
%MEND KEEPVAR;

***** 2 ******;
%MACRO SET_VAR;
 %DO N=1 %TO &I;
  %UPCASE(&&V&N)
 %END;;
%MEND SET_VAR;

*********** 3 ************;
 %MACRO SET_DATA(DATA=,I=);
 %DO N=1 %TO &I;
  &DATA&N
 %END;;
 %MEND SET_DATA;
```

```
******* 4 *********;
%MACRO STD(VAR=,J=);
 %IF &VAR NE  %THEN %DO;
   %DO N=1 %TO &J;
    DATA STD_DA&N(KEEP=_NAME_ VARIANCE);
     SET  COV;
       IF  _NAME_=%UPCASE("&&&VAR&N");
    VARIANCE=&&&VAR&N;
  %END;
 %END;
 %ELSE %DO;
       %DO N=1 %TO &J;
              DATA  INCP&N(KEEP=_NAME_
VARIANCE);
            SET  COV;
            IF _NAME_="INTERCP&N";
          VARIANCE=INTERCP&N;
       %END;
  DATA INTERCPT;
  SET %SET_DATA(DATA=INCP,i=&M);
      %END;
%MEND STD;


***** 5 *****;
%MACRO INTCEP;
%IF %EVAL(&ORDINAL) %THEN %DO;
 DATA CONSTANT;
  SET  COV;
   NAME=SUBSTR(_NAME_,1,7);
     IF NAME='INTERCP' ;
%GLOBAL M;
DATA _NULL_;
IF  0  THEN  SET  CONSTANT  POINT=_N_
NOBS=COUNT;
CALL SYMPUT('M',LEFT(PUT(COUNT,2.)));
STOP;
   %STD(VAR=,J=&M)
  RUN;
%END;
%ELSE
%DO;
  DATA CONSTANT(KEEP=_NAME_ INTERCEP);
   SET  COV ;
    IF _NAME_='INTERCPT';
      DATA INTERCPT;
      SET  CONSTANT;
    _NAME_='INTERCEP';
  RENAME INTERCEP=VARIANCE;
 %END;
%MEND INTCEP;

**************************     MAIN   PROGRAM
******************************;
%MACRO
LOGIT(DATA=,DEV=,V1=,V2=,V3=,V4=,V5=,V6
=,V7=,V8=,V9=,V10=,K=,ORDINAL=);
*-------------------------------------------------------------------;
* use SAS/STAT logist procedure to generate odds
ratio and
* 95% convidence interval
*
* Where:
*   data = SAS data set you want analyzed,
*   dev = dependent variable (ordianl or binary),
*   v1, --- V10, = independent variable,
*   k = # of independent var had value,
*   ordinal = 1 = = > dependent variable is ordinal,
*   ordinal = 0 = = > dependent variable is binary.
*
*
*programmer: Eric Yu I Wang, Aili Gong, DAVID P.
MACKINNON
*Institute for Health Promotion and Disease
Prevention Research
*  University of Southern California
*
**************************************************
******************************;

**************************************************
****
  KEEP THOSE VARIABLES IN THE LOGIST
MODEL
**************************************************
****;
 %GLOBAL I;
 %LET I=10;
 %let keep= ;
 %KEEPVAR
***********************************************;
 DELETE MISSING VALUE
***********************************************;

 DATA  LOG_DATA(KEEP=  %UPCASE(&DEV)
&KEEP );
 SET  &DATA ;
  %DO N=1 %TO &K;
   IF &&V&N = . THEN DELETE;
  %END;
  IF &DEV=. THEN DELETE;
**************************************************;
 GET STANDARD DEVIATION FOR
 THE INDEPENDENT VARIABLES (SAMPLE
VARIANCE)
**************************************************;

 PROC MEANS MEAN STD N NOPRINT;
 VAR %SET_VAR ;
 OUTPUT OUT=STD_OUT(KEEP = &KEEP)
 STD=%SET_VAR ;
 RUN;

 PROC TRANSPOSE DATA =STD_OUT
             PREFIX=SD
             OUT=S_STD(KEEP=_NAME_ SD1) ;
 RUN;
*********************************************;
  PROC LOGIST AND OUTPUT:
  1. PARAMETER ESTIMATE
  2. COVARIANCE MATRIX
*********************************************;

 PROC  LOGIST  DATA=LOG_DATA  COVOUT
 OUTEST=NEW;
```

```
MODEL &DEV = %SET_VAR;

*********************************************;
  CREATE PARAMETER ESTIMATE DATA SET
*********************************************;

DATA ES;
SET NEW;
IF _NAME_='ESTIMATE';
 PROC TRANSPOSE DATA=ES
OUT=TRANS(KEEP=_NAME_ ESTIMATE);
DATA P_ESTIMA;
SET TRANS;
J+1;
*************************************************
****;
 CREATE STANDARD ERROR OF INTERCEPT
AND
 INDEPENDENT VARIABLES
*************************************************
****;

 DATA COV;
 SET NEW;
 IF _TYPE_='COV';

 %INTCEP
 %STD(VAR=V,J=&K)

 DATA COMBINE ;
   SET INTERCPT
%SET_DATA(DATA=STD_DA,I=&K); J+1;

 PROC SORT DATA=COMBINE; BY _NAME_;
 PROC SORT DATA=S_STD ; BY _NAME_;
 DATA STDMERGE; MERGE COMBINE S_STD; BY
_NAME_;

 PROC SORT DATA=STDMERGE ;   BY j;
 PROC SORT DATA=P_ESTIMA ;   BY j;

*************************************************
*****;
* CALCULATE:
* 1) STANDARD ERROR
* 2) CHI-SQUARE
* 3) P-VALUE
* 4) STANDARDIZED ESTIMATE
* 5) ODDS RATIO
* 6) 95% CONFIDENCE INTERVAL
*************************************************
****;

 DATA BETA ;
 MERGE P_ESTIMA STDMERGE ;   BY j;

 SD_ERROR=SQRT(VARIANCE);
 T_VALUE=ESTIMATE/SD_ERROR;
 CHI_SQRE=(T_VALUE)**2;
 P_VALUE=(1-PROBNORM(ABS(T_VALUE)))*2;

STANDEST=ESTIMATE*SD1/(SQRT((3.14159265
4**2)/3));
 ESTIMATE=-ESTIMATE;
 ODDS=EXP(ESTIMATE);
 UP_LIMIT=EXP(ESTIMATE + 1.96*SD_ERROR);
 LO_LIMIT=EXP(ESTIMATE - 1.96*SD_ERROR);

******************************************;
   STANDARDIZE OUTPUT FORMAT
******************************************;

 PROC PRINT DATA=BETA SPLIT='*' NOOBS;
 VAR _NAME_ ESTIMATE SD_ERROR CHI_SQRE
P_VALUE STANDEST ODDS LO_LIMIT UP_LIMIT ;
label
  _NAME_='Variable'
 ESTIMATE='Paramater* Estimate'
 SD_ERROR='Standard* Error  '
 CHI_SQRE=' Wald* Chi-Square '
 P_VALUE ='Pr > * Chi-Square'
 STANDEST='Standardized*Estimate'
 ODDS   ='Odds*Ratio'
 UP_LIMIT='95% *Ucl'
 LO_LIMIT='95% *Lcl' ;

title1 'Analysis of Maximum Likelihood Estimates';
title2 'Odds Ratio and 95% Confidence Interval  ';
title3 "Response Variable: &dev";
title4 "Independent Variable: %SET_VAR";
title5 '                              ';
RUN;
title1;
%MEND LOGIT;
```

References

Agresti, A. (1984). Analysis of ordinal categorical data. New York: Wiley & Sons, Inc.

Cornfield, J. (1951). A method of estimating comparative rates from clinical data: Applications to cancer of the lung, breast, and cervix. Journal of the National Cancer Institute, 11, 1269-1275.

Hosmer, D. W., and Lemeshow, S. (1989). Applied Logistic Regression, New York: Wiley and Sons.

MacKinnon, D.P., Pentz, M.A, and Stacy, A. (1990) Youth awareness of alcohol risks before warning label legislation. Manuscript submitted for publication.

Pentz, M.A., Dwyer, J.H., MacKinnon, D.P., Flay, B.R., Hansen, W.B., Wang, E. and Johnson, C.A. (1989). A multicommunity trial for primary prevention of adolescent drug abuse: Effects on drug use prevalence. Journal of the American Medical Association, 261, 3259-3266.

SAS Institute, Inc. SAS/STAT™ Guide for personal computers, Version 6, 1987.

SAS® Technical Report P-200 SAS/STAT Software. CALIS and LOGISITC procedures. Release 6.04, 1990.

AUTOMATED GENERATION OF STATISTICAL TABLES:
Integration of Structured Programming and SAS® Macros

Lee-Hwa Jane & Maureen McCormick
Syntex Laboratories, Inc., Palo Alto, California

INTRODUCTION

In the pharmaceutical industry, there is often a need to repetitively create report quality statistical tables of nearly identical formats. The conventional approach to this problem has been to manually transcribe statistical parameters to a preformatted table. This approach is tedious, vulnerable to transcription errors, and requires detailed proofing. We present an alternative approach to this task that integrates the techniques of structured programming with the use of SAS macros and results in the automatic generation of repetitive tables. In addition to the obvious time efficiency benefits of this method, transcription errors are eliminated and future modifications are facilitated.

PURPOSE

The table we want to create presents treatment means, standard deviations, and sample sizes for 10 days of efficacy evaluation. It also reports Cochran-Mantel-Haenszel (CMH) statistics comparing the treatments on each day. The study being presented has four treatments: two active drugs (active 1, active 2) and two placebos (placebo 1, placebo 2). Four comparisons are reported: active 1 vs placebo 1, active 2 vs placebo 2, active 1 vs active 2, and overall treatment differences. There are 10 records per patient, one per day. Each record contains patient number, treatment group, investigator number, day, enrollment stratum, and efficacy rating. Using this input data set, the SAS® program creates Table 1. Further enhancements (underlining, centering titles, bold type) may be made using a word processor. Table 2 is the enhanced version of Table 1 using Microsoft® WORD.

STRUCTURED PROGRAMMING USING SAS MACROS

The top-down approach in structured programming is used to solve complex problems and begins with decomposing a general task into many sub-tasks. A function or subroutine is first assigned to each task with the detailed code for each function/subroutine to be written later. SAS macro language is a vehicle for writing such functions/subroutines, with the macros themselves being used as the building blocks for more complex SAS code.

The following example illustrates the use of the top-down approach in developing the algorithm for generating our statistical table. Flow charts are used to show the directions and relationships of the sub-tasks.

STEP 1- Two general tasks are identified (Table 3):
- 1.1 Generate statistics.
- 1.2 Print the statistics to a DOS file in the appropriate format.

STEP 2- Each task in step 1 is refined into detailed sub-tasks (Table 4):

Step 1.1 consists of two parts:
- 2.1 For each day, get descriptive statistics (means, standard deviations, and sample sizes) for all of the treatment groups.
- 2.2 For each day, get the p-values for the CMH statistics for the overall comparison and the pairwise comparisons.

Step 1.2 consists of three parts:
- 2.3 Print the top of the table, i.e., titles and column headings.
- 2.4 Print the body of the table (statistics).
- 2.5 Print the bottom of the table (footnotes).

STEP 3- More details are added to 2.1 and 2.2 (Table 5):

Step 2.1 is further divided into two steps:
- 3.1 Get the descriptive statistics for each group and save them onto a SAS data set.
- 3.2 Merge (by day) all of the SAS data sets generated in 3.1 into one file.

Step 2.2 is refined into three steps:
- 3.3 For each day, generate CMH statistics for the overall comparison and the three pairwise comparisons and direct the results into four DOS files (one for each comparison).
- 3.4 Read the p-values from the DOS files generated in step 3.3, and save them in four SAS data sets (one for each comparison).
- 3.5 Merge all SAS data sets generated in 3.4.
- 3.6 Merge the data sets generated in 3.2 (summary stats) and 3.5 (p-values) by day.

At this point, we stop further dividing the tasks. SAS macros are defined to accomplish the tasks identified above (Table 6):

MACRO SUMSTATS :
1. MACRO SUMMARY - This macro generates a SAS data set containing descriptive statistics for each treatment group.
2. MACRO SUMMARY is called four times (one for each group).
3. The resulting four SAS data sets are merged.

MACRO PVALCMH :
1. MACRO CMH - This macro directs CMH statistics to a DOS file.
2. MACRO CMH is called four times (one for the overall treatment comparison, three for pairwise comparisons).
3. MACRO PVALUE - This macro gets p-values from the DOS files created by the

above step; the p-values are saved into a SAS data set.
4. MACRO PVALUE is called four times, yielding four SAS data sets.
5. The resulting four SAS data sets are merged.

MACRO PRINTTOP - This macro prints the titles of the tables.
MACRO PRTABLE - This macro prints statistics.
MACRO PRINTBUT - This macro prints footnotes.

MACRO SPECIFICATIONS

MACRO SUMSTATS

MACRO CALL:

%SUMSTATS(OLDDATA,NEWDATA);
where
OLDDATA is the original SAS data set containing the individual observations. This is the data set that is passed to the SUMSTATS macro. NEWDATA is the SAS data set with the summary statistics for each treatment group. This is the data set that is returned by the SUMSTATS macro.

There are four treatment groups in our data set. In order to calculate the summary statistics, PROC SUMMARY is executed four times (once for each group.) To avoid repetition of the code, macro SUMMARY is written and nested under macro SUMSTATS.

MACRO CALL:

%SUMMARY(INDATA,OUTDATA,GROUP);
where
INDATA is the SAS data set containing the individual observations. This is the data set that was previously passed to the SUMSTATS macro and is now passed down to macro SUMMARY. OUTDATA is the SAS data set with the summary statistics for the treatment group. This is the data set that will returned by the SUMMARY macro. GROUP is a constant which indicates the treatment group.

Macro SUMMARY calls PROC SUMMARY and outputs the summary statistics (mean, standard deviation, and sample size) for a specific group to the SAS data set OUTDATA.

The SUMSTATS macro makes one call to macro SUMMARY for each of the treatment groups (a total of four in our sample program). Four SAS data sets containing the summary statistics are created. These files are then merged by day to form the data set NEWDATA.

MACRO PVCMH

MACRO CALL:

%PVALCMH(OLDDATA,NEWDATA);
where
OLDDATA is the original SAS data set containing the individual observations. This is the data set that is passed to the PVALCMH macro. NEWDATA is the SAS data set with the CMH p-values for each comparison. This is the data set that is returned by the PVALCMH macro.

We want to make 4 comparisons, 1 overall and 3 pairwise comparisons. In order to calculate the CMH statistics for the 4 comparisons, PROC FREQ must be executed four times. To avoid repetition of the code, macro CMH is written and nested under macro PVALCMH.

MACRO CALL:

%CMH(INDATA,OUTFILE,TRT1,TRT2,TRT3, TRT4);
where
INDATA is the SAS data set containing the individual observations. This is the data set that was previously passed to the PVALCMH macro and is now passed down to macro CMH. OUTFILE is the DOS file that will contain the PROC FREQ output for the comparison. These files will be read in the PVALUE macro described below. TRT1, TRT2, TRT3, and TRT4 are constants which indicate the treatment groups to be used in the comparison.

Macro CMH calls PROC FREQ and writes the output for a specific comparison to the DOS file OUTFILE.

%PVALUE(OUTFILE,WORK,PV);
where
OUTFILE is the DOS file containing the PROC FREQ output for the comparison created above in the CMH macro. PVALUE macro reads this file and extracts the "Row Mean Scores Differ" p-value statistic for each evaluation day. The desired p-value is located using the INDEX and SUBSTR functions. WORK is the SAS data set containing the CMH statistic p-values extracted from OUTFILE. PV is the variable containing the p-values.

The PVALCMH macro makes one call to macro CMH and macro PVALUE for each of the comparisons (a total of four in our sample program). Four SAS data sets containing the CMH statistic p-values are created. These files are then merged by day to form the data set NEWDATA.

MACRO PRINTTOP

MACRO CALL:

%PRINTTOP(OUTFILE);

This macro takes the values of macro variables TITLE1, TITLE2, TITLE3, and TITLE4 and writes them to OUTFILE. The top of the table, which contains only the titles and column headings of the table, is created and saved onto OUTFILE.

MACRO PRTABLE

MACRO CALL:

%PRTABLE(DATASET,OUTFILE,VAR,VARFMT);

This macro appends the summary statistics and the p-values from macro CMH to OUTFILE. The statistics are printed for each treatment group by day. DATASET is the SAS dataset containing the statistics. VAR is the variable which labels each line of the statistics. VARFMT is the format for VAR.

MACRO PRINTBUT

MACRO CALL:

%PRINTBUT(OUTFILE);

This macro appends the footnotes to the end of OUTFILE.

STUDY NAME
INVESTIGATOR: NAME
TABLE 1

TABLE TITLE

						P-VALUES[b]			
DAY[a]		PLACEBO 1	ACTIVE 1	ACTIVE 2	PLACEBO 2	ACTIVE 1 vs PLACEBO 1	ACTIVE 2 vs PLACEBO 2	ACTIVE 1 vs ACTIVE 2	OVERALL TREATMENT DIFFERENCE
1	Mean (SD)	1.2 (0.9)	1.5 (1.0)	1.5 (1.1)	1.1 (1.0)	0.006	0.005	0.930	0.001
	N	105	323	301	99				
2	Mean (SD)	1.5 (1.0)	1.7 (1.1)	1.7 (1.0)	1.5 (1.1)	0.068	0.079	0.756	0.067
	N	94	297	283	94				
3	Mean (SD)	1.7 (1.1)	1.8 (1.1)	1.8 (1.1)	1.5 (1.1)	0.574	0.036	0.947	0.189
	N	82	244	239	74				
4	Mean (SD)	1.9 (1.0)	1.8 (1.1)	1.8 (1.1)	1.7 (1.1)	0.748	0.650	0.992	0.951
	N	65	199	196	54				
5	Mean (SD)	1.9 (0.9)	1.8 (1.2)	1.9 (1.1)	1.7 (1.3)	0.945	0.125	0.387	0.469
	N	53	169	157	48				
6	Mean (SD)	1.8 (1.0)	1.9 (1.3)	1.9 (1.2)	1.6 (1.2)	0.848	0.242	0.902	0.682
	N	41	146	142	36				
7	Mean (SD)	1.6 (1.3)	1.7 (1.2)	2.1 (1.1)	1.5 (1.1)	0.761	0.017	0.009	0.012
	N	38	106	108	28				
8	Mean (SD)	1.9 (1.1)	1.9 (1.2)	2.2 (1.1)	1.3 (1.3)	0.779	0.002	0.062	0.015
	N	30	98	91	23				
9	Mean (SD)	1.8 (0.9)	1.9 (1.2)	2.2 (1.2)	1.0 (1.2)	0.280	<0.001	0.063	<0.001
	N	26	77	75	20				
10	Mean (SD)	1.7 (1.2)	1.8 (1.3)	2.2 (1.3)	0.9 (1.2)	0.456	0.002	0.029	0.004
	N	18	69	68	16				

a Treatment Effectiveness Scale: 0=Not Effective, 1=Slightly, 2=Somewhat, 3=Very, 4=Completely Effective.
b P-values for daily ratings from Cochran-Mantel-Haenszel test, adjusted for investigator and stratum.

SOURCE: TABLE (Feb 7, 1991)

STUDY NAME
INVESTIGATOR: NAME

TABLE 2

TABLE TITLE

DAY[a]		PLACEBO 1	ACTIVE 1	ACTIVE 2	PLACEBO 2	P-VALUES[b] ACTIVE 1 vs PLACEBO 1	ACTIVE 2 vs PLACEBO 2	ACTIVE 1 vs ACTIVE 2	OVERALL TREATMENT DIFFERENCE
1	Mean (SD)	1.2 (0.9)	1.5 (1.0)	1.5 (1.1)	1.1 (1.0)	0.006	0.005	0.930	0.001
	N	105	323	301	99				
2	Mean (SD)	1.5 (1.0)	1.7 (1.1)	1.7 (1.0)	1.5 (1.1)	0.068	0.079	0.756	0.067
	N	94	297	283	94				
3	Mean (SD)	1.7 (1.1)	1.8 (1.1)	1.8 (1.1)	1.5 (1.1)	0.574	0.036	0.947	0.189
	N	82	244	239	74				
4	Mean (SD)	1.9 (1.0)	1.8 (1.1)	1.8 (1.1)	1.7 (1.1)	0.748	0.650	0.992	0.951
	N	65	199	196	54				
5	Mean (SD)	1.9 (0.9)	1.8 (1.2)	1.9 (1.1)	1.7 (1.3)	0.945	0.125	0.387	0.469
	N	53	169	157	48				
6	Mean (SD)	1.8 (1.0)	1.9 (1.3)	1.9 (1.2)	1.6 (1.2)	0.848	0.242	0.902	0.682
	N	41	146	142	36				
7	Mean (SD)	1.6 (1.3)	1.7 (1.2)	2.1 (1.1)	1.5 (1.1)	0.761	0.017	0.009	0.012
	N	38	106	108	28				
8	Mean (SD)	1.9 (1.1)	1.9 (1.2)	2.2 (1.1)	1.3 (1.3)	0.779	0.002	0.062	0.015
	N	30	98	91	23				
9	Mean (SD)	1.8 (0.9)	1.9 (1.2)	2.2 (1.2)	1.0 (1.2)	0.280	<0.001	0.063	<0.001
	N	26	77	75	20				
10	Mean (SD)	1.7 (1.2)	1.8 (1.3)	2.2 (1.3)	0.9 (1.2)	0.456	0.002	0.029	0.004
	N	18	69	68	16				

[a] Treatment Effectiveness Scale: 0=Not Effective, 1=Slightly, 2=Somewhat, 3=Very, 4=Completely Effective.
[b] P-values for daily ratings from Cochran-Mantel-Haenszel test, adjusted for investigator and stratum.

SOURCE: TABLE (Feb 7, 1991)

Table 3

Generate statistics

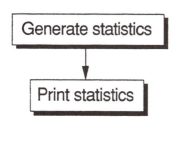

Print statistics

Table 4

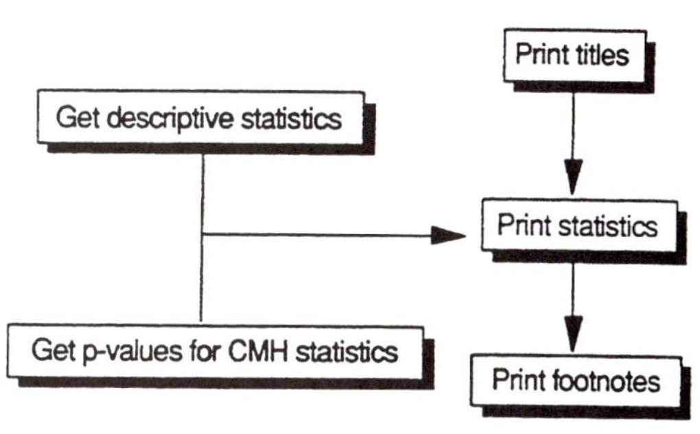

Table 5

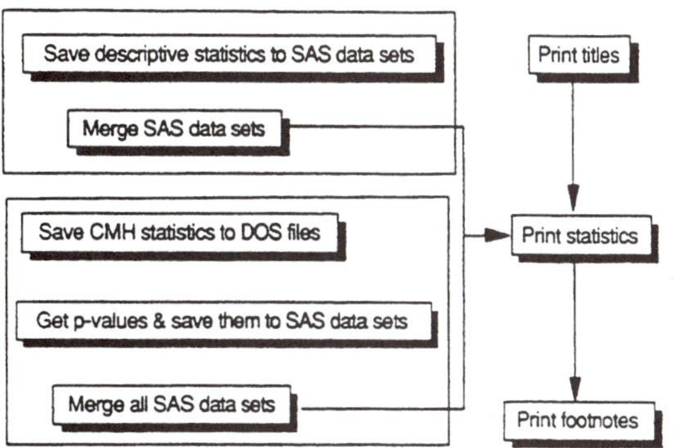

Table 6

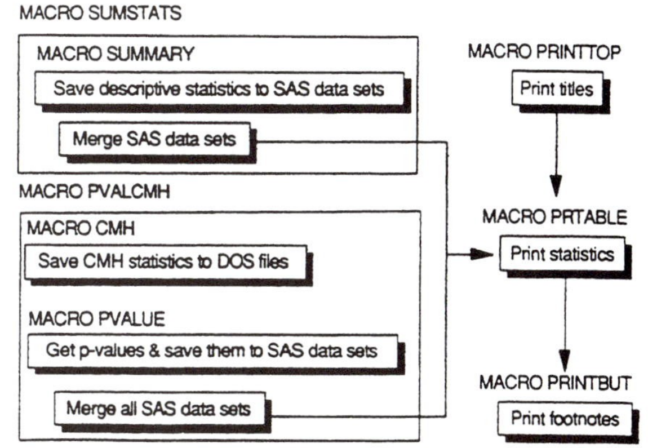

```
*********************************************
PROGRAM:        D:\SUGI\TABLE.SAS
BY:             Lee-Hwa Jane and Maureen McCormick
STUDY:
CREATED:        Aug 1990
REVISED BY:
PURPOSE:        Create efficacy results table.
INPUT DATA:     neweffic.ssd
*********************************************;
%let outfile=TABLE;
%let extensn=.DOC;
%let title1='STUDY NAME';
%let title2='INVESTIGATOR: NAME';
%let title3='TABLE X';
%let title4='TABLE TITLE';
libname in 'd:\sugi\data';
filename &outfile "d:\sugi\&outfile&extensn";
options ps=45 ls=108 nocenter;

***********************************************************
                         MACROS
***********************************************************;
%macro sumstats(olddata,newdata);
    %macro summary(indata,outdata,group,mean,std,n);
           proc summary data=&indata;
             where newrand=&group;
             class day;
             var rating;
             output out=&outdata mean=&mean std=&std n=&n;
           proc print data=&outdata;
    %mend summary;

    %summary(&olddata,trt1,1,mean1,std1,n1);
    %summary(&olddata,trt2,2,mean2,std2,n2);
    %summary(&olddata,trt3,3,mean3,std3,n3);
    %summary(&olddata,trt4,4,mean4,std4,n4);

    data &newdata;
            merge trt1 trt2 trt3 trt4 ;
            by day;
            where _TYPE_ eq 1;
    proc print data=&newdata;
%mend sumstats;

%macro pvalcmh(olddata,newdata);
    %macro cmh(indata,outfile,trt1,trt2,trt3,trt4);
           proc printto print=&outfile new;
           proc freq data=&indata;
             where newrand in (&trt1,&trt2,&trt3,&trt4);
             by day;
             tables stratumc*inv*newrand*rating / noprint cmh;
           proc printto;
    %mend cmh;

    %cmh(&olddata,compare1,1,2,0,0);
    %cmh(&olddata,compare2,3,4,0,0);
    %cmh(&olddata,compare3,2,3,0,0);
    %cmh(&olddata,compare4,1,2,3,4);

    %macro pvalue(outfile,work,pv);
           data &work;
             infile "d:\sugi\&outfile" ls=62;
             input a $char62.;
               keep day &pv;
               retain day 0;
               b='Row Mean Scores Differ';
               x=index(a,b);
               if x ne 0 then do;
                     day=day+1;
                     &pv=substr(a,57,6);
                     if &pv = ' 0.000' then &pv = '<0.001';
                     output;
               end;
    %mend pvalue;

    %pvalue(compare1.lst,work1,pvalue1);
    %pvalue(compare2.lst,work2,pvalue2);
    %pvalue(compare3.lst,work3,pvalue3);
    %pvalue(compare4.lst,work4,pvalue4);

    data &newdata;
      merge work1 work2 work3 work4;
      by day;
%mend pvalcmh;

%macro printtop(outfile);
    data null;
          file &outfile /*print*/ notitle n=1 pagesize=44 linesize=108;
       put @1 &title1/
          @1 &title2/
          @1 &title3//
          @1 &title4/
          @93 'b' /
          @85 'P-VALUES' /
          @67 'ACTIVE 1' @78 'ACTIVE 2' @89 'ACTIVE 1' @100 'OVERALL' /
          @5 'a' @70 'vs' @81 'vs' @92 'vs' @99 'TREATMENT' /
          @2 'DAY' @19 'PLACEBO 1' @31 'ACTIVE 1'
          @43 'ACTIVE 2' @55 'PLACEBO 2' @67 'PLACEBO 1' @78 'PLACEBO 2'
          @89 'ACTIVE 2' @99 'DIFFERENCE' /;
%mend printtop;

%macro prtable(dataset,outfile,var,varfmt);
    data null;
       file &outfile mod /*print*/ notitle n=1 pagesize=44 linesize=108;
       set &dataset;
       left = '(';
       right= ')';
       label1='Mean (SD)';
       label2='N';
       put     @2 &var &varfmt  @6 label1 $9.
               @18 mean1 3.1  @23 left $1. std1 3.1 right $1.
               @30 mean2 3.1  @35 left $1. std2   3.1 right $1.
               @42 mean3 3.1  @47 left $1. std3   3.1 right $1.
               @54 mean4 3.1  @59 left $1. std4 3.1 right $1.
               @68 pvalue1 $char6. @79 pvalue2 $char6.
               @89 pvalue3 $char6. @100 pvalue4 $char6. /
               @6 label2 $1.
               @18 n1 3. @30 n2 3. @42 n3 3. @54 n4 3.;
%mend prtable;


%macro printbut(outfile);
%macro fdate(fmt);
     %global fdate;
     data _null_; call symput("fdate",left(put("&sysdate"d,&fmt))); run;
%mend fdate;
%fdate(worddate12.);
     data null;
         file &outfile mod /*print*/ notitle n=1 pagesize=44 linesize=108;
         put @1 108*'_'/
@1 'a Treatment Effectiveness Scale: 0=Not Effective, 1=Slightly, 2=Somewhat,'
   ' 3=Very, 4=Completely Effective.'/
@1 'b P-values for daily ratings from Cochran-Mantel-Haenszel test, adjusted'
   ' for investigator and stratum.'//
@1 "SOURCE: &OUTFILE (&fdate)";
%mend printbut;
******************************************************************************
                              MACRO CALLS
******************************************************************************;
%sumstats(in.neweffic,statfile);
%pvalcmh(in.neweffic,pvalues);
data statspv; merge statfile pvalues; by day;
%printtop(&outfile);
%prtable(statspv,&outfile,day,2.);
%printbut(&outfile);
```

ACKNOWLEDGEMENTS: The authors would like to express their thanks to Don Young, Mary Lange, and Carol Francisco for their assistance in this paper.

PLOTCORR:A SAS® MACRO FOR APPENDING CORRELATION AND REGRESSION STATISTICS TO THE PLOT OR GPLOT PROCEDURES

Erik J. Bergstralh, Mayo Clinic

Introduction:

When examining the relationship between two continuous variables (x,y) the usual first step is to produce a scatter plot using PROC PLOT or GPLOT. The statistician is often additionally interested in examining the correlation between y and x and/or the simple linear regression of y on x. Also, descriptive statistics for x and y are often of interest. We have found it useful to include some of these statistics on the scatter plot when presenting results to the investigator. In order to avoid transcription errors and save transcription time, we have developed a SAS macro, PLOTCORR, to summarize the relationship between y and x using a scatter plot with these frequently used statistics appended at the bottom. The specific statistics included are the mean, standard deviation, median and range for x and y, the Pearson and Spearman simple linear correlation coefficients and simple linear regression statistics (slope, intercept, R-square and root MSE). If one calls the macro using the SAS/GRAPH® procedure GPLOT, then optionally the regression line along with confidence limits (for either the predicted mean y or predicted individual points) will be included on the scatter plot. An example of how to use PLOTCORR is presented along with the macro code.

Macro Description and Use:

Table 1 provides a listing of PLOTCORR and documentation for input parameter definitions. Note that the descriptive statistics for y and x come from the output dataset in PROC UNIVARIATE. Any observations with missing values for either y or x are deleted prior to calculating the descriptive statistics. The Pearson and Spearman correlation coefficients are retrieved from the PROC CORR output dataset. The p-values for the tests of the true correlation coefficients being significantly different form zero are calculated as described under the PROC CORR documentation (see p. 869 of reference 1). The simple linear regression statistics are calculated from the Pearson correlation coefficients.

To use PLOTCORR one need minimally input only the name of the dataset containing x and y and the names of the x-variable and the y-variable. Optionally one can control the appearance of the horizontal and vertical axis by defining the XAXIS and YAXIS parameters (Table 1). These parameters allow one to define the HAXIS, HREF and HMINOR (plus VAXIS, VREF and VMINOR) options from PLOT or GPLOT. In addition, one can include the regression line and confidence intervals for the mean y or predicted individual values on the plot by using the LINE parameter. This parameter is available only with GPLOT and defines the LINE option for the SYMBOL statement to be used with GPLOT (see p. 69 of reference 2). One should be aware that exchanging x and y will result in different regression statistics, and that the relationship between x and y may be non-linear.

Example:

Figure 1 is an example of PLOTCORR being used with GPLOT to look at a measure of lung function (LF) versus age in men. The code used to generate Figure 1 is given below:

```
%PLOTCORR(DATA=one,YVAR=LF,XVAR=Age,
 XAXIS="haxis=35 to 60 by 5 hminor=4",
 PTYPE=gplot,LINE=rlcli95,PLTDATA=
 ind.plot);
```

Computing Comment:

PLOTCORR is an example of a macro which combines output from several SAS procedures onto a single printed page. This is done by assigning the desired statistics from each procedure to macro variables and including them in FOOTNOTE statements. This has proved to be a useful technique in several other macro applications. However, the method has some limitations. The use of BY variables is not possible as one cannot change the FOOTNOTE as the BY variable changes. Second, it is sometimes rather tedious to produce a report that is appealing to the eye because the length of the macro variables needs to be controlled.

Summary:

We have found PLOTCORR to be very useful in our daily consulting activities. It produces a concise summary of the linear association between two continuous variables, saves transcription time and eliminates transcription errors. Inquiries should be made to the author at the following address:

Erik Bergstralh
Section of Biostatistics
Mayo Clinic
Rochester, MN 55905

References:
1. SAS Institute Inc. (1985),SAS User's Guide: Basics, Version 5 Edition, Cary, NC
2. SAS Institute Inc. (1985), SAS/GRAPH User's Guide, Version 5 Edition, Cary, NC

TABLE 1

```
/*****************************************************************************
   MACRO CALL:     %PLOTCORR(DATA=,YVAR=,XVAR=,YAXIS=,XAXIS=,
                             PTYPE=,LINE=,PLTDATA=);

   PARAMETERS:     DATA=INPUT DATA SET CONTAINING Y & X VARS.

                   YVAR=VARIABLE TO PLOT ON VERTICAL AXIS.

                   XVAR=VARIABLE TO PLOT ON HORIZONTAL AXIS.

                   YAXIS=VAXIS, VREF AND VMINOR OPTIONS FROM PROC
                         PLOT OR GPLOT.  THESE MUST BE ENCLOSED IN
                         DOUBLE QUOTES IF USED.  FOR EXAMPLE,
                            YAXIS="10 TO 20 BY 1 VREF=15  VMINOR=1".

                   XAXIS=HAXIS, HREF AND HMINOR OPTIONS FROM PROC
                         PLOT OR GPLOT.


                   *** THE FOLLOWING PARAMETERS APPLY ONLY FOR GPLOTS**

                   PTYPE=TYPE OF PLOT.  THIS MUST BE SET TO 'GPLOT'
                         IF ONE DESIRES A GRAPHICS PLOT, ELSE LEAVE
                         IT BLANK FOR A STANDARD LINE PRINTER PLOT.

                   LINE=ALLOWS ONE TO INCLUDE THE REGRESSION LINE ON
                        THE PLOT ALONG WITH CONFIDENCE LIMITS IF
                        DESIRED.  THIS IS ONLY APPLICABLE FOR GPLOT.
                        SEE PAGE 69 OF THE SAS/GRAPH USERS GUIDE(V5)
                        FOR DETAILS.  EXAMPLES ARE:
                                LINE=RL        LINEAR REGN LINE ONLY.
                                LINE=RLCLM95   LINEAR REGN WITH CONF.
                                               LIMITS(95%) FOR MEAN Y.
                                LINE=RLCLI95   LINEAR REGN WITH CONF.
                                               LIMITS(95%) FOR INDIVID.
                                               PREDICTED VALUES OF Y.

                   PLTDATA=OUTPUT GRAPHICS CATALOG FOR SAVING THE GPLOT
                          GRAPH.
*****************************************************************************/

OPTIONS NOCENTER DQUOTE ;
 %MACRO PLOTCORR(DATA=,YVAR=,XVAR=,YAXIS=,XAXIS=,
   PTYPE=,LINE=,PLTDATA=WORK);
  DATA __A; SET &DATA(KEEP= &YVAR &XVAR );
   __Y=&YVAR;
   __X=&XVAR;
   IF __Y=. OR __X=. THEN DO; __Y=.; __X=.; END; **IF ONE IS MISSING
                                                    SET BOTH TO BLANK;
  PROC UNIVARIATE NOPRINT; VAR __Y __X;
   OUTPUT OUT=__B N=N MEAN=MEAN_Y MEAN_X STD=SD_Y SD_X
   MEDIAN=MED_Y MED_X MIN=MIN_Y MIN_X MAX=MAX_Y MAX_X;
  DATA _NULL_; SET __B;
   LENGTH _Y _X $8.;
   _Y=SYMGET('YVAR');
   _X=SYMGET('XVAR');
   _YA=SYMGET('YAXIS');
   _XA=SYMGET('XAXIS');
   _YA=COMPRESS(_YA,'"');
   _XA=COMPRESS(_XA,'"');
   CALL SYMPUT('YAXIS',_YA);
   CALL SYMPUT('XAXIS',_XA);
   CALL SYMPUT('YVAR',_Y);
   CALL SYMPUT('XVAR',_X);
   CALL SYMPUT('NUSE',PUT(N,6.) );
   CALL SYMPUT('MNY',PUT(MEAN_Y,BEST8.) );
   CALL SYMPUT('MNX',PUT(MEAN_X,BEST8.) );
   CALL SYMPUT('SDY',PUT(SD_Y,BEST8.) );
   CALL SYMPUT('SDX',PUT(SD_X,BEST8.) );
   CALL SYMPUT('MDY',PUT(MED_Y,BEST8.) );
   CALL SYMPUT('MDX',PUT(MED_X,BEST8.) );
   CALL SYMPUT('MIY',PUT(MIN_Y,BEST8.) );
   CALL SYMPUT('MAY',LEFT(PUT(MAX_Y,BEST8.)) );
   CALL SYMPUT('MIX',PUT(MIN_X,BEST8.) );
   CALL SYMPUT('MAX',LEFT(PUT(MAX_X,BEST8.)) );
  PROC CORR NOPRINT OUTP=__P OUTS=__S DATA=__A; VAR __Y; WITH __X;
  DATA __C; SET __P(IN=INP) __S(IN=INS); IF _N_=1 THEN SET __B;
   IF _TYPE_='CORR';                      ** First obs. is Pearson corr(__Y);
                                          ** 2nd obs. is Spearman corr(__Y);
   T= __Y*SQRT( (N-2)/(1-__Y**2) );       ** T statistic for test of r=0;
   DF=N-2;                                ** Degrees of freedom for T;
   R=ROUND(__Y,.0001);                    ** r=corr. coeff. rounded;
   P=( 1-PROBT(ABS(T),DF) )*2;            ** p-value for test of r=0;
   P=ROUND(P, .0001);
   IF INP THEN DO;                        ** Regression stats;
       S2Y=(N-1)*SD_Y**2;                       **  Corrected ss for y;
       S2X=(N-1)*SD_X**2;                       **  Corrreted ss for x;
       RSQ=__Y**2;                              **  R-square;
       B=__Y*SD_Y/SD_X;                         **  Slope;
       A=MEAN_Y-B*MEAN_X;                       **  Intercept;
       RMSE=SQRT(((1-RSQ)*S2Y)/(N-2));          **  Square root MSE or Sy.x;
       SEB=RMSE*SQRT(1/S2X);                    **  Est. SE slope;
       SEA=RMSE*SQRT(1/N + MEAN_X**2/S2X);**    Est. SE intercept;
       CALL SYMPUT('RHO',PUT(R,6.4   ) );
       CALL SYMPUT('PRHO',PUT(P,5.4   ) );
       CALL SYMPUT('B',PUT(B,BEST8.) );
       CALL SYMPUT('A',PUT(A,BEST8.) );
       CALL SYMPUT('SEB',PUT(SEB,BEST8.) );
       CALL SYMPUT('SEA',PUT(SEA,BEST8.) );
       CALL SYMPUT('SYX',PUT(RMSE,BEST8.) );
       CALL SYMPUT('RSQ',PUT(RSQ,5.4) );
   END;
   IF INS THEN DO;
       CALL SYMPUT('RHOS',PUT(R,6.4 ) );
       CALL SYMPUT('PRHOS',PUT(P,5.4) );
   END;
 %IF %UPCASE(&PTYPE)=GPLOT %THEN %DO;
  SYMBOL1 C=RED  V=PLUS I=&LINE;
  PROC GPLOT DATA=__A GOUT=&PLTDATA;
    PLOT &YVAR*&XVAR / &YAXIS &XAXIS;
 %END;
 %ELSE %DO;
  PROC  PLOT DATA=__A;
    PLOT &YVAR*&XVAR / &YAXIS &XAXIS;
 %END;
 %macro ftn(fn); footnote&fn .j=l .h=.7  %mend  ftn;
 %ftn(1) "DESC. STATS(N=&NUSE):   MEAN      STD      MEDIAN      RANGE";
 %ftn(2) "          &YVAR(Y)      &MNY &SDY &MDY &MIY => &MAY             ";
 %ftn(3) "          &XVAR(X)      &MNX &SDX &MDX &MIX => &MAX             ";
 %ftn(4) "CORRELATIONS:           PEARSON=&RHO(P=&PRHO)  SPEARMAN=&RHOS(P=&P
RHOS)";
 %ftn(5) "REGRESSION(Y=A+BX):  S(Y.X)=&SYX         RSQUARE=&RSQ";
 %ftn(6) "                      A(SE)=&A(&SEA)  B(SE)=&B(&SEB)  ";
  PROC DELETE DATA=__A __B __C __P __S;
  RUN;
  %ftn(1);
 %MEND PLOTCORR;
```

FIGURE 1

Example of PLOTCORR Macro Using GPLOT

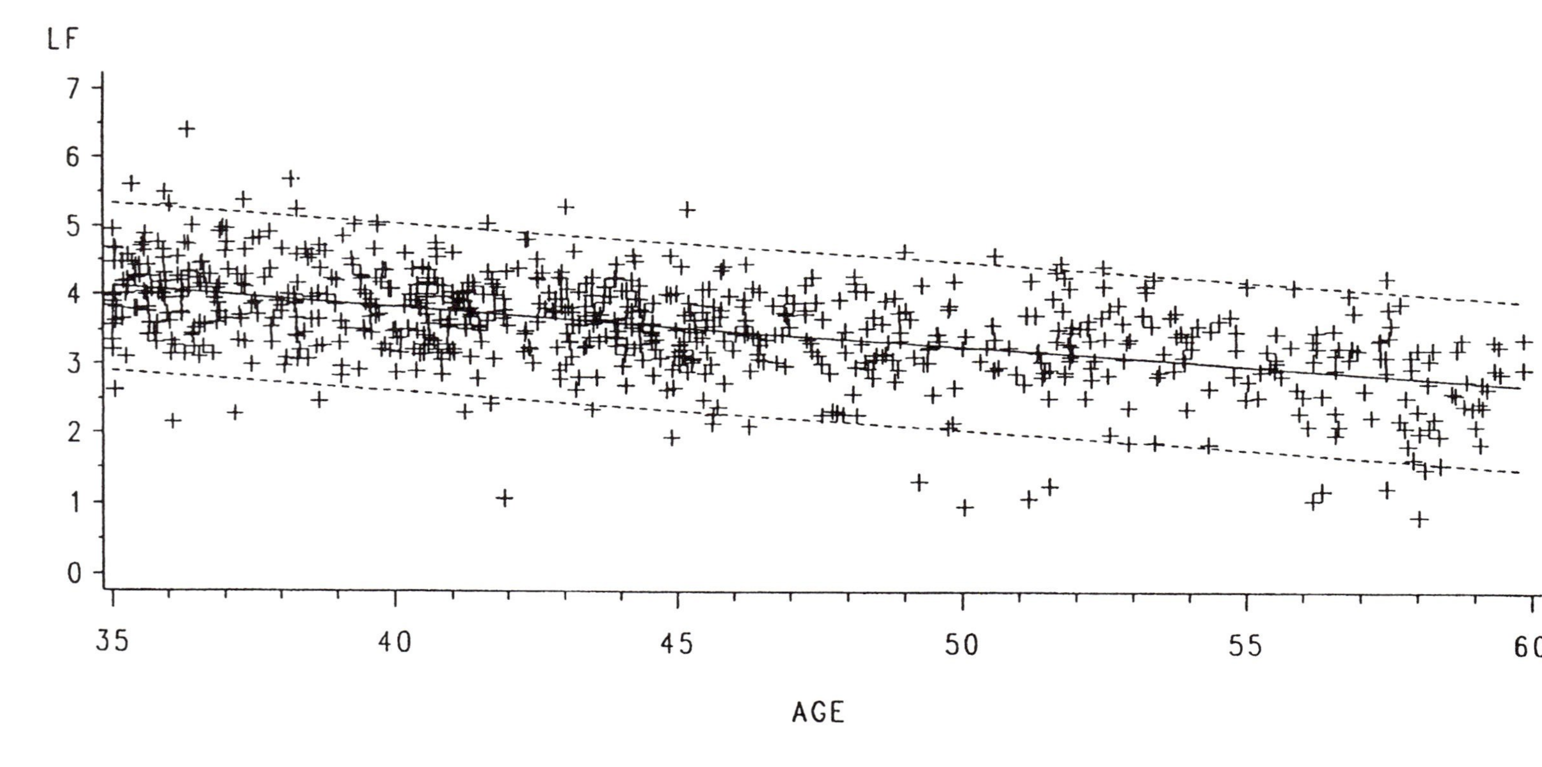


```
DESC. STATS(N=    751):    MEAN       STD        MEDIAN      RANGE
        LF        (Y)       3.5526 0.732163      3.57      0.83 => 6.4
        Age       (X)      44.8487  6.84225      43.9        35 => 59.87
CORRELATIONS:          PEARSON=-.5337(P=.0000)  SPEARMAN=-.5267(P=.0000)
REGRESSION(Y=A+BX):   S(Y.X)=0.619595           RSQUARE=.2848
                       A(SE)= 6.11376(0.150009)  B(SE)=-.057107(.0033066)
```

Using *the* SAS® *System* in the Pharmaceutical Industry: Project Setup and Standardization for the Analysis of Clinical Trial Data

Cam Huffman, Burroughs Wellcome Co.
Carl P. Arneson, Burroughs Wellcome Co.
John Horton, Burroughs Wellcome Co.
John H. King, J. H. King Associates

ABSTRACT

At Burroughs Wellcome Co., statistical programmers in the Clinical Statistics Department generally work on many different projects. Each project requires that different types of data be collected, managed, analyzed and presented. Usually, each project team has its own strategy of dealing with these responsibilities. In the past, this has resulted in programming inconsistencies and duplication of effort among SAS programmers. To overcome this problem, we have implemented a system to standardize SAS programming strategy and report generation within and across projects. The system includes a set of SAS programs and macros for keeping track of titles, pre-processing data to create "analysis data sets" that contain both raw and derived data structured in logical and useful ways, and initializing SAS programs for a particular project. This system has helped us acheive greater programming efficiency and consistency and at the same time, has helped us to improve the quality of our work.

INTRODUCTION

The Clinical Statistics Department at Burroughs Wellcome Co. generates statistical reports containing summary tables, graphics, and data listings which present safety and efficacy analyses for many different pharmaceutical products. The reports are used by clinical groups within the company and are eventually included in a New Drug Application prepared for the Food and Drug Administration.

In the past, we have run into difficulties when many SAS programmers work on the same project. This is usually the result of producing reports without an organized strategy to deal with across-project programming issues. Here are a few problems that can arise:

- There are often differences in the page layout and titles of tabular reports (which makes review of reports across the project difficult).
- Inconsistencies in how programs are named, documented, and tracked (which can lead to frustration when a table, graphic, or listing needs to be reproduced and/or updated or a programmer has to use someone else's code).
- Discrepancy in how derived variables are calculated in programming across the project (which causes inconsistency and error).
- Subtle differences in the way similar analyses are performed (which can lead to misleading conclusions).

These problems are difficult to deal with during the early stages of a project and are often magnified when data and results from different studies must be pooled together for an across-study analysis and review. In the end, these problems can eventually result in: a loss of valuable time, a lack of confidence in programming and output, arrousal of suspicion from reviewers who detect errors in tabular reports, and outright disaster.

In order to avoid these problems, our department is using is a system to standardize SAS programming strategy and report generation within and across projects. Specifically, this paper documents the system and spells out ways to:

- Use SAS programs and macros to consistently keep track of titles and programs across a project.
- Automate as much programing as possible through use of project-specific initialization macros and other programming tools.
- Pre-process data into "analysis data sets" in order to keep complicated analysis and data listing programs short and simple.
- Use project-wide SAS format and macro libraries for centralized organization and programming efficiency.
- Use macro programming to produce listings across studies.
- Make output appearace as consistent as possible through use of PROC REPORT, and other programming utilities.

PROGRAM INITIALIZATION MACROS

Programmers for a particular project often begin all their programs with the same few lines of code. These lines of code are typically used to set SAS system options, define library references, create common header titles, and perhaps to define some global macro variables that can be used later in the program. This can get quite tedious and can present problems when different programmers on the same project set themselves up in different ways. We propose that each project develop its own customized program initialization macro (or "INIT macro"), which every programmer on a project should call at the beginning of every program.

INIT macros replace several lines of code with a single macro call, make it easier for programmers to standardize margins, line size, page size, and other aspects of the appearance of their output, and are also a convenient place to do some more complicated tasks. An example of an INIT macro (called %P*nnn*INIT) is provided in **Appendix A**.

%P*nnn*INIT should be called at the beginning of any program for Project *nnn*. Though it has several key-word parameters, most have useful defaults, and rarely need to be specified. The PS=, LS=, SKIP= and PRINTER= parameters are used to control various SAS system options. The PROT= parameter is used to specify the particular study (or protocol) within a project for which the program is written. The macro uses this information to establish library references to the data for the correct study. If you do not specify the PROT= parameter, the macro will determine the study number from the file name of the program (NOTE: In this example, the %FN macro resolves to the file name of the program). Because of this, you must use a file naming convention for your programs that will include the study number. You can use the VSTOP= parameter to override the SAS version checking feature, which will stop program execution and print a warning in the SASLOG when you use an old release of SAS.

In addition to defining library references, setting SAS system options, and checking the SAS version number, %P*nnn*INIT performs a variety of more specialized functions. For instance, It places several useful special characters (e.g., 0123456789®©™) into global macro variables corresponding to their hex-codes (e.g., the hex character 'B1'x could be referred to as &XB1). It also generates two TITLE statements that will place some study information (including the project number, study number and the creation date of a typical data set), left-justified, in the first two title lines of any output. Finally, it calls a macro that places title lines for each piece of output that the program will generate into global macro variables. This macro is part of a "title management system" that we discuss in the next section.

%P*nnn*INIT would require some customization from project to project, and for different operating systems. We have intended for our example to introduce the concept of INIT macros, and to point out some useful functions that you may want them to perform.

TITLE AND TABLE NUMBER MANAGEMENT

Very often, changes need to be made to the titles or numbering scheme for tables, appendices or figures long after all the programs for a particular study have been completed. It is a nuisance to have to make these changes in each program, especially when there are many programs. This problem can be eliminated by storing all the titles and table numbers for a study in one SAS data set. Each program can then place the appropriate titles and table numbers into macro variables using the CALL SYMPUT routine. Not only can changes be made quickly and easily to many titles at one time, but a table of contents or listing of programs can be produced without having to reenter any information.

Titles and table numbers can be put into SAS data sets in several ways. You could use SAS/FSP® software and SAS/AF® software to build applications for entering and editing the titles directly in SAS data sets. Alternatively, you could keep all your titles in a separate text file and read them into a SAS data set whenever you make changes or additions to the text file. One method may be easier and more efficient than the other, depending on your computing environment.

The %GETTITLE macro (see **Appendix B**) can be used to read titles and table numbers from a specially formatted text file into a SAS data set. To use this macro, you must specify the SAS fileref of the text file, the name of the SAS data set, and your user-ID using the FILE=, DSET= and USER= key-word parameters. Additionally, you may specify the number of variables you wish to maintain in the SAS data set to store the individual title lines using the TITLES= parameter. The default is five, meaning that a maximum of five title lines will be stored in the variables TITLE1-TITLE5. You may need to increase this if you use more than five title lines, or decrease it if you use fewer than five title lines and would like to save space.

To use the %GETTITLE macro, you must organize the text file containing the titles in a specific way. The first line of each entry must contain the table, appendix or figure number in columns 1-9, the type of output (i.e., Appendix, Table or Figure) in columns 10-19, and the file name of the corresponding program in columns 20-27. Follow this line with individual title lines using columns 1-80. An example of a "titles file" is shown below:

```
    5    10   15   20   25   30   35   40
----+----+----+----+----+----+----+----+
B1       Appendix  SUGIPGM1
Listing of Demographic Information
1        Table     SUGIPGM1
Summary of Demographic Information
B2       Appendix  SUGIPGM2
Listing of Medical History Information
2        Table     SUGIPGM2
Summary of Medical History Information
(Part 1 of 2)
2        Table     SUGIPGM2
Summary of Medical History Information
(Part 2 of 2)
```

To simplify the process of getting titles from the text file into a SAS data set, you may want to reduce the necessary steps to a single command that you can issue at the command line of your particular operating system. For example, on the CMS operating system, we have accomplished this using a Rexx EXEC (called NEWTITLE EXEC; see **Appendix C**).

To use NEWTITLE EXEC, you must type

NEWTITLE *filename*

where *filename* is the file name of your text file containing the titles (which must have a file type of "TITLES"). This file name must the same as the file type used for the study's data library. The NEWTITLE EXEC first verifies the existence of the text file and ensures that you have Read/Write access to the output data set. It then puts the file name that you specified, the file mode that contains the data and your user-ID into CMS GLOBALV variables. Finally, it runs the following SAS program that reads the information from the CMS GLOBALV variables and calls %GETTITLE:

```
/* NEWTITLE SAS */

%let user = %sysget(gettitle user) ;
%let  lib = %sysget(gettitle lib)  ;
%let   fm = %sysget(gettitle fm)   ;

libname  out "&lib &fm" ;
filename titles disk "&lib TITLES A" ;

%gettitle(dset=OUT.TITLES,file=titles,
          user=&user) ;
```

Once the titles and table numbers are successfully stored in a SAS data set, you will need to get them into appropriate TITLE statements in all of your programs. You can accomplish this using the %SETTITLE and %PUTTITLE macros (see **Appendix D** and **Appendix E**).

The %SETTITLE macro will place the type of output and output number into the global macro variables &TABNUM1-&TABNUM*n*, and each of the title lines into the global macro variables &TITLE1_1-&TITLE9_*n* (where *n* is the number of observations in the data set containing the titles for a given program). To use this macro, you must specify the file name of the current program and the name of the data set containing the titles using the FN= and DSET= parameters. If you call this macro at the top of a program, you can use the global macro variables that it creates in TITLE statements any time in your program. Alternatively, you can call this macro in an INIT macro (see the previous section on "Program Initialization Macros").

The %PUTTITLE macro will use the global macro variables created by %SETTITLE macro to generate appropriate TITLE statements that correspond to each piece of output in a program. Additionally, it will create a global macro variable (&NEXTT) that resolves to the number of the next available TITLE line. You should call the %PUTTITLE macro anywhere where you would normally place TITLE statements for your output. Usually, you will not need to specify any parameters. By default, it will begin with TITLE3, since TITLE1 and TITLE2 are usually used for "header titles" that are defined in an INIT macro. However, this can be overridden using the STARTN= parameter. If you are using %PUTTITLE with a SAS/GRAPH® procedure, you may specify GRAPHIC=Y, which will allow you to specify a font and height with the FONT= and HEIGHT= parameters.

The following example illustrates the use of %PUTTITLE (where %SETTITLE is called within %P*nnn*INIT; see **Appendix A**):

```
/* SUGIPGM1 SAS */
%pnnninit(prot=ppp) ;
/* Data manipulation */
proc report data=dd01 ;
  /* more PROC REPORT statements */
  %puttitle ;
  title&nextt 'Some extra title line' ;
  run ;
/* More data manipulation */
proc report data=dd01 ;
  /* more PROC REPORT statements */
  %puttitle ;
  run ;
```

In the example above, the first call of %PUTTITLE corresponds to the first entry for SUGIPGM1 in the text file, and the second call corresponds to the second entry. The macro keeps track of the appropriate entry using a global macro variable (&__PTCNT) that is used to count the number of times that %PUTTITLE has been called within a program. If no entry corresponding to the current value of &__PTCNT is found, "dummy" titles will be generated.

The %GETTITLE, %SETTITLE and %PUTTITLE macros provide a convenient method for managing titles and table numbers. They can be easily modified to fit a variety of specialized situations. We have found that long term benefits of using these macros outweigh the small amount of time and effort that it takes to implement them.

DATA PREPARATION PROGRAMS

In general, data we retrieve from our clinical data management system usually needs some manipulation before it is truly ready to use. When working with a single database, some programmers tend to redundantly manipulate data in several programs. Instead of programming in this fashion, data manipulation, where possible, should be performed in one program, and the results should be stored in permanent SAS data sets. If data is retreived and updated often, this manipulation should be performed automatically as part of the data retreival process. This practice will help to keep complicated analysis and listing programs as short and as simple as possible, while decreasing the time you spend on programming.

Since data preparation programs are highly dependent on the study design, we did not include an example. However, here are a few data preparation ideas and concepts you may want to use:

- It is often useful to create a data set which pulls together all key identification, sorting, subsetting, and other often used variables. This "ID" data set should contain one observation per patient.
- Merge the "ID" data set into some or all other data sets (this may save CPU time in the long run, but make sure that storage space is not an issue).
- Set up important analysis data sets and store the results in permanent SAS data sets so they will not have to be recreated every time they are used.
- Sort all data in the order it will most likely be merged and presented.
- Associate formats and labels with key variables.
- Decide on the wording of formats and labels up-front, before the bulk of programming takes place. This will avoid future programming changes.
- If needed, add any information which is not in the database (e.g., patients not treated as randomized).
- Reorganize data that are awkwardly structured.
- If variable names are unsatisfactory, change them.
- If coded data is confusing, change it.
- Check for consistency of units and delete unit variables when all are the same.
- Remove unwanted variables.
- Decide on a method for calculating relative time, and include relative time in listings of data with dates wherever feasible.
- Add relative time or other derived variables to data sets up-front. It's helpful to identify these derived variables added to data sets by using a leading underbar in the variable name.

OTHER PROGRAMMING ISSUES

Besides data manipulation, and specific SAS macro code, there are other simple concepts that can be put into practice to enhance programming productivity. It's often a good idea to meet with the end-user of your output (in our case, our colleagues in Clinical Research and ultimately the FDA) to agree upon the layout of listings, tables and figures up-front. This practice helps to avoid time consuming programming changes at the end of the report generation process. It's also beneficial to standardize items such as column headers, titles, the handling of missing values, variable formats, abbreviations, etc. Other programming issues that could be addressed are:

- Use of %MACPAGE page numbers in a consistent location on the page (see "*MACPAGE - A SAS Macro for Enhancing Reports*", K.D. Edwards & J.H. King, Proceedings of the Fourteenth Annual SUGI Conference, 1989, 1024-1027).
- Use of %JOBID for identification of program, user, and date and time run (see "*SAS Macros for Source Program Tracking*", J.H. King & D.S. Goldstein, Proceedings of the Fifteenth Annual SUGI Conference, 1990, 1206-1208).
- Use the same version of SAS across the project.
- Development of a project macro library containing macros specifcally used for that project.
- Development of a project format library, containing formats for commonly used variables.
- Use of mixed case vs. uppercase in titles, column headers, and formats.
- Suppressing repeated values of sorting variables.
- Use of formatted values. Codes (unformatted values) can force the reviewer to constantly refer to footnotes.
- For data where only the exceptions are interesting (e.g., admission criteria), list only observations with unexpected or missing data.
- Use of a naming convention for program names. The convention could include an indicator of project and may include digits for the study, programmer, data type, and output type.
- Use of across-study programs using the macro facility (i.e., programs that generate output for more than one study).
- Use of PROC REPORT (or PROC PRINT) versus data nulls. The former can save considerable programming and revision time.
- Decide who will maintain project data, who will be allowed to retrieve or modify the data, format libraries and macro libraries and how they will notify others they have done so.

CONCLUSION

By using these programming tools and concepts, our SAS programmers have become more consistent in their programming practices. This makes keeping track of programming setup and analysis strategies across many projects less frustrating. We believe these concepts can be generalized and used in any organization where SAS programming production work takes place. In our case, the use of this system has resulted in greater programming efficiency and consistency, and has improved the quality of our work.

ACKNOWLEDGMENTS

We would like to thank the following members of the "Mean Squares" Quality Circle for their contributions to this paper:

Randall Austin	Erin McDade	Hedy Weissinger
Lynn Dix	Janna Scott	Diane Wold
Suzanne Edwards	Denise Shortino	

The first three authors can be contacted at:
Burroughs Wellcome Co.
3030 Cornwallis Road.
Research Triangle Park, NC 27709

The fourth author can be contacted at:
J. H. King Associates
29 Eastwood Drive
Bryant, AR 72022
(501) 847 - 8247
FAX: (501) 847 - 8871

APPENDIX A:

```
%macro PnnnINIT(prot=,printer=IBM,ps=56,ls=132,
                skip=6,vstop=Y) ;
%*******************************************************
%* PURPOSE: Initialize SAS environment for this project
%*    NOTE: This example is written for the
%*          CMS Operating System
%*******************************************************;
%*-----------------------------------------------------*
%* If PROT= has not been specified, try to get the
%* protocol number from the file name of the program:
%*-----------------------------------------------------;
%if &prot= %then %let prot = %substr(%fn,2,3) ;

%*-----------------------------------------------------*
%* Make sure the correct version of SAS is being used:
%*-----------------------------------------------------;
%if %length(&vstop) %then %let vstop =
%upcase(%substr(&vstop,1,1)) ;
%if &vstop=Y and &sysver~=6.07 %then %do ;
  %put ERROR: Version &sysver of SAS is being used. ;
  %put ERROR: Use Version 6.07. ;
  %if &sysenv=BACK %then %str(;ENDSAS;) ;
%end ;

%*-----------------------------------------------------*
%* Associate the libref "LIBRARY" with the project
%* format library:
%*-----------------------------------------------------;
libname library 'PnnnFMT *' ;

%*-----------------------------------------------------*
%* Associate the librefs "IN" and "OUT" with the
%* appropriate input and output data libraries:
%*-----------------------------------------------------;
libname in  "Pnnn&prot *" ;
libname out "Pnnn&prot A" ;

%*-----------------------------------------------------*
%* Establish a list of hex characters (preceded by an "x")
%* to be placed in global macro variables:
%*-----------------------------------------------------;
%local hexlist ;
%let hexlist=xb1 xb2 xb3 xb4 xb5 xb6 xb7 xb8 xb9 xb0 x8c
             xae xbe xbf ;
%global &hexlist ;

%*-----------------------------------------------------*
%* Read the date from a typical data set from the project
%* data library (in this case, we are using
%* demography data):
%*-----------------------------------------------------;
proc contents data=in.dd01 out=t_e_m_p(keep=crdate)
              noprint ;
  run ;

%*-----------------------------------------------------*
%* Put the data set creation date and the hex characters
%* into macro variables using CALL SYMPUT:
%*-----------------------------------------------------;
%local date ;
data _null_ ;
  set t_e_m_p(obs=1) ;
  if crdate>.Z then
    call symput('date',put(datepart(crdate),worddate18.));
  else call symput('date','Unknown') ;
  i = 1 ;
  w = scan("&hexlist",i,' ') ;
  do while (w~=' ') ;
    hexc = input(substr(w,2,2),$hex2.) ;
    call symput(w,hexc) ;
    i = i + 1 ;
    w = scan("&hexlist",i,' ') ;
  end ;
  run ;

%*-----------------------------------------------------*
%* Create global macro variables HEAD1 and HEAD2 for
%* header titles, and the global macro variable PAD for
%* left justifying titles and footnotes:
%*-----------------------------------------------------;
%global head1 head2 pad ;
%let date = %left(%trim(&date)) ;
%let head1 = Project nnn, Protocol &prot ;
%let head2 = (Data as of: &date) ;
%let pad='                                              ';

%*-----------------------------------------------------*
%* Set SAS options (with printer specific FORMCHARs):
%*-----------------------------------------------------;
options nodate nonumber ls=&ls skip=&skip pagesize=&ps
        missing=' '
  %if %upcase(&printer)=IBM %then %do ;
    formchar='FABFACCCBCEB8FECABCBBB4E7B4F6061E04C6EAF'x
  %end ;
  %else %if %upcase(&printer)=XEROX %then %do ;
    formchar='4F6D5C6D5C4F5C4F5C6D5C4E7B4F6061E04C6E5C'x
  %end ; ;

%*-----------------------------------------------------*
%* Insert header titles:
%*-----------------------------------------------------;
title1 "&head1" &pad &pad &pad ;
title2 "&head2" &pad &pad &pad ;

%*-----------------------------------------------------*
%* Put titles from titles data set into global macro
%* variables:
%*-----------------------------------------------------;
%settitle(fn=%fn) ;
```

APPENDIX B:

```
%macro GETTITLE(dset=,file=,user=,titles=5) ;
%*******************************************************
%* PURPOSE:  Get titles from a text file and store them in
%*           a SAS data set
%*******************************************************;
%*-----------------------------------------------------*
%*  Determine whether the DSET= data set exists yet:
%*-----------------------------------------------------;
%local new lib mem ;
%if %index(&dset,%str(.)) %then %do ;
  %let lib = %upcase(%scan(&dset,1,%str(.))) ;
  %let mem = %upcase(%scan(&dset,2,%str(.))) ;
%end ;
%else %do ;
  %let lib = WORK ;
  %let mem = %upcase(&dset) ;
%end ;

%let new=1 ;
proc contents data=&lib.._all_ out=t_e_m_p(keep=memname)
              noprint ;
  run ;
data _null_ ;
  set t_e_m_p(where=(memname="&mem")) ;
  call symput('NEW','0') ;
  stop ;
  run ;

data t_e_m_p ;
  infile &file end=eof lrecl=80 pad ;
  drop line i titleno ;
  length user $8 ;
  user = "&user" ;
  retain tabnum type program titleno title1-title&titles ;
  array _t (&titles) $80 title1-title&titles ;
  input @1 line $80. @ ;
  if upcase(trim(substr(line,10,8)))
       in('APPENDIX','TABLE','FIGURE') then do ;
    if _n_>1 then do ;
      output ;
      do i = 1 to dim(_t) ;
        _t(i) = ' ' ;
      end ;
    end ;
    titleno = 0 ;
    input @1 tabnum $9. @10 type $9. @20 program $8. ;
    program = upcase(program) ;
  end ;
  else do ;
    titleno + 1 ;
    _t(titleno) = line ;
  end ;
  if eof then output ;
  run ;

data &dset(index=(program)) ;
  set %if &new=0 %then %do ;
        &dset (where=(user~="&user"))
      %end ;
      t_e_m_p ;
  run ;

%mend GETTITLE ;
```

APPENDIX C:

```
/*******************************************************/
/*  This EXEC will run GETTITLE SAS to put titles in   */
/*    a text file into a SAS data set                  */
/*******************************************************/
arg lib .

user = userid()

if lib = '' then do
  say 'You must supply the file name of the TITLES',
      || ' text file'
  exit 8
  end

'SET EMSG OFF'
'STATE' lib 'TITLES A'
ok = rc
'SET EMSG ON'
if ok *= 0 then do
  say lib 'TITLES A not found.'
  exit 8
  end

before = queued()
rwexist = 0
flag = 1
fm = 'A'

'MAKEBUF'

'QUERY DISK (STACK'
do i = 1 to queued() - before
  pull label vaddr mode stat .
  if stat = 'R/W' then do
    mode = substr(mode,1,1)
    'SET EMSG OFF'
```

```
    'STATEW TITLES' lib mode
    ok = rc
    'SET EMSG ON'
    if ok=0 & flag=1 then do
      flag = 0
      fm = mode
      rwexist = 1
      end
    end
  end
'DROPBUF'


if rwexist=0 then do
  'SET EMSG OFF'
  'STATE TITLES' lib '*'
  ok = rc
  'SET EMSG ON'
  if ok=0 then do
    say 'TITLES' lib 'exists only on a read-only',
        || ' file mode.'
    say 'TITLES' lib 'cannot be updated.'
    exit 8
    end
  else say 'NOTE: TITLES' lib 'not found.'
  end

'GLOBALV SELECT GETTITLE PUT LIB FM USER'

'EXEC SAS NEWTITLE'
ok = rc

if ok ^= 0 then do
  say 'NEWTITLE SAS failed (rc=' || ok || ').'
  exit ok
  end

'ERASE NEWTITLE SASLOG A'

say 'TITLES' lib 'has been updated on file mode' fm || '.'

exit
```

APPENDIX D:

```
%macro SETTITLE(fn=,dset=in.titles) ;
%*******************************************************;
%* PURPOSE: Place the titles for the current program
%*          from the titles data set into global macro
%*          variables
%*******************************************************;
%*-----------------------------------------------------*
%* Get only observations for the current program from the
%* titles data set:
%*-----------------------------------------------------;
data t_e_m_p ;
  set &dset (where=(upcase(program)="%upcase(&fn)")) ;
  run ;

%*-----------------------------------------------------*
%* Count the number of title entries for the current
%* program:
%*-----------------------------------------------------;
%local _nobs ;
data _null_ ;
  if 0 then set t_e_m_p nobs=count ;
  call symput('_nobs',left(put(count,8.))) ;
  stop ;
  run ;

%*-----------------------------------------------------*
%* Initialize and globalize the macro variables:
%*   TABNUM1-TABNUMn, TYPE1-TYPEn, NUM1-NUMn,
%*     TITLE1_1-TITLE9_n
%*   where n is the number of observations in the
%*   titles data setfor the current program.
%*-----------------------------------------------------;
%local i j ;
%do i = 1 %to &_nobs ;
  %global tabnum&i type&i num&i ;
  %do j = 1 %to 9 ;
    %global title&j._&i ;
  %end ;
%end ;

%*-----------------------------------------------------*
%* Read the titles data set and use CALL SYMPUT to put
%* the titles and table numbers into the appropriate
%* macro variables:
*------------------------------------------------------;
%if &_nobs>0 %then %do ;
  data _null_ ;
    set t_e_m_p ;
    array _t (9) title1-title9 ;
    call symput('tabnum'!!left(_n_),
                trim(type)!!' '!!trim(tabnum)) ;
    call symput('type'!!left(_n_),substr(type,1,1)) ;
    call symput('num'!!left(_n_),trim(tabnum)) ;
    do i = 1 to dim(_t) ;
      call symput('title'!!left(i)!!'_'!!left(_n_),
                  trim(_t(i))) ;
    end ;
    run ;
%end ;

%mend SETTITLE ;
```

APPENDIX E:

```
%macro
PUTTITLE(startn=3,graphic=N,font=SIMPLEX,height=0.68) ;
%*******************************************************
%* PURPOSE: When used in conjuction with SETTITLE, will
%*          generate appropriate TITLE statements for a
%*          given table or appendix for the current
%*          program
%*******************************************************;
%*-----------------------------------------------------*
%* Update or create a global macro variable to act as
%* a counter for the number of times the macro is called:
%*-----------------------------------------------------;
%global __ptcnt ;
%if &__ptcnt= %then %let __ptcnt = 1 ;
%else %let __ptcnt = %eval(&__ptcnt + 1) ;

%*-----------------------------------------------------*
%* For graphics, build a string of graphics options:
%*-----------------------------------------------------;
%local gopt ;
%if %quote(&graphic)~= %then %do ;
  %if %upcase(%substr(&graphic,1,1))=Y %then %do ;
    %if %quote(&font)~= %then %let gopt = &gopt F=&font ;
    %if %quote(&height)~= %then %let gopt = &gopt H=0.68 ;
    %let gopt = &gopt J=C ;
  %end ;
%end ;

%*-----------------------------------------------------*
%* Calculate the maximum number of title lines:
%*-----------------------------------------------------;
%local titles ;
%let titles = %eval(10 - &startn) ;

%*-----------------------------------------------------*
%* If no titles have been established for the current
%* piece of output, create dummy values:
%*-----------------------------------------------------;
%local i check ;
%let check = 1 ;
%do i = 1 %to &titles ;
  %global title&i._&__ptcnt ;
  %if %nrbquote(&&title&i._&__ptcnt)~= %then %let check=0;
%end ;
%if &check %then %do i = 1 %to 3 ;
  %let title&i._&__ptcnt = Sample title line number &i ;
%end ;

%global tabnum&__ptcnt type&__ptcnt num&__ptcnt ;
%if %nrbquote(&&tabnum&__ptcnt)= %then %do ;
  %let tabnum&__ptcnt = Appendix/Table # ;
  %let type&__ptcnt   = A ;
  %let num&__ptcnt    = 0 ;
%end ;

%*-----------------------------------------------------*
%* Count the non-null titles:
%*-----------------------------------------------------;
%local ntitle ;
%do i = 1 %to &titles ;
  %if %nrbquote(&&title&i._&__ptcnt)~= %then
    %let ntitle = &i ;
%end ;

%*-----------------------------------------------------*
%* Generate TITLE statement for table number:
%*-----------------------------------------------------;
title&startn &gopt "&&tabnum&__ptcnt" ;

%*-----------------------------------------------------*
%* Set the global macro variables TYPE and NUM and
%* initialize the global macro variable TOC:
%*-----------------------------------------------------;
%global type num toc ;
%let type = &&type&__ptcnt ;
%let num = &&num&__ptcnt ;
%let toc = ;

%do i = 1 %to &ntitle ;
  %let startn = %eval(&startn + 1) ;
  %*---------------------------------------------------*
  %* Generate TITLE statements for each title line of
  %* the current for the current set of titles:
  %*---------------------------------------------------;
  title&startn &gopt "&&title&i._&__ptcnt" ;

  %*---------------------------------------------------*
  %* Build the TOC macro variable, excluding
  %* lines of the form:  (Part k of n)
  %*---------------------------------------------------;
  %local key ;
  %let key = (PART ;
  %if %index(%upcase(%nrbquote(&&title&i._&__ptcnt)),
             %nrbquote(&key))=0
  and %nrbquote(&&title&i._&__ptcnt)~= %then
           %let toc = &toc &&title&i._&__ptcnt ;
%end ;

%*-----------------------------------------------------*
%* Set the global macro variable NEXTT:
%*-----------------------------------------------------;
%global nextt ;
%let nextt = %eval(&startn + 1) ;

%mend PUTTITLE ;
```

SAS® Macros for Converting Between ARC/INFO® Import/Export Files and SAS Data Sets

Barbara L. Jackson, Oak Ridge National Laboratory[1]

Abstract

ARC/INFO is a widely used geographic information system by Environmental Systems Research Institute (ESRI). ARC/INFO has powerful spatial analysis and presentation capabilities, but its data management and statistical analysis capabilities are limited. The SAS macros described here facilitate exchange of data between ARC/INFO and SAS.

The SAS macro, ARCTOSAS, creates a SAS data set from an ARC/INFO sequential export file. The SAS data set will have as many variables as there are INFO items, with identical or abbreviated names and appropriate data types.

The SAS macro, QUICKARC, creates a sequential file from a SAS data set. This file can be imported directly into ARC/INFO for use in the geographic information system. All the variables in the SAS data set are included as items in the INFO data set, with the appropriate data types and the same names.

The macros run under SAS version 6 for the PC/DOS and VMS operating systems, and version 5.18 or higher for MVS operating systems.

QUICKARC for SAS Version 6

The QUICKARC macro creates a flat, .E00-type file that can be imported by ARC/INFO from a member of a SAS version 6 data set. (There is also a SAS version 5.18 QUICKARC program that will run on the IBM mainframe.) Some features of QUICKARC are the following:

1. The file name of the .E00 file appears in the first record of the .E00 file. The name of the SAS data set appears in the third record of the .E00 file. This feature will help to keep track of the origin of data sets.

2. All the variables in the SAS member are included as INFO items in the output file. All SAS variables will have their same name in the INFO data set.

3. All numeric variables in the SAS data set will be floating (8-byte) INFO items, regardless of their SAS length. The INFO display format will be (10.4).

4. All character variables in the SAS data set will be character items in the INFO data set, with the same length.

5. SAS numeric variables with a date format will be floating (8-byte) in the INFO data set. Since the SAS date value is not useful in INFO, variables for year, month, and day should be created in SAS as needed.

6. Missing values in the SAS data set will be written as blank in the .E00 file. (OPTIONS MISSING=' '; appears in the macro.) ARC/INFO will read in the blank values as zeros. If this is not acceptable, the missing values in the SAS data set should be modified before invoking the QUICKARC macro.

To summarize, the SAS data set should have exactly the variables and observations of interest with the desired name, type, length, and missing value specification before invoking the QUICKARC macro. It is very tedious to alter the .E00 file after it is created. Instead, the SAS data set should be modified and the QUICKARC macro invoked again.

TSO Interactive

The QUICKARC macro can be "included" into the edit screen of your TSO SAS session in the following manner: Supply the appropriate allocate statements for the output .E00 file, the SAS data set if necessary, and the file for the QUICKARC macro. Code the call statement for QUICKARC with the appropriate arguments, and "submit".

1. Logon to TSO.

2. Invoke SAS.

3. Submit the following to allocate the QUICKARC macro:
   libname arcprog '.arc.prog';

4. Submit the following to allocate the E00 output file:
   filename e00 '.myfile.e00' new lrecl(80);

5. Submit the following to allocate your (existing) SAS data set:
   libname mysas '.mysas.sas' old;

6. Create the SAS data set member(s) with exactly the variables (length and type) and observations desired.

7. On the command line for the edit screen:
   include arcprog(quickarc)

(The entire QUICKARC macro listing will appear in the edit screen.)

Hit the SUBMIT PF key or enter the submit command on the command line. This will compile the QUICKARC macro so that it can be used anytime during the rest of your SAS session.

8. Invoke the macro with a call statement and submit:
   %QUICKARC(SASDATA=mysas.abc,FILE=e00,
   WORKFILE=work2,DUMMY=arra);

where
SASDATA is assigned the name of the input SAS data set member,
FILE is the ddname of the output E00 flat file,
WORKFILE is a (one-level) SAS work data set,
DUMMY is a four-letter (or less) SAS variable name that does not appear in the SASDATA data set.

The default argument values are shown below:

```
%QUICKARC(SASDATA=sasin,FILE=e00,
 WORKFILE=work2,DUMMY=arra);
```

If a parameter is omitted, the default value will be used. The SAS log screen will display the progress of the macro. The output screen will display work data sets.

9. Copy the E00 file to the host computer that has the ARC/INFO software. The following example is for copying from an IBM/MVS® mainframe to a VAX/VMS® using INTERLINK®.

   Log on to the VAX and type the command:

   ```
   $convert/truncate/fdl=anye00.fdl hostibm::"[uid]myfile.e00"
       vaxfile.e00
   ```

Note: The anye00.fdl file can be created from an .e00 file using the ANALYZE/RMS_FILE/FDL command on the VAX.

10. Import the vaxfile.e00 to ARC/INFO.

   ```
   $ARC
   arc: IMPORT INFO VAXFILE.E00 ARCFILE.EXT
   ```

   where
   VAXFILE.E00 is the SAS output file
   ARCFILE.EXT is the INFO data set.

ARCTOSAS for SAS Version 6

The ARCTOSAS macro creates a SAS (version 6) data set from an ARC/INFO export (.E00) file. (There is also an ARCTOSAS program for SAS version 5.18 that runs on the IBM mainframe.) Some features of ARCTOSAS include the following:

1. The SAS data set that is created will have as many variables as there are INFO items in the .E00 file. The names of the SAS variables will be identical or close to the INFO item names. If a set of unique SAS variable names cannot be created from the set of INFO item names, the SAS variable names will be VAR1-VARn, where n is the number of items.

2. The LABEL for the SAS data set will be the name of the .E00 file and the name of the originating ARC file.

3. The LABELs for the SAS variables will be the exact corresponding INFO item names.

4. The length and type of the SAS variables are shown below:

–INFO item–	–SAS variable–
binary (4,8)	numeric (8)
char (1-4096)	char ($1-$200)
date (8)	date (8)
floating (4,8)	numeric (8)
integer (4,8)	numeric (8)

5. The SAS data set will have the same number of observations as the .E00 file.

6. The ARCTOSAS macro will print a PROC CONTENTS and 10 observations of the SAS data set.

Create the ARC/INFO EXPORT File

The ARCTOSAS reads as input an ARC/INFO export file. This file will typically have a name extension of .E00. The export file must be created in ARC. The following example is for ARC/INFO running on a VAX with VMS:

1. Log on to the VAX.

2. Invoke ARC/INFO.
   $ARC

3. Execute the EXPORT command
   arc: EXPORT INFO ARCFILE.EXT OUTNAME NONE

where
   a. ARCFILE.EXT is the INFO data set,
   b. OUTNAME is the name of the export file (OUTNAME.E00),
   c. NONE specifies no compression.

4. Exit from ARC.
   $arc: quit

5. Copy the export file to the computer that has the SAS software. Below are some hints for copying the .E00 file to another computer.

   a. Copy to IBM mainframe with MVS operating system over INTERLINK.

The .E00 file has record length of 80, but is stored as variable length records of undefined length on the VAX. The IBM mainframe with MVS operating system requires that the length of the records be defined as 80 bytes with fixed length. Therefore, you can use the Convert command on the VAX to copy the file to the IBM and, at the same time, convert it to fixed length. Or you can use the Copy command and use switches to specify the length of the file.

```
$convert/truncate/fdl=fix80.fdl
 arcfile.e00 nodename::"[uid]ibmfile.e00"
```

or

```
$copy arcfile.e00
nodename::"[uid]ibmfile.e00/fixed:80/pad:20"
```

   uid is your user id.
   nodename is the name of the IBM host.
   The fix80.fdl file can be created from an existing 80-byte, fixed length record file using the Analyze/rms_file/fdl command.

   b. Copy to an IBM-compatible personal computer. See the documentation for your communications software for downloading the .E00 file to your PC.

TSO Interactive

The ARCTOSAS macro can be "included" into the edit screen of your TSO SAS session. Supply the appropriate allocate statements for the .E00 export file, the SAS data set, and the file containing the ARCTOSAS macro. Code the call statement for ARCTOSAS with the appropriate arguments, and "submit".

1. Log on to TSO.

2. Invoke SAS.

3. Submit the following to allocate your SAS data set:
   libref mysas '\arc\gis';

4. On the command line of the edit screen:
   include '\arc\arctosas.sas'

(The entire ARCTOSAS macro listing will appear in the edit screen.)

Hit the SUBMIT PF key, or enter the submit command on the command line. This will compile the ARCTOSAS macro so that it can be used anytime during the rest of your SAS session.

5. Invoke the macro with a call statement and submit:

   %ARCTOSAS(INFILE='info.e00',OUTSAS=mysas.member,
   WORKFILE=work1,DUMMY=dummy);

   where
   a. INFILE specifies the file name of the ARC/INFO export file, 'C:\ARCDIR\FILE.E00'.
   b. OUTSAS specifies the one-level (temporary) or two-level (permanent) SAS output data set.
   c. WORKFILE specifies a SAS work data set (temporary).
   d. DUMMY specifies a five-character or less SAS variable name that is not the name of an INFO variable in the .E00 data set.

The default values are shown below:

%ARCTOSAS(INFILE='info.e00',OUTSAS=outsas,
WORKFILE=work1,DUMMY=dummy);

If a parameter is omitted from the argument list, the default value will be used.

The SAS log screen will display the progress of the macro. The output screen will display work data sets.

The macro will print a PROC CONTENTS and 10 observations of the SAS data set to the output screen. You may continue the SAS session as desired.

1. SAS is a registered trademark of SAS Institute, Inc., Cary, NC, USA.
2. ARC/INFO is a registered trademark of Environmental Systems Research Institute (ESRI), Redlands, CA, USA.
3. INTERLINK is a registered trademark of Computer Sciences, Inc., Freemont, CA, USA.
4. IBM and MVS are registered trademarks of International Business Machines Corporation.
5. VAX and VMS are registered trademarks of Digital Equipment Corporation.

[1]Managed by Martin Marietta Energy Systems, Inc. under contract DE-AC05-84OR21400 with the U.S. Department of Energy.

Appendix 1 - QUICKARC MACRO

```
%MACRO QUICKARC(SASDATA=sasin,FILE='arcfile.e00',
WORKFILE=work2, DUMMY=arra);
  %* this macro creates an ARC export file (.e00) from a SAS data
  set.
  SASDATA is one- or two- level sas name of input data set.
  FILE is name of the output (flat) arc/info import file.
  WORKFILE is name of temporary SAS work data set (should be
  one-level).
  DUMMY is a SAS variable name of four characters or less that
  does not appear in the SASDATA data set.
  default values for arguments are shown in the argument list;

OPTIONS MISSING = ' ';
%*----CHKSET-------------------------------------------;
%MACRO CHKSET(INDATA);
%* this macro is a PC version of the macro to check
  to see if a SAS data set exists.
  INDATA is one- or two-level SAS data set name (CAPS or lower
  case).
  the macro variable &DAMSG will have value BAD if no data set
  &DAMSG will have value OK if data set exists;
  %LOCAL MEMNAME LIBNAME;
  %GLOBAL DAMSG;
  %LET DAMSG=BAD;
  %IF %INDEX(&INDATA,.) GT 0 %THEN %DO;
  %LET LIBNAME
  =%QUOTE(%UPCASE(%QUOTE(%SCAN(&INDATA,1,.))));
  %LET MEMNAME
  =%QUOTE(%UPCASE(%QUOTE(%SCAN(&INDATA,2,.))));
  %END;
  %ELSE %DO;
  %LET LIBNAME=WORK;
  %LET MEMNAME
  =%QUOTE(%UPCASE(%QUOTE(&INDATA)));
  %END;
  data cout;
  run;
  proc contents data=&INDATA noprint out=cout
  (keep=memname);
  data _null_;
  set cout;
  if memname = "&MEMNAME" then call symput('DAMSG','OK');
  stop;
  run;
%MEND CHKSET;
%*-----------------------------------------------------;
%CHKSET(&SASDATA);
%IF &DAMSG=BAD %THEN %DO;
  %PUT '*********';
  %PUT "SAS data set &SASDATA does not exist - QUICKARC
  terminating";
  %PUT '*********';
  %END;
  %ELSE %DO;
  %*
  create output data set from proc contents of SASDATA;
  proc contents data=&SASDATA out=&WORKFILE;
%*
  create some macro variables from information in contents data
  set.
  NUMVARS has the number of variables in the data set
  ARCREC has the length in bytes of the logical data record
    for FILE
  NUMRECS  number of 80-byte physical records in a logical
  record
  LOGLEN  length of logical data record
  NUMOBS  number of data observations;
  data &WORKFILE;
  set &WORKFILE end = eof;
  retain arcrec loglen boundary;
  if type = 1 then length = 8; /* length is always 8 for numeric*/
  laglen = lag(length);
  if _n_ = 1 then do;
    arcrec = length; /* initialize arcrec */
    boundary = 14;   /* first boundary is always 14  */
    if type = 1 then loglen = 24; /*logical length 24 for numeric*/
    else loglen = length;      /*logical len =length for char*/
    end;
    else do;
    arcrec = arcrec + length;   /* increment arcrec */
    boundary = boundary + laglen*10; /* len of prev var times
    10*/
    if type = 1 then loglen = loglen + 24; /* 24 for numeric var*/
      else loglen = loglen + length;
    end;
    if eof then do;
      call symput('NUMVARS',(put(_n_,3.)));
      call symput('ARCREC',(put(arcrec,4.)));
      call symput('LOGLEN',(put(loglen,4.)));
      call symput('NUMOBS',(put(nobs,8.)));
```

```
      call symput('NUMRECS',left(put(ceil(loglen/80),5.)));
      end;
    keep length name type boundary;
  run;
proc print data=&WORKFILE;
%PUT number of variables is **&NUMVARS**;
%PUT length of arc records is **&ARCREC**;
%PUT length of physical data records is **&LOGLEN**;
%PUT number of phys records in a logical record is
**&NUMRECS**;
%PUT number of data records is **&NUMOBS**;
  %*
  write header information and variable information to FILE
  create macro variables
    MVi variable name
    FMi output format of variable
    STi starting position of variable in output record
    Wli width of output variable
    ;
  data _null_;
    set &WORKFILE;
    file &FILE;
    retain startpos;
    if _n_ = 1 then do;
      put 'EXP  0' @8 "&FILE";
      put 'IFO  2';
      put @1 "&SASDATA" @36 "&NUMVARS" @40 "&NUMVARS"
        @43 "&ARCREC" @49 "&NUMOBS";
      startpos = 1;
      end;
    call symput('MV'||left(put(_n_,5.)),name);
    call symput('ST'||left(put(_n_,8.)),left(put(startpos,8.)));
    if type=1 then do;              /* numeric variable */
      call symput('FM'||left(put(_n_,5.)),'E24.0');
      put name $8. @17 '  8-1'  boundary 5.  '-1  10 4 60-1  -1
      -1-1' @67 _n_ 3.;
      call symput('WI'||left(put(_n_,5.)),'24');
      startpos = startpos + 24;
      end;
      else if type=2 then do;             /* character variable */
        call symput('FM'||left(put(_n_,5.)),
          '$char'||compress(put(length,5.))||'.');
        call symput('WI'||left(put(_n_,5.)),left(put(length,8.)));
        startpos = startpos + length;
        put name $8. @17 length 3. '-1'  boundary 5.  '-1 '  length
        3.  '-1 20-1  -1  -1-1' @67 _n_ 3.;
        end;
    run;

%DO i = 1 %TO &NUMVARS;
  %PUT mv&i=*&&MV&i*   fm&i=*&&FM&i*   st&i=*&&ST&i*
  wi&i=*&&WI&i*;
  %END;
%*----PUTSTMTS-----------------------------------------;
%MACRO PUTSTMTS;
  %* this macro generates put statements for writing data records;
  %LOCAL i;
  %DO i = 1 %TO &NUMRECS;
    put (arra%EVAL((&i-1)*80+1) - arra%EVAL(&i*80) ) ($char1.);
    %END;
%MEND PUTSTMTS;
%*-------------------------------------------------;
%*
  write data records to FILE
  there are NUMRECS physical records for each logical record;
  data _null_;
    set &SASDATA end=eof;
    file &FILE mod;
      attrib &DUMMY.x length=$200;
      array &DUMMY{%EVAL(&NUMRECS*80)} $1
        &DUMMY.1-&DUMMY%EVAL(&NUMRECS*80) ;
    %* load variables into array 1 character at a time;
    %DO i = 1 %TO &NUMVARS;
      &DUMMY.x = put(&&MV&i,&&FM&i);
      do j = 1 to &&WI&i;
        &DUMMY{&&ST&i + j -1} = substr(&DUMMY.x,j,1);
        end;
      %END;
    %PUTSTMTS;
    if eof then do;
      put 'EOI';
      put 'EOS';
      end;
run;
run;
%END;
%MEND QUICKARC;

 /* calling example for SAS PC /*
*options mprint ;
*libname arc 'c:\sas\arci\';       /* define libname */
*%quickarc(SASDATA=arc.data1,FILE='arcfile2.e00');     /* call
quickarc */
*run;
```

Appendix 2 - ARCTOSAS MACRO

```
%MACRO ARCTOSAS(INFILE='info.e00',
OUTSAS=outsas,WORKFILE=work1, DUMMY=dummy);
%*
this macro creates a SAS data set from an ARC/INFO export file.
```

1. create an ARC/INFO export (.e00) file,
   $ARC
   arc: EXPORT INFO ARCFILE.EXT OUTNAME NONE

   where
   ARCFILE.EXT is ARC file,
   OUTNAME is export file name (OUTNAME.E00),
   NONE specifies no compression.

2. download the export (.e00) file to the PC.

3. a. invoke SAS on the PC.
   b. allocate SAS library, filenames.
   c. include the file that contains the ARCTOSAS macro.
   d. supply the ARCTOSAS macro call with the following arguments:
      INFILE is the ARC/INFO export file name
      OUTSAS is the one-level (temporary) or two-level (permanent) SAS output data set
      WORKFILE is a SAS work data set (temporary)
      DUMMY is a five-character or less SAS variable name that is not the name of an INFO variable in the .e00 data set (the default values are shown in the argument list of the macro statement).
   e. submit.

the resulting SAS data set will have as many variables as there are INFO items. the macro will attempt to give SAS names that are identical or close to the INFO item names. if it fails, the SAS names will be VAR1-VARn.
the LABEL for the SAS data set will be the value of the INFILE parameter (the .e00 data set name).
the LABELS for the SAS variables will be the exact corresponding INFO item names.

```
   the length and type of the SAS variables are shown below:

      --info item--              --SAS variable--
      binary (4,8)               real (8)
      char (1-4096)              char ($1-$200)
      date (8)                   date (8)
      floating (4,8)             real (8)
      integer (4,8)              real (8)

   good luck !

Program developed by Barbara Jackson, C&TD, (615) 574-8680,
2/90, Martin Marietta Energy Systems, Inc., P.O. Box 2008,
MS 6038, Oak Ridge, TN 37831-6038.
;

  data _null_;
    %GLOBAL NUMVARS INFOLINS DATALIN NUMDATA;
    infile &INFILE firstobs=3 obs=3;
%PUT you have chosen infile = &INFILE;
%PUT you have chosen outfile = &OUTSAS;
%PUT work file is &WORKFILE;
%PUT dummy variable name is &DUMMY;
    input numvars 39-42 numdata 52-56;
    /* numvars includes redefined items*/
    infolins = numvars + 3;        /* last information record */
    datalin = infolins + 1;        /* first data record */
    call symput('NUMVARS' ,left(put(numvars,5.)));
    call symput('INFOLINS',left(put(infolins,5.)));
    call symput('DATALIN' ,left(put(datalin,5.)));
    call symput('NUMDATA' ,left(put(numdata,5.)));
  run;
%PUT number of variables = &NUMVARS;
  data &WORKFILE;
    infile &INFILE firstobs=4 obs=&infolins;
    attrib sasname length=$8;
    attrib fmt length=$10;
    retain startcol endcol;
    input varname $16. arclen $3. @30 len $3. @34 dec_n $1. @36
    type 1.;
    nochars = length(varname);
    count = _n_;
    if _n_ = 1 then endcol = 0;
    sasname = substr(varname,1,8);
    %* replace invalid characters in sasname with '_' ;
    if indexc(sasname,'#-/*()\|$@!%&.?<>') gt 0 then
      sasname = translate
      (sasname,'_________________','#-/+()\|$@!%&.?<>');
    if indexc(sasname,"'") gt 0 then
      sasname = translate(sasname,'_',"'");
    %* assign a format value according to type
      assign the width of this field;
    select (type);
      when (1) do;                        /* date */
        fmt = 'yymmdd8.';
        width = 8;
        end;
      when (2) do;                        /* char */
        %*character variable is max length of 200;
        fmt = '$char'||compress(min(200,len))||'.';
        width = len;
        end;
      when (3) do;                        /*integer*/
        fmt = compress(arclen)||'.';
        width = arclen;
        end;
      when (5) do;                        /*binary */
        fmt = '11.'||left(dec_n);
        width = 11;
        end;
      when (6) if arclen='4' then do;     /*floating*/
        fmt = '14.'||left(dec_n);
        width = 14;
        end;
      else if arclen='8' then do;
        fmt = '24.'||left(dec_n);
        width = 24;
        end;
      end;
      %* assign the start and end column number for this field;
      startcol = endcol + 1;
      endcol = startcol + width -1;
%*
  sort the sasnames according to length of name and alphabetical
  order. if any names are duplicates, then append an integer to
  the end of the name. a name may have up to 8 characters.
  ;
  proc sort data=&WORKFILE;
    by nochars sasname;
  data &WORKFILE;
    set &WORKFILE;
    retain i;
    if _n_ = 1 then i = 0;
    if sasname = lag(sasname) then do;
      i = i + 1;
      if nochars <= 7 then
        sasname = compress(sasname)||left(put(i,3.));
        else
        sasname = substr(sasname,1,7)||left(put(i,3.));
      end;
      else i = 0;
%*
  check to see if there are still duplicate sasnames
  if so, set a macro variable to flag this condition;
  proc sort data=&WORKFILE;
    by sasname;
  %LET FLAG=good;
  data _null_;
    set &WORKFILE;
    if sasname = lag(sasname) then
      call symput ('FLAG','bad');
run;
%*
  sort the workfile data set back to its orginal order;
  proc sort data=&WORKFILE;
    by count;
  proc print data=&WORKFILE;
%*
create macro variables
  MVi from sas variable names
  FMi from formats
  TYi from data type
  STi start column for this field logical record
  SCi start column for this field physical record
  WIi for width of this field
  SRi first 80-col record for this variable
  NRi SRi + 1
  LRi last 80-col record for this variable
  LAi label for this variable
  NUMBYTES total width of the logical record
  NUMRECS number of physical records in a logical record
  ENDDATA number of last physical data record
  ;
  data _null_;
    set &WORKFILE end = eof;
    call symput ('MV'||left(put(_n_,3.)),sasname);
```

```
    call symput ('LA'||left(put(_n_,3.)),varname);
    call symput ('FM'||left(put(_n_,3.)),fmt);
    call symput ('TY'||left(put(_n_,3.)),type);
    call symput ('ST'||left(put(_n_,5.)),left(put(startcol,8.)));
    sc1 = mod(startcol,80);
     if sc1 = 0 then sc1 = 80;
    call symput ('SC'||left(put(_n_,3.)),left(put(sc1,8.)));
    call symput ('WI'||left(put(_n_,3.)),left(put(width,8.)));
    call symput ('SR'||left(put(_n_,3.)),left(put(ceil(startcol/80),8.)));
    st1 = ceil(startcol/80) + 1;
    call symput ('NR'||left(put(_n_,3.)),left(put(st1,8.)));
    call symput ('LR'||left(put(_n_,3.)),
     left(put(ceil((startcol+width-1)/80),8.)));
    if eof then do;
     call symput ('NUMBYTES',endcol);
     call symput ('NUMRECS',compress(ceil(endcol/80)));
     call symput
      ('ENDDATA',ceil(endcol/80)*&NUMDATA+&INFOLINS);
     end;
run;
%DO i = 1 %TO &NUMVARS;
%PUT MVi *&&MV&i* STi *&&ST&i* SCi *&&SC&i* WIi
*&&WI&i* SRi *&&SR&i* NRi *&&NR&i* LRi *&&LR&i*;
%END;
%*******************************************************;
%MACRO INPUTEM;
%* this macro generates an input statement;
 %IF &NUMRECS = 1 %THEN
  %STR(input &DUMMY.1 $char80.;);
  %ELSE   %STR(input   (&DUMMY.1-&DUMMY&NUMRECS)
   ($char80.););
%MEND INPUTEM;
%*******************************************************;
%MACRO GETREC(l);
%* this macro concatenates physical records together
 to make the big logical record;
 %LOCAL j;
 &DUMMY&&SR&l
 %IF &&LR&l > &&SR&l %THEN
  %DO j = &&NR&l %TO &&LR&l;
   ||&DUMMY&j
   %END;
%MEND GETREC;
%*******************************************************;
%MACRO VARS2;
%* this macro extracts variables from big logical record string;
 options symbolgen;
 %DO i = 1 %TO &NUMVARS;
  %IF &&TY&i = 1 %THEN
   %STR( var&i = input(translate(substr(%GETREC(&i),
    &&SC&i,&&WI&i),'0',' '),&&FM&i); );
   %ELSE
    %STR(var&i = input(substr(%GETREC(&i),
     &&SC&i,&&WI&i),&&FM&i); );
  %END;
options nosymbolgen;
%MEND VARS2;
%*******************************************************;
%MACRO VARS;
%* this macro extracts variables from big logical record string;
 %LOCAL i;
 %DO i = 1 %TO &NUMVARS;
  %IF &&TY&i = 1 %THEN
   %STR(var&i = input(translate(substr
    (&BIGREC,&&ST&i,&&WI&i),'0',' '),&&FM&i););
   %ELSE
    %STR(var&i =
     input(substr(&BIGREC,&&ST&i,&&WI&i),&&FM&i););
   %END;
 %MEND VARS;
%*******************************************************;
 %MACRO CONCAT;
 %* this macro concatenates physical records together
  to make the big logical record;
  %LOCAL i;
  &DUMMY.1
  %IF &NUMRECS > 1 %THEN %DO i = 2 %TO &NUMRECS;
   ||&&DUMMY&i
   %END;
 %MEND CONCAT;
%*******************************************************;
 %MACRO LABELEM;
 %* this macro generates a label statement;
  %LOCAL i;
  label
  %DO i = 1 %TO &NUMVARS;
   var&i = "&&LA&i"
   %END;
   ;
 %MEND LABELEM;
%*******************************************************;
 %MACRO RENAMEM;
 %* this macro generates rename statement;
  %LOCAL i;
   rename
   %DO i = 1 %TO &NUMVARS;
    var&i = &&MV&i
    %END;
   ;
 %MEND RENAMEM;
%*******************************************************;
%* read the arc/info input file and create SAS output file;
 data &OUTSAS (label = "&INFILE");
  infile &INFILE firstobs=&DATALIN flowover
   lrecl=80 linesize=80 obs = &ENDDATA;
  %LABELEM;        /* generate label statment */
  %INPUTEM;        /* input physical records */
  %VARS2;          /* input variables from string */
  drop &DUMMY.1-&DUMMY&NUMRECS;
  run;
 proc print data=&OUTSAS;
 proc contents data=&OUTSAS;
run;
%* if sasnames are valid rename all the variables;
%IF &FLAG=good %THEN %DO;
 data &OUTSAS (label = "&INFILE");
  set &OUTSAS;
  %RENAMEM;           /* rename variables to sasname */
 proc contents data=&OUTSAS;
 proc print data=&OUTSAS (obs=10);
 run;
%END;
run;
%MEND ARCTOSAS;

/* example call to ARCTOSAS */
*libname arc 'c:\sas\arci\';
*options mprint;
*%arctosas(INFILE='arcfile1.e00',OUTSAS=arctemp);
```

SAS® Macros For Source Program Tracking

John Henry King and Donna S. Goldstein
Burroughs Wellcome Co.

This paper describes a macro system designed to reduce confusion over the origin of output. It is primarily designed for CMS SAS users and for jobs submitted to OS from CMS. Using the macro system, output can be annotated so that one can easily determine the origin of the source program producing the output, and the date and time it was run. Specifically, the macro traces the CMS Userid, the CMS minidisk file that created the output, and the date and time the output was produced. Output from SAS procedures, PUT statements, and SAS/GRAPH® can be annotated using this system composed of two EXECs and a SAS macro.

To initiate the source program tracking system, users must modify their SAS EXEC and write a QUERYCON EXEC to communicate with VMBATCH©. Changes to the EXECs are made once, and saved permanently on the user's minidisk for future use.

The following changes should be made to the SAS EXEC:

replace:
```
parse upper ARG ARGSTRING
```
with:
```
parse upper ARG fn others '(' options
if fn = '' then sysparm = ''
else sysparm = 'SYSPARM' fn
```

replace:
```
'SAS' ARGSTRING
```
with:
```
'SAS' fn others '(' sysparm options
```

The QUERYCON EXEC is listed below:

```
/* querycon exec */
'EXECIO * CP (STEM CON. STRING QUERY CONS'
parse var con.3 addr how userid
push userid
return rc
```

The JOBID SAS macro is listed in Appendix A. It can be saved as a SAS source file and brought into the program using %INCLUDE, or for ease of use, it can be added to the user's AUTOCALL macro library. The Source Program Tracking System is now ready for use.

Initiation of the Source Program Tracking System is done from within the program whose output is to be annotated. Specifications for the JOBID macro are dependent on the type of output to be annotated (i.e., is the output generated by SAS procedures, PUT statements, or SAS/GRAPH?). Once the type of output has been determined, the appropriate positional/keyword parameters can be included in the macro call from within the program.

The JOBID macro is easy to use. Table 1 lists available parameters and their default values. The following examples illustrate its use for three types of output.

Examples

Ex 1. For procedures that produce printed output, use the FOOTNOTE option in the macro call, e.g.
the macro call:
```
%JOBID(FOOTNOTE)
```
generates:
```
FOOTNOTE "USERID(FILENAME) 04/03/90 11:15"
'                                   '
'                                   '
'                                   ';
```
In this example the user supplies the option FOOTNOTEn, where n = 1 by default and may take on values n = 1 to 10. The JOBID macro generates a footnote that is LEFT justified. A useful strategy is to place a macro call of this form at the beginning of a program. Because footnote statements are global statements, all subsequent output is annotated with the JOBID output string.

Ex 2. For graphics procedures, use the GRAPHICS option in the JOBID macro call, e.g.
the macro call:
```
%JOBID(GRAPHICS,HEIGHT = 1.25)
```
generates:
```
NOTE MOVE = (0.0 IN, 0.01 IN)
    F = SIMPLEX
    H = 1.25
    C = BLACK
    "USERID(FILENAME) 04/03/90 11:17";
```
The macro generates a complete NOTE statement with the appropriate subcommand to place the JOBID output string in the lower left corner of the graphics output. The JOBID macro call must be placed within the SAS/GRAPH PROC whose output is to be annotated, as NOTE statements are not global.

Ex 3. For FILE PRINT output, use a PUT statement with pointer control commands in the argument of the JOBID macro call, e.g.
the macro call:
```
PUT %JOBID(#60);
```
generates:
```
PUT #60 "USERID(FILENAME) 04/03/90 11:19";
```
In this example the JOBID macro generates the pointer control to place the JOBID output string on line 60 of each page of the output.

The authors may be reached at:
Burroughs Wellcome Co.
3030 Cornwallis Road
Research Triangle Park, NC 27709

SAS and SAS/GRAPH are registered trademarks of SAS Institute, Inc., Cary, NC USA.

Table 1

JOBID MACRO PARAMETERS

Parameter	Default Value	Description of Use
arg	FOOTNOTE	This positional parameter is used to define the action the macro will take to annotate the output. Other options include: GRAPHICS, TITLE, and pointer control commands.
DATEFMT	= MDY	Keyword parameter used to define date style. Other options include: DMY, YMD, and DATE7.
TIME	= YES	Keyword parameter to specify inclusion of the time the job executed. To suppress the inclusion of time, specify NO.
BEFORE	=	Keyword parameter specifying character constants to be placed before the JOBID output string.
AFTER	=	Keyword parameter specifying character constants to be placed after the JOBID output string.

The following keyword parameters are relevant only when GRAPHICS options are specified, and affect only the JOBID output string on graphics output:

Parameter	Default Value	Description of Use
FONT	= SIMPLEX	Keyword parameter specifying graphics font.
HEIGHT	= 0.5	Keyword parameter specifying font height.
COLOR	= BLACK	Keyword parameter specifying font color of the JOBID output string.
MOVE	= (0.0 IN, 0.01 IN)	Keyword parameter specifying the location of the JOBID output string on the graph.

```
%macro jobid(arg, /* FOOTNOTE, TITLE, GRAPHICS, pointer control */
       datefmt=MDY, /* date style MDY, DMY, YMD, DATE7 */
          time=YES, /* include time of day? */
        before=,    /* character constant "before" jobid string */
         after=,    /* character constant "after"  jobid string */
                                /* Options for Graphics only */
          font=SIMPLEX,            /* graphics font */
        height=0.5,                /* font height */
         color=BLACK,              /* font color */
          move=(0.0 IN, 0.01 IN)); /* location of id string */
  /*-------------------------------------------------------------------*/
  /* E X A M P L E S:                                                  */
  /*                                                                   */
  /*  %jobid(FOOTNOTEn)           >> Procedures                        */
  /*  %jobid(GRAPHICS)            >> Graphics                          */
  /*  PUT %jobid(#60);            >> File Print                        */
  /*-------------------------------------------------------------------*/
  %let arg = %upcase(&arg);
  %if "&arg"="" %then %let arg=FOOTNOTE1;
  %local date time;
  %let datefmt=%upcase(&datefmt);
  %if %index(&datefmt,DATE) %then %let date=&sysdate;
  %else %do;
     %local mm dd yy ml;
     %let mm=%scan(&sysdate,1,0123456789);
     %let dd=%substr(&sysdate,1,%index(&sysdate,&mm)-1);
     %let yy=%substr(&sysdate,%index(&sysdate,&mm)+3);
     %let ml=%str(XX JAN FEB MAR APR MAY JUN JUL AUG SEP OCT NOV DEC);
     %let mm=%eval(%index(&ml,&mm)/4);
     %let mm=%substr(0&mm,%length(&mm),2);
     %let dd=%substr(0&dd,%length(&dd),2);
     %if       "&datefmt"="YMD" %then %let date=&yy/&mm/&dd;
     %else %if "&datefmt"="DMY" %then %let date=&dd..&mm..19&yy;
     %else                            %let date=&mm/&dd/&yy;
     %end;
  %let time = %upcase(&time);
  %if %substr(&time,1,1)=Y %then %let time=%str( )&systime;
  %else                          %let time=;
  %local userid pgm;
  %if &sysscp=CMS %then %do;
     %let userid=&sysjobid;
     %let pgm   =&sysparm;
     %if %substr(&sysjobid,1,3)=VMB %then %do;
        %cms STATE QUERYCON EXEC *;
        %if &sysrc=0 %then %do;
           %cms EXEC QUERYCON;
           %cms SENTRIES;
           %if &sysrc>0 %then %input userid;
           %end;
        %end;
     %end;
  %else %if &sysscp=OS %then %do;
     %let userid=&sysparm;
     %let pgm   =&sysjobid;
     %end;
  %let userid=%substr(&userid%str(         ),1,
            %index(&userid%str( ),%str( ))-1);
  %let pgm=%substr(&pgm%str(        ),1,%index(&pgm%str( ),%str( ))-1);
  %let pad='                                                             ';
  %if %index(&arg,FOOTNOTE) | %index(&arg,TITLE) %then %do;
     &arg &before "&userid(&pgm) &date&time" &after &pad &pad &pad;
     %end;
  %else %if %index(GRAPHICS,&arg) %then %do;
     %if %length(&font)  =0 %then %let font   =SIMPLEX;
     %if %length(&height)=0 %then %let height=0.5;
     %if %length(&color) =0 %then %let color =BLACK;
     %if %length(&move)  =0 %then %let move  =(0.0 IN, 0.01 IN);
     NOTE MOVE=&move F=&font H=&height  C=&color
          &before "&userid(&pgm) &date&time" &after;
     %end;
  %else %do;
     &arg &before "&userid(&pgm) &date&time" &after %str( )
     %end;
  %mend jobid;
```

Index

C

D

J

K

L

M

N

O

P

Q

R

S

T

U

V

W

Y

Special Characters

Your Turn

If you have comments or suggestions about *SAS Macro Facility Tips and Techniques, Version 6, First Edition*, please send them to us on a photocopy of this page or send us electronic mail.

For comments about this book, please return the photocopy to

SAS Institute Inc.
Publications Division
SAS Campus Drive
Cary, NC 27513
email: yourturn@unx.sas.com

For suggestions about the software, please return the photocopy to

SAS Institute Inc.
Technical Support Division
SAS Campus Drive
Cary, NC 27513
email: suggest@unx.sas.com